1989 THE COMPLETE HANDBOOK OF BASEBALL

1989 THE COMPLETE HANDBOOK OF BASEBALL

EDITED BY ZANDER HOLLANDER

AN ASSOCIATED FEATURES BOOK

A SIGNET BOOK
NEW AMERICAN LIBRARY
A DIVISION OF PENGUIN BOOKS USA INC.

ACKNOWLEDGMENTS

It'll never replace "Take Me Out To The Ball Game," but don't be surprised if ballpark organists add the "Wiffenpoof" to their repertoire this season. The celebrated Yale song will have its most strident chorus in new commissioner Bart Giamatti, ex-Yale president, and Yalies Eli Jacobs, Lawrence Lucchino, Sargent Shriver and son Robert, the new owners of the Baltimore Orioles. For backup, count on an ex-Yale first baseman named George Bush and another Boola Boola product, Ron Darling.

For this 19th edition of *The Complete Handbook of Baseball*, we acknowledge the support of contributing editor Howard Blatt, the writers listed on the contents page and Lee Stowbridge, Richard Rossiter, Eric Compton, David Kaplan, Linda Spain, Phyllis Merhige, John Maroon, Katy Feeney, Jim Trdinich, Kevin Mulroy, Elias Sports Bureau, MLB-IBM Baseball Information System, Dot Gordineer of Libra Graphics and the staff at Westchester Book Composition.

Zander Hollander

PHOTO CREDITS: Covers—Focus on Sports. Inside photos —George Gojkovich, Ira Golden, Vic Milton, Mitch Reibel, Michigan State, AP/Wide World, UPI and the major-league team photographers.

SIGNET TRADEMARK REG. U.S. PAT. OFF. AND FOREIGN COUNTRIES
REGISTERED TRADEMARK—MARCA REGISTRADA
HECHO EN DRESDEN, TN

SIGNET, SIGNET CLASSIC, MENTOR, ONYX, PLUME, MERIDIAN and NAL BOOKS are published by
New American Library, a division of Penguin Books USA, Inc.,
1633 Broadway, New York, New York 10019

First Printing, March, 1989

1 2 3 4 5 6 7 8 9

PRINTED IN THE UNITED STATES OF AMERICA

CONTENTS

Orel & Kirk:
The Dodgers' Odd Couple .... By Ken Gurnick 6

Jose Canseco's 40-40 Vision .... By Kit Stier 16

The Adventures of David Cone .... By Steve Marcus 24

Stunning, Silly, Significant Stats .... By Marty Noble 32

Inside the National League
By Barry Bloom and Bob Hertzel 40

Chicago Cubs 42
Montreal Expos 52
New York Mets............. 62
Philadelphia Phillies......... 73
Pittsburgh Pirates 83
St. Louis Cardinals 93
Atlanta Braves 103
Cincinnati Reds 113
Houston Astros 123
Los Angeles Dodgers....... 134
San Diego Padres 145
San Francisco Giants 156

Inside the American League.............. By Tom Pedulla 168

Baltimore Orioles.......... 170
Boston Red Sox........... 180
Cleveland Indians.......... 190
Detroit Tigers............. 200
Milwaukee Brewers 210
New York Yankees 220
Toronto Blue Jays 232
California Angels 242
Chicago White Sox......... 252
Kansas City Royals 263
Minnesota Twins 274
Oakland A's 285
Seattle Mariners........... 297
Texas Rangers 306

Major League Year-by-Year Leaders 318

All-Time Records.................................... 337

World Series Winners 338

1988 World Series Summary........................... 340

Official 1988 American League Statistics 342

Official 1988 National League Statistics 366

National League Schedule............................. 392

American League Schedule............................ 396

Editor's Note: The material herein includes trades and rosters up to final printing deadline.

Orel historians will toast ace who iced A's in Game 5.

OREL & KIRK: THE DODGERS' ODD COUPLE

By KEN GURNICK

When playwright Neil Simon wrote *The Odd Couple*, he could have had the Dodgers' Kirk Gibson and Orel Hershiser in mind.

Gibson is worn blue jeans, the bulldozer he wheels around his 100-acre Michigan spread, a spike haircut, a three-day-old beard and a fiery foul-mouthed intensity approaching the lunatic fringe.

Ken Gurnick, a Dodger beat writer for the Los Angeles Herald Examiner *since 1981, was on the scene all the way during the championship season.*

Kirk Gibson's homeric feat in 12th turned NLCS around.

Hershiser is wire-rim glasses, tailored suits, a lap-top computer, lunch at the country club, hymn-humming in the dugout and a face that doesn't look old enough to shave.

Their common ground is baseball, where they both display extraordinary ability, determination and a will to win. In Gibson and Hershiser last season, the Dodgers had the National League's Most Valuable Player and Cy Young Award winner. Thanks to Gibson and Hershiser, the Dodgers were world champs.

To better understand the Dodger achievement of 1988, momentarily consider 1987. Los Angeles finished 16 games below .500 for the second consecutive year, displaying the worst offense in the league and an attitude to match. There were fights in the dugout, discord in the clubhouse, a crowd in the trainer's room. Peter O'Malley's club, among the richest in the game, was a shambles and the bottom line didn't look so good, either. Attendance dipped below three million and O'Malley drew unprecedented heat from fans and media for ignoring free agent Tim Raines.

O'Malley was convinced by executive vice president Fred Claire that the Dodgers had holes their farm system couldn't fill and the coffers were opened when Gibson became a free agent through the collusion ruling of arbitrator Tom Roberts, who probably deserved Executive of the Year honors as much as Claire.

Quickly, Gibson became a Dodger by signing a three-year,

$4.5-million contract and the sudden move by management to infuse talent wasn't overlooked by Hershiser.

The pitcher has more than a strong arm. He has a sharp mind and a tongue to match. One winter earlier, he had led a group of teammates into Claire's office to lobby for the signing of Raines. All along, Hershiser had complained the loudest that the Dodgers' problems in 1986 and 1987 were not because of injuries or bad luck. He blamed a lack of talent.

So it was fitting on the night that Hershiser won his 20th game last season that he issued a compliment to Dodger management. "I made a statement over the winter that we needed more players to give me a chance to win and Fred Claire did that and Peter O'Malley paid the price," he said. "Those guys gave me the opportunity to do this."

Upon seeing so many new faces in the Dodger clubhouse last spring, Hershiser joked that he felt like he had been traded. And the new face that was the focus of the most uncertainty was Gibson's. Teammates had heard the stories and now they wanted to see for themselves. "The Animal," as Gibson often is called, was in their zoo. Would he take charge?

He waited until the first game of the preseason. Jesse Orosco didn't do much else for the Dodgers last year, but he helped Gibson set a no-nonsense tone with a bit of nonsense, smearing eye-black on the inside band of Gibson's cap. "The Animal" stormed off into the sunset. He is coy when asked if his temper tantrum was planned or spontaneous. Either way, it had a lasting effect.

"I definitely think it was a positive experience," Gibson said later. "I don't think it hurt. It was good to defuse the bomb right away, so to speak."

Hershiser liked Gibson's response, because he suspected the Dodgers had gotten a little soft after two years of losing and needed a swift kick.

"Kirk takes intensity to a different level and I think what he did made some of us examine ourselves," Hershiser said. "Not a lot of guys would get away with that or would even try it. Most would just laugh along with the joke. To Kirk, it was unacceptable."

As the season went along, so much credit was heaped on Gibson for turning up the club's intensity that a backlash resulted from some teammates who felt their attitude wasn't the cause of earlier problems. Manager Tommy Lasorda defended Mike Scioscia and Steve Sax and Mike Marshall, insisting they were just as competitive as Gibson. Scioscia took offense at the notion that the team cared more about winning now that it was winning than

Hershiser was Mr. October with pair of MVP trophies.

it did when it was losing.

Regardless of those comments, it was apparent to everyone that a new spirit arrived along with Gibson and it translated into a team that played the game harder and dug a little deeper, coming up with wins instead of excuses.

And the biggest winner of the bunch was Hershiser, who capped the winningest season for a Dodger pitcher since 1965 with a late-season roll the likes of which has never been seen in baseball.

He broke Don Drysdale's consecutive scoreless innings record—one which baseball scholars believed would never be broken—and he ran out of regular season at 59 and counting. He won the NL Championship Series MVP award with a remarkable performance and then added the World Series MVP award, even though unsung Mickey Hatcher might have deserved it more.

It was the type of season that made Hershiser as valuable to Madison Avenue as he is to the Dodgers, triggering an avalanche of endorsement offers. He made an All-Star tour of Japan, play-

Orel says thanks after leaving Mets without a prayer.

ing to his hosts by suggesting he might play there someday. Just imagine: Hershiser the Ham Fighter.

Ever the politician, he cut short that trip and was home in time for a press conference the day the Cy Young Award was announced.

He has cultivated a rare image for today's ballplayer: courteous, cooperative, kind (even with reporters), although teammates noticed his late-season success was just about matched by his ego.

On the other hand, there was Gibson. While Hershiser monitored his Cy Young race with Cincinnati's Danny Jackson over the waning weeks of the season with statistical updates, Gibson refused to acknowledge the existence of an NL MVP award. "All I care about is winning," he would say, eventually snapping at reporters when pressed.

Cliche or not, all he really did care about was winning—and he proved it by celebrating unashamedly following the World Series clincher, even though he hadn't played since Game 1.

Of course, his lone at-bat won't ever be forgotten. A real-life

Roy Hobbs, he limped to the plate with battered legs with two out in the bottom of the ninth inning and wristed a game-winning, pinch-hit, two-run home run off Dennis Eckersley, a blast that will go down as one of the great moments in World Series history.

"I wanted to go out and kiss the guy," said Hatcher. "But he never shaves and I could have hurt myself."

It was a magical moment and typical of Gibson, who bills himself as "an impact player" and lives up to the billing. Even at $1.5 million a year, he proved a bargain to Dodger management, which had shunned free agents after making disastrous investments in Don Stanhouse and Dave Goltz.

So, clearly, what the Dodgers have here is a pair of players who are good and know it, and there is nothing wrong with that. And they are living proof there is more than one path to success.

Gibson, 31, is the only son and youngest child of two Michigan school teachers. A two-sport star at Michigan State, he played four years of football as a nationally acclaimed wide receiver and only one season of baseball, but rejected the football Cardinals and chose baseball when drafted by his home-state Tigers in June 1978.

His early years in the Detroit organization were marked by ridiculous expectations that went unfulfilled and a bad attitude.

"I've said more than once I was a self-centered, egotistical jerk in those days and I was," he said.

His plight was not made easier when a quote from Tigers' manager Sparky Anderson was embellished, resulting in Gibson being labeled as "the next Mickey Mantle."

It might as well have been Babe Ruth, because his relationship with Detroit fans was equal parts love and hate—and he didn't deal with either very well. He claims to have reached a magical insight in the winter following the 1983 season while riding a horse in the snow, a realization he was "headed in the wrong direction." He sought a motivation specialist in Seattle and worked on concentration and self-concept. In 1984, he was named World Series MVP as the Tigers beat the Padres in five games.

"I learned not to be afraid of screwing up. I can screw up," he said, "but it doesn't mean I am a screw-up."

He was a victim of owner collusion when he was a free agent after the 1985 season, eventually accepting a three-year, $4-million deal that Roberts subsequently voided. Prior to that, though, Gibson experienced the reality of the baseball business when the Tigers tried to trade him to the Dodgers for Pedro Guerrero. So much for the dream of being a Tiger forever.

When granted his free agency, Gibson received an offer from the Tigers of $2.8 million, which didn't compare to the Dodger bonanza of $4.5 million. He accepted the challenge of a city not at all like Detroit, knowing there would be a culture shock. But he welcomed a new start where he wouldn't be hammered in the newspapers by an owner who made his fortune by selling pizzas.

"I've gotten away from the distractions in Detroit. I needed the change," he said. "I feel a lot of the burden is off me. What I did in Detroit was never good enough. There was a certain stagnation being a hometown boy, a savior one time and a goat another time."

He became an immediate hero in the city of glitz and glitter and mineral water and he wasn't as out of place as his midwest critics predicted. He even showed up once at the trendy Spagos restaurant on Sunset Boulevard, the quintessence of L.A. life and a favorite eatery of the Robin Leach set. He lived in Pacific Palisades, only a short jog from Malibu.

"Everything worked out even better than I could have imagined," he said. "The reason I'm playing well here is that I feel comfortable. Tommy has been great and I'm surrounded by a lot of good players, and they're as much a reason for our success as I am."

But you can't take the country out of the boy, and all that. He still spends the offseason on his Lapeer spread, which is run by brother-in-law and former teammate Dave Rozema. He has a real estate and investment office in Grosse Pointe, having already started his post-baseball career. He is right where he wants to be.

"I couldn't live in Los Angeles all year," he said. "I can't stand to wake up and see it 70 degrees and a clear blue sky every day."

That's Kirk Gibson, right there. Don't try to figure him out. Sometimes, he's a little stubborn, but he knows what he likes.

Hershiser adapts to the situation, a talent acquired through a childhood spent in five hometowns before he graduated from Cherry Hill (N.J.) East High School. His father was a salesman for a printing business who later owned it and became wealthy. Hershiser, 30, points out his upbringing was strictly middle class.

The former youth hockey player was a late bloomer in baseball. He was cut from his high school team as well as his college squad at Bowling Green. He has been a Dodger since being drafted in the 17th round in June 1979, but he seems eager at the chance for free agency following 1989. He earned $1.1 million last year, will probably double it this year and wouldn't mind someday becoming the highest-paid player in the game.

While Gibson's rugged look has epitomized his animal reputa-

Gibby spurned NFL Cardinals for home-state Tigers.

tion, Hershiser has had to live down an appearance that flies in the face of a rough-and-tough sports hero.

"I look like a guy who was probably a straight-A student, but I was academically ineligible my first year in college. I look like a guy who would probably be weak, but I am actually pretty strong for my body composition. I look like a guy who doesn't have a whole lot of heart and would fold under pressure, but I feel I can hold up to whatever you want to give me. I look like someone who doesn't have a whole lot of pain tolerance, but I have never missed a start.

"I don't really look the part of some tough, aggressive pitcher who goes out to the mound and gets people out. I don't look like a guy who would pitch inside, but I seem to lead our team and most of the league in hitting batters every year. I've never hit one intentionally, but I intentionally throw inside and it's kind of nice. Batters look at me and don't expect it. People looked at my boyish face and concluded I wasn't aggressive enough to pitch in the majors."

People were wrong, as were those who thought he was too religious to succeed in baseball, a misconception that prompted his famous 1985 quote: "Just because you're religious doesn't mean you have to be a wimp."

No wimp, Hershiser showed he could pitch by the middle of 1984, following the legendary "Bulldog" pep talk Lasorda gave him to bring out his aggressiveness. He went 19-3 with a 2.03 ERA in 1985, but was overshadowed by greater seasons from Dwight Gooden and John Tudor. He had a .500 record in 1986 and 1987, but it wasn't fair to call him a .500 pitcher. In each of his five seasons, his winning percentage has exceeded that of his club, a pretty good indication of his superior performance.

Finally in 1988, he broke free of the enormous shadow of Fernando Valenzuela and emerged as the Dodger ace, which wasn't easy.

"Since I became a Dodger, Fernando was the criteria by which all pitchers were judged," he said last April. "Fernando could pitch, he could hit, he could bunt, he could field, he could strike people out, he pitched complete games, he never missed a start and he was a media draw. That made him the standard I strived for. I didn't look to be like Jerry Reuss or Rick Honeycutt or Bob Welch. In Los Angeles, Fernando has represented what good pitching is all about. Fernando has achieved greatness. Where there is a goal, I will follow. I've strived for that and, most times, accomplished that."

His methods are not always conventional. Consider his fascination with computers, for example. Most pitchers keep a "book" on opposing hitters. Hershiser keeps a floppy disk.

"I know it's really against the grain of baseball tradition. The image is a guy on the bench, chewing tobacco, going out and pitching and just throwing hard," he told the *Los Angeles Times*. "This is a little high-tech. My computer replaces the old pitcher's book, only I put more into it. I keep a record of how I felt on the mound each game, my physical status, the adjustments I made on the mound.

"It's mostly for learning about hitters and about myself, recording the feelings I have on a daily basis. Like maybe I

Once upon a time, Kirk was a clean-shaven Spartan.

warmed up really well, seemed to have all my pitches working, but when the game started, I wasn't making the pitches. What did it feel like? What adjustments did I make? Did they bring me back in line? I'll write down a key pitch sequence that worked or a change in the philosophy of the hitter. In general, I'm really mechanically conscious out there. That's where the computer helps. My recall is so much better. If you've just studied on the computer adjustments you made in the past, it's easier to have them at the top of your mind when you're out there pitching, instead of having to search for ideas."

The computer has paid off in another way. He's now endorsing the product.

Gibson turns down most endorsements and appearances. When the team went to the White House for a congratulatory meeting with President Reagan, Hershiser served as spokesman for the Oval Office meeting. Gibson skipped the trip altogether, remaining on the farm.

It said something about the two players and the two personalities. An odd couple, to be sure.

JOSE CANSECO'S 40-40 VISION

By KIT STIER

It would be foolish to place limits upon what Jose Canseco may yet accomplish on the diamond. He is already a superstar, though still a novice by baseball standards.

"You've seen just a brief introduction of what Jose Canseco can do," the Athletics' veteran slugger Dave Parker said after his teammate was the unanimous choice as AL Most Valuable Player last November. "He's the best player in this league. And he might be the best player in baseball."

Baseball's stage is already too small to hold Canseco. He is handsome enough to sell products and has corporations knocking at his door. Even Hollywood isn't out of the question. In just three major-league seasons, the Athletics' right fielder has become one of those rare sports stars who has crossed the boundaries of his game and become a household name. He has gone prime time, to the point that his stardom has become a burden at times.

"Everyone knows who I am, even in Hawaii," said Canseco during his honeymoon in the islands in November. "A couple of years ago, people would walk up to me and then turn away and say, 'That's not Canseco, it doesn't even look like him.' But I do like talking with people, especially the kids."

However, he has found fame does have a price.

"I was eating at a place I won't mention and, just when I am about to eat some soup, a drunk comes up and tries to talk to me, but spits all over me and my soup," said Canseco.

Some people never doubted this 24-year-old, Cuban-born, 20th-century Hercules would achieve stardom quickly and show maturity in his ability to handle it.

Kit Stier, a native Californian who grew up abroad as the son of an American diplomat, spends his days—and nights—covering the Oakland A's for the Oakland Tribune *and* The Sporting News.

Jose's World Series began with slam, ended with whimper.

"The trick to me is how he can handle the attention, all the distractions of being a major-league player," said Karl Kuehl, A's director of player development, before Canseco began his successful quest to become AL Rookie of the Year in 1986. "He has been very good in the local theaters and now he is going to Carnegie Hall. But I think he'll handle it all. He is going to put some big numbers on the board."

Kuehl hadn't gazed into a crystal ball, but he had watched this 6-3, 230-pounder develop during four minor-league seasons. Still, the veteran baseball man had no idea it was in the stars that Canseco would have editors working overtime updating the record books by 1988.

But Jose's mother, Barbara, knew.

Before she died of a brain hemorrage in April 1984, Barbara Canseco consulted a psychic in Miami to see what course life would take for her twin sons, Jose and Ozzie.

"She didn't go to a fortune teller or anyone like that," Canseco's father, Jose Sr., told *Sports Illustrated* in June 1986. "No, the woman she saw was more serious than that, a real psychic. And she told my wife that both of our boys would become popular in sports, but that one of them would get there first and would become very famous. It has all happened."

It has happened so quickly the head spins and the mind races. Canseco was being likened to "The Natural" before he ever put on an Oakland uniform. One look at Canseco in the batting cage had people associating his name with Babe Ruth, Mickey Mantle, Roberto Clemente and other greats. Canseco didn't just hit home runs, he put the baseball into orbit.

Canseco's rapid rise to stardom has been phenomenal, but it probably shouldn't have come as a huge surprise. He has always had the physical tools, the smarts and the desire to be the best.

Last year, he became the first player in history to hit at least 40 home runs and steal 40 bases in a single season with 42 and 40 respectively, accomplishing most of those numbers before his 24th birthday July 2. He became the first player to hit at least 30 home runs and drive in at least 100 runs in each of his first three seasons.

While Canseco has matured on the field, he has grown to manhood off it. He has learned to accept his immense popularity and now rates darling status with the media. He is greeted with squeals of delight from women of all ages.

"I never realized in the minor leagues what all this was like," Canseco said. "I never realized how much the fans got into it, and all that's required."

Handsome Jose won $10,000 bet by marrying Esther Haddad.

The foundation of Canseco's legend was built on a monster 1985 season, when he was named Minor League Player of the Year, and his tremendous batting practice power displays that left fans and peers oohing and aahing. However, his development into one of the game's best all-around players has been the result of hard work.

Canseco was nine months old when his father, now an area manager for an oil company, moved the family—wife, daughter and the twins—from Havana to Miami in 1965.

Jose Sr. said he made the move because "communism is a rotten thing." The family first settled in the Opa Locka area of Miami and later moved to the southwest area of the city. It was there, while Jose was attending Coral Park High School, that A's scout Camilo Pasqual noticed the youngster.

The A's weren't interested in Canseco at first. He weighed only 170 pounds at the time and his skills were undeveloped. But Pasqual insisted, actually offering to pay the young man's bonus. Finally, in the 15th round of the June 1982 draft, the A's took the bait.

Canseco struggled at first, then finally showed some signs of blossoming in his third year in the minors, batting .276 with 15 homers and 73 RBI for Modesto (A) in the California League.

Weight training became a major factor in Canseco's life shortly after he began his pro career and, by the time 1985 rolled around, he had grown to his present size. He started that year in Double-A and hit 25 homers, drove in 80 runs and batted .318 in just 58 games for Huntsville (Ala.) in the Southern League. He was promoted to Tacoma (AAA), where he batted .348, hit 11 homers and drove in 47 runs in 60 games before getting a call to finish the season in Oakland.

As soon as Canseco arrived in the majors, he began to draw rave reviews. He finished 1985 with five homers and 13 RBI in 29 games, but he was shy, a trait that led some to conclude he was also unfriendly. There was also a quiet confidence about him that could have been mistaken for arrogance.

"I think whatever is going to happen in the future will happen," he said before embarking on his first full major-league season as Oakland's left fielder in 1986. "Regardless of what they say I can't do, regardless of what they say I can do, whatever is going to happen is predetermined."

There was a bumper crop of talented rookies in the AL, but Canseco—who hit 33 homers and drove in 117 runs while batting .240 and striking out 175 times—edged the Angels' Wally Joyner to become the first of Oakland's three consecutive Rookies of the Year.

Canseco's home run and RBI totals dipped a bit to 31 and 113 in 1987, but his batting average climbed to .257 and he cut his strikeout total to 157. He was working, he was learning, he was maturing as a human being.

In 1988, Canseco drew the most votes of any AL player during the All-Star Game balloting. And, when he arrived in Cincinnati, he became a favorite with the press, too, telling media members that he fully intended to have fun playing his game and that they were to be a part of that fun. Canseco gave freely of his time, as he had since late 1987. His remarks were thought out, yet spontaneous, and colorful.

Perhaps the most amazing aspect of Canseco's 1988 season was that he accomplished the 40-40 feat after he said he would in spring training. What he didn't know when he uttered his personal challenge was that no one in the game had ever turned the trick. It was also during spring training that he broke thousands of hearts by announcing that he would marry Esther Haddad, a former Miss Miami, once the season had ended.

No one challenged Canseco on his 40-40 prediction, but teammate Dave Stewart, knowing that Canseco had arrived at two previous spring trainings engaged to different women, bet the outfielder $10,000 he wouldn't carry out his wedding plans with Haddad.

Stewart's bank account is now $10,000 lighter and Canseco is the founding father of the 40-40 Club, after becoming only the 11th member to join the 30-30 Club.

But there was more to his season than a major-league-leading 42 homers. He also led the majors in RBI with 124 and in slugging percentage at .569. He was among the league leaders in nearly every offensive category.

He became a fine clutch hitter, slugging 27 homers that either tied a game or gave the A's the lead. His .307 average rated ninth in the league and he cut his strikeout total to 128.

"I think the way to look at it would be to break it down," said Athletics' manager Tony La Russa. "Batting average, he's capable of hitting .300. And, if he decided to make every swing a base-hit swing, he's capable of challenging for the batting title."

Canseco laughed when asked about the possibility of winning a triple crown some day. "Wade Boggs would have to retire," he said. "Kirby Puckett and a couple of other players, too."

However, La Russa was serious. "Home runs," continued the manager. "He's so amazing that if he made consistent contact and it was the kind of year where the ball was carrying, he might do something that's never been done.

"Stolen bases. I think there's a limit to what he can get, because he won't push it. Defensively, he could become outstanding in right field or he could become a center fielder."

Canseco, nurtured as a right fielder, spent his first two years with the A's in left. When Mike Davis departed after the 1987

Thanks to Mark McGwire and Canseco, A's were awesome.

season, Canseco moved back to his natural spot and led all A's outfielders with 11 assists.

"I think, more than anything else, this guy likes to have the game on the line," La Russa said. "He's not afraid at all of being in the pressure situation. That's where his potential is the greatest."

His MVP season, for which he was paid $325,000, didn't pass without controversy. The first pitch of the playoffs had hardly crossed home plate when Red Sox fans in Fenway began shouting, "Steroids, steroids, steroids," following up on columnist Thomas Boswell's suggestion that Canseco had achieved his impressive mass of muscle by using the controversial drug.

Canseco stood in right field at Fenway and flexed his muscles with a wide smile as the fans taunted him. The young man had grown up.

"Anybody who used any common sense would back me up," said Canseco. "People who know me know I don't indulge in steroids. You wouldn't believe how hard I worked in the offseason. I took no vacation. I didn't drink or party. I came to spring training in better shape than I'm in now."

Canseco had a fine playoff series, then went hitless in 18 at-bats after hitting the first grand slam of his career off Tim Belcher in Game 1 of the World Series against the Dodgers. And, even though he and the powerful Athletics faltered against the Dodgers, Canseco continued to stand up and take his medicine from inquiring members of the media.

Canseco is looking forward to having his brother Ozzie, an outfielder now at the Double-A level in the A's system, join him in the majors. And that could well happen since Ozzie is about the same size as Jose and is just now making up for time lost when the Yankees insisted he could become a pitcher after they drafted him.

Jose will undoubtedly be a millionaire before the next time he takes the field. He has already contracted to do some national advertisements and the A's will need armored cars to cover his paychecks in 1989.

So, the obvious question is where does he go from here?

"You're the one in command out there," Canseco said. "You're the one who sets the time to sign the autographs, the time to talk to reporters.

"All that is for you to decide. And I decided a long time ago that I'd never stop doing the hard work it took to get me here. It's hard work that brings success and, without that hard work, there wouldn't be any of this."

THE ADVENTURES OF DAVID CONE

By STEVE MARCUS

Before last year, the sound of David Cone's name conjured in the minds of many New Yorkers the image of a nice Jewish boy from Brooklyn, not a baby-faced Irish pitcher from Kansas City with an assortment of nasty stuff. But, by the end of an extraordinary 1988 season that began in the bullpen and ended in the spotlight, David Cone was a household name not only among Met fans, but across the country.

The slender right-hander's seven-month odyssey from the obscurity of middle relief to recognition as one of the game's dominant starters was nothing if not eventful. In becoming the first 20-game winner to begin the year in the bullpen since the Orioles' Wayne Garland in 1976, Cone was nearly decapitated by a bat thrown at him by Pedro Guerrero, narrowly missed pitching no-hitters twice, pitched a scoreless inning in the All-Star Game and weathered a storm created by a ghost-written column appearing under his name that made him a marked man with the Dodgers after Game 1 of the NLCS.

Cone came out of the shadows to blend an overpowering fastball, a sharp curve, a splitter and a nasty drop-down slider he called "Laredo" with devastating results. En route to the sixth-highest winning percentage in history by a 20-game winner (.870 at 20-3), Cone was second in the NL in ERA (2.22) and strikeouts (213) and held opposing hitters to a .213 batting average.

If Orel Hershiser had chosen another year to stamp as his own personal showcase, Cone's numbers would have meant more than token support in the Cy Young race. As it was, Cone finished third, behind the unanimously endorsed Dodger right-hander and Reds' 23-game-winner Danny Jackson.

Veteran baseball writer Steve Marcus of Newsday *eyewitnessed David Cone and Conehead-mania.*

David Cone achieved vindication with Game 6 gem.

"I'm very happy for Coney. We're all very proud," said Gary Carter, his catcher. "It's just a shame Orel had the kind of year he did. David, in any other year, probably would be the Cy Young winner."

Cone's first full year as a starter—he was limited to 13 starts for the Mets in 1987 due mostly to injury—compared favorably to the debut seasons of such greats as Vida Blue (24-8 for the A's in 1971), Doc Gooden (17-9 for the Mets in 1984), Fernando Valenzuela (13-7 for the Dodgers in 1981) and Steve Carlton (14-9 for the Cards in 1967).

"I'm thrilled to be considered with the league's best pitchers," said Cone the day the Cy Young voting was announced. "But doing it once doesn't mean anything. I have to go out and do it three, four or five years. In this game, you are only recognized if you do it on a consistent basis and that's what I still have to prove."

Having something to prove is nothing new for Cone.

Rockhurst, his high school in Kansas City, didn't have a baseball team, so he starred as a football quarterback and basketball guard instead and earned the scouts' attention in American Legion ball. When the Royals made him their third-round pick in June 1981, he was glad to accept the chance to play for the franchise in the city of his birth, Jan. 2, 1963.

But there were obstacles and finally a detour in this local-boy-makes-good story. After a couple of promising years in the lower minors, Cone suffered severed ligaments in his left knee while covering the plate on a wild pitch in a spring game in 1983. His season was over before it had begun—and maybe his career, too.

"It was one of the most devastating knee injuries I'd ever seen, a real mess," said KC GM John Schuerholz. "But David worked harder than anyone I had ever seen in rehab."

Cone took his inspiration from a partner in rehab, former 20-game-winner Dennis Leonard. "I was a 19-year-old who hadn't made it to the majors yet and here was a guy who was making $2 million a year, who could afford to walk away, but was working harder than I did to make it back. I learned from that," he said.

Cone endured losing seasons in Double-A in 1984 and Triple-A in 1985 before regaining his form while going 8-4 with a 2.79 ERA for Omaha (AAA) in 1986. Then a funny thing happened only a week before he was set to go north with the Royals as their No. 5 starter the next spring. He was traded to the Mets with catcher Chris Jelic for catcher Ed Hearn and pitchers Rick Anderson and Mauro Gozzo in a deal that Keith Hernandez later called "the steal of the century."

"It's very unusual to get the top pitching prospect in an organization," said Met VP Joe McIlvaine, who would settle for no one else. "And it is rare to get universal agreement on [the potential of] a player. But we had it."

"I rank it as one of my very best deals," said Schuerholz with an uncomfortable laugh. Actually, the Royals' GM felt Hearn would be the catcher who could make his team a pennant winner in 1987. He couldn't have known that a torn rotator cuff would render Hearn almost useless within months of the deal. And it's not like he offered Cone around to any club that would have him.

"Dave was a highly regarded prospect and we hated to give him up, but there's not many people who thought he was ready to have this kind of year," said Schuerholz.

Things weren't easy for Cone at first. He was joining a team that was defending a world championship and was careful not to say or do anything to make waves. "I didn't know anyone and no one knew me," he recalled. "I was real quiet, because I was afraid of how I might be viewed. I just sat in the corner and waited for my chance to pitch. I wasn't even sure I'd make the staff."

Cone made the team, but didn't set the baseball world on fire immediately. In fact, in his first major-league start April 27, the Astros tortured him for 10 runs in five innings as he fidgeted his way to six walks and three balks.

"It was the most embarrassing night of my life," he said. "I didn't sleep that night at all . . . I had finally gotten a major-league start—something I always wanted—and I didn't think I'd get another one."

He did, though, and showed far better command and glimpses of his talent—before breaking the index finger on his pitching hand during a bunt attempt May 27. He returned to the Mets Aug. 13, but his 5-6 record and 3.71 ERA in 1987 gave no hint of his potential and didn't do much to help his chances of cracking the vaunted Met starting five last spring.

"I knew I could control my own destiny, once I got into the rotation," said Cone, who began the season as Davey Johnson's middle-inning guy while Rick Aguilera filled the No. 5 starter's role. "All I needed was a chance."

He got it when Aguilera's elbow troubles flared up again. Cone made his first 1988 start May 3 and gained his first major-league shutout with an 8-0 blanking of the Braves. As Cone rang up five wins in his first five starts to push his overall mark to 7-0, a smiling Johnson observed, "In a sense, I was hoping he wouldn't do this. He gives me quality innings in the bullpen."

His May 22 confrontation with then-Dodger slugger Guerrero at Dodger Stadium further established Cone as a gutsy competitor who would back down to no one. After Cone hit Guerrero with what he called "a helicopter curve", Pedro threw his bat at Cone.

"I don't think it will ever be forgotten, but I think it will be a positive thing for my career," said Cone, who stood his ground as the muscular slugger headed toward the mound. "Now people know I'm going to pitch my game, do what I have to do to win."

Guerrero, who later told reporters he was trying to "brush back" the pitcher rather than part his hair with the bat, wound up with a $1,000 fine and a four-day suspension. Cone wound up with new-found respect from his teammates and opposing hitters around the league.

Still, the pitcher's goals remained modest. "Winning 20 never entered my mind," he would later reflect. "I thought if I got into the rotation, I could win 15."

Twice, he threw 10 innings of one-run ball and got no-decisions. He no-hit the Phillies for 7⅔ innings June 19—the longest no-hit bid by a Met since Pat Zachry came within four outs in April 1972—but shortstop Steve Jeltz spoiled it with a single. "I suppose I should be happy, but I'm a little disappointed," he said after settling for a two-hit shutout. "Not to be demeaning to the Phillies, but I had a chance to finish it."

He threw a one-hitter at the Padres Aug. 29 in a 6-0 victory, but this time the hit came in the fourth. It was a double by NL batting champ Tony Gwynn, who earlier in the season had described Cone's varied repertoire of pitches as "an arsenal." Cone was on a roll that prompted teammate Ron Darling to reach for a musical analogy. "Coney has come out of the Royals the way George Michael came out of WHAM," he said.

And the pitcher wasn't afraid to show his feelings on the mound, a quality at which Darling marvelled. "Coney doesn't conceal his emotions. I was always taught to keep my emotions in and I've tried to do it," Darling said. "I've never seen a pitcher who lets the other team know how he's feeling as much as Coney does. They can tell when he's happy and they can see when they've got to him.

"The public sees that, too, and I think they like it. A guy sees Coney squatting on the mound [in disgust] after [Cubs' catcher Damon] Berryhill took him deep [to break open a scoreless duel in the 10th June 2] and knows that's the way he felt in Sunday morning softball . . . Coney's just a normal guy pitching for the Mets."

Cone won 20, though he didn't make first start until May.

"I'm a regular dude," agreed Cone. A regular dude with a special arm and a special following.

As his victory total grew last season, a group of Met fans took to wearing Cones on their heads in the style made famous in the 1970s by "The Coneheads" of the original *Saturday Night Live* television show. They called their little spot in the upper deck "Cone's Co'ner." The pitcher, whom *The Jerusalem Post* had insisted upon interviewing a year earlier because they couldn't believe he wasn't Jewish, began to discover the price of fame.

"I'm having lunch in this fancy French restaurant, where I'm pretty sure they don't know who I am," said Cone in September. "Then the waiter comes to the table and he's wearing a cone."

Conehead-mania reached a fever pitch when Dave reeled off seven wins in as many starts between Aug. 23 to Sept. 25 to raise his season mark to 19-3. He needed one more victory to join Tom Seaver, Jerry Koosman and Gooden as the only 20-game winners in Met history and to tie Seaver's club record for consecutive victories by a pitcher. He even had a shot at the ERA title—if he could shut out the Cards Sept. 30—but had to settle for a 4-2 victory instead. He had his 20—exactly one-fifth the win total that his playoff-bound team achieved in the regular season.

Just before the postseason began in Los Angeles, Cone accepted a gig as a guest columnist for the tabloid *New York Daily News*, figuring it would be a useful experience for him because he'd always wanted to be a sportswriter in the days before he became a sports star. It turned out to be a mistake more glaring than any he had committed on the mound for a long time.

Someone forgot to tell the kid from Kansas City that he should be careful about what he said to his ghostwriter. After the Mets' dramatic 3-2 Game 1 victory on a ninth-inning rally capped by a Gary Carter hit off Jay Howell, Cone ridiculed the Dodger relief ace for throwing so many curves, calling him "a high school pitcher."

It was in print the next day and on the Dodger bulletin board, courtesy of manager Tom Lasorda. Cone, who got paid for the column by the newspaper, got paid back for what he said by the Dodgers, who rallied around the rag and pummelled him for five runs in only four innings of what became a 6-3 Met defeat in Game 2.

"I take full responsibility for what I said," said Cone before ending his postseason writing career the next day. "For me to belittle an outstanding pitcher like Jay Howell . . . I would not do that. I didn't mean to offend anybody. I said those things facetiously. It was a lack of communication of my part with the writer."

When he got a chance to redeem himself in Game 6, he shook free of a first-inning jam and kept the Mets alive with a 5-1, five-hit, complete-game victory. "It was the biggest game of my career," said Cone. Added teammate Bobby Ojeda, "He knew it was do or die."

The next night, in Game 7, the Mets died. Cone soon left for a postseason tour of Japan with other major-league stars, bringing with him the memories of a season in which he was a singular sensation.

"It seems like everything came out of nowhere," he reflected. "I was a Royals' pitcher, then I was a Mets' pitcher, a reliever and spot starter type. Then I was in the rotation. And now we've got Coneheads in the stands.

"I've always had the same type of stuff I have now. Ability has never been a question. It's always been the mental part and the experience part. With the Royals, I never got the chance to get the experience. They knew I had potential, but they weren't sure I could put the mental and the physical together . . . Coming to New York and being able to be around guys like Darling, Gooden and Ojeda and having Mel Stottlemyre [as a pitching coach] is a very positive influence. You can't help but learn."

And Cone was a quick study.

STUNNING, SILLY SIGNIFICANT STATS

By MARTY NOBLE

By now our memories have been saturated with certain numbers produced during the 1988 season. We are overfamiliar with the significance of number 59 as it relates to the accomplishments of Orel Hershiser. We now associate 40-40 with Jose Canseco as readily as we pair 20-20 with eyesight. And who among us can see 0-21 and not relate it to the season-opening losing streak that distinguished the O-rioles from every other major-league team in history?

Even casual fans are aware of those numbers and know who won the batting titles and home-run championships and perhaps which pitchers allowed the fewest walks. You might even know journeyman infielder Jim Morrison pitched 3⅔ innings for the Braves in three appearances and allowed no runs; that Oil Can Boyd allowed 25 home runs in 129⅓ innings and wasn't the most generous pitcher on the Red Sox staff; and that the Twins completed as many triple plays (2) as the other 25 teams combined.

Baseball always produces seas of statistics on an annual basis. But, in recent years, with computers facilitating procedures, all sorts of new, esoteric and sometimes bewildering stats have been developed.

What follows is a mixture of statistics produced last season.

Some are stunning. Did you know, for example, that Ozzie Smith committed 22 errors, only seven fewer than the two shortstops who led the NL in errors?

Some are silly. Mets' left fielder Kevin McReynolds was rated lower than the Reds' Kal Daniels among NL outfielders in the complex ranking statistics produced for major-league baseball.

And some are significant. Did you know that the Mets' pitchers nearly outhit the Rangers' designated hitters?

Between innings, Newsday *baseball writer Marty Noble voyages in a sea of statistics and a trove of trivia.*

Cards' Ozzie Smith committed un-Wizardly 22 errors.

E-GADS

We've all heard a manager explain his team's hitting streak by saying "hitting is contagious." But can defense be catching? Apparently, poor defense can be. With the Braves' infield, not catching is contagious.

Braves' first baseman Gerald Perry, second baseman Ron Gant and shortstop Andres Thomas either led the NL or tied for the league leadership in errors at their respective positions.

The league leaders at all positions follow:

National League

Pitcher—Doug Drabek, Pirates, 6
Orel Hershiser, Dodgers, 6
Dennis Martinez, Expos, 6

Catcher—Benito Santiago, Padres, 12
First base—Mark Grace, Cubs, 17
Gerald Perry, Braves, 17
Third base—Bobby Bonilla, Pirates, 32
Shortstop—Barry Larkin, Reds, 29
Andres Thomas, Braves, 29
Outfield—Kirk Gibson, Dodgers, 12
Candy Maldonado, Giants, 10
Phil Bradley, Phillies, 9
Vince Coleman, Cardinals, 9
Willie McGee, Cardinals, 9
Darryl Strawberry, Mets, 9

American League

Pitcher—Jack McDowell, White Sox, 5
Jeff Russell, Rangers, 5
Dave Stewart, Athletics, 5
Catcher—Andy Allanson, Indians, 11
Don Slaught, Yankees, 11
First base—Willie Upshaw, Indians, 12
Second base—Harold Reynolds, Mariners, 18
Third base—Kevin Seitzer, Royals, 26
Shortstop—Dale Sveum, Brewers, 27
Outfield—Chili Davis, Angels, 19
George Bell, Blue Jays, 15
Rickey Henderson, Yankees, 12

E-NOUGH

As poor as the Braves' infield defense was, it wasn't a liability compared to the handicap that third-base defense was to the White Sox. The White Sox were guilty of a whopping 46 E-5s.

Contributors to that defensive breakdown were Steve Lyons (25), Carlos Martinez (14), Kenny Williams (14), Donnie Hill (2) and Kelly Paris (1).

CASE OF THE RUNS

You might have known that the Expos' Otis Nixon began the 1988 season as the only player in the majors who had more career runs than hits. But did you know that, in September, his brother Donell of the Giants put together a streak of four games in which his boxscore line was 0-1-0-0? That's no at-bats, one run, no hits and no RBI.

THE LATE SHOW

Sometimes it was a lament and sometimes Mets' manager Davey Johnson made the observation proudly: "We don't score until after 10 o'clock." Davey was right. The Mets were definitely at their best late in games. They were an after-hours club.

Indeed, no one should have been surprised when the Mets scored three times in the ninth inning to win Game 1 of the NLCS playoffs. During the season, they had scored 79 runs in the ninth inning, the most in the NL. What makes that figure more remarkable is that the Mets batted in the ninth inning only 114 times, which means they averaged .693 runs per ninth inning. Aside from the 14th inning—they scored twice in their only 14-inning game—the ninth was their most productive inning by far.

	R	Inn.	Runs/Inning
1st	77	160	.481
2nd	66	160	.412
3rd	57	160	.356
4th	69	160	.431
5th	83	160	.519
6th	93	160	.581
7th	81	159	.509
8th	83	159	.522
9th	79	114	.693
10th	6	14	.429
11th	4	6	.667
12th	1	6	.167
13th	2	4	.500
14th	2	1	2.000
Totals	703	1409	.499

(Note: Inn. represents the number of times the Mets batted in a particular inning. They played 160 games. One was ended after six innings because of rain. They batted in the ninth inning in 114 games, in the 10th in 14 games, in the 11th in six games, in the 12th in six games, in the 13th in four games and in the 14th in two games.)

FEAST AND FAMINE

No, this is not a line score left over from the 1945 World

Series. It is a comparison of the runs the Tigers scored in nine innings against the White Sox May 20 and the runs the Cubs scored in nine games May 11-20.

Tigers	211	043	030	—	14
Cubs	122	120	112	—	12

NO OFFENSE

The word offense often was spelled with a zero rather than a O last season. Production was down dramatically throughout the game. The average major-league batting average for 1988 was .254, nine points lower than in 1987. Only five teams—the Red Sox, Angels, Twins, Yankees and Athletics—compiled 1988 averages higher than their '87 marks. And 16 teams experienced drops of more than 10 points.

No team equalled its run production of 1987 and the Blue Jays were the only team that experienced an increase in earned-run average. The average major-league ERA decreased from 4.28 in 1987 to 3.72 last season. Strange, isn't it, that the lower ERA was accomplished while strikeouts also decreased?

The following chart illustrates the decline in offense in four telling categories and also shows the decline in strikeouts.

National League

Year	BA	Runs	HR	Total Bases	SO
1987	.261	8,771	1,824	26,743	11,651
1988	.248	7,522	1,279	23,772	11,032
Pct. of Decline	4.98%	14.24%	29.88%	11.11%	5.36%

American League

Year	BA	Runs	HR	Total Bases	SO
1987	.265	11,112	2,634	33,111	13,442
1988	.259	9,858	1,901	30,079	12,324
Pct. of Decline	2.26%	11.29%	27.83%	9.16%	8.32%

BRIDESMAIDS WEAR RED

The Reds placed second in the NL West for the fourth successive season. They might have won a division championship in one of those seasons if they had fared better against the eventual champion. Consider Cincinnati's records against the teams it had to beat:

1985—7-11 vs. Dodgers
1986—4-14 vs. Astros
1987—7-11 vs. Giants
1988—7-11 vs. Dodgers

NO-CAL DIET

On April 9, Orioles' manager Cal Ripken ordered pitcher Mark Williamson to intentionally walk Willie Upshaw of the Indians and load the bases. That brought up Pat Tabler, who at the time had a career BA of .527 with the bases loaded. Even worse, Ripken allowed Williamson to face Tabler. In 1987, Williamson allowed eight hits with the bases loaded: the most in baseball.

The results: Tabler singled. And Ripken was fired.

ALMOSTS

The Cubs fell just short of leading the NL in complete games. They pitched 30, one less than the Mets and two fewer than the Dodgers. The last time the Cubs led the league in complete games was 1971, when Ferguson Jenkins pitched 30 and the Cubs had a total of 75 . . . By allowing 404 walks last season, the Mets just missed becoming the fourth post-expansion team to strike out more than 1,000 and walk fewer than 400. The last team to do so was the 1967 Twins (1,089 strikeouts, 396 walks). The Mets struck out 1,100.

ODDS 'N ENDS

The Astros, White Sox and Rangers didn't have a player bat as high as .280 (400 at-bats minimum) . . . The NL East compiled a 214-213 record against the West, despite the Phillies' 25-46 record against the West . . . The Zero Factor: The Blue Jays led the AL with 17 shutouts and they were shut out the fewest times in the league (3) . . . The Mariners' Harold Reynolds led the AL in stolen bases in 1987 with 60 in 80 attempts. He was thrown out 29 times in 64 attempts last season . . . The Rangers' designated hitters combined to bat .197, one point higher than the Mets' pitchers.

Brave first baseman Gerald Perry was the first to accomplish this dubious triple double: 10 caught stealing, 10 errors and 10 GIDPs (grounded into double plays). He completed the feat in the third week of August . . . The Rangers' Bobby Valentine was ejected four times last season and has been ejected 17 times in his managerial career by 17 different umpires . . . When infielder Jeff

Kunkel pitched for the Rangers Aug. 31, he became the first non-pitcher ever to pitch for the Washington-Texas franchise. The Mets are the only existing major-league franchise that has never used a non-pitcher to pitch.

Not until the Phillies defeated the Cardinals Aug. 11 did every team have a victory on every day of the week . . . The White Sox' Kelly Paris was a high school teammate of Milwaukee's Robin Yount. Yount hit his first major-league home run in 1974. Paris hit his last August . . . Andre Dawson became the first player in history to hit 10 or more home runs and steal 10 or more bases in 12 consecutive seasons . . . The Dodgers were the only team not to lose more than four straight games.

Philadelphia's Juan Samuel, Von Hayes and Mike Schmidt had a total of 84 home runs in 1987 and 30 last season . . . The Indians had a 36-21 record June 8 and finished six games under .500 . . . The Rangers' Jeff Russell allowed three grand slams last season, two in Boston, by Mike Greenwell and Ellis Burks, and one by Darryl Boston of the White Sox . . . The Cardinals didn't score in their first 25 extra innings last year.

Frequent fliers: From April 1 through May 1, the Cubs traveled 9,461 miles as a team . . . Vince Coleman of the Cardinals and Gerald Young of the Astros, who placed first and second respectively in NL stolen bases, shared the league leadership in being caught (27 times each) . . . The Padres committed 60 fewer balks than the A's . . . The Giants batted .000 in 35 at-bats against Met reliever Randy Myers . . . One year after establishing a record for most grand slams in a season (6), the Yankees' Don Mattingly matched the record for least grand slams (0).

In the 43 years of post-World War II baseball, four players have batted higher than .350, with 200 or more hits, 40 or more doubles, 20 or more home runs, 100 or more RBI and 100 or more runs—Mattingly in 1986, Henry Aaron in 1959, Stan Musial in 1948 and the Twins' Kirby Puckett last year . . . Puckett's .356 average was the highest by an AL player since 1941, when Joe DiMaggio batted .357 . . . The Giants' Will Clark was walked intentionally 27 times, an NL high. The Mariners received 24 intentional walks.

THE TOP 25

0—The number of game-winning RBI produced by Cub outfielder Rafael Palmeiro.

1—The number of NL players with 100 or more walks (Giants' Will Clark, 100).

2—The number of Yankee managers fired in 1988.

3—The highest total of grand slams by a single player (Royal outfielder Danny Tartabull).

4—The number of voters who omitted the Mets' Kevin McReynolds from their NL MVP ballots.

5—The number of errors committed by Blue Jay pitchers, the lowest total in the majors.

6—The number of successive shutouts by Orel Hershiser during The Streak.

7—The number of categories in which Oriole pitchers placed last in the AL (victories, ERA, saves, innings pitched, runs allowed, earned runs and strikeouts.)

8—The number of unintentional walks drawn by Cub shortstop Shawon Dunston. That's the fewest ever by a player who appeared at least 150 games.

9—The Cardinals' Jose Oquendo has now played all nine positions after catching against the Mets last October.

10—The longest winning streak by a pitcher in the NL (Astros' Juan Agosto).

11—The highest total of pinch-hit RBI in the AL (Royals' Bill Buckner).

12—The Cardinals' rank in total bases in the NL.

13—The highest total of pinch-hit RBI in the NL (Expos' Graig Nettles).

14—The Orioles' rank in AL in average, runs, hits, total bases, doubles, RBI and slugging percentage.

15—Cub Greg Maddux' victory total at All-Star break.

16—The number of balks called on the Athletics' Dave Stewart and the entire Padres' staff.

17—The number of AL players batting higher than .300. The NL had four.

18—Greg Maddux' final victory total.

19—The difference between the A's league-leading balk total (76) and the second-highest total (the Rangers' 57).

20—(Actually 19$\frac{1}{2}$ rounded off) The total games behind of the five teams that finished behind Boston in the AL East.

21—The number of grand slams hit in the NL (19 fewer than in the AL).

22—The number of consecutive games in which the Indians' Julio Franco hit safely, the AL high. The second-highest streak in the league was 21, also by Franco.

23—The number of times Boston's Wade Boggs grounded into double plays, the AL high.

24—Brave Dale Murphy's NL-leading total of GIDP (grounded into double plays).

25—The Braves' NL-low saves total.

INSIDE THE NATIONAL LEAGUE

By BOB HERTZEL and BARRY BLOOM
Pittsburgh Press *San Diego Tribune*

PREDICTED ORDER OF FINISH

East	West
New York Mets	San Diego Padres
Montreal Expos	Cincinnati Reds
St. Louis Cardinals	Los Angeles Dodgers
Pittsburgh Pirates	San Francisco Giants
Chicago Cubs	Houston Astros
Philadelphia Phillies	Atlanta Braves

Playoff winner: San Diego

EAST DIVISION		Owner		Morning Line Manager
1	**METS** Orange, white & blue Always the horse to beat	N. Doubleday/F. Wilpon	1988 W 100 L 60	2-1 Davey Johnson
2	**EXPOS** Scarlet, white & royal blue Making strides	Charles Bronfman	1988 W 81 L 81	3-1 Buck Rodgers
3	**CARDINALS** Red & white Dangerous when healthy	August A. Busch Jr.	1988 W 76 L 86	7-2 Whitey Herzog
4	**PIRATES** Old gold, white & black Losing ground by standing still	Douglas Danforth	1988 W 85 L 75	8-1 Jim Leyland
5	**CUBS** Royal blue & white Still lack the horsepower	Tribune Co.	1988 W 77 L 85	20-1 Don Zimmer
6	**PHILLIES** Crimson & white Not a contender	Bill Giles	1988 W 65 L 96	80-1 Nick Leyva

METS will go wire-to-wire if they stay hungry. **EXPOS** make real run, along with resurgent **CARDS.** Young **BUCS** fall out of the money. **CUBS** can't muster closing kick. **PHILS** get lapped.

Coast-To-Coast Stakes

113th Running. National League Race. Distance: 162 games plus playoff. Payoff (based on '88): $108,665 per winning player, World Series; $86,221 per losing player, World Series. A field of 12 entered in two divisions.

Track Record: 116 wins—Chicago, 1906

WEST DIVISION		Owner		Morning Line Manager
1	**PADRES** New blood makes them favorite	Joan Kroc Brown, gold & white	1988 W 83 L 78	**2-1** Jack McKeon
2	**REDS** Seems like their spot	Marge Schott Red & white	1988 W 87 L 74	**3-1** Pete Rose
3	**DODGERS** Can't reenact last run	Peter O'Malley Royal blue & white	1988 W 94 L 67	**4-1** Tommy Lasorda
4	**GIANTS** Slippin' and slidin'	Bob Lurie White, orange & black	1988 W 83 L 79	**15-1** Roger Craig
5	**ASTROS** Going backwards	John McMullen Orange & white	1988 W 82 L 80	**25-1** Art Howe
6	**BRAVES** Ready for glue factory	W. Bartholomay/S. Kasten Royal blue & white	1988 W 54 L 106	**200-1** Russ Nixon

PADRES, feeling their oats, will have what it takes to ward off hard-charging **DODGERS** and **REDS** in best race since 1982. **GIANTS** have lost too much ground. **ASTROS** and **BRAVES** will be left at the gate.

CHICAGO CUBS

TEAM DIRECTORY: Pres.-Chief Exec. Off.: Donald Grenesko; Exec. VP-Dir. Baseball Operations: Jim Frey; VP-Dir. Scouting: Gordon Goldsberry; VP-Adm.: E.R. Saltwell; Dir. Media Rel./ Publications: Ned Colletti; Trav. Sec.: Peter Durso; Mgr.: Don Zimmer. Home: Wrigley Field (39,600). Field distances: 355, l.f. line; 400, c.f.; 353, r.f. line. Spring training: Mesa, Ariz.

SCOUTING REPORT

HITTING: The Cubs traded Rafael Palmeiro, the NL's second-leading hitter, to the Rangers, which one might expect would weaken the offense, but that may not be the case. Palmeiro went through last season without a game-winning RBI and drove in only 53 runs, despite a .307 average. Whoever wins the job in left figures to be at least that productive.

The Cubs felt secure in trading Palmeiro because first baseman Mark Grace (.296, 7, 57) showed so much promise in finishing second in NL Rookie of the Year voting. Besides, the heart of the Cubs' lineup remains intact and revolves around former NL MVPs Ryne Sandberg (.264, 19, 69) and Andre Dawson (.303, 24, 79), neither of whom had great seasons in 1988. Third baseman Vance Law proved to be a valuable addition in 1988, hitting .293 with 78 RBI, and Shawon Dunston (.249, 9, 56) figures to keep getting better.

PITCHING: The Cubs, who had the second-fewest number of saves in the NL last season with 29 after trading away former closer Lee Smith, tried to shore up their poor pen over the winter by acquiring young, hard-throwing left-hander Mitch Williams (2-7, 4.63, 18 saves) from the Rangers in the Palmeiro deal. Manager Don Zimmer plans to use Williams and Calvin Schiraldi (9-13, 4.38) out of the pen, along with the aging Goose Gossage (4-4, 4.33, 13 saves).

The starting rotation is built around former Cy Young Award winner Rick Sutcliffe (13-14, 3.86) and Greg Maddux (18-8, 3.18), who can become a Cy Young winner if he ever puts two halves of a season together. Last season, Maddux had 15 victories at the All-Star break, but won only three more the rest of the year. Left-hander Paul Kilgus (12-15, 4.16), who came over in the Texas trade, should replace the departed Jamie Moyer in the rotation.

Cubs' amazing Grace was rookie revelation at first.

DEFENSE: Although you don't hear much about it, the Cubs are one of the league's better defensive clubs. Sandberg annually wins the Gold Glove at second and Dawson generally wins one in right field. Catcher Damon Berryhill, whose development enabled the Cubs to deal Jody Davis, has an awesome throwing arm and Dunston, a remarkable shortstop, has an even more awesome one, if he ever learns to control it.

OUTLOOK: Some day, the Cubs are going to return to the World Series, but it will not be this year. They have assembled a nice mix of youngsters (Dunston, Grace, Berryhill and Maddux) and veterans (Sandberg, Dawson and Sutcliffe), but they still lack the talent of the Mets, the Expos and the Cards.

CHICAGO CUBS 1989 ROSTER

MANAGER Don Zimmer
Coaches—Joe Altobelli, Chuck Cottier, Larry Cox, Jose Martinez, Dick Pole

PITCHERS

No.	Name	1988 Club	W-L	IP	SO	ERA	B-T	Ht.	Wt.	Born
36	Bielecki, Mike	Iowa	3-2	55	50	2.63	R-R	6-3	195	7/31/59 Baltimore, MD
		Chicago (NL)	2-2	48	33	3.35				
51	Blankenship, Kevin	Greenville	13-9	177	127	2.34	R-R	6-0	185	1/26/63 Anaheim, CA
		Atl.-Chi. (NL)	1-1	16	9	4.60				
39	Boskie, Shawn	Winston-Salem	12-7	186	164	3.39	R-R	6-3	205	3/28/67 Hawthorne, NV
42	Coffman, Kevin	Atlanta	2-6	67	24	5.78	R-R	6-3	206	1/19/65 Austin, TX
		Richmond	1-1	19	18	4.19				
		Durham	1-1	10	10	4.50				
54	Gossage, Rich	Chicago (NL)	4-4	44	30	4.33	R-R	6-3	226	7/5/51 Colorado Springs, CO
22	Harkey, Mike	Pittsfield	9-2	86	73	1.37	R-R	6-5	220	10/25/66 San Diego, CA
		Iowa	7-2	79	62	3.55				
		Chicago (NL)	0-3	35	18	2.60				
—	Kilgus, Paul	Texas	12-15	203	88	4.16	L-L	6-1	175	2/2/62 Bowling Green, KY
50	Lancaster, Les	Chicago (NL)	4-6	86	36	3.78	R-R	6-2	200	4/21/62 Dallas, TX
31	Maddux, Greg	Chicago (NL)	18-8	249	140	3.18	R-R	6-0	170	4/14/66 San Angelo, TX
45	Nipper, Al	Chicago (NL)	2-4	80	27	3.04	R-R	6-0	194	4/2/59 San Diego, CA
37	Perry, Pat	Cin.-Chi. (NL)	4-4	59	35	4.14	L-L	6-1	190	2/4/59 Taylorville, IL
		Iowa	0-0	3	4	0.00				
41	Pico, Jeff	Iowa	5-2	68	40	2.24	R-R	6-2	170	2/12/66 Antioch, CA
		Chicago (NL)	6-7	113	57	4.15				
21	Sanderson, Scott	Chicago (NL)	1-2	15	6	5.28	R-R	6-5	200	7/22/56 Dearborn, MI
32	Schiraldi, Calvin	Chicago (NL)	9-13	166	140	4.38	R-R	6-4	200	6/16/62 Houston, TX
40	Sutcliffe, Rick	Chicago (NL)	13-14	226	144	3.86	L-R	6-7	215	6/21/56 Independence, MO
33	Wilkins, Dean	Pittsfield	5-7	72	59	1.63	R-R	6-1	170	8/24/66 Blue Island, IL
—	Williams, Mitch	Texas	2-7	68	61	4.63	L-L	6-4	200	11/17/64 Santa Ana, CA
—	Wilson, Steve	Tulsa	15-7	165	132	3.16	L-L	6-4	195	12/13/64 Canada

CATCHERS

No.	Name	1988 Club	H	HR	RBI	Pct.	B-T	Ht.	Wt.	Born
9	Berryhill, Damon	Iowa	16	2	11	.219	S-R	6-0	210	12/3/63 South Laguna, CA
		Chicago (NL)	80	7	38	.259				
7	Girardi, Joe	Pittsfield	97	7	41	.272	R-R	5-11	195	10/14/64 Peoria, IL
10	Mann, Kelly	Winston-Salem	84	8	40	.274	R-R	6-3	215	8/17/67 Santa Monica, CA
		Pittsfield	10	0	3	.196				
—	McClendon, Lloyd	Nashville	1	0	0	.143	R-R	5-11	195	1/11/59 Gary, IN
		Cincinnati	30	3	14	.219				

INFIELDERS

No.	Name	1988 Club	H	HR	RBI	Pct.	B-T	Ht.	Wt.	Born
12	Dunston, Shawon	Chicago (NL)	143	9	56	.249	R-R	6-1	175	3/21/63 Brooklyn, NY
17	Grace, Mark	Iowa	17	0	14	.254	L-L	6-2	190	6/28/64 Winston-Salem, NC
		Chicago (NL)	144	7	57	.296				
2	Law, Vance	Chicago (NL)	163	11	78	.293	R-R	6-1	190	10/1/56 Boise, ID
23	Sandberg, Ryne	Chicago (NL)	163	19	69	.264	R-R	6-2	180	9/18/59 Spokane, WA
16	Smith, Greg	Winston-Salem	101	4	29	.280	S-R	5-11	170	4/5/67 Baltimore, MD
11	Stephenson, Phil	Iowa	125	22	81	.293	L-L	6-1	195	9/19/60 Guthrie, OK
—	Wilkerson, Curtis	Texas	99	0	28	.293	S-R	5-9	160	4/26/61 Petersburg, VA

OUTFIELDERS

No.	Name	1988 Club	H	HR	RBI	Pct.	B-T	Ht.	Wt.	Born
29	Dascenzo, Doug	Iowa	149	6	49	.295	S-L	5-8	160	6/30/64 Cleveland, OH
		Chicago (NL)	16	0	4	.213				
8	Dawson, Andre	Chicago (NL)	179	24	79	.303	R-R	6-3	195	7/10/54 Miami, FL
30	Jackson, Darrin	Chicago (NL)	50	6	20	.266	R-R	6-0	185	8/22/63 Los Angeles, CA
—	May, Derrick	Winston-Salem	148	8	65	.305	L-R	6-4	210	7/14/68 Rochester, NY
15	Smith, Dwight	Iowa	148	9	48	.293	L-R	5-11	175	11/8/63 Tallahassee, FL
24	Varsho, Gary	Iowa	65	4	26	.278	L-R	5-11	190	6/20/61 Marshfield, WI
		Chicago (NL)	20	0	5	.274				
20	Walton, Jerome	Pittsfield	137	3	49	.331	R-R	6-1	175	7/8/65 Newnan, GA
28	Webster, Mitch	Mont.-Chi. (NL)	136	6	39	.260	S-L	6-1	185	5/16/59 Larned, KS

CUB PROFILES

ANDRE DAWSON 34 6-3 195 **Bats R Throws R**

Numbers were down from his 1987 NL MVP season standards, but then again they almost had to be . . . A .287 average with 49 homers and 137 RBI is one tough act to follow . . . Finished third in league in hitting at .303 last year, but slipped to 24 homers and 79 RBI . . . Second in NL in hits with 179 and in total bases with 298 . . . Right fielder has hit 10 or more homers and stolen 10 or more bases in each of last 12 seasons . . . Cubs signed him prior to 1987 season, after he had left Montreal as a free agent and received no offers . . . Wound up signing a blank contract with Cubs, because he wanted to play on natural grass, to ease the demands on his knees, and during the day, when he has been most productive . . . Nicknamed "Hawk" . . . Born July 11, 1954, in Miami, Fla. . . . Attended Florida A&M for three years . . . Expos' 11th-round pick in June 1975 draft . . . Enjoys deep-sea fishing.

Year	Club	Pos.	G	AB	R	H	2B	3B	HR	RBI	SB	Avg.
1976	Montreal	OF	24	85	9	20	4	1	0	7	1	.235
1977	Montreal	OF	139	525	64	148	26	9	19	65	21	.282
1978	Montreal	OF	157	609	84	154	24	8	25	72	28	.253
1979	Montreal	OF	155	639	90	176	24	12	25	92	35	.275
1980	Montreal	OF	151	577	96	178	41	7	17	87	34	.308
1981	Montreal	OF	103	394	71	119	21	3	24	64	26	.302
1982	Montreal	OF	148	608	107	183	37	7	23	83	39	.301
1983	Montreal	OF	159	633	104	189	36	10	32	113	25	.299
1984	Montreal	OF	138	533	73	132	23	6	17	86	13	.248
1985	Montreal	OF	139	529	65	135	27	2	23	91	13	.255
1986	Montreal	OF	130	496	65	141	32	2	20	78	18	.284
1987	Chicago (NL).....	OF	153	621	90	178	24	2	49	137	11	.287
1988	Chicago (NL).....	OF	157	591	78	179	31	8	24	79	12	.303
	Totals		1753	6840	996	1932	350	77	298	1054	276	.282

RYNE SANDBERG 29 6-2 180 **Bats R Throws R**

Generally considered the best second baseman in league . . . Won his sixth straight Gold Glove last year . . . Had rough start in 1988, but recovered to bat .264 with 19 homers and 69 RBI . . . Named NL MVP in 1984, when he hit .314 with 200 hits and led league with 114 runs . . . Born Sept. 18, 1959, in Spokane, Wash. . . . Signed a letter of intent to play football at Washington State just four days before signing a contract with Phillies, who had drafted him in the 20th round in June

1978 . . . Was part of trade that helped the Cubs win the NL East championship in 1984, as he and shortstop Larry Bowa went to Cubs for shortstop Ivan DeJesus prior to the 1982 season . . . Nicknamed "Ryno" and authored a book by that title after the 1984 season.

Year	Club	Pos.	G	AB	R	H	2B	3B	HR	RBI	SB	Avg.
1981	Philadelphia......	SS-2B	13	6	2	1	0	0	0	0	0	.167
1982	Chicago (NL).....	3B-2B	156	635	103	172	33	5	7	54	32	.271
1983	Chicago (NL).....	2B-SS	158	633	94	165	25	4	8	48	37	.261
1984	Chicago (NL).....	2B	156	636	114	200	36	19	19	84	32	.314
1985	Chicago (NL).....	2B-SS	153	609	113	186	31	6	26	83	54	.305
1986	Chicago (NL).....	2B	154	627	68	178	28	5	14	76	34	.284
1987	Chicago (NL).....	2B	132	523	81	154	25	2	16	59	21	.294
1988	Chicago (NL).....	2B	155	618	77	163	23	8	19	69	25	.264
	Totals		1077	4287	652	1219	201	49	109	473	235	.284

SHAWON DUNSTON 26 6-1 175 **Bats R Throws R**

Biggest problem has been living up to potential that forecast superstardom . . . Manager Don Zimmer has made him a personal project . . . Strikeout-walk ratio was one of game's worst, as he fanned 108 times and walked just 16 times (eight intentional) in 1988 . . . Got off to a fast start, especially in power categories, but did very little the second half, finishing with nine homers and a .249 batting average . . . Has one of strongest throwing arms of any shortstop and Cubs have been working on harnessing that sometimes erratic gun . . . After a senior season in high school that saw him steal 37 bases in 37 attempts and bat .790, he was first player selected in the June 1982 draft . . . Born March 21, 1963, in Brooklyn, N.Y.

Year	Club	Pos.	G	AB	R	H	2B	3B	HR	RBI	SB	Avg.
1985	Chicago (NL).....	SS	74	250	40	65	12	4	4	18	11	.260
1986	Chicago (NL).....	SS	150	581	66	145	36	3	17	68	13	.250
1987	Chicago (NL).....	SS	95	346	40	85	18	3	5	22	12	.246
1988	Chicago (NL).....	SS	155	575	69	143	23	6	9	56	30	.249
	Totals		474	1752	215	438	89	16	35	164	66	.250

MARK GRACE 24 6-2 190 **Bats L Throws R**

First baseman came out of nowhere to become one of the league's top rookies . . . Recalled from Iowa (AAA) May 2 to take Leon Durham's job . . . Was hitting .254 with no homers and 14 RBI in minors . . . Went on to bat .296 with seven homers and 57 RBI in first major-league season . . . His average was the highest by a Cub rookie since Bill Madlock batted .313 in 1974 . . . Was sixth in the league in hitting and on-base percentage (.371) . . . His 60 walks led the Cubs . . . Struck out just 43 times in 550 plate appearances . . . Collected first major-league hit off San Diego's Jimmy Jones on the day he was recalled and hit first major-league home run off Keith Comstock May 4 . . . Did not hit a home run at Wrigley Field . . . Was 24th-round draft pick in June 1985, out of San Diego State . . . Led the Midwest League in hitting with a .342 average at Peoria (A) in 1986, then won Eastern League MVP award for Pittsfield (AA) in 1987 . . . Born June 28, 1964, in Winston-Salem, N.C. . . . Idolizes Met first baseman Keith Hernandez and wears his number.

Year	Club	Pos.	G	AB	R	H	2B	3B	HR	RBI	SB	Avg.
1988	Chicago (NL)	1B	134	486	65	144	23	4	7	57	3	.296

DAMON BERRYHILL 25 6-0 210 **Bats S Throws R**

His progress allowed the Cubs to trade veteran catcher Jody Davis to the Braves for a pair of young pitching prospects late in 1988 . . . Batting .259 in first full major-league season with seven homers and 38 RBI . . . Owns extremely strong throwing arm . . . Threw out nearly 40 percent of would-be base-stealers in 1988 . . . Was an American Association All-Star at Iowa (AAA) in 1987, batting .287 and throwing out 50 of 120 would-be base-stealers . . . First major-league hit came off Cincinnati's Rob Murphy . . . Born Dec. 3, 1963, in South Laguna, Cal. . . . Originally picked by the White Sox in the 13th round of the January 1983 draft, but did not sign . . . Crosstown Cubs drafted him in the first round in January 1984, as the fourth player chosen overall . . . Attended Orange Coast College in Costa Mesa, Cal.

Year	Club	Pos.	G	AB	R	H	2B	3B	HR	RBI	SB	Avg.
1987	Chicago (NL)	C	12	28	2	5	1	0	0	1	0	.179
1988	Chicago (NL)	C	95	309	19	80	19	1	7	38	1	.259
	Totals		107	337	21	85	20	1	7	39	1	.252

GREG MADDUX 22 6-0 170 **Bats R Throws R**

Spectacular first half put him on NL All-Star team . . . Was 15-4 at the All-Star break, but ran out of gas in second half, just as he did in 1987, when he was youngest player in league . . . Finished the 1988 season with an 18-8 record, so he won just three games after break . . . In 1987, he was 1-7 after the All-Star break . . . His 3.18 ERA was best among Cubs starters last year . . . Selected by Cubs in second round of June 1984 draft . . . Younger brother of Phillies' Mike Maddux, whom he outdueled, 8-3, Sept. 29, 1986, in first brother pitching confrontation in majors since the Niekros had faced each other in 1982 . . . Born April 14, 1966, in San Angelo, Tex.

Year	Club	G	IP	W	L	Pct.	SO	BB	H	ERA
1986	Chicago (NL)	6	31	2	4	.333	20	11	44	5.52
1987	Chicago (NL)	30	155⅔	6	14	.300	101	74	181	5.61
1988	Chicago (NL)	34	249	18	8	.692	140	81	230	3.18
	Totals	70	435⅔	26	26	.500	261	166	455	4.21

MITCH WILLIAMS 24 6-4 200 Bats L Throws L

Cubs counting on him to be closer . . . Acquired from Rangers with Paul Kilgus, Steve Wilson, Curtis Wilkerson and two minor leaguers for Rafael Palmeiro, Jamie Moyer and Drew Hall in December . . . Despite ragged finish, he led Rangers last year with 18 saves in 27 chances . . . Converted first nine save chances through May 14 . . . Did not earn a save after Aug. 27, failing in final three opportunities . . . Ranked third in AL with 67 appearances last year, giving him league-leading 232 appearances over the last three years . . . Walked 479 batters in 504 minor-league innings, leading to 28-36 minor-league mark . . . Born Nov. 17, 1964, in Santa Ana, Cal. . . . Originally drafted by Padres in eighth round in June 1982.

Year	Club	G	IP	W	L	Pct.	SO	BB	H	ERA
1986	Texas	80	98	8	6	.571	90	79	69	3.58
1987	Texas	85	108⅔	8	6	.571	129	94	63	3.23
1988	Texas	67	68	2	7	.222	61	47	48	4.63
	Totals	232	274⅔	18	19	.486	280	220	180	3.70

RICK SUTCLIFFE 32 6-7 215 Bats L Throws R

When the topic of conversation is the top pitchers in the game, this guy is seldom mentioned, but he should be . . . Won NL Rookie of the Year honors in 1979, the AL ERA title in 1982, the NL Cy Young Award in 1984 and the NL Comeback Player of the Year Award in 1987, when he narrowly missed a second Cy Young endorsement . . . Last season, he struggled to a 13-14 record with a 3.86 ERA and was the subject of numerous trade rumors . . . Has won the Roberto Clemente Award for humanitarian service . . . Born June 21, 1956, in Independence, Mo., and still makes his home there . . . Came from Indians with Ron Hassey and George Frazier for Mel Hall, Joe Carter, Don Schulze and Darryl Banks, June 13, 1984 . . . Notoriously slow worker, particularly when he is concentrating on holding a runner close . . . Originally drafted by Dodgers as 21st player taken overall in June 1974.

Year	Club	G	IP	W	L	Pct.	SO	BB	H	ERA
1976	Los Angeles	1	5	0	0	.000	3	1	2	0.00
1978	Los Angeles	2	2	0	0	.000	0	1	2	0.00
1979	Los Angeles	39	242	17	10	.630	117	97	217	3.46
1980	Los Angeles	42	110	3	9	.250	59	55	122	5.56
1981	Los Angeles	14	47	2	2	.500	16	20	41	4.02
1982	Cleveland	34	216	14	8	.636	142	98	174	2.96
1983	Cleveland	36	243⅓	17	11	.607	160	102	251	4.29
1984	Cleveland	15	94⅓	4	5	.444	58	46	111	5.15
1984	Chicago (NL).	20	150⅓	16	1	.941	155	39	123	2.69
1985	Chicago (NL).	20	130	8	8	.500	102	44	119	3.18
1986	Chicago (NL).	28	176⅔	5	14	.263	122	96	166	4.64
1987	Chicago (NL).	34	237⅓	18	10	.643	174	106	223	3.68
1988	Chicago (NL).	32	226	13	14	.481	144	70	232	3.86
	Totals	317	1880	117	92	.560	1252	775	1783	3.83

CALVIN SCHIRALDI 26 6-4 200 Bats R Throws R

Key man in major trade with Boston Red Sox at winter meetings of 1987, but he did not live up to expectations . . . Cubs gave up Lee Smith to obtain this tall right-hander and Al Nipper . . . Managed to go just 9-13 with a 4.38 ERA, splitting time between the rotation and the bullpen . . . Did strike out 140 in 166.1 innings . . . Born June 16, 1962, in Houston . . . First-round pick of the Mets in June 1983 draft . . . Went to Boston in multi-player exchange for Bob Ojeda prior to 1986 season . . . In 1983, he helped Texas into College World Series with 12-1 record and was MVP as Longhorns won NCAA title . . . Had nightmarish 1986 World Series vs. former Met teammates.

Year	Club	G	IP	W	L	Pct.	SO	BB	H	ERA
1984	New York (NL)	5	17⅓	0	2	.000	16	10	20	5.71
1985	New York (NL)	10	26⅓	2	1	.667	21	11	43	8.89
1986	Boston	25	51	4	2	.667	55	15	36	1.41
1987	Boston	62	83⅔	8	5	.615	93	40	75	4.41
1988	Chicago (NL).	29	166⅓	9	13	.409	140	63	166	4.38
	Totals	131	344⅔	23	23	.500	325	139	340	4.36

TOP PROSPECT

TY GRIFFIN 21 5-10 175 Bats S Throws R

Gained greatest fame when he hit two-run homer with two out in bottom of ninth inning to lift Team USA to victory over Cuba in 1987 Pan Am Games . . . Cubs' No. 1 draft selection in June 1988, after All-American career at Georgia Tech . . . Did not play professionally, opting to compete in the Olympics . . . In 53-game tour leading up to Olympics, this second baseman led Team USA with .416 average, 16 home runs, 52 RBI, 21 steals and 69 runs . . . In the Olympics, he helped the U.S. to the gold medal by hitting .333 with two homers, four RBI and three steals . . . Born Sept. 5, 1967, in Ft. Campbell, Ky., but raised in Tampa, Fla. . . . As a junior, he led ACC with 38 steals and set school record with 127 for career.

MANAGER DON ZIMMER: Entering his 40th season in pro ball after leading Cubs to 77-85 finish in 1988 . . . Attended Cincinnati's Western Hills High School, which also produced Reds' manager Pete Rose, Braves' manager Russ Nixon and Zim's long-time friend, Cubs' GM Jim Frey . . . Managing his fourth major-league team, having already been in San Diego, Boston and Texas . . . His teams in Boston won 91 or more games for three straight years . . . His lifetime major-league managerial record is 697-685 . . . A third baseman during a 12-year career with the Dodgers, the original Mets, the Reds and the Senators . . . Finished playing career in 1966 with Japan . . . Had two career-threatening head injuries . . . Was beaned while in the minors by Columbus' Jim Kirk in 1953 and by Cincinnati's Hal Jeffcoat in 1956 . . . Has metal plate in his head . . . One of game's great characters with a round face that prompted pitcher Bill Lee to nickname him "The Gerbil" . . . Born Jan. 17, 1931, in Cincinnati.

GREATEST FIRST BASEMAN

By the 1960s, baseball had changed from a sport to a business. Night baseball had devoured the game, expansion had come and plastic grass had taken root. There remained, however, one bastion of real baseball—Wrigley Field. That was the place you could see day ball, played on grass, with an original team led by an American classic, Ernie Banks, who always greeted folks with a smile and by saying, "It's a beautiful day. Let's play two."

There were lots of beautiful days for Banks, who left the Negro Leagues as a 22-year-old shortstop in 1953 and became one of the game's greatest hitters with the Cubs.

Moved to first base midway through his career, he wound up hitting 512 home runs, tying Eddie Mathews for 12th on the all-time list. From 1957 through 1960, he averaged 44 homers per season. In 1958 and 1959, he was named the NL MVP.

ALL-TIME CUB SEASON RECORDS

BATTING: Rogers Hornsby, .380, 1929
HRs: Hack Wilson, 56, 1930
RBIs: Hack Wilson, 190, 1930
STEALS: Frank Chance, 67, 1903
WINS: Mordecai Brown, 29, 1908
STRIKEOUTS: Ferguson Jenkins, 274, 1970

MONTREAL EXPOS

TEAM DIRECTORY: Chairman: Charles Bronfman; Pres.-Chief Oper. Off.: Claude Brochu; VP-Baseball Oper.: Bill Stoneman; VP-Player Pers.: Dave Dombrowski; Publicists: Monique Giroux, Richard Griffin; Trav. Sec.: Erik Ostling; Mgr.: Buck Rodgers. Home: Olympic Stadium (59,149). Field distances: 325, l.f. line; 375, l.c.; 404, c.f.; 375, r.c.; 325, r.f. line. Spring training: West Palm Beach, Fla.

SCOUTING REPORT

HITTING: The Expos managed to do a lot of offseason wheeling and dealing without breaking up the heart of a productive lineup that should have been able to generate more than 628 runs last season.

Tim Raines (.270, 12, 48, 33 steals) remains the ultimate offensive player and should regain his form now that the shoulder problem that hampered him last season has been corrected by surgery. The Expos have awesome right-handed power in Andres Galarraga (.302, 29, 92), Hubie Brooks (.279, 20, 90) and Tim Wallach (.257, 12, 69), who is coming off a poor season. In an effort to locate some lefty punch, Mike Aldrete (.267, 3, 50) was acquired from the Giants for Tracy Jones last winter.

Unhappy with their shortstop situation, the Expos traded for the Red Sox' Spike Owen and, while he has some shortcomings, remember that Boston went to the World Series with Owen at short in 1986.

PITCHING: The Expos' 3.08 team ERA ranked third in the league last year and their pitching could be even better in 1989 with the addition of veteran Kevin Gross (12-14, 3.69) from the Phillies. This gives Montreal arguably the league's best rotation: Pascual Perez (12-8, 2.44), Dennis Martinez (15-13, 2.72), Bryn Smith (12-10, 3.00), Gross and 6-10 rookie Randy Johnson. Drug-plagued Floyd Youmans, sent to the Phils in the Gross deal, and promising John Dopson, traded to the Red Sox in the package for Owen, shouldn't be missed.

Montreal's bullpen did suffer somewhat with the dealing of Jeff Parrett to the Phils, but not too much. Manager Buck Rodgers likes to go with a bullpen-by-committee approach anyway and still has the perfect man to close in Tim Burke (3-5, 3.40, 18 saves). Andy McGaffigan and lefties Neal Heaton and Joe Hesketh provide better-than-adequate support.

Andres Galarraga hit .302, despite 153 strikeouts.

FIELDING: The Expos are neither the NL's best nor its worst defensive team. Galarraga may be the equal of Keith Hernandez at first and Wallach has no peer at third. However, up the middle, they are little more than average. Shortstop Owen must prove he can cover enough ground on Astroturf, while second basemen Johnny Paredes and Tim Foley, catchers Nelson Santovenia and Mike Fitzgerald and center fielders Dave Martinez and Otis Nixon are nothing special.

OUTLOOK: The Expos believe they can win this year and took steps during the offseason aimed at erasing their weaknesses. By adding a veteran starting pitcher in Gross and an established shortstop in Owen, Buck Rodgers' Expos should be ready to improve on last year's 81-81 finish. However, they still lack a left-handed power bat to balance Brooks, Galarraga and Wallach.

MONTREAL EXPOS 1989 ROSTER

MANAGER Buck Rodgers

Coaches—Larry Bearnarth, Ron Hansen, Rafael Landestoy, Ken Macha, Jackie Moore, Joe Sparks

PITCHERS

No.	Name	1988 Club	W-L	IP	SO	ERA	B-T	Ht.	Wt.	Born
44	Burke, Tim	Montreal	3-5	82	42	3.40	R-R	6-3	200	2/19/59 Omaha, NE
64	Bottenfield, Kent	West Palm Beach	10-8	181	120	3.33	S-R	6-3	215	11/4/68 Portland, OR
56	Gardner, Mark	Jacksonville	6-3	112	130	1.60	R-R	6-1	190	3/1/62 Los Angeles, CA
		Indianapolis	4-2	84	71	2.77				
—	Gross, Kevin	Philadelphia	12-14	232	162	3.69	R-R	6-5	215	6/8/61 Downey, CA
61	Harris, Gene	Jacksonville	9-5	127	103	2.63	R-R	5-11	190	12/5/64 Sebring, FL
26	Heaton, Neal	Montreal	3-10	97	43	4.99	L-L	6-1	195	3/3/60 Jamaica, NY
38	Hesketh, Joe	Indianapolis	0-0	11	16	3.27	L-L	6-2	170	2/15/59 Lackawanna, NY
		Montreal	4-3	73	64	2.85				
59	Holman, Brian	Indianapolis	8-1	91	70	2.36	R-R	6-4	185	1/25/65 Denver, CO
		Montreal	4-8	100	58	3.23				
51	Johnson, Randy	Indianapolis	8-7	113	111	3.26	R-L	6-10	225	9/10/63 Walnut Creek, CA
		Montreal	3-0	26	25	2.42				
63	Leon, Danilo	Jamestown	10-3	116	100	1.16	R-R	6-1	150	4/3/67 Venezuela
		West Palm Beach	0-0	14	15	3.21				
32	Martinez, Dennis	Montreal	15-13	235	120	2.72	R-R	6-1	183	5/14/55 Nicaragua
27	McGaffigan, Andy	Montreal	6-0	91	71	2.76	R-R	6-3	190	10/25/56 West Palm Beach, FL
47	Pacillo, Pat	Nash.-Ind.	3-4	75	62	3.86	R-R	6-2	210	7/23/63 Jersey City, NJ
		Cincinnati	1-0	11	11	5.06				
34	Perez, Pascual	Montreal	12-8	188	131	2.44	R-R	6-3	180	5/17/57 Dominican Republic
39	Sauveur, Rich	Jacksonville	0-2	7	8	4.05	L-L	6-4	170	11/23/63 Arlington, VA
		Indianapolis	7-4	81	58	2.43				
		Montreal	0-0	3	3	6.00				
28	Smith, Bryn	Montreal	12-10	198	122	3.00	R-R	6-2	200	8/11/55 Marietta, GA
46	Valdez, Sergio	Indianapolis	5-4	84	61	3.43	R-R	6-1	190	9/7/65 Dominican Republic

CATCHERS

No.	Name	1988 Club	H	HR	RBI	Pct.	B-T	Ht.	Wt.	Born
20	Fitzgerald, Mike	Montreal	42	5	23	.271	R-R	5-11	190	7/13/60 Long Beach, CA
		Indianapolis	24	1	13	.250				
22	Santovenia, Nelson	Indianapolis	28	2	13	.308	R-R	6-3	220	7/27/61 Cuba
		Montreal	73	8	41	.236				

INFIELDERS

62	Blowers, Mike	Jacksonville	115	15	60	.250	R-R	6-2	190	4/24/65 Germany
16	Foley, Tom	Montreal	100	5	43	.265	L-R	6-1	180	9/9/59 Columbus, GA
14	Galarraga, Andres	Montreal	184	29	92	.302	R-R	6-3	235	6/18/61 Venezuela
25	Hudler, Rex	Indianapolis	71	7	25	.303	R-R	6-2	180	9/2/60 Tempe, AZ
		Montreal	59	4	14	.273				
15	Huson, Jeff	Jacksonville	118	0	34	.251	L-R	6-3	170	8/15/64 Scottsdale, AZ
		Montreal	13	0	3	.310				
6	Johnson, Wallace	Montreal	29	0	3	.309	S-R	5-11	185	12/25/56 Gary, IN
23	O'Malley, Tom	Oklahoma City	152	9	72	.291	L-R	6-0	190	12/25/60 Orange, NJ
		Montreal	7	0	2	.259				
—	Owen, Spike	Boston	64	5	18	.249	S-R	5-10	167	4/19/61 Cleburne, TX
5	Paredes, Johnny	Indianapolis	118	4	46	.295	R-R	5-11	165	9/2/62 Venezuela
		Montreal	17	1	10	.187				
29	Wallach, Tim	Montreal	152	12	69	.257	R-R	6-3	200	9/14/57 Huntington Park, CA

OUTFIELDERS

—	Aldrete, Mike	San Francisco	104	3	50	.267	L-L	5-11	185	1/29/61 Carmel, CA
7	Brooks, Hubie	Montreal	164	20	90	.279	R-R	6-0	190	9/24/56 Los Angeles, CA
57	Dean, Kevin	Jacksonville	127	7	48	.256	R-R	6-1	190	12/7/67 Vallejo, CA
60	Hernandez, Cesar	Rockford	101	19	60	.246	R-R	6-0	160	9/28/66 Dominican Republic
1	Martinez, Dave	Chi. (NL)-Mon.	114	6	46	.255	L-L	5-10	150	9/26/64 New York, NY
35	Nixon, Otis	Indianapolis	67	0	19	.285	S-R	6-2	180	1/9/59 Evergreen, NC
		Montreal	66	0	15	.244				
21	Powell, Alonzo	Indianapolis	74	4	39	.262	R-R	6-2	195	12/12/64 San Francisco, CA
30	Raines, Tim	Montreal	116	12	48	.270	S-R	5-8	180	9/16/59 Sanford, FL
55	Walker, Larry	Montreal	Injured				L-R	6-2	185	12/1/66 Canada

EXPO PROFILES

TIM RAINES 29 5-8 180 **Bats S Throws R**

A shoulder injury sabotaged, then curtailed his '88 season as he underwent surgery in September . . . Average fell to .270 last year after four consecutive .300-plus seasons . . . Left fielder won NL batting title in '86 . . . For the first time in his career, "Rock" stole fewer than 50 bases, finishing with 33 . . . As one of the free agents frozen out by owners' collusion, he did not re-sign with Expos until May 1, 1987. But he still went on to hit .330 and lead league with 123 runs . . . Born Sept. 16, 1959, in Sanford, Fla., he was the Expos' fifth-round draft choice in June 1977 . . . Led NL in steals from 1981-84 and is all-time leader in stolen-base percentage with .899 . . . Remains close friend of former teammate Andre Dawson . . . Brother Ned played in Giants' system for two years . . . One of the few switch-hitters equally dangerous from both sides.

Year	Club	Pos.	G	AB	R	H	2B	3B	HR	RBI	SB	Avg.
1979	Montreal	PR	6	0	3	0	0	0	0	0	2	.000
1980	Montreal	2B-OF	15	20	5	1	0	0	0	0	5	.050
1981	Montreal	OF-2B	88	313	61	95	13	7	5	37	71	.304
1982	Montreal	OF-2B	156	647	90	179	32	8	4	43	78	.277
1983	Montreal	OF-2B	156	615	133	183	32	8	11	71	90	.298
1984	Montreal	OF-2B	160	622	106	192	38	9	8	60	75	.309
1985	Montreal	OF	150	575	115	184	30	13	11	41	70	320
1986	Montreal	OF	151	580	91	194	35	10	9	62	70	.334
1987	Montreal	OF	139	530	123	175	34	8	18	68	50	.330
1988	Montreal	OF	109	429	66	116	19	7	12	48	33	.270
	Totals		1130	4331	793	1319	233	70	78	430	544	.305

ANDRES GALARRAGA 27 6-3 235 **Bats R Throws R**

"The Cat" merits his nickname as he is extremely quick and agile for a big man . . . Emerged from the shadows to become the best player on the Expos in 1988 . . . Had MVP-type season with a .302 average, 99 runs, 92 RBI and 29 home runs and earned an All-Star berth for the first time . . . Must cut down on strikeouts, which numbered 153 in 609 at-bats last year . . . Relaxes by painting . . . His defensive prowess as a right-handed first baseman prompted Cards' manager Whitey Herzog to compare him to the late Gil Hodges . . . Born June 18, 1961, in Caracas, Venezuela . . . Signed as free agent by Felipe Alou in January 1979 . . . At that time, some scouts thought this

17-year-old power-hitting prodigy was too fat to play professionally.

Year	Club	Pos.	G	AB	R	H	2B	3B	HR	RBI	SB	Avg.
1985	Montreal	1B	24	75	9	14	1	0	2	4	1	.187
1986	Montreal	1B	105	321	39	87	13	0	10	42	6	.271
1987	Montreal	1B	147	551	72	168	40	3	13	90	7	.305
1988	Montreal	1B	157	609	99	184	42	8	29	92	13	.302
	Totals		433	1556	219	453	96	11	54	228	27	.291

TIM WALLACH 31 6-3 200 **Bats R Throws R**

Never really recovered from a slow start and finished with a .257 average, only 12 homers and 69 RBI . . . One year earlier, he had established himself as league's premier third baseman with 26 homers and a club-record 123 RBI to go with a .298 average . . . Hard-nosed guy who has played in more than 150 games in six of last seven seasons . . . Expos' first-round draft pick and 10th player taken overall in June 1979 draft, after being named the Sporting News Collegiate Player of the Year at Cal State-Fullerton . . . Never played third base before turning pro . . . One of the NL's best defensive third basemen, but he committed 18 errors last year . . . Born Sept. 14, 1957, in Huntington Park, Cal. . . . Expos traded productive veteran Larry Parrish to make room for him in spring 1982.

Year	Club	Pos.	G	AB	R	H	2B	3B	HR	RBI	SB	Avg.
1980	Montreal	OF-1B	5	11	1	2	0	0	1	2	0	.182
1981	Montreal	OF-1B-3B	71	212	19	50	9	1	4	13	0	.236
1982	Montreal	3B-OF-1B	158	596	89	160	31	3	28	97	6	.268
1983	Montreal	3B	156	581	54	156	33	3	19	70	0	.269
1984	Montreal	3B-SS	160	582	55	143	25	4	18	72	3	.246
1985	Montreal	3B	155	569	70	148	36	3	22	81	9	.260
1986	Montreal	3B	134	480	50	112	22	1	18	71	8	.233
1987	Montreal	3B-P	153	593	89	177	42	4	26	123	9	.298
1988	Montreal	3B	159	592	52	152	32	5	12	69	2	.257
	Totals		1152	4216	479	1100	230	24	148	598	37	.261

HUBIE BROOKS 32 6-0 190 **Bats R Throws R**

Rebounded from two injury-riddled seasons to become one of league's better power hitters . . . Injuries to left thumb and right wrist limited him to total of only 192 games in 1986 and 1987 . . . However, after being moved from shortstop to right field last year, he hit 20 homers and had 90 RBI in 151 games . . . Was shifted from third base to short after he was acquired from the Mets with Floyd Youmans, Mike Fitzgerald and Herm Winningham in the Gary Carter trade, following the 1984 season . . . In 1985, he became first 100-RBI shortstop in NL since Ernie Banks did it for Cubs in 1960 . . . Born Sept. 24,

1956, in Los Angeles . . . Starred at Arizona State, alongside Bob Horner, and Mets made him the third player selected in the June 1978 draft, behind Horner and Lloyd Moseby.

Year	Club	Pos.	G	AB	R	H	2B	3B	HR	RBI	SB	Avg.
1980	New York (NL)	3B	24	81	8	25	2	1	1	10	1	.309
1981	New York (NL)	3B-OF-SS	98	358	34	110	21	2	4	38	9	.307
1982	New York (NL)	3B	126	457	40	114	21	2	2	40	6	.249
1983	New York (NL)	3B-2B	150	586	53	147	18	4	5	58	6	.251
1984	New York (NL)	3B-SS	153	561	61	159	23	2	16	73	6	.283
1985	Montreal	SS	156	605	67	163	34	7	13	100	6	.269
1986	Montreal	SS	80	306	50	104	18	5	14	58	4	.340
1987	Montreal	SS	112	430	57	113	22	3	14	72	4	.263
1988	Montreal	OF	151	588	61	164	35	2	20	90	7	.279
	Totals		1050	3972	431	1099	194	28	89	539	49	.277

MIKE ALDRETE 28 5-11 185 Bats L Throws L

Acquired from Giants for Tracy Jones in December . . . Became Giants' starting left fielder June 8 last season, when Giants traded Jeff Leonard to Milwaukee for Earnest Riles, but that designation didn't last . . . Earned $160,000 in 1988, his second full year in majors . . . Hit .325 in limited 1987 action with nine homers and 51 RBI in 357 at-bats . . . Hit just .267 with three homers and 50 RBI in 389 at-bats last season . . . An adequate outfielder, he's not fast but he gets the job done . . . Born Jan. 29, 1961, in Carmel, Cal. . . . Giants' seventh selection in June 1983 draft . . . Can play all three outfield spots and first base, his natural position . . . Led Stanford to NCAA College World Series in 1982 . . . Brother Rich plays in Giants' system.

Year	Club	Pos.	G	AB	R	H	2B	3B	HR	RBI	SB	Avg.
1986	San Francisco	1B-OF	84	216	27	54	18	3	2	25	1	.250
1987	San Francisco	1B-OF	126	357	50	116	18	2	9	51	6	.325
1988	San Francisco	OF-1B	139	389	44	104	15	0	3	50	6	.267
	Totals		349	962	121	274	51	5	14	126	13	.285

PASCUAL PEREZ 31 6-3 180 Bats R Throws R

This animated veteran gets opposition angry with his hot-dogging antics on the mound, but he emerged as one of NL's best pitchers last season . . . Frustrates opponents with a blooper pitch and a hesitation pitch reminiscent of Satchel Paige . . . Went 12-8 and ranked among league ERA leaders with 2.44 mark . . . Famous for missing a start because he got lost driving to Fulton County Stadium back in his days with the Braves, he still wears a warmup jacket inscribed with "I-285", the road on which he was lost . . . Missed part of last season with a finger injury . . . Born May 17, 1957, in San Cristobal, Dominican Republic . . . Originally signed by Pirates as free agent in 1976 . . . Traded to Braves with Carlos Rios for Larry McWilliams, June 30, 1982 . . . Expos signed him to a minor-league contract in February 1987, following his release by Braves in April 1986 . . . Since joining Expos in August 1987, he has gone 19-8 . . . Brother Melido pitches for White Sox.

Year	Club	G	IP	W	L	Pct.	SO	BB	H	ERA
1980	Pittsburgh	2	12	0	1	.000	7	2	15	3.75
1981	Pittsburgh	17	86	2	7	.222	46	34	92	3.98
1982	Atlanta	16	79⅓	4	4	.500	29	17	85	3.06
1983	Atlanta	33	215⅓	15	8	.652	144	51	213	3.43
1984	Atlanta	30	211⅔	14	8	.636	145	51	208	3.74
1985	Atlanta	22	95⅓	1	13	.071	57	57	115	6.14
1987	Montreal	10	70⅓	7	0	1.000	58	16	52	2.30
1988	Montreal	27	188	12	8	.600	131	44	133	2.44
	Totals	157	958	55	49	.529	617	272	913	3.51

DENNIS MARTINEZ 33 6-1 183 Bats R Throws R

Recycled veteran has battled back from alcohol and shoulder problems to be as dominant a pitcher in the NL as he was with the Orioles when they were on top of the AL . . . This notoriously slow worker was Expos' top winner with hard-luck 15-13 record and 2.72 ERA . . . Obtained by Expos for Rene Gonzalez, June 16, 1986 . . . Like Tim Raines, he was a free agent prior to 1987 season and could not re-sign with Expos until May 1, but he stayed in shape by working out with Class-A Miami team . . . Originally signed as free agent by Baltimore in December 1973 . . . On Sept. 14, 1976, this curveballer became the first Nicaraguan-born player in major-league history, striking out the first three Detroit players he faced . . . Among the best-fielding pitchers in the league . . . Owns a tricky pickoff move . . . Born May 14, 1955, in Granada, Nicaragua . . . Represented Nicaragua in Amateur World Series in 1972 and 1973.

Year	Club	G	IP	W	L	Pct.	SO	BB	H	ERA
1976	Baltimore	4	28	1	2	.333	18	8	23	2.57
1977	Baltimore	42	167	14	7	.667	107	64	157	4.10
1978	Baltimore	40	276	16	11	.593	142	93	257	3.25
1979	Baltimore	40	292	15	16	.484	132	78	279	3.67
1980	Baltimore	25	100	6	4	.600	42	44	103	3.96
1981	Baltimore	25	179	14	5	.737	88	62	173	3.32
1982	Baltimore	40	252	16	12	.571	111	87	262	4.21
1983	Baltimore	32	153	7	16	.304	71	45	209	5.53
1984	Baltimore	34	141⅔	6	9	.400	77	37	145	5.02
1985	Baltimore	33	180	13	11	.542	68	63	203	5.15
1986	Baltimore	4	6⅔	0	0	.000	2	2	11	6.75
1986	Montreal	19	98	3	6	.333	63	28	103	4.59
1987	Montreal	22	144⅔	11	4	.733	84	40	133	3.30
1988	Montreal	34	235⅓	15	13	.536	120	55	215	2.72
	Totals	394	2253⅓	137	116	.542	1125	706	2273	3.97

KEVIN GROSS 27 6-5 215 **Bats R Throws R**

Acquired from Phils for Floyd Youmans and Jeff Parrett in December swap of right-handers . . . Specialized in close contests while leading Phils in wins last season . . . Twelve of his 34 starts were one-run decisions . . . Phils scored just 21 runs in his 14 losses, but 67 in his 12 wins . . . Suffered longest losing streak of career, six games, from Aug. 18-Sept. 13 . . . Pitched one inning for NL in All-Star Game . . . Most famous for being suspended after being caught with sandpaper in his glove, Aug. 10, 1987 . . . Born June 8, 1961, in Downey, Cal. . . . Phils' first pick in January 1981 secondary draft . . . Owns one of the best curves in the game . . . An accomplished artist, specializing in nature scenes, who has sold many of his paintings.

Year	Club	G	IP	W	L	Pct.	SO	BB	H	ERA
1983	Philadelphia	17	96	4	6	.400	66	35	100	3.56
1984	Philadelphia	44	129	8	5	.615	84	44	140	4.12
1985	Philadelphia	38	205⅔	15	13	.536	151	81	194	3.41
1986	Philadelphia	37	241⅔	12	12	.500	154	94	240	4.02
1987	Philadelphia	34	200⅔	9	16	.360	110	87	205	4.35
1988	Philadelphia	33	231⅔	12	14	.462	162	89	209	3.69
	Totals	203	1104⅔	60	66	.476	727	430	1088	3.87

TIM BURKE 30 6-3 200 **Bats R Throws R**

Lost closer's role for awhile, then regained it when Jeff Parrett was injured . . . Wound up leading Expos with 18 saves for second straight year and has career total of 48 . . . Had been extremely consistent before struggling at times last season . . . May have been best unknown pitcher in game in 1987, with 7-0 record and 1.19 ERA . . . Born Feb. 19, 1959, in Omaha, Neb. . . . Pirates' sixth-round draft pick in June 1980 . . . Traded to Yankees with Jose Rivera, John Holland and Jerry Aubin for Lee Mazzilli after the 1982 season . . . Came to Expos the following winter for outfielder Pat Rooney . . . Attended University of Nebraska.

Year	Club	G	IP	W	L	Pct.	SO	BB	H	ERA
1985	Montreal	78	120⅓	9	4	.692	87	44	86	2.39
1986	Montreal	68	101⅓	9	7	.563	82	46	103	2.93
1987	Montreal	55	91	7	0	1.000	58	17	64	1.19
1988	Montreal	61	82	3	5	.375	42	25	84	3.40
	Totals	262	394⅔	28	16	.636	269	132	337	2.46

BRYN SMITH 33 6-2 200 **Bats R Throws R**

One of the great comeback stories . . . Elbow problem almost ended his career in 1987, but he rebounded to win 10 games that year and had solid season last year, too, with 12-10 record and 3.00 ERA . . . Has outstanding control, walking only 32 and striking out 122 in 1988 . . . He is the only man to drive a ball out of Olympic Stadium in fair territory . . . The catch is it was a golf ball . . . He is a two-handicap player who wants to join the senior circuit when he turns 50 . . . His parents met while working at RKO Studios in Hollywood and were introduced to each other by Jane Russell. His mother, Meg, had been dating Cary Grant . . . Born Aug. 11, 1955, in Marietta, Ga. . . . Orioles signed him as a free agent in December 1974 . . . Acquired from Baltimore with outfielder Gary Roenicke and pitchers Joe Kerrigan and Don Stanhouse for pitchers Rudy May and Randy Miller after the 1977 season . . . His first name is composed from maternal grandfather's initials.

Year	Club	G	IP	W	L	Pct.	SO	BB	H	ERA
1981	Montreal	7	13	1	0	1.000	9	3	14	2.77
1982	Montreal	47	79⅓	2	4	.333	50	23	81	4.20
1983	Montreal	49	155⅓	6	11	.353	101	43	142	2.49
1984	Montreal	28	179	12	13	.480	101	51	178	3.32
1985	Montreal	32	222⅓	18	5	.783	127	41	193	2.91
1986	Montreal	30	187⅓	10	8	.555	105	63	182	3.94
1987	Montreal	26	150⅓	10	9	.526	94	31	164	4.37
1988	Montreal	32	198	12	10	.545	122	32	179	3.00
	Totals	251	1184⅔	71	60	.542	709	287	1133	3.37

MANAGER BUCK RODGERS: This veteran of 32 years in pro ball is one of the most affable of major-league managers . . . Survived injuries to key personnel to nurse Expos to an 81-81 record—a drop of 10 victories from 1987, when he was named NL Manager of the Year . . . His four-year record as Expos' manager is 334-314 and his overall record in the majors is 458-415 . . . In 1984, he was named Minor League Manager of the Year by the Sporting News for managing Indianapolis (AAA) to the American Association championship . . . Replaced George Bamberger as interim Milwaukee manager from March 6 to June 6 in 1980, then was named full-time manager of Brewers Sept. 9 . . . In 1981, Brewers won the second-half title in the strike-shortened split season . . . When Brewers got off to 23-24 start in 1982, he was replaced by Harvey Kuenn, who led club to

AL pennant . . . Played nine seasons as a switch-hitting catcher with Angels, batting .232 . . . Born Aug. 16, 1938, in Delaware, Ohio . . . Attended Ohio Wesleyan.

TOP PROSPECT

RANDY JOHNSON 25 6-10 225 **Bats R Throws L**

When he made his debut against the Pirates in late September, he became the tallest pitcher in major-league history . . . Attended USC on a baseball and basketball scholarship, but opted to play only baseball by his junior year . . . Expos' second-round selection in June 1985 draft . . . His fastball has been clocked at 95 mph and he has just enough of a control problem to keep batters honest . . . Expected to pitch his way into the Expos' rotation this spring . . . Went 8-7 with 3.26 ERA for Indianapolis (AAA) in 1988, striking out 111 and walking 72 in 113 innings, and 3-0 for Expos . . . Born Sept. 10,1963, Walnut Creek, Cal.

GREATEST FIRST BASEMAN

Through the years, the Expos have done more shuffling at first base than a Las Vegas dealer. Bob Bailey, Mike Jorgensen, Rusty Staub, Tony Perez, Ron Fairly, Dan Driessen, Al Oliver, Terry Francona, Jason Thompson all came and went. Then along came Andres Galarraga to put an end to the Montreal shuffle at first base. All indications are the big Venezuelan will man the position for a long, long time.

A smooth fielder who is likely to win his share of Gold Gloves once Keith Hernandez hangs up his spikes, Galarraga is a power hitter who can hit for average. A friendly, quiet giant who enjoys painting in his spare time, he has been a regular at first base for three years now and has twice batted .300, twice driven in more than 90 runs and twice hit at least 40 doubles. Last year, he clubbed 29 homers. And he's only 27.

ALL-TIME EXPO SEASON RECORDS

BATTING: Tim Raines, .334, 1986
HRs: Andre Dawson, 32, 1983
RBIs: Tim Wallach, 123, 1987
STEALS: Ron LeFlore, 97, 1980
WINS: Ross Grimsley, 20, 1978
STRIKEOUTS: Bill Stoneman, 251, 1971

NEW YORK METS

TEAM DIRECTORY: Chairman: Nelson Doubleday; Pres.: Fred Wilpon; VP-GM: Frank Cashen; VP-Baseball Oper.: Joe McIlvaine; Sr. VP-Adm.: Al Harazin; Dir. Scouting: Roland Johnson; Dir. Minor League Oper.: Gerry Hunsicker; Minor League Coordinator: Bobby Floyd; Dir. Publ. Rel.: Jay Horwitz; Asst. GM-Trav. Sec.: Arthur Richman; Mgr.: Davey Johnson. Home: Shea Stadium (55,300). Field distances: 338, l.f. line; 371, l.c.; 410, c.f.; 371, r.c.; 338, r.f. line. Spring training: Port St. Lucie, Fla.

SCOUTING REPORT

HITTING: No NL team scored as many runs (703) or hit as many home runs (152) as Davey Johnson's Mets did last year and they can expect to be even more productive in '89 if Keith Hernandez stays healthy. Remember, the Mets' No. 3 hitter spent a good part of last summer on the disabled list with a pulled hamstring, hog-tying the offense.

The full-season availability of super rookie Gregg Jefferies (.321, 6, 17 in 109 late-season at-bats), a postseason regular last

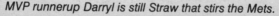

MVP runnerup Darryl is still Straw that stirs the Mets.

fall, should make the Mets' attack even more awesome. His presence near the top of the lineup should provide additional RBI opportunities for Hernandez (.276, 11, 55), NL MVP runnerup Darryl Strawberry (.269, 39, 101), Kevin McReynolds (.288, 27, 99, 21 steals in 21 tries) and fading Gary Carter (.242, 11, 46).

The Mets were shopping for a right-handed power bat last winter, dangling third baseman Howard Johnson and center fielder Len Dykstra in their quest. Their expendability was an indication of the talent depth in this organization.

PITCHING: The Mets' continued domination of NL hitters depends greatly on left-hander Bob Ojeda's ability to come back from that freak gardening accident in which he cut off the tip of his left index finger last September. Last season, the Mets' staff ERA of 2.91 was the league's lowest and the club averaged a shutout every eight games.

Just the names in the rotation are enough to strike fear in the hearts of hitters: Dwight Gooden (18-9, 3.19), Ron Darling (17-9, 3.25), David Cone (20-3, 2.22), Sid Fernandez (12-10, 3.03) and the hard-luck Ojeda (10-13, 2.88). If Ojeda doesn't regain his form, there's always comebacking Rick Aguilera or highly regarded prospect Dave West.

The bullpen is built around the talents of left-hander Randy Myers (7-3, 1.72, 26 saves), who struck out 69 in 68 innings, and sinkerballing right-hander Roger McDowell (5-5, 2.63, 16 saves).

FIELDING: Because of their awesome offense and pitching, the Mets' defense goes unnoticed, but the club finished second in the league in fielding percentage, just a notch below the Cards at .981, in '88.

Hernandez remains the prototypical first baseman with 11 Gold Gloves, Carter is still the game's best at calling a game behind the plate, McReynolds (a league-leading 18 assists) is the NL's best left fielder and Kevin Elster boosted the defense at shortstop. The weak link is the lackadaisical, fundamentally poor Strawberry in right.

OUTLOOK: The Mets, coming off a 100-60 season and an NL East title, are aware of how difficult repeating has become in any sport. The way to combat complacency is with new blood, like Jefferies and scrappy Keith Miller, who was given the second-base job when Wally Backman was sent to the Twins last winter. So, the onus remains on the other contenders to prove they're better than the Mets, with or without the old Ojeda.

NEW YORK METS 1989 ROSTER

MANAGER Davey Johnson

Coaches—Bud Harrelson, Greg Pavlick, Sam Perlozzo, Bill Robinson, Mel Stottlemyre

PITCHERS

No.	Name	1988 Club	W-L	IP	SO	ERA	B-T	Ht.	Wt.	Born
15	Aguilera, Rick	St. Lucie	0-0	7	5	1.29	R-R	6-5	200	12/31/61 San Gabriel, CA
		Tidewater	0-0	6	4	1.50				
		New York (NL)	0-4	25	16	6.93				
64	Beatty, Blaine	Jackson	16-8	209	103	2.46	L-L	6-2	185	4/25/64 Victoria, TX
55	Bross, Terry	Little Falls	2-1	55	59	3.09	R-R	6-9	234	3/30/66 El Paso, TX
62	Brown, Kevin	Jackson	1-2	33	24	2.20	L-L	6-1	185	3/5/66 Oroville, CA
		St. Lucie	5-7	134	113	1.81				
44	Cone, David	New York (NL)	20-3	231	213	2.22	L-R	6-1	185	1/2/63 Kansas City, MO
12	Darling, Ron	New York (NL)	17-9	241	161	3.25	R-R	6-3	200	8/19/60 Honolulu, HI
63	Drummond, Tim	Tidewater	6-3	82	62	3.28	R-R	6-3	170	12/24/64 La Plata, MD
50	Fernandez, Sid	New York (NL)	12-10	187	189	3.03	L-L	6-1	230	10/12/62 Honolulu, HI
36	Givens, Brian	Jackson	6-14	164	156	3.78	R-L	6-5	220	11/6/65 Lompoc, CA
16	Gooden, Dwight	New York (NL)	18-9	248	175	3.19	R-R	6-3	198	11/16/64 Tampa, FL
26	Leach, Terry	New York (NL)	7-2	92	51	2.54	R-R	6-0	191	3/13/54 Selma, AL
43	Mitchell, John	Tidewater	10-9	190	65	2.84	R-R	6-2	195	8/11/65 Dickson, TN
		New York (NL)	0-0	1	1	0.00				
48	Myers, Randy	New York (NL)	7-3	68	69	1.72	L-L	6-1	190	9/19/62 Vancouver, WA
42	McDowell, Roger	New York (NL)	5-5	89	46	2.63	R-R	6-1	185	12/21/60 Cincinnati, OH
45	Nunez, Edwin	Seattle	1-4	29	19	7.98	R-R	6-5	240	5/27/63 Puerto Rico
		New York (NL)	1-0	14	8	4.50				
19	Ojeda, Bob	New York (NL)	10-13	190	133	2.88	L-L	6-1	190	12/17/57 Los Angeles, CA
23	Savage, Jack	Tidewater	5-8	88	46	3.16	R-R	6-0	185	4/22/64 Louisville, KY
65	Tapani, Kevin	St. Lucie	1-0	19	11	1.42	R-R	6-0	180	2/18/64 Des Moines, IA
		Jackson	5-1	62	35	2.74				
46	West, Dave	Tidewater	12-4	160	143	1.80	L-L	6-6	220	9/1/64 Memphis, TN
		New York (NL)	1-0	6	3	3.00				
47	Whitehurst, Wally	Tidewater	10-11	165	113	3.05	R-R	6-3	180	4/11/64 Shreveport, LA

CATCHERS

No.	Name	1988 Club	H	HR	RBI	Pct.	B-T	Ht.	Wt.	Born
8	Carter, Gary	New York (NL)	110	11	46	.242	R-R	6-2	210	4/8/54 Culver City, CA
39	Lombardi, Phil	Tidewater	90	9	44	.308	R-R	6-2	205	2/20/63 Abilene, TX
33	Lyons, Barry	New York (NL)	21	0	11	.231	R-R	6-1	202	6/30/60 Biloxi, MS
2	Sasser, Mackey	New York (NL)	35	1	17	.285	L-R	6-1	210	8/3/62 Ft. Gaines, GA

INFIELDERS

21	Elster, Kevin	New York (NL)	87	9	37	.214	R-R	6-2	195	8/3/64 San Pedro, CA
17	Hernandez, Keith	New York (NL)	96	11	55	.276	L-L	6-0	205	10/20/53 San Francisco, CA
9	Jefferies, Gregg	Tidewater	142	7	61	.282	S-R	5-10	175	8/1/67 Burlingame, CA
		New York (NL)	35	6	17	.321				
20	Johnson, Howard	New York (NL)	114	24	68	.230	S-R	5-10	175	11/29/60 Clearwater, FL
29	Magadan, Dave	New York (NL)	87	1	35	.277	L-R	6-3	195	9/30/62 Tampa, FL
25	Miller, Keith	Tidewater	48	1	15	.281	R-R	5-11	180	6/12/63 Midland, MI
		New York (NL)	15	1	5	.214				
35	Shipley, Craig	Jackson	88	6	41	.263	S-R	6-0	170	1/7/63 Australia
		Tidewater	41	1	13	.272				
11	Teufel, Tim	New York (NL)	64	4	31	.234	R-R	6-0	174	7/7/58 Greenwich, CT

OUTFIELDERS

32	Carreon, Mark	Tidewater	96	14	55	.263	R-L	6-0	194	7/19/63 Chicago, IL
		New York (NL)	5	1	1	.556				
4	Dykstra, Lenny	New York (NL)	116	8	33	.270	L-L	5-10	170	2/10/63 Santa Ana, CA
13	Mazzilli, Lee	New York (NL)	17	0	12	.147	S-R	6-1	195	3/25/55 New York, NY
22	McReynolds, Kevin	New York (NL)	159	27	99	.288	R-R	6-1	210	10/16/59 Little Rock, AR
47	Reed, Darren	Tidewater	83	9	47	.241	R-R	6-1	190	10/16/65 Ventura, CA
18	Strawberry, Darryl	New York (NL)	146	39	101	.269	L-L	6-6	190	3/12/62 Los Angeles, CA
1	Wilson, Mookie	New York (NL)	112	8	41	.296	S-R	5-10	174	2/9/56 Bamberg, SC

MET PROFILES

KEVIN McREYNOLDS 29 6-1 210 — Bats R Throws R

Left fielder enjoyed finest major-league season with career highs in RBI with 99 and game-winning RBI with 19 . . . Finished fifth in NL with 27 homers, including two grand slams . . . Led NL outfielders with 18 assists . . . Also succeeded in 21-of-21 stolen-base attempts during '88 and has stolen 31 straight in regular-season play . . . Had big September, hitting .345 with seven homers and 22 RBI . . . Strong, silent type . . . Obtained from the Padres with Gene Walter and Adam Ging for Kevin Mitchell, Shawn Abner, Stan Jefferson, Kevin Armstrong and Kevin Brown following the 1986 season . . . Born Oct. 16, 1959, in Little Rock, Ark., where he still resides . . . Padres made him the sixth player taken overall in June 1981 draft . . . Had great career at University of Arkansas, helping the Razorbacks reach NCAA World Series in 1979 . . . Went 4-for-4 with homer in Game 6 of NLCS, but was 3-for-24 in the other six playoff games.

Year	Club	Pos.	G	AB	R	H	2B	3B	HR	RBI	SB	Avg.
1983	San Diego	OF	39	140	15	31	3	1	4	14	2	.221
1984	San Diego	OF	147	525	68	146	26	6	20	75	3	.278
1985	San Diego	OF	152	564	61	132	24	4	15	75	4	.234
1986	San Diego	OF	158	560	89	161	31	6	26	96	8	.288
1987	New York (NL)....	OF	151	590	86	163	32	5	29	95	14	.276
1988	New York (NL)....	OF	147	552	82	159	30	2	27	99	21	.288
	Totals		794	2931	401	792	146	24	121	454	52	.270

DARRYL STRAWBERRY 27 6-6 190 — Bats L Throws L

Earned NL MVP honors with spectacular season . . . Led NL in home runs with 39, tying his own club record set in 1987 . . . Became the Mets' all-time leader in home runs, surpassing Dave Kingman's 154 . . . Led NL in slugging percentage at .545 and was second in RBI with 101 . . . His legend continues to grow . . . Hit homer off Montreal's Olympic Stadium roof Opening Day . . . Homered in first at-bat of '88, the third time in his career he has homered in his opening at-bat of a season . . . Most dramatic hit of season was two-out, two-run, 10th-inning homer off Reds' John Franco that gave Mets 4-3 victory May 6 . . . Has 18 multi-homer games in his career . . . Struggled defensively in right field . . . Started in All-Star Game for fifth straight year . . . Born March 12, 1962, in Los Angeles . . . Mets made him the No. 1 pick in the nation in June 1980 draft . . . Made headlines on eve of NLCS when he suggested he and childhood friend Eric Davis of the Reds might want to return home and play for the Dodgers when they become free agents . . . Hit .300 with six RBI in playoffs vs. LA.

Year	Club	Pos.	G	AB	R	H	2B	3B	HR	RBI	SB	Avg.
1983	New York (NL)....	OF	122	420	63	108	15	7	26	74	19	.257
1984	New York (NL)....	OF	147	522	75	131	27	4	26	97	27	.251
1985	New York (NL)....	OF	111	393	78	109	15	4	29	79	26	.277
1986	New York (NL)....	OF	136	475	76	123	27	5	27	93	28	.259
1987	New York (NL)....	OF	154	532	108	151	32	5	39	104	36	.284
1988	New York (NL)....	OF	153	543	101	146	27	3	39	101	29	.269
	Totals		823	2885	501	768	143	28	186	548	165	.266

GARY CARTER 34 6-2 210 **Bats R Throws R**

It took almost three months, but he finally hit career home run No. 300, Aug. 11 off Cubs' Al Nipper . . . Had gone homerless since May 16, a span of 225 at-bats . . . Became 59th major leaguer to hit 300 homers . . . Has 278 home runs as a catcher, ranking fourth behind Johnny Bench, Yogi Berra and Carlton Fisk . . . Has 12 straight years with 100 games caught and the major-league record is 13, shared by Yankees' Bill Dickey and Bench . . . From July 27, 1977 through start of last season, he was 0-for-27 as pinch-hitter, but he went 4-for-7 with four RBI in that capacity in 1988 . . . Seems destined for Hall of Fame . . . Born April 8, 1954, in Culver City, Cal. . . . Chosen by Expos in third round of June 1972 draft . . . Traded to Mets for Hubie Brooks, Floyd Youmans, Herm Winningham and Mike Fitzgerald following the '84 season . . . Nickname "Kid" reflects his boyish enthusiasm for game . . . Once owned imposing throwing skills, but opponents have run wild on him the last few years . . . Mets gave up most stolen bases of any major-league team (204) in 1988 . . . No longer a big power threat, but still a savvy receiver.

Year	Club	Pos.	G	AB	R	H	2B	3B	HR	RBI	SB	Avg.
1974	Montreal	C-OF	9	27	5	11	0	1	1	6	2	.407
1975	Montreal	OF-C-3B	144	503	58	136	20	1	17	68	5	.270
1976	Montreal	C-OF	91	311	31	68	8	1	6	38	0	.219
1977	Montreal	C-OF	154	522	86	148	29	2	31	84	5	.284
1978	Montreal	C-1B	157	533	76	136	27	1	20	72	10	.255
1979	Montreal	C	141	505	74	143	26	5	22	75	3	.283
1980	Montreal	C	154	549	76	145	25	5	29	101	3	.264
1981	Montreal	C-1B	100	374	48	94	20	2	16	68	1	.251
1982	Montreal	C	154	557	91	163	32	1	29	97	2	.293
1983	Montreal	C-1B	145	541	63	146	37	3	17	79	1	.270
1984	Montreal	C-1B	159	596	75	175	32	1	27	106	2	.294
1985	New York (NL)....	C-1B-OF	149	555	83	156	17	1	32	100	1	.281
1986	New York (NL)....	C-1B-3B-OF	132	490	81	125	14	2	24	105	1	.255
1987	New York (NL)....	C-1B-OF	139	523	55	123	18	2	20	83	0	.235
1988	New York (NL)....	C-1B-3B	130	455	39	110	16	2	11	46	0	.242
	Totals		1958	7041	941	1879	321	30	302	1128	36	.267

KEITH HERNANDEZ 35 6-0 205 Bats L Throws L

Co-captain's torn hamstring resulted in first trips to disabled list of his career and held him to fewer than 100 games for first time since 1975 . . . Biggest game in '88 occurred the day after his divorce came through, as he drove in career-high seven runs and hit his seventh career grand slam vs. Braves April 26 . . . Those seven RBI gave him exactly 1,000 for his career . . . Owns a .301 average as a Met, tops on club's all-time list . . . Has 129 game-winning RBI, the most of any player in history . . . Obtained from Cards for pitchers Neil Allen and Rick Ownbey, June 15, 1983 . . . Born Oct. 20, 1953, in San Francisco . . . A Civil War buff . . . Father John and brother Gary played in Cards' organization . . . Was a 40th-round pick of Cards in June 1971 draft . . . Led league in hitting at .344 in 1979 and was co-NL MVP with Pirates' Willie Stargell that season . . . Still a defensive force at first base, though he has lost a step . . . Hit .269 with a homer and five RBI in playoffs.

Year	Club	Pos.	G	AB	R	H	2B	3B	HR	RBI	SB	Avg.
1974	St. Louis	1B	14	34	3	10	1	2	0	2	0	.294
1975	St. Louis	1B	64	188	20	47	8	2	3	20	0	.250
1976	St. Louis	1B	129	374	54	108	21	5	7	46	4	.289
1977	St. Louis	1B	161	560	90	163	41	4	15	91	7	.291
1978	St. Louis	1B	159	542	90	138	32	4	11	64	13	.255
1979	St. Louis	1B	161	610	116	210	48	11	11	105	11	.344
1980	St. Louis	1B	159	595	111	191	39	8	16	99	14	.321
1981	St. Louis	1B-OF	103	376	65	115	27	4	8	48	12	.306
1982	St. Louis	1B-OF	160	579	79	173	33	6	7	94	19	.299
1983	St.L.-NY (NL)	1B	150	538	77	160	23	7	12	63	9	.297
1984	New York (NL)....	1B	154	550	83	171	31	0	15	94	2	.311
1985	New York (NL)....	1B	158	593	87	183	34	4	10	91	3	.309
1986	New York (NL)....	1B	149	551	94	171	34	1	13	83	2	.310
1987	New York (NL)....	1B	154	587	87	170	28	2	18	89	0	.290
1988	New York (NL)....	1B	95	348	43	96	16	0	11	55	2	.276
	Totals		1970	7025	1099	2106	416	60	157	1044	98	.300

HOWARD JOHNSON 28 5-10 175 Bats S Throws R

Increased value by starting 34 games at shortstop in addition to 109 games at third base . . . Slipped badly after becoming second infielder in history to join 30-30 club in 1987, when he hit 36 homers and stole 32 bases . . . Tied for ninth in NL with 24 homers and stole 23 bases last year . . . Was fourth in league with 86 walks and second with 25 intentional walks . . . His dramatic two-out, two-strike, game-tying, ninth-inning homer off Pirates' Jim Gott June 28 led to an extra-inning victory that was vital to the Mets' divisional title run . . . Had hits in seven consecutive at-bats in September . . . Tigers' first-round pick in June 1979 draft . . . Obtained from Detroit for pitcher Walt Terrell following the 1984 season . . . Was 1-for-18 in NLCS and spent final two games on bench . . . Future as a Met in doubt with the arrival of prospect Gregg Jefferies . . . Struggles vs. lefties and breaking balls and curves . . . Born Nov. 29,1960, in Clearwater, Fla.

Year	Club	Pos.	G	AB	R	H	2B	3B	HR	RBI	SB	Avg.
1982	Detroit..........	3B-OF	54	155	23	49	5	0	4	14	7	.316
1983	Detroit..........	3B	27	66	11	14	0	0	3	5	0	.212
1984	Detroit..........	3B-SS-1B-OF	116	355	43	88	14	1	12	50	10	.248
1985	New York (NL)....	3B-SS	126	389	38	94	18	4	11	46	6	.242
1986	New York (NL)....	3B-SS-OF	88	220	30	54	14	0	10	39	8	.245
1987	New York (NL)....	3B-SS-OF	157	554	93	147	22	1	36	99	32	.265
1988	New York (NL)....	3B-SS	148	495	85	114	21	1	24	68	23	.230
	Totals		716	2234	323	560	94	7	100	321	86	.251

RANDY MYERS 26 6-1 190 **Bats L Throws L**

His development allowed the Mets to trade Jesse Orosco following the 1987 season . . . Hard thrower became king of the Met bullpen as he converted 26 of 29 save opportunities . . . Allowed only 10 of 52 inherited runners to score . . . Went one 11-inning stretch in which he allowed only one hit, two walks and no runs while striking out 11 . . . Born Sept. 19, 1962, in Vancouver, Wash. . . . Mets' No. 1 pick in secondary phase of June 1982 draft . . . Had pitched less than 20 games when drafted, spending most of his time in the outfield during high school and at Clark Community College . . . One of the most interesting characters in the Met clubhouse . . . Wears camouflage T-shirts and regards himself as a blue-collar worker . . . Held opponents to .190 batting average . . . Was winning pitcher in NLCS Game 1 and was unscored upon in 4.2 innings during playoffs.

Year	Club	G	IP	W	L	Pct.	SO	BB	H	ERA
1985	New York (NL)	1	2	0	0	.000	2	1	0	0.00
1986	New York (NL)	10	10⅔	0	0	.000	13	9	11	4.22
1987	New York (NL)	54	75	3	6	.333	92	30	61	3.96
1988	New York (NL)	55	68	7	3	.700	69	17	45	1.72
	Totals	120	155⅔	10	9	.526	176	57	117	2.95

DAVID CONE 26 6-1 185 **Bats L Throws R**

Just the fourth 20-game winner in Met history, joining Tom Seaver, Jerry Koosman and Dwight Gooden . . . His 20-3 record gave him the sixth-best winning percentage (.870) in history for pitchers with 20 or more victories . . . First seven outings of the season were in relief . . . Started for the first time May 3 and threw his first major-league shutout, vs.

Braves . . . Was 7-0 before suffering first loss, May 28 to Padres . . . Worked perfect inning of relief in the All-Star Game . . . Hit double figures in strikeouts six times . . . Threw a one-hitter vs. Padres Aug. 29 . . . Won club-record eight straight to close out regular season . . . Caused stir when he took shots at Dodger reliever Jay Howell in ghost-written newspaper column on eve of NLCS Game 2 start . . . Was then routed for five runs in two innings in 6-3 Game 2 loss before beating Dodgers, 5-1, with complete-game effort in Game 6 . . . Wants to be a sportswriter . . . Born Jan. 2, 1963, in Kansas City . . . Royals, in need of a catcher, traded him and Chris Jelic to Mets for catcher Ed Hearn and pitchers Rick Anderson and Mauro Gozzo, March 27, 1987, a deal KC deeply regrets . . . Throws nasty drop-down fastball and slider he calls "Laredo" to right-handed hitters, who hit only .165 against him last season.

Year	Club	G	IP	W	L	Pct.	SO	BB	H	ERA
1986	Kansas City..........	11	22⅔	0	0	.000	21	13	29	5.56
1987	New York (NL)	21	99⅓	5	6	.455	68	44	87	3.71
1988	New York (NL)	35	231⅓	20	3	.870	213	80	178	2.22
	Totals	67	353⅓	25	9	.735	302	137	294	2.85

DWIGHT GOODEN 24 6-3 198 Bats R Throws R

Got off to big start by winning first eight decisions . . . Did not lose until May 26 vs. Giants . . . Mets won 24 of the 34 games he started . . . Was starting and losing pitcher in All-Star Game as he gave up a home run to Oakland's Terry Steinbach . . . Had 1,067 strikeouts prior to 24th birthday. Only Bert Blyleven had more . . . Mets made him the fifth player selected overall in June 1982 draft . . . Had spectacular high-school career in Tampa, where he was born, Nov. 16, 1964 . . . Named NL Rookie of the Year in 1984 and NL Cy Young Award winner at 24-4 in 1985 . . . Averaged 11.39 strikeouts per nine innings in 1984, but only 6.3 per nine last year . . . Despite his dominance, he has won 20 games only once in five-year career . . . Came back in 1987 from drug rehabilitation to carry Mets in second half of season . . . "Doc" remains winless in postseason play after yielding NLCS-turning, game-tying homer to Mike Scioscia in ninth inning of Game 4.

Year	Club	G	IP	W	L	Pct.	SO	BB	H	ERA
1984	New York (NL)	31	218	17	9	.654	276	73	161	2.60
1985	New York (NL)	35	276⅔	24	4	.857	268	69	198	1.53
1986	New York (NL)	33	250	17	6	.739	200	80	197	2.84
1987	New York (NL)	25	179⅔	15	7	.682	148	53	162	3.21
1988	New York (NL)	34	248⅓	18	9	.667	175	57	242	3.19
	Totals	158	1172⅔	91	35	.722	1067	332	960	2.62

RON DARLING 28 6-3 200 **Bats R Throws R**

Had career-high 17 victories, seven complete games and four shutouts . . . Pitched division-clinching 3-1 victory vs. Phillies Sept. 22 . . . Pitched shutout vs. Expos in Mets' home opener . . . Lasted more than seven innings in 25 of 34 starts, a testament to his consistency . . . Experienced elbow problems for a stretch during midseason . . . Fifth on Mets' all-time victory list with 73 . . . Acquired from Rangers in one of Mets' best deals, coming with Walt Terrell in exchange for Lee Mazzilli, April 1, 1982 . . . Born Aug. 19, 1960, in Honolulu, but grew up in Massachusetts . . . Attended Yale, where he was a football and baseball star . . . Got no-decision in Game 3 of NLCS, then lost Game 7 as he failed to make it out of the second inning in 6-0 defeat.

Year	Club	G	IP	W	L	Pct.	SO	BB	H	ERA
1983	New York (NL)	5	35⅓	1	3	.250	23	17	31	2.80
1984	New York (NL)	33	205⅔	12	9	.571	136	104	179	3.81
1985	New York (NL)	36	248	16	6	.727	167	114	214	2.90
1986	New York (NL)	34	237	15	6	.714	184	81	203	2.81
1987	New York (NL)	32	207⅔	12	8	.600	167	96	183	4.29
1988	New York (NL)	34	240⅔	17	9	.654	161	60	218	3.25
	Totals	174	1174⅓	73	41	.640	838	472	1028	3.36

BOBBY OJEDA 31 6-1 190 **Bats L Throws L**

Hard-luck season ended in a nightmare Sept. 21, when he nearly severed the tip of the middle finger on his pitching hand with an electric hedge-clipper . . . Mets have fingers crossed that five hours of microsurgery, during which the finger was re-attached at an angle that would allow him to grip a curve, will save his career . . . His absence hurt Mets during NLCS . . . Was enjoying strong comeback following elbow surgery in 1987, even though his 10-13 won-lost record didn't show it . . . Pitched five shutouts, matching a career high, and won four of those games, 1-0 . . . From June 25 through his final start of the year Sept. 16, he posted a 2.25 ERA and gave up only 83 hits in 104.2 innings, but had only a 5-7 record and three no-decisions to show for it . . . Obtained from Red Sox with Tom McCarthy, John Mitchell and Chris Bayer for Calvin Schiraldi, Wes Gardner, John Christensen and LaSchelle Tarver following 1985 season . . . Born Dec. 17, 1957, in Los Angeles . . . Red Sox had signed him as free agent in May 1978, out of College of the

Sequoias . . . Led NL in winning percentage (.783 at 18-5) and was second in ERA in '86, when he was 2-0 with 2.33 ERA in postseason . . . Best pitch is "dead fish" changeup.

Year	Club	G	IP	W	L	Pct.	SO	BB	H	ERA
1980	Boston	7	26	1	1	.500	12	14	39	6.92
1981	Boston	10	66	6	2	.750	28	25	50	3.14
1982	Boston	22	78⅓	4	6	.400	52	29	95	5.63
1983	Boston	29	173⅔	12	7	.632	94	73	173	4.04
1984	Boston	33	216⅔	12	12	.500	137	96	211	3.99
1985	Boston	39	157⅔	9	11	.450	102	48	166	4.00
1986	New York (NL)	32	217⅓	18	5	.783	148	52	185	2.57
1987	New York (NL)	10	46⅓	3	5	.375	21	10	45	3.88
1988	New York (NL)	29	190⅓	10	13	.435	133	33	158	2.88
	Totals	211	1172⅓	75	62	.547	727	380	1122	3.68

TOP PROSPECT

GREGG JEFFERIES 21 5-10 170 — Bats S Throws R

One of the greatest minor-league players of recent years, he was named *Baseball America*'s Minor League Player of the Year in 1986 and 1987 . . . Got off to slow start at Tidewater (AAA) last year and was hitting just .153 May 14 . . . Went on 24-game hitting streak and was hitting .282 with 32 steals in 38 attempts when recalled Aug. 27 . . . Started for Mets Aug. 28, becoming the 84th third baseman in club history . . . In just over a month with Mets, he had one four-hit game, five three-hit games and four two-hit games . . . Mets made him the No. 1 pick in the nation in June 1985 draft . . . Born Aug. 1, 1967, in Burlingame, Cal. . . . Father Rich, a high school coach, had him swing bat underwater to improve bat speed . . . Struggled defensively at shortstop in minors . . . Played third and second for Mets, hitting .321 with six homers and 17 RBI in 109 at-bats during regular season and .333 in NLCS.

MANAGER DAVEY JOHNSON: Mets won 100 games for second time in his five years as manager and have won 90 or more in each of his first five seasons, a feat never before accomplished . . . With 488-320 career record, he has more victories in his first five seasons than any manager in history . . . Has never won Manager of the Year honors . . . Named manager Oct. 13, 1983, after winning three championships in

three seasons in the minors . . . Excellent second baseman who played in four All-Star Games and four World Series during 13-year career with Orioles, Braves, Phillies and Cubs . . . Also played in Japan . . . Tied Hall of Famer Rogers Hornsby's record for a second baseman when he hit 42 homers in 1973 for Atlanta . . . Has mathematics degree from Trinity University . . . Was re-signed to three-year pact during winter . . . Born Jan. 30, 1943, in Orlando, Fla.

GREATEST FIRST BASEMAN

The Mets, who have been in existence only since 1962, do not have a rich history of quality first basemen—unless you recognize Ed Kranepool for his longevity or Donn Clendenon for his MVP effort in the 1969 World Series. But, even if the franchise had been around longer, it's hard to imagine a greater Met first baseman than the guy who is playing for them now—Keith Hernandez.

In four-plus years as the club's regular first baseman—the longest uninterrupted run of any first baseman in team history—Hernandez has been one of the game's great hitters, the accepted defensive master at the position and also an inspirational leader.

A lifetime .300 hitter and the NL co-MVP as a Cardinal in 1979, Hernandez has won 11 consecutive Gold Gloves and the Mets have won two divisional titles, a pennant and a World Series since his arrival in June 1983.

ALL-TIME MET SEASON RECORDS

BATTING: Cleon Jones, .340, 1969
HRs: Darryl Strawberry, 39, 1987, 1988
RBIs: Rusty Staub, 105, 1975
Gary Carter, 105, 1986
STEALS: Mookie Wilson, 58, 1982
WINS: Tom Seaver, 25, 1969
STRIKEOUTS: Tom Seaver, 289, 1971

PHILADELPHIA PHILLIES

TEAM DIRECTORY: Pres. William Y. Giles; Exec. VP: David Montgomery; VP/GM: Lee Thomas; VP-Baseball: Tony Siegle; VP-Pub. Rel.: Larry Shenk; Dir. Publicity: Vince Nauss; Trav. Sec.: Eddie Ferenz; Mgr.: Nick Leyva. Home: Veterans Stadium (64,538). Field Distances: 330, l.f. line; 408, c.f.; 330, r.f. line. Spring training: Clearwater, Fla.

SCOUTING REPORT

HITTING: Every year, it seems the Phillies are loaded with hitting talent, but wind up near the bottom in most offensive departments. Last year, they generated only 597 runs, fewer than all but two other NL teams, and posted the lowest team batting average in the NL at .240.

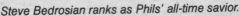

Steve Bedrosian ranks as Phils' all-time savior.

The lineup has to be better in 1989 with the full-season availability of rookie Ricky Jordan, the first baseman who came up late last summer and hit .308 with 11 homers and 43 RBI in just 69 games. If he and good-looking outfield prospect Ron Jones (.290, 8, 26 in 124 at-bats) are for real and veterans Von Hayes (.272, 6, 45) and Mike Schmidt (.249, 12, 62) can stay healthy, the Phillies shouldn't lack punch. Of course, Schmidt is coming off rotator-cuff surgery that ended his 1988 season in August.

At the top of the lineup will be Juan Samuel (.243, 12, 67, 33 steals) and Tommy Herr (.263, 1, 21 with the Twins), who was acquired for Shane Rawley last winter. Talented Chris James (.242, 19, 66) will serve as protection for the men in the middle.

With the exile of Lance Parrish to the Angels, the problem areas in terms of production are catcher and shortstop. Maybe Steve Lake (.278,1,4), the catcher imported from the Cards along with Curt Ford in the Milt Thompson deal last December, will hit enough to finally nail down a starting job.

PITCHING: The Phillies posted the NL's most bloated ERA last season with a staff mark of 4.14. Because of that, they took a gamble, trading veteran Kevin Gross to the Expos for 24-year-old Floyd Youmans (3-6, 3.21), who showed flashes of brilliance before being derailed by drugs.

It will be difficult to recognize the Phillies' rotation with Gross and Rawley gone. If Youmans makes it back, he will join left-handers Don Carman (10-14, 4.29) and Bruce Ruffin (6-10, 4.43), who had to fight his control last season. Ex-Dodger Ken Howell (0-1, 6.39) was acquired from the Orioles for Phil Bradley last winter and may be converted into a starter.

If it is ever given a lead, the Phils' bullpen should be able to hold it. Steve Bedrosian, the 1987 Cy Young Award winner, was 6-6 with a 3.75 ERA and 28 saves despite missing the early part of 1988. He is now teamed with Jeff Parrett (12-4, 2.65, 6 saves), who came from Montreal along with Youmans in the Gross deal.

FIELDING: Catching and throwing the ball has been a major problem for the Phillies, who committed 145 errors in 1988, more than every other NL club except the Braves. The Phils hope they took steps to correct this failing by acquiring Herr and moving Samuel to center, but they still will never be mistaken for the Cardinals when it comes to leather.

Schmidt, once a Gold Glove third baseman, has slowed and an outfield of James, Samuel and Hayes is geared to produce offense, not defense.

PHILADELPHIA PHILLIES 1989 ROSTER

MANAGER Nick Leyva
Coaches—Larry Bowa, Darold Knowles, Denis Menke, Mike Ryan, Tony Taylor, John Vukovich

PITCHERS

No.	Name	1988 Club	W-L	IP	SO	ERA	B-T	Ht.	Wt.	Born
40	Bedrosian, Steve	Philadelphia	6-6	74	61	3.75	R-R	6-3	205	12/6/57 Methuen, MA
—	Brantley, Cliff	Clearwater	8-11	167	124	2.59	R-R	6-1	195	4/12/68 Staten Island, NY
		Reading	1-0	6	5	6.00				
34	Brink, Brad	Maine	5-5	86	58	4.29	R-R	6-2	195	1/20/65 Roseville, CA
42	Carman, Don	Philadelphia	10-14	201	116	4.29	L-L	6-3	195	8/14/59 Oklahoma City, OK
48	Freeman, Marvin	Maine	5-5	74	37	4.62	R-R	6-6	200	4/10/63 Chicago, IL
		Philadelphia	2-3	52	37	6.10				
52	Frohwirth, Todd	Philadelphia	1-2	12	11	8.25	R-R	6-4	195	9/28/62 Milwaukee, WI
		Maine	7-3	63	39	2.44				
—	Grimsley, Jason	Clearwater	4-7	101	90	3.73	R-R	6-3	180	8/7/67 Cleveland, TX
		Reading	1-3	21	14	7.17				
33	Harris, Greg	Philadelphia	4-6	107	71	2.36	L-R	6-0	165	11/2/55 Lynwood, CA
—	Howell, Ken	Albuquerque	10-1	107	95	3.27	R-R	6-3	225	11/28/60 Detroit, MI
		Los Angeles	0-1	13	12	6.39				
44	Maddux, Mike	Maine	0-2	24	18	4.18	L-R	6-2	180	8/27/61 Dayton, OH
		Philadelphia	4-3	89	59	3.76				
34	Madrid, Alex	Denver	5-2	89	52	4.06	R-R	6-2	198	4/18/63 Springerville, AZ
		Maine	0-0	11	9	2.31				
		Philadelphia	1-1	16	2	2.76				
—	Magee, Warren	Reading	6-6	109	90	3.81	R-R	6-0	195	5/26/66 Seaford, DE
—	Malone, Chuck	Reading	12-7	127	107	3.92	R-R	6-7	250	7/8/65 Harrisburg, AR
		Maine	1-4	28	38	6.83				
—	McElroy, Chuck	Reading	9-12	161	93	4.50	L-L	6-0	160	10/1/67 Galveston, TX
59	Moore, Brad	Reading	4-6	71	39	3.06	R-R	6-1	185	6/21/64 Loveland, CO
		Philadelphia	0-0	6	2	0.00				
—	Parrett, Jeff	Montreal	12-4	92	62	2.65	R-R	6-3	200	8/26/61 Indianapolis, IN
47	Ruffin, Bruce	Philadelphia	6-10	144	82	4.43	R-R	6-2	205	10/4/63 Lubbock, TX
41	Scanlan, Bob	Maine	5-18	161	79	5.59	R-R	6-7	200	8/9/66 Los Angeles, CA
37	Sebra, Bob	Indianapolis	12-6	174	126	2.94	R-R	6-2	195	12/11/61 Ridgewood, NJ
		Philadelphia	1-1	11	7	7.94				
39	Service, Scott	Reading	3-4	57	39	2.86	R-R	6-6	225	7/27/67 Cincinnati, OH
		Maine	8-8	110	87	3.67				
		Philadelphia	0-0	5	6	1.69				
—	Youmans, Floyd	Montreal	3-6	84	54	3.21	R-R	6-1	200	5/11/64 Tampa, FL
		Indianapolis	0-0	3	1	3.00				

CATCHERS

No.	Name	1988 Club	H	HR	RBI	Pct.	B-T	Ht.	Wt.	Born
10	Daulton, Darren	Philadelphia	30	1	12	.208	L-R	6-2	190	1/3/62 Arkansas City, KS
—	Lake, Steve	St. Louis	15	1	4	.278	R-R	6-1	190	3/14/57 Inglewood, CA
—	Nieto, Tom	Portland	44	3	21	.278	R-R	6-1	205	10/27/60 Downey, CA
		Minnesota	4	0	0	.067				
6	Russell, John	Maine	29	7	24	.203	R-R	6-0	195	1/5/61 Oklahoma City, OK
		Philadelphia	9	3	8	.145				

INFIELDERS

14	Barrett, Tommy	Maine	111	1	33	.285	S-R	5-10	170	6/15/65 Baytown, TX
		Philadelphia	11	0	3	.204				
28	Herr, Tom	St. Louis	13	1	3	.260	S-R	6-0	185	4/4/56 Lancaster, PA
		Minnesota	80	1	21	.263				
18	James, Chris	Philadelphia	137	19	66	.242	R-R	6-1	190	10/4/62 Rusk, TX
30	Jeltz, Steve	Philadelphia	71	0	27	.187	S-R	5-11	180	5/28/59 France
17	Jordan, Ricky	Maine	104	7	36	.308	R-R	6-3	210	5/26/65 Richmond, CA
		Philadelphia	84	11	43	.308				
—	Parker, Rick	Reading	93	3	47	.257	R-R	6-0	185	4/20/63 Kansas City, MO
8	Samuel, Juan	Philadelphia	153	12	67	.243	R-R	5-11	170	12/9/60 Dominican Republic
20	Schmidt, Mike	Philadelphia	97	12	62	.249	R-R	6-2	203	9/27/49 Dayton, OH

OUTFIELDERS

—	Bullock, Eric	Portland	134	2	46	.309	L-L	5-11	185	2/16/60 Los Angeles, CA
		Minnesota	5	0	3	.294				
22	Dernier, Bob	Philadelphia	48	1	10	.289	R-R	6-0	165	1/5/57 Kansas City, MO
—	Ford, Curt	St. Louis	25	1	18	.195	L-R	5-10	150	10/11/60 Jackson, MS
9	Hayes, Von	Philadelphia	100	6	45	.272	L-R	6-5	180	8/31/58 Stockton, CA
26	Jones, Ron	Maine	119	16	75	.267	L-R	5-10	200	6/11/64 Seguin, TX
		Philadelphia	36	8	26	.290				

OUTLOOK: Despite efforts by new GM Lee Thomas to make big changes, the Phillies remain a team with gaping holes at shortstop and catcher and in the starting rotation. No team can overcome those kind of shortcomings and, unless Schmidt can summon one last 40-homer season from his aging body, the Phillies are in for another very long season in 1989.

PHILLIE PROFILES

VON HAYES 30 6-5 180 **Bats L Throws R**

Underwent surgery July 18 to remove bone chips from right elbow and did not play again until Sept. 2 . . . Hit .385 on grass, .327 against right-handers, .313 on road and .362 in day games . . . Obtained from Indians in shocking five-for-one trade that sent Manny Trillo, George Vukovich, Julio Franco, Jay Baller and Gerry Willard to Cleveland following the 1982 season . . . Deal was criticized in 1983, when he drove in only 32 runs, but he has been one of NL's best offensive players since '84 . . . Hit .305 and led NL with 107 runs and 46 doubles in '86 . . . Indians' seventh-round pick in June 1979 draft . . . Has played center field and first base for Phils . . . Born Aug. 31, 1958, in Stockton, Cal. . . . Became only player in history to hit two homers in first inning of a game, June 11, 1985 vs. Mets . . . Attended St. Mary's College.

Year	Club	Pos.	G	AB	R	H	2B	3B	HR	RBI	SB	Avg.
1981	Cleveland	OF-3B	43	109	21	28	8	2	1	17	8	.257
1982	Cleveland	OF-3B-1B	150	527	65	132	25	3	14	82	32	.250
1983	Philadelphia......	OF	124	351	45	93	9	5	6	32	20	.265
1984	Philadelphia......	OF	152	561	85	164	27	6	16	67	48	.292
1985	Philadelphia......	OF	152	570	76	150	30	4	13	70	21	.263
1986	Philadelphia......	1B-OF	158	610	107	186	46	2	19	98	24	.305
1987	Philadelphia......	1B-OF	158	556	84	154	36	5	21	84	16	.277
1988	Philadelphia......	1B-OF	104	367	43	100	28	2	6	45	20	.272
	Totals		1041	3651	526	1007	209	29	96	495	189	.276

MIKE SCHMIDT 39 6-2 203 **Bats R Throws R**

Season ended Aug. 12, after he hit home run off Pirates' John Smiley . . . Underwent arthroscopic surgery Sept. 7 for torn rotator cuff . . . Has more homers, RBI and extra-base hits than any third baseman in history . . . Ranks seventh all time in home runs with 542 and 20th in RBI with 1,567 . . . Hit 500th career homer at Pittsburgh, April 18, 1987, a game-winning blow off Don Robinson in the ninth inning . . . Only

Babe Ruth, Harmon Killebrew, Jimmie Foxx and Mickey Mantle reached 500 plateau in fewer at-bats than he did . . . Has had 11 seasons with 35 or more homers. Only Babe Ruth had more . . . Born Sept. 27, 1949, in Dayton, Ohio . . . Attended Ohio University . . . Phils' second-round pick in June 1971 draft . . . Won World Series MVP honors in 1980 . . . Has won three NL MVP awards (1980, '81 and '86), a feat previously accomplished by only Roy Campanella and Stan Musial . . . Has been awarded 10 Gold Gloves at third base, the most in NL history . . . Phils re-signed him for one year at $2 million last December.

Year	Club	Pos.	G	AB	R	H	2B	3B	HR	RBI	SB	Avg.
1972	Philadelphia......	3B-2B	13	34	2	7	0	0	1	3	0	.206
1973	Philadelphia......	3B-2B-1B-SS	132	367	43	72	11	0	18	52	8	.196
1974	Philadelphia......	3B	162	568	108	160	28	7	36	116	23	.282
1975	Philadelphia......	3B-SS	158	562	93	140	34	3	38	95	29	.249
1976	Philadelphia......	3B	160	584	112	153	31	4	38	107	14	.262
1977	Philadelphia......	3B-SS-2B	154	544	114	149	27	11	38	101	15	.274
1978	Philadelphia......	3B-SS	145	513	93	129	27	2	21	78	19	.251
1979	Philadelphia......	3B-SS	160	541	109	137	25	4	45	114	9	.253
1980	Philadelphia......	3B	150	548	104	157	25	8	48	121	12	.286
1981	Philadelphia......	3B	102	354	78	112	19	2	31	91	12	.316
1982	Philadelphia......	3B	148	514	108	144	26	3	35	87	14	.280
1983	Philadelphia......	3B-SS	154	534	104	136	16	4	40	109	7	.255
1984	Philadelphia......	3B-1B-SS	151	528	93	146	23	3	36	106	5	.277
1985	Philadelphia......	1B-3B-SS	158	549	89	152	31	5	33	93	1	.277
1986	Philadelphia......	3B-1B	160	552	97	160	29	1	37	119	1	.290
1987	Philadelphia......	3B-1B-SS	147	522	88	153	28	0	35	113	2	.293
1988	Philadelphia......	3B-1B	108	390	52	97	21	2	12	62	3	.249
	Totals		2362	8204	1487	2204	401	59	542	1567	174	.269

RICKY JORDAN 23 6-5 210 — Bats R Throws R

First baseman was a rookie sensation after joining Phils July 15 . . . At the time of his recall, he was batting .308 with seven homers and 36 RBI and leading the International League with 104 hits for Maine (AAA) . . . Became 31st player in major-league history to hit a homer in first official at-bat, victimizing Astros' Bob Knepper for three-run job after walking in first plate appearance . . . Hit three homers in his first 17 at-bats . . . Had an 18-game hitting streak, the fifth-longest by a Phil rookie and five short of the NL rookie record . . . Hit .331 at home and .390 in day games . . . Born May 26, 1965, in Richmond, Cal. . . . Phils' first pick in June 1983 draft . . . Was named top player in Phils' farm system in 1987, when he hit .316 with 16 homers and 95 RBI for Reading (AA).

Year	Club	Pos.	G	AB	R	H	2B	3B	HR	RBI	SB	Avg.
1988	Philadelphia......	1B	69	273	41	84	15	1	11	43	1	.308

JUAN SAMUEL 28 5-11 170 **Bats R Throws R**

Had down season in 1988, but still led Phils in hits, total bases, doubles, triples, RBI and stolen bases . . . Put together career-high 17-game hitting streak . . . Struck out 151 times and now fanned 613 times in five full seasons . . . Monster season in 1987 gave him star status . . . Had 28 homers, the most by a second baseman since Bobby Grich hit 30 in 1979, amassed 80 extra-base hits and ranked among NL top 10 in 10 offensive categories in '87 . . . First player in history to reach double figures in doubles, triples, home runs and steals in first four seasons and missed doing it again in 1988 by one triple . . . Born Dec. 9, 1960, in San Pedro de Macoris, Dominican Republic . . . Discovered while playing for factory softball team and signed as free agent, April 29, 1980 . . . Might be shifted to center field to accommodate newly acquired second baseman Tommy Herr.

Year	Club	Pos.	G	AB	R	H	2B	3B	HR	RBI	SB	Avg.
1983	Philadelphia......	2B	18	65	14	18	1	2	2	5	3	.277
1984	Philadelphia......	2B	160	701	105	191	36	19	15	69	72	.272
1985	Philadelphia......	2B	161	663	101	175	31	13	19	74	53	.264
1986	Philadelphia......	2B	145	591	90	157	36	12	16	78	42	.266
1987	Philadelphia......	2B	160	655	113	178	37	15	28	100	35	.272
1988	Philadelphia......	2B	157	629	68	153	32	9	12	67	33	.243
	Totals		801	3304	491	872	173	70	92	393	238	.264

CHRIS JAMES 26 6-1 190 **Bats R Throws R**

Phils may convert him from outfielder into Mike Schmidt's successor at third base . . . Played 30 games at third near the end of '88 season, marking first time he had played anywhere but the outfield in majors . . . Led Phils with 19 homers, the first time someone other than Schmidt led club in that department since 1978 . . . Set career high with 66 RBI . . . Born Oct. 4, 1962, in Rusk, Tex. . . . Signed in October 1981 as undrafted free agent . . . Brother Craig is former SMU star who plays for the NFL Patriots . . . Showed power early as he hit 26 homers and drove in 121 runs at Spartanburg (A) in 1983, leading South Atlantic League in homers and total bases . . . First major-league home run came April 26, 1986, off Pirates' Larry McWilliams.

Year	Club	Pos.	G	AB	R	H	2B	3B	HR	RBI	SB	Avg.
1986	Philadelphia......	OF	16	46	5	13	3	0	1	5	0	.283
1987	Philadelphia......	OF	115	358	48	105	20	6	17	54	3	.293
1988	Philadelphia......	OF-3B	150	566	57	137	24	1	19	66	7	.242
	Totals		281	970	110	255	47	7	37	125	10	.263

TOMMY HERR 32 6-0 185 Bats S Throws R

Second baseman has done his share of traveling since April 23 of last season, when he was dealt to Twins for Tom Brunansky after spending at least part of 10 seasons as Cardinal... Acquired by Phillies along with Tom Nieto and Eric Bullock for Shane Rawley after the conclusion of the 1988 season... Gritty, clutch performer who is rumored to have lost a step defensively... In 1985, he became first player in 35 years to drive in 100 runs without hitting at least 10 homers and only the seventh second baseman in history to top 100 RBI... Born April 4, 1956, in Lancaster, Pa.... Attended University of Delaware ... Cards signed him as free agent in August 1974... Tested free-agent waters after being dealt to Phils.

Year	Club	Pos.	G	AB	R	H	2B	3B	HR	RBI	SB	Avg.
1979	St. Louis........	2B	14	10	4	2	0	0	0	1	1	.200
1980	St. Louis........	2B-SS	76	222	29	55	12	5	0	15	9	.248
1981	St. Louis........	2B	103	411	50	110	14	9	0	46	23	.268
1982	St. Louis........	2B	135	493	83	131	19	4	0	36	25	.266
1983	St. Louis........	2B	89	313	43	101	14	4	2	31	6	.323
1984	St. Louis........	2B	145	558	67	154	23	2	4	49	13	.276
1985	St. Louis........	2B	159	596	97	180	38	3	8	110	31	.302
1986	St. Louis........	2B	152	559	48	141	30	4	2	61	22	.252
1987	St. Louis........	2B	141	510	73	134	29	0	2	83	19	.263
1988	St. Louis........	2B	15	50	4	13	0	0	1	3	3	.260
1988	Minnesota.......	2B	86	304	42	80	16	0	1	21	10	.263
	Totals..........		1115	4026	540	1101	195	31	20	456	162	.273

DON CARMAN 29 6-3 195 Bats L Throws L

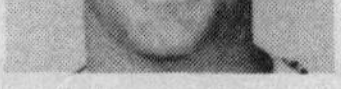

Suffered through disappointing year in fourth full season with Phillies, finishing under .500 for first time at 10-14... ERA has gone up each season since rookie year in 1985, mostly as a result of his propensity for giving up home runs... Last year, he allowed 20, ranking among top 10 most-victimized pitchers in NL... Born Aug. 14, 1959, in Oklahoma City, Okla.... Phillies signed him as undrafted free agent in August 1978... Attended University of Oklahoma... Bounced back from broken left thumb that hampered him early in 1987 to close out that year with six wins in his last nine starts... Pitched one-hitter vs. Mets, Sept. 29, 1987... Joined parent club as a reliever... Owns decent fastball and biting slider.

Year	Club	G	IP	W	L	Pct.	SO	BB	H	ERA
1983	Philadelphia	1	1	0	0	.000	0	0	0	0.00
1984	Philadelphia	11	13⅓	0	1	.000	16	6	14	5.40
1985	Philadelphia	71	86⅓	9	4	.692	87	38	52	2.08
1986	Philadelphia	50	134⅓	10	5	.667	98	52	113	3.22
1987	Philadelphia	35	211	13	11	.542	125	69	194	4.22
1988	Philadelphia	36	201⅓	10	14	.417	116	70	211	4.29
	Totals	204	647⅓	42	35	.545	442	235	584	3.77

STEVE BEDROSIAN 31 6-3 205 **Bats R Throws R**

Coming off a remarkable season in 1987, "Bedrock" missed the first 6½ weeks of 1988, while he recovered from pneumonia and pleurisy . . . Still saved 28 games in 36 opportunities . . . Among his 138 career saves are 97 saves for the Phils, shattering Tug McGraw's club record of 94 . . . Won closest race in Cy Young history in 1987, edging Cubs' Rick Sutcliffe by two points in balloting . . . Led majors in saves with 40 in '87, including NL-record 13 straight . . . Picked up from Braves along with Milt Thompson for Ozzie Virgil and Pete Smith after the 1985 season . . . Braves' third-round pick in June 1978 draft . . . Born Dec. 6, 1957, in Methuen, Mass. . . . Was named NL Rookie Pitcher of the Year by the Sporting News in 1982 . . . A big Boston Celtics fan.

Year	Club	G	IP	W	L	Pct.	SO	BB	H	ERA
1981	Atlanta	15	24	1	2	.333	9	15	15	4.50
1982	Atlanta	64	137⅔	8	6	.571	123	57	102	2.42
1983	Atlanta	70	120	9	10	.474	114	51	100	3.60
1984	Atlanta	40	83⅔	9	6	.600	81	33	65	2.37
1985	Atlanta	37	206⅔	7	15	.318	134	111	198	3.83
1986	Philadelphia	68	90⅓	8	6	.571	82	34	79	3.39
1987	Philadelphia	65	89	5	3	.625	74	28	79	2.83
1988	Philadelphia	57	74⅓	6	6	.500	61	27	75	3.75
	Totals	416	825⅔	53	54	.495	678	356	713	3.27

JEFF PARRETT 27 6-3 200 **Bats R Throws R**

Acquired from Expos with Floyd Youmans in December deal that sent Kevin Gross to Montreal . . . Had emerged as Expos' bullpen stopper before injury took him out of action in August and part of September . . . Hard thrower finished with 12-4 record, six saves and 2.65 ERA . . . His victory total led NL relief pitchers in 1988 . . . Ninth-round draft selection by Milwaukee in June 1983, out of the University of Kentucky . . . Converted into reliever in second pro season, at Beloit (A) . . . Drafted by Expos off the Vancouver roster in December 1985 . . . Spent three years in Class A, then jumped to majors . . . Born Aug. 26, 1961, in Indianapolis.

Year	Club	G	IP	W	L	Pct.	SO	BB	H	ERA
1986	Montreal	12	20⅓	0	1	.000	21	13	19	4.87
1987	Montreal	45	62	7	6	.538	56	30	53	4.21
1988	Montreal	61	91⅔	12	4	.750	62	45	66	2.65
	Totals	118	174	19	11	.633	139	88	138	3.47

TOP PROSPECT

RON JONES 24 5-10 200 Bats L Throws R
Outfielder showed power and an ability to hit for average after recall by Phils late last season . . . Played in 33 games in majors and batted .290 with eight homers and 26 RBI . . . A free swinger, he walked only twice in 129 major-league plate appearances . . . Born June 11, 1964, in Seguin, Tex. . . . Signed as a free agent by the Phils in October 1984, though he was previously drafted by the Blue Jays and Expos . . . In 1986, he was voted the top prospect in the Phil organization after hitting .371 at Clearwater (A) to lead Florida State League . . . Jumped from Class A to majors in less than two full seasons . . . Hit .267 with 16 homers and 75 RBI in 445 at-bats for Maine (AAA) prior to joining Phils last season.

MANAGER NICK LEYVA: This 35-year-old became the

youngest manager in the majors when he was named to replace Lee Elia after the 1988 season . . . Has coached under Cards' manager Whitey Herzog since 1984, handling first base for two seasons and third base for three . . . Spent six years as manager in Cards' system, almost exclusively in Class A, posting 350-340 record . . . Worked with new Phils' GM Lee Thomas when the latter was director of player personnel in St. Louis . . . Born Aug. 16, 1953, in Ontario, Cal. . . . An infielder who was Cards' 24th-round pick in June 1975 draft, out of LaVerne College . . . Ended pro playing career at Arkansas (AA) in 1977 . . . Managed Mayaguez club in Puerto Rican Winter League for three seasons.

GREATEST FIRST BASEMAN

This one is going to surprise you. The greatest first baseman in Phillies' history is a Hall of Famer who isn't primarily associated with the club. But he certainly earned a niche in Phils' history. His name is Peter Edward Rose, baseball's all-time hit leader with 4,256.

First basemen haven't lasted long with the Phillies. In fact,

Rose stands fifth among first basemen on the club's all-time list in games played, behind such household names as Fred Luderus, Sid Farrar, Don Hurst and Kitty Bransfield.

Signed as a free agent when Cincinnati refused to make him an adequate offer in 1979, Rose promised a pennant to the Phils and he delivered in 1980. Though he was past his prime by the time he came to town, Rose did hit .300 three times and led the NL in hits once and doubles twice as a Phil.

ALL-TIME PHILLIE SEASON RECORDS

BATTING: Frank O'Doul, .398, 1929
HRs: Mike Schmidt, 48, 1980
RBIs: Chuck Klein, 170, 1930
STEALS: Juan Samuel, 72, 1984
WINS: Grover Alexander, 33, 1916
STRIKEOUTS: Steve Carlton, 310, 1972

PITTSBURGH PIRATES

TEAM DIRECTORY: Chairman: Douglas Danforth; Pres.: Carl Barger; Sr. VP-GM/Baseball Oper.: Larry Doughty; VP-Business Oper.: Bernard Mullin; Dir. Media Rel.: Greg Johnson; Trav. Sec.: Charles Muse; Mgr.: Jim Leyland. Home: Three Rivers Stadium (58,437). Field distances: 335, l.f. line; 375, l.c.; 400, c.f.; 375, r.c.; 335, r.f. line. Spring training: Bradenton, Fla.

Andy Van Slyke was triple-threat Buc with NL-leading 15.

SCOUTING REPORT

HITTING: The Pirates have put together the heart of a lineup that could be one of the NL's most feared for years to come, combining Barry Bonds' ability to score runs with the ability of Andy Van Slyke and Bobby Bonilla to drive them in. Playing with an injured knee that slowed him considerably in 1988, leadoff man Bonds (.283, 24, 58) scored 97 runs, thanks in large part to the efforts of Van Slyke (.288, 25, 100) and Bonilla (.274, 24, 100).

The problem with the lineup is in the seven and eight holes, which provided very little production. Pittsburgh's three starting shortstops managed to drive in a total of 17 runs all year and, though Mike LaValliere (.261, 2, 47) was productive in the seventh spot, his lack of power and speed made it difficult to move him around the bases.

The ineffectiveness of Van Slyke and Sid Bream (.264, 10, 65) vs. left-handed pitching contributed to the Pirates' vulnerability to southpaws last year. The search for one more right-handed bat continues, unless late-season additions Gary Redus or Glenn Wilson can make a difference.

PITCHING: The Pirates go into 1989 with the same starting rotation they had last year and can expect natural maturation to make it better. Certainly young starting pitchers like John Smiley (13-11, 3.25) and Mike Dunne (7-11, 3.92) figure to get better with age.

Doug Drabek (15-7, 3.08) blossomed to become the ace of the staff last year, but, for the second season in a row, he did most of his best work after the All-Star break. Late-blooming veteran Bob Walk (12-10, 2.71) was re-signed to a three-year contract after pitching his way onto the All-Star team last summer with a career high in victories.

The bullpen still lacks a left-hander closer, but the right-handed combination of Jim Gott (6.6, 3.49, club-record 34 saves) and set-up man Jeff Robinson (11-5, 3.03, 9 saves) was very effective.

FIELDING: The Pirates like to believe they are the best defensive club in the league, with one of the three best defenders at each position except third base. LaValliere won a Gold Glove as a catcher in 1987 and Van Slyke won one last season. No second baseman has the range or flair exhibited by the acrobatic Jose Lind and the outfield of Van Slyke in center, Bonds in left and Wilson in right is unmatched defensively.

PITTSBURGH PIRATES 1989 ROSTER

MANAGER Jim Leyland
Coaches—Rich Donnelly, Bruce Kimm, Gene Lamont, Milt May, Ray Miller, Tommy Sandt

PITCHERS

No.	Name	1988 Club	W-L	IP	SO	ERA	B-T	Ht.	Wt.	Born
—	Belinda, Stan	Salem	6-4	72	63	2.76	R-R	6-3	187	8/6/66 State College, PA
15	Drabek, Doug	Pittsburgh	15-7	219	127	3.08	R-R	6-1	185	7/25/62 Victoria, TX
41	Dunne, Mike	Pittsburgh	7-11	170	70	3.92	L-R	6-4	200	10/27/62 South Bend, IN
54	Fisher, Brian	Pittsburgh	8-10	146	66	4.61	R-R	6-4	210	3/18/62 Honolulu, HI
—	Gideon, Brett	Buffalo	1-6	42	41	3.64	R-R	6-2	195	8/8/63 Ozona, TX
		Harrisburg	3-2	40	30	1.36				
35	Gott, Jim	Pittsburgh	6-6	77	76	3.49	R-R	6-4	220	8/3/59 Hollywood, CA
16	Kipper, Bob	Pittsburgh	2-6	65	39	3.74	R-L	6-2	175	7/8/64 Aurora, IL
60	Kramer, Randy	Buffalo	10-8	198	120	3.13	R-R	6-2	180	9/20/60 Palo Alto, CA
		Pittsburgh	1-2	10	7	5.40				
42	Krueger, Bill	Albuquerque	15-5	173	114	3.01	L-L	6-5	210	4/24/58 Waukegan, IL
		Los Angeles	0-0	2	1	11.57				
59	Madden, Morris	Buffalo	5-6	109	56	3.48	L-L	6-0	165	8/31/60 Laurens, SC
		Pittsburgh	0-0	6	3	0.00				
49	Robinson, Jeff	Pittsburgh	11-5	125	87	3.03	R-R	6-4	200	12/13/60 Santa Ana, CA
57	Smiley, John	Pittsburgh	13-11	205	129	3.25	L-L	6-4	195	3/17/65 Phoenixville, PA
—	Smith, Willie	Augusta	1-4	48	48	2.98	R-R	6-5	226	1/27/67 Savannah, GA
17	Walk, Bob	Pittsburgh	12-10	213	81	2.71	R-R	6-4	217	11/26/56 Van Nuys, CA
—	Walker, Mike	Harrisburg	2-7	74	47	3.51	R-R	6-3	205	6/23/65 Houston, TX
		Salem	2-2	37	29	3.16				
		Buffalo	2-3	55	26	2.78				

CATCHERS

No.	Name	1988 Club	H	HR	RBI	Pct.	B-T	Ht.	Wt.	Born
12	LaValliere, Mike	Pittsburgh	92	2	47	.261	L-R	5-8	200	8/18/60 Charlotte, NC
26	Ortiz, Junior	Pittsburgh	33	2	18	.280	R-R	5-11	176	10/24/59 Puerto Rico
3	Rodriquez, Ruben	Harrisburg	44	0	19	.275	R-R	6-0	175	8/4/64 Dominican Republic
		Buffalo	21	0	2	.256				
		Pittsburgh	1	0	1	.200				

INFIELDERS

No.	Name	1988 Club	H	HR	RBI	Pct.	B-T	Ht.	Wt.	Born
6	Belliard, Rafael	Pittsburgh	61	0	11	.213	R-R	5-6	150	10/24/61 Dominican Republic
25	Bonilla, Bobby	Pittsburgh	160	24	100	.274	S-R	6-3	230	2/23/63 New York, NY
5	Bream, Sid	Pittsburgh	122	10	65	.264	L-L	6-4	220	8/3/60 Carlisle, PA
2	Destrade, Orestes	Buffalo	74	12	42	.271	S-R	6-4	220	5/8/62 Cuba
		Pittsburgh	7	1	3	.149				
30	Distefano, Benny	Buffalo	127	19	63	.263	L-L	6-1	200	1/23/62 Brooklyn, NY
		Pittsburgh	10	1	6	.345				
29	Fermin, Felix	Buffalo	92	0	31	.261	R-R	5-11	170	10/9/63 Dominican Republic
		Pittsburgh	24	0	2	.276				
7	Khalifa, Sammy	Buffalo	49	5	21	.228	R-R	5-11	177	12/5/63 Fontana, CA
		Harrisburg	47	2	15	.331				
—	King, Jeff	Harrisburg	105	14	66	.255	R-R	6-1	179	12/26/64 Marion, IN
13	Lind, Jose	Pittsburgh	160	2	49	.262	R-R	5-11	170	5/1/64 Puerto Rico
14	Oberkfell, Ken	Atl.-Pitt.	129	3	42	.271	L-R	6-1	210	5/4/56 Maryville, IL

OUTFIELDERS

No.	Name	1988 Club	H	HR	RBI	Pct.	B-T	Ht.	Wt.	Born
—	Alou, Moises	Augusta	112	7	62	.313	R-R	6-3	178	7/3/66 Atlanta, GA
24	Bonds, Barry	Pittsburgh	152	24	58	.283	L-L	6-1	185	7/24/64 Riverside, CA
44	Cangelosi, John	Pittsburgh	30	0	8	.254	S-L	5-8	150	3/10/63 Brooklyn, NY
		Buffalo	48	0	10	.331				
—	Cook, Jeff	Harrisburg	126	1	29	.257	S-R	6-0	185	12/17/65 Kansas City, MO
19	Redus, Gary	Chicago (AL)	69	6	34	.263	R-R	6-1	185	11/1/56 Athens, AL
		Pittsburgh	14	2	4	.197				
23	Reynolds, R.J.	Pittsburgh	80	6	51	.248	S-R	6-0	183	4/19/60 Sacramento, CA
18	Van Slyke, Andy	Pittsburgh	169	25	100	.288	L-R	6-2	192	12/21/60 Utica, NY
11	Wilson, Glenn	Seattle	71	3	17	.250	R-R	6-1	190	12/22/58 Baytown, TX
		Pittsburgh	34	2	15	.270				

OUTLOOK: Jim Leyland's Pirates, coming off an 85-75 season and a second-place finish, are clearly a team on the rise. But they did little to improve themselves this offseason. Having lost out in a bid for free agent Scott Fletcher, the Pirates still must find a shortstop with some hitting ability to perhaps catch the Mets or even stay ahead of the Cardinals and Expos.

PIRATE PROFILES

ANDY VAN SLYKE 28 6-2 192 **Bats L Throws R**

Center fielder blossomed into one of league's best all-around players and a true NL MVP candidate in 1988 . . . His 15 triples led NL . . . Threw out nine runners at the plate . . . Hit team-leading .288, scored 101 runs and drove in 100 . . . Also stole 30 bases . . . Lone weakness was continued inability to handle left-handed pitching . . . "Psycho" definitely led NL in memorable quotes. A sample: "If I could change places with anyone on earth, it would be my wife, so I could see how great I am to live with." . . . Cards made him sixth player chosen overall in June 1979 draft . . . Never got full-time shot with St. Louis, which played him at third, at first and in right field . . . Acquired along with catcher Mike LaValliere and pitcher Mike Dunne for Tony Pena, April 1, 1987, in move that laid new foundation for Pirates . . . Born Dec. 21, 1960, in Utica, N.Y.

Year	Club	Pos.	G	AB	R	H	2B	3B	HR	RBI	SB	Avg.
1983	St. Louis........	OF-1B-3B	101	309	51	81	15	5	8	38	21	.262
1984	St. Louis........	OF-1B-3B	137	361	45	88	16	4	7	50	28	.244
1985	St. Louis........	OF-1B	146	424	61	110	25	6	13	55	34	.259
1986	St. Louis........	OF-1B	137	418	48	113	23	7	13	61	21	.270
1987	Pittsburgh.......	OF-1B	157	564	93	165	36	11	21	82	34	.293
1988	Pittsburgh.......	OF	154	587	101	169	23	15	25	100	30	.288
	Totals		832	2663	399	726	138	48	87	386	168	.273

BOBBY BONILLA 26 6-3 230 **Bats B Throws R**

Through first half of last season, he was a leading NL MVP candidate and he was starting third baseman in All-Star Game . . . Tailed off after break, but still managed to compile best stats of any third baseman in NL, driving in 100 runs and hitting career-high 24 home runs . . . Discovered by former Pirates' GM Syd Thrift during baseball tour through Scandinavia, he was signed as a free agent by Bucs in 1981 . . . Was drafted out of Bucs' system by White Sox in December 1985, after a broken right leg had ruined his '85 season . . . Reacquired by Thrift for pitcher Jose DeLeon, July 23, 1986 . . . Only Pirate ever to hit homers from both sides of plate in same game, a feat he has done twice . . . Also owns only upper-deck home run hit at Three Rivers Stadium in last decade . . . Born Feb. 23, 1963, in New York, N.Y. . . . Escaped streets of south Bronx to play in major leagues.

Year	Club	Pos.	G	AB	R	H	2B	3B	HR	RBI	SB	Avg.
1986	Chicago (AL)	OF-1B	75	234	27	63	10	2	2	26	4	.269
1986	Pittsburgh	OF-1B-3B	63	192	28	46	6	2	1	17	4	.240
1987	Pittsburgh	3B-OF-1B	141	466	58	140	33	3	15	77	3	.300
1988	Pittsburgh	3B	159	584	87	160	32	7	24	100	3	.274
	Totals		438	1476	200	409	81	14	42	220	14	.277

SID BREAM 28 6-4 220 **Bats L Throws L**

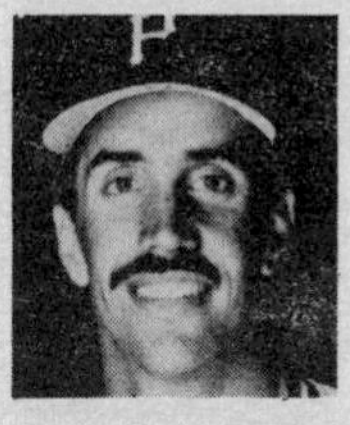

Hustling veteran turned in solid, though unspectacular season . . . Led NL first basemen in fielding percentage and is among best at fielding bunts . . . Hits lots of doubles, leading Pirates with 37 last year . . . Pirates would like to see him improve in power departments, figuring he can do better than 10 home runs and 65 RBI . . . Acquired from Dodgers with Cecil Espy and R.J. Reynolds for Bill Madlock, Aug. 31, 1985 . . . Born Aug. 3, 1960, in Carlisle, Pa. . . . Played for former major-league pitcher Al Worthington at Liberty Baptist College (Va.), where he once hit four homers in one game . . . Dodgers' second-round pick in June 1981 draft.

Year	Club	Pos.	G	AB	R	H	2B	3B	HR	RBI	SB	Avg.
1983	Los Angeles	1B	15	11	0	2	0	0	0	2	0	.182
1984	Los Angeles	1B	27	49	2	9	3	0	0	6	1	.184
1985	L.A.-Pitt.........	1B	50	148	18	34	7	0	6	21	0	.230
1986	Pittsburgh	1B-OF	154	522	73	140	37	5	16	77	13	.268
1987	Pittsburgh	1B	149	516	64	142	25	3	13	65	9	.275
1988	Pittsburgh	1B	148	462	50	122	37	0	10	65	9	.264
	Totals		543	1708	207	449	109	8	45	236	32	.263

BARRY BONDS 24 6-1 185 **Throws L Bats L**

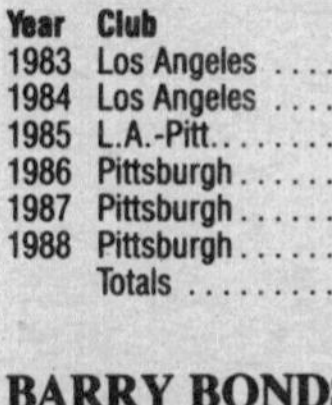

Despite knee injury that bothered him all season and required arthroscopic surgery, this left fielder turned in another solid year and is on verge of stardom . . . Showed awesome power for a leadoff man with 24 homers . . . Scored 97 runs and would have reached 100 if not for injury . . . His .283 average was career high . . . His goal is to become a 30-30 man like his dad, Bobby, who hit 30 or more homers and stole 30 or more bases eight times . . . Born July 24, 1964, in Riverside, Cal., he considers 24 his lucky number. It is his uniform number and the number worn by his godfather, Willie Mays . . . Sixth pick in June 1985 draft, out of Arizona State . . . Has sliced strikeout total each season since debut in 1984, but still fans a lot for a leadoff man.

Year	Club	Pos.	G	AB	R	H	2B	3B	HR	RBI	SB	Avg.
1986	Pittsburgh	OF	113	413	72	92	26	3	16	48	36	.223
1987	Pittsburgh	OF	150	551	99	144	34	9	25	59	32	.261
1988	Pittsburgh	OF	144	538	97	152	30	5	24	58	17	.283
	Totals		407	1502	268	388	90	17	65	165	85	.258

MIKE LaVALLIERE 28 5-8 200 **Bats L Throws R**

One of the best defensive catchers in baseball, he won Gold Glove in 1987 . . . Also handles pitching staff extremely well . . . Hit .337 with runners in scoring position in 1988 . . . Had solid offensive season overall, hitting .261 . . . Known as one of game's slowest runners, he surprised everyone by stealing three bases in 1988—as many as the Padres' fleet center fielder Marvell Wynne . . . Gave up hopes of switch-hitting, but does have a career average of .500 right-handed (1-for-2) . . . Acquired from Cards with Andy Van Slyke and Mike Dunne in Tony Pena trade, April 1, 1987 . . . Originally signed as free agent by Philadelphia in July 1981, after playing hockey and baseball at University of Lowell (Mass.) . . . Nicknamed "Spanky" . . . Born Aug. 18, 1960, in Charlotte, N.C., but grew up in New England.

Year	Club	Pos.	G	AB	R	H	2B	3B	HR	RBI	SB	Avg.
1984	Philadelphia......	C	6	7	0	0	0	0	0	0	0	.000
1985	St. Louis	C	12	34	2	5	1	0	0	6	0	.147
1986	St. Louis	C	110	303	18	71	10	2	3	30	0	.234
1987	Pittsburgh	C	121	340	33	102	19	0	1	36	0	.300
1988	Pittsburgh	C	120	352	24	92	18	0	2	47	3	.261
	Totals		369	1036	77	270	48	2	6	119	3	.261

JOSE LIND 24 5-11 170 **Bats R Throws R**

Greatest claim to fame was jumping over NBC announcer Joe Garagiola's head before nationally televised game . . . Jumping feats are legendary . . . No second baseman has more range . . . Shortly after pitcher Dave LaPoint joined Pirates, this second baseman made a play on shortstop side of second, prompting LaPoint to note, "I looked and no one else budged, I just figured he does that all the time." . . . He does . . . An unselfish player on offense with superior bat control, he finished first full season hitting .262 as Bucs' No. 2 hitter . . . Scored 82 runs . . . Brother Orlando is a pitcher in Pirates' farm system . . . Born May 1, 1964, in Toabaja, Puerto Rico . . . Signed as free agent in December 1982... Not surprisingly, he is an outstanding basketball player, too.

Year	Club	Pos.	G	AB	R	H	2B	3B	HR	RBI	SB	Avg.
1987	Pittsburgh	2B	35	143	21	46	8	4	0	11	2	.322
1988	Pittsburgh	2B	154	611	82	160	24	4	2	49	15	.262
	Totals		189	754	103	206	32	8	2	60	17	.273

JIM GOTT 29 6-4 220 Bats R Throws R

Has overcome career-threatening shoulder injury to become one of league's most feared right-handed relievers... His 34 saves were high among right-handers in NL as he broke Kent Tekulve's club record... Although he's a hard thrower, he exhibits pinpoint control... Walked only 22 and struck out 76 in 1988... Had shoulder surgery to repair torn rotator cuff and was buoyed by encouraging phone conversation with Red Sox' Roger Clemens, who had similar injury... Pirates' player representative was claimed for waiver price, Aug. 3, 1987, after Giants had given up on him... Born Aug. 3, 1959, in Hollywood, Cal.... Cards' fourth-round pick in June 1977 draft... Extremely hard worker... A black belt in Hapikido karate... Father Van pitched in White Sox organization.

Year	Club	G	IP	W	L	Pct.	SO	BB	H	ERA
1982	Toronto	30	136	5	10	.333	82	66	134	4.43
1983	Toronto	34	176⅔	9	14	.391	121	68	195	4.74
1984	Toronto	35	109⅔	7	6	.538	73	49	93	4.02
1985	San Francisco	26	148⅓	7	10	.412	78	51	144	3.88
1986	San Francisco	9	13	0	0	.000	9	13	16	7.62
1987	S.F.-Pit.	55	87	1	2	.333	90	40	81	3.41
1988	Pittsburgh..........	67	77⅓	6	6	.500	76	22	68	3.49
	Totals	256	748	35	48	.422	529	309	731	4.18

BOB WALK 32 6-4 217 Bats R Throws R

Veteran became father figure on Pirates' young staff... Had finest major-league season with career-high 12 victories... Challenged for ERA title, finishing at 2.71... Named to NL All-Star team for first time... Nicknamed "Whirlybird" because he does some strange things, like going to the plate without a bat and to the bullpen without his glove... Reclamation project is 20-12 in last two seasons with Pirates... Born Nov. 26, 1956, in Van Nuys, Cal.... Signed by Pirates as a free agent, April 7, 1984, after Braves had released him... Worked his way back to majors by going 25-10 for Hawaii (AAA) over the next two seasons... Starter and winner of first game of 1980 World Series as a rookie for Philllies, who had drafted him in third round in June 1976.

Year	Club	G	IP	W	L	Pct.	SO	BB	H	ERA
1980	Philadelphia	27	152	11	7	.611	94	71	163	4.56
1981	Atlanta	12	43	1	4	.200	16	23	41	4.60
1982	Atlanta	32	164⅓	11	9	.550	84	59	179	4.87
1983	Atlanta	1	3⅔	0	0	.000	4	2	7	7.36
1984	Pittsburgh	2	10⅓	1	1	.500	10	4	8	2.61
1985	Pittsburgh	9	58⅔	2	3	.400	40	18	60	3.68
1986	Pittsburgh	44	141⅔	7	8	.467	78	64	129	3.75
1987	Pittsburgh	39	117	8	2	.800	78	51	107	3.31
1988	Pittsburgh	32	212⅔	12	10	.545	81	65	183	2.71
	Totals	198	903⅓	53	44	.546	485	357	877	3.83

DOUG DRABEK 26 6-1 185 **Bats R Throws R**

For second year in a row, he started slowly, then blossomed into one of NL's best pitchers . . . Finished with 10 victories in his last 12 decisions . . . Posted 15-7 record, 3.08 ERA . . . Added curve to arsenal, under tutelage of pitching coach Ray Miller, and it made him a complete pitcher . . . In '87, he started 1-8 before winning 10 of last 14 decisions . . . Acquired from Yankees with Brian Fisher and Logan Easley for pitchers Rick Rhoden, Cecilio Guante and Pat Clements, after 1986 season . . . Born July 25, 1962, in Victoria, Tex. . . . Drafted by White Sox in 11th round in June 1983, out of University of Houston.

Year	Club	G	IP	W	L	Pct.	SO	BB	H	ERA
1986	New York (AL)	27	131⅔	7	8	.467	76	50	126	4.10
1987	Pittsburgh	29	176⅓	11	12	.478	120	46	165	3.88
1988	Pittsburgh	33	219⅓	15	7	.682	127	50	194	3.08
	Totals	89	527⅓	33	27	.550	323	146	485	3.60

JOHN SMILEY 24 6-4 195 **Bats L Throws L**

Converted into a starter, this hard-throwing lefty was called "the most pleasant surprise of the season" by manager Jim Leyland . . . Pitched a one-hitter en route to 13-11 record and 3.25 ERA . . . Only Doug Drabek won more games for Bucs and this hard-luck pitcher received the least offensive support of any pitcher on Pirate staff . . . Signed as Pirates' 12th-round draft choice in June 1983 . . . Didn't have much success as a starter early in his minor-league career, forcing Pirates to change him into a reliever at Prince William of Carolina League (AA) . . . He jumped from Double-A to majors, suffering through tough rookie season in relief before pitching coach Ray Miller completely restructured his repertoire . . . Miller told him to file his slider and taught him a curve and changeup to go with a 95-mph fastball . . . Born March 17, 1965, in Phoenixville, Pa. . . . Studies karate and enjoys the beach.

Year	Club	G	IP	W	L	Pct.	SO	BB	H	ERA
1986	Pittsburgh	12	11⅔	1	0	1.000	9	4	4	3.86
1987	Pittsburgh	63	75	5	5	.500	58	50	69	5.76
1988	Pittsburgh	34	205	13	11	.542	129	46	185	3.25
	Totals	109	291⅔	19	16	.543	196	100	258	3.92

TOP PROSPECT

MARK MERCHANT 20 6-2 195 **Bats S Throws R**

Pirates made him No. 2 pick in the nation in the June 1987 draft . . . One veteran scout says "he's the best player ever drafted out of Florida." . . . Had spectacular high school career, hitting .419 in 28 games with five homers, 23 RBI and 48 steals . . . During first professional season at Bradenton (A), he led Gulf Coast League in steals with 33 and was named league's top prospect by *Baseball America* . . . Struggled through injury-marred second season for Augusta (A) in South Atlantic League in 1988 . . . Batted .242 with only two homers and 19 RBI, but played only 60 games . . . Pirates project him as a Mickey Mantle type of player—a switch-hitter with speed and power . . . Born Jan. 23, 1969, in Dunkirk, N.Y.

MANAGER JIM LEYLAND: Received two-year contract as a reward for club's steady progress from last place in 1986 to second in tough NL East last year . . . Extremely popular with his players . . . Had wisdom to turn John Smiley into a starter, make Jim Gott his closer and move Bobby Bonilla from outfield to third base . . . Born Dec. 15, 1944, in Toledo, Ohio, but was raised in nearby Perrysburg . . . Was high-school classmate of Houston Oiler coach Jerry Glanville . . . Was a minor-league catcher, coach and manager in Detroit organization, managing such future stars as Kirk Gibson and Lance Parrish . . . Inability to hit better than .243 rushed him into managing at age 26 . . . Spent four seasons as White Sox' third-base

coach . . . Owns 230-256 lifetime major-league managerial mark after posting first winning mark (85-75) in 1988 . . . Managed Mets' VP Joe McIlvaine at Lakeland in 1976.

GREATEST FIRST BASEMAN

Though he also played the outfield, Wilver Dornel Stargell is fourth on the Pirates' all-time list of games played by a first baseman. He stands first in home runs, ahead of such Hall of Famers as Roberto Clemente and Ralph Kiner, and some of his prodigious blasts were among the most memorable in history.

Stargell, who was inducted into the Hall of Fame in 1987, twice led the NL in homers—with 48 in 1971 and 44 in 1973. He is the only man to hit the ball out of Dodger Stadium, a feat he accomplished twice. He hit one in Olympic Stadium that folks are still talking about and he owns six of the seven upper-deck homers in Three Rivers Stadium history.

Stargell set the Pirates' all-time home run record with 475, but he's best known for his leadership qualities. "Pops" was the inspirational force behind the 1979 world champion Bucs and the MVP in that World Series.

ALL-TIME PIRATE SEASON RECORDS

BATTING: Arky Vaughan, .385, 1935
HRs: Ralph Kiner, 54, 1949
RBIs: Paul Waner, 131, 1927
STEALS: Omar Moreno, 96, 1980
WINS: Jack Chesbro, 28, 1902
STRIKEOUTS: Bob Veale, 276, 1965

ST. LOUIS CARDINALS

TEAM DIRECTORY: Chairman-Pres.: August A. Busch, Jr.; VP/GM: Dal Maxvill; Senior VP: Fred L. Kuhlmann; Dir. Player Pers.: Ted Simmons; Dir. Pub. Rel.: Kip Ingle; Trav. Sec.: C.J. Cherre; Mgr.: Whitey Herzog. Home: Busch Stadium (54,224). Field distances: 330, l.f. line; 414, c.f.; 330, r.f. line. Spring training: St. Petersburg, Fla.

Workhorse Todd Worrell's gas tank is never empty.

SCOUTING REPORT

HITTING: The Cardinals lost Jack Clark to free agency prior to '88, unsuccessfully tried to replace him with Bob Horner and eventually found they could not generate enough offense with their legs alone to win. Now, they've compensated in a big way. They'll go into this year with two big bats in the middle of the order who weren't around at the start of '88: Pedro Guerrero (.286, 10, 65) and Tom Brunansky (.245, 22, 79 as a Cardinal), who have a total of 364 career homers.

Of course, the Cardinals still come at you with their speed, particularly leadoff hitter Vince Coleman (.260, 3, 38), who won his fourth straight stolen-base crown, but failed for the first time to steal 100 bases (he had 81). Ozzie Smith (.270, 3, 51, 57 steals) has become an offensive force, Willie McGee (.292, 3, 50) is capable of bigger things, ex-Phil Milt Thompson (.288, 2, 33, 17 steals) should fit right in among the rabbits and Tony Pena (.263, 10, 51) relocated his stroke in 1988.

One big key to the Cards improving an attack that generated the second-fewest number of runs in the NL (578) last season is the ability of gifted third baseman Terry Pendleton to bounce back from knee surgery that ruined his 1988 season.

PITCHING: This was the Cardinals' Achilles heel last season as injuries once again decimated the pitching staff. Despite playing half their games in spacious Busch Stadium, a pitchers' park, the Cards posted a 3.47 team ERA that ranked ninth in the NL.

Danny Cox (3-8, 3.98) and Greg Mathews (4-6, 4.24) were almost useless to manager Whitey Herzog as the Cardinals dropped to 76-86 last season. If both starters come back in 1989, Herzog feels he can win a title, even without former ace John Tudor. If one comes back, he feels he has a chance to win. But if neither come back, Whitey knows his team is in trouble again.

Joe Magrane (5-9, 2.18), injured much of last year, will join Cox and Mathews in the rotation. Jose DeLeon (13-10, 3.67), long known as an unproductive talent, looks ready to blossom. Scott Terry (9-6, 2.92) also figures to have a spot in the rotation.

The bullpen is anchored by Todd Worrell (5-9, 3.00, 32 saves), who saved more than 30 games for the third straight season, and left-hander Ken Dayley (2-7, 2.77, 5 saves).

FIELDING: The Cardinals are built on defense and led the NL in fielding percentage at .981 last year, but there's reason to suspect they are slipping somewhat. Smith, for example, committed 22 errors at shortstop in 1988, and, though he did win another Gold Glove, he was not the top vote-getter overall, as he usually is. Still, Smith and slick Jose Oquendo make a fine double-play combination and Pendleton has a flair for the spectacular at third base when he is healthy.

The outfield of Coleman, McGee and Brunansky has no holes. The same cannot be said of Guerrero at first base.

OUTLOOK: Give Herzog a contending team and there's no one more likely to win with it. If Cox, who won 18 games three years ago, comes back, he might have one. All the other parts are there

ST. LOUIS CARDINALS 1989 ROSTER

MANAGER Whitey Herzog
Coaches—Rich Hacker, Johnny Lewis, Dave Ricketts, Jim Riggleman, Mike Roarke, Red Schoendienst

PITCHERS

No.	Name	1988 Club	W-L	IP	SO	ERA	B-T	Ht.	Wt.	Born
44	Carpenter, Cris	Louisville	6-2	88	45	2.87	R-R	6-1	185	4/5/65 Gainesville, GA
		St. Louis	2-3	48	38	4.72				
50	Costello, John	Louisville	1-1	29	34	1.84	R-R	6-1	180	12/24/60 New York, NY
		St. Louis	5-2	50	38	1.81				
34	Cox, Danny	St. Louis	3-8	86	47	3.98	R-R	6-4	225	9/21/59 England
		Louisville	0-0	12	7	3.09				
46	Dayley, Ken	St. Louis	2-7	55	38	2.77	L-L	6-0	180	2/25/59 Jerome, ID
48	DeLeon, Jose	St. Louis	13-10	225	208	3.67	R-R	6-3	215	12/20/60 Dominican Republic
—	Di Pino, Frank	Chicago (NL)	2-3	90	69	4.98	L-L	6-0	180	10/22/56 Syracuse, NY
52	Fassero, Jeff	Arkansas	5-5	78	72	3.58	L-L	6-1	180	1/5/63 Springfield, IL
43	Hill, Ken	Arkansas	9-9	115	107	4.92	R-R	6-2	175	12/14/65 Lynn, MA
		St. Louis	0-1	14	6	5.14				
—	Kinzer, Matt	Arkansas	3-0	29	34	3.10	R-R	6-2	210	6/17/63 Indianapolis, IN
		Louisville	6-2	80	53	3.71				
32	Magrane, Joe	St. Louis	5-9	165	100	2.18	R-L	6-6	230	7/2/64 Des Moines, IA
		Louisville	2-1	20	18	3.15				
53	Mathews, Greg	St. Louis	4-6	68	31	4.24	R-L	6-2	180	5/17/62 Harbor City, CA
		Louisville	0-1	16	8	7.31				
40	Quisenberry, Dan	Kansas City	0-1	25	9	3.55	R-R	6-2	185	2/7/53 Santa Monica, CA
		St. Louis	2-0	38	19	6.16				
37	Terry, Scott	St. Louis	9-6	129	65	2.92	R-R	5-11	195	11/21/59 Hobbs, NM
		Louisville	0-0	5	1	0.00				
38	Worrell, Todd	St. Louis	5-9	90	78	3.00	R-R	6-5	210	9/28/59 Arcadia, CA

CATCHERS

No.	Name	1988 Club	H	HR	RBI	Pct.	B-T	Ht.	Wt.	Born
19	Pagnozzi, Tom	St. Louis	55	0	15	.282	R-R	6-1	190	7/30/62 Tucson, AZ
26	Pena, Tony	St. Louis	133	10	51	.263	R-R	6-0	185	6/4/57 Dominican Republic
—	Zeile, Todd	Arkansas	116	19	75	.270	R-R	6-1	190	9/9/65 Van Nuys, CA

INFIELDERS

No.	Name	1988 Club	H	HR	RBI	Pct.	B-T	Ht.	Wt.	Born
10	Booker, Rod	St. Louis	12	0	3	.343	L-R	6-0	175	9/4/58 Los Angeles, CA
		Louisville	96	4	31	.259				
28	Guerrero, Pedro	LA-St. L.	104	10	65	.286	R-R	6-0	197	6/29/56 Dominican Republic
5	*Horner, Bob	St. Louis	53	3	33	.257	R-R	6-1	215	8/6/57 Junction City, KS
22	Jones, Tim	Louisville	95	6	38	.257	L-R	5-10	175	12/1/62 Sumpter, SC
		St. Louis	14	0	3	.269				
12	*Lawless, Tom	St. Louis	10	1	3	.154	R-R	5-11	165	12/19/56 Erie, PA
11	Oquendo, Jose	St. Louis	125	7	46	.277	S-R	5-10	160	7/4/63 Puerto Rico
60	Pena, Geronimo	St. Petersburg	125	4	35	.258	R-R	6-0	184	3/29/67 Dominican Republic
9	Pendleton, Terry	St. Louis	99	6	53	.253	S-R	5-9	180	7/16/60 Los Angeles, CA
1	Smith, Ozzie	St. Louis	155	3	51	.270	S-R	5-10	155	12/26/54 Mobile, AL

OUTFIELDERS

No.	Name	1988 Club	H	HR	RBI	Pct.	B-T	Ht.	Wt.	Born
23	Brunansky, Tom	Minnesota	9	1	6	.183	R-R	6-4	216	8/20/60 W. Covina, CA
		St. Louis	128	22	79	.245				
55	Cole, Alex	Louisville	91	0	24	.232	L-L	6-2	170	8/17/65 Fayetteville, NC
29	Coleman, Vince	St. Louis	160	3	38	.260	S-R	6-0	170	9/22/61 Jacksonville, FL
51	McGee, Willie	St. Louis	164	3	50	.292	S-R	6-1	175	11/2/58 San Francisco, CA
33	Morris, John	St. Louis	11	0	3	.289	L-L	6-1	185	2/23/61 Freeport, NY
		Louisville	4	0	0	.100				
—	Thompson, Milt	Philadelphia	109	2	33	.288	L-R	5-11	170	1/5/59 Washington, DC
21	Walling, Denny	Hou.-St. L.	56	1	21	.239	L-R	6-1	185	4/17/54 Neptune, NJ

*Free agent at press time listed with 1988 team

and this team, which seems to win pennants every other year, should be hungry to prove itself once again.

CARDINAL PROFILES

WILLIE McGEE 30 6-1 175 **Bats S Throws R**

Center fielder continues to be one of the game's most consistent hitters, even though he's lost a step or two to knee surgery . . . His .292 average ranked ninth in NL last season . . . Talk about consistent . . . Owns a .295 lifetime average, a .291 World Series average and a .292 playoff average . . . Selected by the Yankees in the first round of January 1977 draft . . . Traded to Cards for pitcher Bob Sykes in Oct. 21, 1981 trade that eventually drew the ire of Yankee owner George Steinbrenner . . . Born Nov. 2, 1958, in San Francisco . . . Attended Diablo Valley College . . . Was named NL MVP in 1985, when he batted .353 to lead league and had league-leading 216 hits and 18 triples.

Year	Club	Pos.	G	AB	R	H	2B	3B	HR	RBI	SB	Avg.
1982	St. Louis	OF	123	422	43	125	12	8	4	56	24	.296
1983	St. Louis	OF	147	601	75	172	22	8	5	75	39	.286
1984	St. Louis	OF	145	571	82	166	19	11	6	50	43	.291
1985	St. Louis	OF	152	612	114	216	26	18	10	82	56	.353
1986	St. Louis	OF	124	497	65	127	22	7	7	48	19	.256
1987	St. Louis	OF-SS	153	620	76	177	37	11	11	105	16	.285
1988	St. Louis	OF	137	562	73	164	24	6	3	50	41	.292
	Totals		981	3885	528	1147	162	69	46	466	238	.295

OZZIE SMITH 34 5-10 155 **Bats S Throws R**

Hold on to your seat . . . The ultimate shortstop was charged with 22 errors last year, more than double his total in 1987 and the most he has committed since 1980, when he was playing on grass and dirt in San Diego . . . Batting average slipped to .270, lowest it has been since 1984, but "The Wizard" matched his career high in steals with 57 . . . Struck out just 43 times in 639 plate appearances . . . Caused a stir when he criticized umpires and manager Whitey Herzog in *Gentleman's Quarterly* article last spring . . . Also blasted Giants' Jeffrey Leonard during 1987 NLCS . . . One of most popular athletes in St. Louis history . . . Born Dec. 26, 1954, in Mobile, Ala. . . . Padres' fourth-round pick in June 1977 draft . . . Traded to Cards for shortstop Garry Templeton prior to 1982 season.

Year	Club	Pos.	G	AB	R	H	2B	3B	HR	RBI	SB	Avg.
1978	San Diego	SS	159	590	69	152	17	6	1	46	40	.258
1979	San Diego	SS	156	587	77	124	18	6	0	27	28	.211
1980	San Diego	SS	158	609	67	140	18	5	0	35	57	.230
1981	San Diego	SS	110	450	53	100	11	2	0	21	22	.222
1982	St. Louis	SS	140	488	58	121	24	1	2	43	25	.248
1983	St. Louis	SS	159	552	69	134	30	6	3	50	34	.243
1984	St. Louis	SS	124	412	53	106	20	5	1	44	35	.257
1985	St. Louis	SS	158	537	70	148	22	3	6	54	31	.276
1986	St. Louis	SS	153	514	67	144	19	4	0	54	31	.280
1987	St. Louis	SS	158	600	104	182	40	4	0	75	43	.303
1988	St. Louis	SS	153	575	80	155	27	1	3	51	57	.270
	Totals		1628	5914	767	1506	246	43	16	500	403	.255

TOM BRUNANSKY 28 6-4 216 Bats R Throws R

Has hit 20 or more homers in each of the last seven seasons, one of a handful of major leaguers who can make that claim... His 22 homers were most by Cardinal right fielder since George Hendrick hit 25 in 1980... Obtained from Twins for second baseman Tommy Herr April 23, a deal necessitated by Bob Horner's inability to take up power slack left by defection of Jack Clark... Had big first half with a .278 average, 13 homers and 49 RBI... Struggled in second half, hitting .205 with nine homers and 30 RBI... Hit 14 of his 22 homers away from Busch Stadium... Made only one error all year and stole a career-high 16 bases... Born Aug. 20, 1960, in West Covina, Cal.... Twins got "Bruno" from Angels with Mike Walters for Doug Corbett and Rob Wilfong, May 11, 1982.

Year	Club	Pos.	G	AB	R	H	2B	3B	HR	RBI	SB	Avg.
1981	California	OF	11	33	7	5	0	0	3	6	1	.152
1982	Minnesota	OF	127	463	77	126	30	1	20	46	1	.272
1983	Minnesota	OF	151	542	70	123	24	5	28	82	2	.227
1984	Minnesota	OF	155	567	75	144	21	0	32	85	4	.254
1985	Minnesota	OF	157	567	71	137	28	4	27	90	5	.242
1986	Minnesota	OF	157	593	69	152	28	1	23	75	12	.256
1987	Minnesota	OF	155	532	83	138	22	2	32	85	11	.259
1988	Minnesota	OF	14	49	5	9	1	0	1	6	1	.184
1988	St. Louis	OF	143	523	69	128	22	4	22	79	16	.245
	Totals		1070	3869	526	962	176	17	188	554	53	.249

PEDRO GUERRERO 32 6-0 197 Bats R Throws R

Cards were 14-4 in games in which he had an RBI... Obtained from Dodgers for pitcher John Tudor Aug. 16... Dodgers were seeking pennant pitching insurance and Cardinals craved his right-handed power bat... Was the 11th player to play third for the Cards during 1988 season... Also saw action at first and in the outfield... Had 11 hits in 39 at-bats with runners in scoring position as a Cardinal . . . Committed only one error after trade . . . Came back from career-threatening knee surgery in 1986 to have big season for Dodgers in '87, hitting .338 with 27 homers and 89 RBI . . . Has hit more than 30 homers three times in career and driven in more than 100 runs twice . . . Born June 29, 1956, in San Pedro de Macoris, Dominican Republic . . . Indians signed him as a free agent in 1973, when he was 16 . . . Dodgers acquired him for Bruce Ellingsen, April 4, 1974.

Year	Club	Pos.	G	AB	R	H	2B	3B	HR	RBI	SB	Avg.
1978	Los Angeles	1B	5	8	3	5	0	1	0	1	0	.625
1979	Los Angeles	OF-1B-3B	25	62	7	15	2	0	2	9	2	.242
1980	Los Angeles	OF-INF	75	183	27	59	9	1	7	31	2	.322
1981	Los Angeles	OF-3B-1B	98	347	46	104	17	2	12	48	5	.300
1982	Los Angeles	OF-3B	150	575	87	175	27	5	32	100	22	.304
1983	Los Angeles	3B-1B	160	584	87	174	28	6	32	103	23	.298
1984	Los Angeles	OF-3B-1B	144	535	85	162	29	4	16	72	9	.303
1985	Los Angeles	OF-3B-1B	137	487	99	156	22	2	33	87	12	.320
1986	Los Angeles	OF-1B	31	61	7	15	3	0	5	10	0	.246
1987	Los Angeles	OF-1B	152	545	89	184	25	2	27	89	9	.338
1988	L.A.-St.L.	1B-3B-OF	103	364	40	104	14	2	10	65	4	.286
	Totals		1080	3751	577	1153	176	25	176	615	88	.307

VINCE COLEMAN 27 6-0 170 Bats S Throws R

Left fielder stole fewer than 100 bases for first time in any full season in his pro career . . . Still was in a class by himself as he easily bested Astros' Gerald Young for NL lead in steals with 81 . . . Has stolen 407 bases in four years, far ahead of pace set by all-time steal leader Lou Brock . . . Batting average slipped from .289 to .260 and runs fell off from 121 to 77, a reflection of Jack Clark's absence from the Cardinal lineup in 1988 . . . Still strikes out too often for a leadoff hitter—111 times last year—and actually has more strikeouts than steals in his major-league career . . . Born Sept. 22, 1961, in Jacksonville, Fla. . . . Cards' 10th-round pick in June 1982 draft . . . Attended Florida A&M, where he was a football punter like his cousin Greg, who had a long career with NFL Vikings . . . Injured leg in freak tarp mishap that knocked him out of 1985 World Series.

Year	Club	Pos.	G	AB	R	H	2B	3B	HR	RBI	SB	Avg.
1985	St. Louis	OF	151	636	107	170	20	10	1	40	110	.267
1986	St. Louis	OF	154	600	94	139	13	8	0	29	107	.232
1987	St. Louis	OF	151	623	121	180	14	10	3	43	109	.289
1988	St. Louis	OF	153	616	77	160	20	10	3	38	81	.260
	Totals		609	2475	399	649	67	38	7	150	407	.262

TONY PENA 31 6-0 184 **Bats R Throws R**

Became the NL's top offensive catcher again in '88, after a disastrous first season with Cardinals . . . Batted .263 with 10 homers and 51 RBI . . . Obtained by Cards in controversial trade that sent outfielder Andy Van Slyke, catcher Mike LaValliere and pitcher Mike Dunne to Pirates, April 1, 1987 . . . Broke thumb early in '87 season when hit by Brian Fisher pitch in first game back in Pittsburgh . . . Out until May 22 and never got going . . . Finished with career-low average of .214, leading to much criticism of trade . . . Became an even bigger focal point of controversy when Cardinals gave him a multi-million-dollar contract, then let Jack Clark get away to Yanks . . . Won three Gold Gloves with Pittsburgh . . . Born June 4, 1957, in Monte Cristi, Dominican Republic . . . Originally signed by Pirates as free agent in July 1975 . . . Brother Ramon pitched in Tiger organization . . . Mother was outstanding softball player and his baseball mentor.

Year	Club	Pos.	G	AB	R	H	2B	3B	HR	RBI	SB	Avg.
1980	Pittsburgh	C	8	21	1	9	1	1	0	1	0	.429
1981	Pittsburgh	C	66	210	16	63	9	1	2	17	1	.300
1982	Pittsburgh	C	138	497	53	147	28	4	11	63	2	.296
1983	Pittsburgh	C	151	542	51	163	22	3	15	70	6	.301
1984	Pittsburgh	C	147	546	77	156	27	2	15	78	12	.286
1985	Pittsburgh	C-1B	147	546	53	136	27	2	10	59	12	.249
1986	Pittsburgh	C-1B	144	510	56	147	26	2	10	52	9	.288
1987	St. Louis	C-1B-OF	116	384	40	82	13	4	5	44	6	.214
1988	St. Louis	C-1B	149	505	55	133	23	1	10	51	6	.263
	Totals		1066	3761	402	1036	176	20	78	435	54	.275

JOE MAGRANE 24 6-6 230 **Bats R Throws L**

Left-hander led NL in ERA with 2.18 mark, but finished at 5-9 . . . First Cardinal to lead NL in earned-run average since 1976, when John Denny led league at 2.52 . . . Of his five victories, three were shutouts . . . Allowed two or fewer runs in 20 of his 24 starts . . . For second year in a row, he went on the disabled list, this time with torn muscle in rib cage . . . Despite some spectacular pitching, he is just 14-16 for major-league career . . . Born July 2, 1964, in Des Moines, Iowa . . . Cards' top selection in June 1985 draft, out of University of Arizona . . . Colorful personality with good sense of humor.

Year	Club	G	IP	W	L	Pct.	SO	BB	H	ERA
1987	St. Louis	27	170⅓	9	7	.563	101	60	157	3.54
1988	St. Louis	24	165⅓	5	9	.357	100	51	133	2.18
	Totals	51	335⅔	14	16	.467	201	111	290	2.87

JOSE DeLEON 28 6-3 215 **Bats R Throws R**

Began to live up to the big things that were predicted for him when he burst onto major-league scene in spectacular fashion with Pirates in 1983 . . . Was 7-3 that year with a 2.83 ERA and a pair of near no-hitters . . . However, by 1985, his career had hit rock-bottom as he went 2-19 with a 4.70 ERA . . . Traded to the White Sox in 1987 . . . Dealt to the Cards for pitcher Rick Horton and outfielder Lance Johnson prior to 1988 season . . . Went 13-10 with 3.67 ERA, becoming first Cardial to strike out more than 200 batters since Bob Gibson in 1972 . . . Born Dec. 20, 1960, in Rancho Viejo, Dominican Republic . . . Brought up in Perth Amboy, N.J. . . . Selected by Pirates in third round of June 1979 draft.

Year	Club	G	IP	W	L	Pct.	SO	BB	H	ERA
1983	Pittsburgh	15	108	7	3	.700	118	47	75	2.83
1984	Pittsburgh	30	192⅓	7	13	.350	153	92	147	3.74
1985	Pittsburgh	31	162⅔	2	19	.095	149	89	138	4.70
1986	Pittsburgh	9	16⅓	1	3	.250	11	17	17	8.27
1986	Chicago (AL)	13	79	4	5	.444	68	42	49	2.96
1987	Chicago (AL)	33	206	11	12	.478	153	97	177	4.02
1988	St. Louis	34	225⅓	13	10	.565	208	86	198	3.67
	Totals	165	989⅔	45	65	.409	860	470	801	3.86

TODD WORRELL 29 6-5 210 **Bats R Throws R**

One of the hardest throwers in NL . . . Became the first player ever to save 30 or more games in each of his first three full seasons when he notched 32 saves for fifth-place Cardinals in 1988 . . . Only Pirates' Jim Gott had more saves among NL's right-handed relievers last year . . . Allowed just 69 hits in 90 innings and opposition hitters batted .214 against him . . . NL Rookie of the Year in 1986, when he had 36 saves and 2.08 ERA while pitching in 74 games . . . Has 106 saves in three-plus seasons . . . Cards' first-round selection in June 1982 draft and the 21st player taken overall . . . Born Sept. 28, 1959, in Arcadia, Cal. . . . Graduated from Biola College.

Year	Club	G	IP	W	L	Pct.	SO	BB	H	ERA
1985	St. Louis	17	21⅔	3	0	1.000	17	7	17	2.91
1986	St. Louis	74	103⅔	9	10	.474	73	41	86	2.08
1987	St. Louis	75	94⅔	8	6	.571	92	34	86	2.66
1988	St. Louis	68	90	5	9	.357	78	34	69	3.00
	Totals	234	310	25	25	.500	260	116	258	2.58

SCOTT TERRY 29 5-11 195 **Bats R Throws R**

Came literally out of nowhere to post 9-6 record, 2.92 ERA for Cardinals . . . Forced into starting role due to injuries to Joe Magrane, Danny Cox and John Tudor, he ran off a six-game winning streak . . . Acquired from Reds, Sept. 3, 1987, as player to be named later in trade for Pat Perry . . . Had 11-10 season at Nashville (AAA) in 1987 . . . Selected by Reds in 12th round of June 1980 draft as an outfielder after playing three years at Southwestern University in Texas . . . Converted to the mound in 1983 at Tampa (A), following three minor-league seasons in which he hit no better than .259 . . . In first full season as pitcher, he went 14-3 with 1.50 ERA for Vermont (AA) . . . Born Nov. 21, 1959, in Hobbs, N.M.

Year	Club	G	IP	W	L	Pct.	SO	BB	H	ERA
1986	Cincinnati	28	55⅔	1	2	.333	32	32	66	6.14
1987	St. Louis	11	13⅓	0	0	.000	9	8	13	3.38
1988	St. Louis	51	129⅓	9	6	.600	65	34	119	2.92
	Totals	90	198⅓	10	8	.556	106	74	198	3.86

TOP PROSPECT

CRIS CARPENTER 23 6-1 185 **Bats R Throws R**

Reached majors in first full pro season . . . Was 6-2 with 2.87 ERA for Louisville (AAA), where Cards intended him to stay before injuries to the St. Louis pitchers forced club to rush him to the majors . . . Had 2-3 record with 4.72 ERA for St. Louis . . . Drafted by Blue Jays in 1986, but did not sign . . . Cards' No. 1 draft pick and 14th player taken overall in June 1987 draft, after two-sport career at University of Georgia . . . Was 9-4 with 2.66 ERA, 11 saves and 102 strikeouts in 105 innings as a senior, helping Bulldogs into NCAA World Series . . . Was All-SEC and honorable mention All-American as a punter on Georgia football team . . . Born April 5, 1965, in St. Augustine, Fla. . . . Named MVP in Pan American Games.

MANAGER WHITEY HERZOG: Last year was wrong year in every-other-year pattern developing in his managerial career . . . Cardinals have won pennant in odd-numbered years and fallen apart in even years . . . Club was decimated by injuries last year and finished fifth with 76-86 record, the worst mark of any Herzog team since 1973, when Texas finished sixth . . . Has led Cards to three divisional titles in 1980s . . .

One of 38 managers in history with 1,000 or more victories . . . Has won six divisional championships, two pennants and one World Series in 11 full seasons . . . Has managed Texas, Kansas City and St. Louis, owning overall record of 1,162-1,002 . . . Full name is Dorrel Norman Elvert Herzog, but he's known as "The White Rat" . . . Avid skier and fisherman and spends much of off-season in Aspen, Colo. . . . Born Nov. 9, 1931, in New Athens, Ill.

GREATEST FIRST BASEMAN

Leo Durocher said, "Nice guys finish last." Leo must not have met Stan Musial, the greatest first baseman in Cardinal history and maybe the greatest left-handed hitter in NL history.

"Stan The Man" split his time between the outfield and first base in his 22 seasons in St. Louis, where he became the most respected man in the game. Hitting out of a unique peek-a-boo batting stance, he won seven batting titles and three NL MVP awards and finished with a .331 lifetime average. He stands third all time in doubles, fourth in hits, fifth in games played, at-bats and RBI, sixth in runs, eighth in walks and ninth in slugging percentage.

Outside Busch Stadium in St. Louis, there is a statue of Musial, a testament to the love the city feels for him.

ALL-TIME CARDINAL SEASON RECORDS

BATTING: Rogers Hornsby, .424, 1924
HRs: Johnny Mize, 43, 1940
RBIs: Joe Medwick, 154, 1937
STEALS: Lou Brock, 118, 1974
WINS: Dizzy Dean, 30, 1934
STRIKEOUTS: Bob Gibson, 274, 1970

ATLANTA BRAVES

TEAM DIRECTORY: Chairman: Bill Bartholomay; Pres.: Stan Kasten; GM: Bobby Cox; Asst. GM: John Mullen; VP-Dir. Player Dev.: Hank Aaron; Dir. Scouting: Paul Snyder; Dir. Pub. Rel.: Jim Schultz; Trav. Sec.: Bill Acree; Mgr.: Russ Nixon. Home: Atlanta-Fulton County Stadium (52,001). Field distances: 330, l.f. line; 402, c.f.; 330, r.f. line. Spring training: West Palm Beach, Fla.

SCOUTING REPORT

HITTING: The Braves went into the winter meetings hoping to shore up an offense that was near the bottom of the league in hitting (.242), homers (96) and dead last in runs (555) in 1988, but they fell flat on their faces. Negotiations to trade Dale Murphy, their only bonafide star, to the Mets, Padres or Astros for packages of players all fizzled, so the Braves will bring back Murphy (.226, 24, 77) for a 13th season.

They will also bring back Gerald Perry (.300, 8, 74), who made a run at the batting title in 1988, former Cub stalwart Jody

Gerald Perry is at center of Brave new world.

Davis (.230, 7, 36) and productive Andres Thomas (.252, 13, 68). But there isn't much else.

PITCHING: The Braves finished next to last in the NL with a 4.09 team ERA in 1988—and that was down from a league-worst 4.63 in 1987. So what did the Braves do to improve their pitching last winter? They let Rick Mahler (9-16, 3.69) escape to the Reds via free agency.

The potential rotation for 1989 does not look like a Who's Who of pitching. Zane Smith (5-10, 4.30) and Pete Smith (7-15, 3.69) are the head of the class. Then comes Tom Glavine, John Smoltz and Charlie Puleo, who combined for a 14-29 record last season. Reliever Bruce Sutter, immersed in a series of comebacks, will be trying to rebound from knee surgery this year. His 14 saves in 45⅓ innings of work last season seemed to prove that years of shoulder problems are behind him. That's more than you can say about the Braves' woes.

FIELDING: It can't come as any surprise that the Braves committed a league-high 151 errors last season. Bad pitching. No hitting. Porous defense. There have got to be reasons when a team loses 106 games and no big trades plus no free-agent signings obviously equal no improvement.

Thomas has the capability of being one of the top shortstops in the league if he can ever get a second baseman to work with him. Last season, Thomas worked with Ron Gant (31 errors), who so unimpressed management in the pivot there has been talk about moving him to third base.

Other than Murphy in right, the outfield is a catastrophe of inexperience. Catching may be better with Davis having replaced Ozzie Virgil, but who knows? Davis didn't play most of last year in Chicago, before the late-season trade that brought him to Atlanta.

OUTLOOK: Bleak. Only the fall of the Astros could keep the Braves out of the cellar for a second straight season. Sitting in the lobby at the winter meetings, manager Russ Nixon, facing his first full season, looked downcast. He was probably thinking about his pitching rotation and his lineup.

Of course, if the Braves don't improve, Nixon's job will be on the line. Who else? General manager Bobby Cox hasn't proven he can do anything except glad-hand since he jumped back to the Braves from a managing slot in Toronto. The best bet for the Braves this season is that somewhere along the line, we'll see Cox managing again.

ATLANTA BRAVES 1989 ROSTER

MANAGER Russ Nixon
Coaches—Bruce Dal Canton, Clarence Jones, Roy Majtyka, Brian Snitker, Bobby Wine

PITCHERS

No.	Name	1988 Club	W-L	IP	SO	ERA	B-T	Ht.	Wt.	Born
38	*Acker, Jim	Atlanta	0-4	42	25	4.71	R-R	6-2	212	9/24/58 Freer, TX
40	Alvarez, Jose	Richmond	2-1	14	10	1.26	R-R	5-11	175	4/12/56 Tampa, FL
		Atlanta	5-6	102	81	2.99				
30	Assenmacher, Paul	Atlanta	8-7	79	71	3.06	L-L	6-3	200	12/10/60 Detroit, MI
37	Boever, Joe	Richmond	6-3	71	71	2.14	R-R	6-1	200	10/4/60 St. Louis, MO
		Atlanta	0-2	20	7	1.77				
48	Eave, Gary	Richmond	5-9	101	80	3.56	R-R	6-4	190	7/22/63 Monroe, LA
		Atlanta	0-0	5	0	9.00				
47	Glavine, Tom	Atlanta	7-17	195	84	4.56	L-L	6-0	175	3/25/66 Concord, MA
33	Greene, Tommy	Richmond	7-17	177	130	4.77	R-R	6-5	225	4/6/67 Lumberton, NC
50	Mercker, Kent	Durham	11-4	128	159	2.68	L-L	6-1	175	2/1/68 Dublin, OH
		Greenville	3-1	48	60	3.35				
82	Miller, Dave	Greenville	5-4	72	50	2.50	R-R	6-3	200	10/17/64 Jacksonville, FL
		Richmond	11-6	116	67	4.12				
59	Nezelek, Andy	Greenville	7-8	134	89	4.38	L-R	6-6	218	10/24/65 Endicott, NY
45	Puleo, Charlie	Atlanta	5-5	106	70	3.47	R-R	6-3	200	2/7/55 Glen Ridge, NJ
52	Richards, Rusty	Durham	1-0	3	3	0.00	L-R	6-4	200	1/27/65 Houston, TX
		Greenville	10-7	147	96	2.63				
25	Smith, Pete	Atlanta	7-15	195	124	3.69	R-R	6-2	183	2/27/66 Abington, MA
34	Smith, Zane	Atlanta	5-10	140	59	4.30	L-L	6-2	195	12/28/60 Madison, WI
29	Smoltz, John	Richmond	10-5	135	115	2.79	R-R	6-3	185	5/15/67 Detroit, MI
		Atlanta	2-7	64	37	5.48				
43	Stoker, Mike	Durham	8-6	147	111	3.92	R-R	6-3	195	11/11/66 Las Vegas, NV
42	Sutter, Bruce	Atlanta	1-4	45	40	4.76	R-R	6-2	195	1/8/53 Lancaster, PA
61	Weems, Danny	Durham	13-8	191	98	3.29	R-R	6-3	175	8/26/66 Greeenville, TN

CATCHERS

No.	Name	1988 Club	H	HR	RBI	Pct.	B-T	Ht.	Wt.	Born
20	Benedict, Bruce	Atlanta	57	0	19	.242	R-R	6-2	195	8/15/55 Birmingham, AL
8	Davis, Jody	Chi. (NL)-Atl.	59	7	36	.230	R-R	6-3	210	11/12/56 Gainesville, GA
56	Deak, Brian	Burlington	85	20	59	.246	R-R	6-0	183	10/25/67 Harrisburg, PA

INFIELDERS

32	Blauser, Jeff	Richmond	77	5	23	.284	R-R	6-0	170	11/8/65 Los Gatos, CA
		Atlanta	16	2	7	.239				
9	Denson, Andrew	Greenville	136	13	78	.268	R-R	6-5	210	11/16/65 Cincinnati, OH
5	Gant, Ron	Richmond	14	0	4	.311	R-R	6-0	172	3/2/65 Victoria, TX
		Atlanta	146	19	60	.259				
17	Lemke, Mark	Greenville	153	16	80	.270	S-R	5-9	167	8/13/65 Utica, NY
		Atlanta	13	0	2	.224				
28	Perry, Gerald	Atlanta	164	8	74	.300	L-R	6-0	190	10/30/60 Savannah, GA
12	Runge, Paul	Atlanta	16	0	7	.211	R-R	6-0	175	5/21/58 Kingston, NY
14	Thomas, Andres	Atlanta	153	13	68	.252	R-R	6-1	185	11/10/63 Dominican Republic
15	Whited, Ed	Greenville	108	16	62	.252	R-R	6-3	195	2/9/64 Bristol, PA

OUTFIELDERS

19	Blocker, Terry	Atlanta	42	2	10	.212	L-L	6-2	195	8/18/60 Columbia, SC
		Richmond	60	2	9	.226				
16	Gregg, Tommy	Pitt.-Atl.	13	1	7	.295	L-L	6-1	190	7/29/63 Boone, NC
1	Hall, Albert	Bradenton	2	0	1	.250	S-R	5-11	158	3/7/59 Birmingham, AL
		Atlanta	57	1	15	.247				
64	Hood, Dennis	Greenville	135	14	47	.257	R-R	6-2	170	7/3/66 Glendell, CA
10	James, Dion	Atlanta	99	3	30	.256	L-L	6-1	170	11/9/62 Philadelphia, PA
57	Jones, Barry	Greenville	109	16	55	.284	L-R	6-2	197	2/14/65 Jackson, AL
		Richmond	35	3	10	.278				
63	Justice, David	Greenville	55	9	37	.278	L-L	6-3	195	4/14/66 Cincinnati, OH
		Richmond	46	8	28	.203				
3	Murphy, Dale	Atlanta	134	24	77	.226	R-R	6-4	215	3/12/56 Portland, OR
6	Smith, Lonnie	Richmond	87	9	51	.300	R-R	5-9	170	12/22/55 Chicago, IL
		Atlanta	27	3	9	.237				

*Free agent at press time listed with 1988 team

BRAVE PROFILES

DALE MURPHY 33 6-4 215 **Bats R Throws R**

Two-time NL MVP suffered through his worst season since 1978, his first full year in big leagues . . . Batted .226 with 24 homers and 77 RBI as compared to .295 with 44 homers and 105 RBI in 1987 . . . Right fielder went 1-for-4 Opening Night, marking only time all season his average was as high as .250 . . . Signed three-year, $6-million contract after '87 season . . . Has hit 334 homers in 11-year career, all with the Braves . . . Born March 12, 1956, in Portland, Ore. . . . Braves' No. 1 choice and the fifth selection overall in June 1974 draft . . . Was rumored to be on trading block last winter . . . Seven-time All-Star has suffered from lack of protection in lineup . . . Attended Brigham Young . . . Became one of four NL players to win back-to-back MVPs in 1982 and 1983, joining Ernie Banks, Joe Morgan and Mike Schmidt.

Year	Club	Pos.	G	AB	R	H	2B	3B	HR	RBI	SB	Avg.
1976	Atlanta..........	C	19	65	3	17	6	0	0	9	0	.262
1977	Atlanta..........	C	18	76	5	24	8	1	2	14	0	.316
1978	Atlanta..........	C-1B	151	530	66	120	14	3	23	79	11	.226
1979	Atlanta..........	1B-C	104	384	53	106	7	2	21	57	6	.276
1980	Atlanta..........	OF-1B	156	569	98	160	27	2	33	89	9	.281
1981	Atlanta..........	OF-1B	104	369	43	91	12	1	13	50	14	.247
1982	Atlanta..........	OF	162	598	113	168	23	2	36	109	23	.281
1983	Atlanta..........	OF	162	589	131	178	24	4	36	121	30	.302
1984	Atlanta..........	OF	162	607	94	176	32	8	36	100	19	.290
1985	Atlanta..........	OF	162	616	118	185	32	2	37	111	10	.300
1986	Atlanta..........	OF	160	614	89	163	29	7	29	83	7	.265
1987	Atlanta..........	OF	159	566	115	167	27	1	44	105	16	.295
1988	Atlanta..........	OF	156	592	77	134	35	4	24	77	3	.226
	Totals		1675	6175	1005	1689	276	37	334	1004	148	.274

GERALD PERRY 28 6-0 190 **Bats L Throws R**

Flirted with batting title until mid-September . . . First baseman wound up hitting .300, good for fifth in league, and was one of only five NL players to hit .300 or better last season . . . Broke index finger on left hand Aug. 13 and played remainder of season with injury . . . Batted .216 from Sept. 1 on . . . Also spent time on disabled list with shoulder separation . . . Braves' 11th-round selection in June 1978 draft . . . Was Braves' only representative on All-Star team last year . . . Born Oct. 30, 1960, in Savannah, Ga. . . . Came up as an outfielder . . . Nephew of former major leaguer Dan Driessen.

Year	Club	Pos.	G	AB	R	H	2B	3B	HR	RBI	SB	Avg.
1983	Atlanta..........	1B-OF	27	39	5	14	2	0	1	6	0	.359
1984	Atlanta..........	1B-OF	122	347	52	92	12	2	7	47	15	.265
1985	Atlanta..........	1B-OF	110	238	22	51	5	0	3	13	9	.214
1986	Atlanta..........	OF-1B	29	70	6	19	2	0	2	11	0	.271
1987	Atlanta..........	1B-OF	142	533	77	144	35	2	12	74	42	.270
1988	Atlanta..........	1B	141	547	61	164	29	1	8	74	29	.300
	Totals		571	1774	223	484	85	5	33	225	95	.273

ANDRES THOMAS 25 6-1 185 — Bats R Throws R

Led all NL shortstops with 13 homers and 68 RBI . . . RBI total was the best in history for an Atlanta shortstop and most for franchise since Johnny Logan drove in 83 runs for Milwaukee Braves in 1955 . . . Homers were most by an Altanta shortstop since Denis Menke hit 20 in 1966 . . . Signed as free agent out of the Dominican Republic in 1981 . . . Embarking on fourth full major-league season . . . Hit .306 with four homers and 20 RBI during June . . . Had pair of 10-game hitting streaks, in May and late June . . . Born Nov. 10, 1963, in Santo Domingo, Dominican Republic . . . His 153 hits last year were second-highest on team . . . Committed 29 errors last season.

Year	Club	Pos.	G	AB	R	H	2B	3B	HR	RBI	SB	Avg.
1985	Atlanta..........	SS	15	18	6	5	0	0	0	2	0	.278
1986	Atlanta..........	SS	102	323	26	81	17	2	6	32	4	.251
1987	Atlanta..........	SS	82	324	29	75	11	0	5	39	6	.231
1988	Atlanta..........	SS	153	606	54	153	22	2	13	68	7	.252
	Totals		352	1271	115	314	50	4	24	141	17	.247

RON GANT 24 6-0 172 — Bats R Throws R

Called up from Richmond (AAA) and took over at second base April 20 . . . Struggled until May 29, hitting .183 with two homers and 13 RBI in his first 33 games . . . Hit a creditable .279 after that and batted .259 for season . . . Was shifted to third base, where he played 22 games late in season . . . Was guilty of 31 errors . . . Played third base in Puerto Rican Winter League and is expected to start at that position for Braves in 1989 . . . Atlanta's fourth-round selection in June 1983 draft . . . Hottest month last season was June, when he hit .294 with five homers and 16 RBI . . . Born March 2, 1965, in Victoria, Tex. . . . Stole 19 bases . . . Had 26 homers, 102 RBI and 35 steals for Durham (AA) in 1986.

Year	Club	Pos.	G	AB	R	H	2B	3B	HR	RBI	SB	Avg.
1987	Atlanta..........	2B	21	83	9	22	4	0	2	9	4	.265
1988	Atlanta..........	2B-3B	146	563	85	146	28	8	19	60	19	.259
	Totals		167	646	94	168	32	8	21	69	23	.260

JODY DAVIS 32 6-3 210 **Bats R Throws R**

Obtained from Cubs Sept. 29 for pitchers Kevin Blankenship and Kevin Coffman... Was immediately signed to two-year, $1.2-million contract... Caught two games for the Braves on final weekend of season... Hit three-run homer vs. Reds' Tom Browning in his third at-bat for Braves Sept. 30... Expected to be Braves' starting catcher in 1989, with backup help from Bruce Benedict... Was left to wallow on Cubs' bench last season as new manager Don Zimmer went with Damon Berryhill... Batted just .229 with six homers and 33 RBI in 88 games... Born Nov. 12, 1956, in Gainesville, Ga.... Became only second Gold Glove catcher in Cub history in 1986... Mets' third-round choice in January 1976 draft.

Year	Club	Pos.	G	AB	R	H	2B	3B	HR	RBI	SB	Avg.
1981	Chicago (NL).....	C	56	180	14	46	5	1	4	21	0	.256
1982	Chicago (NL).....	C	130	418	41	109	20	2	12	52	0	.261
1983	Chicago (NL).....	C	151	510	56	138	31	2	24	84	0	.271
1984	Chicago (NL).....	C	150	523	55	134	24	2	19	94	5	.256
1985	Chicago (NL).....	C	142	482	47	112	30	0	17	58	1	.232
1986	Chicago (NL).....	C-1B	148	528	61	132	27	2	21	74	0	.250
1987	Chicago (NL).....	C	125	428	57	106	12	2	19	51	1	.248
1988	Chi (NL)-Atl......	C	90	257	21	59	9	0	7	36	0	.230
	Totals		992	3326	352	836	158	11	123	470	7	.251

TOMMY GREGG 25 6-1 190 **Bats L Throws L**

Acquired from Pirates as player to be named later in Aug. 28 deal for Ken Oberkfell... Is targeted to start in either left field or center field in 1989... Played just 25 major-league games last season, 11 of them for the Braves ... Started five games in left and two in center... Led Eastern League with .371 average in 1987, prior to being called up by Bucs for 10 games... Hit .294 with six homers and 27 RBI in 72 games for Buffalo (AAA) last season... Born July 29, 1963, in Boone, N.C.... Hit .345 (10-for-29) with four RBI in 11 games for Braves... Pirates' seventh-round pick in June 1985 draft, out of Wake Forest.

Year	Club	Pos.	G	AB	R	H	2B	3B	HR	RBI	SB	Avg.
1987	Pittsburgh.......	OF	10	8	3	2	1	0	0	0	2	.250
1988	Pitt.-Atl.........	OF	25	44	5	13	4	0	1	7	0	.295
	Totals		35	52	8	15	5	0	1	7	2	.288

Braves need Zane Smith to bounce back from bleak '88.

ZANE SMITH 28 6-2 195 Bats L Throws L

Underwent arthroscopic surgery to remove bone spurs from left elbow Sept. 1 and missed final month of season . . . Subject of great interest in trade talks, he never won back-to-back games all year . . . Beat Dodgers April 17 in Los Angeles, ending Braves' season-opening, NL-record 10-game losing streak . . . Missed a July 19 start in Philly because his foot fell asleep on the airplane the day before . . . Braves' third-round selection in June 1982 draft . . . His 15-10 record in 1987 made him second-highest winning lefty in NL behind Phillies' Shane Rawley . . . His 15 wins was most ever by an Atlanta left-hander and most for franchise lefty since 1965, when Milwaukee

Braves' Don Blasingame won 16 . . . Born Dec. 28, 1960, in Madison, Wis. . . . Gets lots of ground-ball outs.

Year	Club	G	IP	W	L	Pct.	SO	BB	H	ERA
1984	Atlanta	3	20	1	0	1.000	16	13	16	2.25
1985	Atlanta	42	147	9	10	.474	85	80	135	3.80
1986	Atlanta	38	204⅔	8	16	.333	139	105	209	4.05
1987	Atlanta	36	242	15	10	.600	130	91	245	4.09
1988	Atlanta	23	140⅓	5	10	.333	59	44	159	4.30
	Totals	142	754	38	46	.452	429	333	764	4.01

PETE SMITH 23 6-2 183 **Bats R Throws R**

Rookie evolved into a competent starter during second half . . . Before All-Star break, he was 3-9 with 5.14 ERA in 18 games . . . After the break, he was 4-6 with 2.27 ERA in 14 games . . . Obtained from Phillies with Ozzie Virgil for Steve Bedrosian and Milt Thompson following 1985 season . . . Led Braves in complete games with five and shutouts with three . . . Was only Brave starter to throw a shutout . . . His back-to-back shutouts against Cubs Aug. 21 and Aug. 26 were part of a 21⅔-inning scoreless streak . . . Born Feb. 27, 1966, in Abington, Mass. . . . Lost seven straight games from May 3 through June 24 . . . Phils' first-round pick in June 1984.

Year	Club	G	IP	W	L	Pct.	SO	BB	H	ERA
1987	Atlanta	6	31⅔	1	2	.333	11	14	39	4.83
1988	Atlanta	32	195⅓	7	15	.318	124	88	183	3.69
	Totals	38	227	8	17	.320	135	102	222	3.85

BRUCE SUTTER 36 6-2 195 **Bats R Throws R**

Has undergone three sets of surgery on his right shoulder since 1986, a year after signing six-year, $40-million contract with Braves . . . Pitched in 16 games in 1986 and did not play in 1987, when it appeared his career might be over . . . Made a stunning first-half comeback in 1988 . . . From May 9 through June 8, he compiled eight saves in nine opportunities . . . Felled by Bell's palsy for second time in his life and went on disabled list July 24 . . . Was not reactivated until Aug. 19 . . . Had 12 of his 14 saves before All-Star break . . . His final save of season, Sept. 9 in San Diego, was the 300th of his career, placing him third on all-time list . . . Born Jan. 8, 1953, in Lancaster, Pa. . . . Won NL Cy Young Award for Cubs in 1979 and was named Fireman of the Year four times . . . Had arthroscopic surgery to clean up his right knee Sept. 26.

Year	Club	G	IP	W	L	Pct.	SO	BB	H	ERA
1976	Chicago (NL)..........	52	83	6	3	.667	73	26	63	2.71
1977	Chicago (NL)..........	62	107	7	3	.700	129	23	69	1.35
1978	Chicago (NL)..........	64	99	8	10	.444	106	34	82	3.18
1979	Chicago (NL)..........	62	101	6	6	.500	110	32	67	2.23
1980	Chicago (NL)..........	60	102	5	8	.385	76	34	90	2.65
1981	St. Louis.............	48	82	3	5	.375	57	24	64	2.63
1982	St. Louis.............	70	102⅓	9	8	.529	61	34	88	2.90
1983	St. Louis.............	60	89⅓	9	10	.474	64	30	90	4.23
1984	St. Louis.............	71	122⅔	5	7	.417	77	23	109	1.54
1985	Atlanta	58	88⅓	7	7	.500	52	29	91	4.48
1986	Atlanta	16	18⅔	2	0	1.000	16	9	17	4.34
1987	Atlanta...............					Injured				
1988	Atlanta	38	45⅓	1	4	.200	40	11	49	4.76
	Totals	661	1040⅔	68	71	.489	861	309	879	2.84

TOP PROSPECT

JOHN SMOLTZ 21 6-3 185 Bats R Throws R

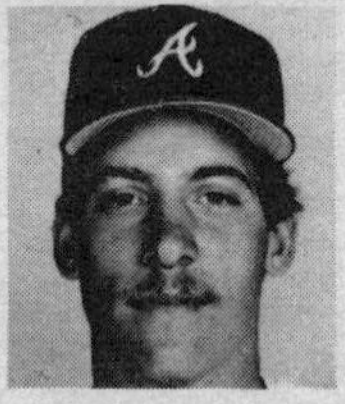

Was called up from Richmond (AAA) July 23 and made a major splash that day . . . Pitched eight innings of four-hit, one-run ball and beat Mets, 6-1 . . . Stayed in the major leagues and made total of 12 starts for Braves . . . Was obtained from Tigers for pitcher Doyle Alexander, Aug. 12, 1987 . . . Was pitching for Class-A Glens Falls at time of the trade and was jumped immediately to Triple-A in Braves' system . . . Made only 23 Triple-A starts before arriving in Braves' starting rotation . . . Born May 15, 1967, in Detroit . . . Tigers signed him as free agent in September 1985 . . . Was 10-5, 2.79 with 115 strikeouts in 135 innings for Richmond and 2-7, 5.48 for Braves.

MANAGER RUSS NIXON: When he took over for Chuck Tanner May 22, the last-place Braves were drifting along at 12-27 . . . Led them to 42-79 record the rest of the way . . . Was told just after the All-Star break that he'd be returning for 1989, but didn't sign a contract until Nov. 1 . . . Wanted two-year contract, but settled for one year . . . Was manager of Greenville (AA) at time of Tanner's firing . . . Greenville was 22-21 and in first-place tie under Nixon . . . Was Tanner's third-base coach in 1986 and 1987 . . . Embarking on his 36th season in pro baseball . . . Previous major-league managerial experience includes a season-plus in Cincinnati . . . Managed Reds to 101-131

record and two sixth-place finishes in 1982 and 1983 . . . Has posted 143-210 record overall . . . Was catcher with 12 years of major-league experience for Cleveland, Boston, Toronto and Minnesota . . . Born Feb. 19, 1935, in Cleveland.

GREATEST FIRST BASEMAN

The Braves' franchise, which moved from Boston to Milwaukee in 1953 and from Milwaukee to Atlanta in 1966, is not replete with great first basemen. During the Atlanta era, Dale Murphy, Bob Horner, Orlando Cepeda, Hank Aaron, Willie Montanez and Chris Chambliss all planted their feet on the first sack for a time.

However, the most productive first baseman in franchise history was unquestionably Joe Adcock, whose career began at County Stadium in 1953, when bratwurst became the club's official sausage. The Braves have only been in the World Series four times and Adcock was the first baseman on the two Milwaukee teams that played in the Series, in 1957 and 1958.

During Adcock's 10-year tenure as a Brave, which ended in 1962, he hit .285 and amassed 239 of his 336 career homers, including many prodigious blows. He was one of only three men to reach the center-field bleachers at the Polo Grounds in New York, nearly 600 feet from home plate. On July 31, 1954, he hit four homers in a game, against the Dodgers at Ebbets Field. And at County Stadium, May 26, 1959, his 13th-inning homer off the Pirates' Harvey Haddix broke up the longest perfect-game effort in history.

ALL-TIME BRAVE SEASON RECORDS

BATTING: Rogers Hornsby, .387, 1928
HRs: Eddie Mathews, 47, 1953
Hank Aaron, 47, 1971
RBIs: Eddie Mathews, 135, 1953
STEALS: Ralph Myers, 57, 1913
WINS: Vic Willis, 27, 1902
Charles Pittinger, 27, 1902
Dick Rudolph, 27, 1914
STRIKEOUTS: Phil Niekro, 262, 1977

CINCINNATI REDS

TEAM DIRECTORY: Principal Owner-Pres.: Marge Schott; Exec. VP: Stephen Schott; GM: Murray Cook; Dir. Scouting: John Cox; VP-Player Pers.: Sheldon Bender; VP-Publicity: Jim Ferguson; Trav. Sec.: Dan Lunetta; Mgr.: Pete Rose. Home: Riverfront Stadium (52,392). Field distances: 330, l.f. line; 404, c.f.; 330, r.f. line. Spring training: Plant City, Fla.

SCOUTING REPORT

HITTING: Trying to fill a hole at first base, the Reds picked up Todd Benzinger (.254, 13, 70) from Boston for Nick Esasky (.243, 15, 62) and valuable lefty reliever Rob Murphy last winter. Who got the better of that deal? Probably the Red Sox. And, despite the rumors that either Kal Daniels (.291, 18, 64) or

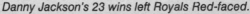

Danny Jackson's 23 wins left Royals Red-faced.

Eric Davis (.273, 26, 93) would be dealt, they're back to lead the Reds' attack for another season.

The Reds finished ninth in the NL in average at .246, but were second behind the Mets in total homers with 122 last season. In 1989, they'll need even better years from Daniels, Davis and Chris Sabo (.271, 11, 44), who was Rookie of the Year despite tailing off seriously in the second half.

PITCHING: The staff seems pretty solvent. Danny Jackson (23-8, 2.73), Tom Browning (18-5, 3.41) and Jose Rijo (13-8, 2.39) give the Reds a potent trifecta right off the top. Rick Mahler (9-16, 3.69 for the Braves) was signed as a free agent and Jeff Sellers (1-7, 4.83) was imported from the Red Sox. Left-hander John Franco (6-6, 1.57, 39 saves) has evolved into perhaps the most reliable closer in the league.

The Reds' 3.35 ERA was good for fifth in the league last year and was nearly a full run less than the 4.24 club mark recorded in 1987. Credit for that can be given to Jackson, who solidified the staff in 1988 after the trade that brought him over from the pitching-rich Royals. But management made a big mistake in June, when left-hander Dennis Rasmussen (16-10, 3.43) was sent to the Padres for right-hander Candy Sierra.

FIELDING: The Reds' infield is one of the youngest and toughest in the game. Shortstop Barry Larkin and third baseman Sabo create a potent left side that could be together for a long time. Both are future Gold Glovers. The right side has been more patchwork. Ron Oester, who blew out a knee midway through 1987, could be back at second base after a season of auditioning Jeff Treadway. Benzinger ought to be a stark improvement over Esasky at first.

The outfield is good, particularly if center fielder Davis stays away from walls and left fielder Daniels can stay motivated. Catcher Bo Diaz is adequate at best, so the Reds should have been in the market for another catcher. They weren't.

OUTLOOK: One gets the feeling that, after four consecutive fourth-place finishes under legend Pete Rose, the Reds must make their move to the top. Still, the perception is that something is seriously missing. Certainly, the Reds must avoid another disastrous start like they've had the last two seasons to have a serious chance. It doesn't help that the Reds essentially stood still while the Dodgers and Padres enjoyed major offseason tune-ups.

Bet that if the Reds fell flat again, the street outside Riverfront Stadium named after Rose will be re-christened.

CINCINNATI REDS 1989 ROSTER

MANAGER Pete Rose

Coaches—Scott Breeden, Tommy Helms, Jim Lett, Lee May, Tony Perez

PITCHERS

No.	Name	1988 Club	W-L	IP	SO	ERA	B-T	Ht.	Wt.	Born
40	Armstrong, Jack	Nashville	5-5	120	116	3.00	R-R	6-5	220	3/7/65 Englewood, NJ
		Cincinnati	4-7	65	45	5.79				
48	Birtsas, Tim	Nashville	1-3	50	48	3.08	L-L	6-7	240	9/6/60 Pontiac, MI
		Cincinnati	1-3	64	38	4.20				
38	Brown, Keith	Chattanooga	9-1	70	34	1.42	S-R	6-4	205	2/14/64 Flagstaff, AZ
		Nashville	6-3	85	43	1.90				
		Cincinnati	2-1	16	6	2.76				
32	Browning, Tom	Cincinnati	18-5	251	124	3.41	L-L	6-1	190	4/28/60 Casper, WY
37	Charlton, Norm	Nashville	11-10	182	161	3.02	S-L	6-3	195	1/6/63 Ft. Polk, LA
		Cincinnati	4-5	61	39	3.96				
49	Dibble, Rob	Nashville	2-1	35	41	2.31	L-R	6-4	235	1/24/64 Bridgeport, CT
		Cincinnati	1-1	59	59	1.82				
31	Franco, John	Cincinnati	6-6	86	46	1.57	L-L	5-10	185	9/17/60 Brooklyn, NY
—	Hammond, Chris	Chattanooga	16-5	183	127	1.72	L-L	6-1	190	1/21/66 Atlanta, GA
20	Jackson, Danny	Cincinnati	23	261	161	2.73	R-L	6-0	195	1/5/62 San Antonio, TX
—	Kaiser, Keith	Greensboro	11-9	186	159	2.52	S-R	6-4	200	5/24/67 San Antonio, TX
—	Mahler, Rick	Atlanta	9-16	249	131	3.69	R-R	6-1	202	8/5/53 Austin, TX
—	Moscrey, Mike	Cedar Rapids	11-8	191	143	2.74	R-L	6-1	195	12/15/67 Dallas, TX
27	Rijo, Jose	Cincinnati	13-8	162	160	2.39	R-R	6-2	185	5/13/65 Dominican Republic
33	Robinson, Ron	Nashville	0-0	4	4	7.36	R-R	6-4	230	3/24/62 Woodlake, CA
		Cincinnati	3-7	79	38	4.12				
55	Roesler, Mike	Chattanooga	1-1	20	13	2.21	R-R	6-5	195	9/12/63 Ft. Wayne, IN
		Nashville	3-2	41	31	5.01				
—	Scudder, Scott	Cedar Rapids	7-3	102	126	2.02	R-R	6-2	180	2/14/68 Paris, TX
		Chattanooga	7-0	70	52	2.96				
—	Sellers, Jeff	Pawtucket	1-1	15	9	5.52	R-R	6-0	195	5/11/64 Compton, CA
		Boston	1-7	86	70	4.83				
35	St. Claire, Randy	Ind.-Nash.	0-3	40	27	2.68	R-R	6-2	190	8/23/60 Glens Falls, NY
		Mont.-Cin.	1-0	21	14	3.86				
47	*Williams, Frank	Nashville	0-0	3	1	9.00	R-R	6-1	205	2/13/58 Seattle, WA
		Cincinnati	3-2	63	43	2.59				

CATCHERS

No.	Name	1988 Club	H	HR	RBI	Pct.	B-T	Ht.	Wt.	Born
6	Diaz, Bo	Cincinnati	69	10	35	.219	R-R	5-11	205	3/23/53 Venezuela
3	McGriff, Terry	Cincinnati	19	1	4	.198	R-R	6-2	195	9/23/63 Ft. Pierce, FL
		Nashville	21	1	12	.216				
7	Oliver, Joe	Chattanooga	26	3	12	.248	R-R	6-3	215	7/24/65 Memphis, TN
		Nashville	45	4	24	.205				
34	Reed, Jeff	Indianapolis	7	0	1	.318	L-R	6-2	190	11/12/62 Joliet, IL
		Mont.-Cin.	60	1	16	.226				
—	Taubensee, Eddie	Greensboro	85	10	41	.258	L-R	6-3	200	10/31/68 Beeville, TX
		Chattanooga	2	1	1	.167				

INFIELDERS

No.	Name	1988 Club	H	HR	RBI	Pct.	B-T	Ht.	Wt.	Born
—	Benzinger, Todd	Boston	103	13	70	.254	S-R	6-1	185	2/11/63 Dayton, KY
51	Brown, Marty	Nashville	128	7	55	.264	R-R	6-1	195	1/23/63 Lawton, OK
		Cincinnati	3	0	2	.188				
56	Harris, Lenny	Glens Falls	22	1	7	.338	L-R	5-10	200	10/28/64 Miami, FL
		Nashville	117	0	35	.277				
		Cincinnati	16	0	8	.372				
—	Jefferson, Reggie	Cedar Rapids	149	18	90	.288	S-L	6-4	210	9/25/68 Tallahassee, FL
11	Larkin, Barry	Cincinnati	174	12	56	.296	R-R	6-0	185	4/28/64 Cincinnati, OH
16	Oester, Ron	Cincinnati	42	0	10	.280	S-R	6-2	190	5/5/56 Cincinnati, OH
9	Quinones, Luis	Nashville	115	9	53	.276	S-R	5-11	175	4/28/62 Puerto Rico
		Cincinnati	12	1	11	.231				
17	Sabo, Chris	Cincinnati	146	11	54	.271	R-R	6-0	185	1/19/62 Detroit, MI
15	Treadway, Jeff	Cincinnati	76	2	23	.252	L-R	5-11	170	1/22/63 Columbus, GA
—	Trillo, Manny	Chicago (NL)	41	1	14	.250	R-R	6-1	164	12/25/50 Venezuela

OUTFIELDERS

No.	Name	1988 Club	H	HR	RBI	Pct.	B-T	Ht.	Wt.	Born
22	Collins, Dave	Cincinnati	41	0	14	.236	S-L	5-10	175	10/20/52 Rapid City, SD
28	Daniels, Kal	Cincinnati	144	18	64	.291	L-R	5-11	195	8/20/63 Vienna, GA
44	Davis, Eric	Cincinnati	129	26	93	.273	R-R	6-3	185	5/29/62 Los Angeles, CA
25	*Griffey, Ken	Atl.-Cin.	62	4	23	.255	L-L	6-0	210	4/10/50 Donora, PA
21	O'Neill, Paul	Cincinnati	122	16	73	.252	L-L	6-4	210	2/25/63 Columbus, OH
—	Roomes, Rolando	Iowa	126	16	66	.301	R-R	6-3	180	2/15/62 Jamaica
		Chicago (NL)	3	0	0	.188				
57	Snider, Van	Nashville	152	23	73	.290	L-R	6-3	205	8/11/63 Birmingham, AL
		Cincinnati	6	1	6	.214				
29	Winningham, Herm	Indianapolis	2	0	1	.200	L-R	5-11	175	12/1/61 Orangeburg, SC
		Mont.-Cin.	47	0	21	.232				
—	Youngblood, Joel	San Francisco	31	0	16	.252	R-R	5-11	175	8/28/51 Houston, TX

*Free agent at press time listed with 1988 team

RED PROFILES

ERIC DAVIS 26 6-3 185 **Bats R Throws R**

Was virtually invisible for the opening two months of 1988 season . . . Through May 31, he was batting .220 with six homers and 23 RBI . . . Picked up his numbers substantially after that . . . From June 1 on, he hit 20 homers and knocked in 70 runs in 86 games . . . Still, the center fielder experienced dip in production from an All-Star 1987 season as his average fell from .293 to .273, his homers from 37 to 26 and his RBI from 100 to 93 . . . His early lack of production was a big reason Reds finished second for fourth straight year instead of first . . . Reds' eighth-round draft pick in June 1980 draft . . . Missed 27 games with nagging injuries, including bruised hamstring, sprained ankle, bruised elbow, bruised knee and shin splints . . . Born May 29, 1962, in Los Angeles . . . Earned $899,000 last year, his third full major-league season . . . Stole 35 bases in 38 attempts last season, but struck out 124 times . . . Remains close to boyhood friend Darryl Strawberry of Mets . . . A remarkable athlete with 40-40 club potential.

Year	Club	Pos.	G	AB	R	H	2B	3B	HR	RBI	SB	Avg.
1984	Cincinnati	OF	57	174	33	39	10	1	10	30	10	.224
1985	Cincinnati	OF	56	122	26	30	3	3	8	18	16	.246
1986	Cincinnati	OF	132	415	97	115	15	3	27	71	80	.277
1987	Cincinnati	OF	129	474	120	139	23	4	37	100	50	.293
1988	Cincinnati	OF	135	472	81	129	18	3	26	93	35	.273
	Totals		509	1657	357	452	69	14	108	312	191	.273

KAL DANIELS 25 5-11 195 **Bats L Throws L**

Known as "Mr. Sweetness" because of his dour temperament . . . Set tempo for 1988 with his production in first five games, in which he went 12-for-20 with four homers and 10 RBI . . . Tossed his bat into the visitors' dugout at Wrigley Field Sept. 2, barely missing manager Pete Rose, coach Tommy Helms and the batboy . . . Was suspended for one game without pay and didn't play in next three . . . Was involved in postgame shouting match with pitcher Danny Jackson after botching a play in left field . . . Was second on club with 18 homers, third with a .291 average and third with 64 RBI . . . Reds' first pick in secondary phase of June 1982 draft . . . Born Aug. 20, 1963, in

Vienna, Ga. . . . Had arthroscopic surgery on left knee July 7, 1987 and missed a month . . . Earned $185,000 in 1988.

Year	Club	Pos.	G	AB	R	H	2B	3B	HR	RBI	SB	Avg.
1986	Cincinnati	OF	74	181	34	58	10	4	6	23	15	.320
1987	Cincinnati	OF	108	368	73	123	24	1	26	64	26	.334
1988	Cincinnati	OF	140	495	95	144	29	1	18	64	27	.291
	Totals		322	1044	202	325	63	6	50	151	68	.311

BARRY LARKIN 24 6-0 185 **Bats R Throws R**

Concluded the season on a 21-game hitting streak, the second-longest in majors last year . . . Went from his low-water mark of .281 at start of streak to season-ending average of .296 . . . One of three Reds on All-Star team . . . Made 29 errors in 1988, his first full season as starting shortstop . . . Was hurt in April 1987, when Padres' Stan Jefferson took him out in the pivot on a double play . . . Missed a month with a hyperextended left knee . . . Reds' No. 1 choice and fourth player chosen overall in June 1985 draft . . . Earned $152,500 last season, including incentives . . . Born April 28, 1964, in Cincinnati . . . Member of 1984 U.S. Olympic team . . . Brother Mike played football for Notre Dame and brother Byron plays basketball for Xavier University . . . Attended University of Michigan and was Big Ten MVP twice.

Year	Club	Pos.	G	AB	R	H	2B	3B	HR	RBI	SB	Avg.
1986	Cincinnati	SS-2B	41	159	27	45	4	3	3	19	8	.283
1987	Cincinnati	SS	125	439	64	107	16	2	12	43	21	.244
1988	Cincinnati	SS	151	588	91	174	32	5	12	56	40	.296
	Totals		317	1186	182	326	52	10	27	118	69	.275

CHRIS SABO 27 6-0 185 **Bats R Throws R**

Named NL Rookie of the Year despite his second-half disappearance . . . Earned a place on All-Star team with huge first half . . . At the break, he was batting .312 with 10 homers, 32 doubles and 35 RBI . . . Had one homer, eight doubles and nine RBI the rest of the way and finished with .271 average . . . Limited to one pinch-hit appearance in club's final 13 games because of groin injury . . . Earned the minimum of $62,500 last season . . . Was the first of two second-round picks in June 1983 draft . . . Had Gold Glove-type season at third base, committing just 14 errors—six after the break . . . Tied major-league record with 11 assists at third base in his second game April 6 . . . Born Jan. 19, 1962, in Detroit . . . University of Michigan product played youth hockey and dreamed of playing in the NHL . . . His emergence allowed club to deal Buddy Bell.

Year	Club	Pos.	G	AB	R	H	2B	3B	HR	RBI	SB	Avg.
1988	Cincinnati	3B	137	538	74	146	40	2	11	44	46	.271

JEFF TREADWAY 26 5-11 170 **Bats L Throws R**

Finished rookie season as starting second baseman, but faces possibility of losing job to comebacking veteran Ron Oester in 1989 . . . Played 23 games in late 1987 and batted .333, making Kurt Stillwell expendable . . . Started strong in 1988 . . . Went on early 14-game hitting streak in May that brought his average to a season-high .318 . . . Floundered after that and wound up hitting .252 . . . Signed out of University of Georgia as free agent in January 1984 . . . Earned $65,000 last season . . . Strong defensively . . . Committed only seven errors last season . . . Born Jan. 22, 1963, in Columbus, Ga. . . . Separated left shoulder in collision with Cardinals' Tom Pagnozzi Aug. 28 and it ended his season . . . Was replaced by Oester, who was making comeback from reconstructive surgery on left knee . . . Never hit less than .300 on any level of pro ball prior to last season.

Year	Club	Pos.	G	AB	R	H	2B	3B	HR	RBI	SB	Avg.
1987	Cincinnati	2B	23	84	9	28	4	0	2	4	1	.333
1988	Cincinnati	2B	103	301	30	76	19	4	2	23	2	.252
	Totals		126	385	39	104	23	4	4	27	3	.270

DANNY JACKSON 27 6-0 195 **Bats R Throws L**

Would have been the first Cy Young Award winner in franchise history had it not been for the record 59-inning scoreless streak compiled by Dodgers' Orel Hershiser . . . Was never below .500 in first season for Reds . . . Obtained from Royals with Angel Salazar for Kurt Stillwell and Ted Power following 1987 season . . . Earned $390,000 last season . . . Was tied with Hershiser for league lead in wins (23) and complete games (15) . . . Was second in innings pitched (260⅔) and shutouts (six) . . . Made All-Star team, but did not get to pitch . . . From June 28 through Aug. 22, he was 11-1 in 13 starts and he pitched three shutouts and allowed just 18 earned runs during the period . . . Born Jan. 5, 1962, in San Antonio, Tex. . . . Helped world champion Royals stave off postseason elimination in 1985 by winning Game 5 of both playoffs and World Series . . . Was first player chosen in secondary phase of January 1982 draft . . .

Royals scored only 37 runs for him in his 18 losses in 1987.

Year	Club	G	IP	W	L	Pct.	SO	BB	H	ERA
1983	Kansas City..........	4	19	1	1	.500	9	6	26	5.21
1984	Kansas City..........	15	76	2	6	.250	40	35	84	4.26
1985	Kansas City..........	32	208	14	12	.538	114	76	209	3.42
1986	Kansas City..........	32	185⅔	11	12	.478	115	79	177	3.20
1987	Kansas City..........	36	224	9	18	.333	152	109	219	4.02
1988	Cincinnati...........	35	260⅔	23	8	.742	161	71	206	2.73
	Totals.............	154	973⅓	60	57	.513	591	376	921	3.43

RICK MAHLER 35 6-1 202 **Bats R Throws R**

Signed two-year, $1.5-million deal with Reds as free agent after posting second straight losing season for Braves . . . From May 9 through June 1, he had a streak of seven straight wins and a 2.87 ERA . . . Was 2-12 the rest of the way and finished 9-16 . . . Talk about tough luck: From July 26 through Sept. 24, he went 1-7 with five no-decisions in 13 starts despite a 2.45 ERA . . . Born Aug. 5, 1953, in Austin, Tex. . . . Originally signed with Atlanta as free agent in June 1975, out of Trinity University.

Year	Club	G	IP	W	L	Pct.	SO	BB	H	ERA
1979	Atlanta	15	22	0	0	.000	12	11	28	6.14
1980	Atlanta	2	4	0	0	.000	1	0	2	2.25
1981	Atlanta	34	112	8	6	.571	54	43	109	2.81
1982	Atlanta	39	205⅓	9	10	.474	105	62	213	4.21
1983	Atlanta	10	14⅓	0	0	.000	7	9	16	5.02
1984	Atlanta	38	222	13	10	.565	106	62	209	3.12
1985	Atlanta	39	266⅔	17	15	.531	107	79	272	3.48
1986	Atlanta	39	237⅔	14	18	.438	137	95	283	4.88
1987	Atlanta	39	197	8	13	.381	95	85	212	4.98
1988	Atlanta	39	249	9	16	.360	131	42	279	3.69
	Totals	294	1530	78	88	.470	755	488	1623	3.97

TOM BROWNING 28 6-1 190 **Bats L Throws L**

Pitched third complete perfect game in NL history and first in franchise history when he stilled Dodgers, 1-0, in Cincinnati Sept. 16, a game that was delayed two hours by rain . . . Club owner Marge Schott, who left after six innings, gave Tom's wife Debbi a full-length mink coat as gift for his gem . . . Almost threw another no-hitter in San Diego June 6, but Tony Gwynn singled to left with one out in ninth to spoil the bid . . . Began his 1988 run June 6 . . . Was 16-2 from that date until end of the season, finishing 18-5 overall . . . Earned

$442,000 last season . . . Was NL Rookie of the Year in 1985, when he finished 20-9 with 3.55 ERA, but was sent back to minors for stretch in 1987 . . . Born April 28, 1960, in Casper, Wyo. . . . Reds' ninth pick in June 1982 draft . . . Attended LeMoyne and Tennessee Wesleyan . . . Has nasty screwball.

Year	Club	G	IP	W	L	Pct.	SO	BB	H	ERA
1984	Cincinnati	3	23⅓	1	0	1.000	14	5	27	1.54
1985	Cincinnati	38	261⅓	20	9	.690	155	73	242	3.55
1986	Cincinnati	39	243⅓	14	13	.519	147	70	225	3.81
1987	Cincinnati	32	183	10	13	.435	117	61	201	5.02
1988	Cincinnati	36	250⅔	18	5	.783	124	64	205	3.41
	Totals	148	961⅔	63	40	.612	557	273	900	3.81

JOHN FRANCO 28 5-10 185 Bats L Throws L

Named NL Fireman of the Year for league-leading 39 saves in 41 opportunites . . . Set major-league record with 13 saves in as many chances in July, when he was named Pitcher of the Month . . . Blew first save opportunity of year May 6 in New York on a Darryl Strawberry homer in the 10th, then began a streak of 28 in row that ended Sept. 11 in Los Angeles . . . In the game that eliminated Reds from division race, he blew a 3-2, ninth-inning lead and lost on Jeff Hamilton's two-run homer . . . Earned $675,000 last season . . . Has 116 saves in his career with Reds, including 32 in 1987 and 29 in 1986 . . . Born Sept. 17, 1960, in Brooklyn, N.Y. . . . Obtained from Dodgers with Brett Wise for Rafael Landestoy, May 9, 1983 . . . Dodgers' fifth-round choice in June 1981 draft, out of St. John's.

Year	Club	G	IP	W	L	Pct.	SO	BB	H	ERA
1984	Cincinnati	54	79⅓	6	2	.750	55	36	74	2.61
1985	Cincinnati	67	99	12	3	.800	61	40	83	2.18
1986	Cincinnati	74	101	6	6	.500	84	44	90	2.94
1987	Cincinnati	68	82	8	5	.615	61	27	76	2.52
1988	Cincinnati	70	86	6	6	.500	46	27	60	1.57
	Totals	333	447⅓	38	22	.633	307	174	383	2.37

JOSE RIJO 23 6-2 185 Bats R Throws R

Began 1988 season in middle relief . . . Moved into rotation June 8 and wound up as one of Reds' most effective starters . . . Ended up 13-8 with 2.39 ERA, fifth-best mark in league . . . Had eight-game winning streak, matching the third-longest in NL, from April 9 through June 14 . . . Struck out 160 batters in 162 innings, and average of 8.9 strikeouts per nine innings, the third-best mark in league and the fourth-best in majors . . . Allowed only 120 hits as opponents hit only .209 against him . . . Three of his losses came by scores of 1-0, 1-0 and

2-0 . . . Went on DL in mid-August with right elbow tendinitis that limited him to brief late-season appearances . . . Acquired from Athletics with Tim Birtsas for Dave Parker after the 1987 season . . . Athletics had gotten him from Yankees in Rickey Henderson deal prior to 1985 season . . . Born May 13, 1965, in San Cristobal, Dominican Republic . . . Yankees signed him as free agent at age 16 . . . His father-in-law is Hall of Fame pitcher Juan Marichal.

Year	Club	G	IP	W	L	Pct.	SO	BB	H	ERA
1984	New York (AL)	24	62⅓	2	8	.200	47	33	74	4.76
1985	Oakland	12	63⅔	6	4	.600	65	28	57	3.53
1986	Oakland	39	193⅔	9	11	.450	176	108	172	4.65
1987	Oakland	21	82⅓	2	7	.222	67	41	106	5.90
1988	Cincinnati	49	162	13	8	.619	160	63	120	2.39
	Totals	145	564	32	38	.457	515	273	529	4.07

TOP PROSPECT

LEN HARRIS 24 5-10 195 **Bats L Throws R**

Middle infielder came up from Nashville (AAA) and played 16 games in September . . . Went 16-for-43 (.372) with eight RBI . . . Could be backup shortstop in 1989, replacing released veteran Davey Concepcion . . . Reds' fifth choice in June 1983 draft . . . Played first four minor-league seasons at third base . . . Born Oct. 28, 1964, in Miami . . . Batted .463 and stole 22 straight bases for Jackson High School in Miami as a senior . . . Hit .277 with 45 steals for Nashville last season.

MANAGER PETE ROSE: Cincinnati's favorite native son

spent much of 1988 on hot seat after it became obvious that the Reds were not going to win division title . . . Had to settle for fourth straight second-place finish in his fourth full season as manager . . . Was finally signed to a $1-million, two-year contract extension near the end of last season . . . Took over as player-manager when he returned to Reds Aug. 16, 1984 . . . Was traded by Expos for Tom Lawless . . . Fond of saying that he took over a last-place team that was drawing 1.2 million people and turned it into one of baseball's most profitable franchises . . . Born April 14, 1941, in Cincinnati . . . Baseball's all-time hit leader began stellar playing career with Reds in 1963 . . . Departed for Phillies as free agent in 1979 . . . Concluded his playing career with a strikeout vs. Padres' Goose Gossage, Aug. 17, 1986 . . . Managerial record is 365-322, a .560 winning percentage . . . Won 87 games last year, but still finished seven games behind first-place Los Angeles.

GREATEST FIRST BASEMAN

There can be no question that Peter Edward Rose is the top first baseman in Cincinnati history. Of course, one might consider him for the same honor at second base, third base and in the outfield. That's how versatile Rose was during his 24-year playing career. His selection to the Hall of Fame is such a sure bet when he becomes eligible in 1991 that they might as well clear out a section for him right now.

Of his myriad accomplishments, Rose will always be remembered for surpassing Ty Cobb's all-time record of 4,192 hits. The record-setting hit came at Riverfront Stadium, Sept. 11, 1985, when he lined a single to left off San Diego right-hander Eric Show. Rose, who was 44 years old at the time, concluded his career with 4,256 hits. He added 45 more hits in the playoffs, 35 more in the World Series and seven more during 16 All-Star appearances.

Above all, Rose was a winner. He played on seven division champions, five pennant winners and three world champions, including the dominant Big Red Machines of 1975 and 1976 and the 1980 Phillies, the only world championship team in the history of that franchise. He was the NL MVP in 1973 and MVP of the Reds' seven-game victory over Boston in the 1975 World Series.

Aside from the all-time hit mark, Rose holds the record for most games played (3,562), most at-bats (14,053), most singles (3,215), most 200-hit seasons (10) and most winning games (1,972).

The street outside Riverfront Stadium is aptly named "Pete Rose Way."

ALL-TIME RED SEASON RECORDS

BATTING: Cy Seymour, .377, 1905
HRs: George Foster, 52, 1977
RBIs: George Foster, 149, 1977
STEALS: Bob Bescher, 81, 1911
WINS: Adolfo Luque, 27, 1923
Bucky Walters, 27, 1939
STRIKEOUTS: Mario Soto, 274, 1982

HOUSTON ASTROS

TEAM DIRECTORY: Chairman: Dr. John J. McMullen; GM: Bill Wood; Asst. GM: Bob Watson; Special Asst.: Donald Davidson; Coordinator Minor League Instruction: Jimmy Johnson; Dir. Pub. Rel.: Rob Matwick; Trav. Sec.: Barry Waters; Mgr.: Art Howe. Home: Astrodome (45,000). Field distances: 330, l.f. line; 380, l.c.; 400, c.f.; 380, r.c.; 330, r.f. line. Spring training: Kissimmee, Fla.

Even the Dome can't hold Glenn Davis' Astro projections.

SCOUTING REPORT

HITTING: Just a few seasons after winning a division title in 1986, the Astros are looking to totally revamp a batting order that finished 10th in the NL in average (.244), tied for ninth in homers (96) and in the middle of the pack in runs (617) last year. They dangled almost everyone except their only powerhouse—Glenn Davis (.271, 30, 99)—but came up empty in their quests for the Braves' Dale Murphy, the Red Sox' Wade Boggs or the Royals' Danny Tartabull.

So, the Astros will have to steal their way around the bases again in 1989, counting on the legs of Gerald Young (65 steals), Billy Hatcher (32 steals) and Kevin Bass (31 steals) to generate a threat. Last year, this club went into fitful scoring droughts and it doesn't appear things should be much better this season.

PITCHING: This is the usual Astro strong point. But the club received a real blow in December, when 43-year-old Nolan Ryan (12-11, 3.52, 228 strikeouts) turned down a million dollars a year and signed as a free agent with neighboring Texas, leaving the Astros Ryan-less for the first time in this decade.

Mike Scott (14-8, 2.92, 190 Ks), Bob Knepper (14-5, 3.14) and Jim Deshaies (11-14, 3.00) are going to have to pick up the slack along with Rick Rhoden (12-12, 4.20, 197 innings as a Yankee), acquired in January. Free agent import Jim Clancy (11-13, 4.49 with Toronto), Danny Darwin (8-13, 3.84) and Bob Forsch (10-8, 4.29) seem to be the pick of the litter.

The bullpen is good, with Juan Agosto (10-2, 2.26, 4 saves) and Dave Smith (4-5, 2.67, 27 saves) forming a potent one-two punch.

FIELDING: Houston did not distinguish itself in this category last season, as one of five NL teams to commit more than 130 errors with 138. The Astros must play better defense to have any chance of being competitive. The middle-infield play is beginning to yellow around the edges with shortstop Rafael Ramirez and second baseman Bill Doran on the down sides of their careers. Third base remains a real question mark. Last season, the Astros picked up Buddy Bell (.241, 7, 40) from the Reds to fill the void, but that void still needs to be filled.

The outfield of Hatcher, Young and Bass, from left to right, is one of the league's swiftest and is perfect for closing the gaps in the wide-open spaces of the Astrodome. But could it really be that Alan Ashby and Alex Trevino are back as catchers?

OUTLOOK: Last year's second-half fade and listless play was the death knell for manager Hal Lanier, who was replaced by the inexperienced Art Howe. This club, which slipped from the first division last season, could slip even further this year—into last place. This team needs a total transplant of heart and talent.

The Astros probably hit their apex when they took the Mets to six games in the 1986 NLCS. Since then, the club has made few significant moves toward improving itself and now the Astros seem on a collision course with disaster.

HOUSTON ASTROS 1989 ROSTER

MANAGER Art Howe
Coaches—Yogi Berra, Matt Galante, Phil Garner, Les Moss

PITCHERS

No.	Name	1988 Club	W-L	IP	SO	ERA	B-T	Ht.	Wt.	Born
49	Agosto, Juan	Houston	10-2	92	33	2.26	L-L	6-2	190	2/23/58 Puerto Rico
42	Andersen, Larry	Houston	2-4	83	66	2.94	R-R	6-3	205	5/6/53 Portland, OR
—	August, Sam	Osceola	2-0	30	28	1.50	R-R	6-2	170	11/24/67 Huntington Beach, CA
50	Childress, Rocky	Houston	1-0	23	24	6.17	R-R	6-2	195	2/18/62 Santa Rosa, CA
		Tucson	6-4	97	57	3.33				
—	Clancy, Jim	Toronto	11-13	196	118	4.49	R-R	6-4	220	12/18/55 Chicago, IL
—	Costello, Fred	Asheville	6-7	76	64	3.55	R-R	6-4	190	10/1/66 Clearlake, CA
44	Darwin, Danny	Houston	8-13	192	129	3.84	R-R	6-3	190	10/25/55 Bonham, TX
43	Deshaies, Jim	Houston	11-14	207	127	3.00	L-L	6-4	220	6/23/60 Massena, NY
31	Forsch, Bob	St. L-Hou.	10-8	136	54	4.29	R-R	6-3	215	1/13/50 Sacramento, CA
—	Heathcock, Jeff	Houston	0-5	31	12	5.81	R-R	6-4	195	11/18/59 Covina, CA
		Tucson	3-5	80	49	5.08				
—	Ilsley, Blaise	Columbus	3-1	39	38	5.95	L-L	6-1	185	4/9/64 Alpena, MI
37	Kerfeld, Charley	Columbus	2-7	64	63	4.50	R-R	6-7	250	9/28/63 Knob Noster, MO
39	Knepper, Bob	Houston	14-5	175	103	3.14	L-L	6-2	210	5/25/54 Akron, OH
53	Meads, Dave	Houston	3-1	40	27	3.18	L-L	6-0	175	1/7/64 Monclair, NJ
		Tucson	3-4	46	48	1.96				
35	Meyer, Brian	Columbus	4-3	83	68	2.27	R-R	6-1	190	1/29/63 Camden, NJ
		Houston	0-0	12	10	1.46				
—	Portugal, Mark	Portland	2-0	20	9	1.37	R-R	6-0	200	10/30/62 Los Angeles, CA
		Minnesota	3-3	58	31	4.53				
—	Rhoden, Rick	New York (AL)	12-12	197	94	4.20	R-R	6-4	203	5/16/53 Boynton Beach, FL
33	Scott, Mike	Houston	14-8	219	190	2.92	R-R	6-3	215	4/26/55 Santa Monica, CA
45	Smith, Dave	Houston	4-5	57	38	2.67	R-R	6-1	195	1/21/55 San Francisco, CA

CATCHERS

No.	Name	1988 Club	H	HR	RBI	Pct.	B-T	Ht.	Wt.	Born
14	Ashby, Alan	Tucson	0	0	0	.000	S-R	6-2	195	7/8/51 Long Beach, CA
		Houston	54	7	33	.238				
4	Biggio, Craig	Tucson	90	3	39	.320	R-R	5-11	180	12/14/65 Smithtown, NY
		Houston	26	3	5	.211				
—	Eusebio, Raul	Osceola	96	0	40	.245	R-R	6-2	179	4/27/67 Dominican Republic
9	Trevino, Alex	Houston	48	2	13	.249	R-R	5-11	179	8/26/57 Mexico

INFIELDERS

25	*Bell, Buddy	Cin.-Hou.	78	7	40	.241	R-R	6-3	200	8/27/51 Pittsburgh, PA
11	Caminiti, Ken	Tucson	113	5	66	.272	S-R	6-0	200	4/21/63 Hanford, CA
		Houston	15	1	7	.181				
1	Candaele, Casey	Indianapolis	63	2	36	.264	S-R	5-9	165	1/12/61 Lompoc, CA
		Mont.-Hou.	25	0	5	.170				
		Tucson	17	0	5	.258				
27	Davis, Glenn	Houston	152	30	99	.271	R-R	6-3	200	3/28/61 Jacksonville, FL
19	Doran, Bill	Houston	119	7	53	.248	S-R	6-0	175	5/28/58 Cincinnati, OH
23	Jackson, Chuck	Tucson	45	2	11	.298	R-R	6-0	185	3/19/63 Seattle, WA
		Houston	19	1	8	.229				
16	Ramirez, Rafael	Houston	156	6	59	.276	R-R	5-11	190	2/18/59 Dominican Republic
12	Reynolds, Craig	Houston	41	1	14	.255	L-R	6-1	175	12/27/52 Houston, TX

OUTFIELDERS

—	Anthony, Eric	Asheville	120	29	89	.273	L-L	6-2	195	11/8/67 San Diego, CA
17	Bass, Kevin	Houston	138	14	72	.255	S-R	6-0	180	5/12/59 Redwood City, CA
28	Hatcher, Billy	Houston	142	7	52	.268	R-R	5-9	175	10/4/60 Williams, AZ
26	Meadows, Louie	Tucson	71	5	43	.254	L-L	5-11	190	4/29/61 Onslow County, NC
		Houston	8	2	3	.190				
21	Puhl, Terry	Houston	71	3	19	.303	L-R	6-2	200	7/8/56 Canada
—	Rhodes, Karl	Osceola	128	1	34	.283	L-L	5-11	170	8/21/68 Cincinnati, OH
2	Young, Gerald	Houston	148	0	37	.257	S-R	6-2	185	10/22/64 Honduras

*Free agent at press time listed with 1988 team

ASTRO PROFILES

GLENN DAVIS 28 6-3 200 **Bats R Throws R**

Was one of only two NL players to hit 30 or more homers last season . . . His 30 was second to Darryl Strawberry's 39 for Mets . . . Drove in 99 runs . . . Power numbers have been remarkably consistent his last three big-league seasons . . . First baseman had 31 homers with 101 RBI in 1986 and 27 homers with 93 RBI in 1987 . . . Was runnerup to Mike Schmidt in 1986 NL MVP voting . . . Earned $340,000 last season . . . Became only the second Astro to hit 30 homers twice in his career . . . Was hit by pitches 11 times, a club record . . . Born March 28, 1961, in Jacksonville, Fla. . . . Selected by Astros in secondary phase of January 1981 draft . . . Was NL All-Star in 1986 . . . Attended University of Georgia.

Year	Club	Pos.	G	AB	R	H	2B	3B	HR	RBI	SB	Avg.
1984	Houston	1B	18	61	6	13	5	0	2	8	0	.213
1985	Houston	1B-OF	100	350	51	95	11	0	20	64	0	.271
1986	Houston	1B	158	574	91	152	32	3	31	101	3	.265
1987	Houston	1B	151	578	70	145	35	2	27	93	4	.251
1988	Houston	1B	152	561	78	152	26	0	30	99	4	.271
	Totals		579	2124	296	557	109	5	110	365	11	.262

BILL DORAN 30 6-0 175 **Bats S Throws R**

Underwent arthroscopic surgery on right shoulder to repair rotator-cuff damage . . . Played in 132 games at second base last season, despite injuries to shoulder, back and hamstring . . . Signed through 1990 at $830,000 a year . . . Led all NL second baseman with .988 fielding percentage in 1988 . . . Committed just eight errors . . . However, his .248 average was his lowest in six full years as major leaguer . . . Astros' sixth-round selection in June 1979 draft . . . Stands 71 hits shy of 1,000 plateau . . . Was club MVP in 1987, when he played in all 162 games with career highs of .283, 177 hits, 16 homers and 79 RBI . . . Born May 28, 1958, in Cincinnati . . . Had career-high 42 steals in 1986 . . . Teammate of current Royal Charlie Leibrandt at Miami-Ohio.

Year	Club	Pos.	G	AB	R	H	2B	3B	HR	RBI	SB	Avg.
1982	Houston	2B	26	97	11	27	3	0	0	6	5	.278
1983	Houston	2B	154	535	70	145	12	7	8	39	12	.271
1984	Houston	2B-SS	147	548	92	143	18	11	4	41	21	.261
1985	Houston	2B	148	578	84	166	31	6	14	59	23	.287
1986	Houston	2B	145	550	92	152	29	3	6	37	42	.276
1987	Houston	2B-SS	162	625	82	177	23	3	16	79	31	.283
1988	Houston	2B	132	480	66	119	18	1	7	53	17	.248
	Totals		914	3413	497	929	134	31	55	314	151	.272

RAFAEL RAMIREZ 30 5-11 190 **Bats R Throws R**

Came over from Altanta prior to last season in deal for minor-leaguers Mike Stoker and Ed Whited . . . Had a strong comeback year following an injury-plagued 1987 season . . . Played just 56 games for Braves in 1987 and was on the disabled list from July 2 to Sept. 25 because of partially torn ligaments in his left knee . . . Last year, he led Astro regulars with .276 average, 156 hits and 30 doubles . . . Currently on final year of two-year contract for $900,000 a year . . . His 23 errors at shortstop were a career low . . . Born Feb. 18, 1959, in San Pedro de Macoris, Dominican Republic . . . Batted career-high .297 for the Braves in 1983 . . . Hit first career grand slam last May 29 at Chicago . . . Originally signed by Braves as free agent in September 1976.

Year	Club	Pos.	G	AB	R	H	2B	3B	HR	RBI	SB	Avg.
1980	Atlanta..........	SS	50	165	17	44	6	1	2	11	2	.267
1981	Atlanta..........	SS	95	307	30	67	16	2	2	20	7	.218
1982	Atlanta..........	SS	157	609	74	169	24	4	10	52	27	.278
1983	Atlanta..........	SS	152	622	82	185	13	5	7	58	16	.297
1984	Atlanta..........	SS	145	591	51	157	22	4	2	48	14	.266
1985	Atlanta..........	SS	138	568	54	141	25	4	5	58	2	.248
1986	Atlanta..........	SS-3B-OF	134	496	57	119	21	1	8	33	19	.240
1987	Atlanta..........	SS-3B	56	179	22	47	12	0	1	21	6	.263
1988	Houston	SS	155	566	51	156	30	5	6	59	3	.276
	Totals		1082	4103	438	1085	169	26	43	360	96	.264

BILLY HATCHER 28 5-9 175 **Bats R Throws R**

Left fielder had first five-hit game of his career May 20 vs. Cardinals . . . Tied Gerald Young for team lead in runs with 79 . . . Played in career-high 145 games . . . Was obtained from the Cubs with Steve Engel for Jerry Mumphrey, following 1985 season . . . Was second on club with 32 steals last year, well below his 53 steals in 1987 . . . Earned $225,000 last season . . . Came up with the Cubs to stay June 25, 1985, when he replaced the injured Bob Dernier in center . . . Born Oct. 4, 1960, in Williams, Ariz. . . . Career highlight is 14th-inning, game-tying homer vs. Mets' Jesse Orosco in Game 6 of 1986 NLCS . . . Cubs' sixth-round pick in January 1981 draft.

Year	Club	Pos.	G	AB	R	H	2B	3B	HR	RBI	SB	Avg.
1984	Chicago (NL).....	OF	8	9	1	1	0	0	0	0	2	.111
1985	Chicago (NL).....	OF	53	163	24	40	12	1	2	10	2	.245
1986	Houston	OF	127	419	55	108	15	4	6	36	38	.258
1987	Houston	OF	141	564	96	167	28	3	11	63	53	.296
1988	Houston	OF	145	530	79	142	25	4	7	52	32	.268
	Totals		474	1685	255	458	80	12	26	161	127	.272

GERALD YOUNG 24 6-2 185 **Bats S Throws R**

Took over center-field duties in first full season . . . Stole a club-record 65 bases, breaking Astro mark of 61 set by Cesar Cedeno in 1977 . . . Was in contention for NL stolen-base crown for much of last season, but wound up second to Cards' Vince Coleman, who finished with 81 . . . Earned $90,000 last season . . . Obtained from Mets with Manny Lee and Mitch Cook in Sept. 1, 1984 deal for Ray Knight . . . Went 576 at-bats without hitting a homer in 1988, the longest stretch in the NL . . . Born Oct. 22, 1964, in Tela, Honduras . . . Has stolen 91 bases in 220 big-league games . . . Mets' fifth-round pick in June 1982 draft.

Year	Club	Pos.	G	AB	R	H	2B	3B	HR	RBI	SB	Avg.
1987	Houston	OF	71	274	44	88	9	2	1	15	26	.321
1988	Houston	OF	149	576	79	148	21	9	0	37	65	.257
	Totals		220	850	123	236	30	11	1	52	91	.278

KEVIN BASS 29 6-0 180 **Bats S Throws R**

Was mentioned in trade talks all last season . . . Early on, he was supposedly on his way to Yankees for Dave Winfield, but Winfield turned down the deal . . . Later was offered to Montreal for Hubie Brooks and Toronto for Jesse Barfield, but the swaps never happened . . . Right fielder experienced dip in average (.284 to .255), homers (19 to 14) and RBI (85 to 72) compared to 1987 . . . Stole career-high 31 bases . . . Acquired from Brewers with pitchers Mike Madden and Frank DiPino for Don Sutton, Aug. 30, 1982 . . . Earned $780,000 last season . . . Born May 12, 1959, in Redwood City, Cal. . . . Was NL All-Star in 1986 and batted .292 in the Astros' six-game 1986 NLCS loss to Mets . . . Brewers' second-round pick in June 1977 draft.

Year	Club	Pos.	G	AB	R	H	2B	3B	HR	RBI	SB	Avg.
1982	Milwaukee.......	OF	18	9	4	0	0	0	0	0	0	.000
1982	Houston	OF	12	24	2	1	0	0	0	0	0	.042
1983	Houston	OF	88	195	25	46	7	3	2	18	2	.236
1984	Houston	OF	121	331	33	86	17	5	2	29	5	.260
1985	Houston	OF	150	539	72	145	27	5	16	68	19	.269
1986	Houston	OF	157	591	83	184	33	5	20	79	22	.311
1987	Houston	OF	157	592	83	168	31	5	19	85	21	.284
1988	Houston	OF	157	541	57	138	27	2	14	72	31	.255
	Totals		860	2822	359	768	142	25	73	352	100	.272

Mike Scott came within two outs of a second no-hitter.

MIKE SCOTT 33 6-3 215 **Bats R Throws R**

Led club with 14 wins, eight complete games, five shutouts and 2.92 ERA . . . Master of the split finger or the sandpaper fastball . . . Held hitters to a .204 average last year . . . Has won 66 games for Astros in last four years . . . Just missed tossing his second career no-hitter June 12, when Braves' Ken Oberkfell singled with one out in the ninth . . . Threw his no-hitter Sept. 25, 1986 in 2-0 victory over Giants and clinched division title for Astros in process . . . Won 1986 Cy Young Award and NL Pitcher of the Year honors for 18-10 season and league-leading 2.22 ERA and 306 strikeouts . . . Obtained from Mets for Danny Heep, Dec. 10, 1982 . . . On final year of contract, he'll earn $1.3 million in 1989 . . . Born April 26, 1955, in Santa Monica, Cal. . . . Missed three weeks with pulled left hamstring last season . . . Mets' second-round pick in June 1976.

Year	Club	G	IP	W	L	Pct.	SO	BB	H	ERA
1979	New York (NL)	18	52	1	3	250	21	20	59	5.37
1980	New York (NL)	6	29	1	1	.500	13	8	40	4.34
1981	New York (NL)	23	136	5	10	.333	54	34	130	3.90
1982	New York (NL)	37	147	7	13	.350	63	60	185	5.14
1983	Houston	24	145	10	6	.625	73	46	143	3.72
1984	Houston	31	154	5	11	.313	83	43	179	4.68
1985	Houston	36	221⅔	18	8	.692	137	80	194	3.29
1986	Houston	37	275⅓	18	10	.643	306	72	182	2.22
1987	Houston	36	247⅔	16	13	.552	233	79	199	3.23
1988	Houston	32	218⅔	14	8	.636	190	53	162	2.92
	Totals	280	1626⅓	95	83	.534	1173	495	1473	3.53

RICK RHODEN 35 6-4 203 **Bats R Throws R**

Is an Astro after the Yankees unloaded him and his $900,000 salary for three minor leaguers in January . . . Had not emerged as the ace the Yankees sought when they obtained him from Pirates with Cecilio Guante and Pat Clements for Doug Drabek, Brian Fisher and Logan Easley following the 1986 season . . . Can't stay away from nagging injuries . . . Muscle strain in lower back led to 1-3 start and caused him to be disabled from April 29 to May 21 . . . Failed to win consecutive decisions until a four-game winning streak in July . . . Followed that with four-game losing streak from Aug. 5-21, then won five in row from Aug. 31 to Sept. 20 before dropping final two decisions . . . Accused of scuffing balls, but has never been caught . . . Born May 16, 1953, in Boynton Beach, Fla. . . . Dodgers' first-round pick in June 1971 draft . . . Excellent hitter who was actually used as DH by Billy Martin early last season.

Year	Club	G	IP	W	L	Pct.	SO	BB	H	ERA
1974	Los Angeles	4	9	1	0	1.000	7	4	5	2.00
1975	Los Angeles	26	99	3	3	.500	40	32	94	3.09
1976	Los Angeles	27	181	12	3	*.800	77	53	165	2.98
1977	Los Angeles	31	216	16	10	.615	122	63	223	3.75
1978	Los Angeles	30	165	10	8	.556	79	51	160	3.65
1979	Pittsburgh	1	5	0	1	.000	2	2	5	7.20
1980	Pittsburgh	20	127	7	5	.583	70	40	133	3.83
1981	Pittsburgh	21	136	9	4	.692	76	53	147	3.90
1982	Pittsburgh	35	230⅓	11	14	.440	128	70	239	4.14
1983	Pittsburgh	36	244⅓	13	13	.500	153	68	256	3.09
1984	Pittsburgh	33	238⅓	14	9	.609	136	62	216	2.72
1985	Pittsburgh	35	213⅓	10	15	.400	128	69	254	4.47
1986	Pittsburgh	34	253⅔	15	12	.556	159	76	211	2.84
1987	New York (AL)	30	181⅔	16	10	.615	107	61	184	3.86
1988	New York (AL)	30	197	12	12	.500	94	56	206	4.20
	Totals	393	2496⅔	149	119	.556	1378	760	2498	3.56

DAVE SMITH 34 6-1 195 **Bats R Throws R**

Set a club record with his 432nd appearance, June 9 vs. Dodgers . . . Finished with 27 saves in 32 chances . . . His 151 career saves make him one of only 12 relief pitchers in history to save more than 150 games . . . Since 1985, he has registered 111 saves in 130 opportunities —an 85 percent success ratio . . . Has saved more games during last four years than Jeff Reardon, Dave Righetti, Lee Smith or John Franco . . . His career high was 33 saves in 1986 . . . Is signed through 1990 at $1.1 million a year . . . Was Houston's eighth-round selection in June 1976 draft . . . Didn't allow a home run during the 1987 season

...Born Jan. 21, 1955, in San Francisco...Astros' eighth-round pick in June 1976 draft, out of San Diego State.

Year	Club	G	IP	W	L	Pct.	SO	BB	H	ERA
1980	Houston	57	103	7	5	.583	85	32	90	1.92
1981	Houston	42	75	5	3	.625	52	23	54	2.76
1982	Houston	49	63⅓	5	4	.556	28	31	69	3.84
1983	Houston	42	72⅔	3	1	.750	41	36	72	3.10
1984	Houston	53	77⅓	5	4	.556	45	20	60	2.21
1985	Houston	64	79⅓	9	5	.643	40	17	69	2.27
1986	Houston	54	56	4	7	.364	46	22	39	2.73
1987	Houston	50	60	2	3	.400	73	21	39	1.65
1988	Houston	51	57⅓	4	5	.444	38	19	60	2.67
	Totals	462	644	44	37	.543	448	221	552	2.53

JUAN AGOSTO 31 6-2 190 **Bats L Throws L**

Developed into club's top left-handed reliever in 1988...Established club record with 75 appearances...Broke Joe Niekro's club record with 10 straight victories...Opened the season 10-0 and finished 10-2 with a 2.26 ERA and four saves...Signed to minor-league contract April 27, 1987 and was called up from Tucson (AAA) July 31...Came up in the Red Sox system and pitched for White Sox and Twins before joining Astros...His 10 wins was most by an Astro left-hander since Hal Woodeshick set the club record with an 11-9 record in 1967...Born Feb. 23, 1958, in Rio Piedras, Puerto Rico... Originally signed with Red Sox as free agent in August 1974.

Year	Club	G	IP	W	L	Pct.	SO	BB	H	ERA
1981	Chicago (AL)	2	6	0	0	.000	3	0	5	4.50
1982	Chicago (AL)	1	2	0	0	.000	1	0	7	18.00
1983	Chicago (AL)	39	41⅔	2	2	.500	29	11	41	4.10
1984	Chicago (AL)	49	55⅓	2	1	.667	26	34	54	3.09
1985	Chicago (AL)	54	60⅓	4	3	.571	39	23	45	3.58
1986	Chi. (AL)-Minn.	26	25	1	4	.200	12	18	49	8.64
1987	Houston	27	27⅓	1	1	.500	6	10	26	2.63
1988	Houston	75	91⅔	10	2	.833	33	30	74	2.26
	Totals	273	309⅓	20	13	.606	149	126	301	3.61

JIM CLANCY 33 6-4 220 **Bats R Throws R**

Free agent signed three-year, $3.45-million contract with the Astros after experiencing roller-coaster 1988 season with the Blue Jays ...Finished on rise by winning eight of last 10 decisions following brief demotion to bullpen ...Did not have an ERA below 5.00 in three of first four months and struggled to 2-6 start ...Born Dec. 18, 1955, in Chicago...Blue Jays acquired him from Rangers in AL expansion draft in November 1976 . . . Rangers' fourth-round pick in June 1974 . . . Was only Blue Jay to play in Toronto for each of franchise's 12 seasons.

Year	Club	G	IP	W	L	Pct.	SO	BB	H	ERA
1977	Toronto	13	77	4	9	.308	44	47	80	5.03
1978	Toronto	31	194	10	12	.455	106	91	199	4.08
1979	Toronto	12	64	2	7	.222	33	31	65	5.48
1980	Toronto	34	251	13	16	.448	152	128	217	3.30
1981	Toronto	22	125	6	12	.333	56	64	126	4.90
1982	Toronto	40	266⅔	16	14	.533	139	77	251	3.71
1983	Toronto	34	223	15	11	.577	99	61	238	3.91
1984	Toronto	36	219⅔	13	15	.464	118	88	249	5.12
1985	Toronto	23	128⅔	9	6	.600	66	37	117	3.78
1986	Toronto	34	219⅓	14	14	.500	126	63	202	3.94
1987	Toronto	37	241⅓	15	11	.577	180	80	234	3.54
1988	Toronto	36	196⅓	11	13	.458	118	47	207	4.49
	Totals	352	2206	128	140	.478	1237	814	2185	4.10

TOP PROSPECT

BRIAN MEYER 26 6-1 190 **Bats R Throws R**

Made eight relief appearances for Astros late last season and posted a 1.46 ERA . . . Allowed nine hits, two earned runs and 10 strikeouts in 12⅓ innings . . . Was 4-3 with 2.27 ERA and 25 saves for Columbus (AA) in 1988 . . . Astros' 16th pick in June 1986 draft . . . Born Jan. 29, 1963, in Camden, N.J. . . . In first two seasons of Class-A ball, he never posted an ERA higher than 2.00 . . . Was 5-2 with a 1.43 ERA and a New York-Penn League-leading 32 appearances for Auburn (A) in 1986 . . . Followed that with 52 appearances and a 1.99 ERA for Osceola (A) of Florida State League in 1987.

MANAGER ART HOWE: Beginning his first season as a manager . . . Was signed to a two-year contract to replace Hal Lanier during offseason . . . Beginning his 19th season in pro ball . . . Big-league playing career as an infielder spanned 11 years, six of them with the Astros . . . Was appointed to the Ranger coaching staff under manager Bobby Valentine, May 21, 1985 . . . Spent last three seasons as Rangers' hitting instructor . . . Managed Rangers during Valentine's four-game suspension in 1986 . . . Spent four winters managing in Puerto Rican Winter League and was named Manager of the Year in 1980 . . . One of the youngest managers in baseball . . . Born Dec.

15, 1946, in Pittsburgh . . . Played on the Astros' 1980 division title winner . . . Missed entire 1983 season, his last in Houston, recovering from surgery on his ankle and elbow . . . Batted .260 with 43 home runs in 891 big-league games . . . Came up with the Pirate organization, but was traded to Houston for Tommy Helms, prior to 1976 season . . . His playing career ended when he was released by Cards in April 1985.

GREATEST FIRST BASEMAN

First base in Houston has been manned by such players as Walt Bond, Nate Colbert, Curt Blefary, Jim Gentile, Keith Lampard, John Mayberry, Danny Walton and Bob Watson. One would be hard-pressed to argue, though, that the man who currently makes his home there—Glenn Davis—is not the best first baseman this franchise has ever had.

When Davis hit 30 homers this part season, he became just the second Astro in the club's 27-year history to hit at least 30 in two seasons. Furthermore, Davis has hit at least 20 homers for four straight seasons, matching the club mark established by Jim Wynn from 1967-70. With 96 homers to show for his 659 big-league games, Davis is as powerful as they come in Houston. He is already fifth on the Astros' all-time homer list behind Wynn (223), Cesar Cedeno (163), Watson (139), Jose Cruz (138) and Doug Rader (128).

ALL-TIME ASTRO SEASON RECORDS

BATTING: Rusty Staub, .333, 1967
HRs: Jimmy Wynn, 37, 1967
RBIs: Bob Watson, 110, 1977
STEALS: Gerald Young, 65, 1988
WINS: Joe Niekro, 21, 1979
STRIKEOUTS: J. R. Richard, 313, 1979

LOS ANGELES DODGERS

TEAM DIRECTORY: Pres.: Peter O'Malley; Exec. VP Player Pers.: Fred Claire; VP-Marketing: Merritt Willey; VP-Communications: Tommy Hawkins: Dir. Minor League Oper.: Charlie Blaney; Trav. Sec.: Bill DeLury; Mgr. Tom Lasorda. Home: Dodger Stadium (56,000). Field distances: 330, l.f. line; 370, l.c.; 395, c.f.; 370, r.c.; 330, r.f. line. Spring training: Vero Beach, Fla.

SCOUTING REPORT

HITTING: The Dodgers won it all without real power last season. They were one of five NL teams to hit less than 100 home runs, with 99. But NL MVP Kirk Gibson (.290, 25, 76) and Mike Marshall (.277, 20, 82) finally have some help now—from former Oriole Eddie Murray, who brings his 28-homer, 84-RBI bat to the Dodger lineup. That's the good news.

The bad news is that Steve Sax, the leadoff hitter and catalyst, left Los Angeles to sign with the Yankees. He will be replaced at second base by ex-Yankee Willie Randolph (.230, 2, 34), a free-agent signee who does not have Sax' offensive tools. Look for Alfredo Griffin to get a shot at the leadoff spot, even though he hit only .199 with seven steals during an injury-plagued 1988.

PITCHING: Tommy Lasorda's staff recorded a 2.96 ERA, second to the Mets' 2.91 mark last season, and should be just as strong this year. If left-hander Fernando Valenzuela (5-8, 4.24) can make it back from last season's shoulder problems, the Dodgers should remain the team to beat. In fact, if everyone is healthy, what will the Dodgers do with John Tudor (10-8, 2.32) when he returns from offseason elbow surgery in the summer? It could get crowded behind Cy Young winner Orel Hershiser (23-8, 2.26), Tim Belcher (12-6, 2.91) and Tim Leary (17-11, 2.91).

Certainly no one expects Hershiser to continue his roll, but he does go into the season on a record 59-inning scoreless streak. The bullpen is strong, thanks to Jay Howell (5-3, 2.08, 21 saves), although the boys who bleed blue will miss Brian Holton (7-3, 1.70), sent to the Orioles in the Murray deal.

FIELDING: The Dodgers will never be confused with a team of defensive artists. Said one NL general manager after the Murray trade, "Well, he fits right in defensively." Murray replaces Franklin (No Hands) Stubbs, who made 13 errors last season. The

Tim Belcher came of age with three postseason wins.

defense at first base doesn't figure to get any better with the aging former Gold Glover Murray holding forth. Likewise, second baseman Randolph was a whiz with the glove during his salad days, but at 34, the salad seems all but wilted. Griffin and Jeff Hamilton are more than adequate, though, on the left side of the infield.

The outfield remains average with Gibson, John Shelby and Marshall trying to stay out of each other's way from left to right. Mike Scioscia still rates with the best plate blockers and top defensive catchers in the game.

OUTLOOK: After taking the Dodgers to their first world championship since 1981, Executive of the Year Fred Claire did not stand still. But will the additions of Murray, who essentially replaces Pedro Guerrero, and Randolph, who replaces Sax, mean an improvement on last year's 94 wins? The guess is no. The guess is also that the Dodgers will find the gap closed by San Diego and Cincinnati. And, in 1989, 94 wins may not be enough to win the division.

There has been no pennant race in the NL West since Atlanta backed into the title when they lost to the Padres and the Giants beat the Dodgers on the final day of the 1982 season. Expect one this year.

LOS ANGELES DODGERS 1989 ROSTER

MANAGER Tom Lasorda
Coaches—Joe Amalfitano, Mark Cresse, Joe Ferguson, Ben Hines, Manny Mota, Ron Perranoski, Bill Russell

PITCHERS

No.	Name	1988 Club	W-L	IP	SO	ERA	B-T	Ht.	Wt.	Born
49	Belcher, Tim	Los Angeles	12-6	180	152	2.91	R-R	6-3	210	10/19/61 Mt. Gilead, OH
—	Brennan, William	Albuquerque	14-8	167	83	3.82	R-R	6-3	194	1/15/63 Tampa, FL
		Los Angeles	0-1	9	7	6.75				
52	Crews, Tim	Albuquerque	1-1	13	7	2.70	R-R	6-0	192	4/3/61 Tampa, FL
		Los Angeles	4-0	72	45	3.14				
—	Hartley, Mike	San Antonio	5-1	45	57	0.80	R-R	6-1	192	8/31/61 Hawthorne, CA
		Albuquerque	2-2	21	16	4.35				
55	Hershiser, Orel	Los Angeles	23-8	267	178	2.26	R-R	6-3	192	9/16/58 Buffalo, NY
29	Horton, Ricky	Chicago (AL)	6-10	109	28	4.86	L-L	6-2	195	7/30/59 Poughkeepsie, NY
		Los Angeles	1-1	9	8	5.00				
50	Howell, Jay	Los Angeles	5-3	65	70	2.08	R-R	6-3	205	11/26/55 Miami, FL
54	Leary, Tim	Los Angeles	17-11	229	180	2.91	R-R	6-3	208	12/23/58 Santa Monica, CA
48	Martinez, Ramon	San Antonio	8-4	95	89	2.46	R-R	6-4	172	3/22/68 Dominican Republic
		Albuquerque	5-2	59	49	2.76				
		Los Angeles	1-3	36	23	3.79				
—	Munoz, Mike	San Antonio	7-2	72	71	1.00	L-L	6-2	190	7/12/65 Baldwin Park, CA
26	Pena, Alejandro	Los Angeles	6-7	94	83	1.91	R-R	6-1	204	6/25/59 Dominican Republic
—	Searage, Ray	Albuquerque	2-3	60	58	5.10	R-R	6-1	180	5/1/55 Freeport, NY
30	Tudor, John	St. L-LA	10-8	198	87	2.32	L-L	6-0	185	2/2/54 Schenectady, NY
34	Valenzuela, Fernando	Los Angeles	5-8	142	64	4.24	L-L	5-11	202	11/1/60 Mexico
—	Wetteland, John	San Antonio	10-8	162	140	3.88	R-R	6-2	195	8/22/66 San Mateo, CA

CATCHERS

No.	Name	1988 Club	H	HR	RBI	Pct.	B-T	Ht.	Wt.	Born
17	Dempsey, Rick	Los Angeles	42	7	30	.251	R-R	6-0	185	9/13/49 Fayetteville, TN
—	Hernandez, Carlos	Bakersfield	103	5	52	.309	R-R	5-11	185	5/24/67 Venezuela
		Albuquerque	1	0	1	.125				
15	Reyes, Gilberto	Albuquerque	93	12	66	.292	R-R	6-2	199	12/10/63 Dominican Republic
		Los Angeles	1	0	0	.111				
14	Scioscia, Mike	Los Angeles	105	3	35	.257	L-R	6-2	230	11/27/58 Upper Darby, PA

INFIELDERS

10	Anderson, Dave	Los Angeles	71	2	20	.249	R-R	6-2	191	8/1/60 Louisville, KY
25	Duncan, Mariano	Albuquerque	65	0	25	.286	S-R	6-0	190	3/13/63 Dominican Republic
7	Griffin, Alfredo	Los Angeles	63	1	27	.199	S-R	5-11	165	3/6/57 Dominican Republic
33	Hamilton, Jeff	Los Angeles	73	6	33	.236	R-R	6-3	214	3/19/64 Flint, MI
—	Hansen, Dave	Vero Beach	149	7	81	.291	L-R	6-0	180	11/24/68 Long Beach, CA
9	Hatcher, Mickey	Los Angeles	56	1	25	.293	R-R	6-2	202	3/15/55 Cleveland, OH
—	Murray, Eddie	Baltimore	171	28	84	.284	S-R	6-2	225	2/24/56 Los Angeles, CA
—	Randolph, Willie	New York (AL)	93	2	34	.230	R-R	5-11	170	7/6/54 Holly Hill, SC
27	Sharperson, Mike	Albuquerque	67	0	30	.319	R-R	6-3	185	10/4/61 Orangeburg, SC
		Los Angeles	16	0	4	.271				
22	Stubbs, Franklin	Los Angeles	54	8	34	.223	L-L	6-2	218	10/21/60 Laurinburg, NC
—	Vizcaino, Jose	Bakersfield	126	0	38	.290	S-R	6-1	150	3/26/68 Dominican Republic
21	Woodson, Tracy	Albuquerque	100	17	73	.319	R-R	6-3	215	10/5/62 Richmond, VA
		Los Angeles	43	3	15	.249				

OUTFIELDERS

37	Davis, Mike	Los Angeles	55	2	17	.196	L-L	6-3	185	6/11/59 San Diego, CA
40	Devereaux, Mike	Albuquerque	144	13	76	.340	R-R	6-0	195	4/10/63 Casper, WY
		Los Angeles	5	0	2	.116				
23	Gibson, Kirk	Los Angeles	157	25	76	.290	L-L	6-3	215	5/28/57 Pontiac, MI
38	Gonzalez, Jose	Albuquerque	88	5	22	.306	R-R	6-2	196	11/23/64 Dominican Republic
		Los Angeles	2	0	0	.083				
—	Gwynn, Chris	Albuquerque	123	5	61	.299	L-L	6-0	200	10/13/64 Los Angeles, CA
		Los Angeles	2	0	0	.182				
12	*Heep, Danny	Los Angeles	36	0	11	.242	L-L	5-11	177	7/3/57 San Antonio, TX
5	Marshall, Mike	Los Angeles	150	20	82	.277	R-R	6-5	218	1/12/60 Libertyville, IL
31	Shelby, John	Los Angeles	130	10	64	.263	S-R	6-1	175	2/23/58 Lexington, KY

*Free agent at press time listed with 1988 team

DODGER PROFILES

KIRK GIBSON 31 6-3 215 **Bats L Throws L**

Had only one at-bat during Dodgers' World Series victory over Athletics last fall and made it count with a two-run, two-out, pinch-hit homer off Dennis Eckersley in the bottom of the ninth to win Game 1 . . . His 12th-inning homer off Roger McDowell gave Dodgers 5-4 victory over Mets in Game 4 of NLCS . . . Had just five hits in postseason play—three of them homers . . . Was hobbled during Dodgers' upset of Mets with a pulled hamstring in left leg . . . A bruised right knee limited his role in World Series . . . Left fielder left Detroit and signed with Dodgers as a free agent in February 1988, after an arbitrator allowed all 1985 free agents back into the market in his Collusion I ruling . . . Signed a three-year deal worth $4.5 million . . . Born May 28, 1957, in Pontiac, Mich. . . . His 25 homers led the team and his 76 RBI ranked second only to Mike Marshall's 82 . . . Credited with being no-nonsense inspiration of Dodgers' championship run, he was named NL MVP . . . Tigers' first-round pick in June 1978 draft . . . Standout wide receiver for Michigan State who could've played in NFL . . . Won 1984 World Series MVP award, hitting .333 with two homers and seven RBI.

Year	Club	Pos.	G	AB	R	H	2B	3B	HR	RBI	SB	Avg.
1979	Detroit..........	OF	12	38	3	9	3	0	1	4	3	.237
1980	Detroit..........	OF	51	175	23	46	2	1	9	16	4	.263
1981	Detroit..........	OF	83	290	41	95	11	3	9	40	17	.328
1982	Detroit..........	OF	69	266	34	74	16	2	8	35	9	.278
1983	Detroit..........	OF	128	401	60	91	12	9	15	51	14	.227
1984	Detroit..........	OF	149	531	92	150	23	10	27	91	29	.282
1985	Detroit..........	OF	154	581	96	167	37	5	29	97	30	.287
1986	Detroit..........	OF	119	441	84	118	11	2	28	86	34	.268
1987	Detroit..........	OF	128	487	95	135	25	3	24	79	26	.277
1988	Los Angeles	OF	150	542	106	157	28	1	25	76	31	.290
	Totals		1043	3752	634	1042	168	36	175	575	197	.278

MIKE MARSHALL 29 6-5 218 **Bats R Throws R**

Rebounded from a 1987 season in which he played only 104 games because of back and hand injuries . . . Played 144 games in 1988 and led club with 82 RBI . . . Was second with 20 homers . . . Hit three-run homer off Oakland's Storm Davis in second inning of World Series Game 2 to key a 6-0 victory . . . Has been tabbed at times as a malingerer and was involved in a celebrated 1987 fight with then-teammate Phil

Garner . . . Very average defensive right fielder . . . Moved back to right early last season after he complained that playing first base hurt his back . . . Was plagued by back trouble during World Series . . . Born Jan. 12, 1960, in Libertyville, Ill. . . . Dodgers' sixth selection in June 1978 draft . . . Nicknamed "Big Foot" . . . Dodgers re-signed him last winter after he had declared himself a free agent.

Year	Club	Pos.	G	AB	R	H	2B	3B	HR	RBI	SB	Avg.
1981	Los Angeles	1B-OF	14	25	2	5	3	0	0	1	0	.200
1982	Los Angeles	OF-1B	49	95	10	23	3	0	5	9	2	.242
1983	Los Angeles	OF-1B	140	465	47	132	17	1	17	65	7	.284
1984	Los Angeles	1B-OF	134	495	69	127	27	0	21	65	4	.257
1985	Los Angeles	OF-1B	135	518	72	152	27	2	28	95	3	.293
1986	Los Angeles	OF	103	330	47	77	11	0	19	53	4	.233
1987	Los Angeles	OF	104	402	45	118	19	0	16	72	0	.294
1988	Los Angeles	OF-1B	144	542	63	150	27	2	20	82	4	.277
	Totals		823	2872	355	784	134	5	126	442	24	.273

MIKE SCIOSCIA 30 6-2 230 **Bats L Throws R**

Catcher is unpopular with runners for his style of blocking the plate without the ball . . . He's the best in the business at that technique . . . Was bowled over by Mets' Kevin McReynolds for the run that decided Game 1 of the playoffs . . . But his ninth-inning homer off Doc Gooden in Game 4 erased a 4-2 Met lead and changed course of the NLCS . . . Had hit just three homers during season . . . Dodgers' top selection in June 1976 draft . . . Threw out 34 percent of would-be basestealers (38 of 111) . . . Born Nov. 27, 1958, in Upper Darby, Pa. . . . Banged up his right knee sliding into second base on a failed hit-and-run attempt in World Series Game 4 . . . Underwent successful arthroscopic surgery to repair torn cartilage in offseason.

Year	Club	Pos.	G	AB	R	H	2B	3B	HR	RBI	SB	Avg.
1980	Los Angeles	C-3B	54	134	8	34	5	1	1	8	1	.254
1981	Los Angeles	C	93	290	27	80	10	0	2	29	0	.276
1982	Los Angeles	C	129	365	31	80	11	1	5	38	2	.219
1983	Los Angeles	C	12	35	3	11	3	0	1	7	0	.314
1984	Los Angeles	C	114	341	29	93	18	0	5	38	2	.273
1985	Los Angeles	C	141	429	47	127	26	3	7	53	3	.296
1986	Los Angeles	C	122	374	36	94	18	1	5	26	3	.251
1987	Los Angeles	C	142	461	44	122	26	1	6	38	7	.265
1988	Los Angeles	C	130	408	29	105	18	0	3	35	0	.257
	Totals		937	2837	254	746	135	7	35	272	18	.263

WILLIE RANDOLPH 34 5-11 170 Bats R Throws R

Wrist and rib-cage injuries hampered veteran second baseman for second straight year and Yankees deemed him expendable free agent when they signed Dodger second-baseman Steve Sax Nov. 23 . . . Two weeks later, Dodgers signed him to a two-year contract worth $1.75 million . . . Despite the injuries, 13-year Yankee had one of his best seasons defensively in 1988, going 40 games without making an error late in year . . . Born July 6, 1954, in Holly Hill, S.C., but grew up in Brooklyn, N.Y. . . . Yanks got him from Pirates with Ken Brett and Dock Ellis for Doc Medich, following 1975 season . . . Pirates' seventh-round pick in June 1972 draft.

Year	Club	Pos.	G	AB	R	H	2B	3B	HR	RBI	SB	Avg.
1975	Pittsburgh	2B-3B	30	61	9	10	1	0	0	3	1	.164
1976	New York (AL)....	2B	125	430	59	115	15	4	1	40	37	.267
1977	New York (AL)....	2B	147	551	91	151	28	11	4	40	13	.274
1978	New York (AL)....	2B	134	499	87	139	18	6	3	42	36	.279
1979	New York (AL)....	2B	153	574	98	155	15	13	5	61	33	.270
1980	New York (AL)....	2B	138	513	99	151	23	7	7	46	30	.294
1981	New York (AL)....	2B	93	357	59	83	14	3	2	24	14	.232
1982	New York (AL)....	2B	144	553	85	155	21	4	3	36	16	.280
1983	New York (AL)....	2B	104	420	73	117	21	1	2	38	12	.279
1984	New York (AL)....	2B	142	564	86	162	24	2	2	31	10	.287
1985	New York (AL)....	2B	143	497	75	137	21	2	5	40	16	.276
1986	New York (AL)....	2B	141	492	76	136	15	2	5	50	15	.276
1987	New York (AL)....	2B	120	449	96	137	24	2	7	67	11	.305
1988	New York (AL)....	2B	110	404	43	93	20	1	2	34	8	.230
	Totals		1724	6364	1036	1741	260	58	48	552	252	.274

EDDIE MURRAY 33 6-2 225 Bats S Throws R

New start for this stagnating old pro . . . Acquired from Orioles last winter for Ken Howell, Brian Holton and Juan Bell . . . Turned his 1988 season around in June . . . Was batting .231 with four home runs and 19 RBI through first 54 games, then manager Frank Robinson pulled him from first base and started using him as a DH . . . Veteran responded by hitting 19 home runs in next 63 games . . . Slammed nine homers in 22 games from July 23 until Aug. 16 . . . Former Gold Glover had made six errors in first 54 games at first . . . Collected 2,000th hit Sept. 12 in Boston, joining Brooks Robinson as the only Orioles to achieve that milestone . . . Born Feb. 24, 1956, in Los

Angeles . . . Selected by Orioles in third round of June 1973 draft . . . Natural right-handed hitter who began to switch-hit in 1975, his third pro season . . . Younger brother Rich played for Giants and three other brothers played minor-league ball . . . Attended UCLA.

Year	Club	Pos.	G	AB	R	H	2B	3B	HR	RBI	SB	Avg.
1977	Baltimore	OF-1B	160	611	81	173	29	2	27	88	0	.283
1978	Baltimore	1B-3B	161	610	85	174	32	3	27	95	6	.285
1979	Baltimore	1B	159	606	90	179	30	2	25	99	10	.295
1980	Baltimore	1B	158	621	100	186	36	2	32	116	7	.300
1981	Baltimore	1B	99	378	57	111	21	2	22	78	2	.294
1982	Baltimore	1B	151	550	87	174	30	1	32	110	7	.316
1983	Baltimore	1B	156	582	115	178	30	3	33	111	5	.306
1984	Baltimore	1B	162	588	97	180	26	3	29	110	10	.306
1985	Baltimore	1B	156	583	111	173	37	1	31	124	5	.297
1986	Baltimore	1B	137	495	61	151	25	1	17	84	3	.305
1987	Baltimore	1B	160	618	89	171	28	3	30	91	1	.277
1988	Baltimore	1B	161	603	75	171	27	2	28	84	5	.284
	Totals		1820	6845	1048	2021	351	25	333	1190	61	.295

ALFREDO GRIFFIN 32 5-11 165 Bats S Throws R

Steady shortstop was out for 57 games from May 21 until July 25 with broken bone in right hand, suffered when he was hit by a Doc Gooden fastball . . . Obtained from Oakland in December 1987 in three-way deal with Mets. A's received pitchers Bob Welch and Matt Young and the Dodgers netted Griffin and relievers Jay Howell and Jesse Orosco . . . Didn't hit much in first NL season, but did have 12-game hitting streak between Aug. 29 and Sept. 13 . . . Born March 6, 1957, in Santo Domingo, Dominican Republic . . . Batted just .160 in the playoffs and .188 in the World Series . . . Batted .199 during regular season, but helped solidify Dodger infield.

Year	Club	Pos.	G	AB	R	H	2B	3B	HR	RBI	SB	Avg.
1976	Cleveland	SS	12	4	0	1	0	0	0	0	0	.250
1977	Cleveland	SS	14	41	5	6	1	0	0	3	2	.146
1978	Cleveland	SS	5	4	1	2	1	0	0	0	0	.500
1979	Toronto	SS	153	624	81	179	22	10	2	31	21	.287
1980	Toronto	SS	155	653	63	166	26	15	2	41	18	.254
1981	Toronto	SS-3B-2B	101	388	30	81	19	6	0	21	8	.209
1982	Toronto	SS	162	539	57	130	20	8	1	48	10	.241
1983	Toronto	SS-2B	162	528	62	132	22	9	4	47	8	.250
1984	Toronto	SS-2B	140	419	53	101	8	2	4	30	11	.241
1985	Oakland.........	SS	162	614	75	166	18	7	2	64	24	.270
1986	Oakland.........	SS	162	594	74	169	23	6	4	51	33	.285
1987	Oakland.........	SS-2B	144	494	69	130	23	5	3	60	26	.263
1988	Los Angeles	SS	95	316	39	63	8	3	1	27	7	.199
	Totals		1467	5218	609	1326	191	71	23	423	168	.254

OREL HERSHISER 30 6-3 192 **Bats R Throws R**

Capped off an amazing career Cy Young Award-winning season by capturing final game of World Series . . . Pitched back-to-back postseason shutouts—NLCS Game 7 against the Mets and World Series Game 2 vs. Oakland—and he also became the first pitcher in 64 years to have three hits in a World Series game . . . Came on in relief to record final out of NLCS Game 4 with the bases loaded and earned save . . . Was MVP of both playoffs and World Series . . . Finished the season with an incredible 59-inning consecutive scoreless streak to break Don Drysdale's 20-year-old record . . . Streak began Aug. 30 in Montreal and included five of his league-leading eight shutouts . . . Record was set in Sept. 28 in San Diego, when he threw 10 innings' worth of zeroes vs. Padres . . . Born Sept. 16, 1958, in Buffalo, N.Y. . . . Dodgers' 17th selection in June 1979 draft . . . Signed through 1989, he hinted he might play in Japan for season if Dodgers don't give him long-term deal he covets.

Year	Club	G	IP	W	L	Pct.	SO	BB	H	ERA
1983	Los Angeles	8	8	0	0	.000	5	6	7	3.38
1984	Los Angeles	45	189⅔	11	8	.579	150	50	160	2.66
1985	Los Angeles	36	239⅔	19	3	.864	157	68	179	2.03
1986	Los Angeles	35	231⅓	14	14	.500	153	86	213	3.85
1987	Los Angeles	37	264⅔	16	16	.500	190	74	247	3.06
1988	Los Angeles	35	267	23	8	.742	178	73	208	2.26
	Totals	196	1200⅓	83	49	.629	833	357	1014	2.77

TIM BELCHER 27 6-3 210 **Bats R Throws R**

Splashed onto the national scene last fall with rousing postseason performance . . . Won Games 2 and 5 of NLCS vs. Mets and Game 4 of World Series vs. Oakland . . . Was the player to be named later in Aug. 29, 1987 trade that sent left-hander Rick Honeycutt to A's . . . Began 1988 season as a reliever, but was forced into a starting role when injuries decimated Dodger rotation . . . Made final relief appearance July 5 and finished with four saves . . . Won seven in row at one point, tying Orel Hershiser for longest winning streak by a Dodger pitcher last season . . . Won nine of his last 11 . . . Born Oct. 19, 1961, in Mt. Gilead, Ohio . . . Pitched a three-hitter, but was the losing pitcher in Cincinnati Sept. 16, when Tom Browning tossed his perfect game . . . Yanks' first-round pick in January 1984, he went to Oakland as compensation draft pick after first pro season.

Year	Club	G	IP	W	L	Pct.	SO	BB	H	ERA
1987	Los Angeles	6	34	4	2	.667	23	7	30	2.38
1988	Los Angeles	36	179⅔	12	6	.667	152	51	143	2.91
	Totals	42	213⅔	16	8	.667	175	58	173	2.82

FERNANDO VALENZUELA 28 5-11 202 Bats L Throws L

Suffered first serious injury of his career last season . . . Was placed on the disabled list July 31 because of a stretched anterior capsule in his left shoulder . . . Missed almost two months . . . Returned Sept. 26 and made two appearances, but was not on postseason roster . . . It marked the first time he missed a turn since becoming a Dodger starter on Opening Day in 1981 . . . Had made 255 straight starts . . . Avoided free agency last winter when he agreed to a pay cut and signed a one-year contract worth $1.85 million . . . Created Fernando-mania in 1981, when he won both NL Rookie of the Year and Cy Young awards . . . High pitch counts may have caught up with him . . . Born Nov. 1, 1960, in Navajoa, Mexico . . . Dodgers purchased his contract from Puebla of Mexican League, July 6, 1979 . . . Owns nasty screwball.

Year	Club	G	IP	W	L	Pct.	SO	BB	H	ERA
1980	Los Angeles	10	18	2	0	1.000	16	5	8	0.00
1981	Los Angeles	25	192	13	7	.650	180	61	140	2.48
1982	Los Angeles	37	285	19	13	.594	199	83	247	2.87
1983	Los Angeles	35	257	15	10	.600	189	99	245	3.75
1984	Los Angeles	34	261	12	17	.414	240	106	218	3.03
1985	Los Angeles	35	272⅓	17	10	.630	208	101	211	2.45
1986	Los Angeles	34	269⅓	21	11	.656	242	85	226	3.14
1987	Los Angeles	34	251	14	14	.500	190	124	254	3.98
1988	Los Angeles	23	142⅓	5	8	.385	64	76	142	4.24
	Totals	267	1948	118	90	.567	1528	740	1691	3.16

JAY HOWELL 33 6-3 205 Bats R Throws R

Received more publicity for less action than any player in postseason history . . . Was called a "high school pitcher" in a column ghosted for Mets' right-hander David Cone after NLCS Game 1, which he lost . . . Was ejected from Game 3 in New York, when umpires found pine tar smeared on his glove, and was suspended for two games . . . Was called "gutless" by former teammate Don Baylor just prior to the World Series . . . Allowed the two-out, ninth-inning homer by Mark McGwire that won Game 3 for Athletics, but came back the next night to earn save in Game 4 . . . Obtained by Dodgers from Oakland in December 1987 three-way deal with Mets . . . Born Nov. 26, 1955, in Miami . . . Became the mainstay of the bullpen during regular season . . . Posted 21 saves, the most by a Dodger since Terry Forster's 22 in 1978 . . . Has 92 career saves . . . Reds' 31st-round pick in June 1976 draft.

Year	Club	G	IP	W	L	Pct.	SO	BB	H	ERA
1980	Cincinnati	5	3	0	0	.000	1	0	8	15.00
1981	Chicago (NL)	10	22	2	0	1.000	10	10	23	4.91
1982	New York (AL)	6	28	2	3	.400	21	13	42	7.71
1983	New York (AL)	19	82	1	5	.167	61	35	89	5.38
1984	New York (AL)	61	103⅔	9	4	.692	109	34	86	2.69
1985	Oakland	63	98	9	8	.529	68	31	98	2.85
1986	Oakland	38	53⅓	3	6	.333	42	23	53	3.38
1987	Oakland	36	44⅓	3	4	.429	35	21	48	5.89
1988	Los Angeles	50	65	5	3	.625	70	21	44	2.08
	Totals	288	499⅓	34	33	.507	417	188	491	3.89

TOP PROSPECT

MIKE SHARPERSON 27 6-3 185 Bats R Throws R
Infielder flew the shuttle back and forth between Los Angeles and Albuquerque (AAA) all last season . . . Was on the playoff roster and had one at-bat in NLCS . . . Did not appear in World Series . . . Was obtained from Toronto for pitcher Juan Guzman, Sept. 21, 1987 . . . Can be used at second base or third base . . . Batted .299 for Syracuse (AAA) in 1987 . . . Was also in Pittsburgh, Montreal and Detroit organizations . . . Played in 31 games after his final recall from Albuquerque Sept. 1 . . . Had three multiple-hit games in majors last season . . . Born Oct. 4, 1961, in Orangeburg, S.C. . . . Hit .271 in 59 at-bats for Dodgers and .319 for Albuquerque in 1988.

MANAGER TOMMY LASORDA: Promised in February that

his lightly regarded team would win NL West and defied long odds to deliver much more . . . His Dodgers went 94-68, upset Mets in NLCS and stunned A's in World Series to win the franchise's sixth world championship . . . Won Manager of the Year honors for accomplishing what few experts predicted . . . Has won six division titles, four pennants and two championships since he replaced the late Walter Alston as Dodger manager in 1977 . . . His clubs' four division titles in the 1980s is most by any major-league team during this decade . . . His overall record with Dodgers is 1,020-872 for a .539 winning percentage, placing him third behind Alston and Wilbert Robinson on franchise's all-time win list . . . Club has had only four losing seasons during his 12-year tenure . . . Also had the Dodgers in contention to win West on last days of both the 1980 and 1982 seasons . . . Has been on the Dodger payroll for 39 years as a pitcher, coach, minor-league manager and major-league manager . . . His $500,000-per-year contract was renewed for another two years . . . Born Sept. 22, 1927, in Norristown, Pa. . . . Has that Hollywood flair and that legendary appetite.

GREATEST FIRST BASEMAN

Trolley tracks still remained on the streets of Brooklyn and Ebbets Field still stood on the corners of Flatbush and Bedford Avenues when Gil Hodges joined the bums for good as a catcher in 1947. He switched to first base in 1948 and it was there that he etched his place in Dodger history.

Steve Garvey was the greatest first baseman during the Dodgers' era in L.A., but the mark Hodges left on this franchise cannot be ignored. Playing with Jackie Robinson, Pee Wee Reese, Don Newcombe and Duke Snider, Hodges led the Dodgers to pennants in 1947, 1949, 1952, 1953, 1955 and 1956 and he also played on the Los Angeles team that beat the White Sox in the 1959 World Series.

Hodges hit 42 homers in 1954, one shy of the club record set by Snider in 1956 and the most by any Dodger first baseman. He reached the 100-RBI plateau seven times in his career, including a career-high 130 during 1954, when he batted .304. Hodges returned to New York in the expansion draft in 1962 and concluded his career in 1963 with the bumbling, young Mets. But he'll be remembered forever as the Dodgers' quiet strong man, the greatest first baseman in franchise history.

ALL-TIME DODGER SEASON RECORDS

BATTING: Babe Herman, .393, 1930
HRs: Duke Snider, 43, 1956
RBIs: Tommy Davis, 153, 1962
STEALS: Maury Wills, 104, 1962
WINS: Joe McGinnity, 29, 1900
STRIKEOUTS: Sandy Koufax, 382, 1965

SAN DIEGO PADRES

TEAM DIRECTORY: Owner: Joan Kroc; Exec. VP-Dick Freeman; Dir. Minor Leagues: Tom Romensko; Dir. Scouting: Randy Smith; Dir. Pub. Rel.: Bill Beck; Trav. Sec.: John Mattei; Mgr.: Jack McKeon. Home: San Diego Jack Murphy Stadium (58,433). Field distances: 327, l.f. line; 405, c.f.; 327, r.f. line. Spring training: Yuma, Ariz.

SCOUTING REPORT

HITTING: The Padres' offseason aim was to shore up an offense that produced just 94 homers last season, ranking second to last in the NL for the second straight year. They accomplished that goal immediately after the World Series by acquiring Jack Clark (.242, 27, 93) from the Yankees for non-essential pitching. The Padres have had just one 20-homer man in the last two years (John Kruk with 20 in 1987) and Clark should fix that.

With Clark, the Padres have finally found protection in the

Tony Gwynn sets his sights on third straight batting title.

lineup for Tony Gwynn, whose average slipped from a league-leading .370 in 1987 to a league-leading .313 in 1988. Look for Gwynn to have another big year, Benito Santiago (.248, 10, 46) to shake the sophomore jinx and the Padres to produce far more than 594 runs this season.

PITCHING: The Padres pulled the coup of the winter when they signed ex-Red Sox lefty Bruce Hurst (18-6, 3.66) as a free agent. This followed an offseason deal that brought Walt Terrell (7-16, 3.97) from the Tigers. Even with the departure of Andy Hawkins, Jimmy Jones and Lance McCullers, a strong staff that was fourth in the NL with a 3.28 ERA last season figures to be even stronger now.

At the outset of last year, the Padres had no left-handers in the starting rotation and only one on the staff. Now the rotation boasts Hurst and former Red Dennis Rasmussen (16-10, 3.43). Bullpen ace Mark Davis is coming off his finest year, with 28 saves and a 2.01 ERA. But the loss of McCullers to the Yanks in the Clark deal leaves the Padres searching for a right-handed set-up man.

FIELDING: The addition of rookie second baseman Roberto Alomar last season ended a long search for a middle infielder. Alomar combined with shortstops Garry Templeton and Dickie Thon to tighten up the Padres' inner defense. Templeton signed for another season and is adequate, despite his arthritic left knee. Third base continues to be a big hole and super subs Tim Flannery and Randy Ready will be asked to fill it.

The outfield is a quagmire, with Gwynn having been shifted to center field late last year after two consecutive Gold Glove seasons in right. Carmelo Martinez will never dazzle anybody in left field and Kruk is severely out of position in right.

Behind the plate, Santiago, a Gold Glove winner, may already be the best-throwing catcher ever. He could throw out 50 percent of all would-be base-stealers and that's never been done before.

OUTLOOK: The Padres, with the addition of Clark, Terrell and Hurst, are the most improved team in the division. Last year's 83-78 mark was the third-best in club history, but San Diego still finished 11 games behind the division-winning Dodgers. The new blood should be enough to close the gap.

What Jack McKeon's Padres must avoid at all costs is the dreadful starts that plagued them in 1987 (12-42) and 1988 (16-31). It will help that they are opening at home for the first time since 1984, the Padres' only pennant-winning season.

SAN DIEGO PADRES 1989 ROSTER

MANAGER Jack McKeon
Coaches—Sandy Alomar, Pat Dobson, Amos Otis, Greg Riddoch, Dennis Sommers

PITCHERS

No.	Name	1988 Club	W-L	IP	SO	ERA	B-T	Ht.	Wt.	Born
56	Bones, Ricky	Riverside	15-6	175	129	3.64	R-R	5-10	175	4/7/69 Puerto Rico
51	Booker, Greg	San Diego	2-2	64	43	3.39	R-R	6-6	245	6/22/60 Lynchburg, VA
38	Clements, Pat	Columbus	6-7	144	69	2.75	R-L	6-0	180	2/2/62 McCloud, CA
		New York (AL)	0-0	8	3	6.48				
48	Davis, Mark	San Diego	5-10	98	102	2.01	L-L	6-4	200	10/19/60 Livermore, CA
55	Grant, Mark	San Diego	2-8	98	61	3.69	R-R	6-2	205	10/24/63 Aurora, IL
46	Harris, Greg W.	Las Vegas	9-5	160	147	4.11	R-R	6-2	190	12/1/63 Greensboro, NC
		San Diego	2-0	18	15	1.50				
—	Hurst, Bruce	Boston	18-6	217	166	3.66	L-L	6-3	214	3/24/58 St. George, UT
51	Leiper, Dave	San Diego	3-0	54	33	2.17	L-L	6-1	160	6/18/62 Whittier, CA
49	Maysey, Matt	Wichita	9-9	187	120	3.71	R-R	6-4	210	1/8/67 Canada
37	Nolte, Eric	San Diego	0-0	3	1	6.00	L-L	6-3	200	4/28/64 Canoga Park, CA
		Las Vegas	8-7	128	68	6.03				
43	Rasmussen, Dennis	Cin.-SD	16-10	205	112	3.43	L-L	6-7	225	4/18/59 Los Angeles, CA
30	Show, Eric	San Diego	16-11	235	144	3.26	R-R	6-1	190	5/19/56 Riverside, CA
35	Terrell, Walt	Detroit	7-16	206	84	3.97	L-R	6-2	205	5/11/58 Jeffersonville, IN
31	Whitson, Ed	San Diego	13-11	205	118	3.77	R-R	6-3	195	5/19/55 Johnson City, TN

CATCHERS

No.	Name	1988 Club	H	HR	RBI	Pct.	B-T	Ht.	Wt.	Born
17	Alomar, Sandy, Jr.	Las Vegas	100	16	71	.297	R-R	6-5	200	6/18/66 Puerto Rico
		San Diego	0	0	0	.000				
27	Parent, Mark	San Diego	23	6	15	.195	R-R	6-5	224	9/16/61 Ashland, OR
9	Santiago, Benito	San Diego	122	10	46	.248	R-R	6-1	185	3/9/65 Puerto Rico

INFIELDERS

12	Alomar, Roberto	Las Vegas	10	2	14	.270	S-R	6-0	155	2/5/68 Puerto Rico
		San Diego	145	9	41	.266				
53	Baerga, Carlos	Wichita	121	12	65	.273	S-R	5-11	165	11/4/68 Puerto Rico
18	Brumley, Mike	Las Vegas	134	3	41	.315	S-R	5-10	165	4/9/63 Oklahoma City, OK
25	Clark, Jack	New York (AL)	120	27	93	.242	R-R	6-3	205	11/10/55 New Brighton, PA
4	Cora, Joey	Las Vegas	136	3	55	.296	S-R	5-8	150	5/14/65 Puerto Rico
11	Flannery, Tim	San Diego	45	0	19	.265	L-R	5-11	181	9/29/57 Tulsa, OK
7	Nelson, Rob	Las Vegas	101	23	77	.260	L-L	6-4	215	5/17/64 Pasadena, CA
		San Diego	4	1	3	.190				
5	Ready, Randy	San Diego	88	7	39	.266	R-R	5-11	180	1/8/60 San Mateo, CA
10	Roberts, Bip	Las Vegas	121	7	51	.353	S-R	5-7	160	10/27/63 Berkeley, CA
		San Diego	3	0	0	.333				
1	Templeton, Garry	San Diego	90	3	36	.249	S-R	6-0	192	3/24/57 Lockey, TX
21	Thon, Dickie	San Diego	68	1	18	.264	R-R	5-11	178	6/20/58 South Bend, IN

OUTFIELDERS

28	Abner, Shawn	Las Vegas	64	4	34	.254	R-R	6-1	190	6/17/66 Hamilton, OH
		San Diego	15	2	5	.181				
47	Byers, Randell	Las Vegas	96	6	55	.267	L-L	6-2	180	10/2/64 Bridgeton, NJ
		San Diego	2	0	0	.200				
24	Clark, Jerald	Las Vegas	123	9	67	.301	R-R	6-4	189	8/10/63 Crockett, TX
		San Diego	3	0	3	.200				
19	Gwynn, Tony	San Diego	163	7	70	.313	L-L	5-11	199	5/9/60 Los Angeles, CA
33	Howard, Tom	Las Vegas	42	0	15	.251	S-R	6-0	198	12/11/64 Middletown, OH
		Wichita	31	0	16	.301				
8	Kruk, John	San Diego	91	9	44	.241	L-L	5-10	195	2/9/61 Charleston, WV
23	Mack, Shane	Las Vegas	68	10	40	.347	R-R	6-0	185	12/7/63 Los Angeles, CA
		San Diego	29	0	12	.244				
14	Martinez, Carmelo	San Diego	86	18	65	.236	R-R	6-2	220	7/28/60 Puerto Rico
16	Wynne, Marvell	San Diego	88	11	42	.264	L-L	5-11	185	12/17/59 Chicago, IL

PADRE PROFILES

TONY GWYNN 28 5-11 199 **Bats L Throws L**

Won second consecutive batting title and third of his career with a .313 mark, the lowest league-leading average in NL history . . . His .370 average in 1987 was the highest by an NL batting champ since Stan Musial hit .376 in 1948 . . . Won title last season despite severe finger and thumb injuries . . . Underwent surgery March 11 to repair tendon damage at the base of his left index finger and complained about soreness in his hand throughout the year . . . Jammed his right thumb during a May 7 base-running mishap and was placed on the 21-day disabled list . . . Was moved from right field, where he had won consecutive Gold Gloves, to center Aug. 21 and remained there for the rest of the season . . . Born May 9, 1960, in Los Angeles . . . Signed a contract extension prior to the 1988 season and is earning $1 million a year through 1990 . . . Brother Chris plays in Dodger system . . . Padres' third-round pick in June 1981 draft, out of San Diego State . . . Also drafted by San Diego Clippers of NBA.

Year	Club	Pos.	G	AB	R	H	2B	3B	HR	RBI	SB	Avg.
1982	San Diego	OF	54	190	33	55	12	2	1	17	8	.289
1983	San Diego	OF	86	304	34	94	12	2	1	37	7	.309
1984	San Diego	OF	158	606	88	213	21	10	5	71	33	.351
1985	San Diego	OF	154	622	90	197	29	5	6	46	14	.317
1986	San Diego	OF	160	642	107	211	33	7	14	59	37	.329
1987	San Diego	OF	157	589	119	218	36	13	7	54	56	.370
1988	San Diego	OF	133	521	64	163	22	5	7	70	26	.313
	Totals		902	3474	535	1151	165	44	41	354	181	.331

JACK CLARK 33 6-3 205 **Bats R Throws R**

Slugger was acquired from Yankees with left-hander Pat Clements for right-handers Lance McCullers and Jimmy Jones and outfielder Stanley Jefferson in October . . . A designated hitter last year, he is ticketed to play first base for Padres . . . Was told by Cardinals after the 1987 season to go out and find a better contract as a free agent, so he did . . . Yankees signed him to huge two-year deal . . . His salary in 1989 will be $1.6 million, plus $400,000 in incentives . . . Hit 27 homers for the Yanks, marking the eighth time in his career he has hit 20 or more in a season . . . Born Nov. 10, 1955, in New Brighton, Pa. . . . Missed final six weeks of the 1987 season and was useless during World Series and playoffs because of torn ligaments in his right ankle . . . Giants' 13th-round pick in June 1973 made no secret of his hatred for Candlestick . . . Hit .381 with key homer in Cards' 1985 NLCS victory over Dodgers.

Year	Club	Pos.	G	AB	R	H	2B	3B	HR	RBI	SB	Avg.
1975	San Francisco	OF-3B	8	17	3	4	0	0	0	2	1	.235
1976	San Francisco	OF	26	102	14	23	6	2	2	10	6	.225
1977	San Francisco	OF	136	413	64	104	17	4	13	51	12	.252
1978	San Francisco	OF	156	592	90	181	46	8	25	98	15	.306
1979	San Francisco	OF-3B	143	527	84	144	25	2	26	86	11	.273
1980	San Francisco	OF	127	437	77	124	20	8	22	82	2	.284
1981	San Francisco	OF	99	385	60	103	19	2	17	53	1	.268
1982	San Francisco	OF	157	563	90	154	30	3	27	103	6	.274
1983	San Francisco	OF-1B	135	492	82	132	25	0	20	66	5	.268
1984	San Francisco	OF-1B	57	203	33	65	9	1	11	44	1	.320
1985	St. Louis	1B-OF	126	442	71	124	26	3	22	87	1	.281
1986	St. Louis	1B	65	232	34	55	12	2	9	23	1	.237
1987	St. Louis	1B-OF	131	419	93	120	23	1	35	106	1	.286
1988	New York (AL)	OF-1B	150	496	81	120	14	0	27	93	3	.242
	Totals		1516	5320	876	1453	272	36	256	904	66	.273

ROBERTO ALOMAR 21 6-0 155 **Bats S Throws R**

Was brought up from Las Vegas (AAA) April 19 and became the Padres' starting second baseman . . . Joined father Sandy Sr., the Padres' third-base coach and was joined in September by older brother Sandy Jr., a coveted catcher . . . Played in 143 games and batted .266 after struggling at the plate early . . . Was platooned briefly with Randy Ready just after the All-Star break . . . Has such a wide range his accomplishments at his position reminded people of what a young Ozzie Smith did at shortstop for Padres . . . Was the main reason the Padres led the NL in double plays for the first time with 147, as he participated in 88 of them . . . Born Feb. 5, 1968, in Salinas, Puerto Rico . . . Hit in 18 of his final 19 games, including 13 straight, and is the probable choice to lead off in 1989 . . . Padres signed him as free agent in February 1985 . . . Hit no less than .293 in each of his three minor-league seasons.

Year	Club	Pos.	G	AB	R	H	2B	3B	HR	RBI	SB	Avg.
1988	San Diego	2B-SS	143	545	84	145	24	6	9	41	24	.266

CARMELO MARTINEZ 28 6-2 220 **Bats R Throws R**

Enjoyed late-season offensive spurt after he was finally placed in the lineup regularly . . . Led the club with 18 homers and was second to Tony Gwynn with 65 RBI, despite having only 365 at-bats . . . Was signed to a two-year contract worth $900,000 prior to the 1988 season . . . Was obtained by the Padres from the Cubs in a three-way deal that also included the Expos in December 1983 as Padres obtained pitcher Scott Sanderson from Montreal and shipped Sanderson to Chicago for pitcher Craig Lefferts and this strapping, lumbering slugger . . . Has hit 76 homers in his five seasons with Padres . . . Improved defensive skills in left field last season, but still prefers to play his natural position of first base . . . Born July 28, 1960, in Dorado, Puerto Rico . . . Started his first game ever in right Aug. 19 . . . Cubs signed him as free agent in December 1978 . . . Attended Central College of Bayamon, P.R.

Year	Club	Pos.	G	AB	R	H	2B	3B	HR	RBI	SB	Avg.
1983	Chicago (NL).....	1B-3B-OF	29	89	8	23	3	0	6	16	0	.258
1984	San Diego	OF-1B	149	488	64	122	28	2	13	66	1	.250
1985	San Diego	OF-1B	150	514	64	130	28	1	21	72	0	.253
1986	San Diego	OF-1B-3B	113	244	28	58	10	0	9	25	1	.238
1987	San Diego	OF-1B	139	447	59	122	21	2	15	70	5	.273
1988	San Diego	OF-1B	121	365	48	86	12	0	18	65	1	.236
	Totals		701	2147	271	541	102	5	82	314	8	.252

DICKIE THON 30 5-11 178 — Bats R Throws R

Former Astros' shortstop made remarkable comeback from vision problems . . . Was signed as a free agent in February to a contract that could have paid him as much as $500,000, including incentives . . . By midseason, he was platooning with Garry Templeton . . . Houston tried to place him on retired list during 1987, when he left the club in July because of psychological reasons relating to problems in his left eye . . . Injury occurred when he was beaned by a fastball from Mets' Mike Torrez, April 8, 1984 . . . The former All-Star, who had 20 homers and 79 RBI in 1983, played just five games in 1984 and 84 in 1985 . . . Born June 20, 1958, in South Bend, Ind., but he is of Puerto Rican descent . . . Hit .264 for the Padres and was third on the club with 19 stolen bases . . . Originally signed by Angels as free agent in November 1975.

Year	Club	Pos.	G	AB	R	H	2B	3B	HR	RBI	SB	Avg.
1979	California........	2B-SS-3B	35	56	6	19	33	0	0	8	0	.339
1980	California........	SS-2B-3B-1B	80	267	32	68	12	2	0	15	7	.255
1981	Houston	2B-SS-3B	49	95	13	26	6	0	0	3	6	.274
1982	Houston	SS-3B-2B	136	496	73	137	31	10	3	36	37	.276
1983	Houston	SS	154	619	81	177	28	9	20	79	34	.286
1984	Houston	SS	5	17	3	6	0	1	0	1	0	.353
1985	Houston	SS	84	251	26	63	6	1	6	29	8	.251
1986	Houston	SS	106	278	24	69	13	1	3	21	6	.248
1987	Houston	SS	32	66	6	14	1	0	1	3	3	.212
1988	San Diego	SS-3B-2B	95	258	36	68	12	2	1	18	19	.264
	Totals		776	2403	300	647	112	26	34	213	120	.269

BENITO SANTIAGO 24 6-1 185 **Bats R Throws R**

Slumped badly at the plate after wonderful 1987 NL Rookie of the Year season . . . Numbers diminished in all categories . . . Average fell from .300 to .248, homers from 18 to 10 and RBI from 79 to 46 . . . Assembled 34-game hitting streak, a record for catchers, rookies and Latin players, in 1987 . . . After his streak was stopped Oct. 3 by Dodgers' Orel Hershiser, he got a hit in final game of season . . . Though offensive numbers decreased last year, his defensive skills were never better . . . Threw out 45 percent (35 of 77) of would-be base-stealers (35 of 77), including Eric Davis, Vince Coleman and Tim Raines from a kneeling or squat position . . . Born March 9, 1965, in Ponce, Puerto Rico . . . Errors and passed balls decreased markedly from rookie season . . . Padres signed him as free agent in September 1982 . . . Pitched nine no-hitters in Little League.

Year	Club	Pos.	G	AB	R	H	2B	3B	HR	RBI	SB	Avg.
1986	San Diego	C	17	62	10	18	2	0	3	6	0	.290
1987	San Diego	C	146	546	64	164	33	2	18	79	21	.300
1988	San Diego	C	139	492	49	122	22	2	10	46	15	.248
	Totals		302	1100	123	304	57	4	31	131	36	.276

BRUCE HURST 31 6-3 214 **Bats L Throws L**

Left Red Sox as free agent to sign three-year, $5.25-million deal with Padres after winning career-high 18 games in 1988 . . . Might actually miss pitching at Fenway . . . Went 13-2 with 3.33 ERA while working in front of the Green Monster, becoming the first lefty to win that many at Fenway since Mel Parnell in 1949 . . . His 18 victories marked the highest total by Red Sox lefty since Parnell in 1953 . . . Finished second in AL to Minnesota's Frank Viola with .750 winning percentage . . . Came to be regarded as Red Sox' stopper, ahead of Roger Clemens . . . Was 11-2 in games following Boston loss . . . Was 0-2 in ALCS, despite 2.77 ERA . . . Born March 24, 1958, in St. George, Utah . . . Red Sox' first pick in June 1976 draft.

Year	Club	G	IP	W	L	Pct.	SO	BB	H	ERA
1980	Boston	12	31	2	2	.500	16	16	39	9.00
1981	Boston	5	23	2	0	1.000	11	12	23	4.30
1982	Boston	28	117	3	7	.300	53	40	161	5.77
1983	Boston	33	211⅓	12	12	.500	115	62	241	4.09
1984	Boston	33	218	12	12	.500	136	88	232	3.92
1985	Boston	35	229⅓	11	13	.458	189	70	243	4.51
1986	Boston	25	174⅓	13	8	.619	167	50	169	2.99
1987	Boston	33	238⅔	15	13	.536	190	76	239	4.41
1988	Boston	33	216⅔	18	6	.750	166	65	222	3.66
	Totals	237	1459⅓	88	73	.547	1043	479	1569	4.23

ERIC SHOW 32 6-1 190 **Bats R Throws R**

Avoided free agency when Padres signed him to a new two-year, $2-million contract just prior to the start of World Series . . . Had his most productive season in 1988 with a 16-11 record and 3.26 ERA . . . His wins, complete games (13), innings pitched (234.2) and strikeouts (144) were all career highs . . . Walked just 53 batters, an average of 2.03 walks per nine innings . . . All this came after he opened the season 1-4 . . . Won his last five decisions . . . Complete-game total was second-best in club history, behind the 25 by Randy Jones in 1976 . . . Finally shed the residue of arm problems that caused him to miss the final five weeks of 1986 . . . Was diagnosed as having tendinitis of the right elbow . . . Winningest right-hander in club history with 86 . . . Born May 19, 1956, in Riverside, Cal. . . . Came up through the Padres' system after becoming club's 18th-round pick in June 1978 . . . A physics major at California-Riverside.

Year	Club	G	IP	W	L	Pct.	SO	BB	H	ERA
1981	San Diego	15	23	1	3	.250	22	9	17	3.13
1982	San Diego	47	150	10	6	.625	88	48	117	2.64
1983	San Diego	35	200⅔	15	12	.556	120	74	201	4.17
1984	San Diego	32	206⅔	15	9	.625	104	88	175	3.40
1985	San Diego	35	233	12	11	.522	141	87	212	3.09
1986	San Diego	24	136⅓	9	5	.643	94	69	109	2.97
1987	San Diego	34	206⅓	8	16	.333	117	85	188	3.84
1988	San Diego	32	234⅔	16	11	.593	144	53	201	3.26
	Totals	254	1390⅔	86	73	.541	830	513	1220	3.37

DENNIS RASMUSSEN 29 6-7 225 **Bats L Throws L**

Stolen from Reds June 8 for right-hander Candy Sierra, who didn't make it out of Cincinnati's minor-league system last season . . . Arrived with a 2-6 record, but, after a short session with pitching coach Pat Dobson in the bullpen, this big lefty made some vital mechanical adjustments . . . Went 14-4 with the Padres and won his first five games in a San Diego uniform . . . This is his second tour of duty with the Padres . . . Was first acquired from the Yankees for right-hander John Montefusco, Sept. 12, 1983 . . . Was returned to the Yankees the following March in deal that brought third baseman Graig Nettles to San Diego . . . Born April 18, 1959, in Los Angeles . . . Became Padres' first left-handed starter since Dave Dravecky was traded to San Francisco, July 4, 1987 . . . Angels' first-round pick and seventh player taken overall in June 1980, out of

Creighton University . . . Grandfather Bill Brubaker played for Pirates and Braves.

Year	Club	G	IP	W	L	Pct.	SO	BB	H	ERA
1983	San Diego	4	13⅔	0	0	.000	13	8	10	1.98
1984	New York (AL)	24	147⅔	9	6	.600	110	60	127	4.57
1985	New York (AL)	22	101⅔	3	5	.375	63	42	97	3.98
1986	New York (AL)	31	202	18	6	.750	131	74	160	3.88
1987	New York (AL)	26	146	9	7	.563	89	55	145	4.75
1987	Cincinnati	7	45⅓	4	1	.800	39	12	39	3.97
1988	Cin.-SD	31	204⅔	16	10	.615	112	58	199	3.43
	Totals	145	861	59	35	.628	557	309	777	4.02

MARK DAVIS 28 6-0 200 **Bats L Throws L**

Finally blossomed into a star reliever in 1989 . . . Was Padres' only representative on All-Star team in 1988, allowing one hit in two-thirds of an inning . . . Had 16 of his club-leading 28 saves prior to the break . . . Acquired from Giants with pitchers Mark Grant and Keith Comstock and third baseman Chris Brown for pitchers Craig Lefferts and Dave Dravecky and third baseman Kevin Mitchell, July 4, 1987 . . . Born Oct. 19, 1960, in Livermore, Cal. . . . Was among the group of major-league All-Stars who toured Japan after last season . . . Is under contract through 1989 . . . Originally signed by Phils in secondary phase of January 1979 draft . . . Had only 13 career saves prior to last season.

Year	Club	G	IP	W	L	Pct.	SO	BB	H	ERA
1980	Philadelphia	2	7	0	0	.000	5	5	4	2.57
1981	Philadelphia	9	43	1	4	.200	29	24	49	7.74
1983	San Francisco	20	111	6	4	.600	83	50	93	3.49
1984	San Francisco	46	174⅔	5	17	.227	124	54	201	5.36
1985	San Francisco	77	114⅓	5	12	.294	131	41	89	3.54
1986	San Francisco	67	84⅓	5	7	.417	90	34	63	2.99
1987	S.F.-S.D.	63	133	9	8	.529	98	59	123	3.99
1988	San Diego	62	98⅓	5	10	.333	102	42	70	2.01
	Totals	346	765⅔	36	62	.367	662	309	692	4.00

TOP PROSPECT

SANDY ALOMAR Jr. 22 6-5 220 **Bats R Throws R**

Named Minor League Player of the Year in recognition of his play behind the plate coupled with a .297 average, 16 homers and 71 RBI in 92 games for Las Vegas (AAA) . . . Season ended Aug. 9, when he suffered torn cartilage in his left knee during a collision at home plate . . . Ensuing arthroscopic surgery was a complete success . . . Joined Padres in September, but was limited to rehab activity . . . His first major-league at-bat—a strikeout—

came during the last weekend of the season . . . Born June 18, 1966, in Salinas, Puerto Rico . . . Object of numerous winter trade rumors . . . Padres signed him as free agent in October 1983.

MANAGER JACK McKEON: Took over club from fired Larry

Bowa on interim basis May 28 after the Padres had gotten off to 16-30 start . . . Led team to a surprising 83-78, third-place finish, a half-game ahead of Giants . . . Club played 67-48 ball under this guy, who was given a three-year contract extension to manage the club through 1991 Sept. 14. His contract is worth $1.5 million . . . Managed Royals from start of the 1973 season until July 24, 1975, compiling a 215-205 record . . . Managed Oakland for parts of the 1977 and 1978 seasons . . . Began managerial career at age 23 and spent 20 years in minors before he was given his first shot at majors . . . Joined Padres in September 1979 as an assistant to then-general manager Bob Fontaine and has played a major role in organization since . . . Built his reputation as "Trader Jack" by helping to put together the 1984 pennant winners . . . Doubled as manager and general manager from the day he replaced Bowa through the winter meetings . . . Padres' 1988 record was third-best in the 20-year history of the franchise . . . Born Nov. 23, 1930, in South Amboy, N.J. . . . Owns 353-358 record as major-league manager.

GREATEST FIRST BASEMAN

One memorable swing on an unforgettable October evening in 1984 forever etched Steve Garvey's name in the annals of San Diego sports history. Garvey's ninth-inning homer in Game 4 of the NLCS vs. the Cubs helped the Padres toward the only pennant in club history and capped a four-hit, five-RBI evening for the player who was named MVP of that series.

It was not the only highlight of Garvey's five-year stay in San Diego, which began when he signed as a free agent in 1983 after 12 brilliant years at first base for the Dodgers. On April 16, 1983, Garvey returned to Dodger Stadium, where he broke Billy

Williams' NL mark for most consecutive games played. His streak of 1,207 games—the third-longest in history—ended July 29, 1983, when Garvey dislocated his left thumb. In 1984, Garvey played 159 straight games at first base without committing an error to set a major-league record.

Although his greatest years came as a Dodger, as NL MVP in 1974, All-Star Game MVP in 1974 and 1978 and NLCS MVP in 1978, Garvey established himself as the greatest first baseman in Padres' history before his career came to an untimely end in 1987 because of a torn biceps tendon in his left shoulder.

ALL-TIME PADRE SEASON RECORDS

BATTING: Tony Gwynn, .370, 1987
HRs: Nate Colbert, 38, 1970, 1972
RBIs: Dave Winfield, 118, 1979
STEALS: Alan Wiggins, 70, 1984
WINS: Randy Jones, 22, 1976
STRIKEOUTS: Clay Kirby, 231, 1971

SAN FRANCISCO GIANTS

TEAM DIRECTORY: Owner: Bob Lurie; Pres.-GM: Al Rosen; Exec. VP-Adm.: Corey Busch; VP-Baseball Oper.: Bob Kennedy; Sr. VP-Business Oper.: Pat Gallagher; Asst. GM: Ralph Nelson; VP-Scouting: Bob Fontaine; VP-Pub. Rel.: Duffy Jennings; Dir. Community Services: Dave Craig; Trav. Sec.: Dirk Smith; Mgr.: Roger Craig. Home: Candlestick Park (58,000). Field distances: 335, l.f. line; 365, l.c.; 400, c.f.; 365, l.c.; 335, r.f. line. Spring training: Scottsdale, Ariz.

SCOUTING REPORT

HITTING: The Giants' response to their 1988 offensive woes was to deal another member of their 1987 outfield, Mike Aldrete, to the Expos for Tracy Jones (.295, 3, 24). That's not going to help reverse last season's power slippage. Without Jeff Leonard and Chili Davis, the Giants went from 205 homers during their division-winning 1987 season to just 113 homers in 1988.

Will (The Thrill) Clark (.282, 29, 109) obviously cannot carry the club by himself. He needs more help from Kevin Mitchell (.251, 19, 80) and Candy Maldonado (.255, 12, 68). With Brett Butler (43 steals) leading the way, the Giants have to depend more on a running game. Stay tuned.

PITCHING: A mystery. Five starters—Mike Krukow, Kelly Downs, Dave Dravecky, Terry Mulholland and Mike LaCoss—finished the season with injuries. Dravecky (offseason surgery to remove a cancerous growth in his arm) and Krukow (arm surgery) may never be back.

Don Robinson (10-5, 2.45) began last season as the Giants' top reliever and ended the season as a starter. He'll be back in the rotation along with Rick Reuschel (19-11, 3.12). Scott Garrelts (5-9, 3.58, 13 saves), who disgraced himself in the bullpen last year, may find himself starting this season. Downs (13-9, 3.32), LaCoss (7-7, 3.62) and Mulholland (2-1, 3.72) should all be back.

The Giants' 3.68 team ERA was good enough to lead the league in 1987 and, even with all the injuries, that number went down to 3.39 in 1988, so there's hope for split-finger master Roger Craig's staff.

FIELDING: When it is healthy, the Giants' infield still may be the best in the league. They are particularly strong up the middle

Will Clark's 109 RBI made a Giant impact.

with Jose Uribe at shortstop and Robby Thompson at second base, but they don't know where they're going at third. Matt Williams? Mitchell?

With the trade of Aldrete, Mitchell could find himself anchored in left field, where he is simply adequate. Butler has range, but the worst throwing arm of any regular center fielder in the NL. Jones could find himself usurping Maldonado's time in right.

The catcher's position is a nightmare. Craig keeps trying to move veteran Bob Brenly out, but can't find anyone to take the job. Bob Melvin has proven he is not a regular and Kurt Manwaring, who will probably start, has yet to develop.

OUTLOOK: Not too good. While the Dodgers and Padres made significant offseason gains, the Giants stood still. Could it be they traded themselves too thin to put together that 1987 division-winning team? Who wants Maldonado or a batch of injured pitchers, anyway? The Giants' biggest stab was at 43-year-old free agent Nolan Ryan, who wound up signing with Texas.

What does it all mean? Well it was 16 years between division titles the last time and it could very well be the next century before the Giants are winners again.

SAN FRANCISCO GIANTS 1989 ROSTER

MANAGER Roger Craig

Coaches—Dusty Baker, Bill Fahey, Wendell Kim, Bob Lillis, Norm Sherry

PITCHERS

No.	Name	1988 Club	W-L	IP	SO	ERA	B-T	Ht.	Wt.	Born
—	Best, Karl	Port.-Phoe.	0-3	42	34	4.32	R-R	6-4	210	3/6/59 Aberdeen, WA
41	Burkett, John	Phoenix	5-11	114	74	5.21	R-R	6-2	180	11/28/64 New Brighton, PA
		Shreveport	5-1	51	34	2.13				
36	Cook, Dennis	Phoenix	11-9	141	110	3.88	L-L	6-3	185	10/4/62 Lamarque, TX
		San Francisco	2-1	22	13	2.86				
37	Downs, Kelly	San Francisco	13-9	168	118	3.32	R-R	6-4	200	10/25/60 Ogden, UT
43	Dravecky, Dave	San Francisco	2-2	37	19	3.16	R-L	6-1	200	2/14/56 Youngstown, OH
		Phoenix	0-1	3	1	16.88				
50	Garrelts, Scott	San Francisco	5-9	98	86	3.58	R-R	6-4	205	10/30/61 Urbana, IL
14	Hammaker, Atlee	San Francisco	9-9	145	65	3.73	S-L	6-2	200	1/24/58 Carmel, CA
39	Krukow, Mike	San Francisco	7-4	125	75	3.54	R-R	6-4	205	1/21/52 Long Beach, CA
		Phoenix	1-0	5	5	0.00				
29	LaCoss, Mike	San Francisco	7-7	114	70	3.62	R-R	6-4	200	5/30/56 Glendale, CA
32	Lefferts, Craig	San Francisco	3-8	92	58	2.92	L-L	6-1	210	9/29/57 West Germany
—	McClellan, Paul	Shreveport	10-12	167	128	4.04	R-R	6-2	180	2/8/66 San Mateo, CA
45	Mulholland, Terry	Phoenix	7-3	101	57	3.58	R-L	6-3	200	3/9/63 Uniontown, PA
		San Francisco	2-1	46	18	3.72				
47	Price, Joe	San Francisco	1-6	62	49	3.94	R-L	6-4	215	11/29/56 Inglewood, CA
48	Reuschel, Rick	San Francisco	19-11	245	92	3.12	R-R	6-3	240	5/16/49 Quincy, IL
—	Robertson, Doug	San Jose	7-5	78	103	1.26	S-R	6-1	185	4/15/63 Upland, CA
40	Robinson, Don	San Francisco	10-5	177	122	2.45	R-R	6-4	235	6/8/57 Ashland, KY
58	Samuels, Roger	Phoenix	3-2	48	33	2.63	L-L	6-5	210	1/3/61 San Jose, CA
		San Francisco	1-2	23	22	3.47				
—	Swan, Russ	San Jose	7-0	77	62	2.23	L-L	6-4	210	1/3/64 Fremont, CA
—	Tate, Stu	Shreveport	3-2	40	45	2.03	R-R	6-3	205	6/17/62 Huntsville, AL
		Phoenix	2-4	47	45	5.89				
52	Wilson, Trevor	Shreveport	5-4	73	53	1.86	L-L	6-0	175	6/7/66 Torrance, CA
		Phoenix	2-3	52	49	5.05				
		San Francisco	0-2	22	15	4.09				

CATCHERS

No.	Name	1988 Club	H	HR	RBI	Pct.	B-T	Ht.	Wt.	Born
15	*Brenly, Bob	San Francisco	39	5	22	.189	R-R	6-2	205	2/25/54 Coshocton, OH
17	Manwaring, Kirt	Phoenix	77	2	35	.282	R-R	5-11	185	7/15/65 Elmira, NY
		San Francisco	29	1	15	.250				
7	Melvin, Bob	San Francisco	64	8	27	.234	R-R	6-4	205	10/28/61 Palo Alto, CA
		Phoenix	23	2	9	.307				
—	Pena, Jose	Shreveport	77	4	36	.245	R-R	6-0	190	4/24/65 Dominican Republic
—	Tejada, Wil	Indianapolis	40	1	19	.233	R-R	6-0	185	11/12/62 Dominican Republic
		Montreal	4	0	2	.267				

INFIELDERS

22	Clark, Will	San Francisco	162	29	109	.282	L-L	6-1	190	3/13/64 New Orleans, LA
53	Hayes, Charlie	Phoenix	151	7	71	.307	R-R	6-0	190	5/29/65 Hattiesburg, MS
		San Francisco	1	0	0	.091				
18	Melendez, Francisco	Phoenix	133	4	58	.361	L-L	6-0	185	1/25/64 Puerto Rico
		San Francisco	5	0	3	.192				
—	Perezchica. Tony	Phoenix	158	9	64	.306	R-R	5-11	175	4/20/66 Mexico
		San Francisco	1	0	1	.125				
1	Riles, Ernest	Milwaukee	32	1	9	.252	L-R	6-1	180	10/2/60 Bainbridge, GA
		San Francisco	55	3	28	.294				
—	Santana, Andres	Clinton	126	0	24	.280	S-R	5-11	165	3/19/68 Dominican Republic
		Shreveport	6	0	3	.167				
35	Speier, Chris	San Francisco	37	3	18	.216	R-R	6-1	180	6/28/50 Alameda, CA
6	Thompson, Robby	San Francisco	126	7	48	.264	R-R	5-11	170	5/10/62 West Palm Beach, FL
23	Uribe, Jose	San Francisco	124	3	35	.252	S-R	5-10	165	1/21/60 Dominican Republic
10	Williams, Matt	Phoenix	83	12	51	.271	R-R	6-2	205	11/28/65 Bishop, CA
		San Francisco	32	8	19	.205				

OUTFIELDERS

2	Butler, Brett	San Francisco	163	6	43	.287	L-L	5-10	160	6/15/57 Los Angeles, CA
—	Jones, Tracy	Cin.-Mont.	66	3	24	.295	R-R	6-3	220	3/31/61 Inglewood, CA
21	Maldonado, Candy	San Francisco	127	12	68	.255	R-R	6-0	195	9/5/60 Puerto Rico
9	Mitchell, Kevin	San Francisco	127	19	80	.251	R-R	5-11	210	1/13/62 San Diego, CA
30	Nixon, Donell	Calgary	45	3	10	.281	R-R	6-1	185	12/31/61 Evergreen, NC
		San Francisco	27	0	6	.346				

GIANT PROFILES

WILL CLARK 25 6-1 190 **Bats L Throws L**

"The Natural" developed into a bonafide star in his third full year in the big leagues . . . Led NL with 109 RBI and paced Giants with 29 homers . . . RBI total was the most for a Giant since Willie McCovey had 126 in 1970 . . . Became only the fourth Giant to reach the 100-RBI plateau in last 18 years . . . Was a real bargain last season at a salary of $325,000 . . . Became the Giants' first baseman in 1986, after playing just 65 games of Class-A ball for Fresno the previous season . . . Homered in his first major-league at-bat, April 8, 1986 off Nolan Ryan . . . Born March 13, 1964, in New Orleans . . . Was the second pick overall in the June 1985 draft . . . Became the first San Francisco Giant to play in all 162 games last season . . . Winner of Golden Spikes Award as best collegiate player in the country when he led Mississippi State into College World Series in 1985 . . . Starred for U.S. Olympic team in 1984 . . . As slick with the glove as he is with the bat.

Year	Club	Pos.	G	AB	R	H	2B	3B	HR	RBI	SB	Avg.
1986	San Francisco	1B	111	408	66	117	27	2	11	41	4	.287
1987	San Francisco	1B	150	529	89	163	29	5	35	91	5	.308
1988	San Francisco	1B	162	575	102	162	31	6	29	109	9	.282
	Totals	1B	423	1512	257	442	87	13	75	241	18	.292

KEVIN MITCHELL 27 5-11 210 **Bats R Throws R**

Underwent successful offseason arthroscopic surgery to clean up loose cartilage in his right knee . . . Refused to undergo surgery during September, although the Giants faded from the NL West race . . . Earned $237,500 in his third major-league season . . . Hit just one of his 19 homers after Aug. 12, but missed only 14 games because of the injury . . . Joined the Giants July 4, 1987, along with Dave Dravecky and Craig Lefferts, in deal that sent Chris Brown, Mark Davis, Keith Comstock and Mark Grant to Padres . . . It marked the second time he had been moved in a matter of months. The Mets had traded him to San Diego in December 1986 . . . Responded immediately to his new surroundings after coming to Giants . . . Hit 15 homers, drove in 44 runs and batted .306 in 69 games for them during 1987 . . . Born Jan. 13, 1962, in San Diego . . . Was moved from third base to left field Aug. 13 to make way for Matt Williams . . . Played six positions for Mets as a rookie in 1986 . . . Originally signed by Mets as free agent in November 1980.

Year	Club	Pos.	G	AB	R	H	2B	3B	HR	RBI	SB	Avg.
1984	New York (NL)	3B	7	14	0	3	0	0	0	1	0	.214
1986	New York (NL)	OF-SS-3B-1B	108	328	51	91	22	2	12	43	3	.277
1987	S.D.-S.F.	3B-SS-OF	131	464	68	130	20	2	22	70	9	.280
1988	San Francisco	3B-OF	148	505	60	127	25	7	19	80	5	.251
	Totals		394	1311	179	351	67	11	53	194	17	.268

ROBBY THOMPSON 26 5-11 170 **Bats R Throws R**

Second baseman suffered from a congenital back problem most of last season and missed 24 games . . . Missed the last three games of the season with a broken finger sustained diving for a grounder . . . Opted for therapy on back rather than surgery during offseason . . . Earned $257,000 in his third major-league season . . . Teamed with shortstop Jose Uribe to turn a franchise-record and league-high 187 double plays in 1987 . . . Virtually matched his .262 offensive output in 1987 with a .264 season last year . . . Failed to become a solid No. 2 hitter, however . . . Struck out 111 times in 477 at-bats and has fanned 324 times in his short career . . . Born May 10, 1962, in West Palm Beach, Fla. . . . Giants' top selection in the secondary phase of the June 1983 draft . . . Attended University of Florida . . . A scrappy player and a skilled bunter.

Year	Club	Pos.	G	AB	R	H	2B	3B	HR	RBI	SB	Avg.
1986	San Francisco	2B-SS	149	549	73	149	27	3	7	47	12	.271
1987	San Francisco	2B	132	420	62	110	26	5	10	44	16	.262
1988	San Francisco	2B	138	477	66	126	24	6	7	48	14	.264
	Totals		419	1446	201	385	77	14	24	139	42	.266

BRETT BUTLER 31 5-10 160 **Bats L Throws L**

Arguably the best leadoff man in baseball in debut season as Giant . . . Led NL in walks with career-high 97 in 1988 . . . Combined that with 163 hits and a .287 average . . . Stole 43 bases, the most by a Giant since 1980 . . . His speed was vital to Giants, considering that, prior to his arrival, three players led the club in steals with only 16 each in 1987 . . . Left Indians as free agent to sign a two-year contract worth $1.8 million in December 1987 . . . Covers decent ground in center field, but possesses awful throwing arm, helping to explain why Giant outfielders threw out only four runners at the plate in all of 1988 . . . Born June 15, 1957, in Los Angeles . . . Came up in the Braves' organization as 23rd-round pick in June 1979 . . . Was traded to Cleveland with Brook Jacoby and Rick Behenna for pitcher Len Barker, Aug. 28, 1983 . . . Another skilled bunter . . . Attended Southern Oklahoma State . . . Led majors in triples in 1983 and 1986.

Year	Club	Pos.	G	AB	R	H	2B	3B	HR	RBI	SB	Avg.
1981	Atlanta.	OF	40	126	17	32	2	3	0	4	9	.254
1982	Atlanta.	OF	89	240	35	52	2	0	0	7	21	.217
1983	Atlanta.	OF	151	549	84	154	21	13	5	37	39	.281
1984	Cleveland	OF	159	602	108	162	25	9	3	49	52	.269
1985	Cleveland	OF	152	591	106	184	28	14	5	50	47	.311
1986	Cleveland	OF	161	587	92	163	17	14	4	51	32	.278
1987	Cleveland	OF	137	522	91	154	25	8	9	41	33	.295
1988	San Francisco	OF	157	568	109	163	27	9	6	43	43	.287
	Totals		1046	3785	642	1064	147	70	32	282	276	.281

JOSE URIBE 29 5-10 165 **Bats S Throws R**

Smooth shortstop went through a season of terrible tragedy in 1988 . . . Was with the club in Montreal May 31 when his wife Sara died during the birth of the couple's third child in San Francisco . . . Was placed on the disabled list and returned home to the Dominican Republic to bury his wife . . . Missed 14 games and returned to action June 17 . . . Never really got it going offensively in a 1988 season during which he earned $535,000 . . . Was batting .243 with seven RBI the day his wife passed away . . . Just after his return, he went on a 10-game hitting streak, raising his average to a high-water mark of .266 . . . His .252 average was 39 points below his .291 mark in 1987, but his '87 average was 68 points higher than his 1986 production . . . Born Jan. 21, 1960, in San Cristobal, Dominican Republic . . . Came to Giants with Dave LaPoint, David Green and Gary Rajsich in trade that sent Jack Clark to St. Louis prior to the 1985 season . . . Formerly known as Jose Gonzalez . . . Originally signed as free agent by Yankees in February 1977, but they released him three months later.

Year	Club	Pos.	G	AB	R	H	2B	3B	HR	RBI	SB	Avg.
1984	St. Louis.	SS-2B	8	19	4	4	0	0	0	3	1	.211
1985	San Francisco	SS-2B	147	476	46	113	20	4	3	26	8	.237
1986	San Francisco	SS	157	453	46	101	15	1	3	43	22	.223
1987	San Francisco	SS	95	309	44	90	16	5	5	30	12	.291
1988	San Francisco	SS	141	493	47	124	10	7	3	35	14	.252
	Totals		548	1750	187	432	61	17	14	137	57	.247

CANDY MALDONADO 28 6-0 195 Bats R Throws R

Suffered the most from the absence of Chili Davis and Jeff Leonard from the Giant lineup in 1988, as his offensive numbers were down from 1987 . . . Experienced drop from .292 to .255, from 20 homers to 12, from 86 RBI to 68 . . . His error total in right field went up from five to 10 . . . His misplay in right field in Game 6 of the 1987 NLCS may have cost the Giants the pennant . . . His inability to handle Tony Pena's second-inning triple led to the Cardinals' only run in a 1-0 contest and the Giants lost that series in seven games . . . Was acquired from the Dodgers for Alex Trevino in December 1985 . . . Had 38 homers and 170 RBI in his first two seasons in San Francisco . . . Earned $750,000 last year . . . Born Sept. 5, 1960, in Humacao, Puerto Rico . . . Signed by Los Angeles as free agent in June 1978.

Year	Club	Pos.	G	AB	R	H	2B	3B	HR	RBI	SB	Avg.
1981	Los Angeles	OF	11	12	0	1	0	0	0	0	0	.083
1982	Los Angeles	OF	6	4	0	0	0	0	0	0	0	.000
1983	Los Angeles	OF	42	62	5	12	1	1	1	6	0	.194
1984	Los Angeles	OF-3B	116	254	25	68	14	0	5	28	0	.268
1985	Los Angeles	OF	121	213	20	48	7	1	5	19	1	.225
1986	San Francisco	OF-1B	133	405	49	102	31	3	18	85	4	.252
1987	San Francisco	OF	118	442	69	129	28	4	20	85	8	.292
1988	San Francisco	OF	142	499	53	127	23	1	12	68	6	.255
	Totals		689	1891	221	487	104	10	61	291	19	.258

RICK REUSCHEL 39 6-3 240 Bats R Throws R

"Big Daddy" turned out to be the mainstay of a crippled Giant rotation last season as Dave Dravecky, Mike Krukow, Mike LaCoss, Kelly Downs and Terry Mulholland all suffered serious injuries . . . This control artist, who had rotator-cuff surgery in 1982, made a whopping 36 starts last year . . . Won 19 games and could have become the first pitcher to have two 20-win years 11 seasons apart, but failed to reach that coveted plateau when Giants could manage just four runs for him in his last three starts . . . Has one year remaining on his contract at $800,000 . . . Was obtained from Pirates for Jeff Robinson and Scott Medvin, Aug, 21, 1987 . . . Born May 16, 1949, in Quincy, Ill. . . . Missed entire 1982 season after the shoulder surgery . . .

Picked up off the scrap heap by Pittsburgh in 1985, he went on to win 14 games . . . Drafted by Cubs in third round in June 1970, out of Western Illinois . . . Brother Paul was teammate during early years with Cubs . . . Needs only six wins to reach 200 . . . Helps himself with glove and bat.

Year	Club	G	IP	W	L	Pct.	SO	BB	H	ERA
1972	Chicago (NL).	21	129	10	8	.556	87	29	127	2.93
1973	Chicago (NL).	36	237	14	15	483	168	62	244	3.00
1974	Chicago (NL).	41	241	13	12	.520	160	83	262	4.29
1975	Chicago (NL).	38	234	11	17	.393	155	67	244	3.73
1976	Chicago (NL).	38	260	14	12	.538	146	64	260	3.46
1977	Chicago (NL).	39	252	20	10	.667	166	74	233	2.33
1978	Chicago (NL).	35	243	14	15	.483	115	54	235	3.41
1979	Chicago (NL).	36	239	18	12	.600	125	75	251	3.62
1980	Chicago (NL).	38	257	11	13	.458	140	76	281	3.40
1981	Chicago (NL).	13	86	4	7	.364	53	23	87	3.45
1981	New York (AL).	12	71	4	4	.500	22	10	75	2.66
1982	New York (AL)					Did Not Play				
1983	Chicago (NL).	4	20⅔	1	1	.500	9	10	18	3.92
1984	Chicago (NL).	19	92⅓	5	5	.500	43	23	123	5.17
1985	Pittsburgh	31	194	14	8	.636	138	52	153	2.27
1986	Pittsburgh	35	215⅔	9	16	.360	125	57	232	3.96
1987	Pitt.-S.F.	34	227	13	9	.591	107	42	207	3.09
1988	San Francisco	36	245	19	11	.633	92	42	242	3.12
	Totals	506	3243⅔	194	175	.526	1851	843	3274	3.38

DON ROBINSON 31 6-4 235 **Bats R Throws R**

Began season in bullpen, but was moved into the starting rotation for good after the Giants' run of pitching injuries . . . Made his first start June 27 after 31 relief appearances had produced six saves . . . Was 8-4 as a starter with wins in five of his last six decisions . . . Threw a complete-game shutout against the Dodgers on the final day of the regular season . . . Obtained from Pirates for catcher Mackey Sasser, July 31, 1987 . . . Had seven saves and five wins to aid Giants' drive to the 1987 NL West title . . . Hit the game-winning homer and was the winning pitcher in San Diego Sept. 28, 1987, the day the Giants won their first title since 1971 . . . Signed through 1989 at $900,000 . . . Born June 8, 1957, in Ashland, Ky. . . . Expected to be back in the rotation in 1989 . . . Pirates' third-round pick in June 1975 . . . A dangerous hitter who toyed with idea of becoming an outfielder when arm problems troubled him in 1983 . . .

Only active pitcher to be walked intentionally, when he pinch-hit vs. Phils, June 22, 1984.

Year	Club	G	IP	W	L	Pct.	SO	BB	H	ERA
1978	Pittsburgh	35	228	14	6	.700	135	57	203	3.47
1979	Pittsburgh	29	161	8	8	.500	96	52	171	3.86
1980	Pittsburgh	29	160	7	10	.412	103	45	157	3.99
1981	Pittsburgh	16	38	0	3	.000	17	23	47	5.92
1982	Pittsburgh	38	227	15	13	.536	165	103	213	4.28
1983	Pittsburgh	9	36⅓	2	2	.500	28	21	43	4.46
1984	Pittsburgh	51	122	5	6	.455	110	49	99	3.02
1985	Pittsburgh	44	95⅓	5	11	.313	65	42	95	3.87
1986	Pittsburgh	50	69⅓	3	4	.429	53	27	61	3.38
1987	Pitt.-S.F.	67	108	11	7	.611	79	40	105	3.42
1988	San Francisco	51	176⅔	10	5	.667	122	49	152	2.45
	Totals	419	1421⅔	80	75	.516	973	508	1346	3.65

SCOTT GARRELTS 27 6-4 205 — Bats R Throws R

Had such a dreadful season in the bullpen that manager Roger Craig is thinking about moving him into the starting rotation in 1989 . . . Has made 21 starts in his major-league career, 18 of them in 1986 . . . Failed in 11 of 24 save opportunities this past season . . . Allowed 27 of 63 inherited base-runners to score in 1988 and 16 of 37 to score in 1987 . . . Reached his low-water mark June 10 in Cincinnati, when he allowed six runs in 1.1 innings . . . Was 1-4 with a 6.21 ERA after that outing . . . His last save came Aug. 20 vs. Phillies as he blew his last six opportunities . . . Born Oct. 30, 1961, in Urbana, Ill. . . . All this heartbreak cost the Giants $625,000 last season . . . Giants' top selection and 15th pick overall in June 1979 draft . . . Hard thrower has 48 career saves, but struggles to control nasty split-finger pitch.

Year	Club	G	IP	W	L	Pct.	SO	BB	H	ERA
1982	San Francisco	1	2	0	0	.000	4	2	3	13.50
1983	San Francisco	5	35⅔	2	2	.500	16	19	33	2.52
1984	San Francisco	21	43	2	3	.400	32	34	45	5.65
1985	San Francisco	74	105⅔	9	6	.600	106	58	76	2.30
1986	San Francisco	53	173⅔	13	9	.591	125	74	144	3.11
1987	San Francisco	64	106⅓	11	7	.611	127	55	70	3.22
1988	San Francisco	65	98	5	9	.357	86	46	80	3.58
	Totals	283	564⅓	42	36	.538	496	288	451	3.25

TOP PROSPECT

MATT WILLIAMS 23 6-2 205 — Bats R Throws R

Despite his two disappointing major-league showings—he hit

.188 in 1987 and .205 last year—the Giants still hope he'll be their third baseman of the future . . . Has only 16 homers and 109 strikeouts to show for 401 major-league at-bats . . . Made two trips to majors from Phoenix (AAA) last year . . . Was brought up May 31, when Jose Uribe left the team after his wife died, but was sent back June 16 . . . Came up for good Aug. 11 . . . Hit four homers in a game for Phoenix last season . . . Born Nov. 25, 1965, in Bishop, Cal. . . . Was picked third overall by Giants in June 1986 draft, out of Nevada-Las Vegas . . . Hit .271 with 12 homers and 51 RBI in 306 at-bats for Phoenix and .205 with light homers and 19 RBI for Giants in 1988.

MANAGER ROGER CRAIG: May be most famous for his phrase "Hummm Baby," which was the trademark of the Giants' 1987 NL West title-winning season . . . Predicted his club would win the world championship in 1988, but Giants finished fourth . . . Was named Giants' manager Sept. 18, 1985, handling the club for the final 18 games of a 100-loss season . . . It was his second major-league managerial job, the first since he was fired by the Padres in 1979 . . . Was the pitching coach for Sparky Anderson on Detroit's 1984 world champions . . . Has managed the Giants to a pair of 83-79 finishes sandwiched around a 90-72 division-winning 1987 season . . . His lifetime managerial record is 414-413, 262-242 with the Giants and 152-171 with the Padres . . . His 84-78 finish with Padres in 1978 still stands as the second-best season in the 20-year history of that franchise . . . Born Feb. 17, 1930, in Durham, N.C. . . . Had a 12-year major-league career as a pitcher . . . Was a member of the 1955 and the 1959 champion Dodgers and the 1964 champion Cardinals . . . Lost 24 games and then 22 games for the expansionist Mets in 1962 and 1963 . . . Claim to fame as both a pitching coach and a manager has been his ability to teach the split-finger fastball to his pitching staffs.

GREATEST FIRST BASEMAN

Five first basemen who wore the Giant uniform in New York or San Francisco have been enshrined in the Hall of Fame, in-

Veteran Rick Reuschel, nearing 40, won 19 games in '88.

cluding Bill Terry, a .341 career hitter, and Johnny Mize, who hit 157 of his 359 career homers as a Giant.

But arguably at the top of the list is a man who hit all but 52 of his 521 career homers for the Giants—Willie Lee McCovey. At 6-4, 200 pounds, McCovey was a silent mountain of a man who led with his towering presence and powerful bat. During a 22-year career that spanned four decades, McCovey hit 30 or more homers seven times and 40 or more homers twice, with 45 in 1969 and 44 in 1963.

"Stretch" splashed upon the San Francisco scene at old Seals Stadium in the Mission District in July 1959. He had four hits in four at-bats vs. Phils' ace Robin Roberts in his first game and he went on to hit .354 with 13 homers in 52 games and win the Rookie of the Year award.

McCovey won the NL Most Valuable Player award in 1969, when he batted .320, hit 45 homers and knocked in 126 runs. He was traded to the Padres after the 1973 season, but made a glorious return to the Giants in 1977 and played the final four years of his career in San Francisco. He retired at 42 and was inducted into the Hall of Fame in 1986.

ALL-TIME GIANT SEASON RECORDS

BATTING: Bill Terry, .401, 1930
HRs: Willie Mays, 52, 1965
RBIs: Mel Ott, 151, 1929
STEALS: George Burns, 62, 1914
WINS: Christy Mathewson, 37, 1908
STRIKEOUTS: Christy Mathewson, 267, 1903

INSIDE THE AMERICAN LEAGUE

By TOM PEDULLA
Gannett Newspapers

PREDICTED ORDER OF FINISH	*East*	*West*
	Milwaukee Brewers	Minnesota Twins
	Toronto Blue Jays	Oakland A's
	New York Yankees	Kansas City Royals
	Detroit Tigers	Texas Rangers
	Boston Red Sox	Chicago White Sox
	Cleveland Indians	California Angels
	Baltimore Orioles	Seattle Mariners

Playoff winner: Minnesota

EAST DIVISION		Owner		Morning Line Manager
1	**BREWERS** Ripe for the winner's circle	Bud Selig Blue, gold & white	1988 W 87 L 75	5-2 Tom Trebelhorn
2	**BLUE JAYS** Still on the outside	Peter Hardy Blue & white	1988 W 87 L 75	3-1 Jimy Williams
3	**YANKEES** Always a contender	George Steinbrenner Navy blue pinstripes	1988 W 85 L 76	4-1 Dallas Green
4	**TIGERS** Can't keep pace	Tom Monaghan Navy, orange & white	1988 W 88 L 74	9-2 Sparky Anderson
5	**RED SOX** No threat to repeat	Jean Yawkey Red, white & blue	1988 W 89 L 73	5-1 Joe Morgan
6	**INDIANS** Keep improving	Richard & David Jacobs Red, white & blue	1988 W 78 L 84	20-1 Doc Edwards
7	**ORIOLES** Don't have the horses	Eli Jacobs Black & orange	1988 W 54 L 107	50-1 Frank Robinson

Fast-closing **BREWERS** make it to the wire as **BLUE JAYS** and **YANKEES** have trouble in the stretch. **TIGERS** show life, but not enough. Defending champ **RED SOX** aren't as strong as last time out. **INDIANS** need more races over the course. **ORIOLES** stumble out of the gate and never recover.

Twin Brew Futurity

89th Running. American League Race. Distance: 162 games plus playoff. Payoff (based on '88): $108,665 per winning player, World Series; $86,221 per losing player, World Series. A field of 14 entered in two divisions.

Track Record: 111 wins—Cleveland, 1954

WEST DIVISION

	Team	Owner	1988	Morning Line Manager
1	**TWINS** Back on top	Carl Pohlad; Scarlet, white & blue	1988 W 91 L 71	**2-1** Tom Kelly
2	**A's** Can't repeat	Walter A. Haas Jr.; Forest green, gold & white	1988 W 104 L 58	**5-2** Tony La Russa
3	**ROYALS** Notch below top two	Ewing Kauffman; Royal blue & white	1988 W 84 L 77	**4-1** John Wathan
4	**RANGERS** Winter transfusion	Eddie Chiles; Red, white & blue	1988 W 70 L 91	**10-1** Bobby Valentine
5	**WHITE SOX** New jockey will help	R. Einhorn/J. Reinsdorf; Navy, white & scarlet	1988 W 71 L 90	**20-1** Jeff Torborg
6	**ANGELS** Out of their class	Gene Autry; Red, white & navy	1988 W 75 L 87	**30-1** Doug Rader
7	**MARINERS** Can see them all	George Argyros; Blue, gold & white	1988 W 68 L 93	**40-1** Jim Lefebvre

TWINS and defending champs **A's** match strides before **TWINS** take it by a nose. **ROYALS** falter at start, but late kick brings third-place money. **RANGERS** can't keep up with leaders. **WHITE SOX** and **ANGELS** drop back quickly and **MARINERS** don't get a call.

BALTIMORE ORIOLES

TEAM DIRECTORY: President: Lawrence Lucchino; VP-Baseball Operations: Roland Hemond; VP-Adm. Pers.: Calvin Hill; VPs: Joseph Hamper Jr., Robert Aylward; Farm Dir.: Doug Melvin; Dir. Pub. Rel.: Rick Vaughn; Trav. Sec.: Philip Itzoe; Mgr.: Frank Robinson. Home: Memorial Stadium (54,017). Field distances: 309, l.f. line; 385, l.c.; 405, c.f.; 385, r.c.; 309, r.f. line. Spring training: Sarasota and Miami, Fla.

SCOUTING REPORT

HITTING: With Eddie Murray now batting cleanup for Los Angeles, the Orioles' offense is in deep trouble. Even with Murray, it was woeful last year as Baltimore scored just 550 runs and compiled a meager .238 team batting average. Both were major-league lows.

The trading of Murray puts even more pressure on Cal Ripken Jr. (.264, 23, 81). He and Murray combined to score or drive in 253 of the club's 550 runs last year. However, the acquisition of outfielder Phil Bradley (.264, 11, 56), a disappointment with Philadelphia in his only NL season, may help. Plus, there is hope that Larry Sheets (.230, 10, 47) can regain his form of 1987, when he hit 31 home runs.

More consistency is needed from Joe Orsulak (.288, 8, 27). Orsulak and Bradley provide some speed in an otherwise lumbering lineup. Baltimore ranked next to last in the AL with 69 steals in 1988.

PITCHING: Some good young arms provide hope after a season in which the Orioles went through 21 pitchers, including 15 different starters.

The staff suffered during all that shuffling in 1988, surrendering a major-league-high 789 runs and posting an unsightly 4.54 ERA. That will happen when rookies make 49 starts. But there is no progress without pain.

Jose Bautista (6-15, 4.30), Jeff Ballard (8-12, 4.40) and top prospect Bob Milacki (2-0, 0.72 in three major-league starts) are among the promising youngsters whom the Birds hope will learn from their mistakes. Dave Schmidt (8-5, 3.40) is a reliable veteran, although the Orioles shopped him this past winter as part of their rebuilding program. Brian Holton (7-3, 1.70), acquired from the Dodgers in the Murray deal, should get an opportunity

As power-hitting shortstop, Cal Ripken Jr. is rare Bird.

to be the bullpen closer with the defection of former closer Tom Niedenfuer to Seattle.

FIELDING: The development of Juan Bell, the 20-year-old shortstop who was the key to the Murray deal, is expected to allow Cal Ripken, an All-Star shortstop, to move to third base and solve the persistent problems at that position. The O's have gone through 34 different third basemen since Brooks Robinson retired in 1977.

Mickey Tettleton's acquisition last year helped solidify the catching situation as he represented a defensive improvement over Terry Kennedy. Billy Ripken is a smooth second baseman.

OUTLOOK: From May of last year through the end of the season, Orioles' general manager Roland Hemond traded or released six players 30 or older. The massive overhaul is far from complete, so you can expect manager Frank Robinson's patience to be tested once again. At least times can't get tougher after a club-record 107 losses in 1988, the most defeats for any major-league team this decade.

BALTIMORE ORIOLES 1989 ROSTER

MANAGER Frank Robinson
Coaches—Elrod Hendricks, Al Jackson, Tom McCraw, Johnny Oates, Cal Ripken Sr.

PITCHERS

No.	Name	1988 Club	W-L	IP	SO	ERA	B-T	Ht.	Wt.	Born
29	Ballard, Jeff	Rochester	4-3	61	32	2.97	L-L	6-2	205	8/13/63 Billings, MT
		Baltimore	8-12	153	41	4.40				
48	Bautista, Jose	Baltimore	6-15	172	76	4.30	R-R	6-2	195	7/25/64 Dominican Republic
—	Bowden, Mark	Rochester	9-5	96	94	3.38	L-L	6-0	175	10/10/60 Ridgewood, NJ
—	Habyan, John	Rochester	9-9	147	91	4.46	R-R	6-2	195	1/29/64 Bayshore, NY
		Baltimore	1-0	15	4	4.30				
42	Harnisch, Pete	Charlotte	7-6	132	141	2.58	R-R	6-0	195	9/23/66 Commack, NY
		Rochester	4-1	58	43	2.16				
		Baltimore	0-2	13	10	5.54				
—	Holton, Brian	Los Angeles	7-3	85	49	1.70	R-R	6-0	195	11/29/59 McKeesport, PA
—	Mejia, Cesar	Glens Falls	14-5	163	99	2.43	R-R	6-2	160	10/10/66 Dominican Republic
—	Mesa, Jose	Rochester	0-3	16	15	8.62	R-R	6-3	210	5/22/66 Dominican Republic
52	Milacki, Bob	Charlotte	3-1	38	29	2.39	R-R	6-4	220	7/28/64 Trenton, NJ
		Rochester	12-8	177	103	2.70				
		Baltimore	2-0	25	18	0.72				
12	Morgan, Mike	Baltimore	1-6	71	29	5.43	R-R	6-2	215	10/8/59 Tulare, CA
		Rochester	0-2	17	7	4.76				
30	Olson, Gregg	Hagerstown	1-0	9	9	2.00	R-R	6-4	211	10/11/66 Omaha, NE
		Charlotte	0-1	15	22	5.87				
		Baltimore	1-1	11	9	3.27				
23	Peraza, Oswaldo	Baltimore	5-7	86	61	5.55	R-R	6-4	209	10/19/62 Venezuela
		Rochester	3-0	44	36	2.89				
43	Schilling, Curt	New Britain	8-5	106	62	2.97	R-R	6-4	215	11/14/66 Anchorage, AK
		Charlotte	5-2	45	32	3.18				
		Baltimore	0-3	15	4	9.82				
24	Schmidt, Dave	Baltimore	8-5	130	67	3.40	R-R	6-1	188	4/22/57 Niles, MI
—	Smith, Mike	Indianapolis	5-1	63	55	2.57	R-R	6-1	195	2/23/61 Jackson, MS
		Montreal	0-0	9	4	3.12				
21	Thurmond, Mark	Baltimore	1-8	75	29	4.58	L-L	6-0	193	9/12/58 Houston, TX
		Rochester	5-3	54	25	2.65				
53	Tibbs, Jay	Rochester	3-1	25	18	2.84	R-R	6-1	175	1/4/62 Birmingham, AL
		Baltimore	4-15	159	82	5.39				
32	Williamson, Mark	Baltimore	5-8	118	69	4.90	R-R	6-0	171	7/21/59 Corpus Christi, TX
		Rochester	2-3	30	25	3.34				

CATCHERS

No.	Name	1988 Club	H	HR	RBI	Pct.	B-T	Ht.	Wt.	Born
—	Hoiles, Chris	Toledo	11	2	6	.159	R-R	6-0	195	3/20/65 Bowling Green, OH
		Glens Falls	102	17	73	.283				
15	Kennedy, Terry	Baltimore	60	3	16	.226	L-R	6-4	226	6/4/56 Euclid, OH
26	Nichols, Carl	Baltimore	9	0	1	.191	R-R	6-0	192	10/14/62 Los Angeles, CA
		Rochester	44	3	16	.228				
14	Tettleton, Mickey	Rochester	10	1	4	.244	S-R	6-2	200	9/16/60 Oklahoma City, OK
		Baltimore	74	11	37	.261				

INFIELDERS

—	Bell, Juan	San Antonio	60	5	21	.279	R-R	5-11	172	3/22/68 Dominican Republic
		Albuquerque	77	8	45	.300				
—	Gomez, Leo	Charlotte	26	1	10	.292	R-R	6-0	180	3/2/67 Puerto Rico
88	Gonzales, Rene	Baltimore	51	2	15	.215	R-R	6-2	189	9/3/61 Austin, TX
—	Milligan, Randy	Pittsburgh	18	3	8	.220	R-R	6-2	225	11/27/61 San Diego, CA
		Buffalo	61	2	30	.276				
7	Ripken, Bill	Baltimore	106	2	34	.207	R-R	6-1	178	12/16/64 Havre de Grace, MD
8	Ripken Jr., Cal	Baltimore	152	23	81	.264	R-R	6-4	225	8/24/60 Havre de Grace, MD
13	Schu, Rick	Baltimore	69	4	20	.256	R-R	6-0	194	1/26/62 Philadelphia, PA
28	Traber, Jim	Baltimore	78	10	45	.222	L-L	6-0	213	12/26/61 Columbus, OH
		Rochester	41	6	23	.285				
3	Worthington, Craig	Rochester	105	16	73	.244	R-R	6-0	190	4/17/65 Los Angeles, CA
		Baltimore	15	2	4	.185				

OUTFIELDERS

16	Anderson, Brady	Bos.-Balt.	69	1	21	.212	L-L	6-1	186	1/18/64 Silver Spring, MD
		Pawtucket	48	4	19	.287				
—	Bradley, Phil	Philadelphia	150	11	56	.264	R-R	6-0	185	3/11/59 Bloomington, IN
38	Gerhart, Ken	Charlotte	2	1	1	.154	R-R	6-1	197	5/19/61 Charleston, SC
		Baltimore	51	9	23	.195				
35	Hughes, Keith	Rochester	74	7	49	.270	L-L	6-3	209	9/12/63 Bryn Mawr, PA
		Baltimore	21	2	14	.194				
6	Orsulak, Joe	Baltimore	109	8	27	.288	L-L	6-1	190	5/31/62 Glen Ridge, NJ
19	Sheets, Larry	Baltimore	104	10	47	.230	L-R	6-3	235	12/6/59 Staunton, VA
—	Skeete, Rafel	Charlotte	117	3	29	.237	L-L	5-10	175	4/24/66 Netherlands Antilles
17	Stanicek, Pete	Rochester	12	2	8	.174	S-R	5-11	183	4/18/63 Harvey, IL
		Baltimore	60	4	17	.230				

ORIOLE PROFILES

CAL RIPKEN JR. 28 6-4 225 — Bats R Throws R

This iron man continued to be productive as he extended his string of consecutive games to 1,088, the sixth-longest in history . . . The streak began May 30, 1982 . . . Became second shortstop in history to hit 20 or more home runs in seven consecutive seasons. Ernie Banks did it from 1955-62 . . . Joined Dwight Evans, Tom Brunansky, Fred Lynn and Dale Murphy as the only active players to have accomplished such a stretch . . . Produced only two hits in his first 43 at-bats, easily the worst start of his career . . . Followed that with his best spurt of the season, batting .538 with six homers and 13 RBI over the next 16 games . . . Finished poorly, failing to hit a home run in 29 games from Aug. 27 until Sept. 29, the longest drought of his career . . . Had consecutive-inning string snapped at 8,243, Sept. 14, 1987 . . . Born Aug. 24, 1960, in Havre de Grace, Md. . . . Selected by Orioles in second round of June 1978 draft . . . Son of former manager Cal Sr. and brother of Oriole second baseman Billy . . . Won AL Rookie of the Year in 1982 and AL MVP in 1983 . . . May go back to third to accommodate Juan Bell.

Year	Club	Pos.	G	AB	R	H	2B	3B	HR	RBI	SB	Avg.
1981	Baltimore	SS-3B	23	39	1	5	0	0	0	0	0	.128
1982	Baltimore	SS-3B	160	598	90	158	32	5	28	93	3	.264
1983	Baltimore	SS	162	663	121	211	47	2	27	102	0	.318
1984	Baltimore	SS	162	641	103	195	37	7	27	86	2	.304
1985	Baltimore	SS	161	642	116	181	32	5	26	110	2	.282
1986	Baltimore	SS	162	627	98	177	35	1	25	81	4	.282
1987	Baltimore	SS	162	624	97	157	28	3	27	98	3	.252
1988	Baltimore	SS	161	575	87	152	25	1	23	81	2	.264
	Totals		1153	4409	713	1236	236	24	183	651	16	.280

JOE ORSULAK 26 6-1 190 — Bats L Throws L

Provided Orioles with needed help in leadoff spot . . . Streaky hitter endured 0-for-18 slump in April . . . Responded to increased playing time by displaying surprising power . . . Slugged seven homers in 79 at-bats from Aug. 13 to Sept. 9 after generating only three homers in first 1,127 career at-bats . . . Also hit for average in August, compiling .386 mark with four homers and 12 RBI from Aug. 6 to Sept. 2 . . . Was great disappointment as an outfielder . . . Has good range, but doesn't always come up with the ball . . . Possesses strong but inaccurate arm . . . Born May 31, 1962, in Glen Ridge, N.J. . . . Acquired from Pittsburgh for Terry Crowley and Rico Rossy, after the 1987 season . . . Chosen by Pirates in sixth round of June 1980 draft.

Year	Club	Pos.	G	AB	R	H	2B	3B	HR	RBI	SB	Avg.
1983	Pittsburgh	OF	7	11	0	2	0	0	0	1	0	.182
1984	Pittsburgh	OF	32	67	12	17	1	2	0	3	3	.254
1985	Pittsburgh	OF	121	397	54	119	14	6	0	21	24	.300
1986	Pittsburgh	OF	138	401	60	100	19	6	2	19	24	.249
1988	Baltimore	OF	125	379	48	109	21	3	8	27	9	.288
	Totals		423	1255	174	347	55	17	10	71	60	.276

BILLY RIPKEN 24 6-1 178 **Bats R Throws R**

Fine glove man at second base must show he can handle major-league pitching . . . Engaged in constant struggle to keep his average above .200 . . . Hit .179 in April, .167 in May and .208 in June before picking up the pace a bit . . . With Cal Jr., he forms the fourth brother keystone combination in history and the first since Milt and Frank Bolling teamed briefly for Detroit in 1958 . . . Has outgoing personality, unlike his serious-minded brother . . . Born Dec. 16, 1964, in Havre de Grace, Md. . . . Orioles' 11th-round choice in June 1982 draft.

Year	Club	Pos.	G	AB	R	H	2B	3B	HR	RBI	SB	Avg.
1987	Baltimore	2B	58	234	27	72	9	0	2	20	4	.308
1988	Balitimore	2B	150	512	52	106	18	1	2	34	8	.207
	Totals		208	746	79	178	27	1	4	54	12	.239

MICKEY TETTLETON 28 6-2 200 **Bats S Throws R**

Orioles' most pleasant surprise . . . This catcher was signed by Birds the day after Opening Day, following his release from Oakland . . . Hit .244 in 19 games at Rochester (AAA) before being called up May 9 . . . Responded with nine homers and 23 RBI in first 40 games . . . Finished with career highs in homers (11), RBI (37), runs (31) and hits (74) . . . Nine of his homers came from the right side, but he usually hits for a better average left-handed . . . Homered from both sides of plate June 13 at Detroit, becoming fourth Oriole to do so and first since Eddie Murray did it in 1987 . . . Born Sept. 16, 1960, in Oklahoma City, Okla. . . . Drafted by Oakland in fifth round in June 1981, out of Oklahoma State.

Year	Club	Pos.	G	AB	R	H	2B	3B	HR	RBI	SB	Avg.
1984	Oakland.........	C	33	76	10	20	2	1	1	5	0	.263
1985	Oakland.........	C	78	211	23	53	12	0	3	15	2	.251
1986	Oakland.........	C	90	211	26	43	9	0	10	35	7	.204
1987	Oakland.........	C-1B	82	211	19	41	3	0	8	26	1	.194
1988	Baltimore	C	86	283	31	74	11	1	11	37	0	.261
	Totals		369	992	109	231	37	2	33	118	10	.233

LARRY SHEETS 29 6-3 235 Bats L Throws R

Fortunes plunged after he seemed to have established himself in 1987 . . . Went 25 games without a homer from April 21 to May 21 . . . Endured another 24-game long-ball drought from May 23 to June 18 . . . Hit .192 in 66 games from April 22 to July 7, including a .176 May and a .213 June . . . Only success came during eight-game stretch in July when he went 12-for-29 (.414) with one homer and four RBI . . . Terrible outfielder who has made no improvement . . . Can only help as a DH . . . Born Dec. 6, 1959, in Staunton, Va. . . . Selected by Orioles in second round of June 1978 draft . . . Attended Eastern Mennonite College . . . Played basketball against Ralph Sampson in high school.

Year	Club	Pos.	G	AB	R	H	2B	3B	HR	RBI	SB	Avg.
1984	Baltimore	OF	8	16	3	7	1	0	1	2	0	.438
1985	Baltimore	OF-1B	113	328	43	86	8	0	17	50	0	.262
1986	Baltimore	OF-1B-3B-C	112	338	42	92	17	1	18	60	2	.272
1987	Baltimore	OF-1B	135	469	74	148	23	0	31	94	1	.316
1988	Baltimore	OF-1B	136	452	38	104	19	1	10	47	1	.230
	Totals		504	1603	200	437	68	2	77	253	4	.273

PHIL BRADLEY 30 6-0 185 Bats R Throws R

Left fielder had trouble adjusting to NL early in '88 and asked Phils to trade him . . . Got wish in December when he came to Orioles in exchange for Ken Howell . . . Batted only .223 in first half, but raised batting average 41 points with a .305 second half . . . Finished third in NL with 14 outfield assists . . . Hit by pitch a club-record 16 times . . . Crowds plate, so pitchers try to jam him . . . Led Phillies with 77 runs . . . Phils got him from Mariners with Tim Fortugno in controversial trade for Glenn Wilson, Mike Jackson and Dave Brundage after 1987 season . . . Born March 11, 1959, in Bloomington, Ind. . . . Attended University of Missouri, where he was three-time All-Big Eight quarterback and conference all-time total yardage leader with 6,457 . . . Mariners' third-round pick in June 1981 draft . . . In 1987, he was only AL player to record double figures in doubles, triples and homers.

Year	Club	Pos.	G	AB	R	H	2B	3B	HR	RBI	SB	Avg.
1983	Seattle..........	OF	23	67	8	18	2	0	0	5	3	.269
1984	Seattle..........	OF	124	322	49	97	12	4	0	24	21	.301
1985	Seattle..........	OF	159	641	100	192	33	8	26	88	22	.300
1986	Seattle..........	OF	143	526	88	163	27	4	12	50	21	.310
1987	Seattle..........	OF	158	603	101	179	38	10	14	67	40	.297
1988	Philadelphia......	OF	154	569	77	150	30	5	11	56	11	.264
	Totals		761	2728	423	799	142	31	63	290	118	.293

JOSE BAUTISTA 24 6-2 195 **Bats R Throws R**

Young pitcher worth keeping an eye on . . . Performed far better than his 6-15 record indicates . . . Although his 15 losses were two more than the previous club record, the Birds scored only 68 runs in his 25 starts and tallied two or fewer runs for him 14 times . . . Went just 1-9 after July 10, but got just 25 runs of support in those unlucky 13 starts . . . Defeated Boston ace Roger Clemens, 6-2, June 24 and Red Sox didn't lose again at Fenway until Aug. 13 . . . Born July 25, 1964, in Bani, Dominican Republic and still lives there . . . Acquired from Mets in the major-league draft in December 1987, he was the first player selected by Baltimore in that draft in 10 years . . . Mets had signed him as free agent in April 1981 and his best year for that organization was 1985, when he went 15-8 with 2.34 ERA at Lynchburg (A).

Year	Club	G	IP	W	L	Pct.	SO	BB	H	ERA
1988	Baltimore	33	171⅔	6	15	.286	76	45	171	4.30

DAVE SCHMIDT 31 6-1 188 **Bats R Throws R**

Has proven a fine acquisition since signing with Baltimore prior to 1987 season, after playing out option with White Sox . . . Orioles' winningest pitcher over last two years with combined mark of 18-10 . . . Set career high in innings pitched for second straight year with 129⅔ . . . Began season in bullpen and didn't force his way into rotation until Aug. 4 . . . In his last nine appearances, all starts, he fashioned 5-2 mark with

2.63 ERA . . . Missed last two turns with stiff lower back . . . Born April 22, 1957, in Niles, Mich. . . . Teammate of current Dodger Tim Leary at UCLA . . . Chosen by Rangers in 26th round of June 1979 draft . . . Has excellent control.

Year	Club	G	IP	W	L	Pct.	SO	BB	H	ERA
1981	Texas	14	32	0	1	.000	13	11	31	3.09
1982	Texas	33	109⅔	4	6	.400	69	25	118	3.20
1983	Texas	31	46⅓	3	3	.500	29	14	42	3.88
1984	Texas	43	70⅓	6	6	.500	46	20	69	2.56
1985	Texas	51	85⅔	7	6	.538	46	22	81	3.15
1986	Chicago (AL)	49	92⅓	3	6	.333	67	27	94	3.31
1987	Baltimore	35	124	10	5	.667	70	26	128	3.77
1988	Baltimore	41	129⅔	8	5	.615	67	38	129	3.40
	Totals	297	690	41	38	.519	407	183	692	3.33

JEFF BALLARD 25 6-2 205 **Bats L Throws L**

Improved stock with strong performance late in season . . . Recalled from Rochester (AAA) May 20 after posting 4-3 record and 2.97 ERA there . . . Suffered nightmarish July, going 0-5 with 6.26 ERA . . . Rebounded to go 3-2 with 2.20 ERA in August . . . Finished as Orioles' leader with six complete games . . . Celebrated 25th birthday Aug. 13 by blanking Milwaukee, 5-0, on three hits . . . Stopped Oakland, 10-1, on four-hitter in next start, becoming second Oriole starter to notch back-to-back complete-game wins in the last three years . . . Born Aug. 13, 1963, in Billings, Mont. . . . Orioles' seventh-round pick in June 1985 draft, out of Stanford University.

Year	Club	G	IP	W	L	Pct.	SO	BB	H	ERA
1987	Baltimore	14	69⅔	2	8	.200	27	35	100	6.59
1988	Baltimore	25	153⅓	8	12	.400	41	42	167	4.40
	Totals	39	223	10	20	.333	68	77	267	5.09

TOP PROSPECT

BOB MILACKI 24 6-4 220 **Bats R Throws R**

Burst onto major-league scene with 2-0 record and 0.72 ERA in three September starts . . . Capped his year by earning his first major-league shutout, a three-hitter vs. the Yankees Sept. 28 . . . Finished third in International League with 12 victories and fourth with 2.70 ERA for Rochester (AAA) after beginning 1988 at Charlotte (AA) . . . Born July 28, 1964, in Trenton, N.J. . . . Orioles' second-round pick in June 1983 draft.

Frank Robinson is Baltimore's link to better days.

MANAGER FRANK ROBINSON: Holds prominent place in baseball history as first black manager . . . Gained that distinction when Cleveland named him player-manager on Oct. 4, 1974 . . . Made debut unforgettable by homering in first at-bat on Opening Day, April 8, 1975, and helping his team to a 5-3 triumph over the Yankees . . . Managed Cleveland from 1975-77 . . . Piloted San Francisco from 1981-84 . . . Named to replace Cal Ripken Sr. as Baltimore manager after 0-6 start in 1988 . . . O's went on to lose 15 more consecutive games at start of season . . . Robinson must keep club together during process of major reconstruction . . . Composite major-league managerial record stands at 504-567 after 54-101 mark in '88 . . . Best showing as manager was third place with San Francisco in 1982 . . . One of the few managers who excelled as a player . . . Hall of Fame career covered 21 major-league seasons . . . Best years were spent with Cincinnati (1956-65) and Baltimore (1966-71) . . . Ranks as fourth-leading home-run hitter with 586 . . . Only man to be named MVP in each league, including Triple Crown year with Baltimore in 1966, when he batted .316 with 49 home runs, 122 RBI . . . Was NL MVP with Cincinnati in 1961 . . . Born Aug. 31, 1935, in Beaumont, Tex.

GREATEST FIRST BASEMAN

There was a time when fans at Baltimore's Memorial Stadium held Eddie Murray responsible for the Orioles' recent decline and booed him. But, by the end of the 1988 season that will be remembered as his Baltimore swan song, a revived Murray had reminded Bird watchers that he was the best first baseman the club has ever had.

In 1988, Murray topped the Orioles in batting average (.284), home runs (28) and RBI (84), the fifth time he won the club's triple crown. Murray's run production was remarkably consistent. He hit 20 or more home runs in each of his first nine seasons and reached the 30-home-run mark a club-record five times.

Murray's place in club history is secure. He is the Orioles' all-time leader with 333 home runs and ranks second to Brooks Robinson with 1,190 RBI. Murray also ranks as one of the most prolific switch-hitters of all time. He stands second to Mickey Mantle (536) in home runs and is third all time in RBI behind Mantle (1,509) and Ted Simmons (1,378).

A three-time Gold Glove winner at first base, Murray was dealt to the Dodgers last December. But his decade of contributions to the Orioles won't soon be forgotten.

ALL-TIME ORIOLE SEASON RECORDS

BATTING: Ken Singleton, .328, 1977
HRs: Frank Robinson, 49, 1966
RBIs: Jim Gentile, 141, 1961
STEALS: Luis Aparicio, 57, 1964
WINS: Steve Stone, 25, 1980
STRIKEOUTS: Ferguson Jenkins, 225, 1974

BOSTON RED SOX

TEAM DIRECTORY: Pres.: Jean R. Yawkey; Chief Exec. Off.-Chief Oper. Off.: Haywood C. Sullivan; Sr. VP-GM: Lou Gorman; VP-Player Dev.: Edward F. Kennedy; Dir. Scouting: Eddie Kasko; Dir. Minor League Oper.: Edward P. Kenney; VP-Pub. Rel.: Dick Bresciani; VP-Transportation: Jack Rogers; Mgr.: Joe Morgan. Home: Fenway Park (33,583). Field distances: 315, l.f. line; 379, l.c.: 390, c.f.; 420, r.c. corner; 380, r.c.; 302, r.f. line. Spring training: Winter Haven, Fla.

SCOUTING REPORT

HITTING: For pure hitting ability, no club can match the Red Sox. Five-time batting champion Wade Boggs (.366, 5, 58), Mike Greenwell (.325, 22, 119) and Dwight Evans (.293, 21, 111) head an offense that compiled a league-leading .283 team mark last year, a whopping nine points higher than runnerup

Mike Greenwell used Monster stroke to notch 119 RBI.

Minnesota. Boston also led the league in runs generated with 813, 13 more than the muscle-bound Athletics.

The Red Sox' secret is no secret: their hitters put the ball in play. Second baseman Marty Barrett (.283, 1, 65), for instance, fanned only 35 times in 612 at-bats. The Sox posted the lowest strikeout total in the majors for the third straight year, with 728.

Center fielder Ellis Burks (.294, 18, 92, 25 steals) is a rising star and the only real base-stealing threat on a club that ranked last in the AL with 65 steals. Fading Jim Rice (.264, 15, 72) and former Reds' first baseman Nick Esasky (.243, 15, 62) are among the plodders.

PITCHING: Two-time Cy Young Award winner Roger Clemens (18-12, 2.93) will have to be greater than ever to help compensate for the loss of free agent Bruce Hurst to San Diego.

In truth, there is no replacing Hurst, who won a career-high 18 games last season and was nearly unbeatable at Fenway Park, where he went 13-2. He was 11-2 when he pitched after a Sox defeat.

Big things will be expected from former Oriole Mike Boddicker (13-15, 3.39) in his first full season in Beantown. Talented John Dopson, acquired from Montreal after a hard-luck 3-11, 3.04 rookie season, ex-reliever Wes Gardner (8-6, 3.50) and the unpredictable Dennis (Oil Can) Boyd (9-7, 5.34) will be asked to pick up the rest of the slack. Lee Smith (29 saves) anchors the bullpen, which was bolstered by the addition of lefty Rob Murphy from the Reds last winter.

FIELDING: Boston has a nice mix of veterans and young players. The veterans' presence—Barrett at second, Evans in right, the re-signed Rich Gedman behind the plate—helps account for the Red Sox' defensive excellence. They ranked second in the AL with a .984 fielding percentage in 1988.

Young shortstop Jody Reed has the tools, but needs time to develop. With Reed and Barrett working together for the first time last year, the Red Sox turned the fewest double plays in the AL with 123.

OUTLOOK: With Hurst, the Red Sox loomed as keen contenders in the AL East, a division they have won two of the last three years. With Hurst gone, the injury-plagued Boyd and the unproven Gardner loom as even greater question marks.

Hurst's family is happier now that he is playing in San Diego, closer to his Utah home, but the Red Sox and miracle-working manager Joe Morgan are likely to mourn his absence in 1989.

BOSTON RED SOX 1989 ROSTER

MANAGER Joe Morgan

Coaches—Dick Berardino, Al Bumbry, Bill Fischer, Richie Hebner, Rac Slider

PITCHERS

No.	Name	1988 Club	W-L	IP	SO	ERA	B-T	Ht.	Wt.	Born
52	Boddicker, Mike	Balt.-Bos.	13-15	236	156	3.39	R-R	5-11	186	8/23/57 Cedar Rapids, IA
50	Bolton, Tom	Pawtucket	3-0	19	15	2.79	L-L	6-3	175	5/6/63 Nashville, TN
		Boston	1-3	30	21	4.75				
23	Boyd, Oil Can	Boston	9-7	130	71	5.34	R-R	6-1	160	10/6/59 Meridian, MS
21	Clemens, Roger	Boston	18-12	264	291	2.93	R-R	6-4	220	8/4/62 Dayton, OH
—	Curry, Steve	Pawtucket	11-9	146	110	3.08	R-R	6-6	217	9/13/65 Winter Park, FL
		Boston	0-1	11	4	8.18				
—	Dopson, John	Indianapolis	0-0	18	15	3.50	L-R	6-4	205	7/14/63 Baltimore, MD
		Montreal	3-11	169	101	3.04				
—	Ellsworth, Steve	Boston	1-6	36	16	6.75	R-R	6-8	220	7/30/60 Chicago, IL
		Pawtucket	7-7	108	58	3.74				
44	Gardner, Wes	Boston	8-6	149	106	3.50	R-R	6-4	203	4/29/61 Benton, AR
—	Hetzel, Eric	Pawtucket	6-10	127	122	3.96	R-R	6-3	175	9/25/63 Crowley, LA
15	Lamp, Dennis	Boston	7-6	83	49	3.48	R-R	6-3	215	9/23/52 Los Angeles, CA
—	Murphy, Rob	Cincinnati	0-6	85	74	3.08	L-L	6-2	205	5/26/60 Miami, FL
—	Rochford, Mike	Pawtucket	1-5	82	47	3.09	L-L	6-4	205	3/14/63 Methuen, MA
		Boston	0-0	2	1	0.00				
48	Smith, Lee	Boston	4-5	84	96	2.80	R-R	6-6	245	12/4/57 Jamestown, LA
41	Smithson, Mike	Boston	9-6	127	73	5.97	R-L	6-8	215	1/21/55 Centerville, TN
46	Stanley, Bob	Winter Haven	0-1	10	3	7.20	R-R	6-4	225	11/10/54 Portland, ME
		Pawtucket	1-0	11	6	0.82				
		Boston	6-4	102	57	3.19				
—	Vasquez, Luis	New Britain	3-9	112	97	2.48	R-R	6-1	170	3/23/67 Venezuela
		Pawtucket	5-4	75	73	3.58				
—	Woodward, Rob	Pawtucket	1-4	44	53	3.86	R-R	6-3	212	9/28/62 Hanover, NH
		Boston	0-0	1	0	13.50				

CATCHERS

No.	Name	1988 Club	H	HR	RBI	Pct.	B-T	Ht.	Wt.	Born
6	Cerone, Rick	Boston	71	3	27	.269	R-R	5-11	195	5/19/54 Newark, NJ
10	Gedman, Rich	Pawtucket	7	1	1	.467	L-R	6-0	215	9/26/59 Worcester, MA
		Boston	69	9	39	.231				
—	Marzano, John	Pawtucket	22	0	5	.198	R-R	5-11	197	2/14/63 Philadelphia, PA
		New Britain	23	0	5	.205				
		Boston	4	0	1	.138				

INFIELDERS

No.	Name	1988 Club	H	HR	RBI	Pct.	B-T	Ht.	Wt.	Born
17	Barrett, Marty	Boston	173	1	65	.283	R-R	5-10	174	6/23/58 Arcadia, CA
26	Boggs, Wade	Boston	214	5	58	.366	L-R	6-2	197	6/15/58 Omaha, NE
—	Cooper, Scott	Lynchburg	148	9	73	.298	L-R	6-3	200	10/13/67 St. Louis, MO
—	Esasky, Nick	Cincinnati	95	15	62	.243	R-R	6-3	215	2/24/60 Hialeah, FL
—	Horn, Sam	Boston	9	2	8	.148	L-L	6-5	240	11/2/63 Dallas, TX
		Pawtucket	65	10	31	.233				
3	Reed, Jody	Boston	99	1	28	.293	R-R	5-9	160	7/26/62 Tampa, FL
—	Rivera, Luis	Montreal	83	4	30	.224	R-R	5-9	165	1/3/64 Puerto Rico
11	Romero, Ed	Boston	18	0	5	.240	R-R	5-11	180	12/9/57 Puerto Rico

OUTFIELDERS

No.	Name	1988 Club	H	HR	RBI	Pct.	B-T	Ht.	Wt.	Born
12	Burks, Ellis	Boston	159	18	92	.294	R-R	6-2	188	9/11/64 Vicksburg, MS
24	Evans, Dwight	Boston	164	21	111	.293	R-R	6-3	208	11/3/51 Santa Monica, CA
39	Greenwell, Mike	Boston	192	22	119	.325	L-R	6-0	195	7/18/63 Louisville, KY
—	Kutcher, Randy	Pawtucket	77	4	27	.233	R-R	5-11	175	4/20/60 Anchorage, AK
		Boston	2	0	0	.167				
—	Quintana, Carlos	Pawtucket	134	16	66	.285	R-R	6-2	195	8/26/65 Venezuela
		Boston	2	0	2	.333				
14	Rice, Jim	Boston	128	15	72	.264	R-R	6-2	216	3/8/53 Anderson, SC
16	Romine, Kevin	Pawtucket	53	4	26	.358	R-R	5-11	185	5/23/61 Exeter, NH
		Boston	15	1	6	.192				

RED SOX PROFILES

WADE BOGGS 30 6-2 197 **Bats L Throws R**

Overcame off-the-field turmoil resulting from that $6-million palimony suit filed by Margo Adams, a woman with whom he admitted having an affair . . . Hit .366 to win fourth straight AL batting title and his fifth in six years . . . Became first player since 1900 to have six straight 200-hit seasons and joined Lou Gehrig (1930-32) as the only players to record three consecutive 200-hit, 100-walk seasons . . . By reaching base 342 times with a hit, walk or hit by pitch, he tied Gehrig for sixth-best total ever . . . It was the highest total in majors since Ted Williams reached 358 times in 1949 . . . Led majors with .366 average, 125 walks, 128 runs, 45 doubles and .476 on-base percentage . . . Hit .382 at Fenway Park . . . Compiled best average in ALCS at .385, but was Game 1 goat as he struck out twice to strand five runners . . . Born June 15, 1958, in Omaha, Neb. . . . Red Sox' seventh-round choice in June 1976 draft . . . Hard work has made him into a solid defensive third baseman.

Year	Club	Pos.	G	AB	R	H	2B	3B	HR	RBI	SB	Avg.
1982	Boston	1B-3B-OF	104	338	51	118	14	1	5	44	1	.349
1983	Boston	3B	153	582	100	210	44	7	5	74	3	.361
1984	Boston	3B	158	625	109	203	31	4	6	55	3	.325
1985	Boston	3B	161	653	107	240	42	3	8	78	2	.368
1986	Boston	3B	149	580	107	207	47	2	8	71	0	.357
1987	Boston	3B-1B	147	551	108	200	40	6	24	89	1	.363
1988	Boston	3B	155	584	128	214	45	6	5	58	2	.366
	Totals		1027	3913	710	1392	263	29	61	469	12	.356

MIKE GREENWELL 25 6-0 195 **Bats L Throws R**

Left fielder contended for AL MVP honors in only his second full major-league season . . . Led majors and set AL record with 23 game-winning RBI . . . Ten of his 22 homers put Red Sox ahead . . . Hit .333 (61-for-183) with runners in scoring position . . . Ranked second in majors with .416 on-base percentage and third in batting average (.325), RBI (119), hits (192) and total bases (313) . . . Reached base 288 times via hit, walk or hit by pitch, the second-best total in majors behind Wade Boggs . . . Hit for cycle Sept. 14 vs. Baltimore . . . Failed to assert himself in ALCS, batting .214 with one homer and three RBI

...Born July 18, 1963, in Louisville, Ky....Red Sox' third-round pick in June 1982 draft.

Year	Club	Pos.	G	AB	R	H	2B	3B	HR	RBI	SB	Avg.
1985	Boston	OF	17	31	7	10	1	0	4	8	1	.323
1986	Boston	OF	31	35	4	11	2	0	0	4	0	.314
1987	Boston	OF-C	125	412	71	135	31	6	19	89	5	.328
1988	Boston	OF	158	590	86	192	39	8	22	119	16	.325
	Totals		331	1068	168	348	73	14	45	220	22	.326

DWIGHT EVANS 37 6-3 208 Bats R Throws R

Veteran right fielder pointed way to the division title, collecting eight homers and 24 RBI in September...Earned distinction as only major-league player with eight consecutive 20-home run seasons..."Dewey" produced 2,000th hit May 27 vs. Oakland...Amassed career-high seven RBI Aug. 13 vs. Detroit... Nine of his 21 homers came from the seventh inning on...Was 6-for-12 with 16 RBI with bases loaded... Slumped during ALCS with .167 average, no homers, one RBI and five strikeouts...Still possesses good arm, but it's not nearly as strong as it used to be...Born Nov. 3, 1951, in Santa Monica, Cal....Red Sox' fifth-round choice in June 1969 draft.

Year	Club	Pos.	G	AB	R	H	2B	3B	HR	RBI	SB	Avg.
1972	Boston	OF	18	57	2	15	3	1	1	6	0	.263
1973	Boston	OF	119	282	46	63	13	1	10	32	5	.223
1974	Boston	OF	133	463	60	130	19	8	10	70	4	.281
1975	Boston	OF	128	412	61	113	24	6	13	56	3	.274
1976	Boston	OF	146	501	61	121	34	5	17	62	6	.242
1977	Boston	OF	73	230	39	66	9	2	14	36	4	.287
1978	Boston	OF	147	497	75	123	24	2	24	63	8	.247
1979	Boston	OF	152	489	69	134	24	1	21	58	6	.274
1980	Boston	OF	148	463	72	123	37	5	18	60	3	.266
1981	Boston	OF	108	412	84	122	19	4	22	71	3	.296
1982	Boston	OF	162	609	122	178	37	7	32	98	3	.292
1983	Boston	OF	126	470	74	112	19	4	22	58	3	.238
1984	Boston	OF	162	630	121	186	37	8	32	104	3	.295
1985	Boston	OF	159	617	110	162	29	1	29	78	7	.263
1986	Boston	OF	152	529	86	137	33	2	26	97	3	.259
1987	Boston	1B-OF	154	541	109	165	37	2	34	123	4	.305
1988	Boston	OF-1B	149	559	96	164	31	7	21	111	5	.293
	Totals		2236	7761	1287	2114	429	66	346	1183	70	.272

ELLIS BURKS 24 6-2 188 Bats R Throws R

Center fielder has a chance to be a star... Finished third on Red Sox with .294 average, 18 homers and 92 RBI, despite injuring left wrist in April...Injury nagged him rest of season...Ripped grand slams vs. New York June 15 and vs. Texas July 27...Went 8-for-17 and notched team-leading 22 RBI with bases loaded...Hit 60 points higher in day games (.332) than at night (.272) . . . Hit only .235 in ALCS . . . Born Sept. 11, 1964, in Vicksburg, Miss. . . . Red Sox' first pick in January 1983 draft.

Year	Club	Pos.	G	AB	R	H	2B	3B	HR	RBI	SB	Avg.
1987	Boston	OF	133	558	94	152	30	2	20	59	27	.272
1988	Boston	OF	144	540	93	159	37	5	18	92	25	.294
	Totals		277	1098	187	311	67	7	38	151	52	.283

JIM RICE 36 6-2 216 **Bats R Throws R**

Fading veteran outfielder and DH isn't nearly the threat he used to be . . . Failed to hit a home run until 49th game June 13, when he connected twice off Yankees' Rich Dotson . . . Career average was in danger of dipping below .300 before he singled and homered during final game of regular season to keep it at that level . . . Singled for 2,400th career hit Sept. 29 vs. Cleveland . . . Hit meager .154 in ALCS . . . Eventually apologized for tangling with manager Joe Morgan after being pulled for pinch-hitter, a pivotal show of strength by Morgan . . . Won AL MVP award in 1978, when he led majors with 46 home runs . . . Born March 8, 1953, in Anderson, S.C. . . . Red Sox' first pick in June 1971 draft.

Year	Club	Pos.	G	AB	R	H	2B	3B	HR	RBI	SB	Avg.
1974	Boston	OF	24	67	6	18	2	1	1	13	0	.269
1975	Boston	OF	144	564	92	174	29	4	22	102	10	.309
1976	Boston	OF	153	581	75	164	25	8	25	85	8	.282
1977	Boston	OF	160	644	104	206	29	15	39	114	5	.320
1978	Boston	OF	163	677	121	213	25	15	46	139	7	.315
1979	Boston	OF	158	619	117	201	39	6	39	130	9	.325
1980	Boston	OF	124	504	81	148	22	6	24	86	8	.294
1981	Boston	OF	108	451	51	128	18	1	17	62	2	.284
1982	Boston	OF	145	573	86	177	24	5	24	97	0	.309
1983	Boston	OF	155	626	90	191	34	1	39	126	0	.305
1984	Boston	OF	159	657	98	184	25	7	28	122	4	.280
1985	Boston	OF	140	546	85	159	20	3	27	103	2	.291
1986	Boston	OF	157	618	98	200	39	2	20	110	0	.324
1987	Boston	OF	108	404	66	112	14	0	13	62	1	.277
1988	Boston	OF	135	485	57	128	18	3	15	72	1	.264
	Totals		2033	8016	1227	2403	363	77	379	1423	57	.300

MARTY BARRETT 30 5-10 174 **Bats R Throws R**

Appreciation for second baseman's ability grows every season . . . Collected career-high 65 RBI . . . Struck out only 35 times in 687 plate appearances, the third straight year he has fanned fewer than 40 times . . . Has great sense for the game . . . Stole home vs. Baltimore June 16, making him first Sox to steal that base since Tommy Harper in 1973 . . . Deceived Orioles' Jim Traber with hidden-ball trick Sept. 5 and flipped to shortstop Jody Reed for out . . . Led Red Sox by driving in 27 of 36 runners from third with less than two outs . . . Suffered dismal ALCS, batting .067 . . . Born June 23, 1958, in Arcadia, Cal. . . . Red Sox' first pick in June 1979 draft.

Year	Club	Pos.	G	AB	R	H	2B	3B	HR	RBI	SB	Avg.
1982	Boston	2B	8	18	0	1	0	0	0	0	0	.056
1983	Boston	2B	33	44	7	10	1	1	0	2	0	.227
1984	Boston	2B	139	475	56	144	23	3	3	45	5	.303
1985	Boston	2B	156	534	59	142	26	0	5	56	7	.266
1986	Boston	2B	158	625	94	179	39	4	4	60	15	.286
1987	Boston	2B	137	559	72	164	23	0	3	43	15	.293
1988	Boston	2B	150	612	83	173	28	1	1	65	7	.283
	Totals		781	2867	371	813	140	9	16	271	49	.284

NICK ESASKY 29 6-3 215 — Bats R Throws R

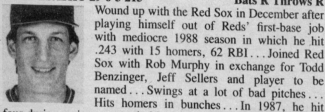

Wound up with the Red Sox in December after playing himself out of Reds' first-base job with mediocre 1988 season in which he hit .243 with 15 homers, 62 RBI . . . Joined Red Sox with Rob Murphy in exchange for Todd Benzinger, Jeff Sellers and player to be named . . . Swings at a lot of bad pitches . . . Hits homers in bunches . . . In 1987, he hit four during a six-game period in June and four in four consecutive games in July . . . Reds' top pick in June 1978 draft . . . Earned $460,000 last season . . . Suffered fractured right wrist when he was hit by a pitch March 16, 1987 and wasn't reactivated until May 19 . . . Still unloaded 22 homers, drove in 59 runs and hit .272 in 100 games in 1987 . . . Born Feb. 24, 1960, in Hialeah, Fla. . . . Missed most of last May, when he was placed on the 21-day disabled list with sprained right ankle.

Year	Club	Pos.	G	AB	R	H	2B	3B	HR	RBI	SB	Avg.
1983	Cincinnati	3B	85	302	41	80	10	5	12	46	6	.265
1984	Cincinnati	3B-1B	113	322	30	62	10	5	10	45	1	.193
1985	Cincinnati	3B-OF-1B	125	413	61	108	21	0	21	66	3	.262
1986	Cincinnati	1B-OF-3B	102	330	35	76	17	2	12	41	0	.230
1987	Cincinnati	1B-3B-OF	100	346	48	94	19	2	22	59	0	.272
1988	Cincinnati	1B-3B-OF	122	391	40	95	17	2	15	62	7	.243
	Totals		647	2104	255	515	94	16	92	319	17	.245

ROGER CLEMENS 26 6-4 220 — Bats R Throws R

Strikeout king had another dazzling season, but "The Rocket" has become hittable . . . His string of Cy Young awards ended at two . . . Was 0-5 with 7.33 ERA in five August starts, the longest losing streak of his career . . . Had been 15-5 with 2.24 ERA to that point . . . Was 6-8 with a 3.91 ERA in 17 starts at Fenway, compared to 12-4, 2.09 on road . . . Led majors with 291 strikeouts and tied Dodgers' Orel Hershiser for major-league lead in shutouts with eight... His 291 strikeouts smashed Red Sox record held since 1912 by Smokey Joe Wood (258) and represented highest total in AL since Nolan Ryan's 341 in 1977... Eight shutouts were most by Red Sox pitcher since Babe Ruth's nine in 1916... Failed to hold 2-0 edge in Game 2 of ALCS and left after seven innings without a decision... In 1986, he won AL MVP, Cy Young and All-Star Game MVP awards... Born Aug. 4, 1962, in Dayton, Ohio... Red Sox' first pick in June 1983 draft, out of the University of Texas.

Year	Club	G	IP	W	L	Pct.	SO	BB	H	ERA
1984	Boston	21	133⅓	9	4	.692	126	29	146	4.32
1985	Boston	15	98⅓	7	5	.583	74	37	83	3.29
1986	Boston	33	254	24	4	.857	238	67	179	2.48
1987	Boston	36	281⅔	20	9	.690	256	83	248	2.97
1988	Boston	35	264	18	12	.600	291	62	217	2.93
	Totals	140	1031⅓	78	34	.696	985	278	873	3.05

MIKE BODDICKER 30 5-11 186 **Bats R Throws R**

Made the difference for Red Sox after they acquired him from Orioles for top prospects Brady Anderson and Curt Schilling July 29 ... Went 7-3 with 2.63 ERA for Red Sox after going 6-12 with 3.86 ERA for Baltimore... Had dropped first eight starts with Orioles... Was 3-0, 1.96 ERA in final six starts for Boston... Allowed three earned runs or less in 13 of 14 starts with Red Sox... Was routed, however, by Athletics in Game 3 of ALCS, surrendering six runs in 2⅔ innings... Born Aug. 23, 1957, in Cedar Rapids, Iowa... Chosen by Orioles in sixth round of June 1978 draft, out of the University of Iowa.

Year	Club	G	IP	W	L	Pct.	SO	BB	H	ERA
1980	Baltimore	1	7	0	1	.000	4	5	6	6.43
1981	Baltimore	2	6	0	0	.000	2	2	6	4.50
1982	Baltimore	7	25⅔	1	0	1.000	20	12	25	3.51
1983	Baltimore	27	179	16	8	.667	120	52	141	2.77
1984	Baltimore	34	261⅓	20	11	.645	128	81	218	2.79
1985	Baltimore	32	203⅓	12	17	.414	135	89	227	4.07
1986	Baltimore	33	218⅓	14	12	.538	175	74	214	4.70
1987	Baltimore	33	226	10	12	.455	152	78	212	4.18
1988	Balt.-Bos.	36	236	13	15	.464	156	77	234	3.39
	Totals	205	1362⅔	86	76	.531	892	470	1283	3.66

LEE SMITH 31 6-6 245 **Bats R Throws R**

Though he fell one save short of becoming first major-league pitcher with 30 saves in five straight seasons, he was a key to Red Sox' division title . . . His 29 saves tied him for the third-highest single-season total by a Red Sox pitcher . . . Recorded 16 saves in last 18 chances, starting July 22 . . . Prevented 28 of 38 inherited runners from scoring . . . Held first batters he faced to a .150 average with 16 strikeouts . . . Ranks ninth all-time with 209 career saves . . . Born Dec. 4, 1957, in Jamestown, La. . . . Acquired from Cubs for Al Nipper and Calvin Schiraldi following the 1987 season . . . Cubs' all-time save leader with 180 . . . Cubs' second-round pick in June 1975 draft.

Year	Club	G	IP	W	L	Pct.	SO	BB	H	ERA
1980	Chicago (NL)	18	22	2	0	1.000	17	14	21	2.86
1981	Chicago (NL)	40	67	3	6	.333	50	31	57	3.49
1982	Chicago (NL)	72	117	2	5	.286	99	37	105	2.69
1983	Chicago (NL)	66	103⅓	4	10	.286	91	41	70	1.65
1984	Chicago (NL)	69	101	9	7	.563	86	35	98	3.65
1985	Chicago (NL)	65	97⅔	7	4	.636	112	32	87	3.04
1986	Chicago (NL)	66	90⅓	9	9	.500	93	42	69	3.09
1987	Chicago (NL)	62	83⅔	4	10	.286	96	32	84	3.12
1988	Boston	64	83⅔	4	5	.444	96	37	72	2.80
	Totals	522	765⅔	44	56	.440	740	301	663	2.90

TOP PROSPECT

CARLOS QUINTANA 23 6-2 195 **Bats R Throws R**

Outfielder distinguished himself during first season in Triple-A . . . Hit .285 with 16 homers and 66 RBI for Pawtucket and led club in homers, RBI and hits (134) in 1988 . . . Went 2-for-6 with two RBI in cup of coffee at major-league level . . . Broken right leg limited him to 56 games at New Britain (AA) in 1987 . . . Born Aug. 26, 1965, in Estado Miranda, Venezuela . . . Signed by Red Sox as free agent, Nov. 26, 1984.

MANAGER JOE MORGAN: Named to replace John McNamara July 14, he enjoyed best managerial start in history and led revived Sox to AL East title . . . Sox won first 12 games and 19 of first 20 under him . . . Went from being interim manager with little chance of survival to recipient of an extension through 1989 . . . Showed he was in command of club by pinch-hitting for veteran Jim Rice, then standing up to Rice

when player threw a temper tantrum in dugout . . . "I'm manager of this nine," Morgan declared at one point . . . Later in season, he used Rice to hit for eventual batting champion Wade Boggs . . . Not at all afraid to make unorthodox moves based on hunches . . . Piloted Sox to 46-31 record as they rallied from nine-game deficit at All-Star break . . . Spent 15 seasons as minor-league infielder-outfielder . . . Had brief stints in majors with Milwaukee Braves, Kansas City A's, Philadelphia, Cleveland and St. Louis . . . Managed in Pittsburgh system from 1966-73 . . . Joined Red Sox organization in 1974 and managed Pawtucket (AAA) until 1982 . . . Used to plow Massachusetts Turnpike in winter to augment meager baseball earnings . . . Born Nov. 19, 1930, in Walpole, Mass.

GREATEST FIRST BASEMAN

Bill Dickey, the great Yankee catcher, once said of Jimmie Foxx, "If I were catching blindfolded, I'd always know when it was Jimmie Foxx who connected. He hit the ball harder than anybody else."

Foxx, who anchored first base for the Red Sox from 1936-42, finished with 534 home runs and among them were many prodigious shots. He once slammed a pitch from Lefty Gomez into the third tier in left at Yankee Stadium and the ball landed with such force that it broke the back of a seat.

The 1951 Hall of Fame inductee began his major-league career with the Philadelphia Athletics at age 17. On May 1, 1925, he collected the first of his 2,646 major-league hits, a pinch single against Washington's Vean Gregg.

Foxx' best season with Boston came in 1938, when he led the league in batting average (.349), slugging percentage (.704) and RBI (175). Those statistics would command a whopping contract today, but Foxx' top salary with Boston was $32,000, including attendance bonuses.

ALL-TIME RED SOX SEASON RECORDS

BATTING: Ted Williams, .406, 1941
HRs: Jimmie Foxx, 50, 1938
RBIs: Jimmie Foxx, 175, 1938
STEALS: Tommy Harper, 54, 1973
WINS: Joe Wood, 34, 1912
STRIKEOUTS: Roger Clemens, 291, 1988

CLEVELAND INDIANS

TEAM DIRECTORY: Owners: Richard Jacobs, David Jacobs; Pres.-Chief Oper. Off.: Hank Peters; VP-Baseball Oper./Player Rel.: Dan O'Brien; Dir. Player Dev.: Dan O'Dowd; Dir. Med. Rel.: Rick Minch; Trav. Sec.: Mike Seghi; Mgr.: Doc Edwards. Home: Cleveland Stadium (74,383). Field distances: 320, l.f. line; 377, l.c.; 400, c.f.; 395, r.c.; 320, r.f. line. Spring training: Tucson, Ariz.

SCOUTING REPORT

HITTING: Offense is a concern for manager Doc Edwards as the Indians managed only 666 runs last season, the fifth-lowest total in the AL. Scoring runs probably won't be any easier in 1989, after the trade that sent Julio Franco, a .300 hitter in each of the last three seasons, to the Rangers last winter.

The Indians are counting on another big season from Joe Carter (.271, 27, 98), who just missed his third straight 100 RBI season. The progress of Cory Snyder (.272, 26, 75), who lopped 66 strikeouts off his 1987 club-record total of 166, is encouraging, too.

The acquisition of Pete O'Brien (.272, 16, 71) from Texas will provide increased production at first base. Mel Hall (.280, 6, 71) is another capable hitter, although his lack of power hurts. Also, more sock is needed from Brook Jacoby (.241, 9, 49), who experienced an alarming drop of 23 home runs last year.

PITCHING: Cleveland finally has some pitching. Last season, Greg Swindell (18-14, 3.20), Tom Candiotti (14-8, 3.28) and John Farrell (14-10, 4.24) gave the Indians three pitchers who achieved 14 or more victories for the first time since 1956.

Swindell has 20-victory potential and can already be compared favorably to the best lefties in the AL. Candiotti, the hard-luck knuckleballer, only lacks support and Farrell is valued for his consistency.

Doug Jones is simply the best bullpen stopper Cleveland has ever had and his 37 saves last season—14 more than the previous club mark—proved it. The addition of free agent Jesse Orosco (3-2, 2.72, nine saves with the Dodgers) provides a left-hander to complement the right-handed Jones. Scott Bailes (9-14, 4.90) is useful because he can start or relieve.

FIELDING: The Indians' weakness up in the middle was reflected in their ability to turn only 131 double plays last season,

As a run producer, Joe Carter is Indian chief.

the third-lowest mark in the AL.

The Indians believe Jerry Browne will be an improvement over Franco at second, which is why they acquired him from Texas with O'Brien and outfielder Oddibe McDowell for Franco. The latter two also are valued for their defensive abilities. The front office spent much of the winter attempting to fill the gaping hole at shortstop.

CLEVELAND INDIANS 1989 ROSTER

MANAGER Doc Edwards
Coaches—Jim Davenport, Luis Isaac, Charlie Manuel, Tom Spencer, Mark Wiley

PITCHERS

No.	Name	1988 Club	W-L	IP	SO	ERA	B-T	Ht.	Wt.	Born
43	Bailes, Scott	Cleveland	9-14	145	53	4.90	L-L	6-2	175	12/18/62 Chillicothe, OH
40	Black, Bud	KC-Cle.	4-4	81	63	5.00	L-L	6-2	180	6/30/57 San Mateo, CA
49	Candiotti, Tom	Cleveland	14-8	217	137	3.28	R-R	6-2	200	8/31/57 Walnut Creek, CA
50	Dedmon, Jeff	Cleveland	1-0	34	17	4.54	L-R	6-2	200	3/4/60 Torrance, CA
		Colorado Springs	2-3	41	25	4.35				
52	Farrell, John	Cleveland	14-10	210	92	4.24	R-R	6-4	210	8/4/62 Neptune, NJ
39	Gordon, Don	Colorado Springs	3-3	57	19	4.24	R-R	6-1	185	10/10/59 New York, NY
		Cleveland	3-4	59	20	4.40				
22	Havens, Brad	Los Angeles	0-0	10	8	4.66	L-L	6-1	196	11/17/59 Highland Park, MI
		Colorado Springs	0-0	15	7	2.40				
		Cleveland	2-3	57	30	3.14				
11	Jones, Doug	Cleveland	3-4	83	72	2.27	R-R	6-2	195	6/24/57 Covina, CA
47	Kaiser, Jeff	Colorado Springs	3-2	53	47	3.74	R-L	6-3	195	7/24/60 Wyandotte, MI
		Cleveland	0-0	3	0	0.00				
54	Nichols, Rod	Kingston	3-1	24	19	4.50	R-R	6-2	190	12/29/64 Burlington, IA
		Colorado Springs	2-6	59	43	5.68				
		Cleveland	1-7	69	31	5.06				
—	Orosco, Jesse	Los Angeles	3-2	53	43	2.72	R-L	6-2	185	4/21/57 Santa Barbara, CA
60	Ortiz, Angel	Waterloo	5-5	98	98	2.57	L-L	6-3	170	12/12/67 Puerto Rico
41	Poehl, Michael	Williamsport	5-2	51	27	2.98	R-R	6-5	195	8/28/64 Houston, TX
64	Seanez, Rudy	Waterloo	6-6	113	93	4.69	R-R	6-0	170	10/20/68 Brawley, CA
57	Shaw, Jeff	Williamsport	5-19	164	61	3.63	R-R	6-2	185	7/7/66 Wash. Court House, OH
67	Skalski, Joe	Colorado Springs	10-13	159	117	6.55	R-R	6-3	190	9/26/64 Chicago, IL
21	Swindell, Greg	Cleveland	18-14	242	180	3.20	S-L	6-3	225	1/2/65 Fort Worth, TX
48	Walker, Mike	Williamsport	15-7	164	145	3.72	R-R	6-1	175	10/4/66 Brooksville, FL
		Cleveland	0-1	9	7	7.27				
53	Wickander, Kevin	Williamsport	1-0	29	33	0.63	L-L	6-2	202	1/4/65 Fort Dodge, IA
		Colorado Springs	0-2	33	22	7.16				
42	Yett, Rich	Cleveland	9-6	134	71	4.62	R-R	6-2	187	10/6/62 Pomona, CA
		Williamsport	0-1	3	4	8.10				
		Colorado Springs	0-1	8	5	9.00				

CATCHERS

No.	Name	1988 Club	H	HR	RBI	Pct.	B-T	Ht.	Wt.	Born
6	Allanson, Andy	Cleveland	114	5	50	.263	R-R	6-5	225	12/22/61 Richmond, VA
17	Lampkin, Tom	Williamsport	71	3	23	.270	L-R	5-11	185	4/4/64 Cincinnati, OH
		Colorado Springs	30	0	7	.280				
		Cleveland	0	0	0	.000				
18	Tingley, Ron	Colorado Springs	37	3	20	.285	R-R	6-2	180	5/27/59 Presque Isle, ME
		Cleveland	4	1	2	.167				

INFIELDERS

No.	Name	1988 Club	H	HR	RBI	Pct.	B-T	Ht.	Wt.	Born
—	Aguayo, Luis	Philadelphia	24	3	5	.247	R-R	5-9	195	3/13/59 Puerto Rico
		New York (AL)	35	3	8	.250				
16	Bell, Jay	Cleveland	46	2	21	.218	R-R	6-1	180	12/11/65 Elgin AFB, FL
		Colorado Springs	50	7	24	.276				
—	Browne, Jerry	Texas	49	1	17	.229	S-R	5-10	170	2/13/66 Virgin Islands
		Oklahoma City	72	5	34	.252				
15	Gonzales, Denny	Buffalo	79	8	39	.296	R-R	5-11	185	7/22/63 Dominican Republic
		Pittsburgh	6	0	1	.188				
1	Hinzo, Tommy	Colorado Springs	104	1	29	.232	S-R	5-10	175	6/18/64 San Diego, CA
26	Jacoby, Brook	Cleveland	133	9	49	.241	R-R	5-11	195	11/23/59 Philadelphia, PA
29	Medina, Luis	Colorado Springs	126	28	81	.310	R-L	6-3	195	3/26/63 Santa Monica, CA
		Cleveland	13	6	8	.255				
—	O'Brien, Pete	Texas	149	16	71	.272	L-L	6-2	205	2/9/58 Santa Monica, CA
34	Williams, Eddie	Colorado Springs	110	12	58	.301	R-R	6-0	175	11/1/64 Shreveport, LA
		Cleveland	4	0	1	.190				
10	Zuvella, Paul	Colorado Springs	67	1	28	.289	R-R	6-0	178	10/31/58 San Mateo, CA
		Cleveland	30	0	7	.231				

OUTFIELDERS

No.	Name	1988 Club	H	HR	RBI	Pct.	B-T	Ht.	Wt.	Born
30	Carter, Joe	Cleveland	168	27	98	.271	R-R	6-3	215	3/7/60 Oklahoma City, OK
8	Castillo, Carmen	Cleveland	48	4	14	.273	R-R	6-1	190	6/8/58 Dominican Republic
25	Clark, David	Cleveland	41	3	18	.263	L-R	6-2	198	9/3/62 Tupelo, MS
		Colorado Springs	49	4	31	.297				
27	Hall, Mel	Cleveland	144	6	71	.280	L-L	6-1	205	9/16/60 Lyons, NY
—	McDowell, Oddibe	Texas	108	6	37	.247	L-L	5-9	160	8/25/62 Hollywood, FL
		Oklahoma City	20	1	6	.286				
28	Snyder, Cory	Cleveland	139	26	75	.272	R-R	6-3	185	11/11/62 Inglewood, CA
36	*Williams, Reggie	Colorado Springs	134	6	58	.294	R-R	5-11	185	8/29/60 Memphis, TN
		Cleveland	7	1	3	.226				

*Free agent at press time listed with 1988 team

OUTLOOK: This is undoubtedly a club on the rise. The Indians' 78-84 record in 1988 represented a 17-game improvement over the year before. Although the Indians finished 11 games behind division-winning Boston, it was the closest they have come to the top since 1959. The wait for the Indians' first pennant since 1954 continues, but now at least there is hope.

INDIAN PROFILES

JOE CARTER 29 6-3 215 — Bats R Throws R

Fell two short in bid for third straight 100 RBI season . . . Did achieve 20 home runs and 20 steals for third consecutive year . . . Became first Indian to notch 100 homers and 100 steals . . . Started very strong with .354 average, seven homers and 21 RBI in April . . . Erupted for five homers and 15 RBI in four-game span during April . . . Moved to center field to compensate for loss of free agent Brett Butler and excelled . . . Paced majors with 121 RBI and 200 runs produced in 1986 . . . Born March 7, 1960, in Oklahoma City, Okla. . . . Acquired from Cubs with Mel Hall, Don Schulze and Darryl Banks for Rick Sutcliffe, Ron Hassey and George Frazier, June 13, 1984 . . . Cubs picked him second overall in June 1981 draft, out of Wichita State.

Year	Club	Pos.	G	AB	R	H	2B	3B	HR	RBI	SB	Avg.
1983	Chicago (NL)	OF	23	51	6	9	1	1	0	1	1	.176
1984	Cleveland	OF-1B	66	244	32	67	6	1	13	41	2	.275
1985	Cleveland	OF-1B-2B-3B	143	489	64	128	27	0	15	59	24	.262
1986	Cleveland	OF-1B	162	663	108	200	36	9	29	121	29	.302
1987	Cleveland	OF-1B	149	588	83	155	27	2	32	106	31	.264
1988	Cleveland	OF	157	621	85	168	36	6	27	98	27	.271
	Totals		700	2656	378	727	133	19	116	426	114	.274

PETE O'BRIEN 31 6-2 205 — Bats L Throws L

First baseman was acquired from Rangers with Oddibe McDowell and Jerry Browne for Julio Franco in December, after finishing 1988 season with 16 homers and 71 RBI, his lowest totals since rookie season in 1983 . . . Hit .437 with five homers and eight RBI in April . . . Dropped to .184 with two homers and 10 RBI in May . . . Finished season poorly, batting .173 in last 31 games . . . Produced just four extra-base hits, all homers, in 33-game span from Aug. 24 through Oct. 1 . . . Born

Feb. 9, 1958, in Santa Monica, Cal. . . . Selected by Rangers in 15th round of June 1979 draft.

Year	Club	Pos.	G	AB	R	H	2B	3B	HR	RBI	SB	Avg.
1982	Texas	OF-1B	20	67	13	16	4	1	4	13	1	.239
1983	Texas	1B-OF	154	524	53	124	24	5	8	53	5	.237
1984	Texas	1B-OF	142	520	57	149	26	2	18	80	3	.287
1985	Texas	1B	159	573	69	153	34	3	22	92	5	.267
1986	Texas	1B	156	551	86	160	23	3	23	90	4	.290
1987	Texas	1B-OF	159	569	84	163	26	1	23	88	0	.286
1988	Texas	1B	156	547	57	149	24	1	16	71	1	.272
	Totals		946	3351	419	914	161	16	114	487	19	.273

CORY SNYDER 26 6-3 185 — Bats R Throws R

Year of progress for former BYU star . . . Cut 65 strikeouts off his club-record total of 166 in 1987 . . . Placed second on club with 26 homers, one behind Joe Carter . . . Became 11th player in club history to belt 20 homers for three straight years . . . Began year by totaling three homers and nine RBI as part of eight-game hitting streak . . . Homered in three successive games from May 19-21 . . . Outfielder possesses powerful, accurate arm . . . At BYU, he became first player in NCAA history to record 20 or more homers three seasons in a row . . . Indians' first-round selection and fourth player taken overall in June 1984 draft . . . Born Nov. 11, 1962, in Inglewood, Cal.

Year	Club	Pos.	G	AB	R	H	2B	3B	HR	RBI	SB	Avg.
1986	Cleveland	OF-SS-3B	103	416	58	113	21	1	24	69	2	.272
1987	Cleveland	OF-SS	157	577	74	136	24	2	33	82	5	.236
1988	Cleveland	OF	142	511	71	139	24	3	26	75	5	.272
	Totals		402	1504	203	388	69	6	83	226	12	.258

MEL HALL 28 6-1 205 — Bats L Throws L

Good contact hitter who contributed offensively, but declined defensively with 10 errors in outfield . . . Put together career-high 16-game hitting streak from July 3-20, going 23-for-66 (.348) with two homers and 13 RBI . . . Went 223 at-bats without a home run . . . Finally connected June 23 at Yankee Stadium and it was his first homer since Oct. 4, 1987 . . . Collected second career home run against a lefty July 6 with an inside-the-parker against Oakland's Rick Honeycutt . . . Marked first inside-the-park homer by an Indian since Joe Carter had one in 1985 . . . Born Sept. 18, 1960, in Lyons, N.Y. . . . Acquired from Cubs with Carter, Don Schulze and Darryl Banks for Rick Sutcliffe, George Frazier and Ron Hassey, June 13, 1984.

Year	Club	Pos.	G	AB	R	H	2B	3B	HR	RBI	SB	Avg.
1981	Chicago (NL).....	OF	10	11	1	1	0	0	1	2	0	.091
1982	Chicago (NL).....	OF	24	80	6	21	3	2	0	4	0	.263
1983	Chicago (NL).....	OF	112	410	60	116	23	5	17	56	6	.283
1984	Chicago (NL).....	OF	48	150	25	42	11	3	4	22	2	.280
1984	Cleveland	OF	83	257	43	66	13	1	7	30	1	.257
1985	Cleveland	OF	23	66	7	21	6	0	0	12	0	.318
1986	Cleveland	OF	140	442	68	131	29	2	18	77	6	.296
1987	Cleveland	OF	142	485	57	136	21	1	18	76	5	.280
1988	Cleveland	OF	150	515	69	144	32	4	6	71	7	.280
	Totals		732	2416	336	678	138	18	71	350	27	.281

BROOK JACOBY 29 5-11 195 Bats R Throws R

Struggled mightily after first month of season . . . Was hitting .343 with three homers and 13 RBI until May 4 . . . Didn't hit his next homer until June 5, 105 at-bats later . . . Dropped 23 home runs from 1987 total, which was highest for any Indian third baseman since Al Rosen led AL with 43 in 1953 . . . Did enjoy 53-game errorless string from May 25 until July 27 . . . Born Nov. 23, 1959, in Philadelphia . . . Obtained with Brett Butler and Rick Behenna as the players to be named later in deal that sent Len Barker to Atlanta, Aug. 28, 1983.

Year	Club	Pos.	G	AB	R	H	2B	3B	HR	RBI	SB	Avg.
1981	Atlanta..........	3B	11	10	0	2	0	0	0	1	0	.200
1983	Atlanta..........	3B	4	8	0	0	0	0	0	0	0	.000
1984	Cleveland	3B-SS	126	439	64	116	19	3	7	40	3	.264
1985	Cleveland	3B-2B	161	606	72	166	26	3	20	87	2	.274
1986	Cleveland	3B	158	583	83	168	30	4	17	80	2	.288
1987	Cleveland	3B-1B	155	540	73	162	26	4	32	69	2	.300
1988	Cleveland	3B	152	552	59	133	25	0	9	49	2	.241
	Totals		767	2738	351	747	126	14	85	326	11	.273

GREG SWINDELL 24 6-3 225 Bats S Throws L

Roaring start enabled him to become first Indian left-hander to win as many as 18 games since Sam McDowell was a 20-game winner in 1970 . . . His 180 strikeouts were the most by an Indian lefty since McDowell's 192 in 1971 . . . Won first seven starts and was 10-1 with 2.11 ERA through May 30 . . . Was first major leaguer to win 10 in 1988 . . . Did sudden reversal in June, when he was 0-5 with 7.00 ERA . . . Dropped eight straight and compiled 6.32 ERA from June 5 to July 19 . . , Best late-season effort was a three-hit, 1-0 shutout of the Yanks Sept. 6 . . . Had earlier thrown pair of two-hitters, May 2 vs. California and May 19 vs. Chicago . . . Four shutouts represented highest total by Indian lefty since McDowell had four in 1969 . . . Born Jan. 2, 1965, in Fort Worth, Tex. . . . Indians' first-round selection and second player picked overall in June 1986 draft . . . Was 43-8 with 1.92 ERA at University of Texas.

Year	Club	G	IP	W	L	Pct.	SO	BB	H	ERA
1986	Cleveland	9	61⅔	5	2	.714	46	15	57	4.23
1987	Cleveland	16	102⅓	3	8	.273	97	37	112	5.10
1988	Cleveland	33	242	18	14	.563	180	45	234	3.20
	Totals	58	406	26	24	.520	323	97	403	3.83

TOM CANDIOTTI 31 6-2 200 **Bats R Throws R**

Used big start to achieve almost half of his victory total . . . Knuckleballer opened with four consecutive complete-game wins in April and posted 2.25 ERA . . . Won six of first seven decisions through May 18, notching six complete games . . . Won only one of his next 12 starts, however, going 1-7 with a 5.38 ERA . . . Bad spell included five-game losing streak from May 23 to June 14 in which Cleveland scored only two runs for him in each game . . . Went on 15-day disabled list Aug. 7 with stiff right shoulder . . . Began developing knuckleball in 1985 with help of 300-game winner Phil Niekro . . . Born Aug. 31, 1957, in Walnut Creek, Cal. . . . Twins' fourth-round pick in June 1984 hooked on with Cleveland when he was signed to a Triple-A contract following the 1985 season.

Year	Club	G	IP	W	L	Pct.	SO	BB	H	ERA
1983	Milwaukee	10	55⅔	4	4	.500	21	16	62	3.23
1984	Milwaukee	8	32⅓	2	2	.500	23	10	38	5.29
1986	Cleveland	36	252⅓	16	12	.571	167	106	234	3.57
1987	Cleveland	32	201⅔	7	18	.280	111	93	193	4.78
1988	Cleveland	31	216⅔	14	8	.636	137	53	225	3.28
	Totals	117	758⅔	43	44	.494	459	278	752	3.86

DOUG JONES 31 6-2 195 **Bats R Throws R**

His outstanding 1988 season was highlighted by a major-league-record 15 saves in 15 consecutive appearances from May 13 until July 2, two more than Steve Bedrosian's 1987 streak . . . His streak ended July 4 vs. Oakland, when he pitched three scoreless innings in a 16-inning game . . . Smashed club record with 37 saves, 14 more than Ernie Camacho's 1984 mark . . . Was scored on only once in first 17 appearances, twice in first 23 . . . Went 48 appearances without yielding a home run before Blue Jays' Nelson Liriano reached second row June 6. Homerless streak spanned 84 innings . . . Born June 24, 1957, in Covina, Cal. . . . Signed by Indians as free agent, April 3, 1985.

Year	Club	G	IP	W	L	Pct.	SO	BB	H	ERA
1982	Milwaukee	4	2⅔	0	0	.000	1	1	5	10.13
1986	Cleveland	11	18	1	0	1.000	12	6	18	2.50
1987	Cleveland	49	91⅓	6	5	.545	87	24	101	3.15
1988	Cleveland	51	83⅓	3	4	.429	72	16	69	2.27
	Totals	115	195⅓	10	9	.526	172	47	193	2.81

JESSE OROSCO 31 6-2 185 Bats R Throws L

Will be wearing his third uniform in three seasons after signing three-year, $2.975-million contract with Indians as free agent . . . Wore out welcome in Los Angeles with his late-season unreliability, though he did finish 1988 with nine saves and a 2.72 ERA . . . Indians hope he'll regain form he showed while becoming Mets' all-time saves leader with 107 . . . Elbow trouble has taken its toll on his slider and fastball . . . Won three games for Mets in 1986 NLCS vs. Astros and won two games in World Series vs. Red Sox . . . Born April 21, 1957, in Santa Barbara, Cal. . . . Twins' second choice in January 1978 draft . . . Inadvertently sparked the Dodgers' turnaround season when he put boot black inside the cap of Kirk Gibson last spring, triggering outburst that set no-nonsense tone for L.A.

Year	Club	G	IP	W	L	Pct.	SO	BB	H	ERA
1979	New York (NL)	18	35	1	2	.333	22	22	33	4.89
1981	New York (NL)	8	17	0	1	.000	18	6	13	1.59
1982	New York (NL)	54	109⅓	4	10	.286	89	40	92	2.72
1983	New York (NL)	62	110	13	7	.650	84	38	76	1.47
1984	New York (NL)	60	87	10	6	.625	85	34	58	2.59
1985	New York (NL)	54	79	8	6	.571	68	34	66	2.73
1986	New York (NL)	58	81	8	6	.571	62	35	64	2.33
1987	New York (NL)	58	77	3	9	.250	78	31	78	4.44
1988	Los Angeles	55	53	3	2	.600	43	30	41	2.72
	Totals	427	648⅓	50	49	.505	549	270	521	2.73

JOHN FARRELL 26 6-4 210 Bats R Throws R

Another Indian pitcher who enjoyed fast start in 1988, but failed to sustain it . . . Went 3-1 with 2.39 ERA in April . . . Earned four complete games in first 10 starts, but didn't finish a game after that . . . Was 7-3 with 4.81 ERA from May 25 until July 26 . . . Had some physical problems late in season . . . Went on 15-day disabled list Aug. 29 with tightness in elbow . . . Born Aug. 4, 1962, in Neptune, N.J. . . . Indians' second-round pick in June 1984 draft, out of Oklahoma State.

Year	Club	G	IP	W	L	Pct.	SO	BB	H	ERA
1987	Cleveland	10	69	5	1	.833	28	22	68	3.39
1988	Cleveland	31	210⅓	14	10	.583	92	67	216	4.24
	Totals	41	279⅓	19	11	.633	120	89	284	4.03

SCOTT BAILES 26 6-2 175 **Bats L Throws L**

Indians must define his role to give him a chance for success . . . Spent third straight season in dual role of starter and reliever . . . Began in rotation and recorded first career shutout in Cleveland's home opener, a three-hitter vs. Baltimore . . . Sustained no-hitter for 6⅔ innings vs. Toronto June 7 before settling for three-hit win . . . Won four in row and posted 3.19 ERA from May 21 to June 7 . . . Followed that by going 1-7 until beginning of August, earning ticket to bullpen . . . Born Dec. 18, 1962, in Chillicothe, Ohio . . . Acquired from Pirates as player to be named later in May 29, 1985 deal for Johnnie Lemaster.

Year	Club	G	IP	W	L	Pct.	SO	BB	H	ERA
1986	Cleveland	62	112⅔	10	10	.500	60	43	123	4.95
1987	Cleveland	39	120⅓	7	8	.467	65	47	145	4.64
1988	Cleveland	37	145	9	14	.391	53	46	149	4.90
	Totals	138	378	26	32	.448	178	136	417	4.83

MANAGER DOC EDWARDS: Indians showed significant improvement in Edwards' first full season as manager . . . Initially hired on interim basis July 16, 1987, to replace fired Pat Corrales . . . Has a lighter touch than tough-guy Corrales and players feel more comfortable playing for him . . . Indians are 108-129 under Edwards . . . Enters 31st season of pro ball . . . Served for 15 years as a player . . . Was in his second season as Indians' bullpen coach when promotion occurred . . . Named Manager of the Year four times in minors . . . Began minor-league managing career in 1973 with Yankees' Eastern League entry . . . Born Dec. 10, 1936, in Red Jacket, W. Va. . . . Managed Indians' Triple-A affiliate for five years . . . Directed Maine Guides to pair of second-place finishes, in 1984 and 1985 . . . Caught for nine minor-league clubs and Cleveland, Philadelphia, Kansas City and the Yankees . . . Acquired nickname "Doc" because of service in Navy Medical Corps from 1954-57 . . . Full name is Howard Rodney Edwards.

TOP PROSPECT

LUIS MEDINA 26 6-3 195 **Bats R Throws L**

First baseman-outfielder has power to spare . . . Paced all Triple-A players with 28 homers for Colorado Springs . . . Despite being disabled from July 21 to Aug. 7 with sprained ligament in right elbow, he was fourth in Pacific Coast League with 81 RBI and batted .310 . . . Hit .255 with six homers and eight RBI in 51 at-bats following September promotion . . . Slammed first two major-league homers Sept. 7 at Yankee Stadium, off Tommy John . . . Born March 26, 1963, in Santa Monica, Cal. . . . Selected by Indians in ninth round of June 1985 draft.

GREATEST FIRST BASEMAN

Hal Trosky manned first base for the Indians from 1933-41, but his legacy endures.

His name still appears among the all-time club leaders in nine offensive categories. Trosky is tops in slugging percentage (.551) and second in home runs with 216, 10 fewer than Earl Averill. Trosky ranks third in RBI (911) and extra-base hits (556).

The native of Norway, Iowa, was a success from the start. He hit .330 with 35 home runs and 142 RBI in his first full major-league season in 1934, beginning a string of six consecutive years in which he knocked in more than 100 runs. He hit 25 or more home runs in five of his seven full seasons with Cleveland.

Trosky's career year occurred in 1936, when he became the first Indian to lead the league in RBI, with a total of 162. In that memorable summer, he also slammed 42 home runs. That still stands as a single-season high for an Indian first baseman.

ALL-TIME INDIAN SEASON RECORDS

BATTING: Joe Jackson, .408, 1911
HRs: Al Rosen, 43, 1953
RBIs: Hal Trosky, 162, 1936
STEALS: Miguel Dilone, 61, 1980
WINS: Jim Bagby, 31, 1920
STRIKEOUTS: Bob Feller, 348, 1946

DETROIT TIGERS

TEAM DIRECTORY: Chairman: John E. Fetzer; Vice-Chairman: Tom Monaghan; Pres.-Chief Exec. Off.: Jim Campbell; VP-Operations: William Haase; VP-GM: William Lajoie; VP-Player Procurement/Dev.: Joe McDonald; VP-Marketing, Radio-TV, Pub. Rel.: Jeff Odenwald; Dir. Pub. Rel.: Dan Ewald; Trav. Sec.: Bill Brown; Mgr.: Sparky Anderson. Home: Tiger Stadium (52, 806). Field distances: 340, l.f. line; 365, l.c.; 440, c.f.; 370, r.c.; 325, r.f. line. Spring training: Lakeland, Fla.

SCOUTING REPORT

HITTING: Alan Trammell (.311, 15, 69) is the player who makes the Tigers go and he wasn't available to make them go often enough last season. The shortstop missed 34 games with injuries, the highest total of his career. Lou Whitaker (.275, 12, 55) was another key Tiger who was sidelined with assorted injuries in 1988. His season came to an embarrassing end when he injured his right knee doing splits at a friend's wedding in early September.

The Tigers are looking for another good season from Chet Lemon (.264, 17, 64) and for Matt Nokes (.251, 16, 53) to rebound after being bitten by the sophomore jinx.

Keith Moreland (.256, 5, 64 with the Padres) is versatile enough to become one of manager Sparky Anderson's favorite role players and, if Anderson can find some way to reach the gifted but troubled Chris Brown, the offseason deal that sent Walt Terrell to San Diego will give the Tiger offense a desperately needed shot in the arm. Last season, the Tigers' .250 team average ranked 12th among the 14 AL clubs and Detroit generated only 703 runs, the club's lowest total for a full season since 1976.

PITCHING: Starting pitching remains one of Detroit's great strengths. Last year, Jack Morris (15-13, 3.94), Doyle Alexander (14-11, 4.32), Frank Tanana (14-11, 4.21) and Jeff Robinson (13-6, 2.98) gave the Tigers four pitchers with at least 13 victories for the first time since 1967.

Morris, the winningest pitcher in baseball during the 1980s, and Robinson can be a potent one-two punch if Robinson is healthy. He missed most of the second half with a circulatory problem in two fingers of his pitching hand.

Mike Henneman (9-6, 1.87, team-high 22 saves) is the mainstay in the bullpen and Guillermo Hernandez (6-5, 3.06, 10 saves) showed there is still some life in his left arm.

Alan Trammell must stay injury-free for toothless Tigers.

FIELDING: Strength up the middle is a Tiger trademark. Shortstop Trammell and second baseman Whitaker will be teaming for a 12th straight season, a major-league record. Wide-ranging Gary Pettis has no equal in center field. Not surprisingly, Detroit tied for fourth in the AL with a .982 fielding percentage.

OUTLOOK: Detroit seemed bound for the AL East title before a devastating late-season slide. That plunge may have been a sign of things to come. Age is beginning to take a toll on the Tigers and this is a poor team offensively.

Worse still, there is no help from the farm system on the horizon. Only Anderson's brilliant touch can keep this club in contention.

DETROIT TIGERS 1989 ROSTER

MANAGER Sparky Anderson
Coaches—Billy Consolo, Alex Grammas, Billy Muffett, Vada Pinson, Dick Tracewski

PITCHERS

No.	Name	1988 Club	W-L	IP	SO	ERA	B-T	Ht.	Wt.	Born
19	Alexander, Doyle	Detroit	14-11	229	126	4.32	R-R	6-3	200	9/4/50 Cordova, AL
42	Beard, Dave	Toledo	6-7	105	76	3.01	L-R	6-5	215	10/2/59 Atlanta, GA
		Glens Falls	3-3	46	41	1.75				
48	Gibson, Paul	Detroit	4-2	92	50	2.93	R-L	6-0	165	1/4/60 Southampton, NY
39	Henneman, Mike	Detroit	9-6	91	58	1.87	R-R	6-4	195	12/11/61 St. Charles, MO
21	Hernandez, Guillermo	Detroit	6-5	68	59	3.06	L-L	6-2	185	11/14/54 Puerto Rico
38	Holman, Shawn	Glens Falls	8-3	92	44	1.87	R-R	6-2	186	11/10/64 Sewickley, PA
27	Huismann, Mark	Toledo	4-6	58	61	1.87	R-R	6-3	195	5/11/58 Lincoln, NE
		Detroit	1-0	5	6	5.06				
45	Hursey, Darren	Lakeland	15-8	166	44	3.39	L-L	6-6	180	8/1/68 Urbana, IL
25	King, Eric	Toledo	3-4	69	51	3.26	R-R	6-2	182	4/10/64 Oxnard, CA
		Detroit	4-1	69	45	3.41				
47	Morris, Jack	Detroit	15-13	235	168	3.94	R-R	6-3	200	5/16/55 St. Paul, MN
37	Nosek, Randy	Lakeland	0-4	31	11	3.82	R-R	6-4	216	1/8/67 Omaha, NE
31	Ritz, Kevin	Glens Falls	8-10	137	75	3.82	R-R	6-4	195	6/8/65 Eatontown, NJ
44	Robinson, Jeff	Detroit	13-6	172	114	2.98	R-R	6-6	210	12/14/61 Ventura, CA
49	Searcy, Steve	Toledo	13-7	170	176	2.59	L-L	6-1	185	6/4/64 Knoxville, TN
		Detroit	0-2	8	5	5.63				
26	Tanana, Frank	Detroit	14-11	203	127	4.21	L-L	6-3	195	7/3/53 Detroit, MI

CATCHERS

No.	Name	1988 Club	H	HR	RBI	Pct.	B-T	Ht.	Wt.	Born
10	Clark, Phil	Lakeland	120	8	66	.298	R-R	6-0	175	5/6/68 Crockett, TX
18	DiMascio, Dan	Glens Falls	59	6	31	.280	R-R	6-1	195	10/8/64 Joliet, IL
8	Heath, Mike	Detroit	54	5	18	.247	R-R	5-11	180	2/5/55 Tampa FL
33	Nokes, Matt	Detroit	96	16	53	.251	L-R	6-1	185	11/31/63 San Diego, CA

INFIELDERS

No.	Name	1988 Club	H	HR	RBI	Pct.	B-T	Ht.	Wt.	Born
29	Austin, Pat	Glens Falls	100	1	29	.297	R-R	6-1	175	2/9/66 Columbus, OH
14	Bergman, Dave	Detroit	85	5	35	.294	L-L	6-2	190	6/6/53 Evanston, IL
16	Brookens, Tom	Detroit	107	5	38	.243	R-R	5-10	170	8/10/53 Chambersburg, PA
35	Brown, Chris	San Diego	58	2	19	.235	R-R	6-2	210	8/15/61 Jackson, MS
23	Lovullo, Torey	Glens Falls	74	9	50	.274	S-R	6-0	180	7/25/65 Santa Monica, CA
		Toledo	41	5	20	.232				
		Detroit	8	1	2	.381				
30	Moreland, Keith	San Diego	131	5	64	.256	R-R	6-0	200	5/2/54 Dallas, TX
—	Pedrique, Al	Pittsburgh	23	0	4	.180	R-R	6-0	155	8/11/60 Venezuela
12	Salazar, Luis	Detroit	122	12	62	.270	R-R	5-9	180	5/19/56 Venezuela
20	Strange, Doug	Toledo	56	6	19	.201	S-R	6-2	170	4/13/64 Greenville, SC
		Glens Falls	61	1	36	.280				
38	Trammell, Alan	Detroit	145	15	69	.311	R-R	6-0	175	2/21/58 Garden Grove, CA
32	Walewander, Jim	Detroit	37	0	6	.211	S-R	5-10	158	5/2/61 Chicago, IL
		Toledo	5	0	2	.455				
1	Whitaker, Lou	Detroit	111	12	55	.275	L-R	5-11	160	5/12/57 New York, NY

OUTFIELDERS

No.	Name	1988 Club	H	HR	RBI	Pct.	B-T	Ht.	Wt.	Born
4	Bean, Billy	Toledo	124	6	40	.256	L-L	6-1	185	5/11/64 Santa Ana, CA
		Detroit	2	0	0	.182				
22	Cuyler, Milt	Lakeland	143	2	32	.296	S-R	5-10	175	10/7/68 Macon, GA
34	Lemon, Chet	Detroit	135	17	64	.264	R-R	6-0	190	2/12/55 Jackson, MS
7	Lusader, Scott	Toledo	86	4	46	.261	L-L	5-10	165	9/30/64 Chicago, IL
		Detroit	1	1	3	.063				
9	Lynn, Fred	Balt.-Det.	96	25	56	.246	L-L	6-1	190	2/3/52 Chicago, IL
40	Murphy, Dwayne	Toledo	38	5	15	.220	L-R	6-1	185	3/18/55 Merced, CA
		Detroit	36	4	19	.250				
24	Pettis, Gary	Detroit	96	3	36	.210	S-R	6-1	160	4/3/58 Oakland, CA
15	Sheridan, Pat	Detroit	88	11	47	.254	L-R	6-3	175	12/4/57 Ann Arbor, MI

*Free agent at press time listed with 1988 team

TIGER PROFILES

ALAN TRAMMELL 31 6-0 175 Bats R Throws R

Tigers' perennial MVP missed 34 games with injuries, the highest total of his career... Was disabled from June 29 to July 17 after being struck on left elbow by pitch from Blue Jays' Todd Stottlemyre... Shortstop played only seven games after being hit near right wrist by Blue Jays' Dave Stieb Sept. 13 and did not appear after Sept. 25... Also had back spasms in early August and a groin pull at the end of the month... Still led Tigers in batting for second straight year, hitting .311... Injuries led to dropoff of 13 home runs and 36 RBI from 1987, when he was second to Blue Jays' George Bell in AL MVP voting... Born Feb. 21, 1958, in Garden Grove, Cal.... Tigers' second-round selection in June 1976 draft... Was World Series MVP in 1984, when he hit .450 with two homers and six RBI.

Year	Club	Pos.	G	AB	R	H	2B	3B	HR	RBI	SB	Avg.
1977	Detroit..........	SS	19	43	6	8	0	0	0	0	0	.186
1978	Detroit..........	SS	139	448	49	120	14	6	2	34	3	.268
1979	Detroit..........	SS	142	460	68	127	11	4	6	50	17	.276
1980	Detroit..........	SS	146	560	107	168	21	5	9	65	12	.300
1981	Detroit..........	SS	105	392	52	101	15	3	2	31	10	.258
1982	Detroit..........	SS	157	489	66	126	34	3	9	57	19	.258
1983	Detroit..........	SS	142	505	83	161	31	2	14	66	30	.319
1984	Detroit..........	SS	139	555	85	174	34	5	14	69	19	.314
1985	Detroit..........	SS	149	605	79	156	21	7	13	57	14	.258
1986	Detroit..........	SS	151	574	107	159	33	7	21	75	25	.277
1987	Detroit..........	SS	151	597	109	205	34	3	28	105	21	.343
1988	Detroit..........	SS	128	466	73	145	24	1	15	69	7	.311
	Totals		1568	5694	884	1650	272	46	133	678	177	.290

LOU WHITAKER 31 5-11 160 Bats L Throws R

Disappointing season ended with embarrassing injury Sept. 4... Tore medial collateral ligament in right knee doing splits while dancing at friend's wedding... Was troubled by a sore back early in season... Also missed three games with sore toe... Desire to play when he's less than 100 percent has been questioned ... Extended major-league record by teaming with keystone partner Alan Trammell for 11th straight season... Still ranks among the best two-way second basemen when healthy... Names AL Rookie of the Year in 1978... Born

May 12, 1957, in New York, N.Y. . . . Selected by Tigers in fifth round of June 1975 draft . . . Began career as third baseman.

Year	Club	Pos.	G	AB	R	H	2B	3B	HR	RBI	SB	Avg.
1977	Detroit..........	2B	11	32	5	8	1	0	0	2	2	.250
1978	Detroit..........	2B	139	484	71	138	12	7	3	58	7	.285
1979	Detroit..........	2B	127	423	75	121	14	8	3	42	20	.286
1980	Detroit..........	2B	145	477	68	111	19	1	1	45	8	.233
1981	Detroit..........	2B	109	335	48	88	14	4	5	36	5	.263
1982	Detroit..........	2B	152	560	76	160	22	8	15	65	11	.286
1983	Detroit..........	2B	161	643	94	206	40	6	12	72	17	.320
1984	Detroit..........	2B	143	558	90	161	25	1	13	56	6	.289
1985	Detroit..........	2B	152	609	102	170	29	8	21	73	6	.279
1986	Detroit..........	2B	144	584	95	157	26	6	20	73	13	.269
1987	Detroit..........	2B	149	604	110	160	38	6	16	59	13	.265
1988	Detroit..........	2B	115	403	54	111	18	2	12	55	2	.275
	Totals		1547	5712	888	1591	258	57	121	636	110	.279

CHET LEMON 34 6-0 190 — Bats R Throws R

Steady outfielder had another solid year . . . Has reached double figures in home runs every full year since rookie season in 1976 . . . Collected more than 60 RBI for fifth time in last six years . . . Made smooth transition from center to right . . . Born Feb. 12, 1955, in Jackson, Miss. . . . Acquired from White Sox for Steve Kemp following 1981 season . . . Attended Pepperdine . . . Athletics' first-round pick in June 1972 draft.

Year	Club	Pos.	G	AB	R	H	2B	3B	HR	RBI	SB	Avg.
1975	Chicago (AL).....	3B-OF	9	35	2	9	2	0	0	1	1	.257
1976	Chicago (AL).....	OF	132	451	46	111	15	5	4	38	13	.246
1977	Chicago (AL).....	OF	150	553	99	151	38	4	19	67	8	.273
1978	Chicago (AL).....	OF	105	357	51	107	24	6	13	55	5	.300
1979	Chicago (AL).....	OF	148	556	79	177	44	2	17	86	7	.318
1980	Chicago (AL).....	OF-2B	147	514	76	150	32	6	11	51	6	.292
1981	Chicago (AL).....	OF	94	328	50	99	23	6	9	50	5	.302
1982	Detroit..........	OF	125	436	75	116	20	1	19	52	1	.266
1983	Detroit..........	OF	145	491	78	125	21	5	24	69	0	.255
1984	Detroit..........	OF	141	509	77	146	34	6	20	76	5	.287
1985	Detroit..........	OF	145	517	69	137	28	4	18	68	0	.265
1986	Detroit..........	OF	126	403	45	101	21	3	12	53	2	.251
1987	Detroit..........	OF	146	470	75	130	30	3	20	75	0	.277
1988	Detroit..........	OF	144	512	67	135	29	4	17	64	1	.264
	Totals		1757	6132	889	1694	361	55	203	805	54	.276

MATT NOKES 25 6-1 185 — Bats L Throws R

Experienced difficult sophomore season . . . Home-run total dropped in half to 16 . . . Fell off 34 RBI from previous year and average declined 38 points . . . Is a better hitter than 1988 dip indicates . . . In 1987, he became first Tiger rookie to hit 30 home runs since Rudy York belted 35 in 1937 . . . Catching skills are very rough . . . Born Oct. 31, 1963, in San

Diego . . . Obtained from San Francisco with Dave LaPoint and Eric King for Juan Berenguer, Scott Medvin and Bob Melvin on Oct. 7, 1985.

Year	Club	Pos.	G	AB	R	H	2B	3B	HR	RBI	SB	Avg.
1985	San Francisco	C	19	53	3	11	2	0	2	5	0	.208
1986	Detroit.	C	7	24	2	8	1	0	1	2	0	.333
1987	Detroit.	C-OF-3B	135	461	69	133	14	2	32	87	2	.289
1988	Detroit.	C-OF	122	382	53	96	18	0	16	53	0	.251
	Totals		283	920	127	248	35	2	51	147	2	.270

JACK MORRIS 33 6-3 200 **Bats R Throws R**

Tigers' ace lost some effectiveness, but maintained his standing as the winningest pitcher of 1980's by boosting his total to 156 . . . Only major leaguer with at least 15 wins in each of last seven years . . . Topped Tigers in victories and innings for record 10th straight time . . . Ended 1988 season by winning last three decisions, including one-hit, 2-1 triumph over Orioles Sept. 25. . . . That no-hit bid ended with one out in seventh on Mickey Tettleton's single . . . Fired no-hitter vs. White Sox, April 7, 1984 . . . Born May 16, 1955, in St. Paul, Minn. . . . Tigers' fifth-round selection in June 1976 draft, out of Brigham Young.

Year	Club	G	IP	W	L	Pct.	SO	BB	H	ERA
1977	Detroit	7	46	1	1	.500	28	23	38	3.72
1978	Detroit	28	106	3	5	.375	48	49	107	4.33
1979	Detroit	27	198	17	7	.708	113	59	179	3.27
1980	Detroit	36	250	16	15	.516	112	87	252	4.18
1981	Detroit	25	198	14	7	.667	97	78	153	3.05
1982	Detroit	37	266⅓	17	16	.515	135	96	247	4.06
1983	Detroit	37	293⅔	20	13	.606	232	83	257	3.34
1984	Detroit	35	240⅓	19	11	.633	148	87	221	3.60
1985	Detroit	35	257	16	11	.593	191	110	212	3.33
1986	Detroit	35	267	21	8	.724	223	82	229	3.27
1987	Detroit	34	266	18	11	.621	208	93	227	3.38
1988	Detroit	34	235	15	13	.536	168	83	225	3.94
	Totals	370	2623⅓	177	118	.600	1703	930	2347	3.59

JEFF ROBINSON 27 6-6 210 **Bats R Throws R**

Potentially big season ended abruptly . . . Missed most of second half with circulatory problem in two fingers of pitching hand . . . Suffered numbness after keeping a ball jammed between the fingers to spread them farther apart for better grip on split-fingered fastball . . . One of AL's top pitchers with 10-3 record and 3.02 ERA in first half, although he was left off All-Star staff . . . Opponents batted only .197 against him . . . Born Dec. 14, 1961, in Ventura, Cal. . . . Tigers' third-round selection in June 1983 draft.

Year	Club	G	IP	W	L	Pct.	SO	BB	H	ERA
1987	Detroit	29	127⅓	9	6	.600	98	54	132	5.37
1988	Detroit	24	172	13	6	.684	114	72	121	2.98
	Totals	53	299⅓	22	12	.647	212	126	253	4.00

GUILLERMO HERNANDEZ 34 6-2 185 Bats L Throws L

Changed name and changed fortunes . . . Was 0-1 with 11.57 ERA and two blown saves when he told club to identify him as Guillermo instead of Willie . . . Pitched 3.1 innings of one-hit, scoreless relief vs. Boston in next outing . . . Re-established himself as useful reliever with eight saves . . . Ranks second to John Hiller on Tigers' all-time save list with 103 and has 130 in his career . . . Won AL Cy Young and MVP awards in 1984, when he converted 32 of 33 save opportunities and nailed down games that clinched division, pennant and World Series. . . . Born Nov. 14, 1954, in Aguada, Puerto Rico . . . Acquired from Phils with Dave Bergman for Glenn Wilson and John Wockenfuss, March 23, 1984 . . . Originally signed by Phils in 1974, then drafted by Cubs in 1976 major-league draft.

Year	Club	G	IP	W	L	Pct.	SO	BB	H	ERA
1977	Chicago (NL)	67	110	8	7	.533	78	28	94	3.03
1978	Chicago (NL)	54	60	8	2	.800	38	35	57	3.75
1979	Chicago (NL)	51	79	4	4	.500	53	39	85	5.01
1980	Chicago (NL)	53	108	1	9	.100	75	45	115	4.42
1981	Chicago (NL)	12	14	0	0	.000	13	8	14	3.86
1982	Chicago (NL)	75	75	4	6	.400	54	24	74	3.00
1983	Chi (NL)-Phil.	74	115⅓	9	4	.692	93	32	109	3.28
1984	Detroit	80	140⅓	9	3	.750	112	36	96	1.92
1985	Detroit	74	106⅔	8	10	.444	76	14	82	2.70
1986	Detroit	64	88⅔	8	7	.533	77	21	87	3.55
1987	Detroit	45	49	3	4	.429	30	20	53	3.67
1988	Detroit	63	67⅔	6	5	.545	59	31	50	3.06
	Totals	712	1013⅔	68	61	.527	758	333	916	3.30

MIKE HENNEMAN 27 6-4 195 Bats R Throws R

Pitched well in second major-league season, recording team-high 22 saves . . . Look for results to get better still . . . Got off to blazing start, racking up seven saves in first seven opportunities . . . Finished April with eight saves . . . Most impressive outing occurred Sept. 11 vs. Yanks, when short man supplied seven scoreless innings in crucial game that Tigers lost in 18th inning. . . . Born Dec. 11, 1961, in St. Charles, Mo. . . . Tigers' third-round selection in June 1984 draft . . . Won first eight decisions and went 11-3 with seven saves in 1987, after starting season at Toledo (AAA) . . . Pitched Oklahoma State to College World Series in 1983 and 1984.

Year	Club	G	IP	W	L	Pct.	SO	BB	H	ERA
1987	Detroit	55	96⅔	11	3	.786	75	30	86	2.98
1988	Detroit	65	91⅓	9	6	.600	58	24	72	1.87
	Totals	120	188	20	9	.690	133	54	158	2.44

FRANK TANANA 35 6-3 195 Bats L Throws L

Big first half combined with dismal second half resulted in disappointing season . . . Won first five starts and was 11-4 at All-Star break, assuring him of reaching double figures in wins for 11th time in 15-year career . . . Failed to win after Aug. 19, however, going 0-4 with four no-decisions in last eight starts . . . Boasts 27-13 career mark vs. AL East . . . Born July 3, 1953, in Detroit . . . Acquired from Rangers for Duane James, June 20, 1985 . . . Began career with Angels as first-round selection in June 1971 draft . . . Led AL in strikeouts with 269 in 1975 . . . Once relied on fire, now depends on finesse.

Year	Club	G	IP	W	L	Pct.	SO	BB	H	ERA
1973	California	4	26	2	2	.500	22	8	20	3.12
1974	California	39	269	14	19	.424	180	77	262	3.11
1975	California	34	257	16	9	.640	269	73	211	2.63
1976	California	34	288	19	10	.655	261	73	212	2.44
1977	California	31	241	15	9	.625	205	61	201	2.54
1978	California	33	239	18	12	.600	137	60	239	3.65
1979	California	18	90	7	5	.583	46	25	93	3.90
1980	California	32	204	11	12	.478	113	45	223	4.15
1981	Boston	24	141	4	10	.286	78	43	142	4.02
1982	Texas	30	194⅓	7	18	.280	87	55	199	4.21
1983	Texas	29	159⅓	7	9	.438	108	49	144	3.16
1984	Texas	35	246⅓	15	15	.500	141	81	234	3.25
1985	Texas-Detroit.	33	215	12	14	.462	159	57	220	4.27
1986	Detroit	32	188⅓	12	9	.571	119	65	196	4.16
1987	Detroit	34	218⅔	15	10	.600	146	56	216	3.91
1988	Detroit	32	203	14	11	.560	127	64	213	4.21
	Totals	474	3180	188	174	.519	2198	892	3025	3.48

DOYLE ALEXANDER 38 6-3 200 Bats R Throws R

Poor second half was a factor in Tigers' inability to hold division lead . . . Earned first career All-Star selection with 8-4 mark and 3.07 ERA at the break . . . Sports 23-8 lifetime record at Tiger Stadium, including 9-5 mark last year . . . Went 5-6 with 5.88 ERA on road in 1988, however . . . Has built reputation as money pitcher . . . Has 26-6 record in September and October since 1983, but was only 3-2 last year . . . Born Sept. 4, 1950, in Cordova, Ala. . . . Acquired from Braves for John Smoltz, Aug. 12, 1987 . . . Keyed Tigers' run to division title by going 9-0 in 11 starts that season . . . One of five major league pitchers to have beaten all 26 teams. The others are Gaylord Perry, Rick Wise, Mike Torrez and Don Sutton . . . Dodgers' 44th-round pick in June 1968 draft.

Year	Club	G	IP	W	L	Pct.	SO	BB	H	ERA
1971	Los Angeles	17	92	6	6	.500	30	18	105	3.82
1972	Baltimore	35	106	6	8	.429	49	30	78	2.46
1973	Baltimore	29	175	12	8	.600	63	52	169	3.84
1974	Baltimore	30	174	6	9	.400	40	43	127	4.03
1975	Baltimore	32	133	8	8	.500	46	47	127	3.05
1976	Balt.-N.Y. (AL)	30	201	13	9	.591	58	63	172	3.36
1977	Texas	34	237	17	11	.607	82	82	221	3.65
1978	Texas	31	191	9	10	.474	81	71	198	3.86
1979	Texas	23	113	5	7	.417	50	69	114	4.46
1980	Atlanta	35	232	14	11	.560	114	74	227	4.19
1981	San Francisco	24	152	11	7	.611	77	44	156	2.90
1982	New York (AL)	16	66⅔	1	7	.125	26	14	81	6.08
1983	N.Y. (AL)-Tor.	25	145	7	8	.467	63	33	157	4.41
1984	Toronto	36	261⅔	17	6	.739	139	59	238	3.13
1985	Toronto	36	260⅔	17	10	.630	142	67	268	3.45
1986	Toronto	17	111	5	4	.556	65	20	120	4.46
1986	Atlanta	17	117⅓	6	6	.500	74	17	135	3.84
1987	Atlanta	16	117⅔	5	10	.333	64	27	115	4.13
1987	Detroit	11	88⅓	9	0	1.000	44	26	63	1.53
1988	Detroit	34	229	14	11	.560	126	46	260	4.32
	Totals	528	3143⅓	188	156	.547	1433	902	3131	3.71

TOP PROSPECT

STEVE SEARCY 24 6-1 185 **Bats L Throws L**

Hard thrower should be ready for majors after being named International League's Most Valuable Pitcher . . . Posted 13-7 record, 2.59 ERA for Toledo (AAA) . . . Topped Triple-A pitchers with 176 strikeouts . . . Lost major-league debut, 3-2, to White Sox Aug. 29, despite allowing only five hits in 7⅔ innings . . . Born June 4, 1964, in Knoxville, Tenn. . . . Selected by Tigers in third round of June 1985 draft, out of University of Tennessee . . . Was 0-2, 5.63 in two late-season starts for Tigers last year.

MANAGER SPARKY ANDERSON: Kept Tigers in hunt despite weak lineup, series of damaging injuries and loss of slugger Kirk Gibson to free agency . . . Has knack for defining roles players are comfortable with . . . Places great emphasis on finding players with strong character who fit in . . . Will not tolerate malcontents . . . First manager to win 100 or more games in a season three times . . . First

manager to win World Series in both leagues . . . Led world champion 1984 Tigers to club-record 104 victories . . . Has won 18 League Championship Series games . . . Has been named Manager of the Year in both leagues . . . First major-league manager to win 700 games with two different teams . . . Boasts 18-year record of 1,699-1,260 . . . Record in Detroit stands at 836-674 . . . Became Tiger manager June 12, 1979 . . . Established winning reputation at Cincinnati . . . Big Red Machine won five NL West titles, four pennants and two World Series under him . . . Named NL Manager of the Year in 1972 and 1973 . . . Born Feb. 22, 1934, in Bridgewater, S.D. . . . Grew up in southern California . . . Played in minors for six seasons as infielder . . . Played for Philadelphia in 1959, lone year as major leaguer . . . Only Los Angeles' Tommy Lasorda has put in more years of continuous service among major-league managers.

GREATEST FIRST BASEMAN

Hank Greenberg had a chance to play for the Yankees but, mindful of Lou Gehrig's presence at first base, opted for a career with the Tigers instead. What a boon that was for Detroit.

Greenberg emerged as the AL Most Valuable Player in 1935, when he was just 24 years old, amassing 36 home runs and 170 RBI. He earned league MVP honors again in 1940 before enlisting in the Army from 1941-45. He returned in July 1945 to help the Tigers to a pennant, smashing a grand slam on the final day of the regular season to clinch the title.

Greenberg's most memorable season was 1938, when he doggedly pursued Babe Ruth's record of 60 home runs. Hammerin' Hank had 58 with five games left.

He had gotten no closer through seven innings in the nightcap of a season-ending doubleheader. With darkness descending, umpire George Moriarty told Greenberg, "I'm sorry, Hank, this is as far as I can go."

"That's all right," Greenberg replied. "This is as far as I can go, too."

ALL-TIME TIGER SEASON RECORDS

BATTING: Ty Cobb, .420, 1911
HRs: Hank Greenberg, 58, 1938
RBIs: Hank Greenberg, 183, 1937
STEALS: Ty Cobb, 96, 1915
WINS: Denny McLain, 31, 1968
STRIKEOUTS: Mickey Lolich, 308, 1971

MILWAUKEE BREWERS

TEAM DIRECTORY: Pres.: Allan (Bud) Selig; Exec. VP-GM: Harry Dalton; Sr. Advisor Baseball Oper.: Walter Shannon; Asst. GM-Farm Dir.: Bruce Manno; VP-Int. Baseball Oper.: Ray Poitevint; Assts. to GM: Dee Fondy, Sal Bando; Dir. Publicity: Tom Skibosh; Trav. Sec.: Jimmy Bank; Mgr.: Tom Trebelhorn. Home: Milwaukee County Stadium (53,192). Field distances: 315, l.f. line; 362, l.f.; 392, l.c.; 402, c.f.; 392, r.c.; 362, r.f.; 315, r.f. line. Spring training: Chandler, Ariz.

SCOUTING REPORT

HITTING: A return to health by Glenn Braggs, who had 10 home runs and 42 RBI in just 72 games during an injury-plagued 1988, and the full-season availability of Rookie of the Year candidate Gary Sheffield in 1989 could lend juice to an offense that struggled last season. Only four AL teams posted averages lower than the Brewers' .257 mark and Milwaukee finished next to last in the AL in home runs with 113, one more than Texas.

Paul Molitor (.312, 13, 60) continues to key an offense that tries to make up in speed what it lacks in muscle. Molitor notched 41 of the Brewers' league-leading 159 steals. Robin Yount (.306, 13, 91) was next with 22 thefts. Strikeout-prone Rob Deer (.252, 23, 85) remains the chief source of power. Better things are expected from B.J. Surhoff (.245, 5, 38), whose average plummeted 54 points in his sophomore season.

Jeffrey Leonard, acquired from the Giants during midseason, had only eight homers and 44 RBI in 374 at-bats as a Brewer in 1988, so his defection to the Mariners as a free agent last winter shouldn't hurt too much.

PITCHING: Teddy Higuera (16-9, 2.45) continues to anchor a strong staff that placed second to AL champ Oakland with a 3.45 team ERA in 1988. The Brewers need Juan Nieves (7-5, 4.08) and relief ace Dan Plesac (1-2, 2.41, team-leading 30 saves), both of whom had injury problems last year, to be at full strength.

There are high hopes for Don August (13-7, 3.09). Bill Wegman (13-13, 4.12) is solid every year. Chuck Crim (7-6, 2.91, nine saves) pitches well and often. He topped the AL with 70 appearances.

The bullpen is underrated. Milwaukee's 51 saves represented the third-highest total in the majors. No AL bullpen had better success in converting save opportunities as the Brewers delivered on 51 of 58 chances, a rate of 88 percent.

Stylish Teddy Higuera was AL ERA runnerup at 2.45.

FIELDING: Manager Tom Trebelhorn looks for continued improvement here. The Brewers made significant strides in 1988, reducing their error total to 120 after making 145 miscues in 1987. Surhoff is getting better all the time behind the plate. Dale Sveum remains erratic with 27 errors, high among AL shortstops. Sveum will be pushed by Sheffield, who might wind up as slick-fielding Jim Gantner's double-play partner.

OUTLOOK: The Brewers are in position to take their first AL East title since 1982. They came on strong late last season despite numerous problems and might have been able to overtake faltering Boston if not for a schedule that had them playing the West in the final weeks. This is an excellent mix of veterans and young players. It is time for this organization's patient rebuilding to be rewarded.

MILWAUKEE BREWERS 1989 ROSTER

MANAGER Tom Trebelhorn

Coaches—Duffy Dyer, Andy Etchebarren, Larry Haney, Chuck Hartenstein, Tony Muser

PITCHERS

No.	Name	1988 Club	W-L	IP	SO	ERA	B-T	Ht.	Wt.	Born
33	Aldrich, Jay	Denver	3-7	72	53	4.63	R-R	6-3	210	4/14/61 Alexandria, LA
38	August, Don	Denver	4-1	72	58	3.52	R-R	6-3	190	7/3/63 Mission Viejo, CA
		Milwaukee	13-7	148	66	3.09				
40	Birbeck, Mike	Milwaukee	10-8	124	64	4.72	R-R	6-2	185	3/10/61 Orrville, OH
		Denver	4-1	45	30	2.01				
29	Bosio, Chris	Milwaukee	7-15	182	84	3.36	R-R	6-3	210	4/3/63 Carmichael, CA
		Denver	1-0	14	12	3.86				
48	Clutterbuck, Bryan	Denver	9-3	131	88	3.44	R-R	6-4	225	12/17/59 Detroit, MI
32	Crim, Chuck	Milwaukee	7-6	105	58	2.91	R-R	6-0	170	7/23/61 Van Nuys, CA
55	Elvira, Narciso	Stockton	7-6	135	161	2.93	L-L	5-10	160	10/29/67 Mexico
39	Filer, Tom	Denver	4-2	56	34	2.10	R-R	6-1	198	12/1/56 Philadelphia, PA
		Milwaukee	5-8	102	39	4.43				
63	Henry, Doug	Stockton	7-1	71	71	1.78	R-R	6-4	185	12/10/63 Sacramento, CA
		El Paso	4-0	46	50	3.15				
49	Higuera, Ted	Milwaukee	16-9	227	192	2.45	S-L	5-10	178	11/9/58 Mexico
41	Knudson, Mark	Denver	11-8	164	66	3.40	R-R	6-5	215	10/28/60 Denver, CO
		Milwaukee	0-0	16	7	1.13				
27	Mirabella, Paul	Denver	0-0	10	7	0.93	L-L	6-2	185	3/20/54 Belleville, NJ
		Milwaukee	2-2	60	33	1.65				
20	Nieves, Juan	Milwaukee	7-5	110	73	4.08	L-L	6-3	190	1/5/65 Puerto Rico
		Denver	0-2	20	14	2.29				
53	Perez, Leo	Beloit	10-8	123	124	2.05	R-R	6-0	180	8/6/66 Mexico
		Stockton	0-0	7	5	2.57				
37	Plesac, Dan	Milwaukee	1-2	52	52	2.41	L-L	6-5	210	2/4/62 Gary, IN
58	Veres, Randy	Stockton	8-4	110	96	3.35	R-R	6-3	189	11/25/65 San Francisco, CA
		El Paso	3-2	39	31	3.66				
56	Watkins, Tim	Denver	6-3	68	50	4.10	R-R	6-4	210	8/14/64 Ogden, UT
46	Wegman, Bill	Milwaukee	13-13	199	84	4.12	R-R	6-5	200	12/19/62 Cincinnati, OH

CATCHERS

No.	Name	1988 Club	H	HR	RBI	Pct.	B-T	Ht.	Wt.	Born
59	McIntosh, Tim	Stockton	147	15	92	.283	R-R	5-11	195	3/21/65 Crystal, MN
22	O'Brien, Charlie	Denver	43	4	25	.281	R-R	6-2	190	5/1/61 Tulsa, OK
		Milwaukee	26	2	9	.220				
5	Surhoff, B.J.	Milwaukee	121	5	38	.245	L-R	6-1	190	8/4/64 Bronx, NY

INFIELDERS

No.	Name	1988 Club	H	HR	RBI	Pct.	B-T	Ht.	Wt.	Born
34	Bates, Billy	Denver	122	2	44	.258	S-R	5-7	155	12/7/63 Houston, TX
9	Brock, Greg	Milwaukee	77	6	50	.212	L-R	6-3	205	6/14/57 McMinnville, OR
61	Canale, George	El Paso	120	23	93	.242	L-R	6-1	190	8/11/65 Memphis, TN
3	Castillo, Juan	Milwaukee	20	0	2	.222	S-R	5-11	155	1/25/62 Dominican Republic
28	Diaz, Edgar	Denver	65	0	21	.234	R-R	6-0	160	2/8/64 Puerto Rico
17	Gantner, Jim	Milwaukee	149	0	47	.276	L-R	5-11	175	1/5/54 Eden, WI
23	Meyer, Joey	Milwaukee	86	11	45	.263	R-R	6-3	260	5/10/62 Honolulu, HI
4	Molitor, Paul	Milwaukee	190	13	60	.312	R-R	6-0	175	8/22/56 St. Paul, MN
—	Polidor, Gus	Edmonton	12	0	7	.364	R-R	6-0	184	10/26/61 Venezuela
		California	12	0	4	.148				
1	Sheffield, Gary	El Paso	93	19	65	.314	R-R	5-11	190	11/18/68 Tampa, FL
		Denver	73	9	54	.344				
		Milwaukee	19	4	12	.238				
7	Sveum, Dale	Milwaukee	113	9	51	.242	S-R	6-3	185	11/23/63 Richmond, CA

OUTFIELDERS

No.	Name	1988 Club	H	HR	RBI	Pct.	B-T	Ht.	Wt.	Born
26	Braggs, Glenn	Milwaukee	71	10	42	.261	R-R	6-3	210	10/17/62 San Bernardino, CA
64	Carrillo, Matias	El Paso	118	12	55	.298	L-L	5-11	185	2/2/64 Mexico
45	Deer, Rob	Milwaukee	124	23	85	.252	R-R	6-3	210	9/29/60 Orange, CA
16	Felder, Mike	Milwaukee	14	0	5	.173	S-R	5-8	160	11/18/62 Richmond, CA
		Denver	21	0	5	.269				
57	Freeman, LaVel	Denver	122	5	59	.318	L-L	5-9	170	2/18/63 Oakland, CA
18	Hamilton, Darryl	Denver	90	0	32	.325	L-R	6-1	180	12/3/64 Baton Rouge, LA
		Milwaukee	19	1	11	.184				
11	Vaughn, Greg	El Paso	152	28	105	.301	R-R	6-0	193	7/3/65 Sacramento, CA
2	Young, Mike	Philadelphia	33	1	14	.226	S-R	6-2	206	3/20/60 Oakland, CA
		Milwaukee	0	0	0	.000				
19	Yount, Robin	Milwaukee	190	13	91	.306	R-R	6-0	180	9/16/55 Danville, IL

BREWER PROFILES

PAUL MOLITOR 32 6-0 175 **Bats R Throws R**

Continues to be an exceptional offensive player who can hurt opponents with his bat and his legs . . . Hit over .300 for fifth time in career and second straight season . . . Ranked sixth in AL at .312 . . . Enjoyed fourth season with 40 or more steals . . . Set club record by swiping 16 straight bases midway through season . . . First Brewer to surpass 300 career steals with 317 . . . Used as a DH in first half of season, he played third base in second half . . . Able to avoid major injury for second straight year . . . His 39-game hitting streak in 1987 was the longest in AL since Joe DiMaggio's record 56-gamer in 1941 . . . Born Aug. 22, 1956, in St. Paul, Minn. . . . Selected by Brewers in first round of June 1977 draft, out of the University of Minnesota.

Year	Club	Pos.	G	AB	R	H	2B	3B	HR	RBI	SB	Avg.
1978	Milwaukee.......	2B-SS-3B	125	521	73	142	26	4	6	45	30	.273
1979	Milwaukee.......	2B-SS	140	584	88	188	27	16	9	62	33	.322
1980	Milwaukee.......	2B-SS-3B	111	450	81	137	29	2	9	37	34	.304
1981	Milwaukee.......	OF	64	251	45	67	11	0	2	19	10	.267
1982	Milwaukee.......	3B-SS	160	666	136	201	26	8	19	71	41	.302
1983	Milwaukee.......	3B	152	608	95	164	28	6	15	47	41	.269
1984	Milwaukee.......	3B	13	46	3	10	1	0	0	6	1	.217
1985	Milwaukee.......	3B	140	576	93	171	28	3	10	48	21	.297
1986	Milwaukee.......	3B-OF	105	437	62	123	24	6	9	55	20	.281
1987	Milwaukee.......	3B-2B	118	465	114	164	41	5	16	75	45	.353
1988	Milwaukee.......	3B-2B	154	609	115	190	34	6	13	60	41	.312
	Totals		1282	5213	905	1557	275	56	108	525	317	.299

ROBIN YOUNT 33 6-0 180 **Bats R Throws R**

Extremely steady offensive player hit better than .300 for third straight season . . . Drove in at least 80 runs for fifth time in last seven years . . . Former shortstop has made himself into a nearly flawless center fielder . . . Became third Brewer to hit for cycle, June 12 at Chicago, as he collected the triple in his last at-bat . . . On Sept. 13 vs. Chicago, he recorded the first inside-the-park homer by a Brewer since he did it in 1982 . . . Was his fifth career inside-the-park homer . . . Second Brewer to play in every game. Gorman Thomas was the other, in 1980 . . . Born Sept. 16, 1955, in Danville, Ill. . . . Brewers' first-round choice in June 1973 draft spent only part of one season in minors . . . Brother Larry pitched in Milwaukee and Houston farm systems.

Year	Club	Pos.	G	AB	R	H	2B	3B	HR	RBI	SB	Avg.
1974	Milwaukee.......	SS	107	344	48	86	14	5	3	26	7	.250
1975	Milwaukee.......	SS	147	558	67	149	28	2	8	52	12	.267
1976	Milwaukee.......	SS-OF	161	638	59	161	19	3	2	54	16	.252
1977	Milwaukee.......	SS	154	605	66	174	34	4	4	49	16	.288
1978	Milwaukee.......	SS	127	502	66	147	23	9	9	71	16	.293
1979	Milwaukee.......	SS	149	577	72	154	26	5	8	51	11	.267
1980	Milwaukee.......	SS	143	611	121	179	49	10	23	87	20	.293
1981	Milwaukee.......	SS	96	377	50	103	15	5	10	49	4	.273
1982	Milwaukee.......	SS	156	635	129	210	46	12	29	114	14	.331
1983	Milwaukee.......	SS	149	578	102	178	42	10	17	80	12	.308
1984	Milwaukee.......	SS	160	624	105	186	27	7	16	80	14	.298
1985	Milwaukee.......	OF-1B	122	466	76	129	26	3	15	68	10	.277
1986	Milwaukee.......	OF-1B	140	522	82	163	31	7	9	46	14	.312
1987	Milwaukee.......	OF	158	635	99	198	25	9	21	103	19	.312
1988	Milwaukee.......	OF	162	621	92	190	38	11	13	91	22	.306
	Totals		2131	8293	1234	2407	443	102	187	1021	207	.290

B. J. SURHOFF 24 6-1 190 — Bats L Throws R

Suffered sophomore jinx and then some . . . Average plunged 54 points to .245 . . . RBI total fell off by 30 after he set Brewer rookie record with 68 . . . His ability to regain his stroke will be a key to Brewer fortunes in 1989 . . . Did improve behind the plate . . . Threw out 33 percent of runners attempting to steal . . . Cut down 15 of last 30 would-be base-stealers . . . Also played handful of games at third base . . . Fine quickness and speed make him very versatile . . . Born Aug. 4, 1964, in Bronx, N.Y. . . . Brewers made him first player selected in June 1985 draft, after a distinguished career at North Carolina.

Year	Club	Pos.	G	AB	R	H	2B	3B	HR	RBI	SB	Avg.
1987	Milwaukee.......	C-3B-1B	115	395	50	118	22	3	7	68	11	.299
1988	Milwaukee.......	C-3B	139	493	47	121	21	0	5	38	21	.245
	totals...........		254	888	97	239	43	3	12	106	32	.269

JIM GANTNER 35 5-11 175 — Bats L Throws R

Lack of power has made him butt of more than a few good-natured jokes around Brewer clubhouse . . . Has not homered in last 618 at-bats . . . Last trot around bases was June 14, 1987, after victimizing Yankees' Tim Stoddard . . . Did fall one shy of club mark for sacrifices with 18 . . . Excelled at second base . . . Guilty of only three errors in final 67 games and one in last 20 . . . Born Jan. 5, 1954, in Eden, Wis. . . . Acquired by Brewers in 12th round of June 1974 draft.

Year	Club	Pos.	G	AB	R	H	2B	3B	HR	RBI	SB	Avg.
1976	Milwaukee.......	3B	26	69	6	17	1	0	0	7	1	.246
1977	Milwaukee.......	3B	14	47	4	14	1	0	1	2	2	.298
1978	Milwaukee.......	2B-3B-SS-1B	43	97	14	21	1	0	1	8	2	.216
1979	Milwaukee.......	3B-2B-SS-P	70	208	29	59	10	3	2	22	3	.284
1980	Milwaukee.......	3B-2B-SS	132	415	47	117	21	3	4	40	11	.282
1981	Milwaukee.......	2B	107	352	35	94	14	1	2	33	3	.267
1982	Milwaukee.......	2B	132	447	48	132	17	2	4	43	6	.295
1983	Milwaukee.......	2B	161	603	85	170	23	8	11	74	5	.282
1984	Milwaukee.......	2B	153	613	61	173	27	1	3	56	6	.282
1985	Milwaukee.......	2B-3B-SS	143	523	63	133	15	4	5	44	11	.254
1986	Milwaukee.......	2B-3B-SS	139	497	58	136	25	1	7	38	13	.274
1987	Milwaukee.......	2B-3B	81	265	37	72	14	0	4	30	6	.272
1988	Milwaukee.......	2B-3B	155	539	67	149	28	2	0	47	20	.276
	Totals		1356	4675	554	1287	197	25	44	444	89	.275

ROB DEER 28 6-3 210 — Bats R Throws R

Outfielder showed improvement at the plate ... Set personal highs in average (.252), hits (124), doubles (24), games (135) and at-bats (492) ... Second Brewer to string together three straight seasons with 20 or more home runs and the first to top club in homers three straight years ... Key to improvement was ability to cut 33 strikeouts from his AL-record total of 186 in 1987 ... Still must learn to be more selective ... Drove in 80-plus runs for third straight season ... Born Sept. 29, 1960, in Orange, Cal. ... Obtained from Giants for Dean Freeland and Eric Pilkington, following 1985 season ... Giants picked him in fourth round of June 1978 draft, out of Fresno City College.

Year	Club	Pos.	G	AB	R	H	2B	3B	HR	RBI	SB	Avg.
1984	San Francisco	OF	13	24	5	4	0	0	3	3	1	.167
1985	San Francisco	OF-1B	78	162	22	30	5	1	8	20	0	.185
1986	Milwaukee.......	OF-1B	134	466	75	108	17	3	33	86	5	.232
1987	Milwaukee.......	OF-1B	134	474	71	113	15	2	28	80	12	.238
1988	Milwaukee.......	OF	135	492	71	124	24	0	23	85	9	.252
	Totals		494	1618	244	379	61	6	95	274	27	.234

TEDDY HIGUERA 30 5-10 178 — Bats S Throws L

Continues to be one of baseball's premier left-handers ... With personal-best 2.45 ERA, he placed second in AL to Minnesota's Allan Anderson ... First Brewer to win 15 or more in four straight seasons ... Boasts .645 career winning percentage, at 69-38 ... Tremendous second-half pitcher ... Owns 40-14 second-half mark for career, including 10-4 record and 2.23 ERA in 1988 ... Tossed four three-hitters ... Starting to show wear and tear from heavy workload ... Failed to record at least 200 strikeouts for first time in three years ... Born Nov. 9,

1958, in Los Mochis, Sinaloa, Mexico . . . Contract was purchased from Juarez of Mexican League, Sept. 13, 1983.

Year	Club	G	IP	W	L	Pct.	SO	BB	H	ERA
1985	Milwaukee	32	212⅓	15	8	.652	127	63	186	3.90
1986	Milwaukee	34	248⅓	20	11	.645	207	74	226	2.79
1987	Milwaukee	35	261⅔	18	10	.643	240	87	236	3.85
1988	Milwaukee	31	227⅓	16	9	.640	192	59	168	2.45
	Totals	132	949⅔	69	38	.645	766	283	816	3.25

DAN PLESAC 27 6-5 210 **Bats L Throws L**

Late-season injury diminished success, but he still had a big year . . . Logged 30 saves in 35 chances, becoming second Brewer to register 30 saves in a season . . . Set club record by reeling off nine saves in as many chances . . . Ranks second on club's all-time list with 67 saves, 30 behind all-time leader Rollie Fingers . . . Led club in saves for unprecedented third straight season . . . Tendinitis in pitching shoulder limited him to two appearances after Aug. 19 . . . Did not work after Sept. 13 . . . Born Feb. 4, 1962, in Gary, Ind. . . . Acquired by Brewers in first round of June 1983 draft.

Year	Club	G	IP	W	L	Pct.	SO	BB	H	ERA
1986	Milwaukee	51	91	10	7	.588	75	29	81	2.97
1987	Milwaukee	57	79⅓	5	6	.455	89	23	63	2.61
1988	Milwaukee	50	52⅓	1	2	.333	52	12	46	2.41
	Totals	158	222⅔	16	15	.516	216	64	190	2.71

JUAN NIEVES 24 6-3 190 **Bats L Throws L**

Strong finish provides hope for future after tired arm cost him most of June and July . . . Brewers believe playing winter ball was responsible for his arm problem last season and he stayed home this past winter . . . Went 3-1 with 2.91 ERA in five second-half starts . . . Was also used in relief . . . Tossed three-hit shutout vs. Chicago Sept. 13 . . . Finished year with three straight victories in final 10 appearances . . . Hurled only no-hitter in majors in 1987, a 7-0 gem vs. Baltimore April 15 . . . Born Jan. 5, 1965, in Santurce, Puerto Rico . . . Signed by Brewers as free agent, July 1, 1983, because he was born in Puerto Rico and wasn't eligible for draft.

Year	Club	G	IP	W	L	Pct.	SO	BB	H	ERA
1986	Milwaukee	35	184⅔	11	12	.478	116	77	224	4.92
1987	Milwaukee	34	195⅔	14	8	.636	163	100	199	4.88
1988	Milwaukee	25	110⅓	7	5	.583	73	50	84	4.08
	Totals	94	490⅔	32	25	.561	352	227	507	4.71

CHUCK CRIM 27 6-0 170 **Bats R Throws R**

Has become valuable set-up man in pen... Topped AL with 70 appearances and tied for second-highest total in club history. Ken Sanders holds club mark with 83 in 1971... Permitted only 18 of 68 inherited runners to score... Had seven wins and nine saves for bullpen that ranked second in majors, after Oakland... A big reason that Brewers' relievers set club record with 51 saves in 1988... Born July 23, 1961, in Van Nuys, Cal.... Chosen by Brewers in 17th round of June 1982 draft, out of the University of Hawaii.

Year	Club	G	IP	W	L	Pct.	SO	BB	H	ERA
1987	Milwaukee...........	53	130	6	8	.429	56	39	133	3.67
1988	Milwaukee...........	70	105	7	6	.538	58	28	95	2.91
	Totals	123	235	13	14	.481	114	67	228	3.33

BILL WEGMAN 26 6-5 200 **Bats R Throws R**

Set personal best with 13 victories, but is getting reputation as .500 pitcher... Finished at .500 by losing last two starts of season... Had also begun year by dropping two straight... Recorded first shutout of career Sept. 2, a four-hitter vs. Detroit... Born Dec. 19, 1962, in Cincinnati... Selected by Brewers in fifth round of June 1981 draft... Led California League in wins with 16 and ERA with a 1.30 mark for Stockton (A) in 1983.

Year	Club	G	IP	W	L	Pct.	SO	BB	H	ERA
1985	Milwaukee...........	3	17⅔	2	0	1.000	6	3	17	3.57
1986	Milwaukee...........	35	198⅓	5	12	.294	82	43	217	5.13
1987	Milwaukee...........	34	225	12	11	.522	102	53	229	4.24
1988	Milwaukee...........	32	199	13	13	.500	84	50	207	4.12
	Totals	104	640	32	36	.471	274	149	670	4.46

TOP PROSPECT

GARY SHEFFIELD 20 5-11 190 **Bats R Throws R**

Nephew of Met ace Dwight Gooden is widely considered either the best or the second-best prospect in the game... Shortstop should play a major role for Brewers this season... Excelled after September promotion to majors... Went hitless in first 10 at-bats, then recovered to bat .271 with four homers and 12 RBI in final 10 games... Class AA Player of the Year as he hit .314 with 19 home runs and 65 RBI in 77 games for El Paso of Texas

League . . . Promoted to Denver and hit .344 with nine homers and 54 RBI in 57 games . . . Born Nov. 18, 1968, in Tampa, Fla. . . . Selected by Brewers in first round of June 1986 draft as the sixth player picked overall.

MANAGER TOM TREBELHORN: Is rapidly building reputation as excellent manager . . . Owns 178-146 record (184-149 overall) in two full seasons at Brewers' helm . . . Has brought promising young talent to majors to create nice blend with veterans . . . Never lost confidence in 1988 Brewers although they hovered around .500 mark for most of season before finishing strong and becoming factor in division race . . . Managed Vancouver (AAA) to Pacific Coast League crown in 1985 . . . Was scheduled to direct Brewers' Helena farm club in Pioneer League in 1986 but became Milwaukee's third-base coach when Tony Muser was injured in clubhouse explosion in spring training . . . Officially named manager, succeeding George Bamberger, Oct. 1, 1986 . . . Born Jan. 27, 1948, in Portland, Ore. . . . Played baseball and basketball at Portland State, where he was a catcher . . . Played in Northwest League in 1971 and 1972 . . . Oakland A's purchased his contract in 1973 and he played two seasons in their system . . . Batted .241 in minor-league career . . . Used to be substitute teacher in Portland system in offseason.

GREATEST FIRST BASEMAN

"C-o-o-o-o-p! C-o-o-o-o-p!"

When that cry used to echo throughout Milwaukee's County Stadium, it meant one thing: Cecil Cooper was coming to bat for the Brewers.

Each of Cooper's at-bats was greeted with high expectations and frequently he delivered. He knocked in more than 100 runs four times and his 126 RBI in 1983 tied for the major-league lead. He was selected as an All-Star first baseman five times.

Cooper heads Milwaukee's all-time list with a .302 batting average and ranks second in 10 other categories: home runs (201), RBI (944), runs (821), hits (1,815), singles (1,234), doubles (345), extra-base hits (579), total bases (2,829), at-bats (6,019) and games (1,490).

The call for Coop is no longer heard, but his accomplishments assure that he will not be forgotten in Milwaukee.

ALL-TIME BREWER SEASON RECORDS

BATTING: Paul Molitor, .353, 1987
HRs: Gorman Thomas, 45, 1979
RBIs: Cecil Cooper, 126, 1983
STEALS: Paul Molitor, 45, 1987
WINS: Mike Caldwell, 22, 1978
STRIKEOUTS: Ted Higuera, 240, 1987

In Milwaukee, Brew-master Paul Molitor is "The Ignitor."

NEW YORK YANKEES

TEAM DIRECTORY: Principal Owner: George Steinbrenner III; VP-GM: Bob Quinn; VP-Dir. Player Dev. and Scouting: George Bradley; Dir. Scouting: Brian Sabean; Dir. Media Rel.: Harvey Greene; Trav. Sec.: Bill Enslie; Mgr.: Dallas Green. Home: Yankee Stadium (57,545). Field distances: 312, l.f. line; 379, l.f.; 411, l.c.; 410, c.f.; 385, r.c.; 310, r.f. line. Spring training: Fort Lauderdale, Fla.

SCOUTING REPORT

HITTING: The Yankees have speed to burn at the top of their lineup with leadoff man Rickey Henderson (.305, 6, 50) and newly acquired second-place hitter Steve Sax (.277, 5, 57).

Henderson has captured the AL stolen-base crown in eight of his nine major-league seasons, including last year, when he had 93 thefts to break his own club mark. Sax, signed as a free agent last winter, ranked among the NL leaders with 42 steals for the Dodgers.

After those two get aboard and go, the Yankees have Don Mattingly (.311, 18, 88) and Dave Winfield (.322, 25, 107) to drive them in. Mattingly is eager to re-establish himself as baseball's best player after a disappointing season in which his production declined by 12 home runs and 27 RBI and his average fell by 25 points from 1987 standards. And how long can Winfield, 37, keep putting up big numbers?

The offseason deal that sent Jack Clark (.242, 27, 93) to San Diego created an offensive void that the Yankees hope will be filled by designated hitter Ken Phelps (.263, 24, 54) and Claudell Washington (.308, 11, 64). But scoring runs is rarely a problem for the Yankees, third in the AL with 772 last year.

PITCHING: The staff underwent a needed overhaul last winter with the signing of former Padre Andy Hawkins (14-11, 3.35) and former Pirate Dave LaPoint (14-13, 3.25) as free agents and the acquisition of Lance McCullers (3-6, 2.49, 10 saves) and Jimmy Jones (9-14, 4.12) from the Padres in the Clark deal.

The quality of the three new starters is questionable as Hawkins, LaPoint and Jones were a combined 37-38 last year. At least they should provide more innings than the Yankees have gotten from their starters in the past. Hawkins (217⅔ innings) and LaPoint (213⅓) would have led last year's Yankee staff and

Dave Winfield's 107 RBI showed George who was Boss.

Jones (179) would have been second behind the departed Rick Rhoden (12-12, 4.20, 197 innings), traded to the Astros in January.

John Candelaria (13-7, 3.38) was the only pitcher to excel on a staff that ranked 12th in the AL with a 4.24 ERA and surrendered a major-league-high 157 home runs last year. McCullers should help relieve the load of bullpen stopper Dave Righetti, who had a career-low 25 saves in 1988 and blew nine save opportunities.

FIELDING: Aside from Mattingly, a perennial Gold Glove first baseman, the Yankees are poor defensively. Shortstop Rafael Santana and third baseman Mike Pagliarulo both have limited range. Catcher Don Slaught made 11 errors and caught only 12 of 72 would-be base-stealers, a dreadful 17 percent. Henderson's carelessness in the outfield was reflected in his 12 errors. Sax, who replaces Willie Randolph at second base, committed twice as many errors as his predecessor with 14.

OUTLOOK: The Yankees make another fresh start with significant changes on and off the field. Principal owner George Steinbrenner has gone away from his list of recycled managers to hire taskmaster Dallas Green. However, it remains to be seen whether Green can get more out of the Yankees, who have been consistently good enough to contend but not quite unified enough to win amid the inevitable tumult.

NEW YORK YANKEES 1989 ROSTER

MANAGER Dallas Green

Coaches—Billy Connors, Pat Corrales, Lee Elia, Charlie Fox, Frank Howard, John Stearns

PITCHERS

No.	Name	1988 Club	W-L	IP	SO	ERA	B-T	Ht.	Wt.	Born
45	Candelaria, John	New York (AL)	13-7	157	121	3.38	R-L	6-6	225	11/6/53 Brooklyn, NY
55	Chapin, Darrin	Ft. Lauderdale	6-4	63	57	0.86	R-R	6-0	170	2/1/66 Warren, OH
		Albany	0-0	4	4	11.25				
36	Dotson, Richard	New York (AL)	12-9	171	77	5.00	R-R	6-0	204	1/10/59 Cincinnati, OH
29	Eiland, David	Albany	9-5	119	66	2.56	R-R	6-3	210	7/5/66 Dade City, FL
		Columbus	1-1	24	13	2.59				
		New York (AL)	0-0	13	7	6.39				
35	Guetterman, Lee	Columbus	9-6	121	46	2.76	L-L	6-8	225	11/22/58 Chattanooga, TN
		New York (AL)	1-2	41	15	4.65				
40	Hawkins, Andy	San Diego	14-11	218	91	3.35	R-R	6-3	205	1/21/60 Waco, TX
41	Hudson, Charles	New York (AL)	6-6	106	58	4.49	R-R	6-3	185	3/16/59 Ennis, TX
38	Jones, Jimmy	San Diego	9-14	179	82	4.12	R-R	6-2	190	4/20/64 Dallas, TX
29	LaPoint, Dave	Chicago (AL)	10-11	161	79	3.40	L-L	6-3	215	7/19/59 Glens Falls, NY
		Pittsburgh	4-2	52	19	2.77				
28	Leiter, Al	Columbus	0-2	13	12	3.46	L-L	6-3	210	10/23/65 Toms River, NJ
		New York (AL)	4-4	57	60	3.92				
34	McCullers, Lance	San Diego	3-6	98	81	2.49	S-R	6-1	218	3/8/64 Tampa, FL
54	Mohorcic, Dale	Tex.-NY (AL)	4-8	75	44	4.22	R-R	6-3	220	1/25/56 Cleveland, OH
43	Pena, Hipolito	Columbus	7-6	105	109	3.87	L-L	6-3	165	1/30/64 Dominican Republic
		New York (AL)	1-1	14	10	2.51				
58	Ridenour, Dana	Albany	5-4	44	56	3.92	R-R	6-2	205	11/15/65 Panorama City, CA
		Columbus	1-2	21	24	2.11				
19	Righetti, Dave	New York (AL)	5-4	87	70	3.52	L-L	6-4	210	11/28/58 San Jose, CA
51	Schulze, Don	Toledo	10-13	185	107	3.11	R-R	6-3	230	9/27/62 Roselle, IL
33	Shields, Steve	Columbus	0-1	25	23	2.52	R-R	6-5	230	11/30/58 Gadsden, AL
		New York (AL)	5-5	82	55	4.37				

CATCHERS

No.	Name	1988 Club	H	HR	RBI	Pct.	B-T	Ht.	Wt.	Born
52	Geren, Bob	Columbus	87	8	35	.271	R-R	6-3	205	9/22/61 San Diego, CA
		New York (AL)	1	0	0	.100				
—	Quirk, Jamie	Kansas City	47	8	25	.240	L-R	6-4	200	10/22/54 Whittier, CA
12	Skinner, Joel	New York (AL)	57	4	23	.227	R-R	6-4	204	2/21/61 La Jolla, CA
11	Slaught, Don	New York (AL)	91	9	43	.283	R-R	6-1	190	9/11/58 Long Beach, CA

INFIELDERS

No.	Name	1988 Club	H	HR	RBI	Pct.	B-T	Ht.	Wt.	Born
53	Maas, Kevin	Prince William	32	12	35	.296	L-L	6-3	195	1/20/65 Castro Valley, CA
		Albany	98	16	55	.263				
23	Mattingly, Don	New York (AL)	186	18	88	.311	L-L	6-0	175	4/20/61 Evansville, IN
57	Meulens, Hensley	Albany	68	13	40	.245	R-R	6-3	190	6/23/67 Curacao
		Columbus	48	6	22	.230				
13	Pagliarulo, Mike	New York (AL)	96	15	67	.216	L-R	6-2	195	6/15/60 Medford, MA
21	Phelps, Ken	Sea.-NY (AL)	78	24	54	.263	L-L	6-1	200	8/6/54 Seattle, WA
17	Santana, Rafael	New York (AL)	115	4	38	.240	R-R	6-1	160	1/31/58 Dominican Republic
8	Sax, Steve	Los Angeles	175	5	57	.277	R-R	5-11	179	1/29/60 Sacramento, CA
2	Tolleson, Wayne	New York (AL)	15	0	5	.254	S-R	5-9	160	9/22/55 Spartanburg, SC
20	Velarde, Randy	Columbus	79	5	37	.270	R-R	6-0	185	11/24/62 Midland, TX
		New York (AL)	20	5	12	.174				

OUTFIELDERS

No.	Name	1988 Club	H	HR	RBI	Pct.	B-T	Ht.	Wt.	Born
61	Azocar, Oscar	Albany	148	6	66	.273	L-L	6-1	170	2/21/65 Venezuela
25	Brower, Bob	Texas	45	1	11	.224	R-R	6-0	190	1/10/60 Queens, NY
—	Fishel, John	Tucson	94	18	68	.261	R-R	5-11	185	11/8/62 Fullerton, CA
		Houston	6	1	2	.231				
24	Henderson, Rickey	New York (AL)	169	6	50	.305	R-L	5-10	195	12/25/58 Chicago, IL
59	Jefferson, Stan	Las Vegas	88	4	33	.317	S-L	5-11	175	12/4/62 New York, NY
		San Diego	16	1	4	.144				
39	Kelly, Roberto	Columbus	40	3	16	.333	R-R	6-4	185	10/1/64 Panama
		New York (AL)	19	1	7	.247				
22	Ward, Gary	New York (AL)	52	4	24	.225	R-R	6-2	202	12/6/53 Los Angeles, CA
18	*Washington, Claudell	New York (AL)	140	11	64	.308	L-L	6-2	195	8/31/54 Los Angeles, CA
25	Williams, Bernabe	Prince William	113	7	45	.338	R-R	6-2	180	9/13/68 Puerto Rico
31	Winfield, Dave	New York (AL)	180	25	107	.322	R-R	6-6	220	10/3/51 St. Paul, MN

*Free agent at press time listed with 1988 team

YANKEE PROFILES

DON MATTINGLY 27 6-0 175 **Bats L Throws L**

Can no longer be called the best player in the game after very disappointing 1988 season... Experienced dip of 12 home runs, 27 RBI and 26 points in batting average compared to 1987 totals... Pitchers capitalized on his willingness to swing at pitches out of the strike zone... Fielding also deteriorated somewhat, although he remains the best first baseman in baseball... Disabled from May 27 to June 14 with strained muscle in right side... Won AL batting championship in 1984, his first full season in majors, with .343 average... Won league MVP honors the following season, collecting 35 homers and 145 RBI... Set club records with 238 hits and 53 doubles in 1986... Hit record-breaking six grand slams and tied record with homers in eight straight games in 1987... Born April 20, 1961, in Evansville, Ind.... Yanks' 19th-round pick in June 1979 draft ... Brother Randy played pro football.

Year	Club	Pos.	G	AB	R	H	2B	3B	HR	RBI	SB	Avg.
1982	New York (AL)....	OF-1B	7	12	0	2	0	0	0	1	0	.167
1983	New York (AL)....	OF-1B-2B	91	279	34	79	15	4	4	32	0	.283
1984	New York (AL)....	1B-OF	153	603	91	207	44	2	23	110	1	.343
1985	New York (AL)....	1B	159	652	107	211	48	3	35	145	2	.324
1986	New York (AL)....	1B-3B	162	677	117	238	53	2	31	113	0	.352
1987	New York (AL)....	1B	141	569	93	186	38	2	30	115	1	.327
1988	New York (AL)....	1B	144	599	94	186	37	0	18	88	1	.311
	Totals		857	3391	536	1109	235	13	141	604	5	.327

DAVE WINFIELD 37 6-6 220 **Bats R Throws R**

Responded to off-the-field controversy with brilliant season and was easily the MVP of this star-studded club in 1988... Was severely criticized by principal owner George Steinbrenner after publication of rather tame autobiography last spring and was forced to head off trade attempts... Drove in more than 100 runs for seventh time in career and sixth time in last seven seasons... Reached base safely in 129 of his 149 games played... Tied Roger Maris for seventh place on all-time Yankee list with 203 homers and has hit 357 in career... Ranks 11th on Yankees' all-time RBI list with 810... Has lost a step, but is still a superior right fielder... Born Oct. 3, 1951, in St. Paul, Minn.... Known as $23-million man because of 10-year contract he signed with Yankees as free agent, following 1980 season . . . Padres made him fourth player taken overall in June 1973 draft, out of University of Minnesota . . . Was chosen in pro football draft by Vikings and in pro basketball draft by Hawks.

Year	Club	Pos.	G	AB	R	H	2B	3B	HR	RBI	SB	Avg.
1973	San Diego	OF-1B	56	141	9	39	4	1	3	12	0	.277
1974	San Diego	OF	145	498	57	132	18	4	20	75	9	.265
1975	San Diego	OF	143	509	74	136	20	2	15	76	23	.267
1976	San Diego	OF	137	492	81	139	26	4	13	69	26	.283
1977	San Diego	OF	157	615	104	169	29	7	25	92	16	.275
1978	San Diego	OF-1B	158	587	88	181	30	5	24	97	21	.308
1979	San Diego	OF	159	597	97	184	27	10	34	118	15	.308
1980	San Diego	OF	162	558	89	154	25	6	20	87	23	.276
1981	New York (AL)	OF	105	388	52	114	25	1	13	68	11	.294
1982	New York (AL)	OF	140	539	84	151	24	8	37	106	5	.280
1983	New York (AL)	OF	152	598	99	169	26	8	32	116	15	.283
1984	New York (AL)	OF	141	567	106	193	34	4	19	100	6	.340
1985	New York (AL)	OF	155	633	105	174	34	6	26	114	19	.275
1986	New York (AL)	OF-3B	154	565	90	148	31	5	24	104	6	.262
1987	New York (AL)	OF	156	575	83	158	22	1	27	97	5	.275
1988	New York (AL)	OF	149	559	96	180	37	2	25	107	9	.322
	Totals		2269	8421	1314	2421	412	74	357	1438	209	.287

RICKEY HENDERSON 30 5-10 195 Bats R Throws L

While his attitude and work habits are frequently questioned, his results cannot be . . . Won AL stolen-base crown for eighth time in nine major-league seasons with 93, breaking own club mark by six . . . Ranks fourth on all-time stolen-base list with 794 . . . Stands as Yankees' all-time leader with 301 steals . . . Left fielder scored 100-plus runs for seventh time in nine seasons . . . Led off July 21 game vs. Kansas City with home run, tying Bobby Bonds' major-league career mark of 35 homers leading off games . . . Reached base safely leading off game 15 consecutive times from July 18 to Aug. 3 . . . Born Dec. 25, 1958, in Chicago . . . Acquired from Oakland with Bert Bradley for Jay Howell, Jose Rijo, Eric Plunk, Tim Birtsas and Stan Javier, following the 1984 season . . . Wears No. 24 because he idolized Willie Mays . . . Oakland's fourth-round pick in June 1976 draft . . . Owns major-league record for steals in a season with 130 in 1982.

Year	Club	Pos.	G	AB	R	H	2B	3B	HR	RBI	SB	Avg.
1979	Oakland	OF	89	351	49	96	13	3	1	26	33	.274
1980	Oakland	OF	158	591	111	179	22	4	9	53	100	.303
1981	Oakland	OF	108	423	89	135	18	7	6	35	56	.319
1982	Oakland	OF	149	536	119	143	24	4	10	51	130	.267
1983	Oakland	OF	145	513	105	150	25	7	9	48	108	.292
1984	Oakland	OF	142	502	113	147	27	4	16	58	66	.293
1985	New York (AL)	OF	143	547	146	172	28	5	24	72	80	.314
1986	New York (AL)	OF	153	608	130	160	31	5	28	74	87	.263
1987	New York (AL)	OF	95	358	78	104	17	3	17	37	41	.291
1988	New York (AL)	OF	140	554	118	169	30	2	6	50	93	.305
	Totals		1322	4983	1058	1455	235	44	126	504	794	.292

Rickey Henderson is on his way to 800th stolen base.

STEVE SAX 29 5-11 179 **Bats R Throws R**

Left Dodgers as free agent and signed three year, $4-million deal with Yankees . . . Has finally evolved into a steady second baseman, having overcome the erratic defensive play that characterized the early years of his career . . . Committed just 14 errors in 1988 . . . Played in career-high 160 games . . . Was fourth in NL with 175 hits . . . His 42 stolen bases was seven short of his career high . . . Had eight hits and three RBI against the Mets in NLCS . . . Batted .300 vs. Oakland in World Series . . . A mainstay for Dodgers at second base since 1982, he will replace Yankee fixture Willie Randolph in 1989 . . . Dodgers' ninth selection in June 1978 draft . . . Born Jan. 29, 1960, in Sacramento, Cal. . . . Finished second to Expos' Tim Raines in NL batting race in 1986.

Year	Club	Pos.	G	AB	R	H	2B	3B	HR	RBI	SB	Avg.
1981	Los Angeles	2B	31	119	15	33	2	0	2	9	5	.277
1982	Los Angeles	2B	150	638	88	180	23	7	4	47	49	.282
1983	Los Angeles	2B	155	623	94	175	18	5	5	41	56	.281
1984	Los Angeles	2B	145	569	70	138	24	4	1	35	34	.243
1985	Los Angeles	2B-3B	136	488	62	136	8	4	1	42	27	.279
1986	Los Angeles	2B	157	633	91	210	43	4	6	56	40	.332
1987	Los Angeles	2B-OF-3B	157	610	84	171	22	7	6	46	37	.280
1988	Los Angeles	2B	160	632	70	175	19	4	5	57	42	.277
	Totals		1091	4312	574	1218	159	35	30	333	290	.282

JOHN CANDELARIA 35 6-6 225 Bats R Throws L

"Candy Man" led poor Yankee staff with 13 victories, despite not pitching after Aug. 24 due to torn cartilage in right knee . . . Team physician insisted he could pitch without risking further injury, but moody lefty refused to work . . . Won six decisions in as many starts from May 4 to June 11, including two-hit, 13-strikeout masterpiece vs. Oakland May 22 . . . Generally has outstanding control . . . Six complete games marked his highest total since 1980 . . . Has great ability, but his mental attitude must be questioned . . . Born Nov. 6, 1953, in Brooklyn, N.Y. . . . Signed with Yankees as free agent prior to last season . . . Didn't get along with manager Lou Piniella last season . . . Pirates' second-round pick in June 1972 draft has been hard to handle throughout his major-league travels.

Year	Club	G	IP	W	L	Pct.	SO	BB	H	ERA
1975	Pittsburgh...........	18	121	8	6	.571	95	36	95	2.75
1976	Pittsburgh...........	32	220	16	7	.696	138	60	173	3.15
1977	Pittsburgh...........	33	231	20	5	.800	133	50	197	*2.34
1978	Pittsburgh...........	30	189	12	11	.522	94	49	191	3.24
1979	Pittsburgh...........	33	207	14	9	.609	101	41	201	3.22
1980	Pittsburgh...........	35	233	11	14	.440	97	50	246	4.02
1981	Pittsburgh...........	6	41	2	2	.500	14	11	42	3.51
1982	Pittsburgh...........	31	174⅔	12	7	.632	133	37	166	2.94
1983	Pittsburgh...........	33	197⅔	15	8	.652	157	45	191	3.23
1984	Pittsburgh...........	33	185⅓	12	11	.522	133	34	179	2.72
1985	Pittsburgh...........	37	54⅓	2	4	.333	47	14	57	3.64
1985	California	13	71	7	3	.700	53	24	70	3.80
1986	California	16	91⅔	10	2	.833	81	26	68	2.55
1987	California	20	116⅔	8	6	.571	74	20	127	4.71
1987	New York (AL)........	3	12⅓	2	0	1.000	10	3	17	5.84
1988	New York (AL)........	25	157	13	7	.650	121	23	150	3.38
	Totals	398	2302⅔	164	102	.617	1481	523	2170	3.23

DAVE RIGHETTI 30 6-4 210 **Bats L Throws L**

Reliever who racked up major-league-record 46 saves in 1986 suffered dramatic loss of form . . . His 25 saves represented his lowest total since he went to the bullpen five years ago . . . Blew nine save opportunities, although Yanks went 29-5 in games in which he entered in save situation . . . Missed four consecutive saves from April 20 to May 2 and endured 12-day layoff after that as then-manager Billy Martin lost confidence in him . . . Earned 151st save July 24 in Kansas City and surpassed Rich Gossage as Yankees' all-time saves leader . . . Now has 163 career saves . . . Heavy workload has caused him to lose zip on fastball . . . Also got himself into trouble with walks . . . Born Nov. 28, 1958, in San Jose, Cal. . . . Obtained from Rangers with Mike Griffin, Paul Mirabella, Juan Beniquez and Greg Jemison for Sparky Lyle, Larry McCall, Dave Rajsich, Mike Heath, Domingo Ramos and cash, following 1978 season . . . Rangers made him ninth player taken in January 1977 draft . . . Threw no-hitter vs. Red Sox, July 4, 1983 . . . May wind up back in rotation in 1989.

Year	Club	G	IP	W	L	Pct.	SO	BB	H	ERA
1979	New York (AL)	3	17	0	1	.000	13	10	10	3.71
1981	New York (AL)	15	105	8	4	.667	89	38	75	2.06
1982	New York (AL)	33	183	11	10	.524	163	108	155	3.79
1983	New York (AL)	31	217	14	8	.636	169	67	194	3.44
1984	New York (AL)	64	96⅓	5	6	.455	90	37	79	2.34
1985	New York (AL)	74	107	12	7	.632	92	45	96	2.78
1986	New York (AL)	74	106⅔	8	8	.500	83	35	88	2.45
1987	New York (AL)	60	95	8	6	.571	77	44	95	3.51
1988	New York (AL)	60	87	5	4	.556	70	37	86	3.52
	Totals	414	1014	71	54	.568	846	421	878	3.10

DAVE LaPOINT 29 6-3 215 **Bats L Throws L**

Yankees signed him to three-year, $2.5-million pact as free agent last winter and plan on using him in their rotation . . . Has done lots of traveling since Brewers made him 10th-round pick in June 1977 draft . . . Last season, he was 10-11 with a 3.40 ERA for White Sox and 4-2 with 2.77 ERA for Pirates after being dealt back to the NL in September . . . Has pitched for seven major-league clubs, including Cards twice . . . Born July 29, 1959, in Glens Falls, N.Y. . . . Has been used as starter and reliever . . . Out pitch is his changeup, which is one of the best in the game . . . Describes himself as "years younger Tommy John" . . . Notched career-high 213⅓ innings last year, easily more than any Yankee starter managed in 1988.

Year	Club	G	IP	W	L	Pct.	SO	BB	H	ERA
1980	Milwaukee	5	15	1	0	1.000	5	13	17	6.00
1981	St. Louis	3	11	1	0	1.000	4	2	12	4.09
1982	St. Louis	42	152⅔	9	3	.750	81	52	170	3.42
1983	St. Louis	37	191⅓	12	9	.571	113	84	191	3.95
1984	St. Louis	33	193	12	10	.545	130	77	205	3.96
1985	San Francisco	31	206⅔	7	17	.292	122	74	215	3.57
1986	Detroit	16	67⅔	3	6	.333	36	32	85	5.72
1986	San Diego	24	61⅓	1	4	.200	41	24	67	4.26
1987	St. Louis	6	16	1	1	.500	8	5	26	6.75
1987	Chicago (AL)	14	82⅔	6	3	.667	43	31	69	2.94
1988	Chicago (AL)	25	161⅓	10	11	.476	79	47	151	3.40
1988	Pittsburgh	8	52	4	2	.667	19	10	54	2.77
	Totals	244	1210⅔	67	66	.504	681	451	1262	3.81

RICHARD DOTSON 30 6-0 204 **Bats R Throws R**

Failed to provide the consistency or the innings the Yankees hoped when they acquired him from White Sox with Scott Nielsen for Dan Pasqua, Mark Salas and Steve Rosenberg, following 1987 season . . . Suffered five-game losing streak while posting 7.84 ERA at critical point in season, from Aug. 13 to Sept. 9 . . . Very vulnerable to home run, allowing 27 of them in 1988 . . . Got off to the best start of his career at 5-0 and did reach double figures in victories for seventh time . . . May respond better to different handling . . . Born Jan. 10, 1959, in Cincinnati . . . Angels made him seventh player selected in June 1977 draft . . . In 1983, he became youngest White Sox 20-game winner since Reb Russell did it in 1913.

Year	Club	G	IP	W	L	Pct.	SO	BB	H	ERA
1979	Chicago (AL)	5	24	2	0	1.000	13	6	28	3.75
1980	Chicago (AL)	33	198	12	10	.545	109	87	185	4.27
1981	Chicago (AL)	24	141	9	8	.529	73	49	145	3.77
1982	Chicago (AL)	34	196⅔	11	15	.423	109	73	219	3.84
1983	Chicago (AL)	35	240	22	7	.759	137	106	209	3.23
1984	Chicago (AL)	32	245⅔	14	15	.483	120	103	216	3.59
1985	Chicago (AL)	9	52⅓	3	4	.429	33	17	53	4.47
1986	Chicago (AL)	34	197	10	17	.370	110	69	226	5.48
1987	Chicago (AL)	31	211⅓	11	12	.478	114	86	201	4.17
1988	New York (AL)	32	171	12	9	.571	77	72	178	5.00
	Totals	269	1677	106	97	.522	895	668	1660	4.13

ANDY HAWKINS 29 6-3 217 **Bats R Throws R**

Signed to a three-year, $3.6-million deal as a free agent last winter, this former Padre is expected to anchor Yankee rotation . . . Bounced back from dreadful 3-10 mark in 1987 to post double figures in victories for the third time in his career last season . . . Showed no signs of shoulder problems that ruined 1987 . . . Born Jan. 21, 1960, in Waco, Tex. . . . Padres made him fifth player taken overall in June 1978 draft . . . Came into his own during 1984 postseason, when he posted 0.57 ERA, then reeled off a club-record 11 consecutive wins at start of 1985 . . . Not overpowering despite his size, but he has learned to pitch more aggressively since the days former manager Dick Williams labeled him "a pussycat."

Year	Club	G	IP	W	L	Pct.	SO	BB	H	ERA
1982	San Diego	15	63⅔	2	5	.286	25	27	66	4.10
1983	San Diego	21	119⅔	5	7	.417	59	48	106	2.93
1984	San Diego	36	146	8	9	.471	77	72	143	4.68
1985	San Diego	33	228⅔	18	8	.692	69	65	229	3.15
1986	San Diego	37	209⅓	10	8	.556	117	75	218	4.30
1987	San Diego	24	117⅔	3	10	.231	51	49	131	5.05
1988	San Diego	33	217 ⅔	14	11	.440	91	76	196	3.35
	Totals	199	1103⅔	60	58	.508	489	412	1098	3.84

LANCE McCULLERS 25 6-1 218 **Bats S Throws R**

Acquired from Padres with Jimmy Jones and Stan Jefferson for Jack Clark and Pat Clements just weeks after the conclusion of last season . . . Hard thrower who served as a set-up man for Goose Gossage and then Mark Davis in San Diego . . . Converted 10 of 16 save opportunities in 1988, boosting career save total to 36 . . . Allowed 15 of 35 inherited runners to score in 1988 . . . Was Phils' second-round pick in June 1982 draft, but was dealt to Padres in August 1983 . . . Was starter for most of pro career before arriving in majors in August 1985 as replacement for injured Gossage . . . Born March 8, 1964, in Tampa, Fla. . . . Led NL relievers in innings with 123.1 in 1987 and his 60 appearances ranked second on Padre staff last season . . . Might wind up getting a chance to be a closer for Dallas Green this season.

Year	Club	G	IP	W	L	Pct.	SO	BB	H	ERA
1985	San Diego	21	35	0	2	.000	27	16	23	2.31
1986	San Diego	70	136	10	10	.500	92	58	103	2.78
1987	San Diego	78	123⅓	8	10	.444	126	59	115	3.72
1988	San Diego	60	97⅔	3	6	.333	81	55	70	2.49
	Totals	229	392	21	28	.429	326	188	311	2.96

TOP PROSPECT

HENSLEY MEULENS 21 6-3 190 Bats R Throws R
"Bam-Bam" is known for his power, but he remains a raw talent . . . Batted .245 with 13 home runs and 40 RBI for Albany-Colonie (AA) . . . Continued to struggle after being promoted to Columbus (AAA), hitting .230 with six home runs and 22 RBI in 55 games . . . Averaged close to one strikeout every three at-bats at each stop . . . Unpolished defensive third baseman . . . Led Carolina League with 28 homers in 1987 . . . Born June 23, 1967, in Curacao . . . Signed by Yankees as free agent, Oct. 31, 1985.

MANAGER DALLAS GREEN: Represents 16th managerial change in 16 years during wild reign of principal owner George Steinbrenner . . . Is only fourth Yankee manager in past 20 years never to have played for team, however . . . Named Oct. 7 to replace fired Lou Piniella, he was given two-year contract . . . Green is emphasizing discipline and team play to star-studded Yankees . . . Favorite slogan is "We, not I" . . . Used that theme in managing Philadelphia to world championship in 1980, franchise's first such triumph in 97 years . . . In 1983, Phillies' fans chose Green as manager of centennial team . . . Had worked extensively in Phillies' farm system since 1967 after spending chunk of pitching career with organization . . . Compiled lifetime major-league record of 20-22 . . . Major-league managerial mark stands at 169-130 . . . Strong-willed individual figures to have more than a few battles with meddling Steinbrenner . . . Named Executive of the Year in 1984 after rebuilding Cubs into NL East champions as general manager . . . Served in that capacity from 1982-87 before clashes with officials of Tribune Company, which owns Cubs, led to dismissal . . . Considered great judge of young talent . . . Born Aug. 4, 1934, in Newport, Del.

GREATEST FIRST BASEMAN

On June 2, 1925, Wally Pipp had a headache and was told by Yankee manager Miller Huggins to "take the day off." Pipp was replaced at first base by Lou Gehrig.

After Lou played in a record 2,130 consecutive games, Gehrig's place in history was secure and Pipp's was, too. No headache has ever been more infamous.

"The Iron Horse" was as talented as he was durable. In 1931, he set an American League record with 184 RBI and he knocked in more than 100 runs for 13 consecutive years from 1926-38.

But, during the Yankees' 1938 World Series sweep of the Cubs, it was obvious that Gehrig's strength was diminishing. He produced only four singles with no home runs or RBI in the four games. Several months later, he was diagnosed as having lateral sclerosis, since known as Lou Gehrig's Disease.

On July 4, 1939, a dying Gehrig told a huge crowd at Yankee Stadium, "Today, I consider myself the luckiest man on the face of the earth."

The words and the memory of the man will live forever.

ALL-TIME YANKEE SEASON RECORDS

BATTING: Babe Ruth, .393, 1923
HRs: Roger Maris, 61, 1961
RBIs: Lou Gehrig, 184, 1931
STEALS: Rickey Henderson, 93, 1988
WINS: Jack Chesbro, 41, 1904
STRIKEOUTS: Ron Guidry, 248, 1978

TORONTO BLUE JAYS

TEAM DIRECTORY: Honorary Chairman: R. Howard Webster; Chairman/Chief Exec. Off.: N.E. (Peter) Hardy; Exec. VP-Baseball: Pat Gillick; VP-Bus. Oper.: Paul Beeston; VP-Baseball: Al LaMacchia; VP-Baseball: Bob Mattick; VP-Finance: Bob Nicholson; Dir. Pub. Rel.: Howard Starkman; Mgr.: Jimy Williams. Home: Exhibition Stadium (43,737). Field distances: 330, l.f. line; 375, l.c.; 400, c.f.; 375, r.c.; 330 r.f. line; Skydome (52,000). Field distances: 330, l.f. line; 365, l.c.; 400, c.f.; 365, r.c.; 330, r.f. line. Spring training: Dunedin, Fla.

SCOUTING REPORT

HITTING: The Blue Jays aren't lacking for firepower after leading the AL in home runs (158) for the second straight year. They also led in total bases (2,330), triples (47) and slugging percentage (.419) in 1988.

Established slugger George Bell (.269, 24, 97), rising star Fred McGriff (.282, 34, 82), Tony Fernandez (.287, 5, 70) and Kelly Gruber (.278, 16, 81) are among the Blue Jays' heavy hitters.

The season-long conflict between manager Jimy Williams and Bell set a sour tone for 1988 and perhaps prompted management to ponder a large-scale shakeup. Lloyd Moseby (.239, 10, 42), Jesse Barfield (.244, 18, 56) and Bell were among the players shopped in trade talks at the winter meetings.

PITCHING: The biggest key to this staff will be Jimmy Key (12-5, 3.29), who required surgery last May to remove bone chips from his left elbow and was limited to 21 starts. A measure of Key's considerable ability and importance to the Blue Jays was that he held opponents to three earned runs or less in 15 of those 21 starts.

Dave Stieb (16-8, 3.04) is out to prove that last year's comeback season was no fluke. Jim Clancy left the Blue Jays to sign with the Astros as a free agent last winter and veteran Mike Flanagan (13-13, 4.18) is a .500 pitcher at best these days. Tom Henke (25 saves) is a capable bullpen closer, provided the Blue Jays can get to him.

FIELDING: The Jays more than hold their own defensively, ranking fourth in the AL in fielding percentage (.982) in 1988. Fernandez ranked third among shortstops in fielding percentage

Fred McGriff slugged his way to .552 mark, second in AL.

(.981) and total chances (640), McGriff paced all first baseman with a .997 fielding percentage and Ernie Whitt ranked second among catchers with a .994 percentage. The disgruntled Bell was the Jays' only weak link. His 15 errors represented the second-highest total among AL outfielders.

OUTLOOK: The Jays remain an unsolved mystery, a team that is nearly impossible to gauge. They have the talent to win but don't. Injuries took a heavy toll on the fast-closing Jays in '88. They lost players for a total of 285 days. If Toronto doesn't get it done this year, it's time to break up that old gang.

TORONTO BLUE JAYS 1989 ROSTER

MANAGER Jimy Williams

Coaches—Cito Gaston, John McLaren, Mike Squires, John Sullivan, Al Widmar

PITCHERS

No.	Name	1988 Club	W-L	IP	SO	ERA	B-T	Ht.	Wt.	Born
—	Blair, Willie	Dunedin	2-0	7	5	2.70	R-R	6-1	185	12/18/65 Paintsville, KY
		Knoxville	5-5	102	76	3.62				
27	Castillo, Tony	Dunedin	4-3	43	46	1.48	L-L	5-10	177	3/1/63 Venezuela
		Knoxville	1-0	8	11	0.00				
		Toronto	1-0	15	14	3.00				
55	Cerutti, John	Toronto	6-7	124	65	3.13	L-L	6-2	200	4/28/60 Albany, NY
—	Cummings, Steve	Knoxville	14-11	213	131	2.75	S-R	6-2	200	7/15/64 Houston, TX
38	Eichhorn, Mark	Syracuse	4-4	38	34	1.17	R-R	6-3	200	11/21/60 San Jose, CA
		Toronto	0-3	67	28	4.19				
24	*Flanagan, Mike	Toronto	13-13	211	99	4.18	L-L	6-0	195	12/16/51 Manchester, NH
—	Guzman, Juan	Knoxville	4-5	84	90	2.36	R-R	6-0	190	10/28/66 Dominican Republic
—	Hall, Darren	Dunedin	1-1	9	15	1.93	R-R	6-3	205	7/14/64 Marysville, OH
		Knoxville	3-2	40	33	2.23				
50	Henke, Tom	Toronto	4-4	68	66	2.91	R-R	6-5	225	12/21/57 Kansas City, MO
—	Hernandez, Xavier	Myrtle Beach	13-6	148	111	2.49	L-R	6-2	185	8/16/65 Port Arthur, TX
		Knoxville	2-4	68	33	2.90				
—	Jones, Dennis	Knoxville	8-4	84	98	2.58	L-L	6-6	195	7/26/66 Gadsden, AL
22	Key, Jimmy	Toronto	12-5	131	65	3.29	R-L	6-1	190	4/22/61 Huntsville, AL
13	Musselman, Jeff	Dunedin	0-0	6	4	3.18	L-L	6-0	185	6/21/63 Doylestown, PA
		Syracuse	4-1	49	31	2.94				
		Toronto	8-5	85	39	3.18				
45	Nunez, Jose	Syracuse	5-4	71	67	2.90	R-R	6-3	185	1/13/64 Dominican Republic
37	Stieb, Dave	Toronto	16-8	207	147	3.04	R-R	6-0	195	7/22/57 Santa Ana, CA
30	Stottlemyre, Todd	Toronto	4-8	98	67	5.69	L-R	6-3	190	5/20/65 Yakima, WA
		Syracuse	5-0	48	51	2.05				
31	Ward, Duane	Toronto	9-3	112	91	3.30	R-R	6-4	205	5/28/64 Parkview, NM
36	Wells, David	Toronto	3-5	64	56	4.62	L-L	6-4	225	5/20/63 Torrance, CA
		Syracuse	0-0	6	8	0.00				

CATCHERS

No.	Name	1988 Club	H	HR	RBI	Pct.	B-T	Ht.	Wt.	Born
10	Borders, Pat	Toronto	42	5	21	.273	R-R	6-2	205	5/14/63 Columbus, OH
		Syracuse	29	3	14	.242				
—	Cabrera, Francisco	Dunedin	14	1	9	.400	R-R	6-4	195	10/10/66 Dominican Republic
		Knoxville	122	20	54	.284				
52	Myers, Greg	Syracuse	34	7	21	.283	L-R	6-2	202	4/14/66 Riverside, CA
12	Whitt, Ernie	Toronto	100	16	70	.251	L-R	6-2	200	6/13/52 Detroit, MI

INFIELDERS

1	Fernandez, Tony	Toronto	186	5	70	.287	S-R	6-2	175	6/30/62 Dopminican Republic
23	Fielder, Cecil	Toronto	40	9	23	.230	R-R	6-3	216	9/21/63 Los Angeles, CA
17	Gruber, Kelly	Toronto	158	16	81	.278	R-R	6-0	185	2/26/62 Bellaire, TX
14	Infante, Alexis	Syracuse	102	2	28	.300	R-R	5-11	182	12/4/61 Venezuela
		Toronto	3	0	0	.200				
—	Kelly, Jimy	Knoxville	74	3	30	.210	R-R	6-0	150	7/13/70 Dominican Republic
4	Lee, Manny	Toronto	111	2	38	.291	S-R	5-9	161	6/17/65 Dominican Republic
2	Liriano, Nelson	Toronto	73	3	23	.264	S-R	5-10	165	6/3/64 Dominican Republic
		Syracuse	6	0	2	.294				
19	McGriff, Fred	Toronto	151	34	82	.282	L-L	6-3	215	10/31/63 Tampa, FL
5	Mulliniks, Rance	Toronto	101	12	48	.300	L-R	6-0	175	1/15/56 Tulare, CA
—	Sojo, Luis	Myrtle Beach	155	5	56	.289	R-R	5-11	174	1/3/66 Venezuela

OUTFIELDERS

29	Barfield, Jesse	Toronto	114	18	56	.244	R-R	6-1	200	10/29/59 Joliet, IL
—	Batiste, Kevin	Knoxville	85	3	22	.234	R-R	6-1	187	10/21/66 Galveston, TX
		Syracuse	24	1	9	.229				
11	Bell, George	Toronto	165	24	97	.269	R-R	6-1	194	10/21/59 Dominican Republic
40	Ducey, Rob	Syracuse	81	7	42	.256	L-R	6-2	173	5/24/65 Canada
		Toronto	17	0	6	.315				
—	Felix, Junior	Knoxville	91	3	25	.253	S-R	5-11	165	10/3/67 Dominican Republic
15	Moseby, Lloyd	Toronto	113	10	42	.239	L-R	6-3	200	11/5/59 Portland, AR
—	Whiten, Mark	Dunedin	97	7	37	.252	R-R	6-3	210	11/25/66 Pensacola, FL
		Knoxville	28	2	9	.259				

BLUE JAY PROFILES

GEORGE BELL 29 6-1 194 **Bats R Throws R**

Suffered huge drop from AL MVP season in 1987 . . . Collected 23 fewer home runs and 37 fewer RBI and his average plunged 39 points . . . His unhappiness about playing for manager Jimy Williams was overriding factor in decline . . . When Williams attempted to make him the designated hitter in spring training, this proud slugger told reporters, "Me and Jimy, we fight." . . . They clashed verbally several times last year . . . Went 0-for-15 from June 10-13 . . . Endured 20-game homerless drought from Aug. 4-28 . . . Played very poorly in left field, making 15 errors . . . Did come on offensively late in season, hitting safely in 19 of 20 games from Aug. 27 to Sept. 16 . . . Born Oct. 21, 1959, in San Pedro de Macoris, Dominican Republic . . . Acquired from Phillies in major-league draft in December 1980 . . . Phillies purchased his contract from Escogido of Dominican League in 1978 . . . Brother Juan plays for Orioles.

Year	Club	Pos.	G	AB	R	H	2B	3B	HR	RBI	SB	Avg.
1981	Toronto	OF	60	163	19	38	2	1	5	12	3	.233
1983	Toronto	OF	39	112	5	30	5	4	2	17	1	.268
1984	Toronto	OF-3B	159	606	85	177	39	4	26	87	11	.292
1985	Toronto	OF-1B	157	607	87	167	28	6	28	95	21	.275
1986	Toronto	OF-3B	159	641	101	198	38	6	31	108	7	.309
1987	Toronto	OF-2B-3B	156	610	111	188	32	4	47	134	5	.308
1988	Toronto	OF	156	614	78	165	27	5	24	97	4	.269
	Totals		886	3353	486	963	171	30	163	550	52	.287

TONY FERNANDEZ 26 6-2 175 **Bats S Throws R**

Dropped off somewhat from production of previous season, but still had a fine year . . . Average declined 35 points from 1987 and stolen-base total dropped from 32 to 15 . . . Was used as No. 3 hitter the first 10 days of season before going back to familiar leadoff role . . . One of the best-fielding shortstops in either league . . . Enjoyed 65-game errorless streak from June 10 to Aug. 26 . . . Born June 30, 1962, in San Pedro de Macoris, Dominican Republic . . . Signed as free agent, April 24, 1979 . . . Fractured right elbow during 1987 stretch run and his absence cost Blue Jays dearly in final week . . . Twin brother Jose played in Blue Jays' system.

Year	Club	Pos.	G	AB	R	H	2B	3B	HR	RBI	SB	Avg.
1983	Toronto	SS	15	34	5	9	1	1	0	2	0	.265
1984	Toronto	SS-3B	88	233	29	63	5	3	3	19	5	.270
1985	Toronto	SS	161	564	71	163	31	10	2	51	13	.289
1986	Toronto	SS	163	687	91	213	33	9	10	65	25	.310
1987	Toronto	SS	146	578	90	186	29	8	5	67	32	.322
1988	Toronto	SS	154	648	76	186	41	4	5	70	15	.287
	Totals		727	2744	362	820	140	35	25	274	90	.299

ERNIE WHITT 36 6-2 200 **Bats L Throws R**

Catcher's strong second half resulted in usual solid season . . . Slammed five homers in 10 games from Aug. 8-23 . . . Posted .319 average to go with five homers and 15 RBI in August . . . Tied personal high with six RBI vs. Boston Sept. 27 . . . Clubbed two home runs in that game for second time last season . . . Did not hit safely in more than three consecutive games through All-Star break . . . Born June 13, 1952, in Detroit . . . Acquired from Red Sox in AL expansion draft in November 1976 . . . Was Boston's 15th-round pick in June 1972 draft.

Year	Club	Pos.	G	AB	R	H	2B	3B	HR	RBI	SB	Avg.
1976	Boston	C	8	18	4	4	2	0	1	3	0	.222
1977	Toronto	C	23	41	4	7	3	0	0	6	0	.171
1978	Toronto	C	2	4	0	0	0	0	0	0	0	.000
1980	Toronto	C	106	295	23	70	12	2	6	34	1	.237
1981	Toronto	C	74	195	16	46	9	0	1	16	5	.236
1982	Toronto	C	105	284	28	74	14	2	11	42	3	.261
1983	Toronto	C	123	344	53	88	15	2	17	56	1	.256
1984	Toronto	C	124	315	35	75	12	1	15	46	0	.238
1985	Toronto	C	139	412	55	101	21	3	19	64	3	.245
1986	Toronto	C	131	395	48	106	19	2	16	56	0	.268
1987	Toronto	C	135	446	57	120	24	1	19	75	0	.269
1988	Toronto	C	127	398	63	100	11	2	16	70	4	.251
	Totals		1097	3147	386	791	142	14	121	468	17	.251

FRED McGRIFF 25 6-3 215 **Bats L Throws L**

Given first-base job in spring training, this rising star responded by smashing 34 home runs, a club record for a left-handed hitter . . . Finished second in AL in home runs and slugging percentage at .552 . . . He and Braves' Dale Murphy were only major-league regulars to have more extra-base hits than singles . . . Led club in walks (79), but also in strikeouts (149) . . . Born Oct. 31, 1963, in Tampa . . . Yankees' ninth-round pick in June 1981 draft . . . Acquired from Yanks with Dave Collins, Mike Morgan and cash for Dale Murray and Tom Dodd, Oct. 6, 1983.

Year	Club	Pos.	G	AB	R	H	2B	3B	HR	RBI	SB	Avg.
1986	Toronto	1B	3	5	1	1	0	0	0	0	0	.200
1987	Toronto	1B	107	295	58	73	16	0	20	43	3	.247
1988	Toronto	1B	154	536	100	151	35	4	34	82	6	.282
	Totals		264	836	159	225	51	4	54	125	9	.269

KELLY GRUBER 27 6-0 185 **Bats R Throws R**

Replaced injured Rance Mulliniks in first inning of home opener April 11 and took over third-base job . . . Went 4-for-6 with two homers and five RBI in that game . . . Can also play second . . . Put together career-high 12-game hitting streak from June 22 to July 4, batting .392 during that time . . . Born Feb. 26, 1962, in Bellaire, Tex. . . . Obtained from Cleveland in major-league draft in December 1983 . . . Indians' 10th-round pick in June 1980 . . . Attended University of Texas for one semester.

Year	Club	Pos.	G	AB	R	H	2B	3B	HR	RBI	SB	Avg.
1984	Toronto	3B-OF-SS	15	16	1	1	0	0	1	2	0	.063
1985	Toronto	3B-2B	5	13	0	3	0	0	0	1	0	.231
1986	Toronto	3B-2B-OF-SS	87	143	20	28	4	1	5	15	2	.196
1987	Toronto	3B-SS-2B-OF	138	341	50	80	14	3	12	36	12	.235
1988	Toronto	3B-SS-2B-OF	158	569	75	158	33	5	16	81	23	.278
	Totals		403	1082	146	270	51	9	34	135	37	.250

JIMMY KEY 27 6-1 190 **Bats R Throws L**

Underwent arthroscopic surgery May 4 to remove two bone chips from left elbow . . . Pitched well after being activated June 29 . . . Won first four starts and five of first six decisions . . . Held opposition to three earned runs or less in 15 of 21 starts . . . Tossed pair of two-hit, 1-0 shutouts, July 15 vs. Oakland and Sept. 28 vs. Boston . . . Placed second to Boston's Roger Clemens in 1987 Cy Young voting . . . Born April 22, 1961, in Huntsville, Ala. . . . Blue Jays' third-round selection in June 1982 draft.

Year	Club	G	IP	W	L	Pct.	SO	BB	H	ERA
1984	Toronto	63	62	4	5	.444	44	32	70	4.65
1985	Toronto	35	212⅔	14	6	.700	85	50	188	3.00
1986	Toronto	36	232	14	11	.560	141	74	222	3.57
1987	Toronto	36	261	17	8	.680	161	66	210	2.76
1988	Toronto	21	131⅓	12	5	.706	65	30	127	3.29
	Totals	191	899	61	35	.635	496	252	817	3.23

DAVE STIEB 31 6-0 195 **Bats R Throws R**

Finished comeback season with a flourish, tossing two near no-hitters in final two starts . . . Lost both bids in ninth inning on two-out, two-strike hits . . . Biggest heartbreaker was Sept. 24, when Indians' Julio Franco reached on bad-hop single over head of second baseman Manny Lee . . . Finished with one-hitter each time, winning 1-0 over Cleveland and 4-0 over Baltimore Sept. 30 . . . Closed season with club-record 31 shutout innings . . . Tied for second in AL with four shutouts . . . Held opponents to three earned runs or less in 21 of 31 starts . . . Born July 22, 1957, in Santa Ana, Cal. . . . Blue Jays' fifth-round selection in June 1978 draft . . . Attended Southern Illinois . . . Played semi-pro ball in Alaska . . . Has extensive guitar collection . . . Blue Jays' all-time leader in innings (2,251.2), wins (131), strikeouts (1,331), shutouts (26) and complete games (96).

Year	Club	G	IP	W	L	Pct.	SO	BB	H	ERA
1979	Toronto	18	129	8	8	.500	52	48	139	4.33
1980	Toronto	34	243	12	15	.444	108	83	232	3.70
1981	Toronto	25	184	11	10	.524	89	61	148	3.18
1982	Toronto	38	288⅓	17	14	.548	141	75	271	3.25
1983	Toronto	36	278	17	12	.586	187	93	223	3.04
1984	Toronto	35	267	16	8	.667	198	88	215	2.83
1985	Toronto	36	265	14	13	.519	167	96	206	2.48
1986	Toronto	37	205	7	12	.368	127	87	239	4.74
1987	Toronto	33	185	13	9	.591	115	87	164	4.09
1988	Toronto	32	207⅓	16	8	.667	147	79	157	3.04
	Totals	324	2251⅔	131	109	.546	1331	797	1994	3.37

TOM HENKE 31 6-5 225 **Bats R Throws R**

Team failure was reflected in his statistics . . . Save total dropped off by nine from league-leading mark of 34 in 1987 . . . Hard thrower got less work than in previous years, because club was in position to win less often than in past . . . Failed to record 100 strikeouts for first time in three years . . . Earned 100th career save Aug. 12 vs. Kansas City . . . Several hundred family members and friends made three-hour trip from his tiny hometown of Taos, Mo., to be on hand . . . Born Dec. 21, 1957, in Kansas City . . . Rangers' fourth-round pick in June 1980 draft . . . Selected by Blue Jays from Rangers in January 1985 from compensation pool for loss of free agent Cliff Johnson . . . Has 102 career saves, including club-record 99 for Blue Jays . . . Maintains extraordinary strikeouts-to-innings pitched ratio.

Year	Club	G	IP	W	L	Pct.	SO	BB	H	ERA
1982	Texas	8	15⅔	1	0	1.000	9	8	14	1.15
1983	Texas	8	16	1	0	1.000	17	4	16	3.38
1984	Texas	25	28⅓	1	1	.500	25	20	36	6.35
1985	Toronto	28	40	3	3	.500	42	8	29	2.03
1986	Toronto	63	91⅓	9	5	.643	118	32	63	3.35
1987	Toronto	72	94	0	6	.000	128	25	62	2.49
1988	Toronto	52	68	4	4	.500	66	24	60	2.91
	Totals	256	353⅓	19	19	.500	405	121	280	3.03

MIKE FLANAGAN 37 6-0 195 **Bats L Throws L**

Veteran southpaw was of minimal help in first full season with Jays . . . Pitched poorly at critical stage of season, dropping six of seven decisions from July 30 to Sept. 11 . . . Poor control was large part of his problem . . . Issued 79 walks while striking out only 85 in first 90⅔ innings . . . Allowed four walks or more in 11 of 34 starts . . . Born Dec. 16, 1951, in Manchester, N.H. . . . Acquired from Orioles for Oswald Peraza and Jose Mesa, Aug. 31, 1987 . . . Orioles' seventh-round pick in June 1973 draft, out of University of Massachusetts . . . Father Edward pitched for Red Sox.

Year	Club	G	IP	W	L	Pct.	SO	BB	H	ERA
1975	Baltimore	2	10	0	1	.000	7	6	9	2.70
1976	Baltimore	20	85	3	5	.375	56	33	83	4.13
1977	Baltimore	36	235	15	10	.600	149	70	235	3.64
1978	Baltimore	40	281	19	15	.559	167	87	271	4.04
1979	Baltimore	39	266	23	9	.781	190	70	245	3.08
1980	Baltimore	37	251	16	13	.552	128	71	278	4.12
1981	Baltimore	20	116	9	6	.600	72	37	808	4.19
1982	Baltimore	36	236	15	11	.577	103	76	233	3.97
1983	Baltimore	20	125⅓	12	4	.750	50	31	135	3.30
1984	Baltimore	34	226⅔	13	13	.500	115	81	213	3.53
1985	Baltimore	15	86	4	5	.444	42	28	101	5.13
1986	Baltimore	29	172	7	11	.389	96	66	179	4.24
1987	Bal.-Tor.	23	144	6	8	.429	93	51	148	4.06
1988	Toronto	34	211	13	13	.500	99	80	220	4.18
	Totals	385	2445	155	124	.556	1367	787	2458	3.88

TOP PROSPECT

ALEX SANCHEZ 22 6-2 185 **Bats R Throws R**

This strikeout pitcher is on the fast track to majors . . . Fanned 166 batters in 149⅓ innings and posted 12-5 record and a 2.53

ERA in 24 starts for Knoxville (AA) . . . Named Knoxville's Most Valuable Player, even though he didn't finish season with Southern League club . . . Promoted to Syracuse (AAA) July 18 . . . Struck out 49 in 52 innings and went 3-3 with 3.81 ERA in nine starts . . . Born April 8, 1966, in Antioch, Cal. . . . Blue Jays' first-round selection in June 1987 draft, out of UCLA, where he was an All-American in 1986.

MANAGER JIMY WILLIAMS: Has been under gun since he was named manager after 1985 season, when Bobby Cox left to become GM in Atlanta . . . Cox had guided Blue Jays to division title, putting Williams in difficult position of trying to match predecessor . . . Has stormy relationship with several players, particularly slugger George Bell, with whom he has clashed repeatedly . . . Jays surprised many by giving Williams new one-year contract . . . Team morale has deteriorated since Williams took over . . . Served as Blue Jays' third-base coach for six seasons . . . Managed in California organization from 1974-79 . . . Major-league career as shortstop consisted of 14 games in which he hit .214 with St. Louis in 1966 and 1967 . . . Born Oct. 4, 1943, in Arroyo Grande, Cal. . . . Graduated from Fresno State, where he majored in animal science . . . Major-league managerial mark stands at 269-217.

GREATEST FIRST BASEMAN

The Blue Jays created an opening at first base for Willie Upshaw on May 5, 1982, when they traded an aging John Mayberry to the Yankees. Toronto would never regret the move.

That year, Upshaw led the club with 21 home runs, 75 RBI and 14 game-winning RBI and topped all first basemen with

1,556 total chances. He really blossomed in 1983, when he became the first Toronto player to surpass 100 RBI with 104.

Upshaw was dealt to the Indians in 1988, but he remains an integral part of Blue Jays' history. Upshaw ranks second on the club's all-time list in runs (538), games (1,115), at-bats (3,710), doubles (177) and walks (390). He is third in hits (982), fourth in RBI (478) and fifth in home runs (112).

When the Blue Jays reflect on their building years, Upshaw's name will always come to mind.

ALL-TIME BLUE JAY SEASON RECORDS

BATTING: Tony Fernandez, .322, 1987
HRs: George Bell, 47, 1987
RBIs: George Bell, 134, 1987
STEALS: Damaso Garcia, 54, 1982
WINS: Dave Stieb, 17, 1982, 1983
Doyle Alexander, 17, 1984, 1985
Jimmy Key, 17,1987
STRIKEOUTS: Dave Stieb, 198, 1984

CALIFORNIA ANGELS

TEAM DIRECTORY: Chairman-Pres.: Gene Autry; VP: Jackie Autry; GM: Mike Port; Dir. Minor League Oper.: Bill Bavasi; Dir. Pub. Rel.: Tim Mead; Trav. Sec.: Frank Sims; Mgr.: Doug Rader. Home: Anaheim Stadium (65,158). Field distances: 333, l.f. line; 386, l.c.; 404, c.f.; 386, r.c.; 333, r.f. line. Spring training: Mesa, Ariz., and Palm Springs, Cal.

SCOUTING REPORT

HITTING: One of new manager Doug Rader's biggest challenges will be breathing life into an offense that lacks power.

Only three AL teams finished with fewer homers than the Angels' 124 in 1988, which represented a 48-homer plunge from the club's total in 1987. An offensive revival hinges on Wally Joyner (.295, 13, 85) regaining his slugging form of 1987, when he smashed 34 home runs. The Angels also need Devon White (.259, 11, 51) to stay healthier than he did in 1988, when he missed one-quarter of the season with injuries.

The return of Lance Parrish (.215, 15, 60) to the American League may be exactly what he needs to excel again after two nightmarish seasons in Philadelphia. Chili Davis (.268, 21, 93) and Johnny Ray (.306, 6, 83) are two strong offensive players.

PITCHING: The Angels tried hard to improve themselves in this area over the winter, but failed and will have to rely on most of the same pitchers who failed them so miserably last year. In 1988, Angel pitchers compiled a bloated 4.32 ERA and permitted 771 runs, the second-highest total in the majors.

Longtime ace Mike Witt (13-16, 4.15) must find a way to regain his form after surrending a club-record 130 runs. Kirk McCaskill (8-6, 4.31), who once provided a potent one-two combination with Witt, is a huge question mark after two injury-filled seasons. Former Twin Bert Blyleven (10-17, 5.43) may have too much mileage on his arm to help. Chuck Finley (9-15, 4.17) and Willie Fraser (12-13, 5.41, 33 home runs) are two youngsters whose development is essential.

If the starters can do their part, hard-throwing Bryan Harvey (7-5, 2.13, 17 saves) will finish the job.

FIELDING: The Angels' pitching problems are magnified by a porous defense. Ray and Davis are the chief culprits. Ray committed five errors in left field last year and 15 after being moved

Wally Joyner is Angel of death to opposing pitchers.

to second base. Davis set an unwelcome club record with 19 outfield errors.

Joyner and Dick Schofield are bright spots. Joyner led AL first basemen in putouts (1,369), assists (143) and double plays (148). Schofield repeated his 1987 performance by leading AL shortstops in fielding percentage (.983).

OUTLOOK: In December, the Angels tried to buy their way back into contention by vigorously pursuing free-agent pitchers Nolan Ryan and Bruce Hurst. They got neither. This summer, the team will come up as empty as the front office did last winter.

CALIFORNIA ANGELS 1989 ROSTER

MANAGER Doug Rader

Coaches—Joe Coleman, Bobby Knoop, Marcel Lachemann, Jimmie Reese, Moose Stubing

PITCHERS

No.	Name	1988 Club	W-L	IP	SO	ERA	B-T	Ht.	Wt.	Born
28	Blyleven, Bert	Minnesota	10-17	207	145	5.43	R-R	6-3	205	4/6/51 Holland
41	Cedeno, Vinicio	Midland	1-2	76	66	4.48	R-R	5-10	185	4/6/64 Dominican Republic
43	Charland, Colin	Palm Springs	17-5	204	183	2.51	L-L	6-3	205	11/13/65 New York, NY
42	Clark, Terry	Edmonton	7-6	114	59	4.51	R-R	6-2	196	10/10/60 Los Angeles, CA
		California	6-6	94	39	5.07				
33	Cliburn, Stewart	California	4-2	84	42	4.07	R-R	6-0	192	12/19/56 Jackson, MS
36	Corbett, Sherman	Midland	3-2	48	40	3.40	L-L	6-4	203	11/3/62 New Braunfels, TX
		California	2-1	46	28	4.14				
48	Fetters, Mike	Midland	8-8	114	101	5.92	R-R	6-4	200	12/19/64 Van Nuys, CA
		Edmonton	2-0	14	11	1.93				
31	Finley, Chuck	California	9-15	194	111	4.17	L-L	6-6	215	11/26/62 Monroe, LA
27	Fraser, Willie	California	12-13	195	86	5.41	R-R	6-1	208	5/26/64 New York, NY
34	Harvey, Bryan	Edmonton	0-0	6	10	3.18	R-R	6-2	212	6/2/63 Chattanooga, TN
		California	7-5	76	67	2.13				
17	Lazorko, Jack	Edmonton	11-8	149	59	3.87	R-R	5-11	218	3/30/56 Hoboken, NJ
		California	0-1	38	19	3.35				
45	Lovelace, Vance	Edmonton	1-3	69	58	6.10	L-L	6-5	235	8/9/63 Tampa, FL
		California	0-0	1	0	13.50				
18	Lugo, Urbano	Edmonton	9-6	116	69	5.26	R-R	5-11	197	8/12/62 Venezuela
		California	0-0	2	1	9.00				
15	McCaskill, Kirk	California	8-6	146	98	4.31	R-R	6-1	200	4/9/61 Canada
38	Minton, Greg	Palm Springs	0-0	4	4	0.00	S-R	6-2	207	7/29/51 Lubbock, TX
		California	4-5	79	46	2.85				
44	Monteleone, Rich	Edmonton	4-7	122	97	5.08	R-R	6-2	217	3/22/63 Tampa, FL
		California	0-0	4	3	0.00				
46	Petry, Dan	Palm Springs	1-2	15	11	6.60	R-R	6-4	215	11/13/58 Palo Alto, CA
		California	3-9	140	64	4.38				
39	Witt, Mike	California	13-16	250	133	4.15	R-R	6-7	195	7/20/60 Fullerton, CA

CATCHERS

No.	Name	1988 Club	H	HR	RBI	Pct.	B-T	Ht.	Wt.	Born
32	Miller, Darrell	Edmonton	39	4	19	.317	R-R	6-2	210	2/26/59 Washington, DC
		California	31	2	7	.221				
13	Parrish, Lance	Philadelphia	91	15	60	.215	R-R	6-3	220	6/15/56 Clairton, PA
—	Schroeder, Bill	Milwaukee	19	5	10	.156	R-R	6-2	200	9/7/58 Baltimore, MD
		Denver	4	0	3	.235				

INFIELDERS

No.	Name	1988 Club	H	HR	RBI	Pct.	B-T	Ht.	Wt.	Born
7	Eppard, Jim	Edmonton	37	0	16	.262	L-L	6-2	181	4/27/60 South Bend, IN
		California	32	0	14	.283				
16	Howell, Jack	California	127	16	63	.254	L-R	6-0	201	8/18/61 Tucson, AZ
21	Joyner, Wally	California	176	13	85	.295	L-L	6-2	190	6/16/62 Atlanta, GA
35	Manto, Jeff	Midland	123	24	101	.301	R-R	6-3	210	8/23/64 Bristol, PA
37	McCollom, Jim	Midland	155	20	75	.343	R-R	6-1	195	4/23/63 New York, NY
10	McLemore, Mark	California	56	2	16	.240	S-R	5-11	195	10/4/64 San Diego, CA
		Edmonton	12	0	6	.267				
		Palm Springs	15	0	6	.341				
3	Ray, Johnny	California	184	6	83	.306	S-R	5-11	180	3/1/57 Chouteau, OK
22	Schofield, Dick	California	126	6	34	.239	R-R	5-10	178	11/21/62 Springfield, IL
9	Stevens, Lee	Midland	123	23	76	.297	L-L	6-4	205	7/10/67 Kansas City, MO

OUTFIELDERS

No.	Name	1988 Club	H	HR	RBI	Pct.	B-T	Ht.	Wt.	Born
20	Armas, Tony	California	100	13	49	.272	R-R	6-1	220	7/2/53 Venezuela
11	Bichette, Dante	Edmonton	136	14	81	.267	R-R	6-3	212	11/18/63 West Palm Beach, FL
		California	12	0	8	.261				
24	Davis, Chili	California	161	21	93	.268	S-R	6-3	200	1/17/60 Jamaica
5	Downing, Brian	California	117	25	64	.242	R-R	5-10	194	10/9/50 Los Angeles, CA
30	White, Devon	California	118	11	51	.259	S-R	6-2	180	12/29/62 Jamaica

ANGEL PROFILES

WALLY JOYNER 26 6-2 190 **Bats L Throws L**

Continues to reign as one of game's best young players . . . Established career highs in average, games and hits . . . With 176 hits, he became first Angel to register 160 or more hits in three consecutive seasons . . . Produced only one home run against a left-hander . . . Led AL first basemen with 1,369 putouts, 143 assists and 148 double plays . . . Born June 16, 1962, in Atlanta . . . Selected by Angels in third round of June 1983 draft . . . Placed second to Oakland's Jose Canseco in balloting for 1986 Rookie of the Year . . . Became ninth player in history to drive in 100 or more runs his first two seasons . . . Attended Brigham Young.

Year	Club	Pos.	G	AB	R	H	2B	3B	HR	RBI	SB	Avg.
1986	California.	1B	154	593	82	172	27	3	22	100	5	.290
1987	California.	1B	149	564	100	161	33	1	34	117	8	.285
1988	California.	1B	158	597	81	176	31	2	13	85	8	.295
	Totals		461	1754	263	509	91	6	69	302	21	.290

JOHNNY RAY 31 5-11 180 **Bats S Throws R**

Helped Angels offensively, but hurt them defensively . . . Established career highs in hits, doubles and RBI . . . His 42 doubles tied for second-highest total in majors . . . Became first Angel to hit .300 since Rod Carew in 1983 . . . Reached base safely via hit, walk or hit by pitch in 127 of his 153 games . . . Performed poorly in the field . . . Committed five errors in left field, 15 at second base . . . Born March 1, 1957, in Chouteau, Okla. . . . Acquired from Pirates for Bill Merrifield and Mitch Garcia, Aug. 29, 1987 . . . Astros' 12th-round pick in June 1979 draft . . . Tough to fan.

Year	Club	Pos.	G	AB	R	H	2B	3B	HR	RBI	SB	Avg.
1981	Pittsburgh	2B	31	102	10	25	11	0	0	6	0	.245
1982	Pittsburgh	2B	162	647	79	182	30	7	7	63	16	.281
1983	Pittsburgh	2B	151	576	68	163	38	7	5	53	18	.283
1984	Pittsburgh	2B	155	555	75	173	38	6	6	67	11	.312
1985	Pittsburgh	2B	154	594	67	163	33	3	7	70	13	.274
1986	Pittsburgh	2B	155	579	67	174	33	0	7	78	6	.301
1987	Pittsburgh	2B	123	472	48	129	19	3	5	54	4	.273
1987	California.	2B	30	127	16	44	11	0	0	15	0	.346
1988	California.	2B-OF	153	602	75	184	42	7	6	83	4	.306
	Totals		1114	4254	505	1237	255	33	43	489	72	.291

CHILI DAVIS 29 6-3 200 **Bats S Throws R**

Signed as free agent prior to 1988 season, he responded with career highs in games, at-bats, doubles and RBI . . . Recorded 46 multiple-hit games . . . Honored as AL Player of the Month in July, when he hit .376 with seven home runs and 25 RBI . . . Ten of his 21 homers were bases-empty shots . . . Played terribly in outfield, making club-record 19 errors there . . . Born Jan. 17, 1960, in Kingston, Jamaica . . . Giants' 11th-round pick in June 1977 draft . . . Has .444 career mark in 27 at-bats vs. Mets' Dwight Gooden.

Year	Club	Pos.	G	AB	R	H	2B	3B	HR	RBI	SB	Avg.
1981	San Francisco	OF	8	15	1	2	0	0	0	0	2	.133
1982	San Francisco	OF	154	641	86	167	27	6	19	76	24	.261
1983	San Francisco	OF	137	486	54	113	21	2	11	59	10	.233
1984	San Francisco	OF	137	499	87	157	21	6	21	81	12	.315
1985	San Francisco	OF	136	481	53	130	25	2	13	56	15	.270
1986	San Francisco	OF	153	526	71	146	28	3	13	70	16	.278
1987	San Francisco	OF	149	500	80	125	22	1	24	76	16	.250
1988	California.	OF	158	600	81	161	29	3	21	93	9	.268
	Totals		1032	3748	513	1001	173	23	122	511	104	.267

LANCE PARRISH 32 6-3 220 **Bats R Throws R**

Veteran catcher returns to AL after two very disappointing seasons in NL . . . Acquired from Phillies in October for minor-league pitcher David Holdridge . . . Had signed with Philadelphia as a free agent before the 1987 season . . . Poor start led him to quickly fall out of favor with hometown fans . . . Chronic back problems make him question mark at this stage . . . Angels allowed 17-year vet catcher Bob Boone to sign with Kansas City as a free agent, giving Parrish the job . . . Born June 15, 1956, in Clairton, Pa. . . . Passed up football scholarship to UCLA to sign with Detroit as 16th player chosen in June 1974 draft.

Year	Club	Pos.	G	AB	R	H	2B	3B	HR	RBI	SB	Avg.
1977	Detroit.	C	12	46	10	9	2	0	3	7	0	.196
1978	Detroit.	C	85	288	37	63	11	3	14	41	0	.219
1979	Detroit.	C	143	493	65	136	26	3	19	65	6	.276
1980	Detroit.	C-1B-OF	144	553	79	158	34	6	24	82	6	.286
1981	Detroit.	C	96	348	39	85	18	2	10	46	2	.244
1982	Detroit.	C-OF	133	486	75	138	19	2	32	87	3	.284
1983	Detroit.	C	155	605	80	163	42	3	27	114	1	.269
1984	Detroit.	C	147	578	75	137	16	2	33	98	2	.237
1985	Detroit.	C	140	549	64	150	27	1	28	98	2	.273
1986	Detroit.	C	91	327	53	84	6	1	22	62	0	.257
1987	Philadelphia.	C	130	466	42	114	21	0	17	67	0	.245
1988	Philadelphia.	C-1B	123	424	44	91	17	2	15	60	0	.215
	Totals		1399	5163	663	1328	239	25	244	827	22	.257

DEVON WHITE 26 6-2 180 **Bats S Throws R**

Promising young outfielder missed one-quarter of season with various injuries, including rib-cage problem and May 21 surgery on right knee . . . Returned from surgery June 10 and was held hitless in first seven games (0-for-23) . . . Slugged three leadoff home runs . . . Could take better advantage of his speed if he was more patient at plate . . . Drew only 23 walks and had 455 at-bats . . . Born Dec. 29, 1962, in Kingston, Jamaica . . . Selected by Angels in sixth round of June 1981 draft.

Year	Club	Pos.	G	AB	R	H	2B	3B	HR	RBI	SB	Avg.
1985	California........	OF	21	7	7	1	0	0	0	0	3	.143
1986	California........	OF	29	51	8	12	1	1	1	3	6	.235
1987	California........	OF	159	639	103	168	33	5	24	87	32	.263
1988	California........	OF	122	455	76	118	22	2	11	51	17	.259
	Totals		331	1152	194	299	56	8	36	141	58	.260

MIKE WITT 28 6-7 195 **Bats R Throws R**

Heavy workload appears to be taking toll on Angels' ace . . . Strikeout total of 133 was his lowest since 1983 . . . Established club record he could do without, permitting 130 runs . . . Endured rocky 1-6 start with 5.48 ERA . . . Pitched 200-plus innings for fifth straight season . . . Born July 20, 1960, in Fullerton, Cal. . . . Selected by Angels in fourth round of June 1978 draft . . . Threw perfect game vs. Rangers, Sept. 30, 1984.

Year	Club	G	IP	W	L	Pct.	SO	BB	H	ERA
1981	California	22	129	8	9	.471	75	47	123	3.28
1982	California	33	179⅔	8	6	.571	85	47	177	3.51
1983	California	43	154	7	14	.333	77	75	173	4.91
1984	California	34	246⅔	15	11	.577	196	84	227	3.47
1985	California	35	250	15	9	.625	180	98	228	3.56
1986	California	34	269	18	10	.643	208	73	218	2.84
1987	California	36	247	16	14	.533	192	84	252	4.01
1988	California	34	249⅔	13	16	.448	133	87	263	4.15
	Totals	271	1725	100	89	.529	1146	595	1661	3.68

BRYAN HARVEY 25 6-2 212 **Bats R Throws R**

Angels' Minor League Player of the Year in 1987 excelled after promotion to majors April 21 . . . Rang up 17 saves in 24 opportunities . . . Held opponents to .214 average . . . Stranded 34 of 46 inherited runners . . . Angels were 35-15 in games he appeared . . . Underwent arthroscopic surgery to remove two bone chips from right elbow Sept. 21 . . . Born June 2, 1963, in Chattanooga, Tenn. . . . Signed by Angels as free agent Aug. 20, 1984, after impressive workout . . . Went 2-2 with 2.04 ERA and 20 saves for Midland (AA) in 1987.

Year	Club	G	IP	W	L	Pct.	SO	BB	H	ERA
1987	California	3	5	0	0	.000	3	2	6	0.00
1988	California	50	76	7	5	.583	67	20	59	2.13
	Totals	53	81	7	5	.583	70	22	65	2.00

KIRK McCASKILL 28 6-1 200 **Bats R Throws R**

Suffered major injury for second straight season . . . Was disabled Aug. 9 with nerve irritation in right arm . . . A fine pitcher when healthy . . . Fashioned career-high six-game winning streak from June 16 to July 25 and compiled 2.71 ERA in that eight-start span . . . Missed most of 1987 with bone spur . . . Selected by Angels in fourth round of June 1982 draft . . . Born April 9, 1961, in Kapuskasing, Ont. . . . Son of former pro hockey player Ted McCaskill . . . First collegian picked in 1981 NHL draft, selected in fourth round by Winnipeg . . . Attended University of Vermont.

Year	Club	G	IP	W	L	Pct.	SO	BB	H	ERA
1985	California	30	189⅔	12	12	.500	102	64	189	4.70
1986	California	34	246⅓	17	10	.630	202	92	207	3.36
1987	California	14	74⅔	4	6	.400	56	34	84	5.67
1988	California	23	146⅓	8	6	.571	98	61	155	4.31
	Totals	101	657	41	34	.547	458	251	635	4.22

BERT BLYLEVEN 38 6-3 205 **Bats R Throws R**

Last year was a season to forget for this declining veteran whom Twins dealt to Angels for three minor leaguers after the '88 season . . . Won four straight in June to boost record to 7-6 with 4.51 ERA . . . Then went into tailspin that saw him compile 3-11 record with 6.65 ERA in his final 14 decisions . . . Disabled from July 30 to Aug. 15 with sprained right thumb . . . Born April 6, 1951, in Zeist, Holland . . . Reacquired by Twins from Indians for Jay Bell, Jim Weaver, Curt Wardle and Rich Yett, Aug. 1, 1985 . . . Originally drafted by Twins as the third-round pick in June 1969 . . . Owns one of best curves in the game . . . Pitched no-hitter vs. Angels, Sept. 22, 1977.

Year	Club	G	IP	W	L	Pct.	SO	BB	H	ERA
1970	Minnesota	27	164	10	9	.526	135	47	143	3.18
1971	Minnesota	38	278	16	15	.516	224	59	267	2.82
1972	Minnesota	39	287	17	17	.500	228	69	247	2.73
1973	Minnesota	40	325	20	17	.541	258	67	296	2.52
1974	Minnesota	37	281	17	17	.500	249	77	244	2.66
1975	Minnesota	35	276	15	10	.600	233	84	219	3.00
1976	Minn.-Tex.	36	298	13	16	.448	219	81	283	2.87
1977	Texas	30	235	14	12	.538	182	69	181	2.72
1978	Pittsburgh	34	244	14	10	.583	182	66	217	3.02
1979	Pittsburgh	37	237	12	5	.706	172	92	238	3.61
1980	Pittsburgh	34	217	8	13	.381	168	59	219	3.82
1981	Cleveland	20	159	11	7	.611	107	40	145	2.89
1982	Cleveland	4	20⅓	2	2	.500	19	11	16	4.87
1983	Cleveland	24	156⅓	7	10	.412	123	44	160	3.91
1984	Cleveland	33	245	19	7	.731	170	74	204	2.87
1985	Clev.-Minn.	37	293⅔	17	16	.515	206	75	264	3.16
1986	Minnesota	36	271⅔	17	14	.548	215	58	262	4.01
1987	Minnesota	37	267	15	12	.556	196	101	249	4.01
1988	Minnesota	33	207⅓	10	17	.370	145	51	240	5.43
	Totals	611	4462⅓	254	226	.529	3431	1224	4094	3.25

CHUCK FINLEY 26 6-6 215 Bats L Throws L

A season of hard luck and disappointment for this young pitcher . . . His 15 defeats represented the highest total by Angel left-hander since Frank Tanana dropped club-record 19 in 1974 . . . Angels scored two runs or less nine times in his starts . . . Born Nov. 26, 1962, in Monroe, La. . . . Selected by Angels in first round of January 1985 draft . . . Attended Northeast Louisiana State.

Year	Club	G	IP	W	L	Pct.	SO	BB	H	ERA
1986	California	25	46⅓	3	1	.750	37	23	40	3.30
1987	California	35	90⅔	2	7	.222	63	43	102	4.67
1988	California	31	194⅓	9	15	.375	111	82	191	4.17
	Totals	91	331⅓	14	23	.378	211	148	333	4.18

WILLIE FRASER 24 6-1 208 Bats R Throws R

Streaky season was mostly sour . . . Lost 10 of first 16 decisions and ended year with three straight defeats . . . Won six straight from July 29 to Sept. 16 . . . Surrendered team-high 33 home runs . . . Fifty-two of the 129 runs he allowed came on home runs . . . Tossed one-hitter Aug. 10 vs. Seattle . . . Born May 26, 1964, in New York, N.Y. . . . Selected by

Angels in first round of June 1985 draft, out of Concordia College . . . Made rapid climb through Angels' system.

Year	Club	G	IP	W	L	Pct.	SO	BB	H	ERA
1986	California	1	4⅓	0	0	.000	2	1	6	8.31
1987	California	36	176⅔	10	10	.500	106	63	160	3.92
1988	California	34	194⅔	12	13	.480	86	80	203	5.41
	Totals	71	375⅔	22	23	.489	194	144	369	4.74

TOP PROSPECT

DANTE BICHETTE 25 6-3 215 Bats R Throws R

Preston Douglas, the scout who signed him, described him in reports as "a giant sleeper" and he may be right . . . This outfielder, selected by Angels in 17th round of June 1984 draft, hit .267 with 14 home runs and 81 RBI in second full season at Edmonton (AAA) . . . Hit .261 with eight RBI in 46 late-season at-bats with Angels . . . Began pro career as third baseman . . . Born Nov. 18, 1963, in West Palm Beach, Fla.

MANAGER DOUG RADER: Given what he described as a

"dream opportunity" when he was named manager in November, replacing Cookie Rojas . . . Twelfth manager in club's 28-year history . . . Had been employed by Angels as a scout . . . Second chance in the majors . . . Compiled a 155-200 mark as skipper of the Texas Rangers from 1983 until he was fired early in 1985 . . . Prior to that, he managed Triple-A Hawaii for three years . . . Was third-base coach at San Diego in 1978 and '79 and a White Sox coach in 1986 and '87 . . . Made his playing mark as a five-time Gold Glove third baseman in a 10½-year career, all but final two seasons with Houston . . . Had .251 lifetime BA . . . Odd mixture of disciplinarian and practical joker . . . Once crashed his motorcycle into a wall and greeted dinner guests in the nude . . . Born July 30, 1944, in Chicago . . . Played two years at Illinois Wesleyan before signing with Astros as free agent in 1964.

GREATEST FIRST BASEMAN

The Angels didn't get the best years of Rod Carew's professional life. Those came in the first 12 years of his career, which he spent with the Twins. However, the Angels did get seven very good seasons from Carew.

Carew made a big difference in 1979, his first season as an Angel, batting .318 and helping California reach the ALCS, in which he hit .412. The native of Gaton, Panama, then led the Angels in batting average in five of the next six seasons: 1980 (.331), 1981 (.305), 1982 (.319), 1983 (.339) and 1985 (.280).

Carew's .339 mark in 1983 stands as the club record and he is the Angels' career batting leader at .314. He also tops the Angels in games played at first base with 720. His retirement after the 1985 season created an opportunity for current first baseman Wally Joyner, whose early accomplishments indicate he is headed for a distinguished career. But Joyner will have to go some before he can be compared to Carew.

ALL-TIME ANGEL SEASON RECORDS

BATTING: Rod Carew, .339, 1983
HRs: Reggie Jackson, 39, 1982
RBIs: Don Baylor, 139, 1979
STEALS: Mickey Rivers, 70, 1975
WINS: Clyde Wright, 22, 1970
Nolan Ryan, 22, 1974
STRIKEOUTS: Nolan Ryan, 383, 1973

CHICAGO WHITE SOX

TEAM DIRECTORY: Chairman: Jerry Reinsdorf; Pres.: Eddie Einhorn; VP-GM: Larry Himes; Exec. VP: Howard Pizer; VP-Baseball Adm.: Jack Gould; Dir. Scouting-Player Dev.: Al Goldis; VP-Pub. Relations and Community Affairs: Chuck Adams; Trav. Sec.: Glen Rosenbaum; Mgr.: Jeff Torborg. Home: Comiskey Park (44,087). Field distances: 347, l.f. line; 382, l.c.; 409, c.f.; 382, r.c., 347, r.f. line. Spring training: Sarasota, Fla.

SCOUTING REPORT

HITTING: The White Sox don't have the best talent in the league, but, at full strength, their lineup is considerably better than the one that ranked 13th in the AL in batting average (.244) and runs scored (631) in 1988.

Carlton Fisk (.277, 19, 50), Ivan Calderon (.212, 14, 35) and Greg Walker (.247, 8, 42) are all solid players when healthy. However, the 41-year-old Fisk's age, the surgery on Calderon's left shoulder and the near-fatal viral infection that struck Walker make all three questionable contributors in 1989.

Another White Sox concern is the drop in production experienced by Harold Baines (.277, 13, 81), who failed to crack 20 home runs for the first time in seven seasons. Dan Pasqua (.277, 20, 50) still must prove he can handle left-handers, as all of his team-leading 20 homers last year came against righties. Maybe former Indian Ron Kittle (.258, 18, 43), whom the White Sox signed as a free agent, can provide a boost.

PITCHING: New manager Jeff Torborg has the ingredients for a solid pitching staff. Melido Perez (12-10, 3.79) and Jack McDowell (5-10, 3.97) are two young pitchers whom the White Sox can build around. Jerry Reuss (13-9, 3.44) went from a non-roster spring training invitee to a staff leader last year.

Bullpen stopper Bobby Thigpen (5-8, 3.30) was in demand over the winter, which wasn't surprising. He set a club record with 34 saves and figured in 39 of Chicago's 71 victories (a major-league-high 54.9 percent).

FIELDING: The White Sox feature baseball's other Ozzie, Ozzie Guillen. He may not be the equal of St. Louis' wizard, Ozzie Smith, but this guy plays a darn good shortstop, too. Guillen is coming off a 1988 season in which he broke the great Luis Aparicio's club record with 569 assists.

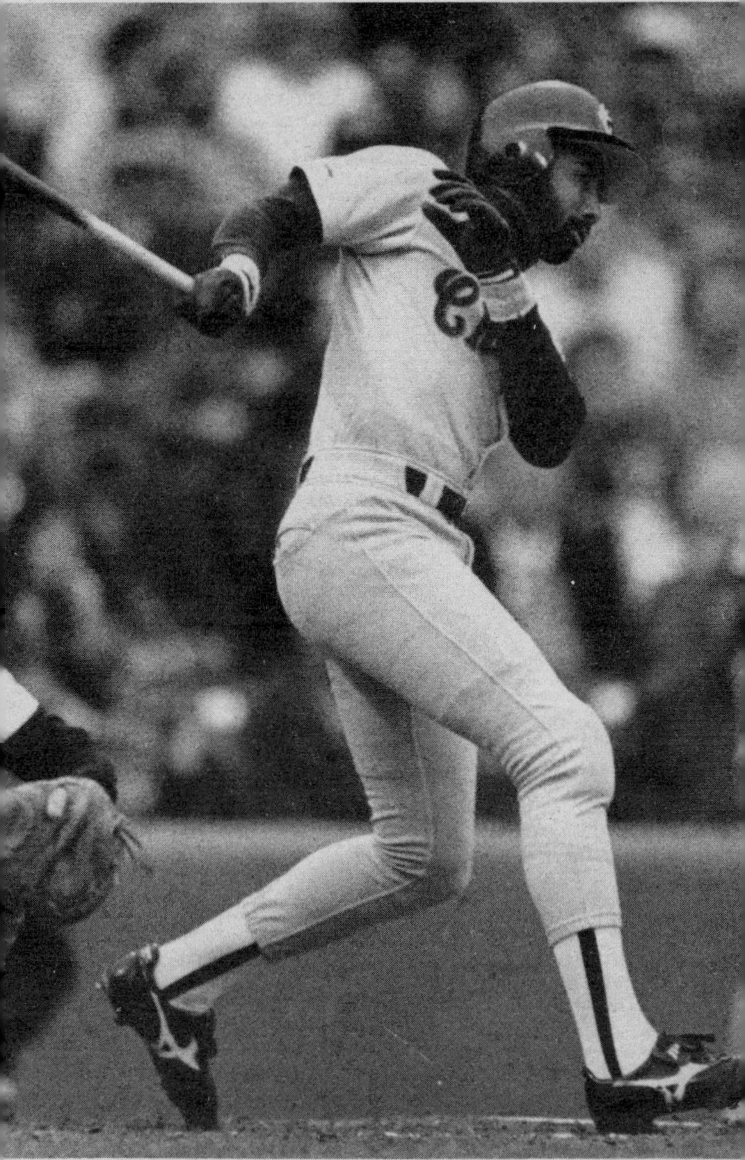

Harold Baines has put sock in the Sox for nine years.

CHICAGO WHITE SOX 1989 ROSTER

MANAGER Jeff Torborg
Coaches—Terry Bevington, Ron Clark, Sammy Ellis, Walt Hriniak, Glen Rosenbaum, Dave LaRoche

PITCHERS

No.	Name	1988 Club	W-L	IP	SO	ERA	B-T	Ht.	Wt.	Born
32	Bittiger, Jeff	Vancouver	4-1	52	49	1.04	R-R	5-10	175	4/13/62 Jersey City, NJ
		Chicago (AL)	2-4	62	33	4.23				
52	Davis, Joel	Vancouver	7-1	96	75	3.75	L-R	6-5	205	1/30/65 Jacksonville, FL
		Chicago (AL)	0-1	16	10	6.75				
31	Davis, John	Chicago (AL)	2-5	64	37	6.64	R-R	6-7	215	1/5/63 Chicago, IL
		Vancouver	1-0	17	9	3.18				
—	Drees, Tom	Birmingham	9-7	158	94	2.79	S-L	6-6	210	6/17/63 Des Moines, IA
—	Edwards, Wayne	Birmingham	9-12	167	136	4.90	L-L	6-5	185	3/7/64 Burbank, CA
		Vancouver	0-0	3	2	0.00				
—	Hibbard, Greg	Vancouver	11-11	144	65	4.12	L-L	6-0	180	9/13/64 New Orleans, LA
45	Hillegas, Shawn	Albuquerque	6-4	101	65	3.49	R-R	6-2	208	8/21/64 Dos Palos, CA
		Los Angeles	3-4	57	30	4.13				
		Chicago (AL)	3-2	40	26	3.15				
38	Jones, Barry	Pittsburgh	1-1	56	31	3.04	R-R	6-4	225	2/15/63 Centerville, IN
		Chicago (AL)	2-2	26	17	2.42				
47	Long, Bill	Chicago (AL)	8-11	174	77	4.03	R-R	6-0	185	2/29/60 Cincinnati, OH
56	Manzanillo, Ravelo	Tampa	10-6	130	140	3.04	L-L	5-10	190	10/17/63 Dominican Republic
		Chicago (AL)	0-1	9	10	5.79				
57	McCarthy, Tom	Tidewater	8-3	57	28	2.67	R-R	6-0	180	6/18/61 West Germany
		Vancouver	1-0	19	11	0.00				
		Chicago (AL)	2-0	13	5	1.38				
40	McDowell, Jack	Chicago (AL)	5-10	159	84	3.97	R-R	6-5	179	1/16/66 Van Nuys, CA
34	Patterson, Ken	Vancouver	6-5	86	89	3.23	L-L	6-4	210	7/8/64 Costa Mesa, CA
		Chicago (AL)	0-2	21	8	4.79				
—	Pawlowski, John	Chicago (AL)	1-0	14	10	8.36	R-R	6-2	175	9/6/63 Johnson City, NY
		Vancouver	0-0	21	11	4.22				
		Birmingham	2-3	27	28	3.29				
33	Perez, Melido	Chicago (AL)	12-10	197	138	3.79	R-R	6-4	180	2/15/66 Dominican Republic
—	Peterson, Adam	Vancouver	14-7	171	103	3.32	R-R	6-3	190	12/11/65 Long Beach, CA
		Chicago (AL)	0-1	6	5	13.50				
41	Reuss, Jerry	Chicago (AL)	13-9	183	73	3.44	L-L	6-5	227	6/19/49 St. Louis, MO
—	Rodriguez, Ricardo	Colorado Springs	8-6	127	55	3.06	R-R	6-2	200	9/21/60 Oakland, CA
		Cleveland	1-2	33	9	7.09				
46	Rosenberg, Steve	Vancouver	2-0	24	17	3.33	L-L	6-0	185	10/31/64 Brooklyn, NY
		Chicago (AL)	0-1	46	28	4.30				
37	Thigpen, Bobby	Chicago (AL)	5-8	90	62	3.30	R-R	6-3	195	7/17/63 Tallahassee, FL
—	Wojna, Ed	Vancouver	10-6	124	73	3.27	R-R	6-1	187	8/20/60 Bridgeport, CT

CATCHERS

No.	Name	1988 Club	H	HR	RBI	Pct.	B-T	Ht.	Wt.	Born
5	Karkovice, Ron	Vancouver	29	2	13	.250	R-R	6-1	215	8/8/63 Union, NJ
		Chicago (AL)	20	3	9	.174				
72	Fisk, Carlton	Chicago (AL)	70	19	50	.277	R-R	6-2	225	12/26/47 Bellows Falls, VT
27	Salas, Mark	Chicago (AL)	49	3	9	.250	L-R	6-0	205	3/8/61 Montebello, CA

INFIELDERS

No.	Name	1988 Club	H	HR	RBI	Pct.	B-T	Ht.	Wt.	Born
20	Diaz, Mike	Pittsburgh	17	0	5	.230	R-R	6-2	220	4/15/60 San Francisco, CA
		Chicago (AL)	36	3	12	.237				
13	Guillen, Ozzie	Chicago (AL)	148	0	39	.261	L-R	5-11	150	1/20/64 Venezuela
15	Hill, Donnie	Chicago (AL)	48	2	20	.217	S-R	5-10	160	11/12/60 Pomona, CA
		Vancouver	9	0	7	.346				
12	Lyons, Steve	Chicago (AL)	127	5	45	.269	L-R	6-3	195	6/3/60 Tacoma, WA
10	Manrique, Fred	Chicago (AL)	81	5	37	.235	R-R	6-1	175	11/5/61 Venezuela
28	Martinez, Carlos	Birmingham	138	14	73	.277	R-R	6-5	175	8/11/65 Venezuela
		Chicago (AL)	9	0	0	.164				
29	Walker, Greg	Chicago (AL)	93	8	42	.247	L-R	6-3	212	10/6/59 Douglas, GA

OUTFIELDERS

No.	Name	1988 Club	H	HR	RBI	Pct.	B-T	Ht.	Wt.	Born
3	Baines, Harold	Chicago (AL)	166	13	81	.277	L-L	6-2	194	3/15/59 Easton, MD
8	Boston, Daryl	Chicago (AL)	61	15	31	.217	L-L	6-3	203	1/4/63 Cincinnati, OH
22	Calderon, Ivan	Chicago (AL)	56	14	35	.212	R-R	6-1	221	3/19/62 Puerto Rico
—	Davis, Mark	Birmingham	72	6	27	.290	R-R	6-0	170	11/25/64 Lemon Grove, CA
		Vancouver	51	4	29	.212				
17	Gallagher, Dave	Vancouver	44	4	27	.336	R-R	6-0	180	9/20/60 Trenton, NJ
		Chicago (AL)	105	5	31	.303				
1	Johnson, Lance	Chicago (AL)	23	0	6	.185	R-R	5-11	155	7/7/63 Cincinnati, OH
		Vancouver	126	2	36	.307				
42	Kittle, Ron	Cleveland	58	18	43	.258	R-R	6-4	220	1/5/58 Gary, IN
44	Pasqua, Dan	Chicago (AL)	96	20	50	.227	L-L	6-0	203	10/17/61 Yonkers, NY
7	Williams, Kenny	Chicago (AL)	35	8	28	.159	R-R	6-1	189	4/6/64 Berkeley, CA
		Vancouver	15	1	6	.250				

OUTLOOK: The White Sox should improve somewhat on last year's 71-90 record, but there is no reason to think they are anything more than a middle-of-the-pack club in the AL West. This team needs further revamping and is a long way away from being able to win a title.

WHITE SOX PROFILES

CARLTON FISK 41 6-2 225 **Bats R Throws R**

"Pudge" enjoyed season of accomplishment despite injury woes in 1988 . . . Established AL record for games caught with his 1,807th, at Detroit Aug. 19, and celebrated with first five-hit game of his career . . . Finished season with 1,838 games caught, fourth on all-time list . . . Has hit 303 of his 323 home runs as a catcher, leaving him three shy of AL record for a catcher, held by Yogi Berra . . . Johnny Bench holds major-league mark with 327 home runs while behind the plate . . . Got off to a fast start, with eight home runs and 17 RBI in 24 games, before breaking hand May 10 on a Jack Clark foul tip . . . Returned July 28 after missing 70 games and collected 11 homers, 33 RBI in his final 52 games . . . Despite missing almost half a season, he placed second on club with 19 homers . . . Averaged one home run per 13.2 at-bats . . . Born Dec. 26, 1947, in Bellows Falls, Vt. . . . Began career with Boston as first-round pick in 1967 winter draft . . . Signed by White Sox as free agent, March 10, 1981 . . . Wears No. 72, reverse of his number with Red Sox.

Year	Club	Pos.	G	AB	R	H	2B	3B	HR	RBI	SB	Avg.
1969	Boston	C	2	5	0	0	0	0	0	0	0	.000
1971	Boston	C	14	48	7	15	2	1	2	6	0	.313
1972	Boston	C	131	457	74	134	28	9	22	61	5	.293
1973	Boston	C	135	508	65	125	21	0	26	71	7	.246
1974	Boston	C	52	187	36	56	12	1	11	26	5	.299
1975	Boston	C	79	263	47	87	14	4	10	52	4	.331
1976	Boston	C	134	487	76	124	17	5	17	58	12	.255
1977	Boston	C	152	536	106	169	26	3	26	102	7	.315
1978	Boston	C-OF	157	571	94	162	39	5	20	88	7	.284
1979	Boston	C-OF	91	320	49	87	23	2	10	42	3	.272
1980	Boston	C-OF-1B-3B	131	478	73	138	25	3	18	62	11	.289
1981	Chicago (AL).....	C-1B-3B-OF	96	338	44	89	12	0	7	45	3	.263
1982	Chicago (AL).....	C-1B	135	476	66	127	17	3	14	65	17	.267
1983	Chicago (AL).....	C	138	488	85	141	26	4	26	86	9	.289
1984	Chicago (AL).....	C	102	359	54	83	20	1	21	43	6	.231
1985	Chicago (AL).....	C	153	543	85	129	23	1	37	107	17	.238
1986	Chicago (AL).....	OF-C	125	457	42	101	11	0	14	63	2	.221
1987	Chicago (AL).....	C-1B-OF	135	454	68	116	22	1	23	71	1	.256
1988	Chicago (AL).....	C	76	253	37	70	8	1	19	50	0	.277
	Totals		2038	7228	1108	1953	346	44	323	1098	116	.270

HAROLD BAINES 30 6-2 194 **Bats L Throws L**

Didn't provide his usual punch, but still posted seventh consecutive season with 80 or more RBI . . . His second-half power shortage, however, ended his club-record streak of consecutive 20-home-run seasons at six . . . Had 10 homers on June 29, but only three in last 84 games . . . Remains White Sox' all-time home-run leader with 173 . . . Put together longest hitting streak of any White Sox player in 1988, 13 games, from April 9-23. He went 17-for-51 (.333) with one home run and eight RBI . . . Average dipped as low as .238 on June 3, but he hit .295 rest of the way . . . Now used almost strictly as a DH, he played only nine games in outfield . . . Born March 15, 1959, in Easton, Md. . . . White Sox made him first pick in nation in June 1977 draft . . . Spotted as 12-year-old Little Leaguer by the late Bill Veeck, a one-time White Sox owner.

Year	Club	Pos.	G	AB	R	H	2B	3B	HR	RBI	SB	Avg.
1980	Chicago (AL)	OF	141	491	55	125	23	6	13	49	2	.255
1981	Chicago (AL)	OF	82	280	42	80	11	7	10	41	6	.286
1982	Chicago (AL)	OF	161	608	89	165	29	8	25	105	10	.271
1983	Chicago (AL)	OF	156	596	76	167	33	2	20	99	7	.280
1984	Chicago (AL)	OF	147	569	72	173	28	10	29	94	1	.304
1985	Chicago (AL)	OF	160	640	86	198	29	3	22	113	1	.309
1986	Chicago (AL)	OF	145	570	72	169	29	2	21	88	2	.296
1987	Chicago (AL)	OF	132	505	59	148	26	4	20	93	0	.293
1988	Chicago (AL)	OF	158	599	55	166	39	1	13	81	0	.277
	Totals		1282	4858	606	1391	247	43	173	763	29	.286

OZZIE GUILLEN 25 5-11 150 **Bats L Throws R**

Though overshadowed by St. Louis wizard Ozzie Smith, this Ozzie showed he can dazzle at shortstop, too . . . Broke White Sox record with 569 assists, six more than the great Luis Aparicio recorded in 1969 . . . He and Smith were only shortstops in majors with 500-plus assists last year . . . Had more total chances than any shortstop with 863 . . . Fielding percentage was a glittering .977 . . . Made first All-Star Game appearance, but didn't play due to leg injury . . . Notched career-high 25 stolen bases for second straight year . . . Went homerless in 1988 for first time in his career. No other American Leaguer went as many at-bats (566) without connecting . . . Born Jan. 20, 1964, in Oculare del Tuy, Venezuela . . . Acquired from the Padres with Tim Lollar, Bill Long and Luis Salazar for LaMarr Hoyt, Todd Simmons and Kevin Kristan after the 1984 season . . . Immediately rewarded White Sox by becoming 1985

AL Rookie of the Year . . . Originally signed by San Diego as a free agent in 1980.

Year	Club	Pos.	G	AB	R	H	2B	3B	HR	RBI	SB	Avg.
1985	Chicago (AL)	SS	150	491	71	134	21	9	1	33	7	.273
1986	Chicago (AL)	SS	159	547	58	137	19	4	2	47	8	.250
1987	Chicago (AL)	SS	149	560	64	156	22	7	2	51	25	.279
1988	Chicago (AL)	SS	156	566	58	148	16	7	0	39	25	.261
	Totals		614	2164	251	575	78	27	5	170	65	.266

IVAN CALDERON 27 6-1 221 **Bats R Throws R**

Fine talent who hasn't been able to overcome chronic shoulder problems . . . Was disabled July 27 and had surgery on left shoulder in attempt to rescue career . . . Outfielder, who has been criticized in the past for poor work habits, faces long road back . . . Before shoulder problem became unbearable, he was disabled from June 30 to July 13 with pulled muscle in rib cage . . . Belted eight homers through 24 games to rank among early league leaders . . . Had 12-game hitting streak from April 9-23, producing five homers and 11 RBI . . . Born March 19, 1962, in Luiza, Puerto Rico . . . Obtained from Mariners as player to be named later in June 26, 1986 trade for Scott Bradley . . . Originally signed by Seattle as a free agent, July 30, 1979.

Year	Club	Pos.	G	AB	R	H	2B	3B	HR	RBI	SB	Avg.
1984	Seattle.	OF	11	24	2	5	1	0	1	1	1	.208
1985	Seattle.	OF-1B	67	210	37	60	16	4	8	28	4	.286
1986	Sea.-Chi. (AL)	OF	50	164	16	41	7	1	2	15	3	.250
1987	Chicago (AL)	OF	144	542	93	159	38	2	28	83	10	.293
1988	Chicago (AL)	OF	73	264	40	56	14	0	14	35	4	.212
	Totals		345	1204	188	321	76	7	53	162	22	.267

GREG WALKER 29 6-3 212 **Bats L Throws R**

Fans everywhere wished this big first baseman well after he suffered a scary seizure that almost cost him his life while taking grounders during batting practice . . . Was hospitalized for 12 days and doctors determined seizure was caused by viral infection in brain . . . Rejoined team after first week of September, but was never activated . . . Participated only in light workouts, but is optimistic he can make it back . . . Hit 20-plus homers three times in five previous seasons, but lacked strength before his illness became known last year . . . Went 170 at-bats without a home run, snapping that drought June 25 at Texas... Born Oct. 6, 1959, in Douglas, Ga., and still lives there.

Year	Club	Pos.	G	AB	R	H	2B	3B	HR	RBI	SB	Avg.
1982	Chicago (AL).....	DH	11	17	3	7	2	1	2	7	0	.412
1983	Chicago (AL).....	1B	118	307	32	83	16	3	10	55	2	.270
1984	Chicago (AL).....	1B	136	442	62	130	29	2	24	75	8	.294
1985	Chicago (AL).....	1B	163	601	77	155	38	4	24	92	5	.258
1986	Chicago (AL).....	1B	78	282	37	78	10	6	13	51	1	.277
1987	Chicago (AL).....	1B	157	566	85	145	33	2	27	94	2	.256
1988	Chicago (AL).....	1B	99	377	45	93	22	1	8	42	0	.247
	Totals		762	2592	341	691	150	19	108	416	18	.267

DAN PASQUA 27 6-0 203 **Bats L Throws L**

Outfielder failed to capitalize on first real opportunity to be a full-time player... Has never shown he can handle left-handed pitching... All of his team-leading 20 homers were off right-handers... Hit .252 (86-for-341) with 20 homers and 44 RBI against righties, .123 (10-for-81) with no homers and six RBI against lefties... This streak hitter had four two-homer games, upping his career total to six... Ran off career-best 12-game hitting streak from June 17 to July 5, going 16-for-40 (.400) with four homers, 10 RBI... Born Oct. 17, 1961, in Yonkers, N.Y.... Obtained from Yankees with Mark Salas and Steve Rosenberg for Richard Dotson and Scott Nielsen, after the 1987 season.

Year	Club	Pos.	G	AB	R	H	2B	3B	HR	RBI	SB	Avg.
1985	New York (AL)....	OF	60	148	17	31	3	1	9	25	0	.209
1986	New York (AL)....	OF-1B	102	280	44	82	17	0	16	45	2	.293
1987	New York (AL)....	OF-1B	113	318	42	74	7	1	17	42	0	.233
1988	Chicago (AL).....	OF-1B	129	422	48	96	16	2	20	50	1	.227
	Totals		404	1168	151	283	43	4	62	162	3	.242

JERRY REUSS 39 6-5 227 **Bats L Throws L**

Extended career as he became one of the biggest surprises in either league... Only non-roster invitee to make White Sox out of spring training... Led staff with 13 wins and 3.44 ERA and was second on club with 183 innings... Gained 200th career victory May 9 at Baltimore, becoming 86th pitcher to reach that plateau... Joined Milt Pappas as only pitchers to attain 200 wins without benefit of a 20-win season... Finished strong, going 4-1 with 1.80 ERA in last seven starts... Permitted three or fewer earned runs in 23 of 29 starts... Born June 19, 1949, in St. Louis... Signed by White

Sox as free agent in February 1988 . . . Began career with Cards as second-round pick in June 1967 draft.

Year	Club	G	IP	W	L	Pct.	SO	BB	H	ERA
1969	St. Louis	1	7	1	0	1.000	3	3	2	0.00
1970	St. Louis	20	127	7	8	.467	74	49	132	4.11
1971	St. Louis	36	211	14	14	.500	131	109	228	4.78
1972	Houston	33	192	9	13	.409	174	83	177	4.17
1973	Houston	41	279	16	13	.552	177	117	271	3.74
1974	Pittsburgh	35	260	16	11	.593	105	101	259	3.50
1975	Pittsburgh	32	237	18	11	.621	131	78	224	2.54
1976	Pittsburgh	31	209	14	9	.609	108	51	209	3.53
1977	Pittsburgh	33	208	10	13	.435	116	71	225	4.11
1978	Pittsburgh	23	83	3	2	.600	42	23	97	4.88
1979	Los Angeles	39	160	7	14	.333	83	60	178	3.54
1980	Los Angeles	37	229	18	6	.750	111	40	193	2.52
1981	Los Angeles	22	153	10	4	.714	51	27	138	2.29
1982	Los Angeles	39	254⅔	18	11	.621	138	510	232	3.11
1983	Los Angeles	32	223⅓	12	11	.522	143	50	233	2.94
1984	Los Angeles	30	99	5	7	.417	44	31	102	3.82
1985	Los Angeles	34	212⅔	14	10	.583	84	58	210	2.92
1986	Los Angeles	19	74	2	6	.250	29	17	96	5.84
1987	L.A.-Cin.	8	36⅔	0	5	.000	12	12	54	7.61
1987	California	17	82⅓	4	5	.444	37	17	112	5.25
1988	Chicago (AL)	32	183	13	9	.591	73	43	183	3.44
	Totals	594	3520⅔	211	182	.537	1866	1090	3555	3.58

BOBBY THIGPEN 25 6-3 195 Bats R Throws R

Achieved status as one of league's premier relievers . . . Set White Sox record with 34 saves, in 43 chances . . . Also had five wins, so he figured in 39 of Chicago's 71 victories (a major-league-high 54.9 percent) . . . Placed second in AL with 68 appearances . . . Converted 26 of first 30 save opportunities, but only eight of last 13 . . . Boasted 2.40 ERA when a save was on the line, but sported 5.08 ERA in non-save situations . . . Born July 17, 1963, in Tallahassee, Fla. . . . Selected by White Sox in fourth round of June 1985 draft.

Year	Club	G	IP	W	L	Pct.	SO	BB	H	ERA
1986	Chicago (AL)	20	35⅔	2	0	1.000	20	12	26	1.77
1987	Chicago (AL)	51	89	7	5	.583	52	24	86	2.73
1988	Chicago (AL)	68	90	5	8	.385	62	33	96	3.30
	Totals	139	214⅔	14	13	.519	134	69	208	2.81

JACK McDOWELL 23 6-5 179 Bats R Throws R

Results weren't there in first full major-league season, but White Sox still have high hopes for this hard thrower . . . Pitched considerably better than 5-10 record would indicate . . . Got no decision against Milwaukee June 10 despite nine innings of six-hit, shutout ball . . . Allowed one run and three hits in eight innings against Yankees July 1 without a decision . . .

His eight innings of shutout ball vs. Seattle July 26 also failed to produce a decision . . . Season ended Aug. 31 because of pulled flexor muscle in right hip . . . Selected by White Sox in first round of June 1987 draft as the fifth pick overall . . . Starred at Stanford, compiling 35-13 record with school-record 337 strikeouts and leading Cardinals to College World Series twice . . . Born Jan. 16, 1966, in Van Nuys, Cal.

Year	Club	G	IP	W	L	Pct.	SO	BB	H	ERA
1987	Chicago (AL)	4	28	3	0	1.000	15	6	16	1.93
1988	Chicago (AL)	26	158⅔	5	10	.333	84	68	147	3.97
	Totals	30	186⅔	8	10	.444	99	74	163	3.66

MELIDO PEREZ 23 6-4 180 **Bats R Throws R**

Showed great promise in becoming first White Sox rookie to win 10 or more games since 1980, when Britt Burns and Rich Dotson both did it . . . Got off to fast start, winning first three decisions . . . Was 5-1 through May 28 with 3.30 ERA . . . Never fell below .500 . . . Went 4-0 in July to improve to 10-5 overall . . . Went 2-5 in last 12 starts, but ERA was still a fine 3.50 . . . Left four of five starts with a lead, but was 0-1 between Aug. 18 and Sept. 4 . . . Of 105 runs scored against him, 22 were unearned . . . Has tendency to let up after errors . . . Born Feb. 15, 1966, in San Cristobal, Dominican Republic . . . Obtained from Royals with John Davis, Chuck Mount and Greg Hibbard for Floyd Bannister and Dave Cochrane, after the 1987 season . . . Younger brother of Montreal's Pascual Perez.

Year	Club	G	IP	W	L	Pct.	SO	BB	H	ERA
1987	Kansas City	3	10⅓	1	1	.500	5	5	18	7.84
1988	Chicago (AL)	32	197	12	10	.545	138	72	186	3.79
	Totals	35	207⅓	13	11	.542	143	77	204	3.99

TOP PROSPECT

LANCE JOHNSON 25 5-10 155 **Bats L Throws L**

Hasn't yet translated minor-league promise as 1987 American Association MVP into major-league production . . . Began season as White Sox' Opening Day center fielder, going 1-for-4 with RBI, but was outrighted to Vancouver (AAA) by May 13 . . . Was hitting .190 at that time . . . Hit .307 in 100 games at Vancouver with two homers, 36 RBI and 49 stolen bases to earn recall Sept. 16 . . . In his first game back, he went 4-for-5 with three RBI and two steals . . . Went 3-for-35 with no stolen bases in last 10 games, however . . . Faces year of reckoning . . . Born July 7, 1963, in Cincinnati . . . Acquired from Cards with Rick Horton for Jose DeLeon, prior to last season . . . Was St. Louis' sixth-round pick in June 1984 . . . Hit .333 for Louisville with 49 steals in 1987.

MANAGER JEFF TORBORG: Got second chance at managing when named to replace fired Jim Fregosi Nov. 3 . . . Received two-year contract to oversee rebuilding effort . . . Former major-league catcher has reputation as handler of pitchers, making him attractive to White Sox as they build around young arms . . . Served as manager of Cleveland Indians from June 19, 1977 until July 23, 1979, compiling 157-201 record with poor club . . . Joined Yankee coaching staff Aug. 1, 1979 and was one of few fixtures in the organization until White Sox hired him . . . Was valued by Yankees as bullpen coach . . . Played 10 major-league seasons, seven with Los Angeles, three with California . . . Caught three no-hitters: Sandy Koufax (1965), Bill Singer (1970) and Nolan Ryan (1973) . . . Ray Schalk holds record for being involved in most no-hitters as a catcher with four . . . Was a member of world champion Dodgers in 1965 . . . Soft-spoken, he nonetheless commands respect . . . Holds bachelor of science degree in education from Rutgers and masters in athletic administration from Montclair State . . . Wrote thesis on effects of platooning in baseball . . . Batted .537 in senior year at Rutgers, setting single-season NCAA mark that still stands . . . Born Nov. 26, 1941, in Westfield, N.J.

GREATEST FIRST BASEMAN

Dick Allen didn't play long for the White Sox, handling first base for them from 1972-74, but he made a tremendous impact in that brief time.

Allen became an instant hero in Chicago in 1972, winning the AL Most Valuable Player Award in convincing fashion. He led the league in home runs (37), RBI (113) and walks (99) to go with a .308 batting average and a lusty .603 slugging percentage.

The 37 home runs stood as a single-season high by a White Sox player until Carlton Fisk matched that total in 1985. Allen's 70 extra-base hits in 1972 rank second on the club's all-time single-season list as two fewer than Joe Jackson's record total in 1920.

Injuries limited Allen to 72 games in 1973, but he followed that disappointing campaign with another big year in 1974, topping the league with 32 home runs and a .563 slugging percentage. At a position that has been home for few memorable White Sox, the power-hitting Allen more than left his mark.

ALL-TIME WHITE SOX SEASON RECORDS

BATTING: Luke Appling, .388, 1936
HRs: Dick Allen, 37, 1972
Carlton Fisk, 37, 1985
RBIs: Zeke Bonura, 138, 1936
STEALS: Rudy Law, 77, 1983
WINS: Ed Walsh, 40, 1908
STRIKEOUTS: Ed Walsh, 269, 1908

KANSAS CITY ROYALS

TEAM DIRECTORY: Chairman: Ewing Kauffman; Vice-Chairman: Avron Fogelman; Pres.: Joe Burke; Exec. VP-GM: John Schuerholz; Exec. VP-Adm.: Spencer Robinson; Dir. Scouting: Art Stewart; Dir. Player Dev.: John Boles; VP-Pub. Rel.: Dean Vogelaar; VP-Marketing, Broadcasting: Dennis Cryder; Trav. Sec.: Dave Witty; Mgr.: John Wathan. Home: Royals Stadium (40,625). Field distances: 330, l.f. line, 385, l.c.; 410, c.f.; 385, r.c.; 330, r.f. line. Spring training: Boardwalk and Baseball, Orlando, Fla.

Mark Gubicza did Royal reversal, from 18 Ls to 20 Ws.

SCOUTING REPORT

HITTING: The Royals will again try to make up in speed what they lack in power.

Willie Wilson (.262, 1, 37) and former Heisman Trophy winner Bo Jackson are the Royals most often on the run. Wilson produced a team-high 35 steals, though that represented a dip of 24 from his total in 1987. Jackson founded Kansas City's 25-25 club with 25 home runs and 27 steals. Their legs helped the Royals to 137 stolen bases, third best in the AL.

Invaluable George Brett (.306, 24, 103) and Danny Tartabull (.274, 26, 102) join Jackson in supplying the Royals with power. The Royals are looking for more punch from Kevin Seitzer (.304, 5, 60), whose home-run total decreased by 10 in his sophomore season. Only two AL teams collected fewer home runs than the Royals, who had 121.

PITCHING: Starting pitching remains the Royals' biggest strength. Last season, Mark Gubicza finally answered questions about when he would come into his own with a stellar year in which he went 20-8 with a 2.70 ERA. It's no secret that Bret Saberhagen is considerably better than last year's 14-16 record and 3.80 ERA would indicate.

Charlie Leibrandt (13-12, 3.19) and Floyd Bannister (12-13, 4.33) give the Royals two more solid starters, although both need to show more consistency. It is a credit to the quality and experience of the Royals' starters that Kansas City allowed fewer home runs (102) than any other AL club.

Top prospect Tom Gordon, *Baseball America*'s Minor League Player of the Year, is an exciting newcomer. Last winter, the Royals gave some thought to putting Gordon in the bullpen, where Steve Farr has been the mainstay. In 1988, Farr accounted for 20 of the Royals' 32 saves, the third-lowest total among AL clubs.

FIELDING: Frank White continues to distinguish himself at second base. He topped AL players at that position with a .994 fielding percentage. The free-agent signing of incomparable veteran Bob Boone, one of the toughest vs. the stolen base, should solve the Royals' catching problem.

OUTLOOK: Kansas City can only be rated third best in the increasingly strong West, behind defending AL champion Oakland and Minnesota. General manager John Schuerholz has not traded well in recent winters and now manager John Wathan faces a win-or-else season.

KANSAS CITY ROYALS 1989 ROSTER

MANAGER John Wathan
Coaches—Glenn Ezell, Frank Funk, Adrian Garrett, Mike Lum, John Mayberry, Bob Schaefer

PITCHERS

No.	Name	1988 Club	W-L	IP	SO	ERA	B-T	Ht.	Wt.	Born
45	Adams, Ken	Baseball City	4-2	58	28	3.43	R-R	6-1	185	6/4/66 Kansas City, MO
27	Aquino, Luis	Omaha	8-3	129	93	2.85	R-R	6-1	175	5/19/65 Puerto Rico
		Kansas City	1-0	29	11	2.79				
19	Bannister, Floyd	Kansas City	12-13	189	113	4.33	L-L	6-1	190	6/10/55 Pierre, SD
53	Crouch, Matt	Memphis	8-5	114	110	2.92	R-R	6-1	170	9/14/64 Rancho Cordova, CA
54	DeJesus, Jose	Memphis	9-9	116	149	3.88	R-R	6-5	175	1/6/65 Brooklyn, NY
		Omaha	2-3	50	57	3.44				
		Kansas City	0-1	3	2	27.00				
26	Farr, Steve	Kansas City	5-4	83	72	2.50	R-R	5-11	200	12/12/56 Cheverly, MD
39	Gleaton, Jerry Don	Omaha	4-2	37	40	1.45	L-L	6-3	210	9/14/57 Brownwood, TX
		Kansas City	0-4	38	29	3.55				
36	Gordon, Tom	Appleton	7-5	118	172	2.06	R-R	5-9	160	11/18/67 Sebring, FL
		Memphis	6-0	47	62	0.38				
		Omaha	3-0	20	29	1.33				
		Kansas City	0-2	16	18	5.17				
23	Gubicza, Mark	Kansas City	20-8	270	183	2.70	R-R	6-5	210	8/14/62 Philadelphia, PA
35	Lee, Mark	Lakeland	1-0	19	15	1.42	L-L	6-3	198	7/20/64 Williston, ND
		Glens Falls	3-0	26	25	2.39				
		Toledo	0-1	19	13	2.79				
		Kansas City	0-0	5	0	3.60				
37	Leibrandt, Charlie	Kansas City	13-12	243	125	3.19	R-L	6-3	200	10/4/56 Chicago, IL
40	Luecken, Rick	Memphis	4-1	25	30	2.19	R-R	6-6	210	11/15/60 McAllen, TX
		Omaha	5-0	40	27	2.03				
21	Montgomery, Jeff	Omaha	1-2	28	36	1.91	R-R	5-11	180	1/7/62 Wellston, OH
		Kansas City	7-2	63	47	3.45				
18	Saberhagen, Bret	Kansas City	14-16	261	171	3.80	R-R	6-1	185	4/11/64 Chicago Heights, IL
31	Sanchez, Israel	Omaha	7-4	102	85	2.91	L-L	5-9	171	8/20/63 Cuba
		Kansas City	3-2	36	14	4.54				
52	Stottlemyre, Mel	Memphis	3-2	45	29	2.40	R-R	6-0	190	12/28/63 Prosser, WA
46	Vasquez, Aguedo	Baseball City	3-2	81	68	1.67	R-R	5-10	160	2/5/67 Dominican Republic
		Omaha	0-0	4	1	9.00				
47	Wagner, Hector	Eugene	4-9	86	67	3.68	R-R	6-3	185	11/26/68 Dominican Republic

CATCHERS

No.	Name	1988 Club	H	HR	RBI	Pct.	B-T	Ht.	Wt.	Born
—	Boone, Bob	California	104	5	39	.295	R-R	6-2	208	11/19/47 San Diego, CA
11	Hearn, Ed	Baseball City	17	0	5	.304	R-R	6-3	210	8/23/60 Stuart, FL
		Kansas City	4	0	1	.222				
8	Macfarlane, Mike	Kansas City	56	4	26	.265	R-R	6-1	200	4/12/64 Stockton, CA
		Omaha	18	2	8	.237				
24	Owen, Larry	Omaha	43	9	32	.215	R-R	5-10	190	5/31/55 Garfield Heights, OH
		Kansas City	17	1	3	.210				
29	Palacios, Rey	Toledo	94	5	27	.230	R-R	5-10	190	11/8/62 Brooklyn, NY
		Kansas City	1	0	0	.091				

INFIELDERS

2	Biancalana, Buddy	Omaha	73	1	37	.248	S-R	5-11	160	2/2/60 Larkspur, CA
5	Brett, George	Kansas City	180	24	103	.306	L-R	6-0	200	5/15/53 Glendale, WV
14	Buckner, Bill	Cal.-KC	71	3	43	.249	L-L	6-1	182	12/14/49 Vallejo, CA
51	de los Santos, Luis	Omaha	164	6	87	.307	R-R	6-5	190	12/29/66 Dominican Republic
		Kansas City	2	0	1	.091				
32	Pecota, Bill	Kansas City	37	1	15	.208	R-R	6-2	190	2/16/60 Redwood City, CA
33	Seitzer, Kevin	Kansas City	170	5	60	.304	R-R	5-11	180	3/26/62 Springfield, IL
1	Stillwell, Kurt	Kansas City	115	10	53	.251	S-R	5-11	175	6/4/65 Glendale, CA
3	Wellman, Brad	Kansas City	29	1	6	.271	R-R	6-0	170	8/17/59 Lodi, CA
20	White, Frank	Kansas City	126	8	58	.235	R-R	5-11	190	9/4/50 Greenville, MS

OUTFIELDERS

58	Brumfield, Jacob	Memphis	98	6	28	.226	R-R	6-0	170	5/27/65 Bogalusa, LA
22	Eisenreich, Jim	Omaha	41	4	14	.289	L-L	5-11	195	4/18/59 St. Cloud, MN
		Kansas City	44	1	19	.218				
16	Jackson, Bo	Kansas City	108	25	68	.246	R-R	6-1	225	11/30/62 Bessemer, AL
30	Tabler, Pat	Cle.-KC	125	2	66	.282	R-R	6-2	198	2/2/58 Hamilton, OH
4	Tartabull, Danny	Kansas City	139	26	102	.274	R-R	6-1	205	10/30/62 Miami, FL
25	Thurman, Gary	Omaha	106	3	40	.251	R-R	5-10	175	11/12/64 Indianapolis, IN
		Kansas City	11	0	2	.167				
59	Watkins, Darren	Appleton	97	4	46	.265	R-R	6-1	185	8/30/66 Everett, WA
		Baseball City	12	0	7	.222				
6	Wilson, Willie	Kansas City	155	1	37	.262	S-R	6-3	195	7/9/55 Montgomery, AL

ROYAL PROFILES

GEORGE BRETT 35 6-0 200 Bats L Throws R

Remains one of baseball's most accomplished hitters . . . Has led league in batting (twice), hits, total bases, doubles, triples, on-base percentage and slugging percentage . . . Only Ty Cobb and Lou Gehrig have won such a variety of titles . . . Did not go more than two games without a hit in '88 . . . Finished above .300 for 10th time in career and knocked in more than 100 runs for fourth time . . . Placed among AL's top 10 in RBI, multi-hit games, total bases, doubles, walks, on-base percentage, slugging percentage and extra-base hits . . . Selected to his 13th All-Star Game, more than any other active player . . . Needs one hit for 2,400 in career . . . Was able to stay away from injuries that have plagued him throughout career . . . Played in 157 games, his high since 1976 . . . Born May 15, 1953, in Glendale, W. Va. . . . Royals' second-round selection in June 1971 draft . . . Has made smooth transition from third base to first the last two seasons.

Year	Club	Pos.	G	AB	R	H	2B	3B	HR	RBI	SB	Avg.
1973	Kansas City	3B	13	40	2	5	2	0	0	0	0	.125
1974	Kansas City	3B-SS	133	457	49	129	21	5	2	47	8	.282
1975	Kansas City	3B-SS	159	634	84	195	35	13	11	89	13	.308
1976	Kansas City	3B-SS	159	645	94	215	34	14	7	67	21	.333
1977	Kansas City	3B-SS	139	564	105	176	32	13	22	88	14	.312
1978	Kansas City	3B-SS	128	510	79	150	45	8	9	62	23	.294
1979	Kansas City	3B-1B	154	645	119	212	42	20	23	107	17	.329
1980	Kansas City	3B-1B	117	449	87	175	33	9	24	118	15	.390
1981	Kansas City	3B	89	347	42	109	27	7	6	43	14	.314
1982	Kansas City	3B-OF	144	552	101	166	32	9	21	82	6	.301
1983	Kansas City	3B-1B-OF	123	464	90	144	38	2	25	93	0	.310
1984	Kansas City	3B	104	377	42	107	21	3	13	69	0	.284
1985	Kansas City	3B	155	550	108	184	38	5	30	112	9	.335
1986	Kansas City	3B-SS	124	441	70	128	28	4	16	73	1	.290
1987	Kansas City	1B-3B	115	427	71	124	18	2	22	78	6	.290
1988	Kansas City	1B	157	589	90	180	42	3	24	103	14	.306
	Totals		2013	7691	1233	2399	488	117	255	1231	161	.312

KEVIN SEITZER 27 5-11 180 Bats R Throws R

Third baseman suffered somewhat from sophomore jinx . . . Home run total dropped by 10 and RBI total dipped by 23 from brilliant rookie season . . . Average fell 19 points to .304, but he still became first player in Royal history to begin career with consecutive .300-plus seasons . . . Very consistent hitter . . . Never went more than two games without a hit and spent just one day below .290 . . . Only Royal other than George Brett to have more walks than strikeouts . . . Runnerup to Oakland's Mark McGwire for 1987 AL Rookie of the Year . . . Became 13th rookie in major-league history to collect 200 hits and first since Tony Oliva and Richie Allen in 1964 . . . Born March 26, 1962, in Springfield, Ill. . . . Selected by Royals in 11th round of June 1983 draft.

Year	Club	Pos.	G	AB	R	H	2B	3B	HR	RBI	SB	Avg.
1986	Kansas City......	1B-OF-3B	28	96	16	31	4	1	2	11	0	.323
1987	Kansas City......	3B-OF-1B	161	641	105	207	33	8	15	83	12	.323
1988	Kansas City......	3B-OF	149	559	90	170	32	5	5	60	10	.304
	Totals		338	1296	211	408	69	14	22	154	22	.315

DANNY TARTABULL 26 6-1 205 Bats R Throws R

Outfielder is building a reputation as a consistent run producer . . . Has knocked in 299 runs in his first three full major-league seasons . . . Became only third player in Royal history to record back-to-back 100 RBI seasons . . . George Brett last accomplished that in 1979 and 1980 . . . Led Royals with 26 homers . . . Led league and set club record with three grand slams . . . Born Oct. 30, 1962, in Miami . . . Obtained from Mariners with Rick Luecken for Scott Bankhead, Mike Kingery and Steve Shields, following 1986 season . . . Son of former Kansas City A's outfielder Jose.

Year	Club	Pos.	G	AB	R	H	2B	3B	HR	RBI	SB	Avg.
1984	Seattle..........	SS-2B	10	20	3	6	1	0	2	7	0	.300
1985	Seattle..........	SS-3B	19	61	8	20	7	1	1	7	1	.328
1986	Seattle..........	OF-2B-3B	137	511	76	138	25	6	25	96	4	.270
1987	Kansas City......	OF	158	582	95	180	27	3	34	101	9	.309
1988	Kansas City......	OF	146	507	80	139	38	3	26	102	8	.274
	Totals		470	1681	262	483	98	13	88	313	22	.287

WILLIE WILSON 33 6-3 195 Bats S Throws R

Season of decline produced worst batting average since his rookie season in 1978 and saw his stolen-base total dip by 24 from 1987 standard . . . His 35 steals nonetheless paced Royals for 11th straight season . . . Very smart base-runner . . . Was caught stealing only seven times . . . Tied for league lead with 11 triples and leads active players with 123 triples . . . Possesses great range in center field . . . Did not commit an error after July 4 . . . Recorded 500th career stolen base July 25, 1987, becoming 32nd major leaguer to achieve that total . . . Born July 9, 1955, in Montgomery, Ala. . . . Passed up scholarship to play football at Maryland to sign with Royals as first-round choice in June 1974 draft . . . Served 32-game drug suspension in 1984.

Year	Club	Pos.	G	AB	R	H	2B	3B	HR	RBI	SB	Avg.
1976	Kansas City......	OF	12	6	0	1	0	0	0	0	2	.167
1977	Kansas City......	OF	13	34	10	11	2	0	0	1	6	.324
1978	Kansas City......	OF	127	198	43	43	8	2	0	16	46	.217
1979	Kansas City......	OF	154	588	113	185	18	13	6	49	83	.315
1980	Kansas City......	OF	161	705	133	230	28	15	3	49	79	.326
1981	Kansas City......	OF	102	439	54	133	10	7	1	32	34	.303
1982	Kansas City......	OF	136	585	87	194	19	15	3	46	37	.332
1983	Kansas City......	OF	137	576	90	159	22	8	2	33	59	.276
1984	Kansas City......	OF	128	541	81	163	24	9	2	44	47	.301
1985	Kansas City......	OF	141	605	87	168	25	21	4	43	43	.278
1986	Kansas City......	OF	156	631	77	170	20	7	9	44	34	.269
1987	Kansas City......	OF	146	610	97	170	18	15	4	30	59	.279
1988	Kansas City......	OF	147	591	81	155	17	11	1	37	35	.262
	Totals		1560	6109	953	1782	211	123	35	424	564	.292

BO JACKSON 26 6-1 225 **Bats R Throws R**

Superb athlete who plays for NFL's Los Angeles Raiders as a "hobby" is making strides in baseball . . . Former Heisman Trophy winner founded Royals' 25-25 club with 25 home runs and 27 stolen bases, despite missing a month with a torn left hamstring . . . Amos Otis is only other Royal to notch more than 20 home runs and 20 steals in same season . . . Left fielder remains raw talent who must learn strike zone . . . Fanned 146 times in 439 at-bats . . . Won Heisman after 1985 season during which he became Auburn's all-time leading rusher with 4,303 yards . . . Has played both baseball and football professionally for last two years . . . Unlikely to realize vast potential in either if he continues to play both . . . Born Nov. 30, 1962, in Bessemer, Ala. . . . Selected by Royals in fourth round of June 1986 draft.

Year	Club	Pos.	G	AB	R	H	2B	3B	HR	RBI	SB	Avg.
1986	Kansas City......	OF	25	82	9	17	2	1	2	9	3	.207
1987	Kansas City......	OF	116	396	46	93	17	2	22	53	10	.235
1988	Kansas City......	OF	124	439	63	108	16	4	25	68	27	.246
	Totals		265	917	118	218	35	7	49	130	40	.238

BOB BOONE 41 6-2 207 **Bats R Throws R**

Remarkable veteran signed with Royals as free agent after extraordinary 1988 season . . . Was selected by Angels Booster Club as California's Most Inspirational Player for second straight year . . . Hit .295, 45 points above previous career high . . . Set major-league record when he caught his 1,919th game, vs. Royals Sept. 16, 1987 . . . Has caught 120-plus games for seven consecutive seasons . . . Very quick release and strong arm allowed him to throw out 37 of 97 (38 percent) would-be base-stealers in 1988 . . . Offseason conditioning program involving martial arts techniques has helped to extend his career . . . Born Nov. 19, 1947, in San Diego . . . Began career with Phillies as sixth-round selection in June 1969 draft, out of Stanford . . . Son of All-Star infielder Ray . . . Began as a third baseman.

Year	Club	Pos.	G	AB	R	H	2B	3B	HR	RBI	SB	Avg.
1972	Philadelphia......	C	16	51	4	14	1	0	1	4	1	.275
1973	Philadelphia......	C	145	521	42	136	20	2	10	61	3	.261
1974	Philadelphia......	C	146	488	41	118	24	3	3	52	3	.242
1975	Philadelphia......	C-3B	97	289	28	71	14	2	2	20	1	.246
1976	Philadelphia......	C	121	361	40	98	18	2	4	54	2	.271
1977	Philadelphia......	C-3B	132	440	55	125	26	4	11	66	5	.284
1978	Philadelphia......	C-1B-OF	132	435	48	123	18	4	12	62	2	.283
1979	Philadelphia......	C-3B	119	398	38	114	21	3	9	58	1	.286
1980	Philadelphia......	C	141	480	34	110	23	1	9	55	3	.229
1981	Philadelphia......	C	76	227	19	48	7	0	4	24	2	211
1982	California........	C	143	472	42	121	17	0	7	58	0	.256
1983	California........	C	142	468	46	120	18	0	9	52	4	.256
1984	California........	C	139	450	33	91	16	1	3	32	3	.202
1985	California........	C	150	460	37	114	17	0	5	55	1	.248
1986	California........	C	144	442	48	98	12	2	7	49	1	.222
1987	California........	C	128	389	42	94	18	0	3	33	0	.242
1988	California........	C	122	352	38	104	17	0	5	39	2	.295
	Totals		2093	6723	635	1699	287	24	104	774	34	.253

MARK GUBICZA 26 6-5 210 Bats R Throws R

Finally gave Royals the stellar season they've been expecting from him . . . Accomplished remarkable turnaround after dismal 18-loss season in 1987 . . . Ranked third in AL with 20 wins and .714 winning percentage . . . Placed fourth with 2.70 ERA and second with 269⅔ innings . . . Earned four shutouts with pair of two-hitters, a three-hitter and a four-hitter . . . AL Pitcher of the Month in June with 5-0 record and 1.18 ERA . . . Born Aug. 14, 1962, in Philadelphia . . . Selected by KC in second round of June 1981 draft as compensation pick for loss of Darrell Porter to free agency.

Year	Club	G	IP	W	L	Pct.	SO	BB	H	ERA
1984	Kansas City..........	29	189	10	14	.417	111	75	172	4.05
1985	Kansas City..........	29	177⅓	14	10	583	99	77	160	4.06
1986	Kansas City..........	35	180⅔	12	6	.667	118	84	155	3.64
1987	Kansas City..........	35	241⅔	13	18	.419	166	120	231	3.98
1988	Kansas City..........	35	269⅔	20	8	.714	183	83	237	2.70
	Totals	163	1058⅓	69	56	.552	677	439	955	3.62

BRET SABERHAGEN 24 6-1 185 **Bats R Throws R**

Pitched far better than losing record would indicate . . . Royals scored more than two runs in only two of his 16 defeats . . . Still managed to post double figures in victories for fourth time in five-year career . . . Hard thrower possesses excellent control . . . Issued only 59 walks in 260⅔ innings . . . Led Royals with nine complete games and ranked fifth in AL in innings pitched . . . Enjoyed dream season in 1985 when, at 21, he became youngest pitcher ever to win Cy Young Award . . . In span of 36 hours, he became a father and won World Series MVP to cap incredible 1985 season . . . Born April 11, 1964, in Chicago Heights, Ill. . . . Selected by Royals in 19th round of June 1982 draft.

Year	Club	G	IP	W	L	Pct.	SO	BB	H	ERA
1984	Kansas City	38	157⅔	10	11	.476	73	36	138	3.48
1985	Kansas City	32	235⅓	20	6	.769	158	38	211	2.87
1986	Kansas City	30	156	7	12	.368	112	29	165	4.15
1987	Kansas City	33	257	18	10	.643	163	53	246	3.36
1988	Kansas City	35	260⅔	14	16	.467	171	59	271	3.80
	Totals	168	1066⅔	69	55	.556	677	215	1031	3.49

CHARLIE LEIBRANDT 32 6-3 200 **Bats R Throws L**

Results were mediocre as brilliant second half of season only salvaged rocky first half . . . Finished with winning record for fifth straight season by winning eight of last nine decisions and 10 of last 12 . . . Lost once after July 15 and fashioned 2.49 ERA in final 18 starts . . . Hurled pair of shutouts, a two-hitter vs. Oakland June 15 and 1-0 blanking of Cleveland Aug. 31 . . . Born Oct. 4, 1956, in Chicago . . . Obtained from Reds for Bob Tufts, June 7, 1983 . . . Cincinnati's ninth-round pick in June 1978 draft.

Year	Club	G	IP	W	L	Pct.	SO	BB	H	ERA
1979	Cincinnati	3	4	0	0	.000	1	2	2	0.00
1980	Cincinnati	36	174	10	9	.526	62	54	200	4.24
1981	Cincinnati	7	30	1	1	.500	9	15	28	3.60
1982	Cincinnati	36	107⅔	5	7	.417	34	48	130	5.10
1984	Kansas City	23	143⅔	11	7	.611	53	38	158	3.63
1985	Kansas City	33	237⅔	17	9	.654	108	68	223	2.69
1986	Kansas City	35	231⅓	14	11	.560	108	63	238	4.09
1987	Kansas City	35	240⅓	16	11	.593	151	74	235	3.41
1988	Kansas City	35	243	13	12	.520	125	62	244	3.19
	Totals	243	1411⅔	87	67	.565	651	424	1458	3.61

FLOYD BANNISTER 33 6-1 190 **Bats L Throws L**

Has never fulfilled expectations and he's with his fourth organization now . . . One of only five major-league pitchers to post 10 or more wins in each of last seven seasons . . . Has produced losing records, however, in four of those seven years . . . Began career with Houston as first player selected overall in June 1976 draft, following sterling 38-6 career at Arizona State . . . Born June 10, 1955, in Pierre, S.D. . . . Obtained from White Sox with Dave Cochrane for Melido Perez, John Davis, Greg Hibbard and Chuck Mount, following 1987 season.

Year	Club	G	IP	W	L	Pct.	SO	BB	H	ERA
1977	Houston	24	143	8	9	.471	112	68	138	4.03
1978	Houston	28	110	3	9	.250	94	63	120	4.83
1979	Seattle	30	182	10	15	.400	115	68	185	4.05
1980	Seattle	32	218	9	13	.409	155	66	200	3.47
1981	Seattle	21	121	9	9	.500	85	39	128	4.46
1982	Seattle	35	247	12	13	.480	209	77	225	3.43
1983	Chicago (AL)	34	217⅓	16	10	.615	193	71	191	3.35
1984	Chicago (AL)	34	218	14	11	.560	152	80	211	4.83
1985	Chicago (AL)	34	210⅔	10	14	.417	198	100	211	4.87
1986	Chicago (AL)	28	165⅓	10	14	.417	92	48	162	3.54
1987	Chicago (AL)	34	228⅔	16	11	.593	124	49	216	3.58
1988	Kansas City	31	189⅓	12	13	.480	113	68	182	4.33
	Totals	365	2250⅓	129	141	.478	1642	797	2169	4.01

STEVE FARR 32 5-11 200 **Bats R Throws R**

Entrusted with closer's role midway through season, he recorded 20 saves in 25 chances . . . Became fifth reliever in club history to reach 20-save level . . . Registered all 14 of club's saves from June 29 to Sept. 14 . . . Led staff in appearances with 62 . . . Was nearly unhittable in May, permitting one earned run and recording 24 strikeouts in 19 innings . . . Born Dec. 12, 1956, in Cheverly, Md. . . . Signed as free agent May 9, 1985, after being released by Cleveland . . . Originally signed by Pirates as free agent in December 1976 and spent six years in their system.

Year	Club	G	IP	W	L	Pct.	SO	BB	H	ERA
1984	Cleveland	31	116	3	11	.214	83	46	106	4.58
1985	Kansas City	16	37⅔	2	1	.667	36	20	34	3.11
1986	Kansas City	56	109⅓	8	4	.667	83	39	90	3.13
1987	Kansas City	47	91	4	3	.571	88	44	97	4.15
1988	Kansas City	62	82⅔	5	4	.556	72	30	74	2.50
	Totals	212	436⅔	22	23	.489	362	179	401	3.61

TOP PROSPECT

TOM GORDON 21 5-9 160 **Bats R Throws R**

The best or the second-best pitching prospect in all of baseball . . . Breaking-ball artist posted combined 16-5 record and 1.55 ERA in minors during season that took him from Class A to majors . . . Notched 263 strikeouts in 185⅔ minor-league innings . . . Eye-opening success included a 6-0 record with a 0.38 ERA in six starts for Memphis (AA), a 3-0 mark with a 1.33 ERA in three starts for Omaha (AAA) . . . Made major-league debut Sept. 8 with two perfect innings against Oakland . . . Ready to try hand at majors after ringing up 29-6 record in minors . . . Born Nov. 18, 1967, in Sebring, Fla. . . . Selected by Royals in sixth round of June 1986 draft . . . Was 0-2 with 5.17 ERA for Royals in '88.

MANAGER JOHN WATHAN: Royals made somewhat surprising move by giving Wathan new one-year contract . . . Has 105-97 composite record in one-plus seasons as Royals' skipper, but team has been troubled . . . Players have scuffled in several instances . . . Royals were never really a factor in 1988 division race, despite strong pitching . . . From all indications, Wathan is in a win-or-else position . . . Has never been with another organization . . . Played in Kansas City from 1976-85, primarily as a catcher . . . Also played some first base and outfield . . . His 36 stolen bases in 1982 established major-league record for catchers . . . Biggest season was 1980, when he set career highs in hits (138), runs (57), home runs (16) and RBI (58) . . . Managed Omaha (AAA) before promotion to Royals . . . American Association club finished with 64-76 mark . . . Served as coach under Dick Howser in 1986 . . . Born Oct. 4, 1949, in Cedar Rapids, Iowa.

GREATEST FIRST BASEMAN

Think of the Royals and George Brett's name invariably comes to mind. Brett, who made the move from third base to first base two seasons ago, is the club's all-time leader in home runs (255), RBI (1,231), hits (2,399), runs (1,233), at-bats (7,691), doubles (488) and triples (117).

The 13-time All-Star has compiled an average of .300 or better in seven of the last 10 seasons, including a .306 mark last year at age 34. He also drove in 103 runs, the fourth time in his career he went over the century mark.

Brett's accomplishments in 16 years in Kansas City have helped the Royals reach the ALCS six times and the World Series twice. When they captured the world championship in 1985, Brett played a leading role with a .370 average in the Series.

ALL-TIME ROYAL SEASON RECORDS

BATTING: George Brett, .390, 1980
HRs: Steve Balboni, 36, 1985
RBIs: Hal McRae, 133, 1982
STEALS: Willie Wilson, 83, 1979
WINS: Steve Busby, 22, 1974
STRIKEOUTS: Dennis Leonard, 244, 1977

MINNESOTA TWINS

TEAM DIRECTORY: Owner: Carl Pohlad; Pres.: Jerry Bell; Exec. VP-GM: Andy MacPhail, VP-Player Pers.: Bob Gebhard; VP-Oper.: Dave Moore; VP-Finance: Jim McHenry; Dir. Media Rel.: Tom Mee; Mgr.: Tom Kelly. Home: Hubert H. Humphrey Metrodome (55, 879). Field distances: 343, l.f. line; 408, c.f.; 327, r.f. line. Spring training: Orlando, Fla.

Little big man Kirby Puckett led majors with 234 hits.

SCOUTING REPORT

HITTING: Kirby Puckett (.356, 24, 121), Kent Hrbek (.312, 25, 76) and Gary Gaetti (.301, 28, 88) do the most damage in a very dangerous lineup. Dan Gladden (.269, 11, 62), who had a team-leading 28 stolen bases in 1988, provides needed speed, along with sparkplug Wally Backman (.303, 0, 17), a winter import from the Mets.

In posting the best average by a right-handed hitter in the AL since Joe DiMaggio finished at .357 in 1941, Puckett helped Minnesota to a .274 team mark that ranked second in the AL behind Boston last season. The Twins were third in the league in homers with 151.

PITCHING: Frank Viola (24-7, 2.64) is in his prime and is coming off a remarkable season in which he paced the majors in victories and winning percentage (.774). He is very capable of winning a second straight Cy Young Award in 1989. Allan Anderson (16-9, 2.45) won the league ERA title and was a huge surprise, so naturally the Twins are looking forward to his first full season in the majors.

Shane Rawley (8-16, 4.18), imported in a deal for Tommy Herr last winter, is a quality left-hander who will benefit from leaving last-place Philadelphia. Charlie Lea (7-7, 4.85) is a question mark because of his history of injury problems.

Jeff Reardon remains among baseball's premier relievers after racking up a club-record 42 saves last year. Juan Berenguer (8-4, 3.96) excels in a supporting role.

FIELDING: No one plays defense nearly as well as the Twins, who made that point with an exclamation point last season, when they set a major-league record for fewest errors with 84. That was a remarkable 11 errors less than the previous standard, accomplished by Baltimore in 1964 and 1980 and Cincinnati in 1977.

Puckett and Gaetti are standouts in center field and at third base, respectively. The acquisition of Backman solidified the second-base position.

OUTLOOK: Tom Kelly's Twins may have finished a distant 13 games behind Oakland last year, but their 91-71 record was six victories better than their mark during their 1987 world championship season. Last year was simply Oakland's year. Now it is talent-laden Minnesota's turn to get back on top.

Frank Viola's 24 wins made him everyone's choice for Cy.

MINNESOTA TWINS 1989 ROSTER

MANAGER Tom Kelly
Coaches—Tony Oliva, Rick Renick, Rick Stelmaszek, Dick Such, Wayne Terwilliger

PITCHERS

No.	Name	1988 Club	W-L	IP	SO	ERA	B-T	Ht.	Wt.	Born
37	Abbott, Paul	Visalia	11-9	172	205	4.18	R-R	6-3	185	9/15/67 Van Nuys, CA
49	Anderson, Allan	Portland	1-1	14	9	1.26	L-L	6-0	186	1/7/64 Lancaster, OH
		Minnesota	16-9	202	83	2.45				
22	Atherton, Keith	Minnesota	7-5	74	43	3.41	R-R	6-4	200	2/19/59 Newport News, VA
40	Berenguer, Juan	Minnesota	8-4	100	99	3.96	R-R	5-11	225	11/30/54 Panama
33	Cook, Mike	Edmonton	5-9	91	84	4.65	R-R	6-3	215	8/14/63 Charleston, SC
		California	0-1	4	2	4.91				
48	Davins, Jim	Portland	0-5	61	55	5.61	R-R	6-3	215	5/23/64 New Haven, CT
39	Dyer, Mike	Orlando	11-13	162	125	3.99	R-R	6-3	195	9/8/66 Upland, CA
36	Galvez, Balvino	Orlando	2-0	24	19	3.04	R-R	6-1	180	3/31/64 Dominican Republic
		Portland	11-7	143	60	3.77				
46	Gonzalez, German	Orlando	2-1	62	69	1.02	R-R	6-0	170	10/3/65 Venezuela
		Minnesota	0-0	21	19	3.38				
53	*Lea, Charlie	Minnesota	7-7	130	72	4.85	R-R	6-4	200	12/25/56 France
50	Pittman, Park	Orlando	8-7	104	103	3.82	R-R	6-0	175	8/5/65 Richmond, IN
18	Rawley, Shane	Philadelphia	8-16	198	87	4.18	R-L	6-0	185	7/27/55 Racine, WI
41	Reardon, Jeff	Minnesota	2-4	73	56	2.47	R-R	6-0	200	10/1/55 Dalton, MA
23	Smith, Roy	Portland	12-9	150	110	4.32	R-R	6-3	217	9/6/61 Mt. Vernon, NY
		Minnesota	3-0	37	17	2.68				
17	Straker, Les	Portland	0-0	20	13	3.20	R-R	6-1	193	10/10/59 Venezuela
		Minnesota	2-5	83	23	3.92				
31	Toliver, Fred	Portland	7-2	95	54	3.13	R-R	6-1	170	2/3/61 Natchez, MS
		Minnesota	7-6	115	69	4.24				
16	Viola, Frank	Minnesota	24-7	255	193	2.64	L-L	6-4	209	4/19/60 Hempstead, NY
38	Williams, Jimmy	Visalia	3-4	51	55	3.71	L-L	6-6	225	5/18/65 Butler, AL

CATCHERS

No.	Name	1988 Club	H	HR	RBI	Pct.	B-T	Ht.	Wt.	Born
12	Harper, Brian	Portland	60	13	42	.353	R-R	6-2	195	10/16/59 Los Angeles, CA
		Minnesota	49	3	20	.295				
15	Laudner, Tim	Minnesota	94	13	54	.251	R-R	6-3	214	6/7/58 Mason City, IA
51	Parks, Derek	Orlando	94	7	42	.235	R-R	6-1	195	9/29/68 Covina, CA
52	Webster, Lenny	Kenosha	134	11	87	.288	R-R	5-9	187	2/10/65 New Orleans, LA

INFIELDERS

No.	Name	1988 Club	H	HR	RBI	Pct.	B-T	Ht.	Wt.	Born
—	Backman, Wally	New York (NL)	89	0	17	.303	S-R	5-9	168	9/22/59 Hillsboro, OR
21	Baker, Doug	Portland	102	2	41	.245	S-R	5-9	165	4/3/61 Fullerton, CA
		Minnesota	0	0	0	.000				
8	Gaetti, Gary	Minnesota	141	28	88	.301	R-R	6-0	200	8/19/58 Centralia, IL
7	Gagne, Greg	Minnesota	109	14	48	.236	R-R	5-11	177	11/12/61 Fall River, MA
14	Hrbek, Kent	Minnesota	159	25	76	.312	L-R	6-4	244	5/21/60 Minneapolis, MN
9	Larkin, Gene	Minnesota	135	8	70	.267	S-R	6-3	212	10/24/62 Astoria, NY
—	Leius, Scott	Visalia	73	3	46	.237	R-R	6-3	185	9/24/65 Yonkers, NY
4	Lombardozzi, Steve	Minnesota	60	3	27	.209	R-R	6-0	183	4/26/60 Malden, MA
26	Newman, Al	Minnesota	58	0	19	.223	S-R	5-9	183	6/30/60 Kansas City, MO
54	Sorrento, Paul	Palm Springs	133	14	99	.286	L-R	6-2	197	11/17/65 Somerville, MA
55	Valdez, Frank	Kenosha	118	8	60	.278	R-R	6-1	160	10/12/68 Dominican Republic

OUTFIELDERS

No.	Name	1988 Club	H	HR	RBI	Pct.	B-T	Ht.	Wt.	Born
56	Brown, Jarvis	Kenosha	156	7	45	.294	R-R	5-7	165	3/26/67 Waukegan, IL
25	Bush, Randy	Minnesota	103	14	51	.261	L-L	6-1	186	10/5/58 Dover, DE
20	*Christensen, John	Calg.-Port.	37	1	14	.264	R-R	6-0	180	9/5/60 Downey, CA
		Minnesota	10	0	5	.263				
27	Davidson, Mark	Portland	18	0	5	.321	R-R	6-2	190	2/15/61 Knoxville, TN
		Minnesota	23	1	10	.217				
59	Delima, Rafael	Orlando	143	3	46	.286	L-L	5-11	175	12/21/67 Venezuela
—	Dwyer, Jim	Balt.-Minn.	24	2	18	.255	L-L	5-10	186	1/3/50 Evergreen Park, IL
32	Gladden, Dan	Minnesota	155	11	62	.269	R-R	5-11	175	7/7/57 San Jose, CA
1	Moses, John	Portland	23	0	6	.348	S-L	5-10	170	8/9/57 Los Angeles, CA
		Minnesota	65	2	12	.316				
34	Puckett, Kirby	Minnesota	234	24	121	.356	R-R	5-8	210	3/14/61 Chicago, IL

*Free agent at press time listed with 1988 team

TWIN PROFILES

KIRBY PUCKETT 28 5-8 210 **Bats R Throws R**

Center fielder would have had a shot at AL MVP award if Minnesota had won . . . Led majors with 73 multi-hit games, 234 hits, 358 total bases . . . Second in majors in batting at .356 and in RBI with 121 . . . Tied for second in majors with 42 doubles and was third with 71 extra-base hits . . . Boasted .545 slugging percentage to tie for fourth in majors . . . Named to All-Star team for third straight year . . . Fashioned two 14-game hitting streaks, April 16 to May 1 and July 9-26 . . . Finished season with 17-game streak that began Sept. 15 . . . Born March 14, 1961, in Chicago . . . Minnesota's first-round selection and third player taken overall in June 1982 draft . . . Attended Bradley . . . One of nine children . . . Got four hits in first big-league game, May 8, 1984 vs. Angels.

Year	Club	Pos.	G	AB	R	H	2B	3B	HR	RBI	SB	Avg.
1984	Minnesota	OF	128	557	63	165	12	5	0	31	14	.296
1985	Minnesota	OF	161	691	80	199	29	13	4	74	21	.288
1986	Minnesota	OF	161	680	119	223	37	6	31	96	20	.328
1987	Minnesota	OF	157	624	96	207	32	5	28	99	12	.332
1988	Minnesota	OF	158	657	109	234	42	5	24	121	6	.356
	Totals		765	3209	467	1028	152	34	87	421	73	.320

KENT HRBEK 28 6-4 244 **Bats L Throws R**

Finished with career-high .312 batting average, but late-season power shortage diminished run production . . . Did not hit another home run after winning recognition as AL Player of the Month in August with .370 average, seven homers and 23 RBI . . . Suffered sprained left wrist Sept. 15 and started only three games after that . . . Ran off 11-game hitting streak from Aug. 27 to Sept. 6, going 19-for-43 (.442) with one home run, eight RBI in that span . . . Stroked 1,000th career hit May 30 against Texas . . . Born May 21, 1960, in Minneapolis . . . Selected in 17th round of June 1978 draft . . . Became 15th Minnesota-born Twin when he debuted with game-winning, 12th-inning homer against Yankees, Aug. 24, 1981 . . . One of AL's slickest first baseman.

Year	Club	Pos.	G	AB	R	H	2B	3B	HR	RBI	SB	Avg.
1981	Minnesota	1B	24	67	5	16	5	0	1	7	0	.239
1982	Minnesota	1B	140	532	82	160	21	4	23	92	3	.301
1983	Minnesota	1B	141	515	75	153	41	5	16	84	4	.297
1984	Minnesota	1B	149	559	80	174	31	3	27	107	1	.311
1985	Minnesota	1B	158	593	78	165	31	2	21	93	1	.278
1986	Minnesota	1B	149	550	85	147	27	1	29	91	2	.267
1987	Minnesota	1B	143	477	85	136	20	1	34	90	5	.285
1988	Minnesota	1B	143	510	75	159	31	0	25	76	0	.312
	Totals		1047	3803	565	1110	207	16	176	640	16	.292

GARY GAETTI 30 6-0 200 — Bats R Throws R

Knee injury cost this third baseman a big season and dealt a severe blow to Twins' chances in 1988 . . . Tore cartilage in left knee Aug. 15 in Detroit while sliding into second base . . . Was hitting .298 with 26 homers and 76 RBI in 117 games when he went on DL Aug. 21, then underwent arthroscopic surgery . . . Returned as pinch-hitter and slugged two-run homer in second appearance Sept. 10 . . . Drilled two-run double as pinch-hitter the following day . . . Started two games at third base in September, before finishing year as a DH and pinch-hitter . . . Full recovery is expected following a winter off . . . Born Aug. 19, 1958, in Centralia, Ill. . . . Minnesota's first-round selection in June 1979 draft . . . Attended Northwest Missouri State.

Year	Club	Pos.	G	AB	R	H	2B	3B	HR	RBI	SB	Avg.
1981	Minnesota	3B	9	26	4	5	0	0	2	3	0	.192
1982	Minnesota	3B-SS	145	508	59	117	25	4	25	84	0	.230
1983	Minnesota	3B-SS	157	584	81	143	30	3	21	78	7	.245
1984	Minnesota	3B-OF-SS	162	588	55	154	29	4	5	65	11	.262
1985	Minnesota	3B-OF-1B	160	560	71	138	31	0	20	63	13	.246
1986	Minnesota	3B-SS-OF-2B	157	596	91	171	34	1	34	108	14	.287
1987	Minnesota	3B	154	584	95	150	36	2	31	109	10	.257
1988	Minnesota	3B	133	468	66	141	29	2	28	88	7	.301
	Totals		1077	3914	522	1019	214	16	166	598	62	.260

DAN GLADDEN 31 5-11 175 — Bats R Throws R

Hard-nosed outfielder provides spark for Twins . . . Notched club-high 28 stolen bases . . . Started triple play Aug. 8 vs. Cleveland by running full speed into left-field wall at Metrodome to make catch, then caroming off wall and firing strike to second baseman Steve Lombardozzi, who threw to first . . . Had consecutive four-hit games April 6 and 8 . . . Born July 7, 1957, in San Jose, Cal. . . . Acquired from Giants with David Blakley for Jose Dominguez, Bryan Hickerson and Ray

Velasquez, March 31, 1987 . . . Attended Fresno State . . . Signed by San Francisco as free agent in June 1979.

Year	Club	Pos.	G	AB	R	H	2B	3B	HR	RBI	SB	Avg.
1983	San Francisco	OF	18	63	6	14	2	0	1	9	4	.222
1984	San Francisco	OF	86	342	71	120	17	2	4	31	31	.351
1985	San Francisco	OF	142	502	64	122	15	8	7	41	32	.243
1986	San Francisco	OF	102	351	55	97	16	1	4	29	27	.276
1987	Minnesota	OF	121	438	69	109	21	2	8	38	25	.249
1988	Minnesota	OF	141	576	91	155	32	6	11	62	28	.269
	Totals		610	2272	356	617	103	19	35	210	147	.272

FRANK VIOLA 29 6-4 209 **Bats L Throws L**

The 1987 World Series MVP produced quite an encore . . . Led majors with 24 wins and .774 winning percentage . . . Ranked third in league with 2.64 ERA and 193 strikeouts . . . Responded to 8-0 shelling from Yankees in season opener by running off nine straight wins from April 10 to June 1, tying a club record . . . Became earliest 10-game winner in Twins' history when he defeated Seattle June 17 . . . Named AL Player of the Month for May with 6-0 mark and 1.53 ERA . . . Tossed consecutive shutouts against Boston May 1 and 6 . . . Starter and winner for AL in 1988 All-Star Game, working two perfect innings . . . Born April 19, 1960, in Hempstead, N.Y. . . . Acquired by Minnesota in second round of June 1981 draft . . . Went 26-2 with 1.67 ERA for St. John's and pitched in 1980 College World Series . . . Winningest pitcher in majors over last five years with 93 . . . Came within a vote of winning 1988 Cy Young unanimously.

Year	Club	G	IP	W	L	Pct.	SO	BB	H	ERA
1982	Minnesota	22	126	4	10	.286	84	38	152	5.21
1983	Minnesota	35	210	7	15	.318	127	92	242	5.49
1984	Minnesota	35	257⅔	18	12	.600	149	73	225	3.21
1985	Minnesota	36	250⅔	18	14	.563	135	68	262	4.09
1986	Minnesota	37	245⅔	16	13	.552	191	83	257	4.51
1987	Minnesota	36	251⅔	17	10	.630	197	66	230	2.90
1988	Minnesota	35	255⅓	24	7	.774	193	54	236	2.64
	Totals	236	1597	104	81	.562	1076	474	1604	3.87

JEFF REARDON 33 6-0 200 **Bats R Throws R**

Achieved distinction as only pitcher to record 40-save season in each league . . . Established club record with 42 saves, second-highest total in majors, three behind Oakland's Dennis Eckersley and four shy of Dave Righetti's major-league record . . . Registered 41 saves with Montreal in 1985 . . . Best stretch came from May 11 to July 1, when he recorded 16 saves in as many chances . . . Named to AL All-Star staff . . . Rolaids Relief Pitcher of the Month for August, when he was 1-1 with seven saves in nine chances . . . Born Oct. 1, 1955, in Dalton, Mass. . . . Acquired from Expos with Tom Nieto for Jeff Reed, Al Cardwood, Neal Heaton and Yorkis Perez, prior to 1987 season . . . Has 235 career saves . . . Attended University of Massachusetts . . . Mets signed him as a free agent in June 1974 . . . Has history of back problems, but he's a workhorse.

Year	Club	G	IP	W	L	Pct.	SO	BB	H	ERA
1979	New York (NL)	18	21	1	2	.333	10	9	12	1.71
1980	New York (NL)	61	110	8	7	.533	101	47	96	2.62
1981	N.Y. (NL)-Mont.	43	70	3	0	1.000	49	21	48	2.19
1982	Montreal	75	109	7	4	.636	86	36	87	2.06
1983	Montreal	66	92	7	9	.438	78	44	87	3.03
1984	Montreal	68	87	7	7	.500	79	37	70	2.90
1985	Montreal	63	87⅔	2	8	.200	67	26	68	3.18
1986	Montreal	62	89	7	9	.438	67	26	83	3.94
1987	Minnesota	63	80⅓	8	8	.500	83	28	70	4.48
1988	Minnesota	63	73	2	4	.333	56	15	68	2.47
	Totals	582	819	52	58	.473	676	289	689	2.93

SHANE RAWLEY 33 6-0 185 — Bats R Throws L

Acquired from Phillies with Tom Nieto and Eric Bullock for Tommy Herr and cash following the end of the '88 season . . . Experienced very disappointing year, yielding 27 homers in 198 innings, so the Homerdome could be a tough home park for him . . . His 8-16 record for the Phillies last year, his first losing season since 1981, left his career mark at exactly .500 . . . Posted 100th career victory with a two-hitter vs. Giants May 16 . . . Lost seven straight from June 23-Aug. 4 . . . Born July 27, 1955, in Racine, Wis. . . . Originally chosen by Expos in secondary phase of January 1974 draft, but was traded to Cincinnati, Seattle, the Yankees and the Phillies . . . Has a pilot's license and flies own plane . . . A free-lance writer who has worked on scripts for movies and television.

Year	Club	G	IP	W	L	Pct.	SO	BB	H	ERA
1978	Seattle	52	111	4	9	.308	66	51	114	4.14
1979	Seattle	48	84	5	9	357	48	40	88	3.86
1980	Seattle	59	114	7	7	.500	68	63	103	3.32
1981	Seattle	46	68	4	6	.400	35	38	64	3.97
1982	New York (AL)........	47	164	11	10	524	111	54	165	4.06
1983	New York (AL)........	34	238⅓	14	14	.500	124	79	246	3.78
1984	New York (AL)........	11	42	2	3	.400	2	227	46	6.21
1984	Philadelphia	18	120⅓	10	6	.625	58	27	117	3.81
1985	Philadelphia	36	198⅔	13	8	.619	106	81	188	3.31
1986	Philadelphia	23	157⅔	11	7	.611	73	50	166	3.54
1987	Philadelphia	36	229⅔	17	11	.607	123	86	250	4.39
1988	Philadelphia	32	198	8	16	.333	87	78	220	4.18
	Totals	442	1725⅔	106	106	.500	923	674	1767	3.92

ALLAN ANDERSON 25 6-0 186 **Bats L Throws L**

Enjoyed remarkable rise, edging Milwaukee lefty Teddy Higuera for league ERA title after beginning season at Portland (AAA) . . . Was called up April 25 and went just 1-3 through May 23 . . . Excelled after that, however, with 15-6 record and 2.01 ERA the rest of the way . . . Was held out of last start to secure ERA title . . . Won six straight starts from July 24 to Aug. 22, posting 1.40 ERA . . . He and Frank Viola tied club record for wins by two pitchers in a single season with 40 and set club mark for a tandem with .714 winning percentage . . . Born Jan. 7, 1964, in Lancaster, Ohio . . . Chosen in second round of June 1982 draft . . . Pitched four no-hitters in high school.

Year	Club	G	IP	W	L	Pct.	SO	BB	H	ERA
1986	Minnesota	21	84⅓	3	6	.333	51	30	106	5.55
1987	Minnesota	4	12⅓	1	0	1.000	3	10	20	10.95
1988	Minnesota	30	202⅓	16	9	.640	83	37	199	2.45
	Totals	55	299	20	15	.571	137	77	325	3.67

JUAN BERENGUER 34 5-11 225 **Bats R Throws R**

Rotund flame-thrower serves as fine complement to Jeff Reardon in pen . . . Takes great pride in strikeouts and racked up 99 in 100 innings . . . Won five straight from May 17 to July 5 . . . Made only start Aug. 3 vs. Toronto, pitching four innings without a decision . . . Gained his only saves June 26 in Oakland and Sept. 25 in California . . . Born Nov. 30, 1954, in Aguadulce, Panama . . . Signed by Twins as free agent prior to 1987 season . . . Originally signed as free agent by Mets back in days he struggled to throw strikes . . . First Panamanian pitcher to appear in a World Series . . . Set-up man has only nine career saves.

Year	Club	G	IP	W	L	Pct.	SO	BB	H	ERA
1978	New York (NL)	5	13	0	2	.000	8	11	17	8.31
1979	New York (NL)	5	31	1	1	.500	25	12	28	2.90
1980	New York (NL)	6	9	0	1	.000	7	10	9	6.00
1981	K.C.-Tor.	20	91	2	13	.133	49	51	84	5.24
1982	Detroit	2	6⅔	0	0	.000	8	9	5	6.75
1983	Detroit	37	157⅔	9	5	.643	129	71	110	3.14
1984	Detroit	31	168⅓	11	10	.524	118	79	146	3.48
1985	Detroit	31	95	5	6	.455	82	48	96	5.59
1986	San Francisco	46	73⅓	2	3	.400	72	44	64	2.70
1987	Minnesota	47	112	8	1	.889	110	47	100	3.94
1988	Minnesota	57	100	8	4	.667	99	61	74	3.96
	Totals	287	857	46	46	.500	707	443	733	3.99

CHARLIE LEA 32 6-4 200 **Bats R Throws R**

Merited AL Comeback Player of the Year consideration for winning spot in rotation after pitching one major-league game in three years . . . Needed that long to recover from arthroscopic surgery on right shoulder performed in May 1985 for rotator-cuff problem . . . Gained spot in spring training with 2.16 ERA in six starts . . . Lost first three regular-season starts before finally winning May 24 to begin five-game streak . . . Compiled 2.35 ERA from June 7 to July 15 . . . Went on disabled list Aug. 28 with strain of right biceps . . . Made two starts after returning, winning one and getting one no-decision . . . Born Dec. 25, 1956, in Orleans, France . . . Signed by Twins as free agent before 1988 season, after Expos had lost patience with him . . . Montreal's ninth-round pick in June 1978 . . . Pitched no-hitter vs. Giants, May 10, 1981.

Year	Club	G	IP	W	L	Pct.	SO	BB	H	ERA
1980	Montreal	21	104	7	5	.583	56	55	103	3.72
1981	Montreal	16	64	5	4	.556	31	26	63	4.64
1982	Montreal	27	177⅔	12	10	.545	115	56	145	3.24
1983	Montreal	33	222	16	11	.593	137	84	195	3.12
1984	Montreal	30	224⅓	15	10	.600	123	68	198	2.89
1987	Montreal	1	1	0	1	.000	1	2	4	36.00
1988	Minnesota	24	130	7	7	.500	72	50	156	4.85
	Totals	152	923	62	48	.564	535	341	864	3.54

TOP PROSPECT

DEREK PARKS 20 6-0 195 **Bats R Throws R**

Needs much work offensively, but has youth on his side . . . Hit .235 with seven homers and 42 RBI in 118 games for Orlando (AA) . . . Has all the defensive skills needed to be a major-league catcher, but is probably a couple of years away . . . Born Sept. 29, 1968, in Covina, Cal. . . . Twins' first-round choice in June 1986 draft.

MANAGER TOM KELLY: Twins failed to repeat as world

champions or even division winners but Kelly again distinguished himself as manager . . . Has fostered great spirit in clubhouse and players enjoy playing for him . . . Handled potentially troublesome pitching staff skillfully . . . Soft-spoken man who shuns spotlight and prefers to give credit to players . . . Has steadied emotional team with emphasis on giving best effort every day no matter what has come before . . . In 1987, he became 18th rookie manager to lead team to World Series and fifth to win it . . . Named to post in late November 1986 after serving on interim basis in place of fired Ray Miller . . . Was minor-league outfielder for 13 years after being Seattle Pilots' fourth-round pick in June 1968 draft . . . Did get to play in majors for 62 games with Twins in 1975 after he signed as a free agent . . . Most productive years as player were at Tacoma (AAA) in Pacific Coast League, where he managed last half of 1977 season . . . Named Manager of the Year in California League in 1979 and 1980 and in Southern League in 1981 . . . In 1983, he became Twins' third-base coach, first Minnesotan to become member of staff . . . Born Aug. 15, 1950, in Graceful, Minn., but makes home in Sayreville, N.J. . . . Father Joe pitched in New York Giants' chain . . . Owns 188-149 major-league managerial record.

GREATEST FIRST BASEMAN

The Minnesota Twins owe thanks for the greatest first baseman in their history to a politician—United States Senator Herman Walker.

It was Walker who wrote a note to Washington Senators' owner Calvin Griffith about a strong young man from Payette, Idaho. That launched the career of Harmon (Killer) Killebrew, the fifth-leading home-run hitter in baseball history.

Killebrew enjoyed his best years after the franchise shifted from Washington to Minnesota. In fact, beginning in 1961, he smashed 46, 48, 45 and 49 home runs in the first four years in the Twin Cities.

Of Killebrew's 573 career home runs, 475 of them came with the Twins. He won five home-run titles in that time, pounding more than 40 homers in each of those seasons.

Killebrew was versatile defensively. He also was used at third base, in the outfield, and as the designated hitter during his distinguished career.

ALL-TIME TWIN SEASON RECORDS

BATTING: Rod Carew, .388, 1977
HRs: Harmon Killebrew, 49, 1964, 1969
RBIs: Harmon Killebrew, 140, 1969
STEALS: Rod Carew, 49, 1976
WINS: Jim Kaat, 25, 1966
STRIKEOUTS: Bert Blyleven, 258, 1973

OAKLAND ATHLETICS

TEAM DIRECTORY: Owner/Managing Partner: Walter A. Haas Jr.; Chief Oper. Off.: Wally Haas; Exec. VP: Roy Eisenhardt; VP-Baseball Oper.: Sandy Alderson; Dir. Player Dev.: Karl Kuehl; Dir. Scouting: Dick Bogard; Dir. Media Rel.: Kathy Jacobson; Dir. Baseball Inf.: Jay Alves; Trav. Sec.: Mickey Morabito; Mgr.: Tony La Russa. Home: Oakland Coliseum (48,219). Field distances: 330, l.f. line; 375, l.c.; 400, c.f.; 375, r.c.; 330, r.f. line. Spring training: Phoenix, Ariz.

Menacing Dennis had Eck of a time as ALCS MVP.

SCOUTING REPORT

HITTING: The Bash Brothers—Jose Canseco and Mark McGwire—form an awesome slugging combination. Canseco (.307, 42, 124) was named the AL's Most Valuable Player in 1988, after founding baseball's 40-40 club with 42 home runs and 40 stolen bases. McGwire (.260, 32, 99) can be just as explosive.

With their bats booming, Oakland placed second in the AL in runs scored (800) and in home runs (156) last year. Pleasant surprise Dave Henderson (.304, 24, 94) and Carney Lansford (.279, 7, 57) will look to make similar contributions in 1989, while Dave Parker (.257, 12, 55) hopes to rebound after a disappointing first season in the AL. However, he is 37 and therefore suspect.

PITCHING: The rich got richer when the A's signed right-hander Mike Moore as a free agent last winter. He is believed to be far better than his 9-15 record and 3.78 ERA with Seattle in 1988 would indicate.

Moore will fit nicely into a rotation that boasted four double-figure winners last year: Dave Stewart (21-12, 3.23), Bob Welch (17-9, 3.64), Storm Davis (16-7, 3.70) and Curt Young (11-8, 4.14). Not surprisingly, Oakland edged Milwaukee for the league ERA crown with a 3.44 mark.

These starters are supported by a superb bullpen that established a major-league record with 64 saves—45 of them by Dennis Eckersley (4-2, 2.35). Eckersley fell one save shy of matching Dave Righetti's record for saves in a single season, set in 1986. Athletics' relievers were 29-13 with a 2.81 ERA overall, thanks to the efforts of Eric Plunk (7-2, 3.00), Gene Nelson (9-6, 3.06) and Greg Cadaret (5-2, 2.89).

FIELDING: Rookie of the Year Walt Weiss spearheads one of the league's best defenses. With Weiss taking over at shortstop, Oakland ranked third in the AL with a .983 fielding percentage and reduced its error total to 105, a dramatic drop of 37 from 1987. Weiss and Co. turned 151 double plays, an increase of 29 over 1987. All-Star Terry Steinbach is a standout behind the plate. Last year, he threw out 28 of 70 would-be base-stealers, a rate of 40 percent.

OUTLOOK: Oakland has the talent to maintain its status as league champion. But the second time won't be as easy as the first, when Tony La Russa's A's ran away with the West on the strength of baseball's best record at 104-58. The young A's already know how to win. Now they will learn how difficult it is to repeat.

OAKLAND A'S 1989 ROSTER

MANAGER Tony La Russa

Coaches—Dave Duncan, Art Kusnyer, Rene Lachemann, Dave McKay, Merv Rettenmund, Tommie Reynolds

PITCHERS

No.	Name	1988 Club	W-L	IP	SO	ERA	B-T	Ht.	Wt.	Born
54	Burns, Todd	Tacoma	4-3	73	59	3.68	R-R	6-2	190	7/6/63 Maywood, CA
		Oakland	8-2	103	57	3.16				
32	Cadaret, Greg	Oakland	5-2	72	65	2.89	L-L	6-3	205	2/27/62 Detroit, MI
41	Corsi, Jim	Tacoma	2-5	59	48	2.75	R-R	6-1	210	9/9/61 Newton, MA
		Oakland	0-1	21	10	3.80				
14	Davis, Storm	Oakland	16-7	202	127	3.70	R-R	6-4	200	12/26/61 Dallas, TX
43	Eckersley, Dennis	Oakland	4-2	73	70	2.35	R-R	6-2	195	10/3/54 Oakland, CA
40	Honeycutt, Rick	Oakland	3-2	80	47	3.50	L-L	6-1	191	6/29/54 Chattanooga, TN
56	Law, Joe	Huntsville	9-3	116	67	2.56	R-R	6-2	200	2/4/62 Pittsburgh, PA
		Tacoma	5-3	66	46	3.93				
—	Moore, Mike	Seattle	9-15	229	182	3.78	R-R	6-4	205	11/26/59 Eakly, OK
19	Nelson, Gene	Oakland	9-6	112	67	3.06	R-R	6-0	175	12/3/60 Tampa, FL
53	*Ontiveros, Steve	Oakland	3-4	55	30	4.61	R-R	6-0	180	3/5/61 Tularosa, NM
38	Otto, Dave	Tacoma	4-9	128	80	3.52	L-L	6-7	210	11/12/64 Chicago, IL
		Oakland	0-0	10	7	1.80				
51	Plunk, Eric	Oakland	7-2	78	79	3.00	R-R	6-5	210	9/3/63 Wilmington, CA
34	Stewart, Dave	Oakland	21-12	276	192	3.23	R-R	6-2	200	2/19/57 Oakland, CA
59	Veres, David	Modesto	4-11	125	91	3.31	R-R	6-2	195	10/19/66 Montgomery, AL
		Huntsville	3-4	39	17	4.15				
35	Welch, Bob	Oakland	17-9	245	158	3.64	R-R	6-3	195	11/3/56 Detroit, MI
29	Young, Curt	Oakland	11-8	156	69	4.14	R-L	6-1	175	10/18/59 Saginaw, MI
20	*Young, Matt	Oakland		Injured			L-L	6-3	205	8/9/58 Pasadena, CA

CATCHERS

No.	Name	1988 Club	H	HR	RBI	Pct.	B-T	Ht.	Wt.	Born
24	Hassey, Ron	Oakland	83	7	45	.257	L-R	6-2	195	2/27/53 Tucson, AZ
49	McGinnis, Russ	Huntsville	20	2	15	.260	R-R	6-3	215	6/18/63 Coffeyville, KS
		Tacoma	47	2	21	.253				
11	Sinatro, Matt	Tacoma	54	2	23	.231	R-R	5-9	175	3/22/60 West Hartford, CT
		Oakland	3	0	5	.333				
36	Steinbach, Terry	Oakland	93	9	51	.265	R-R	6-1	195	3/2/62 New Ulm, MN

INFIELDERS

30	Blankenship, Lance	Tacoma	116	9	52	.265	R-R	6-0	185	12/6/63 Portland, OR
		Oakland	0	0	0	.000				
9	Gallego, Mike	Oakland	58	2	20	.209	R-R	5-8	160	10/31/60 Whittier, CA
57	Hemond, Scott	Huntsville	106	9	53	.220	R-R	6-0	205	11/18/65 Taunton, MA
17	Hubbard, Glenn	Oakland	75	3	33	.255	R-R	5-7	170	9/25/57 Germany
4	Lansford, Carney	Oakland	155	7	57	.279	R-R	6-2	195	2/7/57 San Jose, CA
25	McGwire, Mark	Oakland	143	32	99	.260	R-R	6-5	225	10/1/63 Pomona, CA
2	Phillips, Tony	Oakland	43	2	17	.203	S-R	5-10	175	4/15/59 Atlanta, GA
		Tacoma	16	2	8	.271				
7	Weiss, Walt	Oakland	113	3	39	.250	S-R	6-0	175	11/28/63 Tuxedo, NY

OUTFIELDERS

33	Canseco, Jose	Oakland	187	42	124	.307	R-R	6-3	230	7/2/64 Cuba
46	Canseco, Ozzie	Madison	98	12	68	.273	R-R	6-2	210	7/2/64 Cuba
		Huntsville	22	3	12	.222				
42	Henderson, Dave	Oakland	154	24	94	.304	R-R	6-2	220	7/21/58 Dos Palos, CA
48	Howard, Steve	Huntsville	114	17	78	.247	R-R	6-2	205	12/7/63 Oakland, CA
28	Javier, Stan	Oakland	102	2	35	.257	S-R	6-0	185	9/1/65 Dominican Republic
6	Jose, Felix	Tacoma	160	12	83	.317	S-R	6-1	190	5/8/65 Dominican Republic
		Oakland	2	0	1	.333				
39	Parker, Dave	Oakland	97	12	55	.257	L-R	6-5	230	6/9/51 Jackson, MS
22	Polonia, Luis	Tacoma	85	2	27	.335	L-L	5-8	155	10/12/64 Dominican Republic
		Oakland	84	2	27	.292				

*Free agent at press time listed with 1988 team

ATHLETIC PROFILES

JOSE CANSECO 24 6-3 230 Bats R Throws R

Right fielder achieved greatness predicted for him when he became first player in major-league history to hit 40 home runs and steal 40 bases in same season . . . Led majors with 42 homers, 124 RBI and .569 slugging percentage . . . Finished with exactly 40 stolen bases . . . Twenty-seven of his 42 homers either tied game or put A's in lead . . . Only player in Oakland history to record three consecutive 100-RBI seasons . . . Leading AL All-Star vote-getter . . . Led A's romp over Boston in ALCS, batting .313 with three home runs . . . Huge disappointment in World Series, going 0-for-18 after his second-inning grand slam in Game 1 . . . Born July 2, 1964, in Havana, Cuba . . . Athletics' 15th-round selection in June 1982 draft . . . Twin brother Oswaldo plays in Athletics' system . . . Was AL Rookie of the Year in 1986 and AL MVP last year . . . Won bet with teammate Dave Stewart when he got married during offseason.

Year	Club	Pos.	G	AB	R	H	2B	3B	HR	RBI	SB	Avg.
1985	Oakland	OF	29	96	16	29	3	0	5	13	1	.302
1986	Oakland	OF	157	600	85	144	29	1	33	117	15	.240
1987	Oakland	OF	159	630	81	162	35	3	31	113	15	.257
1988	Oakland	OF	158	610	120	187	34	0	42	124	40	.307
	Totals		503	1936	302	522	101	4	111	367	71	.270

MARK McGWIRE 25 6-5 225 Bats R Throws R

First baseman failed to approach totals of 1987 AL Rookie of the Year season, but did enjoy big season as lesser half of "Bash Brothers" . . . Finished third in AL with 32 homers and eighth with 99 RBI . . . Twenty of his 32 homers came on road . . . Started in All-Star Game . . . Hit .333 with one homer and three RBI in ALCS . . . Belted game-ending solo homer to give Oakland its lone World Series win, a 2-1 decision in Game 3 . . . That was his only hit in 17 at-bats, however, although he made good contact several other times . . . Born Oct. 1, 1963, in Pomona, Cal. . . . Athletics' first-round selection in June 1984 draft.

Year	Club	Pos.	G	AB	R	H	2B	3B	HR	RBI	SB	Avg.
1986	Oakland	3B	18	53	10	10	1	0	3	9	0	.189
1987	Oakland	1B-3B-OF	151	557	97	161	28	4	49	118	1	.289
1988	Oakland	1B-OF	155	550	87	143	22	1	32	99	0	.260
	Totals		324	1160	194	314	51	5	84	226	1	.271

DAVE PARKER 37 6-5 230 **Bats L Throws R**

First AL season for 15-year veteran was disappointing . . . Missed 44 games after tearing ligaments in right thumb while breaking up double play vs. Toronto June 3 . . . A's received only six home runs from left-handed batters while he recovered from surgery . . . Designated hitter had one big stretch from May 13 through June 7, smashing 31 hits in 82 at-bats with four homers and 16 RBI . . . Didn't assert himself in postseason as much as A's had hoped . . . Went 3-for-15 in World Series and did not have a homer or RBI . . . Born June 9, 1951, in Jackson, Miss. . . . Obtained from Reds for Jose Rijo and Tim Birtsas following 1987 season . . . Chosen by Pirates in 15th round of June 1970 draft . . . Led NL in hitting in 1977 and 1978 and was NL MVP in '78 before injuries began to take a toll.

Year	Club	Pos.	G	AB	R	H	2B	3B	HR	RBI	SB	Avg.
1973	Pittsburgh	OF	54	139	17	40	9	1	4	14	1	.288
1974	Pittsburgh	OF-1B	73	220	27	62	10	3	4	29	3	.282
1975	Pittsburgh	OF	148	558	75	172	35	10	25	101	8	.308
1976	Pittsburgh	OF	138	537	82	168	28	10	13	90	19	.313
1977	Pittsburgh	OF-2B	159	637	107	215	44	8	21	88	17	.338
1978	Pittsburgh	OF	148	581	102	194	32	12	30	117	20	.334
1979	Pittsburgh	OF	158	622	109	193	45	7	25	94	20	.310
1980	Pittsburgh	OF	139	518	71	153	31	1	17	79	10	.295
1981	Pittsburgh	OF	67	240	29	62	14	3	9	48	6	.258
1982	Pittsburgh	OF	73	244	41	66	19	3	6	29	7	.270
1983	Pittsburgh	OF	144	552	68	154	29	4	12	69	12	.279
1984	Cincinnati	OF	156	607	73	173	28	0	16	94	11	.285
1985	Cincinnati	OF	160	635	88	198	42	4	34	125	5	.312
1986	Cincinnati	OF	162	637	89	174	31	3	31	116	1	.273
1987	Cincinnati	OF-1B	153	589	77	149	28	0	26	97	7	.253
1988	Oakland.........	OF	101	377	43	97	18	1	12	55	0	.257
	Totals		2033	7693	1098	2270	443	70	285	1245	147	.295

DAVE HENDERSON 30 6-2 220 **Bats R Throws R**

One of baseball's biggest surprises after signing with Athletics as lightly-regarded free agent after the 1987 season . . . His .304 average was 50 points higher than previous career mark . . . Set career highs in average, runs, hits, homers, total bases and doubles . . . A's were 23-1 when he homered . . . Has fine tools as center fielder, but gets careless out there . . . Enhanced reputation as postseason player by hitting .375 in playoffs and .300 in World Series . . . Two-out, two-strike home run in ninth inning of Game 5 of 1986 AL playoffs kept Red Sox alive . . . Born July 21, 1958, in Dos Palos, Cal. . . . Mariners'

first-round choice in June 1977 draft . . . Uncle Joe pitched for White Sox and Reds.

Year	Club	Pos.	G	AB	R	H	2B	3B	HR	RBI	SB	Avg.
1981	Seattle	OF	59	126	17	21	3	0	6	13	2	.167
1982	Seattle	OF	104	324	47	82	17	1	14	48	2	.253
1983	Seattle	OF	137	484	50	130	24	5	17	55	9	.269
1984	Seattle	OF	112	350	42	98	23	0	14	43	5	.280
1985	Seattle	OF	139	502	70	121	28	2	14	68	6	.241
1986	Sea.-Bos	OF	139	388	59	103	22	4	15	47	2	.265
1987	Boston	OF	75	184	30	43	10	0	8	25	1	.234
1987	San Francisco	OF	15	21	2	5	2	0	0	1	2	.238
1988	Oakland	OF	146	507	100	154	38	1	24	94	2	.304
	Totals		926	2886	417	757	167	13	112	394	31	.262

TERRY STEINBACH 27 6-1 195 — Bats R Throws R

Controversial selection to All-Star Game silenced critics by driving in both AL runs in 2-1 victory and winning MVP award . . . Was hitting just .217 at the break, but came on strong to bat .289 over second half . . . Missed 22 games from May 6 until June 1 when he was struck by thrown ball during batting practice and suffered fractured orbital bone around left eye . . . Strong-armed catcher threw out 28 of 70 (40 percent) of would-be base-stealers . . . Was A's best hitter in World Series with .364 average on 4-for-11 . . . Born March 2, 1962, in New Ulm, Minn. . . . Acquired by Athletics in ninth round of June 1983 draft, out of the University of Minnesota.

Year	Club	Pos.	G	AB	R	H	2B	3B	HR	RBI	SB	Avg.
1986	Oakland	C	6	15	3	5	0	0	2	4	0	.333
1987	Oakland	C-3B-1B	122	391	66	111	16	3	16	56	1	.284
1988	Oakland	C-3B	104	351	42	93	19	1	9	51	3	.265
	Totals		232	757	111	209	35	4	27	111	4	.276

WALT WEISS 25 6-0 175 — Bats S Throws R

Could not have responded better after being given shortstop job in offseason when A's dealt veteran Alfredo Griffin to Los Angeles . . . Made dramatic improvement as season progressed . . . Just one of his 15 errors came after July 8 . . . Went 58 consecutive games without an error before miscue Sept. 21 . . . Already ranks among best shortstops in either league . . . Hit .281 from Aug. 1 on . . . Showed youth in World

Series, going 1-for-16 . . . Born Nov. 29, 1963, in Tuxedo, N.Y. . . . Athletics' first-round selection in June 1985 draft, out of the University of North Carolina . . . Won AL Rookie of the Year honors, following in footsteps of Jose Canseco and Mark McGwire.

Year	Club	Pos.	G	AB	R	H	2B	3B	HR	RBI	SB	Avg.
1987	Oakland..........	SS	16	26	3	12	4	0	0	1	1	.462
1988	Oakland..........	SS	147	452	44	113	17	3	3	39	4	.250
	Totals		163	478	47	125	21	3	3	40	5	.262

DENNIS ECKERSLEY 34 6-2 195 **Bats R Throws R**

Entrusted with role of bullpen stopper, he responded with dream season . . . Finished with 45 saves, one short of major-league record set by Dave Righetti in 1986 . . . Named ALCS MVP when he saved all four games in sweep of Boston . . . Failed to convert just nine save opportunities all season . . . Enjoyed blazing start with 20 saves in first 21 chances . . . Pinpoint control has enabled him to make conversion from starter with such great results . . . Only lowlight of season was two-out, two-strike, ninth-inning homer he allowed to Dodgers' gimpy Kirk Gibson to lose World Series opener . . . Born Oct. 3, 1954, in Oakland . . . Acquired from Cubs with Dan Rohn for Dave Wilder, Brian Guinn and Mark Leonette, April 3, 1987 . . . Threw no-hitter vs. Angels, May 30, 1977 . . . Chosen by Indians in third round of June 1972 draft.

Year	Club	G	IP	W	L	Pct.	SO	BB	H	ERA
1975	Cleveland	34	187	13	7	.650	152	90	147	2.60
1976	Cleveland	36	199	13	12	.520	200	75	155	3.44
1977	Cleveland	33	247	14	13	.519	191	54	214	3.53
1978	Boston	35	268	20	8	.714	162	71	258	2.99
1979	Boston	33	247	17	10	.630	150	59	234	2.99
1980	Boston	30	198	12	14	.462	121	44	188	4.27
1981	Boston	23	154	9	8	.529	79	35	160	4.27
1982	Boston	33	224⅓	13	13	.500	127	43	228	3.73
1983	Boston	28	176⅓	9	13	.409	77	39	223	5.61
1984	Boston	9	64⅔	4	4	.500	33	13	71	5.01
1984	Chicago (NL).........	24	160⅓	10	8	.556	81	36	152	3.03
1985	Chicago (NL).........	25	169⅓	11	7	.611	117	19	145	3.08
1986	Chicago (NL).........	33	201	6	11	.353	137	43	226	4.57
1987	Oakland.............	54	115⅔	6	8	.429	113	17	99	3.03
1988	Oakland.............	60	72⅔	4	2	.667	70	11	52	2.35
	Totals	490	2684⅓	161	138	.538	1810	652	2552	3.61

DAVE STEWART 32 6-2 200 **Bats R Throws R**

Career has taken off since he was released by Phillies and signed by Athletics as a free agent, May 23, 1986 . . . Joined Hall of Famer "Catfish" Hunter as only pitchers in A's history to post consecutive 20-win seasons . . . "Smoke" has learned to use forkball to complement hard fastball . . . Finished second in AL to Minnesota Frank Viola with 21 wins . . . Led majors with 275⅔ innings pitched and 37 starts . . . Tied Boston's Roger Clemens for AL lead with 14 complete games . . . Got off to 8-0 start . . . Also had big finish, taking nine of last 11 decisions . . . Continued strong pitching in postseason, going 2-0 with 1.35 ERA in AL playoffs, 0-1 with 3.14 ERA in two World Series starts . . . Born Feb. 19, 1957, in Oakland . . . Chosen by Dodgers in 16th round of June 1975 draft and immediately converted from catcher to pitcher.

Year	Club	G	IP	W	L	Pct.	SO	BB	H	ERA
1978	Los Angeles	1	2	0	0	.000	1	0	1	0.00
1981	Los Angeles	32	43	4	3	.571	29	14	40	2.51
1982	Los Angeles	45	146⅓	9	8	.529	80	49	137	3.81
1983	Los Angeles	46	76	5	2	.714	54	33	67	2.96
1983	Texas	8	59	5	2	.714	24	17	50	2.14
1984	Texas	32	192⅓	7	14	.333	119	87	193	4.73
1985	Texas	42	81⅓	0	6	.000	64	37	86	5.42
1985	Philadelphia	4	4⅓	0	0	.000	2	4	5	6.23
1986	Philadelphia	8	12⅓	0	0	.000	9	4	15	6.57
1986	Oakland	29	149⅓	9	5	.643	102	65	137	3.74
1987	Oakland	37	261⅓	20	13	.606	205	105	224	3.68
1988	Oakland	37	275⅔	21	12	.636	192	110	240	3.23
	Totals	321	1303	80	65	.552	881	525	1195	3.75

BOB WELCH 32 6-3 193 **Bats R Throws R**

Played key role in Oakland's rise by winning career-high 17 games in his first season in AL after 10 years with Dodgers . . . Acquired from Dodgers as part of three-team, seven-player deal that also involved the Mets following the 1987 season . . . Placed second on staff to Dave Stewart in starts, innings and strikeouts . . . Helped A's take early command of division by winning seven straight from April 24 through May 25 . . . Pitched far better at home, posting 13-4 record with 2.56 ERA at the Coliseum, compared to 4-5, 5.29 on road . . . Did not get a decision in two postseason starts . . . Born Nov. 3, 1956, in Detroit . . . Dodgers' first-round pick in June 1977 draft, out of

Eastern Michigan . . . Wrote book about his battle against alcoholism.

Year	Club	G	IP	W	L	Pct.	SO	BB	H	ERA
1978	Los Angeles	23	111	7	4	.636	66	26	92	2.03
1979	Los Angeles	25	81	5	6	.455	64	32	82	4.00
1980	Los Angeles	32	214	14	9	.609	141	79	190	3.28
1981	Los Angeles	23	141	9	5	.643	88	41	141	3.45
1982	Los Angeles	36	235⅔	16	11	.593	176	81	199	3.36
1983	Los Angeles	31	204	15	12	.556	156	72	164	2.65
1984	Los Angeles	31	178⅔	13	13	.500	126	58	191	3.78
1985	Los Angeles	23	167⅓	14	4	.778	96	35	141	2.31
1986	Los Angeles	33	235⅔	7	13	.350	183	55	227	3.28
1987	Los Angeles	35	251⅔	15	9	.625	196	86	204	3.22
1988	Oakland..............	36	244⅔	17	9	.654	158	81	237	3.64
	Totals	328	2064⅔	132	95	.581	1450	646	1868	3.20

MIKE MOORE 29 6-4 205 **Bats R Throws R**

Recovered from slow start to boost stock, then fled Mariners as free agent . . . Received three-year, $4-million deal from Athletics . . . Went 2-6 with 5.54 ERA in first 10 starts and was 4-9 with 4.31 ERA in first half . . . Won three straight from Aug. 9-19 and notched club record-tying 16 strikeouts vs. Yankees Aug. 19 . . . Born Nov. 26, 1959, in tiny Eakly, Okla. . . . First right-handed pitcher to be nation's No. 1 choice as Mariners selected him to kick off June 1981 draft . . . Attended Oral Roberts University.

Year	Club	G	IP	W	L	Pct.	SO	BB	H	ERA
1982	Seattle	28	144⅓	7	14	.333	73	79	159	5.36
1983	Seattle	22	128	6	8	.429	108	60	130	4.71
1984	Seattle	34	212	7	17	.292	158	85	236	4.97
1985	Seattle	35	247	17	10	.630	155	70	230	3.46
1986	Seattle	38	266	11	13	.458	146	94	279	4.30
1987	Seattle	33	231	9	19	.321	115	84	268	4.71
1988	Seattle	37	228⅔	9	15	.375	182	63	196	3.78
	Totals	227	1457	66	96	.407	937	535	1498	4.38

STORM DAVIS 27 6-4 200 **Bats R Throws R**

Produced best results of career in first full season with Athletics . . . Set career highs in wins, starts and strikeouts . . . Acquired from Padres for Dave Leiper and Rob Nelson, Aug. 30, 1987 . . . Helped A's turn division race into runaway by winning 10 consecutive decisions from July 8 to Sept. 5 . . . Generally regarded as a six-inning pitcher . . . Suffered 0-2 record with 11.25 ERA in two World Series starts . . . Born Dec. 26,

1961, in Dallas . . . Chosen by Orioles in seventh round of June 1979 draft . . . High school teammate of current Astros' first baseman Glenn Davis.

Year	Club	G	IP	W	L	Pct.	SO	BB	H	ERA
1982	Baltimore	29	100⅔	8	4	.667	67	28	96	3.49
1983	Baltimore	34	200⅓	13	7	.650	125	64	180	3.59
1984	Baltimore	35	225	14	9	.609	105	71	205	3.12
1985	Baltimore	31	175	10	8	.556	93	70	172	4.53
1986	Baltimore	25	154	9	12	.429	96	49	166	3.62
1987	San Diego	21	62⅔	2	7	.222	37	36	70	6.18
1987	Oakland	5	30⅓	1	1	.500	28	11	28	3.26
1988	Oakland	33	201⅔	16	7	.696	127	91	211	3.70
	Totals	213	1149⅔	73	55	.570	678	420	1128	3.79

TOP PROSPECT

DOUG JENNINGS 24 5-10 165 **Bats L Throws L**

Paid his dues after being plucked out of Angels' system, Dec. 7, 1987 . . . Used in left and right field and at first base in learning year . . . Hit .327 in 49 at-bats for Tacoma (AAA) . . . Topped A's pinch-hitters with five hits and five RBI . . . Went 4-for-4 with double and first major-league homer in first start, April 13 in Seattle . . . Hit .208 with one homer and 15 RBI in 101 at-bats with Oakland . . . Born Sept. 30, 1964, in Atlanta.

MANAGER TONY LA RUSSA: Honored as AL Manager of the Year after leading A's to World Series for first time since 1974 . . . His intensity was reflected in young club as it broke on top early in AL West and continued widening margin . . . Great believer in detail . . . Insists players meet frequently to review approach . . . Gets everyone involved by using entire roster . . . Made debut as Oakland skipper on July 7, 1986 . . . Inherited listless 32-52 last-place club and rallied A's to 76-86 mark and tie for third . . . Became White Sox manager Aug. 2, 1979 . . . Guided Sox to 99 victories and AL West title in 1983, but they failed to maintain that success, dropping off to 74 wins a year later . . . Victim of front-office chaos in Windy City as former GM Ken (Hawk) Harrelson was out not long after firing him . . . Had managed parts of two seasons in minors . . . Signed as shortstop with Kansas City A's in 1962 . . . Spent parts

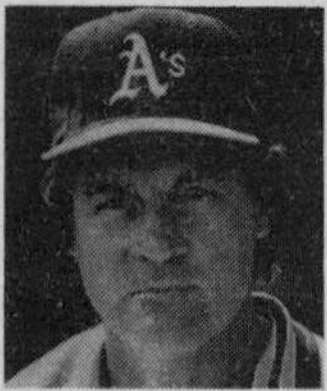

of six years in majors, batting .199 overall in career that spanned 1962-77 . . . Holds law degree from Florida State . . . Born Oct. 4, 1944, in Tampa . . . Has major-league managerial record of 681-611.

Walt Weiss became A's third straight Rookie of Year.

GREATEST FIRST BASEMAN

He has only two full major-league seasons under his belt, but Mark McGwire is an easy choice as the Athletics' best first baseman.

McGwire became the first first baseman to represent the A's in an All-Star Game in 1987, when he enjoyed one of the greatest rookie seasons in history. The 6-foot-5, 225-pound slugger established a rookie record with 49 home runs.

That season, McGwire established Oakland marks in home runs—he hit two more than Reggie Jackson had amassed in 1969—and in slugging percentage with a .618 mark that topped the majors. Then just 23 years old, McGwire was a unanimous choice as AL Rookie of the Year.

McGwire tailed off somewhat in 1988—if 32 home runs and 99 RBI can be called tailing off.

ALL-TIME A's SEASON RECORDS

BATTING: Napoleon Lajoie, .422, 1901
HRs: Jimmie Foxx, 58, 1932
RBIs: Jimmie Foxx, 169, 1932
STEALS: Rickey Henderson, 130, 1982
WINS: John Coombs, 31, 1910
Lefty Grove, 31, 1931
STRIKEOUTS: Rube Waddell, 349, 1904

SEATTLE MARINERS

TEAM DIRECTORY: Owner: George Argyros; Pres.: Chuck Armstrong; VP-Baseball Oper.: Woody Woodward; Dir. Player Dev.: Brian Granger; Dir. Baseball Adm.: Lee Pelekoudas; Dir. Publicity: David Aust; Trav. Sec.: Craig Detwiler; Mgr.: Jim Lefebvre. Home: Kingdome (59,438). Field distances: 316, l.f. line; 357, l.c.; 410, c.f.; 357, r.c.; 316, r.f. line. Spring training: Tempe, Ariz.

Alvin Davis hit remarkable .321 vs. southpaws.

SCOUTING REPORT

HITTING: The Mariners desperately lack a big hitter, in the middle of the order, a glaring weakness evident in the fact that Alvin Davis led the club with just 69 RBI in 1988.

Jay Buhner (.215, 13, 38) has the chance to be a big RBI man, but perhaps not at this stage of his young career. The Mariners hope the free-agent signing of Jeffrey (Hack Man) Leonard will help. He was a considerable disappointment to Milwaukee, batting .235 with eight home runs and 44 RBI there after being acquired from San Francisco during the 1988 season.

Harold Reynolds (.283, 4, 41) and Mickey Brantley (.263, 15, 56) both provide speed. Reynolds recorded a team-high 35 stolen bases and Brantley added 18. But more help is needed as only three AL teams scored fewer runs than Seattle's total of 664 in 1988.

PITCHING: Mark Langston (15-11, 3.34) continues to be one of the best and least appreciated pitchers in either league. Scott Bankhead (7-9, 3.07), Mike Campbell (6-10, 5.89) and highly-regarded Erik Hanson will try to make up for the loss of free-agent defector Mike Moore to the Athletics.

The Mariners signed ex-Oriole Tom Niedenfuer in an attempt to boost a bullpen that finished last in the AL with 28 saves in 1988. Niedenfuer (3-4, 3.51) earned a team-leading 18 saves with Baltimore last season and should help. Mike Schooler (5-8, 3.54, 15 saves) gives the Mariners a second pitcher capable of closing games and Mike Jackson (6-5, 2.63 in 62 appearances) is a fine set-up man.

FIELDING: The Mariners are mediocre defensively. Rey Quinones must develop more consistency after making 23 errors last season, the second-highest total among AL shortstops.

The right side of the infield is strong with Reynolds at second and Davis at first. Reynolds topped AL players at his position with 794 total chances and 112 double plays. Davis ranked fourth among AL first basemen in fielding, committing only six errors in 1,051 chances.

OUTLOOK: The last-place Mariners have not enjoyed a winning season since their inception in 1977 and they have never finished higher than fourth. New manager Jim Lefebvre brings a great deal of enthusiasm to his first major-league managerial post. Maybe that will be enough for the Mariners to escape the AL West cellar. Then again, maybe not.

SEATTLE MARINERS 1989 ROSTER

MANAGER Jim Lefebvre
Coaches—Bob Didier, Rusty Kuntz, Mike Paul, Bill Plummer, Gene Clines

PITCHERS

No.	Name	1988 Club	W-L	IP	SO	ERA	B-T	Ht.	Wt.	Born
15	Bankhead, Scott	Seattle	7-9	135	102	3.07	R-R	5-10	175	7/31/63 Raleigh, NC
27	Campbell, Mike	Seattle	6-10	115	63	5.89	R-R	6-3	210	2/17/64 Seattle, WA
		Calgary	4-4	70	38	4.48				
—	Dobie, Reggie	Tidewater	8-5	112	78	3.86	R-R	6-1	174	8/17/64 Rosedale, MS
39	Hanson, Erik	Calgary	12-7	162	154	4.23	R-R	6-6	205	5/18/65 Kinnelon, NJ
		Seattle	2-3	42	36	3.24				
38	Jackson, Mike	Seattle	6-5	99	76	2.63	R-R	6-0	185	12/22/64 Houston, TX
12	Langston, Mark	Seattle	15-11	261	235	3.34	R-L	6-2	188	8/20/60 San Diego, CA
—	Niedenfuer, Tom	Baltimore	3-4	59	40	3.51	R-R	6-5	227	8/13/59 St. Louis Park, MN
48	Powell, Dennis	Calgary	6-4	108	81	4.17	L-L	6-3	200	8/13/63 Detroit, MI
		Seattle	1-3	19	15	8.68				
31	Reed, Jerry	Seattle	1-1	86	48	3.96	R-R	6-1	190	10/8/55 Bryson City, NC
40	Schooler, Mike	Calgary	4-4	34	47	3.21	R-R	6-3	220	8/10/62 Anaheim, CA
		Seattle	5-8	48	54	3.54				
37	Solano, Julio	Seattle	0-0	22	10	4.09	R-R	6-1	170	1/8/60 Dominican Republic
		Calgary	3-2	35	23	4.89				
18	Swift, Bill	Seattle	8-12	175	47	4.59	R-R	6-0	180	10/27/61 S. Portland, ME
44	Taylor, Terry	Calgary	11-9	134	97	5.64	R-R	6-1	180	7/28/64 Crestview, FL
		Seattle	0-1	23	9	6.26				
34	Trout, Steve	Seattle	4-7	56	14	7.83	L-L	6-4	190	7/30/57 Detroit, MI
32	Walter, Gene	New York (NL)	0-1	17	14	3.78	L-L	6-4	201	11/22/60 Chicago, IL
		Seattle	1-0	26	13	5.13				
		Calgary	0-0	9	11	2.08				
13	Wilkinson, Bill	Seattle	2-2	31	25	3.48	R-L	5-10	160	8/10/64 Greybull, WY
		Calgary	0-4	24	20	9.13				
—	Zavaras, Clint	Vermont	10-7	129	120	3.92	R-R	6-1	175	1/4/67 Denver, CO

CATCHERS

No.	Name	1988 Club	H	HR	RBI	Pct.	B-T	Ht.	Wt.	Born
9	Bradley, Scott	Seattle	86	4	33	.257	L-R	5-11	185	3/22/60 Montclair, NJ
—	Goff, Jerry	San Bernardino	62	13	43	.287	L-R	6-3	205	4/12/64 San Raphael, CA
		Vermont	41	7	23	.210				
35	McGuire, Bill	Vermont	28	5	24	.206	R-R	6-3	215	2/14/64 Omaha, NE
		Calgary	27	2	15	.231				
		Seattle	3	0	2	.188				
10	Valle, David	Seattle	67	10	50	.231	R-R	6-2	200	10/30/60 Bayside, NY

INFIELDERS

No.	Name	1988 Club	H	HR	RBI	Pct.	B-T	Ht.	Wt.	Born
45	Balboni, Steve	KC-Sea.	97	23	66	.235	R-R	6-3	225	1/16/57 Brockton, MA
21	Davis, Alvin	Seattle	141	18	69	.295	L-R	6-1	190	9/9/60 Riverside, CA
—	Diaz, Mario	Seattle	22	0	9	.306	R-R	5-10	160	1/10/62 Puerto Rico
		Calgary	54	1	30	.329				
—	Lennon, Patrick	Vermont	83	9	40	.259	R-R	6-2	200	6/27/68 Whiteville, NC
11	Martinez, Edgar	Calgary	120	8	64	.363	R-R	5-11	175	1/2/63 New York, NY
		Seattle	9	0	5	.281				
17	Presley, Jim	Seattle	125	14	62	.230	R-R	6-1	190	10/23/61 Pensacola, FL
51	Quinones, Rey	Seattle	124	12	52	.248	R-R	5-11	185	11/11/63 Puerto Rico
1	Renteria, Rich	Seattle	18	0	6	.205	R-R	5-9	175	12/25/61 Harbor City, CA
		Calgary	23	4	10	.264				
4	Reynolds, Harold	Seattle	169	4	41	.283	S-R	5-11	165	11/26/60 Eugene, OR
—	Vizquel, Omar	Vermont	95	2	35	.253	S-R	5-9	155	5/15/67 Venezuela
		Calgary	24	1	12	.224				

OUTFIELDERS

No.	Name	1988 Club	H	HR	RBI	Pct.	B-T	Ht.	Wt.	Born
14	Brantley, Mickey	Seattle	152	15	56	.263	R-R	5-10	180	6/17/61 Catskill, NY
8	Briley, Greg	Calgary	139	11	66	.313	L-R	5-8	165	5/24/65 Bethel, NC
		Seattle	9	1	4	.250				
43	Buhner, Jay	Columbus	33	8	18	.256	R-R	6-3	205	8/13/64 Louisville, KY
		NY (AL)-Sea.	56	13	38	.215				
2	Coles, Darnell	Pittsburgh	49	5	36	.232	R-R	6-1	185	6/2/62 San Bernardino, CA
		Seattle	57	10	34	.292				
28	Cotto, Henry	Seattle	100	8	33	.259	R-R	6-2	178	1/5/61 Bronx, NY
20	Hengel, Dave	Calgary	51	6	37	.230	R-R	6-0	195	12/18/61 Oakland, CA
		Seattle	10	2	7	.167				
7	Kingery, Mike	Seattle	25	1	9	.203	L-L	6-0	180	3/29/61 St. James, MN
		Calgary	54	1	14	.318				
—	Leonard, Jeffrey	San Francisco	41	2	20	.256	R-R	6-4	205	9/22/55 Philadelphia, PA
		Milwaukee	88	8	44	.235				

MARINER PROFILES

HAROLD REYNOLDS 28 5-11 165 **Bats S Throws R**

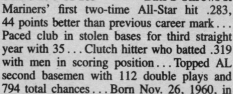

Mariners' first two-time All-Star hit .283, 44 points better than previous career mark . . . Paced club in stolen bases for third straight year with 35 . . . Clutch hitter who batted .319 with men in scoring position . . . Topped AL second basemen with 112 double plays and 794 total chances . . . Born Nov. 26, 1960, in Eugene, Ore. . . . Mariners' first-round selection in June 1980 draft and the second player picked overall . . . Brothers Don and Larry played pro ball . . . Led AL in steals with 60 in 1987, supplanting perennial league leader, Rickey Henderson.

Year	Club	Pos.	G	AB	R	H	2B	3B	HR	RBI	SB	Avg.
1983	Seattle..........	2B	20	59	8	12	4	1	0	1	0	.203
1984	Seattle..........	2B	10	10	3	3	0	0	0	0	1	.300
1985	Seattle..........	2B	67	104	15	15	3	1	0	6	3	.144
1986	Seattle..........	2B	126	445	46	99	19	4	1	24	30	.222
1987	Seattle..........	2B	160	530	73	146	31	8	1	35	60	.275
1988	Seattle..........	2B	158	598	61	169	26	11	4	41	35	.283
	Totals		541	1746	206	444	83	25	6	107	129	.254

ALVIN DAVIS 28 6-1 190 **Bats L Throws R**

Consistent performer hit .295 for second straight year . . . First baseman ranked third in AL with .412 on-base percentage and fourth with 95 walks . . . Led club with 69 RBI . . . Homered in four straight games from May 5-8 . . . Hammered left-handed pitching for .321 average . . . Mariners' all-time leader in eight offensive categories, including home runs (110) and RBI (435) . . . Born Sept. 9, 1960, in Riverside, Cal. . . . Mariners' sixth-round selection in June 1982 draft . . . Named AL Rookie of the Year in 1984 . . . Was standout at Arizona State.

Year	Club	Pos.	G	AB	R	H	2B	3B	HR	RBI	SB	Avg.
1984	Seattle..........	1B	152	567	80	161	34	3	27	116	5	.284
1985	Seattle..........	1B	155	578	78	166	33	1	18	78	1	.287
1986	Seattle..........	1B	135	479	66	130	18	1	18	72	0	.271
1987	Seattle..........	1B	157	580	86	171	37	2	29	100	0	.295
1988	Seattle..........	1B	140	478	67	141	24	1	18	69	1	.295
	Totals		739	2682	377	769	146	8	110	435	7	.287

MICKEY BRANTLEY 27 5-10 180 **Bats R Throws R**

Speedster is coming into his own . . . Set career highs in games, hits, doubles, triples, homers, RBI, walks and stolen bases . . . Played all three outfield positions . . . Ran off career-high 13-game hitting streak in May and hit .370 that month with eight homers and 20 RBI . . . Born June 17, 1961, in Catskill, N.Y., and still lives there . . . Mariners' second-round choice in June 1983 draft, out of Coastal Carolina College . . . Was one of three AL rookies to hit more than .300 in 1987 . . . Had three homers and seven RBI vs. Indians, Sept. 14, 1987.

Year	Club	Pos.	G	AB	R	H	2B	3B	HR	RBI	SB	Avg.
1986	Seattle..........	OF	27	102	12	20	3	2	3	7	1	.196
1987	Seattle..........	OF	92	351	52	106	23	2	14	54	13	.302
1988	Seattle..........	OF	149	577	76	152	25	4	15	56	18	.263
	Totals		268	1030	140	278	51	8	32	117	32	.270

REY QUINONES 25 5-11 185 **Bats R Throws R**

Youngster remains an erratic performer . . . Batted .303 in April, then hit .221 in May . . . Followed that with big June, belting six homers to go with .282 average . . . Made 23 errors at shortstop, but has good tools . . . Born Nov. 11, 1963, in Rio Piedras, Puerto Rico . . . Acquired from Red Sox with John Christensen, Mike Trujillo and Mike Brown for Spike Owen and Dave Henderson, Aug. 17, 1986 . . . Signed by Boston as free agent in 1982.

Year	Club	Pos.	G	AB	R	H	2B	3B	HR	RBI	SB	Avg.
1986	Bos.-Sea........	SS	98	312	32	68	16	1	2	22	4	.218
1987	Seattle..........	SS	135	478	55	132	18	2	12	56	1	.276
1988	Seattle..........	SS	140	499	63	124	30	3	12	52	0	.248
	Totals		373	1289	150	324	64	6	26	130	5	.251

JAY BUHNER 24 6-3 205 **Bats R Throws R**

Acquired from the Yankess with Rick Balabon and Troy Evers for Ken Phelps July 21 and was immediately installed as everyday right fielder . . . Showed considerable potential, batting .306 with five homers and 16 RBI in August . . . Became only fifth player to reach center-field bleachers in Yankee Stadium with mammoth shot Aug. 19 . . . Faltered in September and October, hitting .136 with 27 strikeouts . . . An above-average outfielder with a rifle arm . . . Born Aug. 13,

1964, in Louisville, Ky. . . . Felt he wasn't given a full shot by Yankees, who were troubled by hitch in his swing . . . Pirates drafted him in January 1984, but sent him to Yanks prior to 1985 season . . . Hit 31 home runs for Columbus (AAA) in 1987.

Year	Club	Pos.	G	AB	R	H	2B	3B	HR	RBI	SB	Avg.
1987	New York (AL)	OF	7	22	0	5	2	0	0	1	0	.227
1988	NY (AL)-Sea.	OF	85	261	36	56	13	1	13	38	1	.215
	Totals		92	283	36	61	15	1	13	39	1	.216

MARK LANGSTON 28 6-2 188 **Bats R Throws L**

Led Mariners' pitchers in virtually every category . . . His 235 strikeouts last season ranked second in majors to Red Sox' Roger Clemens . . . Rang up club-record 16 strikeouts vs. Toronto May 10 . . . Went 6-8 with 3.95 ERA in first half, but finished very strong . . . Named AL Pitcher of the Month in September, compiling 5-1 record and 0.50 ERA . . . Born Aug. 20, 1960, in San Diego . . . Mariners' second-round pick in June 1981 draft as compensation selection from Rangers for loss of free agent Bill Stein . . . Clashed with former manager Dick Williams . . . Attended San Jose State . . . Has led AL in strikeouts three times, including rookie season of 1984.

Year	Club	G	IP	W	L	Pct.	SO	BB	H	ERA
1984	Seattle	35	225	17	10	.630	204	118	188	3.40
1985	Seattle	24	126⅔	7	14	.333	72	91	122	5.47
1986	Seattle	37	239⅓	12	14	.462	245	123	234	4.85
1987	Seattle	35	272	19	13	.594	262	114	242	3.84
1988	Seattle	35	261⅓	15	11	.577	235	110	222	3.34
	Totals	166	1124⅓	70	62	.530	1018	556	1008	4.03

MIKE JACKSON 24 6-0 185 **Bats R Throws R**

Excellent pickup for Mariners . . . Acquired from Phils with Dave Brundage and Glenn Wilson for Phil Bradley and Tim Fortugno prior to last season . . . Appeared in club-high 62 games . . . Posted 1.96 ERA over final 16 games . . . Right-handers batted just .169 against him . . . Features fastball clocked as high as 96 mph . . . Born Dec. 22, 1964, in Houston . . . Phils' second-round pick in January 1984.

Year	Club	G	IP	W	L	Pct.	SO	BB	H	ERA
1986	Philadelphia	9	13⅓	0	0	.000	3	4	12	3.38
1987	Philadelphia	55	109⅓	3	10	.231	93	56	88	4.20
1988	Seattle	62	99⅓	6	5	.545	76	43	74	2.63
	Totals	126	222	9	15	.375	172	103	174	3.45

TOM NIEDENFUER 29 6-5 227 **Bats R Throws R**

Left Orioles to sign two-year, $1.75-million deal with Mariners as free agent last winter . . . Recorded 18 saves in 23 chances in 1988 . . . Had allowed just three home runs until Sept. 4, but was hammered for five the rest of the way . . . Was a big part of Orioles' limited success . . . Was finishing pitcher in 26 of Birds' 54 wins . . . One of only four relievers to record at least 10 saves in each of the last six years. Others are Rich Gossage, Lee Smith and Jeff Reardon . . . Born Aug. 13, 1959, in St. Louis Park, Minn. . . . As a Dodger, he lost last two games of 1985 NLCS when he threw gopher balls to Cards' Ozzie Smith and Jack Clark . . . Dodgers signed him as free agent in August 1980 . . . Attended Washington State . . . Has 95 career saves . . . Married to singer/actress Judy Landers.

Year	Club	G	IP	W	L	Pct.	SO	BB	H	ERA
1981	Los Angeles	17	26	3	1	.750	12	6	25	3.81
1982	Los Angeles	55	69⅔	3	4	.429	60	25	71	2.71
1983	Los Angeles	66	94⅔	8	3	.727	66	29	55	1.90
1984	Los Angeles	33	47⅓	2	5	.286	45	23	39	2.47
1985	Los Angeles	64	106⅓	7	9	.438	102	24	86	2.71
1986	Los Angeles	60	80	6	6	.500	55	29	86	3.71
1987	Los Angeles	15	16⅓	1	0	1.000	10	9	13	2.76
1987	Baltimore	45	52⅓	3	5	.375	37	22	55	4.99
1988	Baltimore	52	59	3	4	.429	40	19	59	3.51
	Totals	407	551⅔	36	37	.493	427	186	489	3.05

SCOTT BANKHEAD 25 5-10 175 **Bats R Throws R**

Unable to avoid major injuries for second straight year . . . Opened season on disabled list with injured right shoulder . . . Activated May 14, but did not earn first victory until June 6 . . . Was 4-3 with 3.12 ERA in 11 first-half starts . . . Did not pitch after Aug. 31 due to sore ribs . . . Born July 31, 1963, in Raleigh, N.C. . . . Acquired from Royals with Steve Shields and Mike Kingery for Danny Tartabull and Rick Luecken following the 1986 season . . . Attended University of North Carolina and was member of 1984 U.S. Olympic team . . . Royals' first-round pick in June 1984.

Year	Club	G	IP	W	L	Pct.	SO	BB	H	ERA
1986	Kansas City..........	24	121	8	9	.471	94	37	121	4.61
1987	Seattle	27	149⅓	9	8	.529	95	37	168	5.42
1988	Seattle	21	135	7	9	.438	102	38	115	3.07
	Totals	72	405⅓	24	26	.480	291	112	404	4.40

MIKE SCHOOLER 26 6-3 220 **Bats R Throws R**

Made conversion to relief with very promising results . . . Led club with 15 saves after promotion from Calgary (AAA), where he was 4-4, 3.21 with eight saves . . . Converted first seven save situations . . . Fanned 410 batters in 430 minor-league innings . . . Born Aug. 10, 1962, in Anaheim, Cal. . . . Mariners' second-round selection in June 1985 draft . . . Attended Golden West College and Cal. State-Fullerton.

Year	Club	G	IP	W	L	Pct.	SO	BB	H	ERA
1988	Seattle	40	48⅓	5	8	.385	54	24	45	3.54

TOP PROSPECT

KEN GRIFFEY Jr. 19 6-3 195 **Bats L Throws L**

Center fielder has chance for stardom at a tender age . . . Named *Baseball America*'s Class A Player of the Year after batting .338 with 11 homers and 42 RBI in 58 games for San Bernadino in 1988 . . . Advanced to Vermont (AA) and helped that club reach Eastern League championship series with .279 average, two homers and 10 RBI in 17 games . . . Son of major-league outfielder Ken Sr. . . . Born Nov. 21, 1969, in Charleroi, Pa. . . . Mariners' first-round selection in June 1987 draft . . . Hit .320 with 14 homers, 40 RBI and 13 steals in 178 at-bats for Bellingham (A) in 1987.

MANAGER JIM LEFEBVRE: Contribution as third-base coach with American League champion A's helped him land first major-league managerial job . . . Showed managerial ability with Phoenix, guiding club to Pacific Coast League title in 1985 and to championship series berth in '86 . . . Gained experience as coach from 1978-82, first with Los Angeles and then with San Francisco . . . Served as Giants' director of player development in 1983-84 . . . Enters 26th year in pro ball . . . An infielder, he began major-league playing career with Dodgers in 1965 and was Rookie of the Year . . . Named to NL All-Star team in 1966 and batted .274 with 24 home runs that

year . . . Wound up eight-year career, all as a Dodger, with .251 average . . . Later played for four years with Lotte Orions in Japan . . . Has world championship ring as member of 1965 Dodgers . . . Born Jan. 7, 1942, in Inglewood, Cal. . . . Said he had three goals in 1988: to win the World Series, to have a healthy, new baby and to be named manager of a major-league team . . . He came close as Athletics reached World Series, his wife Ruth gave birth to Brittany Oct. 28 and he became Mariner manager Nov. 7.

GREATEST FIRST BASEMAN

Alvin Davis didn't make the Mariners during spring training in 1984, but an injury presented him with an early opportunity to become the regular first baseman and he seized it.

Davis became the first player in the Mariners' brief history to win a major award when he was honored as AL Rookie of the Year after pounding 27 home runs, knocking in 116 runs and batting .284. His 116 RBI represented the finest rookie total since Al Rosen reached that level in 1950 and Davis achieved an AL rookie mark with 13 game-winning RBI.

Davis was no rookie flash. He continues to be among the Mariners' most productive hitters and heads the club's all-time list with 110 home runs and 435 RBI.

ALL-TIME MARINER SEASON RECORDS

BATTING: Tom Paciorek, .326, 1981
HRs: Gorman Thomas, 32, 1985
RBIs: Alvin Davis, 116, 1984
STEALS: Harold Reynolds, 60, 1987
WINS: Mark Langston, 19, 1987
STRIKEOUTS: Mark Langston, 262, 1987

TEXAS RANGERS

TEAM DIRECTORY: Chairman: Eddie Chiles; Pres.: Mike Stone; VP-GM: Tom Grieve; VP-Fin.: Charles Wangner; Asst. GM-Player Pers./Scouting: Sandy Johnson; Dir. Player Dev.: Marty Scott; Media Rel. Dir.: John Blake; Trav. Sec.: Dan Schimek; Mgr.: Bobby Valentine. Home: Arlington Stadium (43,508). Field distances: 330, l.f. line; 380, l.c.; 400, c.f.; 380, r.c.; 330, r.f. line. Spring training: Port Charlotte, Fla.

SCOUTING REPORT

HITTING: The Rangers were determined to improve their lineup last winter, after compiling a .252 team batting average that ranked 11th in the AL and scoring just 637 runs, fewer than all but two AL teams.

They made some progress by acquiring smooth-swinging Rafael Palmeiro (.307, 8, 53) from the Cubs and Julio Franco, a .300 hitter each of the last three seasons, from the Indians. Neither, however, is likely to provide much power and the Rangers need some after finishing last in the AL with 112 homers, 76 of them bases-empty shots, in 1988.

Obviously, big seasons are needed from holdovers Ruben Sierra (.254, 23, 91), Pete Incaviglia (.249, 22, 54), Steve Buechele (.250, 16, 58) and Scott Fletcher (.276, 0, 47).

PITCHING: The Rangers hope all-time strikeout king and future Hall of Famer Nolan Ryan (12-11, 3.52 with Houston) can provide leadership for an unpredictable young staff that topped the majors in walks (654) for the third straight year in 1988, was first in wild pitches (72) and second in hit batsmen (56) and balks (57).

Ryan, the former Astro who was signed as a free agent, joins knuckleballer Charlie Hough (15-16, 3.32), Bobby Witt (8-10, 3.92), Jose Guzman (11-13, 3.70) and former Cub Jamie Moyer (9-15, 3.48) in an unusual rotation. Ryan and Hough are both over 40, but still going strong.

The Rangers may have huge problems in the bullpen after dealing closer Mitch Williams to the Cubs as part of the nine-player blockbuster for Palmeiro. Williams accounted for 18 of the Rangers' 31 saves. Only two teams finished with fewer saves. Ex-Cub prospect Drew Hall will be given a shot at replacing Williams. Also, Jeff Russell (10-9, 3.82) may make the switch to the bullpen.

At 41, Charlie Hough still makes hitters knuckle under.

FIELDING: Fletcher set a club record for shortstops with a .983 fielding percentage, finishing a hair behind California's Dick Schofield for the league lead. Incaviglia is an improving outfielder. He made only two errors last year, 11 fewer than the previous year, and tied for second in the AL with 12 assists.

As a team, though, Texas needs to tighten up defensively after finishing 11th with a .978 percentage. The Rangers continue to have catching problems. Thanks to the thankless job of catching Hough, Geno Petralli led AL receivers in passed balls (20) for the second straight year.

OUTLOOK: After going three years without making a major trade, the Rangers acknowledged that the rebuilding plan had stalled and shuffled the deck this past winter. Bobby Valentine's revamped club should do better than the 70-91 disaster that spelled the fifth-worst record in the majors in 1988. However, it is not good enough to scare any of the top clubs in the AL West.

TEXAS RANGERS 1989 ROSTER

MANAGER Bobby Valentine
Coaches—Dick Egan, Toby Harrah, Tom House, Davey Lopes, Dave Oliver, Tom Robson

PITCHERS

No.	Name	1988 Club	W-L	IP	SO	ERA	B-T	Ht.	Wt.	Born
24	Akerfelds, Darrel	Colorado Springs	3-7	58	50	4.34	R-R	6-2	210	6/12/62 Denver, CO
27	Barfield, John	Tulsa	9-9	169	125	2.88	L-L	6-1	185	10/15/64 Little Rock, AR
41	Brown, Kevin	Tulsa	12-10	174	118	3.51	R-R	6-4	188	3/14/65 McIntyre, GA
		Texas	1-1	23	12	4.24				
18	Correa, Edwin	Texas		Injured			R-R	6-2	215	4/29/66 Puerto Rico
—	*Guante, Cecilio	NY (AL)-Tex.	5-6	80	65	2.82	R-R	6-3	205	2/2/60 Dominican Republic
23	Guzman, Jose	Texas	11-13	207	157	3.70	R-R	6-3	185	4/9/63 Puerto Rico
44	Hall, Drew	Iowa	4-3	65	75	2.34	L-L	6-4	220	3/27/63 Louisville, KY
		Chicago (NL)	1-1	22	22	7.66				
45	Henry, Dwayne	Oklahoma City	5-5	76	98	5.59	R-R	6-3	205	2/16/62 Elkton, MD
		Texas	0-1	10	10	8.71				
49	Hough, Charlie	Texas	15-16	252	174	3.32	R-R	6-2	190	1/5/48 Honolulu, HI
48	May, Scott	Oklahoma City	8-7	152	103	2.97	R-R	6-0	185	11/11/61 West Bend, WI
		Texas	0-0	7	4	8.59				
38	McMurtry, Craig	Oklahoma City	2-5	50	35	4.35	R-R	6-5	192	11/5/59 Temple, TX
		Texas	3-3	60	35	2.25				
39	Moyer, Jamie	Chicago (NL)	9-15	202	121	3.48	L-L	6-1	170	11/18/62 Sellersville, PA
42	Pavlas, Dave	Oklahoma City	3-1	52	40	4.47	R-R	6-7	180	8/12/62 West Germany
		Tulsa	5-2	77	69	1.98				
46	Raether, Rick	Tulsa	4-1	56	40	0.96	R-R	6-4	192	5/30/64 Milwaukee, WI
61	Rogers, Kenny	Charlotte	2-0	35	26	1.27	L-L	6-1	200	11/10/64 Savannah, GA
		Tulsa	4-6	83	76	4.00				
40	Russell, Jeff	Texas	10-9	189	88	3.82	R-R	6-3	210	9/2/61 Cincinnati, OH
—	Ryan, Nolan	Houston	12-11	220	228	3.52	R-R	6-2	210	1/31/47 Refugio, TX
43	Vande Berg, Ed	Texas	2-2	37	18	4.14	R-L	6-1	170	10/26/58 Redlands, CA
36	Witt, Bobby	Oklahoma City	4-6	77	70	4.34	R-R	6-2	200	5/11/64 Arlington, VA
		Texas	8-10	174	148	3.92				

CATCHERS

No.	Name	1988 Club	H	HR	RBI	Pct.	B-T	Ht.	Wt.	Born
7	Kreuter, Chad	Tulsa	95	3	51	.265	S-R	6-2	190	8/26/64 Marin County, CA
		Texas	14	1	5	.275				
12	Petralli, Geno	Texas	99	7	36	.282	L-R	6-1	180	9/25/59 Sacramento, CA
10	*Sundberg, Jim	Chicago (NL)	13	2	9	.241	R-R	6-0	192	5/18/51 Galesburg, IL
		Texas	26	4	13	.286				

INFIELDERS

22	Buechele, Steve	Texas	126	16	58	.250	R-R	6-2	190	9/26/61 Lancaster, CA
1	Fletcher, Scott	Texas	142	0	47	.276	R-R	5-11	173	7/30/58 Ft. Walton Beach, FL
14	Franco, Julio	Cleveland	186	10	54	.303	R-R	6-0	165	8/23/61 Dominican Republic
20	Kunkel, Jeff	Oklahoma City	44	5	21	.217	R-R	6-2	190	3/25/62 West Palm Beach, FL
		Texas	35	2	15	.227				
19	Meacham, Bobby	New York (AL)	25	0	7	.217	R-R	6-1	180	8/25/60 Los Angeles, CA
16	Palmer, Dean	Charlotte	81	4	35	.266	R-R	6-1	175	12/27/68 Tallahassee, FL
3	Palmeiro, Rafael	Chicago (NL)	178	8	53	.307	L-L	6-0	180	9/24/64 Cuba
8	Sanchez, Rey	Charlotte	128	0	38	.306	R-R	5-10	180	10/5/67 Puerto Rico

OUTFIELDERS

6	Espy, Cecil	Texas	86	2	39	.248	S-R	6-3	195	1/20/63 San Diego, CA
—	Gonzalez, Juan	Charlotte	71	8	43	.256	R-R	6-3	175	10/16/69 Puerto Rico
29	Incaviglia, Pete	Texas	104	22	54	.249	R-R	6-1	220	4/2/64 Pebble Beach, CA
47	Reimer, Kevin	Tulsa	147	21	76	.302	L-R	6-2	215	6/28/64 Macon, GA
		Texas	3	1	2	.120				
21	Sierra, Ruben	Texas	156	23	91	.254	S-R	6-1	175	10/6/65 Puerto Rico
17	Sosa, Sam	Charlotte	116	9	51	.229	R-R	6-0	165	11/10/68 Dominican Republic

*Free agent at press time listed with 1988 team

RANGER PROFILES

RUBEN SIERRA 23 6-1 175 **Bats S Throws R**

Failed to put up the big numbers the Rangers were expecting, but still led club with 23 homers, 91 RBI, 156 hits, 77 runs and 32 doubles . . . Outfielder just missed becoming fourth Ranger to have 20 homers and 20 steals in same season, falling two steals short with career-high 18 in 22 tries . . . First Ranger to have more than 600 at-bats in consecutive seasons . . . Had Ranger season-high 14-game hitting streak from Sept. 4-18, going 20-for-55 (.364) with one home run and 12 RBI . . . Homered from both sides of plate Aug. 27 against Toronto . . . In 1987, he became sixth player in major-league history to hit 30 home runs and drive in 100 runs in a season before turning 22 . . . Born Oct. 6, 1965, in Rio Piedras, Puerto Rico, and still lives there . . . Texas signed him as a free agent, Nov. 21, 1982.

Year	Club	Pos.	G	AB	R	H	2B	3B	HR	RBI	SB	Avg.
1986	Texas.	OF	113	382	50	101	13	10	16	55	7	.264
1987	Texas.	OF	158	643	97	169	35	4	30	109	16	.263
1988	Texas.	OF	156	615	77	156	32	2	23	91	18	.254
	Totals		427	1640	224	426	80	16	69	255	41	.260

PETE INCAVIGLIA 24 6-1 220 **Bats R Throws R**

Injuries and strikeouts combined to cause a disappointing season . . . Missed 29 of Rangers' last 30 games with strained ligaments in right hand . . . Also missed 11 games in late June with a strained lower back, suffered in a car accident in Chicago . . . Back continued to bother him for much of season . . . Still ranked second on club with 22 homers . . . Free swinger tied Milwaukee's Rob Deer for AL lead with 153 strikeouts, despite playing only 116 games . . . Hit eight home runs in May, one shy of club record for that month . . . Outfielder has made great strides defensively, cutting error total from AL high of 13 in 1987 to two last year . . . Set NCAA career records for home runs (100) and slugging percentage (.915) at Oklahoma State . . . Set NCAA single-season marks with 48 homers, 143 RBI, 285 total bases and 1.140 slugging percentage in 1985 . . . Born April 2, 1964, in Pebble Beach, Cal. . . . Selected by Montreal in first round of June 1985 draft . . . The day he signed with

Expos, Nov. 2, 1985, he was traded to Texas for Bob Sebra and Jim Anderson.

Year	Club	Pos.	G	AB	R	H	2B	3B	HR	RBI	SB	Avg.
1986	Texas............	OF	153	540	82	135	21	2	30	88	3	.250
1987	Texas............	OF	139	509	85	138	26	4	27	80	9	.271
1988	Texas............	OF	116	418	59	104	19	3	22	54	6	.249
	Totals		408	1467	226	377	66	9	79	222	18	.257

JULIO FRANCO 27 6-0 165 **Bats R Throws R**

Acquired from Indians for Pete O'Brien, Oddibe McDowell and Jerry Browne during winter meetings . . . Last year, he made smooth transition from shortstop to second base and responded with strong season . . . Compiled AL's two longest hitting streaks—22 games from July 3-27 (.409 on 38-for-93) and 21 games from May 11 to June 3 (.360 on 32-for-89) . . . Surpassed 150 hits for sixth straight year . . . Equalled career high with 10 home runs . . . Notched 1,000th hit July 29 against Minnesota . . . Needs work on double-play pivot . . . Born Aug. 23, 1961, in San Pedro de Macoris, Dominican Republic . . . Originally signed with Phils as free agent in June 1978.

Year	Club	Pos.	G	AB	R	H	2B	3B	HR	RBI	SB	Avg.
1982	Philadelphia......	SS-3B	16	29	3	8	1	0	0	3	0	.276
1983	Cleveland	SS	149	560	68	153	24	8	8	80	32	.273
1984	Cleveland	SS	160	658	82	188	22	5	3	79	19	.286
1985	Cleveland	SS-2B	160	636	97	183	33	4	6	90	13	.288
1986	Cleveland	SS-2B	149	599	80	183	30	5	10	74	10	.306
1987	Cleveland	SS-2B	128	495	86	158	24	3	8	52	32	.319
1988	Cleveland	2B	152	613	88	186	23	6	10	54	25	.303
	Totals		914	3590	504	1059	157	31	45	432	131	.295

STEVE BUECHELE 27 6-2 190 **Bats R Throws R**

Showed more patience at the plate, leading to career highs with .250 average, 58 RBI and 65 walks . . . Walked 30 more times than previous high . . . Hit .318 in May, including 16-game span during which he hit .420 (21-for-50) . . . Played 153 games at third base, most by a Ranger since Buddy Bell in 1983 . . . Born Sept. 26, 1961, in Lancaster, Cal. . . . Selected in fifth round of June 1982 draft . . . Roomed at Stanford with current Denver star quarterback John Elway.

Year	Club	Pos.	G	AB	R	H	2B	3B	HR	RBI	SB	Avg.
1985	Texas............	3B-2B	69	219	22	48	6	3	6	21	3	.219
1986	Texas............	3B-2B-OF	153	461	54	112	19	2	18	54	5	.243
1987	Texas............	3B-2B-OF	136	363	45	86	20	0	13	50	2	.237
1988	Texas............	3B-2B	155	503	68	126	21	4	16	58	2	.250
	Totals		513	1546	189	372	66	9	53	183	12	.241

SCOTT FLETCHER 30 5-11 173 **Bats R Throws R**

Re-signed with Texas for $1.2 million in December . . . Led Rangers in batting average for third consecutive year, at .276 . . . Recovered from slow start during which he hit .163 over first 25 games by batting .373 over next 25 games . . . Was hit by pitch 12 times, a club record . . . Also set another club mark he could do without—going 515 at-bats without a home run in 1988 . . . An underrated defensive player, he finished second among AL shortstops with club-record .983 fielding percentage . . . Missed last two weeks of season with broken right thumb after being hit by pitch Sept. 16 . . . Born July 30, 1958, in Fort Walton Beach, Fla. . . . Acquired from White Sox with Ed Correa for Dave Schmidt and Wayne Tolleson, after the 1985 season.

Year	Club	Pos.	G	AB	R	H	2B	3B	HR	RBI	SB	Avg.
1981	Chicago (NL).....	2B-SS-3B	19	46	6	10	4	0	0	1	0	.217
1982	Chicago (NL).....	SS	11	24	4	4	0	0	0	1	1	.167
1983	Chicago (AL).....	SS-2B-3B	114	262	42	62	16	5	3	31	5	.237
1984	Chicago (AL).....	SS-2B-3B	149	456	46	114	13	3	3	35	10	.250
1985	Chicago (AL).....	3B-SS-2B	119	301	38	77	8	1	2	31	5	.256
1986	Texas...........	SS-2B-3B	147	530	82	159	34	5	3	50	12	.300
1987	Texas...........	SS	156	588	82	169	28	4	5	63	13	.287
1988	Texas...........	SS	140	515	59	142	19	4	0	47	8	.276
	Totals		855	2722	359	737	122	22	16	259	54	.271

RAFAEL PALMEIRO 24 6-0 180 **Bats L Throws L**

Acquired from Cubs with Jamie Moyer and Drew Hall in nine-player deal last December . . . Rangers plan to move him from outfield to first base . . . Led NL in hitting most of 1988 season, but a cut hand put him on the bench in the final weeks while the Padres' Tony Gwynn passed him for the batting title . . . His .307 average was second-best in league . . . Also finished second in the NL with 41 doubles and third with 178 hits . . . Struck out just 34 times in 629 plate apparances, an average of one per 18.5 plate appearances . . . Left fielder had 20-game hitting streak from July 18 until Aug. 11 . . . Born Sept. 24, 1964, in Havana, Cuba . . . Grew up in Miami and attended Mississippi State . . . First-round draft pick of the Cubs in June 1985.

Year	Club	Pos.	G	AB	R	H	2B	3B	HR	RBI	SB	Avg.
1986	Chicago (NL).....	OF	22	73	9	18	4	0	3	12	1	.247
1987	Chicago (NL).....	OF-1B	84	221	32	61	15	1	14	30	2	.276
1988	Chicago (NL).....	OF-1B	152	580	75	178	41	5	8	53	12	.307
	Totals		258	874	116	257	60	6	25	95	15	.294

CHARLIE HOUGH 41 6-2 190 **Bats R Throws R**

Second-winningest pitcher in majors since 1982, with 111 victories, keeps rolling along . . . Knuckleballer led club in wins (15) and innings (252) for seventh straight year . . . Ranked seventh in league in innings and ninth in AL with 174 strikeouts . . . Tied for eighth with 10 complete games . . . His 3.32 ERA was lowest among Texas starters . . . Won four consecutive starts from Sept. 6-23 . . . Only major leaguer to pitch more than nine innings four times—and won three of those games . . . Pitched 11-plus innings in Seattle June 29, the longest outing by any major-league pitcher in 1988 . . . Born Jan. 5, 1948, in Honolulu, Hawaii . . . Purchased from Dodgers, July 11, 1980 . . . Originally selected by Los Angeles in eighth round of June 1966 draft.

Year	Club	G	IP	W	L	Pct.	SO	BB	H	ERA
1970	Los Angeles	8	17	0	0	.000	8	11	18	5.29
1971	Los Angeles	4	4	0	0	.000	4	3	3	4.50
1972	Los Angeles	2	3	0	0	.000	4	2	2	3.00
1973	Los Angeles	37	72	4	2	.667	70	45	52	2.75
1974	Los Angeles	49	96	9	4	.692	63	40	65	3.75
1975	Los Angeles	38	61	3	7	.300	34	34	43	2.95
1976	Los Angeles	77	143	12	8	.600	81	77	102	2.20
1977	Los Angeles	70	127	6	12	.333	105	70	98	3.33
1978	Los Angeles	55	93	5	5	.500	66	48	69	3.29
1979	Los Angeles	42	151	7	5	.583	76	66	152	4.77
1980	Los Angeles	19	32	1	3	.250	25	21	37	5.63
1980	Texas	16	61	2	2	.500	47	37	54	3.98
1981	Texas	21	82	4	1	.800	69	31	61	2.96
1982	Texas	34	228	16	13	.552	128	72	217	3.95
1983	Texas	34	252	15	13	.536	152	95	219	3.18
1984	Texas	36	266	16	14	.533	164	94	260	3.76
1985	Texas	34	250⅓	14	16	.467	141	83	198	3.31
1986	Texas	33	230⅓	17	10	.630	146	89	188	3.79
1987	Texas	40	285⅓	18	13	.581	223	124	238	3.79
1988	Texas	34	252	15	16	.484	174	126	202	3.32
	Totals	683	2706	164	144	.532	1780	1168	2278	3.55

JOSE GUZMAN 25 6-3 185 **Bats R Throws R**

Became first Texas pitcher other than Charlie Hough to win 10 or more games in consecutive seasons since Doc Medich in 1980-81 . . . Finished second on team in innings (206⅔) and strikeouts (157) . . . Set a career high with the strikeouts . . . Won three straight games twice, from April 4-26 and June 28 to July 8 . . . Was 2-7, 4.37 ERA in last 12 starts . . . Bothered last month of season by shoulder problems . . . Missed three of last four scheduled turns . . . Born April 9, 1963, in Santa Isabel, Puerto Rico . . . Signed as free agent, Feb. 10, 1981, at age 17.

Year	Club	G	IP	W	L	Pct.	SO	BB	H	ERA
1985	Texas	5	32⅔	3	2	.600	24	14	27	2.76
1986	Texas	29	172⅓	9	15	.375	87	60	199	4.54
1987	Texas	37	208⅓	14	14	.500	143	82	196	4.67
1988	Texas	30	206⅔	11	13	.458	157	82	180	3.70
	Totals	101	620	37	44	.457	411	238	602	4.21

JEFF RUSSELL 27 6-3 210 **Bats R Throws R**

Blazing start, which led to an All-Star berth, was offset by a poor finish . . . Still set career highs with 10 wins and five complete games . . . Won first seven decisions, six as a starter, the best beginning in club history . . . Joined rotation in mid-May after serving in long relief . . . Was Rangers' All-Star representative with 8-2 mark and 3.16 ERA at break . . . Went just 2-7 with 4.42 ERA in 14 starts thereafter . . . Was 0-4 with 3.98 ERA in his last seven starts . . . Born Sept. 2, 1961, in Cincinnati . . . Acquired from Reds, July 23, 1985, to complete deal that sent Buddy Bell to Cincinnati for Duane Walker.

Year	Club	G	IP	W	L	Pct.	SO	BB	H	ERA
1983	Cincinnati	10	68⅓	4	5	.444	40	22	58	3.03
1984	Cincinnati	33	181⅔	6	18	.250	101	65	186	4.26
1985	Texas	13	62	3	6	.333	44	27	85	7.55
1986	Texas	37	82	5	2	.714	54	31	74	3.40
1987	Texas	52	97⅓	5	4	.556	56	52	109	4.44
1988	Texas	34	188⅔	10	9	.526	88	66	183	3.82
	Totals	179	680	33	44	.429	383	263	695	4.24

BOBBY WITT 24 6-2 200 **Bats R Throws R**

Jolted by early-season demotion, he finally began to realize vast potential . . . Was sent to Oklahoma City (AAA) May 10, after going 0-5 with a 7.68 ERA through six starts . . . Went 4-6 with 4.34 ERA in 11 starts at Oklahoma City . . . Returned to majors with July 10 start and posted 8-5 record with 2.93 ERA and 12 complete games in 16 starts the rest of the way . . . Reeled off complete games in each of his first nine starts after recall, tying club record shared by Ferguson Jenkins and Gaylord Perry . . . Marked only fourth time in 1980's that a pitcher has recorded nine or more successive complete games . . . Finished third in AL with 13 complete games, most by Texas pitcher other than Charlie Hough since 1978 . . . Born May 11, 1964, in Arlington, Va. . . . Chosen by Texas in first round of

June 1985 draft . . . Went 17-6 with 231 strikeouts in 196⅔ innings in two seasons at University of Oklahoma.

Year	Club	G	IP	W	L	Pct.	SO	BB	H	ERA
1986	Texas	31	157⅔	11	9	.550	174	143	130	5.48
1987	Texas	26	143	8	10	.444	160	140	114	4.91
1988	Texas	22	174⅓	8	10	.444	148	101	134	3.92
	Totals	79	475	27	29	.482	482	384	378	4.74

NOLAN RYAN 42 6-2 210 — Bats R Throws R

Rangers won bidding war for this amazing Texan, signing him to one-year pact for $1.6 million plus a $200,000 signing bonus and a $1.4-million option on his services in 1990 . . . Sure to be missed by Astros . . . Last year, he narrowly missed sixth no-hitter of career April 27, when Phillies' Mike Schmidt singled with one out in the ninth . . . Led NL in strikeouts for second year in a row with 228 . . . Was ninth time in 21-year career he has led league in strikeouts . . . Has struck out 200 or more in 12 seasons—a major-league record . . . Tops the all-time strikeout list with 4,775 and could surpass 5,000 whiffs in 1989 . . . A six-time All-Star . . . Jumped the Angels to sign with Astros as free agent after 1979 season and both clubs were among those that pursued him last winter . . . Holds 38 different major-league records, but has never been named winner of the Cy Young Award or MVP . . . Born Jan. 31, 1947, in Refugio, Tex. . . . In 1988, he became the only pitcher other than Cy Young to win 100 games in each league . . . Mets' eighth-round pick in June 1965 . . . No one else has thrown so hard for so long.

Year	Club	G	IP	W	L	Pct.	SO	BB	H	ERA
1966	New York (NL)	2	3	0	1	.000	6	3	5	15.00
1968	New York (NL)	21	134	6	9	.400	133	75	93	3.09
1969	New York (NL)	25	89	6	3	.667	92	53	60	3.54
1970	New York (NL)	27	132	7	11	.389	125	97	86	3.41
1971	New York (NL)	30	152	10	14	.417	137	116	125	3.97
1972	California	39	284	19	16	.543	329	157	166	2.28
1973	California	41	326	21	16	.568	383	162	238	2.87
1974	California	42	333	22	16	.578	367	202	221	2.89
1975	California	28	198	14	12	.538	186	132	152	3.45
1976	California	39	284	17	18	.486	327	183	193	3.36
1977	California	37	299	19	16	.543	341	204	198	2.77
1978	California	31	235	10	13	.435	260	148	183	3.71
1979	California	34	223	16	14	.533	223	114	169	3.59
1980	Houston	35	234	11	10	.524	200	98	205	3.35
1981	Houston	21	149	11	5	.688	140	68	99	1.69
1982	Houston	35	250⅓	16	12	.571	245	109	196	3.16
1983	Houston	29	196⅓	14	9	.609	183	101	134	2.98
1984	Houston	30	183⅔	12	11	.522	197	69	143	3.04
1985	Houston	35	232	10	12	.455	209	95	205	3.80
1986	Houston	30	178	12	8	.600	194	82	119	3.34
1987	Houston	34	211⅔	8	16	.333	270	87	154	2.76
1988	Houston	33	220	12	11	.522	228	87	186	3.52
	Totals	678	4547	273	253	.519	4775	2442	3330	3.15

Nolan Ryan brings his Texas-style heat to Arlington.

JAMIE MOYER 26 6-1 170 **Bats L Throws L**

Acquired with Rafael Palmeiro and Drew Hall in December deal that sent Mitch Williams and five others to Cubs . . . Was the hard-luck pitcher on Cub staff in 1988, receiving less offensive support than any other pitcher on team . . . His 3.48 ERA in friendly confines of Wrigley Field should have helped to make his record 15-9 instead of 9-15 . . . Cut down on walks, which had haunted him in 1987 . . . Born Nov. 18, 1962, in Sellersville, Pa. . . . Attended St. Joseph University in Philadelphia . . . Chosen by Cubs in the sixth round of the June 1984 draft.

Year	Club	G	IP	W	L	Pct.	SO	BB	H	ERA
1986	Chicago (NL)	16	87⅓	7	4	.636	45	42	107	5.05
1987	Chicago (NL)	35	201	12	15	.444	147	97	210	5.10
1988	Chicago (NL)	34	202	9	15	.375	121	55	212	3.48
	Totals	85	490⅓	28	34	.452	313	194	529	4.42

TOP PROSPECT

CHAD KREUTER 24 6-2 190 **Bats S Throws R**

Catcher's strong season allowed him to make jump from Double-A to majors on Sept. 12, after he had helped Tulsa to Texas League title . . . Started 15 of last 18 games for Rangers, hitting .275 with one home run and five RBI . . . Homered off Oakland's Dave Stewart in first major-league game, Sept. 14 . . . Rangers like him defensively, but offensive skills must be refined . . . Was Texas League All-Star catcher . . . Hit .265 at Tulsa with three homers and 51 RBI in 108 games . . . Born Aug. 26, 1964, in Marin County, Cal. . . . Selected in fifth round of June 1985 draft, after playing three seasons at Pepperdine.

MANAGER BOBBY VALENTINE: Losing favor in Lone Star

State after Rangers' second consecutive sixth-place finish . . . Has won more games (285) and managed more games (614) than any manager in Ranger history, but club has gotten off track since showing dramatic improvement in 1986, Valentine's first full season . . . Was Mets' third-base coach until Rangers hired him to manage in May 1985 . . . Took over 9-23 club and compiled 53-79 record rest of way . . . Managerial mark stands at 285-329 . . . Was first-round pick of Los Angeles in 1968 and was mostly an infielder in 10-year career with Dodgers, Angels, Padres, Mets and Mariners . . . Broken leg suffered with California in 1973 prevented him from realizing full potential . . . Hit .260 in 639 games . . . Born May 13, 1950, in Stamford, Conn. . . . Owns restaurants in Connecticut area . . . Wife Mary is daughter of former Dodger pitcher Ralph Branca.

GREATEST FIRST BASEMAN

Although Pete O'Brien didn't receive a great deal of attention outside of Texas, he more than made his mark with the Rangers before being dealt to the Indians last winter.

O'Brien ranks third on the Rangers' all-time list with 114 home runs and rates fourth in RBI (487), hits (914), runs (419) and at-bats (3,351).

He gained the club record for home runs by a left-handed batter and by a first baseman with 23 in 1986, then repeated that total the following season. The steady O'Brien hit 16 or more home runs each of the last five years and knocked in at least 71 runs in each of those seasons.

O'Brien is also a fine defensive first baseman who set a club record for assists at that position with 146 in 1987.

ALL-TIME RANGER SEASON RECORDS

BATTING: Mickey Rivers, .322, 1980
HRs: Larry Parrish, 32, 1987
RBIs: Jeff Burroughs, 118, 1974
STEALS: Bump Wills, 52, 1978
WINS: Ferguson Jenkins, 25, 1974
STRIKEOUTS: Ferguson Jenkins, 235, 1974

MAJOR LEAGUE YEAR-BY-YEAR LEADERS

NATIONAL LEAGUE MVP

Year	Player, Club
1931	Frank Frisch, St. Louis Cardinals
1932	Chuck Klein, Philadelphia Phillies
1933	Carl Hubbell, New York Giants
1934	Dizzy Dean, St. Louis Cardinals
1935	Gabby Hartnett, Chicago Cubs
1936	Carl Hubbell, New York Giants
1937	Joe Medwick, St. Louis Cardinals
1938	Ernie Lombardi, Cincinnati Reds
1939	Bucky Walters, Cincinnati Reds
1940	Frank McCormick, Cincinnati Reds
1941	Dolph Camilli, Brooklyn Dodgers
1942	Mort Cooper, St. Louis Cardinals
1943	Stan Musial, St. Louis Cardinals
1944	Marty Marion, St. Louis Cardinals
1945	Phil Cavarretta, Chicago Cubs
1946	Stan Musial, St. Louis Cardinals
1947	Bob Elliott, Boston Braves
1948	Stan Musial, St. Louis Cardinals
1949	Jackie Robinson, Brooklyn Dodgers
1950	Jim Konstanty, Philadelphia Phillies
1951	Roy Campanella, Brooklyn Dodgers
1952	Hank Sauer, Chicago Cubs
1953	Roy Campanella, Brooklyn Dodgers
1954	Willie Mays, New York Giants
1955	Roy Campanella, Brooklyn Dodgers
1956	Don Newcombe, Brooklyn Dodgers
1957	Hank Aaron, Milwaukee Braves
1958	Ernie Banks, Chicago Cubs
1959	Ernie Banks, Chicago Cubs
1960	Dick Groat, Pittsburgh Pirates
1961	Frank Robinson, Cincinnati Reds

Year	Player, Club
1962	Maury Wills, Los Angeles Dodgers
1963	Sandy Koufax, Los Angeles Dodgers
1964	Ken Boyer, St. Louis Cardinals
1965	Willie Mays, San Francisco Giants
1966	Roberto Clemente, Pittsburgh Pirates
1967	Orlando Cepeda, St. Louis Cardinals
1968	Bob Gibson, St. Louis Cardinals
1969	Willie McCovey, San Francisco Giants
1970	Johnny Bench, Cincinnati Reds
1971	Joe Torre, St. Louis Cardinals
1972	Johnny Bench, Cincinnati Reds
1973	Pete Rose, Cincinnati Reds
1974	Steve Garvey, Los Angeles Dodgers
1975	Joe Morgan, Cincinnati Reds
1976	Joe Morgan, Cincinnati Reds
1977	George Foster, Cincinnati Reds
1978	Dave Parker, Pittsburgh Pirates
1979	Keith Hernandez, St. Louis Cardinals
	Willie Stargell, Pittsburgh Pirates
1980	Mike Schmidt, Philadelphia Phillies
1981	Mike Schmidt, Philadelphia Phillies
1982	Dale Murphy, Atlanta Braves
1983	Dale Murphy, Atlanta Braves
1984	Ryne Sandberg, Chicago Cubs
1985	Willie McGee, St. Louis Cardinals
1986	Mike Schmidt, Philadelphia Phillies
1987	Andre Dawson, Chicago Cubs
1988	Kirk Gibson, Los Angeles Dodgers

AMERICAN LEAGUE MVP

Year	Player, Club
1931	Lefty Grove, Philadelphia Athletics
1932	Jimmy Foxx, Philadelphia Athletics
1933	Jimmy Foxx, Philadelphia Athletics
1934	Mickey Cochrane, Detroit Tigers
1935	Hank Greenberg, Detroit Tigers
1936	Lou Gehrig, New York Yankees
1937	Charley Gehringer, Detroit Tigers
1938	Jimmy Foxx, Boston Red Sox
1939	Joe DiMaggio, New York Yankees
1940	Hank Greenberg, Detroit Tigers
1941	Joe DiMaggio, New York Yankees

Year	Player, Club
1942	Joe Gordon, New York Yankees
1943	Spud Chandler, New York Yankees
1944	Hal Newhouser, Detroit Tigers
1945	Hal Newhouser, Detroit Tigers
1946	Ted Williams, Boston Red Sox
1947	Joe DiMaggio, New York Yankees
1948	Lou Boudreau, Cleveland Indians
1949	Ted Williams, Boston Red Sox
1950	Phil Rizzuto, New York Yankees
1951	Yogi Berra, New York Yankees
1942	Bobby Shantz, Philadelphia Athletics
1953	Al Rosen, Cleveland Indians
1954	Yogi Berra, New York Yankees
1955	Yogi Berra, New York Yankees
1956	Mickey Mantle, New York Yankees
1957	Mickey Mantle, New York Yankees
1958	Jackie Jensen, Boston Red Sox
1959	Nellie Fox, Chicago White Sox
1960	Roger Maris, New York Yankees
1961	Roger Maris, New York Yankees
1962	Mickey Mantle, New York Yankees
1963	Elston Howard, New York Yankees
1964	Brooks Robinson, Baltimore Orioles
1965	Zoilo Versalles, Minnesota Twins
1966	Frank Robinson, Baltimore Orioles
1967	Carl Yastrzemski, Boston Red Sox
1968	Dennis McLain, Detroit Tigers
1969	Harmon Killebrew, Minnesota Twins
1970	Boog Powell, Baltimore Orioles
1971	Vida Blue, Oakland A's
1972	Dick Allen, Chicago White Sox
1973	Reggie Jackson, Oakland A's
1974	Jeff Burroughs, Texas Rangers
1975	Fred Lynn, Boston Red Sox
1976	Thurman Munson, New York Yankees
1977	Rod Carew, Minnesota Twins
1978	Jim Rice, Boston Red Sox
1979	Don Baylor, California Angels
1980	George Brett, Kansas City Royals
1981	Rollie Fingers, Milwaukee Brewers
1982	Robin Yount, Milwaukee Brewers
1983	Cal Ripken Jr., Baltimore Orioles
1984	Willie Hernandez, Detroit Tigers
1985	Don Mattingly, New York Yankees

Year	Player, Club
1986	Roger Clemens, Boston Red Sox
1987	George Bell, Toronto Blue Jays
1988	Jose Canseco, Oakland A's

AMERICAN LEAGUE
Batting Champions

Year	Player, Club	Avg.
1901	Napoleon Lajoie, Philadelphia Athletics	.422
1902	Ed Delahanty, Washington Senators	.376
1903	Napoleon Lajoie, Cleveland Indians	.355
1904	Napoleon Lajoie, Cleveland Indians	.381
1905	Elmer Flick, Cleveland Indians	.306
1906	George Stone, St. Louis Browns	.358
1907	Ty Cobb, Detroit Tigers	.350
1908	Ty Cobb, Detroit Tigers	.324
1909	Ty Cobb, Detroit Tigers	.377
1910	Ty Cobb, Detroit Tigers	.385
1911	Ty Cobb, Detroit Tigers	.420
1912	Ty Cobb, Detroit Tigers	.410
1913	Ty Cobb, Detroit Tigers	.390
1914	Ty Cobb, Detroit Tigers	.368
1915	Ty Cobb, Detroit Tigers	.370
1916	Tris Speaker, Cleveland Indians	.386
1917	Ty Cobb, Detroit Tigers	.383
1918	Ty Cobb, Detroit Tigers	.382
1919	Ty Cobb, Detroit Tigers	.384
1920	George Sisler, St. Louis Browns	.407
1921	Harry Heilmann, Detroit Tigers	.393
1922	George Sisler, St. Louis Browns	.420
1923	Harry Heilmann, Detroit Tigers	.398
1924	Babe Ruth, New York Yankees	.378
1925	Harry Heilmann, Detroit Tigers	.393
1926	Heinie Manush, Detroit Tigers	.377
1927	Harry Heilmann, Detroit Tigers	.398
1928	Goose Goslin, Washington Senators	.379
1929	Lew Fonseca, Cleveland Indians	.369
1930	Al Simmons, Philadelphia Athletics	.381
1931	Al Simmons, Philadelphia Athletics	.390
1932	David Alexander, Detroit Tigers-Boston Red Sox	.367
1933	Jimmy Foxx, Philadelphia Athletics	.356
1934	Lou Gehrig, New York Yankees	.365
1935	Buddy Myer, Washington Senators	.349

Year	Player, Club	Avg.
1936	Luke Appling, Chicago White Sox	.388
1937	Charlie Gehringer, Detroit Tigers	.371
1938	Jimmy Foxx, Boston Red Sox	.349
1939	Joe DiMaggio, New York Yankees	.381
1940	Joe DiMaggio, New York Yankees	.352
1941	Ted Williams, Boston Red Sox	.406
1942	Ted Williams, Boston Red Sox	.356
1943	Luke Appling, Chicago White Sox	.328
1944	Lou Boudreau, Cleveland Indians	.327
1945	Snuffy Stirnweiss, New York Yankees	.309
1946	Mickey Vernon, Washington Senators	.353
1947	Ted Williams, Boston Red Sox	.343
1948	Ted Williams, Boston Red Sox	.369
1949	George Kell, Detroit Tigers	.343
1950	Billy Goodman, Boston Red Sox	.354
1951	Ferris Fain, Philadelphia Athletics	.344
1952	Ferris Fain, Philadelphia Athletics	.327
1953	Mickey Vernon, Washington Senators	.337
1954	Bobby Avila, Cleveland Indians	.341
1955	Al Kaline, Detroit Tigers	.340
1956	Mickey Mantle, New York Yankees	.353
1957	Ted Williams, Boston Red Sox	.388
1958	Ted Williams, Boston Red Sox	.328
1959	Harvey Kuenn, Detroit Tigers	.353
1960	Pete Runnels, Boston Red Sox	.320
1961	Norm Cash, Detroit Tigers	.361
1962	Pete Runnels, Boston Red Sox	.326
1963	Carl Yastrzemski, Boston Red Sox	.321
1964	Tony Oliva, Minnesota Twins	.323
1965	Tony Oliva, Minnesota Twins	.321
1966	Frank Robinson, Baltimore Orioles	.316
1967	Carl Yastrzemski, Boston Red Sox	.326
1968	Carl Yastrzemski, Boston Red Sox	.301
1969	Rod Carew, Minnesota Twins	.332
1970	Alex Johnson, California Angels	.329
1971	Tony Oliva, Minnesota Twins	.337
1972	Rod Carew, Minnesota Twins	.318
1973	Rod Carew, Minnesota Twins	.350
1974	Rod Carew, Minnesota Twins	.364
1975	Rod Carew, Minnesota Twins	.359
1976	George Brett, Kansas City Royals	.333
1977	Rod Carew, Minnesota Twins	.388
1978	Rod Carew, Minnesota Twins	.333
1979	Fred Lynn, Boston Red Sox	.333

Year	Player, Club	Avg.
1980	George Brett, Kansas City Royals	.390
1981	Carney Lansford, Boston Red Sox	.336
1982	Willie Wilson, Kansas City Royals	.332
1983	Wade Boggs, Boston Red Sox	.361
1984	Don Mattingly, New York Yankees	.343
1985	Wade Boggs, Boston Red Sox	.368
1986	Wade Boggs, Boston Red Sox	.357
1987	Wade Boggs, Boston Red Sox	.363
1988	Wade Boggs, Boston Red Sox	.366

NATIONAL LEAGUE
Batting Champions

Year	Player, Club	Avg.
1876	Roscoe Barnes, Chicago	.403
1877	James White, Boston	.385
1878	Abner Dalrymple, Milwaukee	.356
1879	Cap Anson, Chicago	.407
1880	George Gore, Chicago	.365
1881	Cap Anson, Chicago	.399
1882	Dan Brouthers, Buffalo	.367
1883	Dan Brouthers, Buffalo	.371
1884	Jim O'Rourke, Buffalo	.350
1885	Roger Connor, New York	.371
1886	Mike Kelly, Chicago	.388
1887	Cap Anson, Chicago	.421
1888	Cap Anson, Chicago	.343
1889	Dan Brouthers, Boston	.373
1890	Jack Glassock, New York	.336
1891	Billy Hamilton, Philadelphia	.338
1892	Cupid Childs, Cleveland	.335
	Dan Brouthers, Brooklyn	.335
1893	Hugh Duffy, Boston	.378
1894	Hugh Duffy, Boston	.438
1895	Jesse Burkett, Cleveland	.423
1896	Jesse Burkett, Cleveland	.410
1897	Willie Keeler, Baltimore	.432
1898	Willie Keeler, Baltimore	.379
1899	Ed Delahanty, Philadelphia	.408
1900	Honus Wagner, Pittsburgh	.380
1901	Jesse Burkett, St. Louis Cardinals	.382
1902	C.H. Beaumont, Pittsburgh Pirates	.357
1903	Honus Wagner, Pittsburgh Pirates	.355

Year	Player, Club	Avg.
1904	Honus Wagner, Pittsburgh Pirates	.349
1905	J. Bentley Seymour, Cincinnati Reds	.377
1906	Honus Wagner, Pittsburgh Pirates	.339
1907	Honus Wagner, Pittsburgh Pirates	.350
1908	Honus Wagner, Pittsburgh Pirates	.354
1909	Honus Wagner, Pittsburgh Pirates	.339
1910	Sherwood Magee, Philadelphia Phillies	.331
1911	Honus Wagner, Pittsburgh Pirates	.334
1912	Heinie Zimmerman, Chicago Cubs	.372
1913	Jake Daubert, Brooklyn Dodgers	.350
1914	Jake Daubert, Brooklyn Dodgers	.329
1915	Larry Doyle, New York Giants	.320
1916	Hal Chase, Cincinnati Reds	.339
1917	Edd Roush, Cincinnati Reds	.341
1918	Zack Wheat, Brooklyn Dodgers	.335
1919	Edd Roush, Cincinnati Reds	.321
1920	Rogers Hornsby, St. Louis Cardinals	.370
1921	Rogers Hornsby, St. Louis Cardinals	.397
1922	Rogers Hornsby, St. Louis Cardinals	.401
1923	Rogers Hornsby, St. Louis Cardinals	.384
1924	Rogers Hornsby, St. Louis Cardinals	.424
1925	Rogers Hornsby, St. Louis Cardinals	.403
1926	Bubbles Hargrave, Cincinnati Reds	.353
1927	Paul Waner, Pittsburgh Pirates	.380
1928	Rogers Hornsby, Boston Braves	.387
1929	Lefty O'Doul, Philadelphia Phillies	.398
1930	Bill Terry, New York Giants	.401
1931	Chick Hafey, St. Louis Cardinals	.349
1932	Lefty O'Doul, Brooklyn Dodgers	.368
1933	Chuck Klein, Philadelphia Phillies	.368
1934	Paul Waner, Pittsburgh Pirates	.362
1935	Arky Vaughan, Pittsburgh Pirates	.385
1936	Paul Waner, Pittsburgh Pirates	.373
1937	Joe Medwick, St. Louis Cardinals	.374
1938	Ernie Lombardi, Cincinnati Reds	.342
1939	Johnny Mize, St. Louis Cardinals	.349
1940	Debs Garms, Pittsburgh Pirates	.355
1941	Pete Reiser, Brooklyn Dodgers	.343
1942	Ernie Lombardi, Boston Braves	.330
1943	Stan Musial, St. Louis Cardinals	.330
1944	Dixie Walker, Brooklyn Dodgers	.357
1945	Phil Cavarretta, Chicago Cubs	.355
1946	Stan Musial, St. Louis Cardinals	.365
1947	Harry Walker, St. L. Cardinals-Phila. Phillies	.363

Year	Player, Club	Avg.
1948	Stan Musial, St. Louis Cardinals	.376
1949	Jackie Robinson, Brooklyn Dodgers	.342
1950	Stan Musial, St. Louis Cardinals	.346
1951	Stan Musial, St. Louis Cardinals	.355
1952	Stan Musial, St. Louis Cardinals	.336
1953	Carl Furillo, Brooklyn Dodgers	.344
1954	Willie Mays, New York Giants	.345
1955	Richie Ashburn, Philadelphia Phillies	.338
1956	Hank Aaron, Milwaukee Braves	.328
1957	Stan Musial, St. Louis Cardinals	.351
1958	Richie Ashburn, Philadelphia Phillies	.350
1959	Hank Aaron, Milwaukee Braves	.328
1960	Dick Groat, Pittsburgh Pirates	.325
1961	Roberto Clemente, Pittsburgh Pirates	.351
1962	Tommy Davis, Los Angeles Dodgers	.346
1963	Tommy Davis, Los Angeles Dodgers	.326
1964	Roberto Clemente, Pittsburgh Pirates	.339
1965	Roberto Clemente, Pittsburgh Pirates	.329
1966	Matty Alou, Pittsburgh Pirates	.342
1967	Roberto Clemente, Pittsburgh Pirates	.357
1968	Pete Rose, Cincinnati Reds	.335
1969	Pete Rose, Cincinnati Reds	.348
1970	Rico Carty, Atlanta Braves	.366
1971	Joe Torre, St. Louis Cardinals	.363
1972	Billy Williams, Chicago Cubs	.333
1973	Pete Rose, Cincinnati Reds	.338
1974	Ralph Garr, Atlanta Braves	.353
1975	Bill Madlock, Chicago Cubs	.354
1976	Bill Madlock, Chicago Cubs	.339
1977	Dave Parker, Pittsburgh Pirates	.338
1978	Dave Parker, Pittsburgh Pirates	.334
1979	Keith Hernandez, St. Louis Cardinals	.344
1980	Bill Buckner, Chicago Cubs	.324
1981	Bill Madlock, Pittsburgh Pirates	.341
1982	Al Oliver, Montreal Expos	.331
1983	Bill Madlock, Pittsburgh Pirates	.323
1984	Tony Gwynn, San Diego Padres	.351
1985	Willie McGee, St. Louis Cardinals	.353
1986	Tim Raines, Montreal Expos	.334
1987	Tony Gwynn, San Diego Padres	.370
1988	Tony Gwynn, San Diego Padres	.313

NATIONAL LEAGUE
Home Run Leaders

Year	Player, Club	HRs
1900	Herman Long, Boston Nationals	12
1901	Sam Crawford, Cincinnati Reds	16
1902	Tom Leach, Pittsburgh Pirates	6
1903	Jim Sheckard, Brooklyn Dodgers	9
1904	Harry Lumley, Brooklyn Dodgers	9
1905	Fred Odwell, Cincinnati Reds	9
1906	Tim Jordan, Brooklyn Dodgers	12
1907	Dave Brain, Boston Nationals	10
1908	Tim Jordan, Brooklyn Dodgers	12
1909	Jim Murray, New York Giants	7
1910	Fred Beck, Boston Nationals	10
	Frank Schulte, Chicago Cubs	10
1911	Frank Schulte, Chicago Cubs	21
1912	Heinie Zimmerman, Chicago Cubs	14
1913	Gavvy Cravath, Philadelphia Phillies	19
1914	Gavvy Cravath, Philadelphia Phillies	19
1915	Gavvy Cravath, Philadelphia Phillies	24
1916	Dave Robertson, New York Giants	12
	Cy Williams, Chicago Cubs	12
1917	Gavvy Cravath, Philadelphia Phillies	12
	Dave Robertson, New York Giants	12
1918	Gavvy Cravath, Philadelphia Phillies	8
1919	Gavvy Cravath, Philadelphia Phillies	12
1920	Cy Williams, Philadelphia Phillies	15
1921	George Kelly, New York Giants	23
1922	Rogers Hornsby, St. Louis Cardinals	42
1923	Cy Williams, Philadelphia Phillies	41
1924	Jack Fournier, Brooklyn Dodgers	27
1925	Rogers Hornsby, St. Louis Cardinals	39
1926	Hack Wilson, Chicago Cubs	21
1927	Cy Williams, Philadelphia Phillies	30
	Hack Wilson, Chicago Cubs	30
1928	Jim Bottomley, St. Louis Cardinals	31
	Hack Wilson, Chicago Cubs	31
1929	Chuck Klein, Philadelphia Phillies	43
1930	Hack Wilson, Chicago Cubs	56
1931	Chuck Klein, Philadelphia Phillies	31
1932	Chuck Klein, Philadelphia Phillies	38
	Mel Ott, New York Giants	38
1933	Chuck Klein, Philadelphia Phillies	28

Year	Player, Club	HRs
1934	Rip Collins, St. Louis Cardinals	35
	Mel Ott, New York Giants	35
1935	Wally Berger, Boston Braves	34
1936	Mel Ott, New York Giants	33
1937	Joe Medwick, St. Louis Cardinals	31
	Mel Ott, New York Giants	31
1938	Mel Ott, New York Giants	36
1939	Johnny Mize, St. Louis Cardinals	28
1940	Johnny Mize, St. Louis Cardinals	43
1941	Dolph Camilli, Brooklyn Dodgers	34
1942	Mel Ott, New York Giants	30
1943	Bill Nicholson, Chicago Cubs	29
1944	Bill Nicholson, Chicago Cubs	33
1945	Tommy Holmes, Boston Braves	28
1946	Ralph Kiner, Pittsburgh Pirates	23
1947	Ralph Kiner, Pittsburgh Pirates	51
	Johnny Mize, New York Giants	51
1948	Ralph Kiner, Pittsburgh Pirates	40
	Johnny Mize, New York Giants	40
1949	Ralph Kiner, Pittsburgh Pirates	54
1950	Ralph Kiner, Pittsburgh Pirates	47
1951	Ralph Kiner, Pittsburgh Pirates	42
1952	Ralph Kiner, Pittsburgh Pirates	37
	Hank Sauer, Chicago Cubs	37
1953	Eddie Mathews, Milwaukee Braves	47
1954	Ted Kluszewski, Cincinnati Reds	49
1955	Willie Mays, New York Giants	51
1956	Duke Snider, Brooklyn Dodgers	43
1957	Hank Aaron, Milwaukee Braves	44
1958	Ernie Banks, Chicago Cubs	47
1959	Eddie Mathews, Milwaukee Braves	46
1960	Ernie Banks, Chicago Cubs	41
1961	Orlando Cepeda, San Francisco Giants	46
1962	Willie Mays, San Francisco Giants	49
1963	Hank Aaron, Milwaukee Braves	44
	Willie McCovey, San Francisco Giants	44
1964	Willie Mays, San Francisco Giants	47
1965	Willie Mays, San Francisco Giants	52
1966	Hank Aaron, Atlanta Braves	44
1967	Hank Aaron, Atlanta Braves	39
1968	Willie McCovey, San Francisco Giants	36
1969	Willie McCovey, San Francisco Giants	45
1970	Johnny Bench, Cincinnati Reds	45
1971	Willie Stargell, Pittsburgh Pirates	48

Year	Player, Club	HRs
1972	Johnny Bench, Cincinnati Reds	40
1973	Willie Stargell, Pittsburgh Pirates	44
1974	Mike Schmidt, Philadelphia Phillies	36
1975	Mike Schmidt, Philadelphia Phillies	38
1976	Mike Schmidt, Philadelphia Phillies	38
1977	George Foster, Cincinnati Reds	52
1978	George Foster, Cincinnati Reds	40
1979	Dave Kingman, Chicago Cubs	48
1980	Mike Schmidt, Philadelphia Phillies	48
1981	Mike Schmidt, Philadelphia Phillies	31
1982	Dave Kingman, New York Mets	37
1983	Mike Schmidt, Philadelphia Phillies	40
1984	Mike Schmidt, Philadelphia Phillies	36
1984	Dale Murphy, Atlanta Braves	36
1985	Dale Murphy, Atlanta Braves	37
1986	Mike Schmidt, Philadelphia Phillies	37
1987	Andre Dawson, Chicago Cubs	49
1988	Darryl Strawberry, New York Mets	39

AMERICAN LEAGUE
Home Run Leaders

Year	Player, Club	HRs
1901	Napoleon Lajoie, Philadelphia Athletics	13
1902	Ralph Seybold, Philadelphia Athletics	16
1903	John Freeman, Boston Pilgrims	13
1904	Harry Davis, Philadelphia Athletics	10
1905	Harry Davis, Philadelphia Athletics	8
1906	Harry Davis, Philadelphia Athletics	12
1907	Harry Davis, Philadelphia Athletics	8
1908	Sam Crawford, Detroit Tigers	7
1909	Ty Cobb, Detroit Tigers	9
1910	Garland Stahl, Boston Red Sox	10
1911	Frank (Home Run) Baker, Philadelphia Athletics	9
1912	Frank (Home Run) Baker, Philadelphia Athletics	10
1913	Frank (Home Run) Baker, Philadelphia Athletics	12
1914	Frank (Home Run) Baker, Philadelphia Athletics	8
	Sam Crawford, Detroit Tigers	8
1915	Bob Roth, Cleveland Indians	7
1916	Wally Pipp, New York Yankees	12
1917	Wally Pipp, New York Yankees	9
1918	Babe Ruth, Boston Red Sox	11
	Clarence Walker, Philadelphia Athletics	11

Year	Player, Club	HRs
1919	Babe Ruth, Boston Red Sox	29
1920	Babe Ruth, New York Yankees	54
1921	Babe Ruth, New York Yankees	59
1922	Ken Williams, St. Louis Browns	39
1923	Babe Ruth, New York Yankees	41
1924	Babe Ruth, New York Yankees	46
1925	Bob Meusel, New York Yankees	33
1926	Babe Ruth, New York Yankees	47
1927	Babe Ruth, New York Yankees	60
1928	Babe Ruth, New York Yankees	54
1929	Babe Ruth, New York Yankees	46
1930	Babe Ruth, New York Yankees	49
1931	Babe Ruth, New York Yankees	46
1932	Jimmy Foxx, Philadelphia Athletics	58
1933	Jimmy Foxx, Philadelphia Athletics	48
1934	Lou Gehrig, New York Yankees	49
1935	Hank Greenberg, Detroit Tigers	36
	Jimmy Fox, Philadelphia Athletics	36
1936	Lou Gehrig, New York Yankees	49
1937	Joe DiMaggio, New York Yankees	46
1938	Hank Greenberg, Detroit Tigers	58
1939	Jimmy Foxx, Boston Red Sox	35
1940	Hank Greenberg, Detroit Tigers	41
1941	Ted Williams, Boston Red Sox	37
1942	Ted Williams, Boston Red Sox	36
1943	Rudy York, Detroit Tigers	34
1944	Nick Etten, New York Yankees	22
1945	Vern Stephens, St. Louis Browns	24
1946	Hank Greenberg, Detroit Tigers	44
1947	Ted Williams, Boston Red Sox	32
1948	Joe DiMaggio, New York Yankees	39
1949	Ted Williams, Boston Red Sox	43
1950	Al Rosen, Cleveland Indians	37
1951	Gus Zernial, Philadelphia Athletics	33
1952	Larry Doby, Cleveland Indians	32
1953	Al Rosen, Cleveland Indians	43
1954	Larry Doby, Cleveland Indians	32
1955	Mickey Mantle, New York Yankees	37
1956	Mickey Mantle, New York Yankees	52
1957	Roy Sievers, Washington Senators	42
1958	Mickey Mantle, New York Yankees	42
1959	Rocky Colavito, Cleveland Indians	42
	Harmon Killebrew, Washington Senators	42
1960	Mickey Mantle, New York Yankees	40

Year	Player, Club	HRs
1961	Roger Maris, New York Yankees	61
1962	Harmon Killebrew, Minnesota Twins	48
1963	Harmon Killebrew, Minnesota Twins	45
1964	Harmon Killebrew, Minnesota Twins	49
1965	Tony Conigliaro, Boston Red Sox	32
1966	Frank Robinson, Baltimore Orioles	49
1967	Carl Yastrzemski, Boston Red Sox	44
	Harmon Killebrew, Minnesota Twins	44
1968	Frank Howard, Washington Senators	44
1969	Harmon Killebrew, Minnesota Twins	49
1970	Frank Howard, Washington Senators	44
1971	Bill Melton, Chicago White Sox	33
1972	Dick Allen, Chicago White Sox	37
1973	Reggie Jackson, Oakland A's	32
1974	Dick Allen, Chicago White Sox	32
1975	George Scott, Milwaukee Brewers	36
	Reggie Jackson, Oakland A's	36
1976	Graig Nettles, New York Yankees	32
1977	Jim Rice, Boston Red Sox	39
1978	Jim Rice, Boston Red Sox	46
1979	Gorman Thomas, Milwaukee Brewers	45
1980	Ben Oglivie, Milwaukee Brewers	41
	Reggie Jackson, New York Yankees	41
1981	Bobby Grich, California Angels	22
	Eddie Murray, Baltimore Orioles	22
	Dwight Evans, Boston Red Sox	22
	Tony Armas, Oakland A's	22
1982	Reggie Jackson, California Angels	39
	Gorman Thomas, Milwaukee Braves	39
1983	Jim Rice, Boston Red Sox	39
1984	Tony Armas, Boston Red Sox	43
1985	Darrell Evans, Detroit Tigers	40
1986	Jesse Barfield, Toronto Blue Jays	40
1987	Mark McGwire, Oakland A's	49
1988	Jose Canseco, Oakland A's	42

CY YOUNG AWARD WINNERS

(Prior to 1967 there was a single overall major league award.)

Year	Player, Club
1956	Don Newcombe, Brooklyn Dodgers
1957	Warren Spahn, Milwaukee Braves
1958	Bob Turley, New York Yankees

Year	Player, Club
1959	Early Wynn, Chicago White Sox
1960	Vernon Law, Pittsburgh Pirates
1961	Whitey Ford, New York Yankees
1962	Don Drysdale, Los Angeles Dodgers
1963	Sandy Koufax, Los Angeles Dodgers
1964	Dean Chance, Los Angeles Angels
1965	Sandy Koufax, Los Angeles Dodgers
1966	Sandy Koufax, Los Angeles Dodgers

AL CY YOUNG

Year	Player, Club
1967	Jim Lonborg, Boston Red Sox
1968	Dennis McLain, Detroit Tigers
1969	Mike Cuellar, Baltimore Orioles
	Dennis McLain, Detroit Tigers
1970	Jim Perry, Minnesota Twins
1971	Vida Blue, Oakland A's
1972	Gaylord Perry, Cleveland Indians
1973	Jim Palmer, Baltimore Orioles
1974	Jim Hunter, Oakland A's
1975	Jim Palmer, Baltimore Orioles
1976	Jim Palmer, Baltimore Orioles
1977	Sparky Lyle, New York Yankees
1978	Ron Guidry, New York Yankees
1979	Mike Flanagan, Baltimore Orioles
1980	Steve Stone, Baltimore Orioles
1981	Rollie Fingers, Milwaukee Brewers
1982	Pete Vuckovich, Milwaukee Brewers
1983	LaMarr Hoyt, Chicago White Sox
1984	Willie Hernandez, Detroit Tigers
1985	Bret Saberhagen, Kansas City
1986	Roger Clemens, Boston Red Sox
1987	Roger Clemens, Boston Red Sox
1988	Frank Viola, Minnesota Twins

NL CY YOUNG

Year	Player, Club
1967	Mike McCormick, San Francisco Giants
1968	Bob Gibson, St. Louis Cardinals

Dwight Gooden won Cy Young after being Rookie of the Year.

Year	Player, Club
1969	Tom Seaver, New York Mets
1970	Bob Gibson, St. Louis Cardinals
1971	Ferguson Jenkins, Chicago Cubs
1972	Steve Carlton, Philadelphia Phillies
1973	Tom Seaver, New York Mets
1974	Mike Marshall, Los Angeles Dodgers
1975	Tom Seaver, New York Mets
1976	Randy Jones, San Diego Padres
1977	Steve Carlton, Philadelphia Phillies
1978	Gaylord Perry, San Diego Padres
1979	Bruce Sutter, Chicago Cubs
1980	Steve Carlton, Philadelphia Phillies
1981	Fernando Valenzuela, Los Angeles Dodgers
1982	Steve Carlton, Philadelphia Phillies
1983	John Denny, Philadelphia Phillies
1984	Rick Sutcliffe, Chicago Cubs
1985	Dwight Gooden, New York Mets
1986	Mike Scott, Houston Astros
1987	Steve Bedrosian, Philadelphia Phillies
1988	Orel Hershiser, Los Angeles Dodgers

NATIONAL LEAGUE
Rookie of Year

Year	Player, Club
1947	Jackie Robinson, Brooklyn Dodgers
1948	Al Dark, Boston Braves
1949	Don Newcombe, Brooklyn Dodgers
1950	Sam Jethroe, Boston Braves
1951	Willie Mays, New York Giants
1952	Joe Black, Brooklyn Dodgers
1953	Junior Gilliam, Brooklyn Dodgers
1954	Wally Moon, St. Louis Cardinals
1955	Bill Virdon, St. Louis Cardinals
1956	Frank Robinson, Cincinnati Reds
1957	Jack Sanford, Philadelphia Phillies
1958	Orlando Cepeda, San Francisco Giants
1959	Willie McCovey, San Francisco Giants
1960	Frank Howard, Los Angeles Dodgers
1961	Billy Williams, Chicago Cubs
1962	Kenny Hubbs, Chicago Cubs
1963	Pete Rose, Cincinnati Reds
1964	Richie Allen, Philadelphia Phillies

Year	Player, Club
1965	Jim Lefebvre, Los Angeles Dodgers
1966	Tommy Helms, Cincinnati Reds
1967	Tom Seaver, New York Mets
1968	Johnny Bench, Cincinnati Reds
1969	Ted Sizemore, Los Angeles Dodgers
1970	Carl Morton, Montreal Expos
1971	Earl Williams, Atlanta Braves
1972	Jon Matlack, New York Mets
1973	Gary Matthews, San Francisco Giants
1974	Bake McBride, St. Louis Cardinals
1975	John Montefusco, San Francisco Giants
1976	Pat Zachry, Cincinnati Reds
	Butch Metzger, San Diego Padres
1977	Andre Dawson, Montreal Expos
1978	Bob Horner, Atlanta Braves
1979	Rick Sutcliffe, Los Angeles Dodgers
1980	Steve Howe, Los Angeles Dodgers
1981	Fernando Valenzuela, Los Angeles Dodgers
1982	Steve Sax, Los Angeles Dodgers
1983	Darryl Strawberry, New York Mets
1984	Dwight Gooden, New York Mets
1985	Vince Coleman, St. Louis Cardinals
1986	Todd Worrell, St. Louis Cardinals
1987	Benito Santiago, San Diego Padres
1988	Chris Sabo, Cincinnati Reds

AMERICAN LEAGUE
Rookie of Year

Year	Player, Club
1949	Roy Sievers, St. Louis Browns
1950	Walt Dropo, Boston Red Sox
1951	Gil McDougald, New York Yankees
1952	Harry Byrd, Philadelphia Athletics
1953	Harvey Kuenn, Detroit Tigers
1954	Bob Grim, New York Yankees
1955	Herb Score, Cleveland Indians
1956	Luis Aparicio, Chicago White Sox
1957	Tony Kubek, New York Yankees
1958	Albie Pearson, Washington Senators
1959	Bob Allison, Washington Senators
1960	Ron Hansen, Baltimore Orioles
1961	Don Schwall, Boston Red Sox

Reds' Chris Sabo was NL's Rookie of the Year in '88.

Year	Player, Club
1962	Tom Tresh, New York Yankees
1963	Gary Peters, Chicago White Sox
1964	Tony Oliva, Minnesota Twins
1965	Curt Blefary, Baltimore Orioles
1966	Tommie Agee, Chicago White Sox
1967	Rod Carew, Minnesota Twins
1968	Stan Bahnsen, New York Yankees
1969	Lou Piniella, Kansas City Royals
1970	Thurman Munson, New York Yankees
1971	Chris Chambliss, Cleveland Indians
1972	Carlton Fisk, Boston Red Sox
1973	Al Bumbry, Baltimore Orioles
1974	Mike Hargrove, Texas Rangers
1975	Fred Lynn, Boston Red Sox
1976	Mark Fidrych, Detroit Tigers
1977	Eddie Murray, Baltimore Orioles
1978	Lou Whitaker, Detroit Tigers
1979	John Castino, Minnesota Twins
	Alfredo Griffin, Toronto Blue Jays
1980	Joe Charboneau, Cleveland Indians
1981	Dave Righetti, New York Yankees
1982	Cal Ripken, Jr., Baltimore Orioles
1983	Ron Kittle, Chicago White Sox
1984	Alvin Davis, Seattle Mariners
1985	Ozzie Guillen, Chicago White Sox
1986	Jose Canseco, Oakland A's
1987	Mark McGwire, Oakland A's
1988	Walt Weiss, Oakland A's

ALL-TIME MAJOR LEAGUE RECORDS

National	American
Batting (Season)	
Average	
.438 Hugh Duffy, Boston, 1894	.422 Napoleon Lajoie, Phila., 1901
.424 Rogers Hornsby, St. Louis, 1924	
At Bat	
701 Juan Samuel, Phila., 1984	705 Willie Wilson, Kansas City, 1980
Runs	
196 William Hamilton, Phila., 1894	177 Babe Ruth, New York, 1921
158 Chuck Klein, Phila., 1930	
Hits	
254 Frank J. O'Doul, Phila., 1929	257 George Sisler, St. Louis, 1920
254 Bill Terry, New York, 1930	
Doubles	
64 Joseph M. Medwick, St. L., 1936	67 Earl W. Webb, Boston, 1931
Triples	
36 J. Owen Wilson, Pitts., 1912	26 Joseph Jackson, Cleve., 1912
	26 Samuel Crawford, Detroit, 1914
Home Runs	
56 Hack Wilson, Chicago, 1930	61 Roger Maris, New York, 1961 (162-game schedule)
	60 Babe Ruth, New York, 1927
Runs Batted In	
190 Hack Wilson, Chicago, 1930	184 Lou Gehrig, New York, 1931
Stolen Bases	
118 Lou Brock, St. Louis, 1974	130 Rickey Henderson, Oakland, 1982
Bases on Balls	
148 Eddie Stanky, Brooklyn, 1945	170 Babe Ruth, New York, 1923
148 Jim Wynn, Houston, 1969	
Strikeouts	
189 Bobby Bonds, S.F., 1970	186 Rob Deer, Milwaukee, 1987
Pitching (Season)	
Games	
106 Mike Marshall, L.A., 1974	88 Wilbur Wood, Chicago, 1968
Innings Pitched	
434 Joseph J. McGinnity, N.Y., 1903	464 Edward Walsh, Chicago, 1908
Victories	
37 Christy Mathewson, N.Y., 1908	41 Jack Chesbro, New York, 1904
Losses	
29 Victor Willis, Boston, 1905	26 John Townsend, Wash., 1904
	26 Robert Groom, Wash., 1909
Strikeouts (Lefthander)	
382 Sandy Koufax, Los Angeles, 1965	343 Rube Waddell, Phila., 1904
(Righthander)	
313 J.R. Richard, Houston, 1979	383 Nolan Ryan, Cal., 1973
Bases on Balls	
185 Sam Jones, Chicago, 1955	208 Bob Feller, Cleveland, 1938
Earned-Run Average (Minimum 200 Innings)	
1.12 Bob Gibson, St. L., 1968	1.01 Hubert Leonard, Boston, 1914
Shutouts	
16 Grover C. Alexander, Phila., 1916	13 John W. Coombs, Phila., 1910

WORLD SERIES WINNERS

Year	A. L. Champion	N. L. Champion	World Series Winner
1903	Boston Red Sox	Pittsburgh Pirates	Boston, 5-3
1905	Philadelphia Athletics	New York Giants	New York, 4-1
1906	Chicago White Sox	Chicago Cubs	Chicago (AL), 4-2
1907	Detroit Tigers	Chicago Cubs	Chicago, 4-0-1
1908	Detroit Tigers	Chicago Cubs	Chicago, 4-1
1909	Detroit Tigers	Pittsburgh Pirates	Pittsburgh, 4-3
1910	Philadelphia Athletics	Chicago Cubs	Philadelphia, 4-1
1911	Philadelphia Athletics	New York Giants	Philadelphia, 4-2
1912	Boston Red Sox	New York Giants	Boston, 4-3-1
1913	Philadelphia Athletics	New York Giants	Philadelphia, 4-1
1914	Philadelphia Athletics	Boston Braves	Boston, 4-0
1915	Boston Red Sox	Philadelphia Phillies	Boston, 4-1
1916	Boston Red Sox	Brooklyn Dodgers	Boston, 4-1
1917	Chicago White Sox	New York Giants	Chicago, 4-2
1918	Boston Red Sox	Chicago Cubs	Boston, 4-2
1919	Chicago White Sox	Cincinnati Reds	Cincinnati, 5-3
1920	Cleveland Indians	Brooklyn Dodgers	Cleveland, 5-2
1921	New York Yankees	New York Giants	New York (NL), 5-3
1922	New York Yankees	New York Giants	New York (NL), 4-0-1
1923	New York Yankees	New York Giants	New York (AL), 4-2
1924	Washington Senators	New York Giants	Washington, 4-2
1925	Washington Senators	Pittsburgh Pirates	Pittsburgh, 4-3
1926	New York Yankees	St. Louis Cardinals	St. Louis, 4-3
1927	New York Yankees	Pittsburgh Pirates	New York, 4-0
1928	New York Yankees	St. Louis Cardinals	New York, 4-0
1929	Philadelphia Athletics	Chicago Cubs	Philadelphia, 4-2
1930	Philadelphia Athletics	St. Louis Cardinals	Philadelphia, 4-2
1931	Philadelphia Athletics	St. Louis Cardinals	St. Louis, 4-3
1932	New York Yankees	Chicago Cubs	New York, 4-0
1933	Washington Senators	New York Giants	New York, 4-1
1934	Detroit Tigers	St. Louis Cardinals	St. Louis, 4-3
1935	Detroit Tigers	Chicago Cubs	Detroit, 4-2
1936	New York Yankees	New York Giants	New York (AL), 4-2
1937	New York Yankees	New York Giants	New York (AL), 4-1
1938	New York Yankees	Chicago Cubs	New York, 4-0
1939	New York Yankees	Cincinnati Reds	New York, 4-0
1940	Detroit Tigers	Cincinnati Reds	Cincinnati, 4-3
1941	New York Yankees	Brooklyn Dodgers	New York, 4-1
1942	New York Yankees	St. Louis Cardinals	St. Louis, 4-1
1943	New York Yankees	St. Louis Cardinals	New York, 4-1
1944	St. Louis Browns	St. Louis Cardinals	St. Louis (NL), 4-2
1945	Detroit Tigers	Chicago Cubs	Detroit, 4-3
1946	Boston Red Sox	St. Louis Cardinals	St. Louis, 4-3
1947	New York Yankees	Brooklyn Dodgers	New York, 4-3
1948	Cleveland Indians	Boston Braves	Cleveland, 4-2
1949	New York Yankees	Brooklyn Dodgers	New York, 4-1
1950	New York Yankees	Philadelphia Phillies	New York, 4-0
1951	New York Yankees	New York Giants	New York (AL), 4-2
1952	New York Yankees	Brooklyn Dodgers	New York, 4-3
1953	New York Yankees	Brooklyn Dodgers	New York, 4-2
1954	Cleveland Indians	New York Giants	New York, 4-0
1955	New York Yankees	Brooklyn Dodgers	Brooklyn, 4-3

Year	A. L. Champion	N. L. Champion	World Series Winner
1956	New York Yankees	Brooklyn Dodgers	New York, 4-3
1957	New York Yankees	Milwaukee Braves	Milwaukee, 4-3
1958	New York Yankees	Milwaukee Braves	New York, 4-3
1959	Chicago White Sox	Los Angeles Dodgers	Los Angeles, 4-2
1960	New York Yankees	Pittsburgh Pirates	Pittsburgh, 4-3
1961	New York Yankees	Cincinnati Reds	New York, 4-1
1962	New York Yankees	San Francisco Giants	New York, 4-3
1963	New York Yankees	Los Angeles Dodgers	Los Angeles, 4-0
1964	New York Yankees	St. Louis Cardinals	St. Louis, 4-3
1965	Minnesota Twins	Los Angeles Dodgers	Los Angeles, 4-3
1966	Baltimore Orioles	Los Angeles Dodgers	Baltimore, 4-0
1967	Boston Red Sox	St. Louis Cardinals	St. Louis, 4-3
1968	Detroit Tigers	St. Louis Cardinals	Detroit, 4-3
1969	Baltimore Orioles	New York Mets	New York, 4-1
1970	Baltimore Orioles	Cincinnati Reds	Baltimore, 4-1
1971	Baltimore Orioles	Pittsburgh Pirates	Pittsburgh, 4-3
1972	Oakland A's	Cincinnati Reds	Oakland, 4-3
1973	Oakland A's	New York Mets	Oakland, 4-3
1974	Oakland A's	Los Angeles Dodgers	Oakland, 4-1
1975	Boston Red Sox	Cincinnati Reds	Cincinnati, 4-3
1976	New York Yankees	Cincinnati Reds	Cincinnati, 4-0
1977	New York Yankees	Los Angeles Dodgers	New York, 4-2
1978	New York Yankees	Los Angeles Dodgers	New York, 4-2
1979	Baltimore Orioles	Pittsburgh Pirates	Pittsburgh, 4-3
1980	Kansas City Royals	Philadelphia Phillies	Philadelphia, 4-2
1981	New York Yankees	Los Angeles Dodgers	Los Angeles, 4-2
1982	Milwaukee Brewers	St. Louis Cardinals	St. Louis, 4-3
1983	Baltimore Orioles	Philadelphia Phillies	Baltimore, 4-1
1984	Detroit Tigers	San Diego Padres	Detroit, 4-1
1985	Kansas City Royals	St. Louis Cardinals	Kansas City, 4-3
1986	Boston Red Sox	New York Mets	New York, 4-3
1987	Minnesota Twins	St. Louis Cardinals	Minnesota, 4-3
1988	Oakland A's	Los Angeles Dodgers	Los Angeles, 4-1

1988 WORLD SERIES

LOS ANGELES DODGERS

PLAYER	AVG	G	AB	R	H	2B	3B	HR	RBI	GW	SH	SF	HB	BB	SO	SB	CS	E
Anderson	.000	1	1	0	0	0	0	0	0	0	0	0	0	0	1	0	0	0
Davis	.143	4	7	3	1	0	0	1	2	0	0	0	0	4	0	2	0	0
Dempsey	.200	2	5	0	1	1	0	0	1	0	0	0	0	1	2	0	0	0
Gibson	1.000	1	1	1	1	0	0	1	2	1	0	0	0	0	0	0	0	0
Gonzalez	.000	4	2	0	0	0	0	0	0	0	0	0	0	0	2	0	0	0
Griffin T	.188	5	16	2	3	0	0	0	0	0	1	0	0	2	4	0	1	1
Griffin R	.000	—	3	—	0	0	0	0	0	0	0	0	0	0	2	—	—	—
Griffin L	.231	—	13	—	3	0	0	0	0	0	1	0	0	2	2	—	—	—
Hamilton	.105	5	19	1	2	0	0	0	0	0	0	0	0	1	4	0	0	1
Hatcher	.368	5	19	5	7	1	0	2	5	1	0	0	0	1	3	0	0	0
Heep	.250	3	8	0	2	1	0	0	0	0	0	0	0	0	2	0	1	0
Hershiser	1.000	2	3	1	3	2	0	0	1	0	0	0	0	0	0	0	0	0
Marshall	.231	5	13	2	3	0	1	1	3	0	0	0	0	0	5	0	0	0
Sax	.300	5	20	3	6	0	0	0	0	0	0	0	1	1	1	1	1	0
Scioscia	.214	4	14	0	3	0	0	0	1	0	0	0	0	0	2	0	1	1
Shelby T	.222	5	18	0	4	1	0	0	1	0	0	0	0	2	7	1	0	0
Shelby R	1.000	—	1	—	1	1	0	0	0	0	0	0	0	0	0	—	—	—
Shelby L	.176	—	17	—	3	0	0	0	1	0	0	0	0	2	7	—	—	—
Stubbs	.294	5	17	3	5	2	0	0	2	1	0	0	0	1	3	0	0	0
Woodson	.000	4	4	0	0	0	0	0	1	0	0	0	0	0	0	0	0	0
DODGERS	.246	5	167	21	41	8	1	5	19	3	1	0	1	13	36	4	4	3
ATHLETICS	.177	5	158	11	28	3	0	2	11	1	1	1	1	17	41	3	0	2

PITCHER		W	L	ERA	G	GS	CG	SHO	SV	IP	H	R	ER	HR	HB	BB	SO	WP
Belcher	R	1	0	6.23	2	2	0	0	0	8.2	10	7	6	1	1	6	10	0
Hershiser	R	2	0	1.00	2	2	2	1	0	18.0	7	2	2	0	0	6	17	1
Holton	R	0	0	0.00	1	0	0	0	0	2.0	0	0	0	0	0	1	0	0
Howell	R	0	1	3.38	2	0	0	0	1	2.2	3	1	1	1	0	1	2	0
Leary	R	0	0	1.35	2	0	0	0	0	6.2	6	1	1	0	0	2	4	0
Pena	R	1	0	0.00	2	0	0	0	0	5.0	2	0	0	0	0	1	7	0
Tudor	L	0	0	0.00	1	1	0	0	0	1.1	0	0	0	0	0	0	1	0
DODGERS		4	1	2.03	5	5	2	1	1	44.1	28	11	10	2	1	17	41	1
ATHLETICS		1	4	3.92	5	5	0	0	0	43.2	41	21	19	5	1	13	36	1

Game 1
At LOS ANGELES
Saturday, October 15

Oakland	0 4 0	0 0 0	0 0 0	4 7 0
Los Angeles	2 0 0	0 0 1	0 0 2	5 7 0

Stewart, ECKERSLEY (9)
Belcher, Leary (3), Holton (6), PENA (8)
HR: Oakland (1)—Canseco; Los Angeles (2)—Hatcher, Gibson
T—3:04; A—55,983

Game 2
At LOS ANGELES
Sunday, October 16

Oakland	0 0 0	0 0 0	0 0 0	0 3 0
Los Angeles	0 0 5	1 0 0	0 0 x	6 10 1

DAVIS, Nelson (4), C. Young (6), Plunk (7), Honeycutt (8)
HERSHISER
HR: Los Angeles (1)—Marshall
T—2:30; A—56,051

Game 3
At OAKLAND
Tuesday, October 18

Los Angeles	0 0 0	0 1 0	0 0 0	1 8 1
Oakland	0 0 1	0 0 0	0 0 1	2 5 0

Tudor, Leary (2), Pena (6), HOWELL (9)
Welch, Cadaret (6), Nelson (6), HONEYCUTT (8)
HR: Oakland (1)—McGwire
T—3:21; A—49,316

OAKLAND ATHLETICS

PLAYER	AVG	G	AB	R	H	2B	3B	HR	RBI	GW	SH	SF	HB	BB	SO	SB	CS	E
Baylor	.000	1	1	0	0	0	0	0	0	0	0	0	0	0	1	0	0	0
Canseco	.053	5	19	1	1	0	0	1	5	0	0	0	1	2	5	1	0	0
Davis	.000	2	1	0	0	0	0	0	0	0	0	0	0	0	1	0	0	0
Gallego	.000	1	0	0	0	0	0	0	0	0	0	0	0	0	0	0	0	0
Hassey	.250	5	8	0	2	0	0	0	1	0	0	0	0	3	3	0	0	0
Henderson	.300	5	20	1	6	2	0	0	1	0	0	0	0	2	7	0	0	0
Hubbard	.250	4	12	2	3	0	0	0	0	0	0	0	0	1	2	1	0	1
Javier .... T	.500	3	4	0	2	0	0	0	2	0	0	1	0	0	1	0	0	0
Javier .... R	.000	—	0	—	0	0	0	0	0	0	0	0	0	0	0	—	—	—
Javier L	.500	—	4	—	2	0	0	0	2	0	0	1	0	0	1	—	—	—
Lansford	.167	5	18	2	3	0	0	0	1	0	0	0	0	2	2	0	0	0
McGwire	.059	5	17	1	1	0	0	1	1	1	0	0	0	3	4	0	0	0
Parker	.200	4	15	0	3	0	0	0	0	0	0	0	0	2	4	0	0	0
Phillips .... T	.250	2	4	1	1	0	0	0	0	0	0	0	0	1	2	0	0	0
Phillips .... R	.000	—	1	—	0	0	0	0	0	0	0	0	0	0	0	—	—	—
Phillips L	.333	—	3	—	1	0	0	0	0	0	0	0	0	1	2	—	—	—
Polonia	.111	3	9	1	1	0	0	0	0	0	0	0	0	0	2	0	0	0
Steinbach	.364	3	11	0	4	1	0	0	0	0	0	0	0	0	2	0	0	0
Stewart	.000	2	3	1	0	0	0	0	0	0	0	0	0	1	3	0	0	0
Weiss .... T	.063	5	16	1	1	0	0	0	0	0	1	0	0	0	2	1	0	1
Weiss .... R	.000	—	0	—	0	0	0	0	0	0	0	0	0	0	0	—	—	—
Weiss L	.063	—	16	—	1	0	0	0	0	0	1	0	0	0	2	—	—	—
ATHLETICS	.177	5	158	11	28	3	0	2	11	1	1	1	1	17	41	3	0	2
DODGERS	.246	5	167	21	41	8	1	5	19	3	1	0	1	13	36	4	4	3

PITCHER		W	L	ERA	G	GS	CG	SHO	SV	IP	H	R	ER	HR	HB	BB	SO	WP
Burns	R	0	0	0.00	1	0	0	0	0	0.1	0	0	0	0	0	0	0	0
Cadaret	L	0	0	0.00	3	0	0	0	0	2.0	2	0	0	0	0	0	3	0
Davis	R	0	2	11.25	2	2	0	0	0	8.0	14	10	10	3	0	1	7	0
Eckersley	R	0	1	10.80	2	0	0	0	0	1.2	2	2	2	1	0	1	2	0
Honeycutt	L	1	0	0.00	3	0	0	0	0	3.1	0	0	0	0	0	0	5	0
Nelson	R	0	0	1.42	3	0	0	0	0	6.1	4	1	1	0	0	3	3	0
Plunk	R	0	0	0.00	2	0	0	0	0	1.2	0	0	0	0	0	0	3	0
Stewart	R	0	1	3.14	2	2	0	0	0	14.1	12	7	5	1	1	5	5	1
Welch	R	0	0	1.80	1	1	0	0	0	5.0	6	1	1	0	0	3	8	0
Young	L	0	0	0.00	1	0	0	0	0	1.0	1	0	0	0	0	0	0	0
ATHLETICS		1	4	3.92	5	5	0	0	0	43.2	41	21	19	5	1	13	36	1
DODGERS		4	1	2.03	5	5	2	1	1	44.1	28	11	10	2	1	17	41	1

Game 4
At OAKLAND
Wednesday, October 19

Los Angeles	2 0 1	0 0 0	1 0 0	4 8 1
Oakland	1 0 0	0 0 1	1 0 0	3 9 2

BELCHER, Howell (S) (7)
STEWART, Cadaret (7), Eckersley (9)
HR: None
T—3:05; A—49,317

Game 5
At OAKLAND
Thursday, October 20

Los Angeles	2 0 0	2 0 1	0 0 0	5 8 0
Oakland	0 0 1	0 0 0	0 1 0	2 4 0

HERSHISER
DAVIS, Cadaret (5), Nelson (5), Honeycutt (8), Plunk (9), Burns (9)
HR: Los Angeles (2)—Hatcher, M. Davis
T—2:51; A—49,317

SCORE BY INNINGS

Los Angeles	6 0 6	3 1 2	1 0 2	21 41 3
Oakland	1 4 2	0 0 1	1 1 1	11 28 2

OFFICIAL 1988 AMERICAN LEAGUE RECORDS

(Compiled by the MLB-IBM Baseball Information System)

FINAL STANDINGS

AMERICAN LEAGUE EAST

Club	Won	Lost	Pct.	Games Behind
Boston	89	73	.549	....
Detroit	88	74	.543	1
Milwaukee	87	75	.537	2
Toronto	87	75	.537	2
New York	85	76	.528	3½
Cleveland	78	84	.481	11
Baltimore	54	107	.335	34½

AMERICAN LEAGUE WEST

Club	Won	Lost	Pct.	Games Behind
Oakland	104	58	.642	....
Minnesota	91	71	.562	13
Kansas City	84	77	.522	19½
California	75	87	.463	29
Chicago	71	90	.441	32½
Texas	70	91	.435	33½
Seattle	68	93	.422	35½

Championship Series: Oakland defeated Boston, 4 games to 0

Batting

INDIVIDUAL BATTING LEADERS

Batting Average	.366	Boggs, Bos.
Games	162	Yount, Mil.
At Bats	657	Puckett, Min.
Runs	128	Boggs, Bos.
Hits	234	Puckett, Min.
Total Bases	358	Puckett, Min.
Singles	163	Puckett, Min.
Doubles	45	Boggs, Bos.
Triples	11	Reynolds, Sea., Wilson, K.C. & Yount, Mil.
Home Runs	42	Canseco, Oak.
Runs Batted In	124	Canseco, Oak.
Game-Winning RBI	23	Greenwell, Bos.
Sacrifice Hits	20	Barrett, Bos.
Sacrifice Flies	10	C. Davis, Cal. & C. Ripken, Bal.
Hit By Pitch	15	Larkin, Min.
Bases on Balls	125	Boggs, Bos.
Intentional Bases on Balls	18	Boggs, Bos. & Greenwell, Bos.
Strikeouts	153	Deer, Mil. & Incaviglia, Tex.
Stolen Bases	93	Henderson, N.Y.
Caught Stealing	29	Reynolds, Sea.
Grounded Into Double Plays	23	Boggs, Bos.
Slugging Percentage	.569	Canseco, Oak.
On-Base Percentage	.476	Boggs, Bos.
Longest Batting Streak	22	Franco, Cle. (July 3-July 27)

TOP 15 QUALIFIERS FOR BATTING CHAMPIONSHIP

Batter	Team	Bats	Avg	G	AB	R	H	TB	2B	3B	HR	RBI	GW	SH	SF	HB	BB	IBB	SO	SB	CS	GIDP	SLG	OBP	E
Boggs, W.	Bos.	L	.366	155	584	128	214	286	45	6	5	58	2	0	7	3	125	18	34	2	3	23	.490	.476	11
Puckett, K.	Min.	R	.356	158	657	109	234	358	42	5	24	121	14	0	9	2	23	4	83	6	7	17	.545	.375	3
Greenwell, M.	Bos.	L	.325	158	590	86	192	313	39	8	22	119	23	0	7	9	87	18	38	16	8	11	.531	.416	6
Winfield, D.	N.Y.	R	.322	149	559	96	180	296	37	2	25	107	10	0	1	2	69	10	88	9	4	19	.530	.398	3
Molitor, P.	Mil.	R	.312	154	609	115	190	275	34	6	13	60	7	5	3	2	71	8	54	41	10	10	.452	.384	17
Hrbek, K.	Min.	L	.312	143	510	75	159	265	31	0	25	76	12	2	7	0	67	7	54	0	3	9	.520	.387	3
Trammell, A.	Det.	R	.311	128	466	73	145	216	24	1	15	69	11	0	7	4	46	8	46	7	4	14	.464	.373	11
Mattingly, D.	N.Y.	L	.311	144	599	94	186	277	37	0	18	88	13	0	8	3	41	14	29	1	0	13	.462	.353	9
Canseco, J.	Oak.	R	.307	158	610	120	187	347	34	0	42	124	16	1	6	10	78	10	128	40	16	15	.569	.391	7
Yount, R.	Mil.	R	.306	162	621	92	190	289	38	11	13	91	13	2	7	3	63	10	63	22	4	21	.465	.369	2
Ray, J.	Cal.	S	.306	153	602	75	184	258	42	7	6	83	10	9	8	4	36	2	38	4	1	10	.429	.345	20
Brett, G.	K.C.	L	.306	157	589	90	180	300	42	3	24	103	8	0	7	3	82	15	51	14	3	15	.509	.389	10
Henderson, R.	N.Y.	R	.305	140	554	118	169	221	30	2	6	50	7	2	6	3	82	1	54	93	13	6	.399	.394	12
Seitzer, K.	K.C.	R	.304	149	559	90	170	227	32	5	5	60	8	3	3	6	72	4	64	10	8	15	.406	.388	26
Henderson, D.	Oak.	R	.304	146	507	100	154	266	38	1	24	94	11	5	7	4	47	1	92	2	4	14	.525	.363	7

INDIVIDUAL BATTING

Batter	Team	Bats	Avg	G	AB	R	H	TB	2B	3B	HR	RBI	GW	SH	SF	HB	BB	IBB	SO	SB	CS	GI DP	SLG	OBP	E
Adduci, J.	Mil.	L	.266	44	94	8	25	36	6	1	1	15	1	0	3	0	0	0	15	0	1	1	.383	.258	1
Aguayo, L.	N.Y.	R	.250	50	140	12	35	48	4	0	3	8	1	0	1	1	7	1	33	0	2	4	.343	.289	6
Allanson, A.	Cle.	R	.263	133	434	44	114	140	11	0	5	50	8	8	4	3	25	2	63	5	9	6	.323	.305	11
Allen, R.	Cle.	R	.091	5	11	1	1	2	1	0	0	0	0	0	0	0	0	0	2	0	0	0	.182	.091	0
Anderson, B.	Bos.-Bal.	L	.212	94	325	31	69	93	13	4	1	21	2	11	1	4	23	0	75	10	6	3	.286	.272	4
Armas, T.	Cal.	R	.272	120	368	42	100	163	20	2	13	49	5	1	2	0	22	0	87	1	3	13	.443	.311	3
Baines, H.	Chi.	L	.277	158	599	55	166	246	39	1	13	81	7	0	7	1	67	14	109	0	0	21	.411	.347	2
Baker, D.	Min.	S	.000	11	7	1	0	0	0	0	0	0	0	0	0	0	0	0	5	0	0	0	.000	.000	0
Balboni, S.	K.C.-Sea.	R	.235	118	413	46	97	185	17	1	23	66	8	0	2	1	24	2	87	0	1	8	.448	.277	4
Bando, C.	Cle.-Det.	S	.125	33	72	6	9	13	1	0	1	8	2	3	2	1	8	0	12	0	0	4	.181	.217	3
Barfield, J.	Tor.	R	.244	137	468	62	114	199	21	5	18	56	9	4	6	1	41	6	108	7	3	10	.425	.302	4
Barrett, M.	Bos.	R	.283	150	612	83	173	206	28	1	1	65	4	20	8	7	40	1	35	7	3	16	.337	.330	7
Baylor, D.	Oak.	R	.220	92	264	28	58	86	7	0	7	34	3	0	3	12	34	2	44	0	1	7	.326	.332	0
Bean, B.	Det.	L	.182	10	11	2	2	4	0	1	0	0	0	1	0	0	0	0	2	0	0	0	.364	.182	0
Beane, B.	Det.	R	.167	6	6	1	1	1	0	0	0	1	0	0	0	0	0	0	2	0	0	0	.167	.167	0
Bell, G.	Tor.	R	.269	156	614	78	165	274	27	5	24	97	17	0	8	1	34	5	66	4	2	21	.446	.304	15
Bell, J.	Cle.	R	.218	73	211	23	46	59	5	1	2	21	1	1	2	1	21	0	53	4	2	3	.280	.289	10
Beniquez, J.	Tor.	R	.293	27	58	9	17	22	2	0	1	8	1	1	1	0	8	0	6	0	0	4	.379	.373	0
Benzinger, T.	Bos.	S	.254	120	405	47	103	172	28	1	13	70	7	6	2	1	22	4	80	2	3	8	.425	.293	6
Bergman, D.	Det.	L	.294	116	289	37	85	114	14	0	5	35	6	2	4	0	38	2	34	0	2	7	.394	.372	4
Bichette, D.	Cal.	R	.261	21	46	1	12	14	2	0	0	8	0	0	4	0	0	0	7	0	0	0	.304	.240	1
Blankenship, L.	Oak.	R	.000	10	3	1	0	0	0	0	0	0	0	0	0	0	0	0	1	0	1	0	.000	.000	0
Boggs, W.	Bos.	L	.366	155	584	128	214	286	45	6	5	58	2	0	7	3	125	18	34	2	3	23	.490	.476	11
Boone, B.	Cal.	R	.295	122	352	38	104	136	17	0	5	39	2	9	0	2	29	2	26	2	2	9	.386	.352	8
Borders, P.	Tor.	R	.273	56	154	15	42	69	6	3	5	21	1	2	1	0	3	0	24	0	0	5	.448	.285	7
Bosley, T.	K.C.-Cal.	L	.260	50	96	10	25	30	5	0	0	9	1	1	4	0	8	1	18	1	1	2	.313	.306	2
Boston, D.	Chi.	L	.217	105	281	37	61	122	12	2	15	31	0	2	1	0	21	5	44	9	3	5	.434	.271	10
Bradley, S.	Sea.	L	.257	103	335	45	86	117	17	1	4	33	5	3	2	2	17	1	16	1	1	11	.349	.295	6
Braggs, G.	Mil.	R	.261	72	272	30	71	115	14	0	10	42	6	1	2	5	14	0	60	6	4	6	.423	.307	3

Brantley, M. ....Sea.	R	.263	149	577	76	152	230	25	4	15	56	8	5	4	2	26	0	64	18	7	12	.399	.296	6
Brett, G. ..................K.C.	L	.306	157	589	90	180	300	42	3	24	103	8	0	7	3	82	15	51	14	3	15	.509	.389	10
Briley, G..................Sea.	L	.250	13	36	6	9	14	2	0	1	4	1	0	1	0	5	1	6	0	1	0	.389	.333	1
Brock, G..................Mil.	L	.212	115	364	53	77	113	16	1	6	50	5	3	4	3	63	16	48	6	2	11	.310	.329	7
Brookens, T...........Det.	R	.243	136	441	62	107	155	23	5	5	38	4	6	4	3	44	2	74	4	4	9	.351	.313	17
Brower, B. ....Tex.	R	.224	82	201	29	45	55	7	0	1	11	0	6	0	0	27	0	38	10	5	6	.274	.316	3
Brown, M. ....Cal.	R	.220	18	50	4	11	13	2	0	0	3	0	1	0	0	1	0	12	0	0	2	.260	.235	2
Browne, J...............Tex.	S	.229	73	214	26	49	65	9	2	1	17	1	3	1	0	25	0	32	7	5	5	.304	.308	11
Brunansky, T. ....Min.	R	.184	14	49	5	9	13	1	0	1	6	0	0	0	0	7	0	11	1	2	0	.265	.286	3
Buckner, B. ....Cal.-K.C.	L	.249	108	285	19	71	94	14	0	3	43	2	4	5	0	17	5	19	5	1	8	.330	.287	1
Buechele, S............Tex.	R	.250	155	503	68	126	203	21	4	16	58	7	6	0	5	65	6	79	2	4	8	.404	.342	16
Buhner, J. ..............N.Y.-Sea.	R	.215	85	261	36	56	110	13	1	13	38	3	1	3	6	28	1	93	1	1	5	.421	.302	3
Bullock, E. ....Min.	L	.294	16	17	3	5	5	0	0	0	3	0	0	0	0	3	0	1	1	0	0	.294	.400	1
Burks, E. ....Bos.	R	.294	144	540	93	159	260	37	5	18	92	9	4	6	3	62	1	89	25	9	8	.481	.367	9
Bush, R. ....Min.	L	.261	136	394	51	103	171	20	3	14	51	3	0	5	9	58	14	49	8	6	8	.434	.365	4
Butera, S. ....Tor.	R	.233	23	60	3	14	21	2	1	1	6	2	1	0	0	1	0	9	0	0	1	.350	.246	1
Calderon, I.............Chi.	R	.212	73	264	40	56	112	14	0	14	35	4	0	3	0	34	2	66	4	4	6	.424	.299	7
Campusano, S. ......Tor.	R	.218	73	142	14	31	51	10	2	2	12	1	2	1	4	9	0	33	0	0	0	.359	.282	8
Canseco, J..............Oak.	R	.307	158	610	120	187	347	34	0	42	124	16	1	6	10	78	10	128	40	16	15	.569	.391	7
Capra, N.................K.C.	R	.138	14	29	3	4	5	1	0	0	0	0	0	0	0	2	0	3	1	0	3	.172	.194	0
Carter, J.................Cle.	R	.271	157	621	85	168	297	36	6	27	98	13	1	6	7	35	6	82	27	5	6	.478	.314	7
Castillo, C..............Cle.	R	.273	66	176	12	48	68	8	0	4	14	2	0	0	1	5	1	31	6	2	4	.386	.297	5
Castillo, J. ....Mil.	R	.222	54	90	10	20	20	0	0	0	2	0	1	0	0	3	0	14	2	0	1	.222	.247	7
Cerone, R...............Bos.	R	.269	84	264	31	71	95	13	1	3	27	1	1	1	3	20	0	32	0	0	6	.360	.326	0
Chambliss, C. ........N.Y.	L	.000	1	1	0	0	0	0	0	0	0	0	0	0	0	0	0	1	0	0	0	.000	.000	0
Christensen, J.......Min.	R	.263	23	38	5	10	14	4	0	0	5	1	0	0	2	3	1	5	0	0	1	.368	.349	0
Clark, D..................Cle.	L	.263	63	156	11	41	56	4	1	3	18	3	0	1	0	17	2	28	0	2	8	.359	.333	2
Clark, J...................N.Y.	R	.242	150	496	81	120	215	14	0	27	93	16	0	5	2	113	6	141	3	2	14	.433	.381	5
Coles, D. ....Sea.	R	.292	55	195	32	57	99	10	1	10	34	4	2	3	4	17	0	26	3	2	5	.508	.356	1
Cotto, H. ....Sea.	R	.259	133	386	50	100	144	18	1	8	33	4	4	3	2	23	0	53	27	3	8	.373	.302	2
Cruz, J.....................N.Y.	L	.200	38	80	9	16	21	2	0	1	7	0	0	0	0	8	1	8	0	1	2	.263	.273	1
Davidson, M. ....Min.	R	.217	100	106	22	23	33	7	0	1	10	1	1	1	1	10	0	20	3	3	3	.311	.288	5

Batter	Team	Bats	Avg	G	AB	R	H	TB	2B	3B	HR	RBI	GW	SH	SF	HB	BB	IBB	SO	SB	CS	GIDP	SLG	OBP	E
Davis, A.	Sea.	L	.295	140	478	67	141	221	24	1	18	69	5	0	5	4	95	13	53	1	1	14	.462	.412	6
Davis, C.	Cal.	S	.268	158	600	81	161	259	29	3	21	93	9	1	10	0	56	14	118	9	10	13	.432	.326	19
Davis, D.	Cal.	R	.000	6	12	1	0	0	0	0	0	0	0	0	0	1	0	0	3	0	0	0	.000	.077	1
Davis, W.	Bal.	R	.240	13	25	2	6	7	1	0	0	0	0	0	0	0	0	0	8	1	0	2	.280	.240	0
Deer, R.	Mil.	R	.252	135	492	71	124	217	24	0	23	85	12	0	5	7	51	4	153	9	5	4	.441	.328	3
DeJesus, I.	Det.	R	.176	7	17	1	3	3	0	0	0	0	0	3	0	0	1	0	4	0	0	0	.176	.222	3
Delos Santos, L.	K.C.	R	.091	11	22	1	2	5	1	1	0	1	0	0	0	0	4	0	4	0	0	3	.227	.231	0
Diaz, M.	Sea.	R	.306	28	72	6	22	27	5	0	0	9	1	0	1	0	3	0	5	0	0	3	.375	.329	1
Diaz, M.	Chi.	R	.237	40	152	12	36	51	6	0	3	12	3	0	0	1	5	0	30	0	1	5	.336	.266	5
Dodson, P.	Bos.	L	.178	17	45	5	8	16	3	1	1	1	0	0	0	0	6	0	17	0	0	0	.356	.275	0
Dorsett, B.	Cal.	R	.091	7	11	0	1	1	0	0	0	2	0	0	0	0	1	0	5	0	0	0	.091	.167	0
Downing, B.	Cal.	R	.242	135	484	80	117	214	18	2	25	64	12	5	6	14	81	5	63	3	4	12	.442	.362	0
Ducey, R.	Tor.	L	.315	27	54	15	17	23	4	1	0	6	1	2	2	0	5	0	7	1	0	1	.426	.361	0
Dwyer, J.	Bal.-Min.	L	.255	55	94	9	24	31	1	0	2	18	4	0	2	1	25	4	19	0	0	1	.330	.410	0
Eisenreich, J.	K.C.	L	.218	82	202	26	44	57	8	1	1	19	2	2	4	0	6	1	31	9	3	2	.282	.236	4
Eppard, J.	Cal.	L	.283	56	113	7	32	37	3	1	0	14	0	2	0	0	11	0	15	0	0	4	.327	.347	2
Espinoza, A.	N.Y.	R	.000	3	3	0	0	0	0	0	0	0	0	0	0	0	0	0	0	0	0	0	.000	.000	0
Espy, C.	Tex.	S	.248	123	347	46	86	121	17	6	2	39	2	5	3	1	20	1	83	33	10	2	.349	.288	7
Evans, D.	Det.	L	.208	144	437	48	91	166	9	0	22	64	7	0	0	1	84	4	89	1	4	14	.380	.337	4
Evans, D.	Bos.	R	.293	149	559	96	164	272	31	7	21	111	12	2	7	1	76	3	99	5	1	16	.487	.375	9
Felder, M.	Mil.	S	.173	50	81	14	14	15	1	0	0	5	0	3	0	1	0	0	11	8	2	1	.185	.183	1
Fernandez, T.	Tor.	S	.287	154	648	76	186	250	41	4	5	70	5	3	4	4	45	3	65	15	5	9	.386	.335	14
Fielder, C.	Tor.	R	.230	74	174	24	40	75	6	1	9	23	1	0	1	1	14	0	53	0	1	6	.431	.289	1
Fields, B.	Sea.	L	.269	39	67	8	18	26	5	0	1	5	1	2	0	0	4	0	11	0	1	2	.388	.310	0
Firova, D.	Cle.	R	....	1	0	0	0	0	0	0	0	0	0	0	0	0	0	0	0	0	0	0	....	....	0
Fisk, C.	Chi.	R	.277	76	253	37	70	137	8	1	19	50	5	1	2	5	37	9	40	0	0	6	.542	.377	2
Fletcher, S.	Tex.	R	.276	140	515	59	142	169	19	4	0	47	4	15	5	12	62	1	34	8	5	13	.328	.364	11
Franco, J.	Cle.	R	.303	152	613	88	186	251	23	6	10	54	8	1	4	2	56	4	72	25	11	17	.409	.361	14
Francona, T.	Cle.	L	.311	62	212	24	66	77	8	0	1	12	2	2	2	0	5	1	18	0	0	4	.363	.324	1
Gaetti, G.	Min.	R	.301	133	468	66	141	258	29	2	28	88	13	1	6	5	36	5	85	7	4	10	.551	.353	7

Gagne, G.	Min.	R	.236	149	461	70	109	183	20	6	14	48	0	11	1	7	27	2	110	15	7	13	.397	.288	18
Gallagher, D.	Chi.	R	.303	101	347	59	105	141	15	3	5	31	6	6	2	0	29	3	40	5	4	8	.406	.354	0
Gallego, M.	Oak.	R	.209	129	277	38	58	72	8	0	2	20	5	8	0	1	34	0	53	2	3	6	.260	.298	8
Gantner, J.	Mil.	L	.276	155	539	67	149	181	28	2	0	47	12	18	2	3	34	1	50	20	8	9	.336	.322	11
Garbey, B.	Tex.	R	.194	30	62	4	12	14	2	0	0	5	2	0	1	0	4	0	11	0	0	3	.226	.239	1
Gedman, R.	Bos.	L	.231	95	299	33	69	110	14	0	9	39	0	9	3	3	18	2	49	0	0	6	.368	.279	5
Geren, R.	N.Y.	R	.100	10	10	0	1	1	0	0	0	0	0	0	0	0	2	0	3	0	0	0	.100	.250	0
Gerhart, K.	Bal.	R	.195	103	262	27	51	90	10	1	9	23	3	2	4	2	21	0	57	7	3	3	.344	.256	5
Gladden, D.	Min.	R	.269	141	576	91	155	232	32	6	11	62	10	2	5	4	46	4	74	28	8	9	.403	.325	3
Gonzales, R.	Bal.	R	.215	92	237	13	51	63	6	0	2	15	0	5	2	3	13	0	32	2	0	5	.266	.263	8
Greenwell, M.	Bos.	L	.325	158	590	86	192	313	39	8	22	119	23	0	7	9	87	18	38	16	8	11	.531	.416	6
Gruber, K.	Tor.	R	.278	158	569	75	158	249	33	5	16	81	8	5	4	7	38	1	92	23	5	20	.438	.328	16
Guillen, O.	Chi.	L	.261	156	566	58	148	178	16	7	0	39	2	10	3	2	25	3	40	25	13	14	.314	.294	20
Hairston, J.	Chi.	S	.000	2	2	0	0	0	0	0	0	0	0	0	0	0	0	0	0	0	0	0	.000	.000	0
Hall, M.	Cle.	L	.280	150	515	69	144	202	32	4	6	71	5	2	8	0	28	12	50	7	3	8	.392	.312	10
Hamilton, D.	Mil.	L	.184	44	103	14	19	26	4	0	1	11	0	0	1	1	12	0	9	7	3	2	.252	.274	0
Harper, B.	Min.	R	.295	60	166	15	49	71	11	1	3	20	0	2	1	3	10	1	12	0	3	12	.428	.344	2
Hassey, R.	Oak.	L	.257	107	323	32	83	119	15	0	7	45	9	3	5	4	30	1	42	2	0	9	.368	.323	3
Hearn, E.	K.C.	R	.222	7	18	1	4	6	2	0	0	1	1	0	0	0	0	0	1	0	0	1	.333	.222	0
Heath, M.	Det.	R	.247	86	219	24	54	80	7	2	5	18	1	3	0	1	18	0	32	1	0	6	.365	.307	6
Henderson, D.	Oak.	R	.304	146	507	100	154	266	38	1	24	94	11	5	7	4	47	1	92	2	4	14	.525	.363	7
Henderson, R.	N.Y.	R	.305	140	554	118	169	221	30	2	6	50	7	2	6	3	82	1	54	93	13	6	.399	.394	12
Hendrick, G.	Cal.	R	.244	69	127	12	31	41	1	0	3	19	0	1	3	1	7	1	20	0	1	2	.323	.283	3
Hengel, D.	Sea.	R	.167	26	60	3	10	17	1	0	2	7	0	0	1	0	1	0	15	0	0	0	.283	.177	1
Herndon, L.	Det.	R	.224	76	174	16	39	56	5	0	4	20	2	0	3	1	23	0	37	0	1	8	.322	.313	0
Herr, T.	Min.	S	.263	86	304	42	80	99	16	0	1	21	4	1	0	0	40	1	47	10	3	9	.326	.349	4
Hill, D.	Chi.	S	.217	83	221	17	48	62	6	1	2	20	3	3	3	0	26	1	32	3	1	3	.281	.296	8
Horn, S.	Bos.	L	.148	24	61	4	9	15	0	0	2	8	2	0	1	0	11	3	20	0	0	1	.246	.274	0
Howell, J.	Cal.	L	.254	154	500	59	127	211	32	2	16	63	5	4	2	6	46	8	130	2	6	8	.422	.323	17
Hrbek, K.	Min.	L	.312	143	510	75	159	265	31	0	25	76	12	2	7	0	67	7	54	0	3	9	.520	.387	3
Hubbard, G.	Oak.	R	.255	105	294	35	75	100	12	2	3	33	4	10	2	3	33	0	50	1	3	9	.340	.334	6
Hughes, K.	Bal.	L	.194	41	108	10	21	35	4	2	2	14	1	0	2	0	16	1	27	1	0	3	.324	.294	2

Batter	Team	Bats	Avg	G	AB	R	H	TB	2B	3B	HR	RBI	GW	SH	SF	HB	BB	IBB	SO	SB	CS	GIDP	SLG	OBP	E
Incaviglia, P.	Tex.	R	.249	116	418	59	104	195	19	3	22	54	6	0	3	7	39	3	153	6	4	6	.467	.321	2
Infante, A.	Tor.	R	.200	19	15	7	3	3	0	0	0	0	0	0	0	0	2	0	4	0	0	1	.200	.294	1
Jackson, B.	K.C.	R	.246	124	439	63	108	207	16	4	25	68	7	1	2	1	25	6	146	27	6	6	.472	.287	7
Jacoby, B.	Cle.	R	.241	152	552	59	133	185	25	0	9	49	5	0	5	1	48	2	101	2	3	12	.335	.300	10
Javier, S.	Oak.	S	.257	125	397	49	102	127	13	3	2	35	5	6	3	2	32	1	63	20	1	13	.320	.313	5
Jennings, D.	Oak.	L	.208	71	101	9	21	30	6	0	1	15	3	1	3	2	21	1	28	0	1	1	.297	.346	1
Jimenez, A.	Cle.	R	.048	9	21	1	1	1	0	0	0	1	0	1	0	0	0	0	2	0	0	1	.048	.048	1
Johnson, L.	Chi.	L	.185	33	124	11	23	29	4	1	0	6	2	2	0	0	6	0	11	6	2	1	.234	.223	2
Jordan, S.	Cle.	R	.111	7	9	0	1	1	0	0	0	1	0	1	0	0	0	0	3	0	0	0	.111	.111	0
Jose, F.	Oak.	S	.333	8	6	2	2	3	1	0	0	1	0	0	0	0	0	0	1	1	0	0	.500	.333	0
Joyner, W.	Cal.	L	.295	158	597	81	176	250	31	2	13	85	12	0	6	5	55	14	51	8	2	16	.419	.356	8
Jurak, E.	Oak.	R	.000	3	1	1	0	0	0	0	0	0	0	0	0	0	0	0	0	0	0	0	.000	.000	0
Karkovice, R.	Chi.	R	.174	46	115	10	20	33	4	0	3	9	0	3	0	1	7	0	30	4	2	1	.287	.228	1
Kelly, R.	N.Y.	R	.247	38	77	9	19	28	4	1	1	7	0	3	1	0	3	0	15	5	2	0	.364	.272	1
Kemp, S.	Tex	L	.222	16	36	2	8	8	0	0	0	2	0	0	1	0	2	0	9	1	0	1	.222	.256	0
Kennedy, T.	Bal.	L	.226	85	265	20	60	79	10	0	3	16	0	2	2	1	15	0	53	0	0	13	.298	.269	2
Kiefer, S.	Mil.	R	.300	7	10	2	3	7	1	0	1	1	0	0	0	1	2	0	3	0	0	0	.700	.462	1
Kingery, M.	Sea.	L	.203	57	123	21	25	34	6	0	1	9	0	1	1	1	19	1	23	3	1	1	.276	.313	2
Kittle, R.	Cle.	R	.258	75	225	31	58	120	8	0	18	43	3	0	5	8	16	1	65	0	0	0	.533	.323	0
Knight, R.	Det.	R	.217	105	299	34	65	90	12	2	3	33	4	2	3	3	20	0	30	1	1	12	.301	.271	4
Kreuter, C.	Tex.	S	.275	16	51	3	14	21	2	1	1	5	0	0	0	0	7	0	13	0	0	1	.412	.362	1
Kunkel, J.	Tex.	R	.227	55	154	14	35	55	8	3	2	15	3	1	1	1	4	1	35	0	1	5	.357	.250	8
Kutcher, R.	Bos.	R	.167	19	12	2	2	3	1	0	0	0	0	0	0	0	0	0	2	0	1	0	.250	.167	1
Lampkin, T.	Cle.	L	.000	4	4	0	0	0	0	0	0	0	0	0	0	0	1	0	0	0	0	1	.000	.200	0
Landrum, T.	Bal.	R	.125	13	24	2	3	5	0	1	0	2	0	0	0	0	4	0	6	0	0	0	.208	.250	0
Lansford, C.	Oak.	R	.279	150	556	80	155	200	20	2	7	57	5	5	4	7	35	4	35	29	8	17	.360	.327	7
Larkin, G.	Min.	S	.267	149	505	56	135	193	30	2	8	70	11	1	5	15	68	8	55	3	2	12	.382	.368	3
Laudner, T.	Min.	R	.251	117	375	38	94	153	18	1	13	54	6	3	3	1	36	0	89	0	0	14	.408	.316	5
Leach, R.	Tor.	L	.276	87	199	21	55	70	13	1	0	23	1	0	0	0	18	3	27	0	1	8	.352	.336	0
Lee, M.	Tor.	S	.291	116	381	38	111	139	16	3	2	38	4	4	4	0	26	1	64	3	3	13	.365	.333	12

Lemon, C.	Det.	R	.264	144	512	67	135	223	29	4	17	64	10	1	3	7	59	6	65	1	2	18	.436	.346	8
Leonard, J.	Mil.	R	.235	94	374	45	88	131	19	0	8	44	7	1	4	3	16	1	68	10	4	10	.350	.270	3
Liriano, N.	Tor.	S	.264	99	276	36	73	92	6	2	3	23	2	5	1	2	11	0	40	12	5	4	.333	.297	12
Lombardozzi, S.	Min.	R	.209	103	287	34	60	88	15	2	3	27	4	6	5	2	35	2	48	2	5	2	.307	.295	5
Lovullo, T.	Det.	S	.381	12	21	2	8	14	1	1	1	2	0	1	0	0	1	0	2	0	0	1	.667	.409	0
Lowry, D.	Min.	L	.000	7	7	0	0	0	0	0	0	0	0	0	0	0	0	0	2	0	0	0	.000	.000	0
Lusader, S.	Det.	L	.063	16	16	3	1	4	0	0	1	3	0	0	1	0	1	0	4	0	0	1	.250	.111	0
Lynn, F.	Bal.-Det.	L	.246	114	391	46	96	187	14	1	25	56	6	1	6	1	33	1	82	2	2	9	.478	.302	2
Lyons, S.	Chi.	L	.269	146	472	59	127	176	28	3	5	45	8	15	6	1	32	1	59	1	2	6	.373	.313	29
Macfarlane, M.	K.C.	R	.265	70	211	25	56	83	15	0	4	26	4	1	2	1	21	2	37	0	0	5	.393	.332	2
Madison, S.	K.C.	S	.171	16	35	4	6	8	2	0	0	2	0	0	0	0	4	0	5	1	0	0	.229	.256	0
Manrique, F.	Chi.	R	.235	140	345	43	81	118	10	6	5	37	4	16	2	3	21	1	54	6	5	7	.342	.283	13
Martinez, C.	Chi.	R	.164	17	55	5	9	10	1	0	0	0	0	0	0	0	0	0	12	1	0	1	.182	.164	4
Martinez, E.	Sea.	R	.281	14	32	0	9	13	4	0	0	5	0	1	1	0	4	0	7	0	0	0	.406	.351	1
Marzano, J.	Bos.	R	.138	10	29	3	4	5	1	0	0	1	0	0	0	0	1	0	3	0	0	1	.172	.167	0
Mattingly, D.	N.Y.	L	.311	144	599	94	186	277	37	0	18	88	13	0	8	3	41	14	29	1	0	13	.462	.353	9
McDowell, O.	Tex.	L	.247	120	437	55	108	155	19	5	6	37	5	2	5	2	41	2	89	33	10	3	.355	.311	3
McGriff, F.	Tor.	L	.282	154	536	100	151	296	35	4	34	82	11	0	4	4	79	3	149	6	1	15	.552	.376	5
McGuire, B.	Sea.	R	.188	9	16	1	3	3	0	0	0	2	0	1	0	0	3	0	2	0	0	0	.188	.316	0
McGwire, M.	Oak.	R	.260	155	550	87	143	263	22	1	32	99	20	1	4	4	76	4	117	0	0	15	.478	.352	9
McLemore, M.	Cal.	S	.240	77	233	38	56	77	11	2	2	16	1	5	2	0	25	0	28	13	7	6	.330	.312	6
Meacham, B.	N.Y.	R	.217	47	115	18	25	34	9	0	0	7	0	1	2	2	14	0	22	7	1	1	.296	.308	7
Medina, L.	Cle.	R	.255	16	51	10	13	31	0	0	6	8	2	1	0	2	2	0	18	0	0	0	.608	.309	0
Mercado, O.	Oak.	R	.125	16	24	3	3	6	0	0	1	1	0	0	0	0	3	0	8	0	0	0	.250	.222	2
Meyer, J.	Mil.	R	.263	103	327	22	86	137	18	0	11	45	6	0	1	1	23	2	88	0	1	9	.419	.313	3
Miller, D.	Cal.	R	.221	70	140	21	31	43	4	1	2	7	0	3	0	5	9	0	29	2	1	1	.307	.292	4
Molitor, P.	Mil.	R	.312	154	609	115	190	275	34	6	13	60	7	5	3	2	71	8	54	41	10	10	.452	.384	17
Morman, R.	Chi.	R	.240	40	75	8	18	20	2	0	0	3	1	2	0	0	3	0	17	0	0	5	.267	269	2
Morris, H.	N.Y.	L	.100	15	20	1	2	2	0	0	0	0	0	0	0	0	0	0	9	0	0	0	.100	.100	0
Morrison, J.	Det.	R	.216	24	74	7	16	21	5	0	0	6	1	0	0	0	0	0	14	0	2	2	.284	.216	1
Moseby, L.	Tor.	L	.239	128	472	77	113	174	17	7	10	42	2	1	3	6	70	6	93	31	8	8	.369	.343	5
Moses, J.	Min.	S	.316	105	206	33	65	87	10	3	2	12	3	1	1	2	15	2	21	11	6	4	.422	.366	0

Batter	Team	Bats	Avg	G	AB	R	H	TB	2B	3B	HR	RBI	GW	SH	SF	HB	BB	IBB	SO	SB	CS	GI DP	SLG	OBP	E
Mulliniks, R.	Tor.	L	.300	119	337	49	101	160	21	1	12	48	10	2	4	0	56	3	57	1	0	10	.475	.395	0
Murphy, D.	Det.	L	.250	49	144	14	36	53	5	0	4	19	2	2	0	1	24	2	26	1	1	0	.368	.361	0
Murray, E.	Bal.	S	.284	161	603	75	171	286	27	2	28	84	8	0	3	0	75	8	78	5	2	20	.474	.361	11
Nelson, G.	Oak.	R	....	57	0	1	0	0	0	0	0	0	0	0	0	0	0	0	0	1	0	0	....	....	0
Newman, A.	Min.	S	.223	105	260	35	58	65	7	0	0	19	2	6	0	0	29	0	34	12	3	4	.250	.301	6
Nichols, C.	Bal.	R	.191	18	47	2	9	10	1	0	0	1	0	1	1	0	3	0	10	0	0	3	.213	.235	1
Nieto, T.	Min.	R	.067	24	60	1	4	4	0	0	0	0	0	0	0	1	1	0	17	0	0	2	.067	.097	1
Noboa, J.	Cal.	R	.063	21	16	4	1	1	0	0	0	0	0	0	0	0	0	0	1	0	0	2	.063	.063	1
Nokes, M.	Det.	L	.251	122	382	53	96	162	18	0	16	53	6	6	2	1	34	3	58	0	1	11	.424	.313	7
O'Brien, C.	Mil.	R	.220	40	118	12	26	38	6	0	2	9	0	4	0	0	5	0	16	0	1	3	.322	.252	2
O'Brien, P.	Tex.	L	.272	156	547	57	149	223	24	1	16	71	9	1	8	0	72	9	73	1	4	12	.408	.352	8
Ontiveros, S.	Oak.	R	....	13	0	1	0	0	0	0	0	0	0	0	0	0	0	0	0	0	0	0	....	....	0
Orsulak, J.	Bal.	L	.288	125	379	48	109	160	21	3	8	27	4	8	3	3	23	2	30	9	8	7	.422	.331	5
Owen, D.	K.C.	S	.000	7	5	0	0	0	0	0	0	0	0	0	0	0	0	0	3	0	0	0	.000	.000	1
Owen, L.	K.C.	R	.210	37	81	5	17	21	1	0	1	3	0	2	0	2	9	0	23	0	0	0	.259	.304	2
Owen, S.	Bos.	S	.249	89	257	40	64	95	14	1	5	18	2	7	1	2	27	0	27	0	1	7	.370	.324	10
Pagliarulo, M.	N.Y.	L	.216	125	444	46	96	163	20	1	15	67	3	1	6	2	37	9	104	1	0	5	.367	.276	19
Palacios, R.	K.C.	R	.091	5	11	2	1	1	0	0	0	0	0	0	0	0	0	0	4	0	0	1	.091	.091	0
Paris, K.	Chi.	R	.250	14	44	6	11	20	0	0	3	6	1	0	0	0	0	0	6	0	0	1	.455	.250	1
Parker, D.	Oak.	L	.257	101	377	43	97	153	18	1	12	55	8	0	2	0	32	2	70	0	1	3	.406	.314	3
Parrish, L.	Tex.-Bos.	R	.217	120	406	32	88	146	14	1	14	52	8	0	4	3	28	2	111	0	1	8	.360	.270	3
Pasqua, D.	Chi.	L	.227	129	422	48	96	176	16	2	20	50	5	2	2	3	46	5	100	1	0	10	.417	.307	2
Pecota, B.	K.C.	R	.208	90	178	25	37	49	3	3	1	15	3	7	1	2	18	0	34	7	2	1	.275	.286	6
Petralli, G.	Tex.	L	.282	129	351	35	99	138	14	2	7	36	2	1	5	2	41	5	52	0	1	12	.393	.356	10
Pettis, G.	Det.	S	.210	129	458	65	96	127	14	4	3	36	3	6	0	1	47	0	85	44	10	3	.277	.285	5
Phelps, K.	Sea.-N.Y.	L	.263	117	297	54	78	163	13	0	24	54	7	0	3	1	70	5	61	1	0	6	.549	.402	1
Phillips, T.	Oak.	S	.203	79	212	32	43	65	8	4	2	17	0	1	1	1	36	0	50	0	2	6	.307	.320	10
Polidor, G.	Cal.	R	.148	54	81	4	12	15	3	0	0	4	0	3	0	0	3	0	11	0	0	2	.185	.179	1
Polonia, L.	Oak.	L	.292	84	288	51	84	109	11	4	2	27	2	2	2	0	21	0	40	24	9	3	.378	.338	2
Presley, J.	Sea.	R	.230	150	544	50	125	193	26	0	14	62	5	3	5	4	36	1	114	3	5	14	.355	.280	22

Puckett, K.	Min.	R	.356	158	657	109	234	358	42	5	24	121	14	0	9	2	23	4	83	6	7	17	.545	.375	3
Quinones, R.	Sea.	R	.248	140	499	63	124	196	30	3	12	52	6	2	3	3	23	1	71	0	3	12	.393	.284	23
Quintana, C.	Bos.	R	.333	5	6	1	2	2	0	0	0	2	0	0	0	0	2	0	3	0	0	0	.333	.500	0
Quirk, J.	K.C.	L	.240	84	196	22	47	80	7	1	8	25	2	4	3	1	28	2	41	1	5	2	.408	.333	8
Rabb, J.	Sea.	R	.357	9	14	2	5	7	2	0	0	4	2	0	0	0	0	0	1	0	0	0	.500	.357	0
Ramos, D.	Cle.-Cal.	R	.230	32	61	10	14	15	1	0	0	5	1	0	2	1	3	0	7	0	0	2	.246	.269	1
Randall, S.	Chi.	S	.000	4	12	1	0	0	0	0	0	1	0	0	1	0	2	0	3	0	0	0	.000	.133	0
Randolph, W.	N.Y.	R	.230	110	404	43	93	121	20	1	2	34	4	8	5	2	55	2	39	8	4	10	.300	.322	7
Ray, J.	Cal.	S	.306	153	602	75	184	258	42	7	6	83	10	9	8	4	36	2	38	4	1	10	.429	.345	20
Redfield, J.	Cal.	R	.000	1	2	0	0	0	0	0	0	0	0	0	0	0	0	0	0	0	0	0	.000	.000	0
Redus, G.	Chi.	R	.263	77	262	42	69	105	10	4	6	34	3	0	7	2	33	1	52	26	2	5	.401	.342	2
Reed, J.	Bos.	R	.293	109	338	60	99	127	23	1	1	28	5	11	2	4	45	1	21	1	3	5	.376	.380	11
Reimer, K.	Tex.	L	.120	12	25	2	3	6	0	0	1	2	0	0	1	0	0	0	6	0	0	0	.240	.115	0
Renteria, R.	Sea.	R	.205	31	88	6	18	27	9	0	0	6	1	1	0	0	2	0	8	1	3	3	.307	.222	3
Reynolds, H.	Sea.	S	.283	158	598	61	169	229	26	11	4	41	3	10	2	2	51	1	51	35	29	9	.383	.340	18
Rhoden, R.	N.Y.	R	.000	31	1	0	0	0	0	0	0	1	0	0	1	0	0	0	0	0	0	0	.000	.000	0
Rice, J.	Bos.	R	.264	135	485	57	128	197	18	3	15	72	5	0	6	3	48	2	89	1	1	18	.406	.330	1
Riles, E.	Mil.	L	.252	41	127	7	32	43	6	1	1	9	1	1	0	0	7	0	26	2	2	3	.339	.291	4
Ripken, B.	Bal.	R	.207	150	512	52	106	132	18	1	2	34	2	6	3	5	33	0	63	8	2	14	.258	.260	12
Ripken, C.	Bal.	R	.264	161	575	87	152	248	25	1	23	81	7	0	10	2	102	7	69	2	2	10	.431	.372	21
Robidoux, B.	Mil.	L	.253	33	91	9	23	28	5	0	0	5	0	3	2	0	8	3	14	1	1	3	.308	.307	4
Romero, E.	Bos.	R	.240	31	75	3	18	21	3	0	0	5	0	2	2	1	3	0	8	0	0	4	.280	.272	0
Romine, K.	Bos.	R	.192	57	78	17	15	22	2	1	1	6	3	0	0	0	7	0	15	2	0	3	.282	.259	2
Rowdon, W.	Bal.	R	.100	20	30	1	3	3	0	0	0	0	0	0	0	0	0	0	6	1	1	3	.100	.100	1
Russell, J.	Tex.	R	.000	35	1	0	0	0	0	0	0	0	0	0	0	0	0	0	0	0	0	0	.000	.000	5
Salas, M.	Chi.	L	.250	75	196	17	49	65	7	0	3	9	2	0	0	3	12	2	17	0	0	3	.332	.303	6
Salazar, L.	Det.	R	.270	130	452	61	122	174	14	1	12	62	9	10	3	3	21	2	70	6	0	13	.385	.305	10
Santana, R.	N.Y.	R	.240	148	480	50	115	141	12	1	4	38	2	5	2	1	33	0	61	1	2	17	.294	.289	22
Schofield, D.	Cal.	R	.239	155	527	61	126	167	11	6	6	34	1	11	2	9	40	0	57	20	5	5	.317	.303	13
Schroeder, B.	Mil.	R	.156	41	122	9	19	36	2	0	5	10	0	1	0	2	6	0	36	0	0	6	.295	.208	0
Schu, R.	Bal.	R	.256	89	270	22	69	98	9	4	4	20	0	0	0	3	21	0	49	6	4	7	.363	.316	11
See, L.	Tex.	R	.130	13	23	0	3	3	0	0	0	0	0	1	0	0	1	0	8	0	0	0	.130	.167	1

Batter	Team	Bats	Avg	G	AB	R	H	TB	2B	3B	HR	RBI	GW	SH	SF	HB	BB	IBB	SO	SB	CS	GI DP	SLG	OBP	E
Seitzer, K.	K.C.	R	.304	149	559	90	170	227	32	5	5	60	8	3	3	6	72	4	64	10	8	15	.406	.388	26
Sheets, L.	Bal.	L	.230	136	452	38	104	155	19	1	10	47	5	0	4	6	42	4	72	1	6	11	.343	.302	4
Sheffield, G.	Mil.	R	.238	24	80	12	19	32	1	0	4	12	2	1	1	0	7	0	7	3	1	5	.400	.295	3
Sheridan, P.	Det.	L	.254	127	347	47	88	140	9	5	11	47	8	7	2	2	44	4	64	8	6	6	.403	.339	4
Sierra, R.	Tex.	S	.254	156	615	77	156	261	32	2	23	91	10	0	8	1	44	10	91	18	4	15	.424	.301	7
Sinatro, M.	Oak.	R	.333	10	9	1	3	5	2	0	0	5	0	0	1	0	0	0	1	0	0	2	.556	.300	0
Skinner, J.	N.Y.	R	.227	88	251	23	57	84	15	0	4	23	1	6	1	0	14	0	72	0	0	6	.335	.267	4
Slaught, D.	N.Y.	R	.283	97	322	33	91	145	25	1	9	43	4	5	4	3	24	3	54	1	0	10	.450	.334	11
Smith, B.	Sea.	R	.100	4	10	1	1	1	0	0	0	1	1	0	0	0	0	0	1	0	0	0	.100	.100	0
Snyder, C.	Cle.	R	.272	142	511	71	139	247	24	3	26	75	11	0	4	1	42	7	101	5	1	12	.483	.326	5
Stanicek, P.	Bal.	S	.230	83	261	29	60	81	7	1	4	17	2	5	1	4	28	0	45	12	6	9	.310	.313	4
Stanley, M.	Tex.	R	.229	94	249	21	57	74	8	0	3	27	5	1	5	0	37	0	62	0	0	6	.297	.323	4
Steels, J.	Tex.	L	.189	36	53	4	10	11	1	0	0	5	1	0	1	0	0	0	15	2	0	0	.208	.185	1
Steinbach, T.	Oak.	R	.265	104	351	42	93	141	19	1	9	51	6	3	5	6	33	2	47	3	0	13	.402	.334	9
Stillwell, K.	K.C.	S	.251	128	459	63	115	183	28	5	10	53	10	6	3	3	47	0	76	6	5	7	.399	.322	13
Stone, J.	Bal.	L	.164	26	61	4	10	11	1	0	0	1	0	1	0	0	4	0	11	4	1	3	.180	.215	1
Sundberg, J.	Tex.	R	.286	38	91	13	26	42	4	0	4	13	0	3	0	0	5	0	17	0	0	2	.462	.323	0
Surhoff, B.	Mil.	L	.245	139	493	47	121	157	21	0	5	38	6	11	3	3	31	9	49	21	6	12	.318	.292	8
Sveum, D.	Mil.	S	.242	129	467	41	113	162	14	4	9	51	6	3	3	1	21	0	122	1	0	6	.347	.274	27
Tabler, P.	Cle.-K.C.	R	.282	130	444	53	125	159	22	3	2	66	11	0	5	3	46	1	68	3	3	9	.358	.349	5
Tartabull, D.	K.C.	R	.274	146	507	80	139	261	38	3	26	102	9	0	6	4	76	4	119	8	5	10	.515	.369	9
Tettleton, M.	Bal.	S	.261	86	283	31	74	120	11	1	11	37	3	1	2	2	28	2	70	0	1	9	.424	.330	3
Thornton, L.	Tor.	L	.000	11	2	1	0	0	0	0	0	0	0	0	0	0	0	0	0	0	0	0	.000	.000	0
Thurman, G.	K.C.	R	.167	35	66	6	11	12	1	0	0	2	0	0	0	0	4	0	20	5	1	0	.182	.214	2
Tingley, R.	Cle.	R	.167	9	24	1	4	7	0	0	1	2	0	0	0	0	2	0	8	0	0	1	.292	.231	0
Tolleson, W.	N.Y.	S	.254	21	59	8	15	17	2	0	0	5	0	1	1	0	8	0	12	1	0	1	.288	.338	3
Torve, K.	Min.	L	.188	12	16	1	3	6	0	0	1	2	0	0	0	0	1	0	2	0	1	0	.375	.235	0
Traber, J.	Bal.	L	.222	103	352	25	78	114	6	0	10	45	6	1	3	1	19	3	42	1	2	8	.324	.261	6
Trammell, A.	Det.	R	.311	128	466	73	145	216	24	1	15	69	11	0	7	4	46	8	46	7	4	14	.464	.373	11
Upshaw, W.	Cle.	L	.245	149	493	58	121	182	22	3	11	50	4	3	4	2	62	4	66	12	9	10	.369	.330	12

Valle, D.	Sea.	R	.231	93	290	29	67	116	15	2	10	50	5	3	2	9	18	0	38	0	1	13	.400	.295	6
Velarde, R.	N.Y.	R	.174	48	115	18	20	41	6	0	5	12	1	0	0	2	8	0	24	1	1	3	.357	.240	8
Walewander, J.	Det.	S	.211	88	175	23	37	42	5	0	0	6	0	10	1	0	12	0	26	11	4	1	.240	.261	6
Walker, C.	Cal.	S	.154	33	78	8	12	13	1	0	0	2	0	2	0	0	6	0	15	2	1	2	.167	.214	2
Walker, G.	Chi.	L	.247	99	377	45	93	141	22	1	8	42	7	1	2	3	29	3	77	0	1	7	.374	.304	7
Ward, G.	N.Y.	R	.225	91	231	26	52	72	8	0	4	24	3	4	1	2	24	4	41	0	1	8	.312	.302	2
Washington, C.	N.Y.	L	.308	126	455	62	140	201	22	3	11	64	8	0	4	2	24	2	74	15	6	7	.442	.342	5
Washington, R.	Cle.	R	.256	69	223	30	57	81	14	2	2	21	2	3	1	5	9	0	35	3	3	2	.363	.298	17
Weiss, W.	Oak.	S	.250	147	452	44	113	145	17	3	3	39	2	8	7	9	35	1	56	4	4	9	.321	.312	15
Wellman, B.	K.C.	R	.271	71	107	11	29	35	3	0	1	6	0	1	0	2	6	0	23	1	2	1	.327	.322	6
Whitaker, L.	Det.	L	.275	115	403	54	111	169	18	2	12	55	5	6	2	0	66	5	61	2	0	8	.419	.376	8
White, D.	Cal.	S	.259	122	455	76	118	177	22	2	11	51	7	5	1	2	23	1	84	17	8	5	.389	.297	9
White, F.	K.C.	R	.235	150	537	48	126	177	25	1	8	58	10	7	6	4	21	3	67	7	3	16	.330	.266	4
Whitt, E.	Tor.	L	.251	127	398	63	100	163	11	2	16	70	5	2	6	1	61	4	38	4	2	9	.410	.348	4
Wilkerson, C.	Tex.	S	.293	117	338	41	99	121	12	5	0	28	4	3	2	2	26	3	43	9	4	7	.358	.345	15
Williams, E.	Cle.	R	.190	10	21	3	4	4	0	0	0	1	0	1	0	1	0	0	3	0	0	1	.190	.227	0
Williams, K.	Chi.	R	.159	73	220	18	35	67	4	2	8	28	3	3	2	8	10	0	64	6	5	2	.305	.221	17
Williams, R.	Cle.	R	.226	11	31	7	7	12	2	0	1	3	0	0	0	0	0	0	6	0	0	2	.387	.226	0
Wilson, G.	Sea.	R	.250	78	284	28	71	92	10	1	3	17	0	1	2	0	15	0	52	1	1	13	.324	.286	3
Wilson, W.	K.C.	S	.262	147	591	81	155	197	17	11	1	37	6	8	5	2	22	1	106	35	7	5	.333	.289	4
Winfield, D.	N.Y.	R	.322	149	559	96	180	296	37	2	25	107	10	0	1	2	69	10	88	9	4	19	.530	.398	3
Woodard, M.	Chi.	L	.133	18	45	3	6	8	0	1	0	4	0	1	0	1	1	0	5	1	1	1	.178	.170	2
Worthington, C.	Bal.	R	.185	26	81	5	15	23	2	0	2	4	0	0	0	0	9	0	24	1	0	2	.284	.267	3
Wynegar, B.	Cal.	S	.255	27	55	8	14	23	4	1	1	8	2	0	2	0	8	1	7	0	0	2	.418	.338	2
Young, M.	Mil.	S	.000	8	14	2	0	0	0	0	0	0	0	1	0	1	2	1	5	0	0	0	.000	.176	0
Yount, R.	Mil.	R	.306	162	621	92	190	289	38	11	13	91	13	2	7	3	63	10	63	22	4	21	.465	.369	2
Zuvella, P.	Cle.	R	.231	51	130	9	30	37	5	1	0	7	1	8	0	0	8	0	13	0	0	3	.285	.275	8

TOP FIFTEEN DESIGNATED HITTERS
(Minimum: 100 At-Bats)

Batter	Team	Bats	Avg	G	AB	R	H	TB	2B	3B	HR	RBI	GW	SH	SF	HB	BB	IBB	SO	SB	CS	GI DP	SLG	OBP
Brett, G.	K.C.	L	.333	33	123	20	41	64	9	1	4	20	1	0	1	1	22	5	8	1	2	3	.520	.435
Francona, T.	Cle.	L	.331	38	163	22	54	62	5	0	1	8	1	2	2	0	5	1	13	0	0	3	.380	.347
Murray, E.	Bal.	S	.314	58	207	30	65	114	8	1	13	33	2	0	2	0	32	3	35	1	1	1	.551	.402
Mulliniks, R.	Tor.	L	.308	108	318	48	98	155	19	1	12	47	10	2	4	0	55	3	55	1	0	9	.487	.406
Hrbek, K.	Min.	L	.307	37	127	17	39	60	6	0	5	17	3	0	1	0	23	3	20	0	1	1	.472	.411
Molitor, P.	Mil.	R	.305	49	200	33	61	94	15	3	4	14	2	1	0	1	14	1	12	11	2	1	.470	.353
Baines, H.	Chi.	L	.285	147	562	53	160	234	39	1	11	76	6	0	7	1	64	13	103	0	0	20	.416	.355
Tabler, P.	Cle.-K.C.	R	.284	69	257	36	73	93	13	2	1	36	5	0	1	1	31	1	34	3	0	6	.362	.362
Rice, J.	Bos.	R	.263	112	414	53	109	174	16	2	15	65	5	0	5	3	42	2	81	1	1	14	.420	.332
Larkin, G.	Min.	S	.255	86	294	30	75	105	21	0	3	40	7	1	4	10	41	4	31	2	1	6	.357	.361
Phelps, K.	Sea.-N.Y.	L	.255	92	271	48	69	148	10	0	23	48	6	0	3	1	62	3	54	1	0	6	.546	.392
Kittle, R.	Cle.	R	.251	63	215	29	54	110	8	0	16	40	2	0	4	8	15	1	62	0	0	0	.512	.318
Fielder, C.	Tor.	R	.250	50	120	16	30	59	3	1	8	19	1	0	0	1	10	0	42	0	0	2	.492	.313
Parker, D.	Oak.	L	.243	61	239	27	58	87	11	0	6	33	7	0	2	0	18	1	43	0	0	3	.364	.293
Clark, J.	N.Y.	R	.243	112	387	61	94	168	11	0	21	72	13	0	5	1	92	6	113	2	0	12	.434	.386

CLUB BATTING

Club	AVG	G	AB	R	OR	H	TB	2B	3B	HR	GS	RBI	SH	SF	HP	BB	IBB	SO	SB	CS	GI DP	LOB	SHO	SLG	OBP
Boston	.283	162	5545	813	689	1569	2329	310	39	124	4	760	66	55	45	623	53	728	65	36	139	1269	13	.420	.357
Minnesota	.274	162	5510	759	672	1508	2317	294	31	151	3	710	37	50	55	528	52	832	107	63	130	1158	9	.421	.340
Toronto	.268	162	5557	763	680	1491	2330	271	47	158	3	706	34	50	31	521	35	935	107	36	145	1105	3	.419	.332
Oakland	.263	162	5602	800	620	1474	2237	251	22	156	3	752	54	55	65	580	29	926	129	54	142	1158	11	.399	.336
New York	.263	161	5592	772	748	1469	2209	272	12	148	4	713	36	51	30	588	56	935	146	39	130	1170	6	.395	.333
California	.261	162	5582	714	771	1458	2150	258	31	124	1	660	63	52	49	469	48	819	86	52	120	1119	7	.385	.321
Cleveland	.261	162	5505	666	731	1435	2128	235	28	134	4	629	36	51	37	416	43	866	97	50	108	1069	10	.387	.314
Kansas City	.259	161	5469	704	648	1419	2137	275	40	121	3	671	46	51	33	486	44	944	137	54	105	1104	12	.391	.321
Seattle	.257	161	5436	664	744	1397	2166	271	27	148	2	617	40	42	38	461	24	787	95	61	135	1044	14	.398	.317
Milwaukee	.257	162	5488	682	616	1409	2058	258	26	113	2	632	59	41	37	439	55	911	159	55	123	1058	14	.375	.314
Texas	.252	161	5479	637	735	1378	2019	227	39	112	2	589	48	53	35	542	43	1022	130	57	111	1174	9	.368	.320
Detroit	.250	162	5433	703	658	1358	2056	213	28	143	5	650	66	37	29	588	38	841	87	42	136	1124	10	.378	.324
Chicago	.244	161	5449	631	757	1327	2017	224	35	132	3	573	67	43	34	446	50	908	98	46	118	1058	7	.370	.303
Baltimore	.238	161	5358	550	789	1275	1925	199	20	137	1	517	40	45	32	504	31	869	69	44	140	1092	14	.359	.305
Totals	.259	1131	77005	9858	9858	19967	30078	3558	425	1901	40	9179	692	676	550	7191	601	12323	1512	689	1782	15702	139	.391	.324

Pitching

INDIVIDUAL PITCHING LEADERS

Games Won	24	Viola, Min.
Games Lost	17	Blyleven, Min.
Won-Lost Percentage	.774	Viola, Min.
Earned Run Average	2.45	Anderson, Min.
Games	70	Crim, Mil.
Games Started	37	Stewart, Oak.
Complete Games	14	Clemens, Bos. & Stewart, Oak.
Games Finished	59	Thigpen, Chi.
Shutouts	8	Clemens, Bos.
Saves	45	Eckersley, Oak.
Innings	275.2	Stewart, Oak.
Hits	271	Saberhagen, K.C.
Batsmen Faced	1156	Stewart, Oak.
Runs	130	Witt, Cal.
Earned Runs	125	Blyleven, Min.
Home Runs	33	Fraser, Cal.
Sacrifice Hits	14	Flanagan, Tor.
Sacrifice Flies	12	Boddicker, Bal.-Bos.
Hit Batsmen	16	Blyleven, Min.
Bases On Balls	126	Hough, Tex.
Intentional Bases On Balls	10	John Davis, Chi., Henneman, Det., Jackson, Sea. & Minton, Cal.
Strikeouts	291	Clemens, Bos.
Wild Pitches	16	Davis, Oak. & Witt, Tex.
Balks	16	Stewart, Oak.
Games Won, Consecutive	10	Davis, Oak. (July 8-Sept. 5)
Games Lost, Consecutive	11	Bosio, Mil. (May 21-August 26)

TOP 15 QUALIFIERS FOR EARNED RUN AVERAGE CHAMPIONSHIP

Pitcher	Team	Thrs	W	L	ERA	G	GS	CG	SHO	GF	SV	IP	H	TBF	R	ER	HR	SH	SF	HB	BB	IBB	SO	WP	BK	OPP AVG
Anderson, A.	Min.	L	16	9	2.45	30	30	3	1	0	0	202.1	199	815	70	55	14	3	5	7	37	1	83	1	4	.261
Higuera, T.	Mil.	L	16	9	2.45	31	31	8	1	0	0	227.1	168	895	66	62	15	10	7	6	59	4	192	0	6	.207
Viola, F.	Min.	L	24	7	2.64	35	35	7	2	0	0	255.1	236	1031	80	75	20	6	6	3	54	2	193	5	1	.245
Gubicza, M.	K.C.	R	20	8	2.70	35	35	8	4	0	0	269.2	237	1111	94	81	11	3	6	6	83	3	183	12	4	.234
Clemens, R.	Bos.	R	18	12	2.93	35	35	14	8	0	0	264.0	217	1063	93	86	17	6	3	6	62	4	291	4	7	.220
Robinson, J.	Det.	R	13	6	2.98	24	23	6	2	0	0	172.0	121	698	61	57	19	2	6	3	72	5	114	8	1	.197
Stieb, D.	Tor.	R	16	8	3.04	32	31	8	4	1	0	207.1	157	844	76	70	15	0	4	13	79	0	147	4	5	.210
Leibrandt, C.	K.C.	L	13	12	3.19	35	35	7	2	0	0	243.0	244	1002	98	86	20	5	7	4	62	3	125	10	4	.264
Swindell, G.	Cle.	L	18	14	3.20	33	33	12	4	0	0	242.0	234	988	97	86	18	9	5	1	45	3	180	5	0	.252
Stewart, D.	Oak.	R	21	12	3.23	37	37	14	2	0	0	275.2	240	1156	111	99	14	7	9	3	110	5	192	14	16	.234
Candiotti, T.	Cle.	R	14	8	3.28	31	31	11	1	0	0	216.2	225	903	86	79	15	12	5	6	53	3	137	5	7	.272
Hough, C.	Tex.	R	15	16	3.32	34	34	10	0	0	0	252.0	202	1067	111	93	20	8	8	12	126	1	174	10	10	.221
Langston, M.	Sea.	L	15	11	3.34	35	35	9	3	0	0	261.1	222	1078	108	97	32	6	5	3	110	2	235	7	4	.233
Bosio, C.	Mil.	R	7	15	3.36	38	22	9	1	15	6	182.0	190	766	80	68	13	7	9	2	38	6	84	1	2	.268
Boddicker, M.	Bal.-Bos.	R	13	15	3.39	36	35	5	1	0	0	236.0	234	1001	102	89	17	4	12	14	77	6	156	6	4	.262

INDIVIDUAL PITCHING

Pitcher	Team	Thrs	W	L	ERA	G	GS	CG	SHO	GF	SV	IP	H	TBF	R	ER	HR	SH	SF	HB	BB	IBB	SO	WP	BK	OPP AVG
Aase, D.	Bal.	R	0	0	4.05	35	0	0	0	16	0	46.2	40	209	22	21	4	3	2	0	37	5	28	1	0	.240
Alexander, D.	Det.	R	14	11	4.32	34	34	5	1	0	0	229.0	260	985	122	110	30	4	8	5	46	7	126	2	1	.282
Allen, N.	N.Y.	R	5	3	3.84	41	2	0	1	10	0	117.1	121	504	51	50	14	7	6	2	37	7	61	2	0	.268
Anderson, A.	Min.	L	16	9	2.45	30	30	3	1	0	0	202.1	199	815	70	55	14	3	5	7	37	1	83	1	4	.261
Anderson, R.	K.C.	R	2	1	4.24	7	3	0	0	0	0	34.0	41	147	17	16	3	1	3	1	9	2	9	1	0	.308
Aquino, L.	K.C.	R	1	0	2.79	7	5	1	1	0	0	29.0	33	136	15	9	1	0	1	1	17	0	11	1	1	.284

Pitcher	Team	Thrs	W	L	ERA	G	GS	CG	SHO	GF	SV	IP	H	TBF	R	ER	HR	SH	SF	HB	BB	IBB	SO	WP	BK	OPP AVG
Atherton, K.	Min.	R	7	5	3.41	49	0	0	0	13	3	74.0	65	309	29	28	10	5	3	2	22	4	43	1	0	.235
August, D.	Mil.	R	13	7	3.09	24	22	6	1	0	0	148.1	137	614	55	51	12	4	3	0	48	6	66	5	0	.245
Bailes, S.	Cle.	L	9	14	4.90	37	21	5	2	7	0	145.0	149	617	89	79	22	5	4	2	46	0	53	2	3	.266
Bair, D.	Tor.	R	0	0	4.05	10	0	0	0	4	0	13.1	14	55	6	6	2	2	0	0	3	0	8	1	0	.280
Ballard, J.	Bal.	L	8	12	4.40	25	25	6	1	0	0	153.1	167	654	83	75	15	3	3	6	42	2	41	2	2	.278
Bankhead, S.	Sea.	R	7	9	3.07	21	21	2	1	0	0	135.0	115	557	53	46	8	3	1	1	38	5	102	3	1	.224
Bannister, F.	K.C.	L	12	13	4.33	31	31	2	0	0	0	189.1	182	816	102	91	22	8	2	5	68	6	113	6	2	.248
Bautista, J.	Bal.	R	6	15	4.30	33	25	3	0	5	0	171.2	171	721	86	82	21	2	3	7	45	3	76	4	5	.258
Berenguer, J.	Min.	R	8	4	3.96	57	1	0	0	27	2	100.0	74	428	44	44	7	5	4	1	61	7	99	3	5	.207
Best, K.	Min.	R	0	0	6.00	11	0	0	0	8	0	12.0	15	59	9	8	1	1	2	0	7	1	9	0	1	.306
Birkbeck, M.	Mil.	R	10	8	4.72	23	23	0	0	0	0	124.0	141	538	69	65	10	4	2	1	37	1	64	0	11	.285
Bittiger, J.	Chi.	R	2	4	4.23	25	7	0	0	9	0	61.2	59	268	31	29	11	4	4	0	29	2	33	3	2	.255
Black, B.	K.C.-Cle.	L	4	4	5.00	33	7	0	0	9	1	81.0	82	358	47	45	8	6	3	4	34	3	63	5	6	.264
Blyleven, B.	Min.	R	10	17	5.43	33	33	7	0	0	0	207.1	240	895	128	125	21	6	6	16	51	1	145	5	3	.294
Boddicker, M.	Bal.-Bos.	R	13	15	3.39	36	35	5	1	0	0	236.0	234	1001	102	89	17	4	12	14	77	6	156	6	4	.262
Bolton, T.	Bos.	L	1	3	4.75	28	0	0	0	8	1	30.1	35	140	17	16	1	2	1	0	14	1	21	2	1	.285
Bordi, R.	Oak.	R	0	1	4.70	2	2	0	0	0	0	7.2	6	34	6	4	0	0	1	0	5	0	6	1	0	.222
Bosio, C.	Mil.	R	7	15	3.36	38	22	9	1	15	6	182.0	190	766	80	68	13	7	9	2	38	6	84	1	2	.268
Boyd, O.	Bos.	R	9	7	5.34	23	23	1	0	0	0	129.2	147	561	82	77	25	3	6	2	41	2	71	0	5	.289
Brown, K.	Tex.	R	1	1	4.24	4	4	1	0	0	0	23.1	33	110	15	11	2	1	0	1	8	0	12	1	0	.330
Buice, D.	Cal.	R	2	4	5.88	32	0	0	0	18	3	41.1	45	183	29	27	5	5	2	0	19	3	38	3	2	.287
Burns, T.	Oak.	R	8	2	3.16	17	14	2	0	3	1	102.2	93	425	38	36	8	2	2	1	34	1	57	3	6	.241
Cadaret, G.	Oak.	L	5	2	2.89	58	0	0	0	16	3	71.2	60	311	26	23	2	5	3	1	36	1	64	5	3	.226
Campbell, M.	Sea.	R	6	10	5.89	20	20	2	0	0	0	114.2	128	507	81	75	18	2	5	0	43	1	63	4	4	.280
Candelaria, J.	N.Y.	L	13	7	3.38	25	24	6	2	1	1	157.0	150	640	69	59	18	4	6	2	23	2	121	2	12	.248
Candiotti, T.	Cle.	R	14	8	3.28	31	31	11	1	0	0	216.2	225	903	86	79	15	12	5	6	53	3	137	5	7	.272
Carlton, S.	Min.	L	0	1	16.76	4	1	0	0	1	0	9.2	20	54	19	18	5	0	0	0	5	1	5	0	2	.408
Castillo, T.	Tor.	L	1	0	3.00	14	0	0	0	6	0	15.0	10	54	5	5	2	0	2	0	2	0	14	0	0	.200
Cecena, J.	Tex.	R	0	0	4.78	22	0	0	0	7	1	26.1	20	121	16	14	2	0	2	2	23	1	27	3	2	.213
Cerutti, J.	Tor.	L	6	7	3.13	46	12	0	0	11	1	123.2	120	524	56	43	12	8	3	3	42	6	65	7	3	.256
Clancy, J.	Tor.	R	11	13	4.49	36	31	4	0	5	1	196.1	207	827	106	98	26	7	4	9	47	3	118	7	0	.272
Clark, T.	Cal.	R	6	6	5.07	15	15	2	1	0	0	94.0	120	410	54	53	8	2	5	0	31	6	39	5	2	.323

Clear, M. ....Mil.	R	1	0	2.79	25	0	0	0	16	0	29.0	23	130	12	9	4	0	2	0	21	0	26	1	4	.215
Clemens, R. ....Bos.	R	18	12	2.93	35	35	14	8	0	0	264.0	217	1063	93	86	17	6	3	6	62	4	291	4	7	.220
Clements, P. ..........N.Y.	L	0	0	6.48	6	1	0	0	1	0	8.1	12	41	8	6	1	0	2	0	4	0	3	1	0	.343
Cliburn, S. ....Cal.	R	4	2	4.07	40	1	0	0	13	0	84.0	83	361	45	38	11	7	4	6	32	6	42	1	4	.266
Codiroli, C. ....Cle.	R	0	4	9.31	14	2	0	0	4	1	19.1	32	101	22	20	2	2	0	3	10	2	12	2	0	.372
Cook, M. ....Cal.	R	0	1	4.91	3	0	0	0	1	0	3.2	4	15	2	2	0	0	0	1	1	0	2	1	0	.308
Corbett, S. ....Cal.	L	2	1	4.14	34	0	0	0	7	1	45.2	47	204	23	21	2	4	5	0	23	3	28	2	0	.273
Corsi, J. ....Oak.	R	0	1	3.80	11	1	0	0	7	0	21.1	20	89	10	9	1	3	3	0	6	1	10	1	1	.260
Crim, C. ....Mil.	R	7	6	2.91	70	0	0	0	25	9	105.0	95	425	38	34	11	5	6	2	28	3	58	9	2	.247
Crouch, Z. ....Bos.	L	0	0	6.75	3	0	0	0	1	0	1.1	4	9	1	1	0	0	0	0	2	0	0	0	0	.571
Curry, S. ....Bos.	R	0	1	8.18	3	3	0	0	0	0	11.0	15	59	10	10	0	1	2	0	14	2	4	2	1	.357
Davis, Joel ....Chi.	R	0	1	6.75	5	2	0	0	1	0	16.0	21	70	12	12	4	0	1	0	5	0	10	0	0	.328
Davis, John ....Chi.	R	2	5	6.64	34	1	0	0	10	1	63.2	77	319	58	47	5	2	4	4	50	10	37	6	3	.297
Davis, S. ....Oak.	R	16	7	3.70	33	33	1	0	0	0	201.2	211	872	86	83	16	3	8	1	91	2	127	16	2	.274
Dedmon, J. ....Cle.	R	1	0	4.54	21	0	0	0	12	1	33.2	35	157	20	17	3	3	3	3	21	1	17	2	1	.276
DeJesus, J. ..............K.C.	R	0	1	27.00	2	1	0	0	0	0	2.2	6	19	10	8	0	0	0	0	5	1	2	0	0	.429
Dillard, G. ....Bal.	L	0	0	6.00	2	1	0	0	0	0	3.0	3	15	2	2	1	0	0	0	4	0	2	0	0	.273
DiMichele, F. ....Cal.	L	0	0	9.64	4	0	0	0	0	0	4.2	5	21	5	5	2	0	0	0	2	0	1	0	1	.263
Dotson, R. ...............N.Y.	R	12	9	5.00	32	29	4	0	0	0	171.0	178	755	103	95	27	3	7	4	72	3	77	3	3	.266
Eckersley, D. ....Oak.	R	4	2	2.35	60	0	0	0	53	45	72.2	52	279	20	19	5	1	3	1	11	2	70	0	2	.198
Eichhorn, M. ....Tor.	R	0	3	4.19	37	0	0	0	17	1	66.2	79	302	32	31	3	8	1	6	27	4	28	3	6	.304
Eiland, D. ...............N.Y.	R	0	0	6.39	3	3	0	0	0	0	12.2	15	57	9	9	6	0	0	2	4	0	7	0	0	.294
Ellsworth, S. ....Bos.	R	1	6	6.75	8	7	0	0	0	0	36.0	47	168	29	27	7	1	1	1	16	1	16	1	0	.315
Farr, S. ...................K.C.	R	5	4	2.50	62	1	0	0	49	20	82.2	74	344	25	23	5	1	3	2	30	6	72	4	2	.240
Farrell, J. ....Cle.	R	14	10	4.24	31	30	4	0	0	0	210.1	216	895	106	99	15	9	6	9	67	3	92	2	3	.269
Filer, T. ....Mil.	R	5	8	4.43	19	16	2	1	0	0	101.2	108	431	54	50	8	5	7	1	33	4	39	5	0	.281
Finley, C. ....Cal.	L	9	15	4.17	31	31	2	0	0	0	194.1	191	831	95	90	15	7	10	6	82	7	111	5	8	.263
Flanagan, M. ....Tor.	L	13	13	4.18	34	34	2	1	0	0	211.0	220	916	106	98	23	14	4	6	80	1	99	3	4	.271
Fossas, T. ....Tex.	L	0	0	4.76	5	0	0	0	1	0	5.2	11	28	3	3	0	0	0	0	2	0	0	1	0	.423
Fraser, W. ....Cal.	R	12	13	5.41	34	32	2	0	0	0	194.2	203	861	129	117	33	2	9	9	80	7	86	12	6	.267
Garber, G. ...............K.C.	R	0	4	3.58	26	0	0	0	19	6	32.2	29	138	15	13	4	1	0	2	13	2	20	0	2	.238
Gardner, W. ....Bos.	R	8	6	3.50	36	18	1	0	12	2	149.0	119	620	61	58	17	5	6	3	64	2	106	5	0	.220
Gibson, P. ....Det.	L	4	2	2.93	40	1	0	0	18	0	92.0	83	390	33	30	6	3	5	2	34	8	50	3	1	.240
Gladden, D. ....Min.	R	0	0	0.00	1	0	0	0	1	0	1.0	0	3	0	0	0	0	0	0	0	0	0	0	0	.000

Pitcher	Team	Thrs	W	L	ERA	G	GS	CG	SHO	GF	SV	IP	H	TBF	R	ER	HR	SH	SF	HB	BB	IBB	SO	WP	BK	OPP AVG
Gleaton, J.	K.C.	L	0	4	3.55	42	0	0	0	20	3	38.0	33	164	17	15	2	2	0	3	17	1	29	2	0	.232
Gonzalez, G.	Min.	R	0	0	3.38	16	0	0	0	14	1	21.1	20	92	8	8	4	1	0	1	8	1	19	0	0	.244
Gordon, D.	Cle.	R	3	4	4.40	38	0	0	0	15	1	59.1	65	261	33	29	5	6	4	3	19	3	20	2	4	.284
Gordon, T.	K.C.	R	0	2	5.17	5	2	0	0	0	0	15.2	16	67	9	9	1	0	0	0	7	0	18	0	0	.267
Guante, C.	N.Y.-Tex.	R	5	6	2.82	63	0	0	0	40	12	79.2	67	331	26	25	11	2	1	5	26	4	65	0	3	.226
Gubicza, M.	K.C.	R	20	8	2.70	35	35	8	4	0	0	269.2	237	1111	94	81	11	3	6	6	83	3	183	12	4	.234
Guetterman, L.	N.Y.	L	1	2	4.65	20	2	0	0	7	0	40.2	49	177	21	21	2	1	1	1	14	0	15	2	0	.306
Guidry, R.	N.Y.	L	2	3	4.18	12	10	0	0	1	0	56.0	57	239	28	26	7	1	1	2	15	3	32	2	2	.259
Guzman, J.	Tex.	R	11	13	3.70	30	30	6	2	0	0	206.2	180	876	99	85	20	4	6	5	82	3	157	10	12	.231
Habyan, J.	Bal.	R	1	0	4.30	7	0	0	0	1	0	14.2	22	68	10	7	2	0	2	0	4	0	4	1	1	.355
Hanson, E.	Sea.	R	2	3	3.24	6	6	0	0	0	0	41.2	35	168	17	15	4	3	0	1	12	1	36	2	2	.230
Harnisch, P.	Bal.	R	0	2	5.54	2	2	0	0	0	0	13.0	13	61	8	8	1	2	0	0	9	1	10	1	0	.260
Harvey, B.	Cal.	R	7	5	2.13	50	0	0	0	38	17	76.0	59	303	22	18	4	3	3	1	20	6	67	4	1	.214
Havens, B.	Cle.	L	2	3	3.14	28	0	0	0	14	1	57.1	62	248	22	20	7	2	2	0	17	3	30	0	1	.273
Hayward, R.	Tex.	L	4	6	5.46	12	12	1	1	0	0	62.2	63	271	44	38	6	4	4	0	35	0	37	6	4	.276
Heinkel, D.	Det.	R	0	0	3.96	21	0	0	0	9	1	36.1	30	151	17	16	4	0	1	1	12	1	30	3	5	.219
Henke T.	Tor.	R	4	4	2.91	52	0	0	0	44	25	68.0	60	285	23	22	6	4	2	2	24	3	66	0	0	.237
Henneman, M.	Det.	R	9	6	1.87	65	0	0	0	51	22	91.1	72	364	23	19	7	5	2	2	24	10	58	8	1	.218
Henry, D.	Tex.	R	0	1	8.71	11	0	0	0	5	1	10.1	15	59	10	10	1	0	1	3	9	1	10	3	1	.326
Hernandez, W.	Det.	L	6	5	3.06	63	0	0	0	38	10	67.2	50	284	24	23	8	6	3	4	31	6	59	3	3	.208
Higuera, T.	Mil.	L	16	9	2.45	31	31	8	1	0	0	227.1	168	895	66	62	15	10	7	6	59	4	192	0	6	.207
Hillegas, S.	Chi.	R	3	2	3.15	6	6	0	0	0	0	40.0	30	166	16	14	4	0	2	1	18	0	26	0	0	.207
Hoffman, G.	Tex.	L	0	0	5.24	11	0	0	0	2	0	22.1	22	99	14	13	5	0	1	1	8	0	9	1	0	.247
Honeycutt, R.	Oak.	L	3	2	3.50	55	0	0	0	17	7	79.2	74	330	36	31	6	3	6	3	25	2	47	3	8	.253
Horton, R.	Chi.	L	6	10	4.86	52	9	1	0	12	2	109.1	120	471	64	59	6	10	8	5	36	4	28	0	3	.291
Hough, C.	Tex.	R	15	16	3.32	34	34	10	0	0	0	252.0	202	1067	111	93	20	8	8	12	126	1	174	10	10	.221
Hudson, C.	N.Y.	R	6	6	4.49	28	12	1	0	10	2	106.1	93	447	53	53	9	5	7	4	36	4	58	4	1	.235
Huismann, M.	Det.	R	1	0	5.06	5	0	0	0	2	0	5.1	6	23	3	3	0	0	0	0	2	1	6	0	0	.286
Hurst, B.	Bos.	L	18	6	3.66	33	32	7	1	0	0	216.2	222	922	98	88	21	8	5	2	65	1	166	5	3	.264
Jackson, M.	Sea.	R	6	5	2.63	62	0	0	0	29	4	99.1	74	412	37	29	10	3	10	2	43	10	76	6	6	.209
Jeffcoat, M.	Tex.	L	0	2	11.70	5	2	0	0	2	0	10.0	19	52	13	13	1	1	0	2	5	1	5	0	0	.432
John, T.	N.Y.	L	9	8	4.49	35	32	0	0	2	0	176.1	221	776	96	88	11	5	2	6	46	4	81	5	5	.308

Jones, B.	Chi.	R	2	2	2.42	17	0	0	0	10	1	26.0	15	106	7	7	3	0	1	0	17	1	17	6	1	.170
Jones, D.	Cle.	R	3	4	2.27	51	0	0	0	46	37	83.1	69	338	26	21	1	3	0	2	16	3	72	2	3	.218
Jones, O.	Mil.	R	5	0	4.35	28	2	0	0	8	1	80.2	75	339	47	39	8	4	6	1	29	6	48	7	3	.251
Kaiser, J.	Cle.	L	0	0	0.00	3	0	0	0	1	0	2.2	2	11	0	0	0	2	1	0	1	0	0	0	0	.286
Key, J.	Tor.	L	12	5	3.29	21	21	2	2	0	0	131.1	127	551	55	48	13	4	3	5	30	2	65	1	0	.250
Kilgus, P.	Tex.	L	12	15	4.16	32	32	5	3	0	0	203.1	190	871	105	94	18	4	4	10	71	2	88	6	4	.243
King, E.	Det.	R	4	1	3.41	23	5	0	0	8	3	68.2	60	303	28	26	5	5	2	5	34	2	45	4	2	.233
Knudson, M.	Mil.	R	0	0	1.13	5	0	0	0	3	0	16.0	17	63	3	2	1	0	0	0	2	0	7	1	0	.279
Krawczyk, R.	Cal.	R	0	1	4.81	14	1	0	0	6	1	24.1	29	108	13	13	2	0	1	2	8	1	17	2	0	.299
Kunkel, J.	Tex.	R	0	0	0.00	1	0	0	0	1	0	1.0	0	3	0	0	0	0	0	0	0	0	1	0	0	.000
Lamp, D.	Bos.	R	7	6	3.48	46	0	0	0	14	0	82.2	92	350	39	32	3	3	2	2	19	3	49	5	8	.284
Langston, M.	Sea.	L	15	11	3.34	35	35	9	3	0	0	261.1	222	1078	108	97	32	6	5	3	110	2	235	7	4	.233
LaPoint, D.	Chi.	L	10	11	3.40	25	25	1	1	0	0	161.1	151	677	69	61	10	8	3	2	47	1	79	1	5	.245
Laskey, B.	Cle.	R	1	0	5.18	17	0	0	0	6	1	24.1	32	110	16	14	0	1	3	0	6	0	17	0	3	.320
Lazorko, J.	Cal.	R	0	1	3.35	10	3	0	0	1	0	37.2	37	165	15	14	5	2	1	1	16	0	19	0	1	.255
Lea, C.	Min.	R	7	7	4.85	24	23	0	0	0	0	130.0	156	585	79	70	19	6	5	5	50	2	72	6	4	.301
Lee, M.	K.C.	L	0	0	3.60	4	0	0	0	4	0	5.0	6	21	2	2	0	0	0	0	1	0	0	0	0	.300
Leibrandt, C.	K.C.	L	13	12	3.19	35	35	7	2	0	0	243.0	244	1002	98	86	20	5	7	4	62	3	125	10	4	.264
Leiter, A.	N.Y.	L	4	4	3.92	14	14	0	0	0	0	57.1	49	251	27	25	7	1	0	5	33	0	60	1	4	.231
Long, B.	Chi.	R	8	11	4.03	47	18	3	0	14	2	174.0	187	732	89	78	21	8	8	4	43	4	77	2	0	.280
Lovelace, V.	Cal.	L	0	0	13.50	3	0	0	0	2	0	1.1	2	8	2	2	1	0	0	0	3	0	0	0	0	.400
Lugo, U.	Cal.	R	0	0	9.00	1	0	0	0	0	0	2.0	2	9	2	2	1	0	0	0	1	0	1	0	0	.250
Manzanillo, R.	Chi.	L	0	1	5.79	2	2	0	0	0	0	9.1	7	46	6	6	1	0	0	1	12	0	10	1	0	.212
Martinez, T.	Min.	L	0	0	18.00	3	0	0	0	2	0	4.0	8	24	9	8	1	0	2	1	4	0	3	0	1	.471
Mason, M.	Min.	L	0	1	10.80	5	0	0	0	0	0	6.2	8	37	8	8	1	0	0	0	9	0	7	0	0	.286
May, S.	Tex.	R	0	0	8.59	3	1	0	0	0	0	7.1	8	33	7	7	3	0	2	0	4	1	4	0	0	.296
McCarthy, T.	Chi.	R	2	0	1.38	6	0	0	0	4	1	13.0	9	51	2	2	0	0	0	2	2	0	5	0	0	.191
McCaskill, K.	Cal.	R	8	6	4.31	23	23	4	2	0	0	146.1	155	635	78	70	9	1	6	1	61	3	98	13	2	.274
McDowell, J.	Chi.	R	5	10	3.97	26	26	1	0	0	0	158.2	147	687	85	70	12	6	7	7	68	5	84	11	1	.245
McGregor, S.	Bal.	L	0	3	8.83	4	4	0	0	0	0	17.1	27	82	18	17	3	0	2	0	7	0	10	0	0	.370
McMurtry, C.	Tex.	R	3	3	2.25	32	0	0	0	14	3	60.0	37	236	16	15	5	3	3	1	24	4	35	2	2	.180
Milacki, B.	Bal.	R	2	0	0.72	3	3	1	1	0	0	25.0	9	91	2	2	1	0	0	0	9	0	18	0	0	.110
Minton, G.	Cal.	R	4	5	2.85	44	0	0	0	26	7	79.0	67	331	37	25	1	3	3	3	34	10	46	4	1	.233
Mirabella, P.	Mil.	L	2	2	1.65	38	0	0	0	13	4	60.0	44	241	12	11	3	2	2	0	21	5	33	1	0	.204

Pitcher	Team	Thrs	W	L	ERA	G	GS	CG	SHO	GF	SV	IP	H	TBF	R	ER	HR	SH	SF	HB	BB	IBB	SO	WP	BK	OPP AVG
Mohorcic, D.	Tex.-N.Y.	R	4	8	4.22	56	0	0	0	25	6	74.2	83	342	42	35	7	1	6	8	29	7	44	4	0	.279
Monteleone, R.	Cal.	R	0	0	0.00	3	0	0	0	2	0	4.1	4	20	0	0	0	0	0	1	1	1	3	0	1	.222
Montgomery, J.	K.C.	R	7	2	3.45	45	0	0	0	13	1	62.2	54	271	25	24	6	3	2	2	30	1	47	3	6	.231
Moore, D.	Cal.	R	5	2	4.91	27	0	0	0	22	4	33.0	48	150	20	18	4	0	2	0	8	2	22	2	4	.343
Moore, M.	Sea.	R	9	15	3.78	37	32	9	3	3	1	228.2	196	918	104	96	24	3	3	3	63	6	182	4	3	.232
Morgan, M.	Bal.	R	1	6	5.43	22	10	2	0	6	1	71.1	70	299	45	43	6	1	0	1	23	1	29	5	0	.255
Morris, J.	Det.	R	15	13	3.94	34	34	10	2	0	0	235.0	225	997	115	103	20	12	3	4	83	7	168	11	11	.251
Musselman, J.	Tor.	L	8	5	3.18	15	15	0	0	0	0	85.0	80	354	34	30	4	1	2	3	30	2	39	1	2	.252
Nelson, G.	Oak.	R	9	6	3.06	54	1	0	0	20	3	111.2	93	456	42	38	9	3	4	3	38	4	67	4	6	.228
Nichols, R.	Cle.	R	1	7	5.06	11	10	3	0	1	0	69.1	73	297	41	39	5	2	2	2	23	1	31	2	3	.272
Niedenfuer, T.	Bal.	R	3	4	3.51	52	0	0	0	42	18	59.0	59	252	23	23	8	2	1	2	19	3	40	0	0	.259
Niekro, J.	Min.	R	1	1	10.03	5	2	0	0	2	0	11.2	16	59	13	13	2	0	0	0	9	0	7	2	3	.320
Nielsen, S.	N.Y.	R	1	2	6.86	7	2	0	0	1	0	19.2	27	94	16	15	5	0	0	0	13	2	4	1	0	.333
Nieves, J.	Mil.	L	7	5	4.08	25	15	1	1	4	1	110.1	84	458	53	50	13	1	2	1	50	4	73	1	3	.208
Noles, D.	Bal.	R	0	2	24.30	2	2	0	0	0	0	3.1	11	23	10	9	2	0	0	1	0	0	1	0	0	.500
Nunez, E.	Sea.	R	1	4	7.98	14	3	0	0	2	0	29.1	45	145	33	26	4	2	4	2	14	3	19	0	1	.366
Nunez, J.	Tor.	R	0	1	3.07	13	2	0	0	3	0	29.1	28	127	11	10	3	1	0	1	17	3	18	2	1	.259
Olson, G.	Bal.	R	1	1	3.27	10	0	0	0	4	0	11.0	10	51	4	4	1	0	0	0	10	1	9	0	1	.244
Ontiveros, S.	Oak.	R	3	4	4.61	10	10	0	0	0	0	54.2	57	241	32	28	4	5	0	0	21	1	30	5	5	.265
Otto, D.	Oak.	L	0	0	1.80	3	2	0	0	1	0	10.0	9	43	2	2	0	0	0	0	6	0	7	0	1	.243
Pall, D.	Chi.	R	0	2	3.45	17	0	0	0	6	0	28.2	39	130	11	11	1	2	1	0	8	1	16	1	0	.328
Patterson, K.	Chi.	L	0	2	4.79	9	2	0	0	3	1	20.2	25	92	11	11	2	0	0	0	7	0	8	1	1	.294
Pawlowski, J.	Chi.	R	1	0	8.36	6	0	0	0	2	0	14.0	20	65	14	13	2	0	1	0	3	0	10	1	2	.328
Pena, H.	N.Y.	L	1	1	3.14	16	0	0	0	8	0	14.1	10	62	8	5	1	0	1	0	9	1	10	1	0	.192
Peraza, O.	Bal.	R	5	7	5.55	19	15	1	0	0	0	86.0	98	392	62	53	10	3	3	2	37	2	61	4	4	.282
Perez, M.	Chi.	R	12	10	3.79	32	32	3	1	0	0	197.0	186	836	105	83	26	5	8	2	72	0	138	13	3	.248
Perlman, J.	Cle.	R	0	2	5.49	10	0	0	0	5	0	19.2	25	94	12	12	0	2	0	0	11	3	10	1	3	.309
Peterson, A.	Chi.	R	0	1	13.50	2	2	0	0	0	0	6.0	6	31	9	9	0	0	0	0	6	1	5	1	0	.240
Petry, D.	Cal.	R	3	9	4.38	22	22	4	1	0	0	139.2	139	604	70	68	18	5	6	6	59	5	64	5	2	.263
Plesac, D.	Mil.	L	1	2	2.41	50	0	0	0	48	30	52.1	46	211	14	14	2	2	0	0	12	2	52	4	6	.234
Plunk, E.	Oak.	R	7	2	3.00	49	0	0	0	22	5	78.0	62	331	27	26	6	3	2	1	39	4	79	4	7	.217
Portugal, M.	Min.	R	3	3	4.53	26	0	0	0	9	3	57.2	60	242	30	29	11	2	3	1	17	1	31	2	2	.274

Powell, D.	Sea.	L	1	3	8.68	12	2	0	0	1	0	18.2	29	95	20	18	2	0	2	2	11	2	15	0	0	.363
Power, T.	K.C.-Det.	R	6	7	5.91	26	14	2	2	3	0	99.0	121	443	67	65	8	2	4	3	38	7	57	4	2	.306
Quisenberry, D.	K.C.	R	0	1	3.55	20	0	0	0	13	1	25.1	32	110	11	10	0	0	0	0	5	2	9	1	1	.305
Reardon, J.	Min.	R	2	4	2.47	63	0	0	0	58	42	73.0	68	299	21	20	6	4	1	2	15	2	56	0	3	.245
Reed, J.	Sea.	R	1	1	3.96	46	0	0	0	19	1	86.1	82	363	42	38	8	3	5	2	33	7	48	1	7	.256
Reuss, J.	Chi.	L	13	9	3.44	32	29	2	0	1	0	183.0	183	751	79	70	15	5	4	3	43	1	73	3	4	.263
Rhoden, R.	N.Y.	R	12	12	4.29	30	30	5	1	0	0	197.0	206	847	107	94	20	8	8	8	56	4	94	2	6	.269
Righetti, D.	N.Y.	L	5	4	3.52	60	0	0	0	41	25	87.0	86	377	35	34	5	4	0	1	37	2	70	2	4	.257
Robinson, J.	Det.	R	13	6	2.98	24	23	6	2	0	0	172.0	121	698	61	57	19	2	6	3	72	5	114	8	1	.197
Rochford, M.	Bos.	L	0	0	0.00	2	0	0	0	0	0	2.1	4	12	0	0	0	0	0	0	1	0	1	0	0	.364
Rodriguez, R.	Cle.	R	1	2	7.09	10	5	0	0	4	0	33.0	43	156	28	26	4	4	1	1	17	1	9	2	0	.323
Rosenberg, S.	Chi.	L	0	1	4.30	33	0	0	0	18	1	46.0	53	203	22	22	5	3	3	0	19	0	28	1	0	.298
Ross, M.	Tor.	R	0	0	4.91	3	0	0	0	2	0	7.1	5	32	6	4	0	0	1	0	4	1	4	0	0	.185
Russell, J.	Tex.	R	10	9	3.82	34	24	5	0	1	0	188.2	183	793	86	80	15	4	3	7	66	3	88	5	7	.257
Saberhagen, B.	K.C.	R	14	16	3.80	35	35	9	0	0	0	260.2	271	1089	122	110	18	8	10	4	59	5	171	9	0	.269
Sanchez, I.	K.C.	L	3	2	4.54	19	1	0	0	6	1	35.2	36	157	20	18	0	2	1	0	18	2	14	3	1	.265
Schatzeder, D.	Cle.-Min.	L	0	3	6.49	25	0	0	0	10	3	26.1	34	121	21	19	7	1	0	2	7	1	17	0	0	.306
Scherrer, B.	Bal.	L	0	1	13.50	4	0	0	0	0	0	4.0	8	23	6	6	2	0	0	0	3	0	3	0	2	.400
Schilling, C.	Bal.	R	0	3	9.82	4	4	0	0	0	0	14.2	22	76	19	16	3	0	3	1	10	1	4	2	0	.355
Schmidt, D.	Bal.	R	8	5	3.40	41	9	0	0	11	2	129.2	129	541	58	49	14	5	3	3	38	5	67	3	0	.262
Schooler, M.	Sea.	R	5	8	3.54	40	0	0	0	33	15	48.1	45	214	21	19	4	2	3	1	24	4	54	4	1	.245
Scurry, R.	Sea.	L	0	2	4.02	39	0	0	0	18	2	31.1	32	150	16	14	6	2	2	4	18	4	33	2	11	.258
Searcy, S.	Det.	L	0	2	5.63	2	2	0	0	0	0	8.0	8	37	6	5	3	0	0	0	4	0	5	0	0	.242
Segura, J.	Chi.	R	0	0	13.50	4	0	0	0	1	0	8.2	19	52	17	13	1	0	0	0	8	0	2	2	3	.432
Sellers, J.	Bos.	R	1	7	4.83	18	12	1	0	2	0	85.2	89	393	49	46	9	2	0	3	56	3	70	8	7	.268
Shaver, J.	Oak.	R	0	0	0.00	1	0	0	0	1	0	1.0	0	4	0	0	0	1	0	1	0	0	0	0	0	.000
Shields, S.	N.Y.	R	5	5	4.37	39	0	0	0	13	0	82.1	96	362	44	40	8	6	2	2	30	4	55	3	1	.298
Sisk, D.	Bal.	R	3	3	3.72	52	0	0	0	29	0	94.1	109	410	43	39	3	5	2	2	45	6	26	3	0	.306
Smith, L.	Bos.	R	4	5	2.80	64	0	0	0	57	29	83.2	72	363	34	26	7	3	2	1	37	6	96	2	0	.225
Smith, R.	Min.	R	3	0	2.68	9	4	0	0	1	0	37.0	29	152	12	11	3	0	1	1	12	1	17	1	4	.210
Smithson, M.	Bos.	R	9	6	5.97	31	18	1	0	6	0	126.2	149	561	87	84	25	4	3	6	37	1	73	2	6	.292
Solano, J.	Sea.	R	0	0	4.09	17	0	0	0	10	3	22.0	22	98	13	10	3	2	2	0	12	2	10	1	0	.268
Stanley, B.	Bos.	R	6	4	3.19	57	0	0	0	31	5	101.2	90	419	41	36	6	5	6	7	29	7	57	5	1	.242
Stapleton, D.	Mil.	L	0	0	5.93	6	0	0	0	0	0	13.2	20	69	9	9	1	0	0	1	9	1	6	0	1	.339

Pitcher	Team	Thrs	W	L	ERA	G	GS	CG	SHO	GF	SV	IP	H	TBF	R	ER	HR	SH	SF	HB	BB	IBB	SO	WP	BK	OPP AVG
Stewart, D.	Oak.	R	21	12	3.23	37	37	14	2	0	0	275.2	240	1156	111	99	14	7	9	3	110	5	192	14	16	.234
Stieb, D.	Tor.	R	16	8	3.04	32	31	8	4	1	0	207.1	157	844	76	70	15	0	4	13	79	0	147	4	5	.210
Stoddard, T.	N.Y.	R	2	2	6.38	28	0	0	0	9	3	55.0	62	253	41	39	5	1	6	2	27	1	33	3	0	.286
Stottlemyre, T.	Tor.	R	4	8	5.69	28	16	0	0	2	0	98.0	109	443	70	62	15	5	3	4	46	5	67	2	3	.283
Straker, L.	Min.	R	2	5	3.92	16	14	1	1	1	1	82.2	86	341	39	36	8	1	3	0	25	1	23	4	3	.276
Swift, B.	Sea.	R	8	12	4.59	38	24	6	1	4	0	174.2	199	757	99	89	10	5	3	8	65	3	47	6	2	.295
Swindell, G.	Cle.	L	18	14	3.20	33	33	12	4	0	0	242.0	234	988	97	86	18	9	5	1	45	3	180	5	0	.252
Tanana, F.	Det.	L	14	11	4.21	32	32	2	0	0	0	203.0	213	876	105	95	25	6	3	4	64	7	127	6	0	.267
Taylor, T.	Sea.	R	0	1	6.26	5	5	0	0	0	0	23.0	26	101	17	16	2	1	1	0	11	1	9	1	0	.295
Terrell, W.	Det.	R	7	16	3.97	29	29	11	1	0	0	206.1	199	870	101	91	20	13	6	2	78	8	84	7	2	.258
Thigpen, B.	Chi.	R	5	8	3.30	68	0	0	0	59	34	90.0	96	398	38	33	6	4	5	4	33	3	62	6	2	.273
Thurmond, M.	Bal.	L	1	8	4.58	43	6	0	0	15	3	74.2	80	322	43	38	10	0	4	2	27	3	29	0	0	.277
Tibbs, J.	Bal.	R	4	15	5.39	30	24	1	0	1	0	158.2	184	708	103	95	18	6	7	3	63	2	82	8	3	.293
Toliver, F.	Min.	R	7	6	4.24	21	19	0	0	0	0	114.2	116	491	57	54	8	7	1	1	52	1	69	10	1	.270
Trautwein, J.	Bos.	R	0	1	9.00	9	0	0	0	4	0	16.0	26	78	17	16	2	0	0	1	9	0	8	1	0	.382
Trout, S.	Sea.	L	4	7	7.83	15	13	0	0	1	0	56.1	86	278	53	49	6	1	3	5	31	2	14	5	7	.361
Trujillo, M.	Det.	R	0	0	5.11	6	0	0	0	2	0	12.1	11	52	7	7	2	0	0	0	5	2	5	1	0	.234
Vande Berg, E.	Tex.	L	2	2	4.14	26	0	0	0	7	2	37.0	44	159	19	17	2	3	2	0	11	4	18	0	1	.308
Vaughn, D.	Tex.	R	0	0	7.63	8	0	0	0	4	0	15.1	24	75	15	13	4	0	2	0	4	0	8	1	0	.348
Viola, F.	Min.	L	24	7	2.64	35	35	7	2	0	0	255.1	236	1031	80	75	20	6	6	3	54	2	193	5	1	.245
Walker, M.	Cle.	R	0	1	7.27	3	1	0	0	0	0	8.2	8	42	7	7	0	1	0	0	10	0	7	0	0	.258
Walter, G.	Sea.	L	1	0	5.13	16	0	0	0	4	0	26.1	21	115	16	15	0	0	1	2	15	4	13	1	6	.216
Ward, D.	Tor.	R	9	3	3.30	64	0	0	0	32	15	111.2	101	487	46	41	5	4	5	5	60	8	91	10	3	.245
Wegman, B.	Mil.	R	13	13	4.12	32	31	4	1	0	0	199.0	207	847	104	91	24	3	10	4	50	5	84	1	1	.265
Welch, B.	Oak.	R	17	9	3.64	36	36	4	2	0	0	244.2	237	1034	107	99	22	12	8	10	81	1	158	3	13	.257
Wells, D.	Tor.	L	3	5	4.62	41	0	0	0	15	4	64.1	65	279	36	33	12	2	2	2	31	9	56	6	2	.269
Wilkinson, B.	Sea.	L	2	2	3.48	30	0	0	0	9	2	31.0	28	136	14	12	3	0	1	0	15	0	25	3	0	.233
Williams, M.	Tex.	L	2	7	4.63	67	0	0	0	51	18	68.0	48	296	38	35	4	3	4	6	47	3	61	5	6	.203
Williamson, M.	Bal.	R	5	8	4.90	37	10	2	0	11	2	117.2	125	507	70	64	14	4	2	2	40	8	69	5	3	.272
Willis, C.	Chi.	R	0	0	8.25	6	0	0	0	0	0	12.0	17	55	12	11	3	0	1	0	7	1	6	2	0	.362
Wills, F.	Tor.	R	0	0	5.23	10	0	0	0	4	0	20.2	22	89	12	12	2	1	1	0	6	2	19	1	0	.272
Wilson, S.	Tex.	L	0	0	5.87	3	0	0	0	1	0	7.2	7	31	5	5	1	0	0	0	4	1	1	0	0	.259

Winn, J. ....Min.	R	1	0	6.00	9	0	0	0	5	0	21.0	33	104	15	14	4	1	0	0	10	1	9	3	1	.355
Witt, B. ....Tex.	R	8	10	3.92	22	22	13	2	0	0	174.1	134	736	83	76	13	7	6	1	101	2	148	16	8	.216
Witt, M. ....Cal.	R	13	16	4.15	34	34	12	2	0	0	249.2	263	1080	130	115	14	11	10	5	87	7	133	9	2	.272
Woodward, R. ....Bos.	R	0	0	13.50	1	0	0	0	1	0	0.2	2	5	1	1	0	0	0	0	1	0	0	0	0	.500
Yett, R. ....Cle.	R	9	6	4.62	23	22	0	0	0	0	134.1	146	590	72	69	11	2	1	1	55	1	71	4	3	.275
Young, C. ....Oak.	L	11	8	4.14	26	26	1	0	0	0	156.1	162	651	77	72	23	3	5	4	50	3	69	3	6	.275

CLUB PITCHING

Club	W	L	ERA	G	CG	SHO	REL	SV	IP	H	R	ER	HR	HB	BB	IBB	SO	WP	BK	OPP AVG
Oakland	104	58	3.44	162	22	9	290	64	1489.1	1376	620	569	116	29	553	27	983	62	76	.247
Milwaukee	87	75	3.45	162	30	8	252	51	1449.1	1355	616	555	125	19	437	47	832	36	39	.248
Kansas City	84	77	3.65	161	29	12	253	32	1428.1	1415	648	580	102	33	465	39	886	55	27	.258
Detroit	88	74	3.71	162	34	8	220	36	1445.2	1361	658	596	150	32	497	68	890	57	27	.248
Toronto	87	75	3.80	162	16	17	293	47	1449.0	1404	680	611	143	59	528	49	904	48	29	.256
Minnesota	91	71	3.93	162	18	9	265	52	1431.2	1457	672	625	146	42	453	28	897	43	38	.266
Boston	89	73	3.97	162	26	14	250	37	1426.1	1415	689	629	143	37	493	34	1085	45	39	.259
Texas	70	91	4.05	161	41	11	251	31	1438.2	1310	735	647	129	56	654	33	912	72	57	.244
Chicago	71	90	4.12	161	11	9	293	43	1439.0	1467	757	659	138	35	533	34	754	61	30	.266
Seattle	68	93	4.15	161	28	11	291	28	1428.0	1385	744	659	144	36	558	57	981	50	55	.256
Cleveland	78	84	4.16	162	35	10	230	46	1434.0	1501	731	663	120	38	442	28	812	36	38	.270
New York	85	76	4.26	161	16	5	303	43	1456.0	1512	748	689	157	49	487	42	861	36	41	.267
California	75	87	4.32	162	26	9	262	33	1455.2	1503	771	698	135	42	568	67	817	68	37	.270
Baltimore	54	107	4.54	161	20	7	286	26	1416.0	1506	789	714	153	43	523	48	709	42	25	.274
Totals	1131	1131	3.97	1131	352	139	3739	569	20187.0	19967	9858	8894	1901	550	7191	601	12323	711	558	.259

Official 1988 National League Records

(Compiled by the MLB-IBM Baseball Information System)

Final Standings

EASTERN DIVISION

	W	L	Pct.	GB
New York	100	60	.625	....
Pittsburgh	85	75	.531	15
Montreal	81	81	.500	20
Chicago	77	85	.475	24
St. Louis	76	86	.469	25
Philadelphia	65	96	.404	35.5

WESTERN DIVISION

	W	L	Pct.	GB
Los Angeles	94	67	.584	....
Cincinnati	87	74	.540	7
San Diego	83	78	.516	11
San Francisco	83	79	.512	11.5
Houston	82	80	.506	12.5
Atlanta	54	106	.338	39.5

Tie Games: Los Angeles at Chicago, July 16, 8 innings (2-2)
Montreal at Philadelphia, April 23, 7 innings (3-3)

Championship Series: Los Angeles defeated New York, 4 games to 3

Batting

INDIVIDUAL BATTING LEADERS

Batting Average	.313	Gwynn, S.D.
Games	162	Clark, S.F.
At Bats	632	Sax, L.A.
Runs	109	Butler, S.F.
Hits	184	Galarraga, Mon.
Total Bases	329	Galarraga, Mon.
Singles	147	Sax, L.A.
Doubles	42	Galarraga, Mon.
Triples	15	Van Slyke, Pit.
Home Runs	39	Strawberry, N.Y.
Runs Batted In	109	Clark, S.F.
Game-Winning RBI	21	Davis, Cin.
Sacrifice Hits	19	Hershiser, L.A. & Reuschel, S.F.
Sacrifice Flies	13	Van Slyke, Pit.
Hit By Pitch	16	Bradley, Phi.
Bases on Balls	100	Clark, S.F.
Intentional Bases on Balls	27	Clark, S.F.
Strikeouts	153	Galarraga, Mon.
Stolen Bases	81	Coleman, St.L.
Caught Stealing	27	Coleman, St.L. & Young, Hou.
Grounded Into Double Plays	24	Murphy, Atl.
Slugging Percentage	.545	Strawberry, N.Y.
On-Base Percentage	.397	Daniels, Cin.
Longest Batting Streak	24	Shelby, L.A. (May 14-June 9)

TOP FIFTEEN QUALIFIERS FOR BATTING CHAMPIONSHIP

Batter	Team	Bats	Avg	G	AB	R	H	TB	2B	3B	HR	RBI	GW	SH	SF	HB	BB	IBB	SO	SB	CS	GIDP	SLG	OBP	E
Gwynn, T.	S.D.	L	.313	133	521	64	163	216	22	5	7	70	12	4	2	0	51	13	40	26	11	11	.415	.373	5
Palmeiro, R.	Chi.	L	.307	152	580	75	178	253	41	5	8	53	0	2	6	3	38	6	34	12	2	11	.436	.349	5
Dawson, A.	Chi.	R	.303	157	591	78	179	298	31	8	24	79	6	1	7	4	37	12	73	12	4	13	.504	.344	3
Galarraga, A.	Mon.	R	.302	157	609	99	184	329	42	8	29	92	16	0	3	10	39	9	153	13	4	12	.540	.352	15
Perry, G.	Atl.	L	.300	141	547	61	164	219	29	1	8	74	9	1	10	1	36	9	49	29	14	18	.400	.338	17
Grace, M.	Chi.	L	.296	134	486	65	144	196	23	4	7	57	9	0	4	0	60	5	43	3	3	12	.403	.371	17
Larkin, B.	Cin.	R	.296	151	588	91	174	252	32	5	12	56	5	10	5	8	41	3	24	40	7	7	.429	.347	29
Law, V.	Chi.	R	.293	151	556	73	163	229	29	2	11	78	12	4	3	3	55	4	79	1	4	15	.412	.358	19
McGee, W.	St.L.	S	.292	137	562	73	164	209	24	6	3	50	9	2	3	1	32	5	84	41	6	10	.372	.329	9
Daniels, K.	Cin.	L	.291	140	495	95	144	229	29	1	18	64	9	0	4	3	87	10	94	27	6	11	.463	.397	5
Gibson, K.	L.A.	L	.290	150	542	106	157	262	28	1	25	76	9	3	7	7	73	14	120	31	4	8	.483	.377	12
McReynolds, K.	N.Y.	R	.288	147	552	82	159	274	30	2	27	99	19	1	5	4	38	3	56	21	0	6	.496	.336	4
Van Slyke, A.	Pit.	L	.288	154	587	101	169	297	23	15	25	100	16	1	13	1	57	2	126	30	9	8	.506	.345	4
Butler, B.	S.F.	L	.287	157	568	109	163	226	27	9	6	43	3	8	2	4	97	4	64	43	20	2	.398	.393	5
Bonds, B.	Pit.	L	.283	144	538	97	152	264	30	5	24	58	3	0	2	2	72	14	82	17	11	3	.491	.368	6

INDIVIDUAL BATTING

Batter	Team	Bats	Avg	G	AB	R	H	TB	2B	3B	HR	RBI	GW	SH	SF	HB	BB	IBB	SO	SB	CS	GIDP	SLG	OBP	E
Abner, S.	S.D.	R	.181	37	83	6	15	24	3	0	2	5	0	0	1	1	4	1	19	0	1	1	.289	.225	1
Acker, J.	Atl.	R	.400	21	5	0	2	2	0	0	0	0	0	0	0	0	1	0	1	0	0	0	.400	.500	0
Agosto, J.	Hou.	L	.000	75	5	0	0	0	0	0	0	0	0	1	0	0	0	0	0	0	0	0	.000	.000	2
Aguayo, L.	Phi.	R	.247	49	97	9	24	36	3	0	3	5	2	1	0	0	13	2	17	2	0	2	.371	.336	7
Aguilera, R.	N.Y.	R	.250	11	4	1	1	1	0	0	0	0	0	0	0	0	0	0	1	0	0	0	.250	.250	0
Alba, G.	St.L.	L	....	3	0	0	0	0	0	0	0	0	0	0	0	0	0	0	0	0	0	0	....	....	0
Aldrete, M.	S.F.	L	.267	139	389	44	104	128	15	0	3	50	5	1	3	0	56	13	65	6	5	10	.329	.357	4
Alicea, L.	St.L.	S	.212	93	297	20	63	84	10	4	1	24	4	4	2	2	25	4	32	1	1	12	.283	.276	14
Almon, B.	Phi.	R	.115	20	26	1	3	5	2	0	0	1	0	2	0	0	3	0	11	0	0	0	.192	.207	2
Alomar, R.	S.D.	S	.266	143	545	84	145	208	24	6	9	41	9	16	0	3	47	5	83	24	6	15	.382	.328	16
Alomar, S.	S.D.	R	.000	1	1	0	0	0	0	0	0	0	0	0	0	0	0	0	1	0	0	0	.000	.000	0
Alvarez, J.	Atl.	R	.375	61	8	0	3	3	0	0	0	0	0	1	0	0	1	0	0	0	0	0	.375	.444	0
Andersen, L.	Hou.	R	.333	53	6	1	2	2	0	0	0	0	0	0	0	0	0	0	1	0	0	0	.333	.333	2
Anderson, D.	L.A.	R	.249	116	285	31	71	91	10	2	2	20	2	5	2	1	32	4	45	4	2	9	.319	.325	5
Andujar, J.	Hou.	S	.211	23	19	0	4	6	2	0	0	0	0	1	0	0	2	0	9	0	0	0	.316	.286	2
Armstrong, J.	Cin.	R	.095	14	21	0	2	2	0	0	0	0	0	1	0	0	0	0	10	0	0	0	.095	.095	0
Arnold, S.	St.L.	R	....	6	0	0	0	0	0	0	0	0	0	0	0	0	0	0	0	0	0	0	....	....	0
Ashby, A.	Hou.	S	.238	73	227	19	54	85	10	0	7	33	4	1	4	0	29	3	36	0	0	5	.374	.319	4
Assenmacher, P.	Atl.	L	.333	64	3	0	1	2	1	0	0	0	0	1	0	0	0	0	0	0	0	0	.667	.333	0
Backman, W.	N.Y.	S	.303	99	294	44	89	101	12	0	0	17	2	9	2	1	41	1	49	9	5	6	.344	.388	4
Bailey, M.	Hou.	S	.130	8	23	1	3	3	0	0	0	0	0	0	0	0	5	0	6	0	1	1	.130	.286	1
Barojas, S.	Phi.	R	....	6	0	0	0	0	0	0	0	0	0	0	0	0	0	0	0	0	0	0	....	....	1
Barrett, T.	Phi.	S	.204	36	54	5	11	12	1	0	0	3	1	1	0	1	7	0	8	0	0	1	.222	.306	2
Barrett, T.	Mon.	L	.000	4	2	0	0	0	0	0	0	0	0	0	0	0	0	0	2	0	0	0	.000	.000	1
Bass, K.	Hou.	S	.255	157	541	57	138	211	27	2	14	72	7	3	3	6	42	10	65	31	6	16	.390	.314	6
Bedrosian, S.	Phi.	R	.000	57	2	0	0	0	0	0	0	0	0	0	0	0	0	0	2	0	0	0	.000	.000	0
Belcher, T.	L.A.	R	.071	36	56	2	4	9	2	0	1	3	0	5	0	0	0	0	28	0	0	0	.161	.071	0
Bell, B.	Cin.-Hou.	R	.241	95	323	27	78	111	10	1	7	40	6	0	3	0	26	2	32	1	1	10	.344	.295	15
Belliard, R.	Pit.	R	.213	122	286	28	61	69	0	4	0	11	1	5	0	4	26	3	47	7	1	10	.241	.288	9
Benedict, B.	Atl.	R	.242	90	236	11	57	64	7	0	0	19	1	5	2	0	19	1	26	0	2	2	.271	.296	5

Berryhill, D.	Chi.	S	.259	95	309	19	80	122	19	1	7	38	6	3	3	0	17	5	56	1	0	11	.395	.295	9
Bielecki, M.	Chi.	R	.100	19	10	0	1	1	0	0	0	0	0	0	0	0	0	0	7	0	0	0	.100	.100	0
Biggio, C.	Hou.	R	.211	50	123	14	26	43	6	1	3	5	1	1	0	0	7	2	29	6	1	1	.350	.254	3
Birtsas, T.	Cin.	L	.000	36	10	0	0	0	0	0	0	0	0	0	0	0	0	0	2	0	0	0	.000	.000	2
Blankenship, K.	Atl.-Chi.	R	.000	3	6	0	0	0	0	0	0	0	0	0	0	0	0	0	4	0	0	0	.000	.000	0
Blauser, J.	Atl.	R	.239	18	67	7	16	27	3	1	2	7	2	3	1	1	2	0	11	0	1	1	.403	.268	4
Blocker, T.	Atl.	L	.212	66	198	13	42	56	4	2	2	10	1	2	0	0	10	3	20	1	1	6	.283	.250	1
Bockus, R.	S.F.	L	.167	20	6	0	1	1	0	0	0	0	0	0	0	0	0	0	2	0	0	0	.167	.167	0
Boever, J.	Atl.	R	....	16	0	0	0	0	0	0	0	0	0	0	0	0	0	0	0	0	0	0	....	....	0
Bonds, B.	Pit.	L	.283	144	538	97	152	264	30	5	24	58	3	0	2	2	72	14	82	17	11	3	.491	.368	6
Bonilla, B.	Pit.	S	.274	159	584	87	160	278	32	7	24	100	13	0	8	4	85	19	82	3	5	4	.476	.366	32
Booker, G.	S.D.	R	.250	34	8	1	2	3	1	0	0	1	0	0	0	0	0	0	5	0	0	0	.375	.250	0
Booker, R.	St.L.	L	.343	18	35	6	12	15	3	0	0	3	0	0	0	0	4	0	3	2	2	0	.429	.410	2
Bradley, P.	Phi.	R	.264	154	569	77	150	223	30	5	11	56	7	3	6	16	54	0	106	11	9	11	.392	.341	3
Brantley, J.	S.F.	R	.500	9	2	0	1	1	0	0	0	0	0	0	0	0	0	0	0	0	0	0	.500	.500	0
Bream, S.	Pit.	L	.264	148	462	50	122	189	37	0	10	65	7	4	8	1	47	6	64	9	9	11	.409	.328	6
Brenly, B.	S.F.	R	.189	73	206	13	39	61	7	0	5	22	2	2	2	2	20	3	40	1	2	3	.296	.265	6
Brennan, W.	L.A.	R	.000	4	2	0	0	0	0	0	0	0	0	0	0	0	0	0	1	0	0	0	.000	.000	0
Brooks, H.	Mon.	R	.279	151	588	61	164	263	35	2	20	90	11	0	4	1	35	3	108	7	3	21	.447	.318	9
Brown, C	S.D.	R	.235	80	247	14	58	70	6	0	2	19	1	3	2	3	19	3	49	0	0	9	.283	.295	10
Brown, K.	Cin.	S	.000	4	4	0	0	0	0	0	0	0	0	1	0	0	0	0	3	0	0	0	.000	.000	0
Brown, M.	Cin.	R	.188	10	16	0	3	4	1	0	0	2	0	0	0	0	1	0	2	0	1	0	.250	.235	0
Browning, T.	Cin.	L	.145	41	83	7	12	14	2	0	0	4	0	9	0	0	5	0	24	3	0	0	.169	.193	3
Brunansky, T.	St.L.	R	.245	143	523	69	128	224	22	4	22	79	9	1	6	4	79	6	82	16	6	17	.428	.345	1
Burke, T.	Mon.	R	.000	61	2	0	0	0	0	0	0	0	0	0	0	0	0	0	1	0	0	0	.000	.000	0
Butler, B.	S.F.	L	.287	157	568	109	163	226	27	9	6	43	3	8	2	4	97	4	64	43	20	2	.398	.393	5
Byers, R.	S.D.	L	.200	11	10	0	2	3	1	0	0	0	0	0	0	0	0	0	5	0	0	0	.300	.200	0
Calhoun, J.	Phi.	L	....	3	0	0	0	0	0	0	0	0	0	0	0	0	0	0	0	0	0	0	....	....	0
Camacho, E.	Hou.	R	.000	13	1	0	0	0	0	0	0	0	0	0	0	0	0	0	0	0	0	0	.000	.000	0
Caminiti, K.	Hou.	S	.181	30	83	5	15	20	2	0	1	7	0	0	1	0	5	0	18	0	0	3	.241	.225	3
Candaele, C.	Mon.-Hou.	S	.170	57	147	11	25	35	8	1	0	5	0	3	0	0	11	1	17	1	1	7	.238	.228	2
Cangelosi, J.	Pit.	S	.254	75	118	18	30	36	4	1	0	8	0	3	0	1	17	0	16	9	4	0	.305	.353	2
Capel, M.	Chi.	R	.000	22	2	0	0	0	0	0	0	0	0	0	0	0	0	0	2	0	0	0	.000	.000	1
Carman, D.	Phi.	L	.048	36	63	1	3	3	0	0	0	0	0	8	0	0	0	0	19	0	0	1	.048	.048	0

Batter	Team	Bats	Avg	G	AB	R	H	TB	2B	3B	HR	RBI	GW	SH	SF	HB	BB	IBB	SO	SB	CS	GI DP	SLG	OBP	E
Carpenter, C	St.L.	R	.143	8	14	1	2	2	0	0	0	1	0	3	0	0	0	0	3	0	0	0	.143	.143	0
Carreon, M.	N.Y.	R	.556	7	9	5	5	10	2	0	1	1	0	0	0	0	2	0	1	0	0	0	1.111	.636	0
Carter, G.	N.Y.	R	.242	130	455	39	110	163	16	2	11	46	8	1	6	7	34	1	52	0	2	8	.358	.301	10
Cary, C.	Atl.	L	....	7	0	0	0	0	0	0	0	0	0	0	0	0	0	0	0	0	0	0	....	....	0
Charlton, N.	Cin.	S	.000	10	15	1	0	0	0	0	0	0	0	4	0	1	0	0	12	0	0	0	.000	.063	0
Childress, R.	Hou.	R	.250	11	4	0	1	1	0	0	0	0	0	0	0	0	0	0	1	0	0	0	.250	.250	1
Clark, J.	S.D.	R	.200	6	15	0	3	4	1	0	0	3	0	0	0	0	0	0	4	0	0	0	.267	.200	0
Clark, W.	S.F.	L	.282	162	575	102	162	292	31	6	29	109	13	0	10	4	100	27	129	9	1	9	.508	.386	12
Clay, D.	Phi.	R	.000	17	2	0	0	0	0	0	0	0	0	1	0	0	0	0	2	0	0	0	.000	.000	1
Coffman, K.	Atl.	R	.227	19	22	2	5	8	3	0	0	4	0	1	0	1	0	0	6	0	0	0	.364	.261	2
Coleman, V.	St.L.	S	.260	153	616	77	160	209	20	10	3	38	4	8	5	1	49	4	111	81	27	4	.339	.313	9
Coles, D.	Pit.	R	.232	68	211	20	49	79	13	1	5	36	7	0	7	3	20	1	41	1	1	3	.374	.299	2
Collins, D.	Cin.	S	.236	99	174	12	41	51	6	2	0	14	2	0	2	2	11	0	27	7	2	0	.293	.286	4
Comstock, K.	S.D.	L	....	7	0	0	0	0	0	0	0	0	0	0	0	0	0	0	0	0	0	0	....	....	0
Concepcion, D.	Cin.	R	.198	84	197	11	39	48	9	0	0	8	0	1	0	0	18	5	23	3	2	4	.244	.265	2
Cone. D.	N.Y.	L	.150	35	80	2	12	15	3	0	0	2	0	5	0	0	3	0	14	0	1	0	.188	.181	1
Cook, D.	S.F.	L	.000	4	4	1	0	0	0	0	0	0	0	1	0	0	3	0	1	0	0	0	.000	.429	0
Costello, J.	St.L.	R	.000	36	5	0	0	0	0	0	0	0	0	0	0	0	0	0	3	0	0	0	.000	.000	0
Cox, D.	St.L.	R	.043	13	23	0	1	1	0	0	0	0	0	5	0	0	0	0	13	0	0	0	.043	.043	0
Crews, T.	L.A.	R	.200	42	5	1	1	1	0	0	0	0	0	1	0	0	0	0	0	0	0	0	.200	.200	1
Daniels, K.	Cin.	L	.291	140	495	95	144	229	29	1	18	64	9	0	4	3	87	10	94	27	6	11	.463	.397	5
Darling, R.	N.Y.	R	.220	34	82	4	18	26	4	2	0	4	1	9	0	0	1	0	21	0	0	1	.317	.229	3
Darwin, D.	Hou.	R	.071	44	56	3	4	9	2	0	1	7	0	2	1	0	1	0	22	0	0	0	.161	.086	1
Dascenzo, D	Chi.	S	.213	26	75	9	16	19	3	0	0	4	0	1	0	0	9	1	4	6	1	2	.253	.298	0
Daulton, D.	Phi.	L	.208	58	144	13	30	39	6	0	1	12	1	0	2	0	17	1	26	2	1	2	.271	.288	6
Davis, E.	Cin.	R	.273	135	472	81	129	231	18	3	26	93	21	0	3	3	65	10	124	35	3	11	.489	.363	6
Davis, G.	Hou.	R	.271	152	561	78	152	268	26	0	30	99	14	0	9	11	53	20	77	4	3	11	.478	.341	6
Davis, J.	Chi.-Atl.	R	.230	90	257	21	59	89	9	0	7	36	4	2	3	1	29	3	52	0	3	7	.346	.307	2
Davis, M.	S.D.	L	.200	62	10	2	2	5	0	0	1	2	0	1	0	0	1	0	4	1	0	0	.500	.273	1
Davis, M.	L.A.	L	.196	108	281	29	55	76	11	2	2	17	3	2	2	0	25	0	59	7	3	6	.270	.260	5
Davis, R.	S.F.	R	.000	9	2	0	0	0	0	0	0	0	0	0	0	0	0	0	0	0	0	0	.000	.000	1

Dawley, B.	Phi.	R	....	8	0	0	0	0	0	0	0	0	0	0	0	0	0	0	0	0	0	0	....	....	0
Dawson, A.	Chi.	R	.303	157	591	78	179	298	31	8	24	79	6	1	7	4	37	12	73	12	4	13	.504	.344	3
Dayley, K.	St.L.	L	.000	54	4	0	0	0	0	0	0	0	0	0	0	0	0	0	2	0	0	0	.000	.000	0
DeLeon, J.	St.L.	R	.139	35	72	1	10	11	1	0	0	2	0	12	0	1	1	0	19	0	0	1	.153	.162	0
Dempsey, R.	L.A.	R	.251	77	167	25	42	76	13	0	7	30	3	0	6	0	25	0	44	1	0	4	.455	.338	4
Dernier, B.	Phi.	R	.289	68	166	19	48	56	3	1	1	10	2	3	0	1	9	0	19	13	6	2	.337	.330	2
Deshaies, J.	Hou.	L	.048	31	63	1	3	3	0	0	0	3	0	6	0	0	2	0	38	0	1	1	.048	.077	2
Destrade, O.	Pit.	S	.149	36	47	2	7	11	1	0	1	3	0	0	1	0	5	0	17	0	0	0	.234	.226	0
Devereaux, M.	L.A.	R	.116	30	43	4	5	6	1	0	0	2	1	0	0	0	2	0	10	0	1	0	.140	.156	0
Diaz, B.	Cin.	R	.219	92	315	26	69	108	9	0	10	35	3	1	3	1	7	4	41	0	2	16	.343	.236	5
Diaz, M.	Pit.	R	.230	47	74	6	17	20	3	0	0	5	2	0	0	0	16	1	13	0	0	2	.270	.367	0
Dibble, R.	Cin.	L	.000	37	2	0	0	0	0	0	0	0	0	2	0	0	0	0	1	0	0	0	.000	.000	0
DiPino, F.	Chi.	L	.100	63	10	2	1	1	0	0	0	0	0	1	0	0	0	0	4	0	0	0	.100	.100	0
Distefano, B.	Pit.	L	.345	16	29	6	10	18	3	1	1	6	0	0	1	0	3	1	4	0	0	1	.621	.394	0
Dopson, J.	Mon.	L	.059	26	51	0	3	4	1	0	0	1	0	4	0	0	1	0	31	0	0	2	.078	.077	2
Doran, B.	Hou.	S	.248	132	480	66	119	160	18	1	7	53	9	4	2	1	65	3	60	17	4	7	.333	.338	8
Downs, K.	S.F.	R	.167	27	54	7	9	13	2	1	0	3	0	4	0	0	3	0	17	0	0	1	.241	.211	1
Drabek, D.	Pit.	R	.171	33	76	4	13	20	3	2	0	5	0	5	0	2	1	0	25	0	0	0	.263	.203	6
Dravecky, D.	S.F.	R	.100	7	10	2	1	1	0	0	0	0	0	3	0	0	0	0	1	0	0	0	.100	.100	2
Drew, C.	Hou.	L	.188	7	16	1	3	5	0	1	0	1	0	0	0	0	0	0	1	0	0	0	.313	.188	0
Dunne, M.	Pit.	L	.109	34	46	7	5	5	0	0	0	3	1	7	2	0	3	0	12	0	0	0	.109	.157	1
Dunston, S.	Chi.	R	.249	155	575	69	143	205	23	6	9	56	7	4	2	2	16	8	108	30	9	6	.357	.271	20
Durham, L.	Chi.-Cin.	L	.218	45	124	14	27	50	9	1	4	8	0	0	0	0	14	3	32	0	1	0	.403	.297	2
Dykstra, L.	N.Y.	L	.270	126	429	57	116	165	19	3	8	33	5	2	2	3	30	2	43	30	8	3	.385	.321	1
Eave, G.	Atl.	R	....	5	0	0	0	0	0	0	0	0	0	0	0	0	0	0	0	0	0	0	....	....	0
Eichelberger, J.	Atl.	R	.000	20	3	0	0	0	0	0	0	0	0	0	0	1	0	0	2	0	0	0	.000	.250	1
Elster, K.	N.Y.	R	.214	149	406	41	87	127	11	1	9	37	6	6	0	3	35	12	47	2	0	5	.313	.282	13
Engle, D.	Mon.	R	.216	34	37	4	8	11	3	0	0	1	0	0	0	0	5	0	5	0	0	2	.297	.310	0
Esasky, N.	Cin.	R	.243	122	391	40	95	161	17	2	15	62	8	0	7	4	48	4	104	7	2	6	.412	.327	6
Escobar, A.	S.F.	S	.333	3	3	1	1	1	0	0	0	0	0	0	0	0	0	0	0	0	0	0	.333	.333	0
Fermin, F.	Pit.	R	.276	43	87	9	24	28	0	2	0	2	0	1	1	3	8	1	10	3	1	3	.322	.354	6
Fernandez, S.	N.Y.	L	.250	31	56	1	14	16	2	0	0	9	0	7	3	1	5	0	14	0	0	2	.286	.308	0
Fishel, J.	Hou.	R	.231	19	26	1	6	9	0	0	1	2	0	1	0	0	3	0	6	0	0	0	.346	.310	0
Fisher, B.	Pit.	R	.048	33	42	1	2	3	1	0	0	1	0	2	0	0	3	0	24	0	1	0	.071	.111	3

Batter	Team	Bats	Avg	G	AB	R	H	TB	2B	3B	HR	RBI	GW	SH	SF	HB	BB	IBB	SO	SB	CS	GI DP	SLG	OBP	E
Fitzgerald, M.	St.L.	R	.196	13	46	4	9	10	1	0	0	1	0	0	0	1	0	0	9	0	0	0	.217	.213	1
Fitzgerald, M.	Mon.	R	.271	63	155	17	42	65	6	1	5	23	5	4	2	0	19	0	22	2	2	4	.419	.347	6
Flannery, T.	S.D.	L	.265	79	170	16	45	58	5	4	0	19	2	5	2	4	24	1	32	3	2	5	.341	.365	3
Foley, T.	Mon.	L	.265	127	377	33	100	142	21	3	5	43	6	0	3	1	30	10	49	2	7	11	.377	.319	15
Ford, C.	St.L.	L	.195	91	128	11	25	34	6	0	1	18	2	1	2	0	8	1	26	6	1	4	.266	.239	2
Forsch, B.	St.L.-Hou.	R	.250	37	32	3	8	9	1	0	0	5	2	6	0	0	1	0	7	1	0	0	.281	.273	3
Franco, J.	Cin.	L	.000	70	1	0	0	0	0	0	0	0	0	0	0	0	0	0	0	0	0	0	.000	.000	1
Freeman, M.	Phi.	R	.214	11	14	1	3	3	0	0	0	0	0	3	0	0	0	0	9	0	0	0	.214	.214	0
Frohwirth, T.	Phi.	R	....	12	0	0	0	0	0	0	0	0	0	0	0	0	0	0	0	0	0	0	....	....	0
Galarraga, A.	Mon.	R	.302	157	609	99	184	329	42	8	29	92	16	0	3	10	39	9	153	13	4	12	.540	.352	15
Gant, R.	Atl.	R	.259	146	563	85	146	247	28	8	19	60	3	2	4	3	46	4	118	19	10	7	.439	.317	31
Garcia, D.	Atl.	R	.117	21	60	3	7	11	1	0	1	4	1	1	0	0	3	0	10	1	0	4	.183	.159	1
Garcia, L.	Cin.	L	.143	23	28	2	4	5	1	0	0	0	0	0	0	0	4	1	5	0	1	0	.179	.250	0
Garcia, M.	Pit.	L	....	1	0	0	0	0	0	0	0	0	0	0	0	0	0	0	0	0	0	0	....	....	0
Garner, P.	S.F.	R	.154	15	13	0	2	2	0	0	0	1	1	0	0	0	1	0	3	0	1	0	.154	.214	0
Garrelts, S.	S.F.	R	.077	65	13	0	1	1	0	0	0	0	0	0	0	0	0	0	5	0	0	0	.077	.077	2
Gibson, K.	L.A.	L	.290	150	542	106	157	262	28	1	25	76	9	3	7	7	73	14	120	31	4	8	.483	.377	12
Glavine, T.	Atl.	L	.183	42	60	6	11	12	1	0	0	5	1	8	0	0	3	0	15	0	0	0	.200	.222	4
Gonzalez, D.	Pit.	R	.188	24	32	5	6	7	1	0	0	1	0	1	0	0	6	0	10	0	0	1	.219	.316	2
Gonzalez, J.	L.A.	R	.083	37	24	7	2	3	1	0	0	0	0	0	0	0	2	0	10	3	0	0	.125	.154	1
Gooden, D.	N.Y.	R	.178	34	90	8	16	20	1	0	1	9	1	9	1	0	1	0	18	0	0	1	.222	.185	5
Gossage, R.	Chi.	R	.000	46	1	0	0	0	0	0	0	0	0	0	0	0	0	0	0	0	0	0	.000	.000	0
Gott, J.	Pit.	R	.000	67	1	0	0	0	0	0	0	0	0	0	0	0	0	0	1	0	0	0	.000	.000	0
Grace, M.	Chi.	L	.296	134	486	65	144	196	23	4	7	57	9	0	4	0	60	5	43	3	3	12	.403	.371	17
Grant, M.	S.D.	R	.000	33	16	2	0	0	0	0	0	0	0	4	0	0	2	0	7	0	0	0	.000	.111	0
Gray, J.	Cin.	R	.000	5	1	0	0	0	0	0	0	0	0	1	0	0	0	0	0	0	0	0	.000	.000	0
Gregg, T.	Pit.-Atl.	L	.295	25	44	5	13	20	4	0	1	7	0	0	1	0	3	1	6	0	1	1	.455	.333	0
Griffey, K.	Atl.-Cin.	L	.255	94	243	26	62	80	6	0	4	23	3	0	2	0	19	3	31	1	3	5	.329	.307	4
Griffin, A.	L.A.	S	.199	95	316	39	63	80	8	3	1	27	4	11	1	2	24	7	30	7	5	3	.253	.259	15
Gross, G.	Phi.	L	.203	98	133	10	27	28	1	0	0	5	0	0	1	1	16	1	3	0	0	3	.211	.291	1
Gross, K.	Phi.	R	.173	33	75	6	13	14	1	0	0	2	0	8	0	1	2	0	28	0	0	2	.187	.205	2

Guerrero, P.	L.A.-St.L.	R	.286	103	364	40	104	152	14	2	10	65	14	0	7	5	46	9	59	4	1	5	.418	.367	12
Gutierrez, J.	Phi.	R	.247	33	77	8	19	23	4	0	0	9	0	1	2	0	2	0	9	0	0	2	.299	.259	8
Gwynn, C.	L.A.	L	.182	12	11	1	2	2	0	0	0	0	0	0	0	0	1	0	2	0	0	0	.182	.250	0
Gwynn, T.	S.D.	L	.313	133	521	64	163	216	22	5	7	70	12	4	2	0	51	13	40	26	11	11	.415	.373	5
Hall, A.	Atl.	S	.247	85	231	27	57	69	7	1	1	15	2	2	1	2	21	1	35	15	10	4	.299	.314	4
Hall, D.	Chi.	L	.000	18	1	1	0	0	0	0	0	0	0	0	0	0	1	0	1	0	0	0	.000	.500	0
Hamilton, J.	L.A.	R	.236	111	309	34	73	109	14	2	6	33	3	2	2	4	10	1	51	0	2	8	.353	.268	14
Hammaker, A.	S.F.	S	.121	43	33	1	4	4	0	0	0	0	0	4	0	0	2	0	13	0	0	0	.121	.171	0
Harkey, M.	Chi.	R	.091	5	11	1	1	1	0	0	0	0	0	2	0	0	0	0	5	0	0	0	.091	.091	2
Harris, G.	Phi.	S	.333	66	9	2	3	5	0	1	0	0	0	1	0	0	0	0	2	0	0	0	.556	.333	3
Harris, G.	S.D.	R	.000	3	7	0	0	0	0	0	0	0	0	0	0	0	0	0	4	0	0	0	.000	.000	0
Harris, L.	Cin.	L	.372	16	43	7	16	17	1	0	0	8	1	1	2	0	5	0	4	4	1	0	.395	.420	1
Hatcher, B.	Hou.	R	.268	145	530	79	142	196	25	4	7	52	11	8	8	8	37	4	56	32	13	6	.370	.321	5
Hatcher, M.	L.A.	R	.293	88	191	22	56	67	8	0	1	25	6	0	2	2	7	3	7	0	0	7	.351	.322	3
Havens, B.	L.A.	L	.000	9	1	0	0	0	0	0	0	0	0	0	0	0	0	0	0	0	0	0	.000	.000	0
Hawkins, A.	S.D.	R	.113	33	62	3	7	7	0	0	0	3	1	10	1	0	1	0	19	0	0	0	.113	.125	2
Hayes, C.	S.F.	R	.091	7	11	0	1	1	0	0	0	0	0	0	0	0	0	0	3	0	0	0	.091	.091	0
Hayes, V.	Phi.	L	.272	104	367	43	100	150	28	2	6	45	5	1	5	1	49	5	59	20	9	3	.409	.355	9
Heathcock, J.	Hou.	R	.000	17	3	0	0	0	0	0	0	0	0	0	0	0	0	0	1	0	0	0	.000	.000	1
Heaton, N.	Mon.	L	.143	32	21	1	3	3	0	0	0	2	0	4	0	0	0	0	6	0	0	0	.143	.143	1
Heep, D.	L.A.	L	.242	95	149	14	36	38	2	0	0	11	1	0	1	1	22	0	13	2	0	4	.255	.341	3
Henderson, S.	Hou.	R	.217	42	46	4	10	12	2	0	0	5	0	0	0	0	7	1	14	1	1	1	.261	.321	0
Hernandez, K.	N.Y.	L	.276	95	348	43	96	145	16	0	11	55	9	0	4	1	31	3	57	2	1	11	.417	.333	2
Herr, T.	St.L.	S	.260	15	50	4	13	16	0	0	1	3	0	2	0	0	11	3	4	3	0	1	.320	.393	1
Hershiser, O.	L.A.	R	.129	36	85	1	11	15	2	1	0	6	2	19	0	0	1	0	18	0	0	1	.176	.140	6
Hesketh J.	Mon.	L	.000	60	2	1	0	0	0	0	0	0	0	0	0	0	2	0	1	0	0	0	.000	.500	0
Hill, K.	St.L.	R	.000	4	3	0	0	0	0	0	0	0	0	0	0	0	0	0	0	0	0	0	.000	.000	0
Hillegas, S.	L.A.	R	.133	11	15	0	2	2	0	0	0	0	0	2	0	0	1	0	6	0	0	0	.133	.188	1
Holman, B.	Mon.	R	.107	20	28	1	3	3	0	0	0	1	0	4	0	0	1	0	17	0	0	0	.107	.138	1
Holton, B.	L.A.	R	.000	45	10	0	0	0	0	0	0	0	0	0	0	0	1	0	7	0	0	1	.000	.091	0
Horner, B.	St.L.	R	.257	60	206	15	53	73	9	1	3	33	6	0	8	1	32	6	23	0	0	9	.354	.348	5
Horton, R.	L.A.	L	....	12	0	0	0	0	0	0	0	0	0	0	0	0	0	0	0	0	0	0	....	....	0
Hostetler, D.	Pit.	R	.250	6	8	0	2	2	0	0	0	0	0	0	0	0	0	0	3	0	0	0	.250	.250	1
Howell, J.	L.A.	R	.000	50	2	0	0	0	0	0	0	0	0	0	0	0	0	0	1	0	0	0	.000	.000	1

Batter	Team	Bats	Avg	G	AB	R	H	TB	2B	3B	HR	RBI	GW	SH	SF	HB	BB	IBB	SO	SB	CS	GI DP	SLG	OBP	E
Howell, K.	L.A.	R	.000	4	1	0	0	0	0	0	0	0	0	1	0	0	0	0	0	0	0	1	.000	.000	0
Hudler, R.	Mon.	R	.273	77	216	38	59	89	14	2	4	14	1	1	2	0	10	6	34	29	7	2	.412	.303	10
Huson, J.	Mon.	L	.310	20	42	7	13	15	2	0	0	3	1	0	0	0	4	2	3	2	1	2	.357	.370	4
Innis, J.	N.Y.	R	....	12	0	0	0	0	0	0	0	0	0	0	0	0	0	0	0	0	0	0	....	....	0
Jackson C.	Hou.	R	.229	46	83	7	19	29	5	1	1	8	1	2	1	0	7	4	16	1	1	2	.349	.286	7
Jackson, D.	Cin.	R	.144	35	90	11	13	16	3	0	0	6	0	8	1	0	2	0	46	0	0	0	.178	.161	3
Jackson, D.	Chi.	R	.266	100	188	29	50	85	11	3	6	20	1	2	1	1	5	1	28	4	1	3	.452	.287	2
James, C.	Phi.	R	.242	150	566	57	137	220	24	1	19	66	5	0	5	3	31	2	73	7	4	15	.389	.283	9
James, D.	Atl.	L	.256	132	386	46	99	135	17	5	3	30	2	2	2	1	58	5	59	9	9	12	.350	.353	3
Jefferies, G.	N.Y.	S	.321	29	109	19	35	65	8	2	6	17	2	0	1	0	8	0	10	5	1	1	.596	.364	2
Jefferson, S.	S.D.	S	.144	49	111	16	16	24	1	2	1	4	0	2	2	1	9	0	22	5	1	3	.216	.211	0
Jeltz, S.	Phi.	S	.187	148	379	39	71	90	11	4	0	27	1	10	2	0	59	8	58	3	0	11	.237	.295	14
Jimenez, G.	Atl.	L	.059	15	17	0	1	1	0	0	0	1	0	0	0	0	0	0	6	0	0	0	.059	.059	0
Johnson, H.	N.Y.	S	.230	148	495	85	114	209	21	1	24	68	7	2	8	3	86	25	104	23	7	6	.422	.343	18
Johnson, R.	Mon.	R	.111	4	9	1	1	1	0	0	0	0	0	0	0	0	0	0	6	0	0	0	.111	.111	1
Johnson, W.	Mon.	S	.309	86	94	7	29	36	5	1	0	3	2	1	0	0	12	1	15	0	2	2	.383	.387	1
Jones, B.	Pit.	R	.000	42	5	0	0	0	0	0	0	0	0	0	0	0	0	0	2	0	0	0	.000	.000	2
Jones, J.	S.D.	R	.164	32	55	2	9	12	0	0	1	4	0	9	1	0	4	0	12	0	0	0	.218	.217	0
Jones, R.	Phi.	L	.290	33	124	15	36	68	6	1	8	26	1	0	3	0	2	0	14	0	0	2	.548	.295	0
Jones, T.	Cin.-Mon.	R	.295	90	224	29	66	83	6	1	3	24	4	3	0	2	20	3	18	18	6	5	.371	.358	2
Jones, T.	St.L.	L	.269	31	52	2	14	14	0	0	0	3	0	0	0	0	4	0	10	4	1	1	.269	.321	1
Jordan, R.	Phi.	R	.308	69	273	41	84	134	15	1	11	43	8	0	1	0	7	2	39	1	1	5	.491	.324	5
Kipper, B.	Pit.	R	.000	50	4	1	0	0	0	0	0	0	0	1	0	1	0	0	0	0	0	1	.000	.200	0
Knepper, B.	Hou.	L	.125	27	48	1	6	6	0	0	0	3	0	14	1	0	2	0	17	0	0	0	.125	.157	2
Kramer, R.	Pit.	R	.000	5	2	0	0	0	0	0	0	0	0	0	0	0	0	0	1	0	0	0	.000	.000	0
Krueger, B.	L.A.	L	....	1	0	0	0	0	0	0	0	0	0	0	0	0	0	0	0	0	0	0	....	....	0
Kruk, J.	S.D.	L	.241	120	378	54	91	137	17	1	9	44	6	3	5	0	80	12	68	5	3	7	.362	.369	3
Krukow, M.	S.F.	R	.073	20	41	1	3	7	1	0	1	2	0	4	0	0	2	0	8	0	0	0	.171	.116	0
LaCoss, M.	S.F.	R	.242	19	33	3	8	9	1	0	0	2	0	4	0	0	2	0	13	0	0	0	.273	.286	0
Laga, M.	St.L.	L	.130	41	100	5	13	16	0	0	1	4	1	0	0	0	2	0	21	0	0	0	.160	.147	0
Lake, S.	St.L.	R	.278	36	54	5	15	21	3	0	1	4	1	0	0	2	3	0	15	0	0	0	.389	.339	1

Lancaster, L.	Chi.	R	.050	44	20	1	1	1	0	0	0	0	0	3	0	0	0	0	12	0	0	0	.050	.050	0
Landrum, B.	Chi.	R	.000	7	2	0	0	0	0	0	0	0	0	0	0	0	0	0	1	0	0	0	.000	.000	0
LaPoint, D.	Pit.	L	.063	8	16	0	1	1	0	0	0	0	0	1	0	0	0	0	6	0	0	2	.063	.063	0
Larkin, B.	Cin.	R	.296	151	588	91	174	252	32	5	12	56	5	10	5	8	41	3	24	40	7	7	.429	.347	29
LaValliere, M.	Pit.	L	.261	120	352	24	92	116	18	0	2	47	7	1	4	2	50	10	34	3	2	8	.330	.353	8
Law, V.	Chi.	R	.293	151	556	73	163	229	29	2	11	78	12	4	3	3	55	4	79	1	4	15	.412	.358	19
Lawless, T.	St.L.	R	.154	54	65	9	10	17	2	1	1	3	0	7	0	0	7	0	9	6	0	1	.262	.236	0
Leach, T.	N.Y.	R	.143	52	14	1	2	3	1	0	0	3	0	0	0	0	0	0	9	0	0	0	.214	.143	0
Leary, T.	L.A.	R	.269	36	67	4	18	21	3	0	0	9	3	13	1	1	1	0	26	0	1	0	.313	.286	1
Lefferts, C.	S.F.	L	.000	64	9	0	0	0	0	0	0	0	0	0	0	0	0	0	7	0	0	0	.000	.000	0
Leiper, D.	S.D.	L	.500	35	2	0	1	1	0	0	0	1	0	0	0	0	0	0	1	0	0	0	.500	.500	0
Lemke, M.	Atl.	S	.224	16	58	8	13	17	4	0	0	2	0	2	0	0	4	0	5	0	2	1	.293	.274	3
Leonard, J.	S.F.	R	.256	44	160	12	41	57	8	1	2	20	2	0	2	0	9	1	24	7	5	5	.356	.292	1
Lind, J.	Pit.	R	.262	154	611	82	160	198	24	4	2	49	6	12	3	0	42	0	75	15	4	11	.324	.308	11
Lindeman, J.	St.L.	R	.209	17	43	3	9	16	1	0	2	7	0	1	0	0	2	0	9	0	0	1	.372	.244	1
Lyons, B.	N.Y.	R	.231	50	91	5	21	30	7	1	0	11	1	3	1	0	3	0	12	0	0	3	.330	.253	3
Mack, S.	S.D.	R	.244	56	119	13	29	32	3	0	0	12	2	3	1	3	14	0	21	5	1	2	.269	.336	2
Madden, M.	Pit.	L	....	6	0	0	0	0	0	0	0	0	0	0	0	0	0	0	0	0	0	0	....	....	0
Maddux, G.	Chi.	R	.198	37	96	13	19	22	3	0	0	5	1	1	0	0	0	0	22	1	0	1	.229	.198	3
Maddux, M.	Phi.	R	.130	26	23	1	3	4	1	0	0	3	0	2	0	0	1	0	8	0	0	0	.174	.167	4
Madrid, A.	Phi.	S	.000	5	3	0	0	0	0	0	0	0	0	0	0	0	0	0	2	0	0	0	.000	.000	0
Magadan, D.	N.Y.	L	.277	112	314	39	87	105	15	0	1	35	5	1	3	2	60	4	39	0	1	9	.334	.393	10
Magrane, J.	St.L.	R	.167	25	48	2	8	12	1	0	1	3	0	8	0	0	1	0	18	0	0	1	.250	.184	5
Mahler, R.	Atl.	R	.125	39	72	3	9	10	1	0	0	5	1	11	0	1	0	0	20	0	0	1	.139	.137	3
Maldonado, C.	S.F.	R	.255	142	499	53	127	188	23	1	12	68	7	3	6	7	37	1	89	6	5	13	.377	.311	10
Manwaring, K.	S.F.	R	.250	40	116	12	29	39	7	0	1	15	1	1	1	3	2	0	21	0	1	1	.336	.279	4
Marshall, M.	L.A.	R	.277	144	542	63	150	241	27	2	20	82	12	0	4	7	24	7	93	4	1	17	.445	.314	7
Martinez, C.	S.D.	R	.236	121	365	48	86	152	12	0	18	65	12	3	2	0	35	3	57	1	1	10	.416	.301	4
Martinez, D.	Mon.	R	.192	34	78	2	15	17	2	0	0	7	1	10	0	1	1	0	25	0	0	0	.218	.213	6
Martinez, D.	Chi.-Mon.	L	.255	138	447	51	114	157	13	6	6	46	6	2	5	2	38	8	94	23	9	3	.351	.313	6
Martinez, R.	L.A.	R	.000	9	7	0	0	0	0	0	0	0	0	1	0	0	0	0	3	0	0	0	.000	.000	0
Mathews, G.	St.L.	R	.174	13	23	1	4	4	0	0	0	0	0	1	0	1	0	0	7	0	0	1	.174	.208	2
Mazzilli, L.	N.Y.	S	.147	68	116	9	17	19	2	0	0	12	3	0	3	1	12	0	16	4	1	3	.164	.227	3
McClendon, L.	Cin.	R	.219	72	137	9	30	43	4	0	3	14	0	1	2	2	15	1	22	4	0	6	.314	.301	4

Batter	Team	Bats	Avg	G	AB	R	H	TB	2B	3B	HR	RBI	GW	SH	SF	HB	BB	IBB	SO	SB	CS	GI DP	SLG	OBP	E
McClure, B.	Mon.-N.Y.	R	.000	33	2	0	0	0	0	0	0	0	0	0	0	0	0	0	0	0	0	0	.000	.000	0
McCullers, L.	S.D.	S	.250	60	8	0	2	2	0	0	0	0	0	0	0	0	1	0	3	0	0	0	.250	.333	2
McDowell, R.	N.Y.	R	.333	63	9	1	3	6	3	0	0	2	0	0	0	0	0	0	5	0	0	0	.667	.333	1
McGaffigan, A.	Mon.	R	.000	63	5	1	0	0	0	0	0	0	0	0	0	0	1	0	4	0	0	0	.000	.167	1
McGee, W.	St.L.	S	.292	137	562	73	164	209	24	6	3	50	9	2	3	1	32	5	84	41	6	10	.372	.329	9
McGriff, T.	Cin.	R	.198	35	96	9	19	25	3	0	1	4	0	0	1	0	12	0	31	1	0	3	.260	.284	2
McReynolds, K.	N.Y.	R	.288	147	552	82	159	274	30	2	27	99	19	1	5	4	38	3	56	21	0	6	.496	.336	4
McWilliams, L.	St.L.	L	.162	45	37	6	6	7	1	0	0	3	1	1	0	2	0	0	12	0	0	0	.189	.205	2
Meadows, L.	Hou.	L	.190	35	42	5	8	16	0	1	2	3	0	0	0	0	6	0	8	4	2	1	.381	.292	0
Meads, D.	Hou.	L	.250	22	4	1	1	1	0	0	0	0	0	0	0	0	2	0	2	0	0	0	.250	.500	1
Medvin, S.	Pit.	R	.000	17	3	0	0	0	0	0	0	0	0	1	0	0	0	0	0	0	0	0	.000	.000	0
Meier, D.	Chi.	R	.400	2	5	0	2	2	0	0	0	1	0	0	0	0	0	0	1	0	0	0	.400	.400	0
Melendez, F.	S.F.	L	.192	23	26	1	5	5	0	0	0	3	0	0	0	0	3	0	2	0	0	1	.192	.276	0
Melvin, B.	S.F.	R	.234	92	273	23	64	103	13	1	8	27	2	1	1	0	13	0	46	0	2	5	.377	.268	7
Meyer, B.	Hou.	R	....	8	0	0	0	0	0	0	0	0	0	0	0	0	0	0	0	0	0	0	....	....	0
Miller, K.	N.Y.	R	.214	40	70	9	15	21	1	1	1	5	1	3	0	0	6	0	10	0	5	1	.300	.276	5
Miller, K.	Phi.	S	.167	47	48	4	8	11	3	0	0	6	0	0	0	0	5	0	13	0	0	0	.229	.245	1
Milligan, R.	Pit.	R	.220	40	82	10	18	32	5	0	3	8	1	0	0	1	20	0	24	1	2	2	.390	.379	3
Milner, E.	Cin.	L	.176	23	51	3	9	10	1	0	0	2	1	0	0	0	4	0	9	2	2	0	.196	.236	1
Mitchell, J.	N.Y.	R	.000	1	1	0	0	0	0	0	0	0	0	0	0	0	0	0	0	0	0	0	.000	.000	0
Mitchell, K.	S.F.	R	.251	148	505	60	127	223	25	7	19	80	14	1	7	5	48	7	85	5	5	9	.442	.319	22
Moore, B.	Phi.	R	....	5	0	0	0	0	0	0	0	0	0	0	0	0	0	0	0	0	0	0	....	....	0
Moreland, K.	S.D.	R	.256	143	511	40	131	169	23	0	5	64	13	2	9	0	40	6	51	2	3	17	.331	.305	7
Morris, J.	St.L.	L	.289	20	38	3	11	15	2	1	0	3	0	0	0	0	1	0	7	0	0	0	.395	.308	2
Morrison, J.	Atl.	R	.152	51	92	6	14	22	2	0	2	13	3	0	3	0	10	1	13	0	1	2	.239	.229	3
Moyer, J.	Chi.	L	.083	34	60	4	5	6	1	0	0	1	0	8	0	0	3	0	25	0	0	2	.100	.127	1
Mulholland, T.	S.F.	R	.000	9	14	2	0	0	0	0	0	0	0	0	0	0	2	0	9	0	0	0	.000	.125	0
Mumphrey, J.	Chi.	S	.136	63	66	3	9	11	2	0	0	9	2	0	0	0	7	2	16	0	0	3	.167	.219	0
Murphy, D.	Atl.	R	.226	156	592	77	134	249	35	4	24	77	6	0	3	2	74	16	125	3	5	24	.421	.313	3
Murphy, R.	Cin.	L	....	76	0	0	0	0	0	0	0	0	0	0	0	0	0	0	0	0	0	0	....	....	0
Myers, R.	N.Y.	L	.250	55	4	1	1	2	1	0	0	1	0	0	0	0	0	0	2	0	0	0	.500	.250	0

Nelson, R.	S.D.	L	.190	7	21	4	4	7	0	0	1	3	1	0	0	0	2	0	9	0	0	0	.333	.261	1
Nettles, G.	Mon.	L	.172	80	93	5	16	23	4	0	1	14	4	0	2	0	9	2	19	0	0	4	.247	.240	5
Nipper, A.	Chi.	R	.087	22	23	0	2	3	1	0	0	0	0	2	0	0	0	0	6	0	0	1	.130	.087	1
Nixon, D.	S.F.	R	.346	59	78	15	27	30	3	0	0	6	2	1	0	0	10	0	12	11	8	1	.385	.420	1
Nixon, O.	Mon.	S	.244	90	271	47	66	78	8	2	0	15	0	4	2	0	28	0	42	46	13	0	.288	.312	1
Nolte, E.	S.D.	L	....	2	0	0	0	0	0	0	0	0	0	0	0	0	0	0	0	0	0	0	....	....	0
Nunez, E.	N.Y.	R	....	10	0	0	0	0	0	0	0	0	0	0	0	0	0	0	0	0	0	0	....	....	1
Oberkfell, K.	Atl-Pit.	L	.271	140	476	49	129	168	22	4	3	42	4	6	8	2	37	7	34	4	5	8	.353	.321	15
Oester, R.	Cin.	S	.280	54	150	20	42	49	7	0	0	10	2	3	1	0	9	3	24	0	2	2	.327	.319	1
Ojeda, B.	N.Y.	L	.164	30	61	0	10	11	1	0	0	3	0	4	0	0	1	0	22	0	0	0	.180	.177	2
Olwine, E.	Atl.	R	....	16	0	0	0	0	0	0	0	0	0	0	0	0	0	0	0	0	0	0	....	....	0
O'Malley, T.	Mon.	L	.259	14	27	3	7	7	0	0	0	2	0	0	1	0	3	1	4	0	0	0	.259	.323	2
O'Neal, R.	St.L.	R	.000	10	19	0	0	0	0	0	0	0	0	1	0	0	0	0	4	0	0	0	.000	.000	0
O'Neill, P.	Cin.	L	.252	145	485	58	122	201	25	3	16	73	10	3	5	2	38	5	65	8	6	7	.414	.306	6
Oquendo, J.	St.L.	S	.277	148	451	36	125	158	10	1	7	46	2	12	3	0	52	7	40	4	6	8	.350	.350	11
Orosco, J.	L.A.	R	.000	55	2	0	0	0	0	0	0	0	0	0	0	0	0	0	1	0	0	0	.000	.000	0
Ortiz, J.	Pit.	R	.280	49	118	8	33	45	6	0	2	18	2	1	2	2	9	0	9	1	4	6	.381	.336	3
Pacillo, P.	Cin.	R	.000	6	1	0	0	0	0	0	0	0	0	0	0	0	0	0	1	0	0	0	.000	.000	1
Pagnozzi, T.	St.L.	R	.282	81	195	17	55	64	9	0	0	15	1	2	1	0	11	1	32	0	0	5	.328	.319	4
Palacios, V.	Pit.	R	.000	7	8	0	0	0	0	0	0	0	0	0	0	0	1	0	5	0	0	0	.000	.111	0
Palmeiro, R.	Chi.	L	.307	152	580	75	178	253	41	5	8	53	0	2	6	3	38	6	34	12	2	11	.436	.349	5
Palmer, D.	Phi.	R	.256	22	39	6	10	20	4	0	2	6	1	9	0	0	0	0	4	0	0	1	.513	.256	1
Pankovits, J.	Hou.	R	.221	68	140	13	31	46	7	1	2	12	1	2	1	2	8	0	28	2	1	1	.329	.272	11
Pardo, A.	Phi.	S	.000	2	2	0	0	0	0	0	0	0	0	0	0	0	0	0	2	0	0	0	.000	.000	0
Paredes, J.	Mon.	R	.187	35	91	6	17	22	2	0	1	10	1	1	0	3	9	0	17	5	2	1	.242	.282	3
Parent, M.	S.D.	R	.195	41	118	9	23	44	3	0	6	15	2	0	1	0	6	0	23	0	0	1	.373	.232	3
Parrett, J.	Mon.	R	....	61	0	0	0	0	0	0	0	0	0	0	0	0	1	0	0	0	0	0	.000	1.000	1
Parrish, L.	Phi.	R	.215	123	424	44	91	157	17	2	15	60	7	0	5	2	47	7	93	0	0	11	.370	.293	9
Pedrique, A.	Pit.	R	.180	50	128	7	23	28	5	0	0	4	1	0	0	1	8	2	17	0	0	4	.219	.234	5
Pena, A.	L.A.	R	.000	60	6	0	0	0	0	0	0	0	0	0	0	0	0	0	1	0	0	0	.000	.000	2
Pena, T.	St.L.	R	.263	149	505	55	133	188	23	1	10	51	6	3	4	1	33	11	60	6	2	12	.372	.308	6
Pendleton, T.	St.L.	S	.253	110	391	44	99	141	20	2	6	53	6	4	3	2	21	4	51	3	3	9	.361	.293	12
Perez, P.	Mon.	R	.037	41	54	6	2	2	0	0	0	0	0	6	0	1	3	0	25	0	1	0	.037	.103	0
Perezchica, T.	S.F.	R	.125	7	8	1	1	1	0	0	0	1	0	0	1	0	2	0	1	0	0	0	.125	.273	0

Batter	Team	Bats	Avg	G	AB	R	H	TB	2B	3B	HR	RBI	GW	SH	SF	HB	BB	IBB	SO	SB	CS	GI DP	SLG	OBP	E
Perry, G.	Atl.	L	.300	141	547	61	164	219	29	1	8	74	9	1	10	1	36	9	49	29	14	18	.400	.338	17
Perry, P.	Cin.-Chi.	L	.333	47	3	1	1	4	0	0	1	2	0	0	0	0	0	0	0	0	0	0	1.333	.333	0
Peters, S.	St.L.	L	.000	44	3	0	0	0	0	0	0	0	0	0	0	0	0	0	2	0	0	0	.000	.000	1
Pico, J.	Chi.	R	.147	29	34	0	5	5	0	0	0	1	1	2	0	0	1	0	10	0	0	0	.147	.171	1
Price, J.	S.F.	R	.000	38	8	0	0	0	0	0	0	0	0	2	0	0	1	0	4	0	0	0	.000	.111	0
Prince, T.	Pit.	R	.176	29	74	3	13	15	2	0	0	6	3	2	0	0	4	0	15	0	0	5	.203	.218	2
Puhl, T.	Hou.	L	.303	113	234	42	71	91	7	2	3	19	4	1	1	1	35	3	30	22	4	0	.389	.395	2
Puleo, C.	Atl.	R	.231	53	13	1	3	3	0	0	0	1	0	4	0	0	0	0	5	0	1	0	.231	.231	1
Quinones, L.	Cin.	S	.231	23	52	4	12	18	3	0	1	11	2	2	1	0	2	1	11	1	1	0	.346	.255	2
Quisenberry, D.	St.L.	R	.000	33	1	0	0	0	0	0	0	0	0	0	0	0	1	0	0	0	0	0	.000	.500	1
Raines, T.	Mon.	S	.270	109	429	66	116	185	19	7	12	48	6	0	4	2	53	14	44	33	7	8	.431	.350	3
Ramirez, R.	Hou.	R	.276	155	566	51	156	214	30	5	6	59	8	4	6	3	18	6	61	3	2	16	.378	.298	23
Rasmussen, D.	Cin.-S.D.	L	.200	31	70	7	14	16	2	0	0	4	0	6	1	1	4	0	23	0	0	2	.229	.250	0
Rawley, S.	Phi.	R	.105	32	57	0	6	8	2	0	0	1	1	11	0	0	1	0	19	0	0	1	.140	.121	2
Ready, R.	S.D.	R	.266	114	331	43	88	129	16	2	7	39	3	4	3	3	39	1	38	6	2	3	.390	.346	11
Redus, G.	Pit.	R	.197	30	71	12	14	22	2	0	2	4	0	0	1	1	15	0	19	5	2	1	.310	.341	2
Reed, J.	Mon.-Cin.	L	.226	92	265	20	60	76	9	2	1	16	1	1	1	0	28	1	41	1	0	5	.287	.299	3
Reed, R.	Pit.	R	.000	2	4	0	0	0	0	0	0	0	0	0	0	0	0	0	1	0	0	0	.000	.000	0
Reid, J.	S.F.	L	.000	2	2	0	0	0	0	0	0	0	0	0	0	0	0	0	1	0	0	0	.000	.000	0
Reuschel, R.	S.F.	R	.110	36	73	4	8	9	1	0	0	3	0	19	0	0	2	0	25	0	1	1	.123	.133	0
Reyes, G.	L.A.	R	.111	5	9	1	1	1	0	0	0	0	0	0	0	0	0	0	3	0	0	0	.111	.111	0
Reynolds, C.	Hou.	L	.255	78	161	20	41	51	7	0	1	14	2	1	0	0	8	2	23	3	0	1	.317	.290	9
Reynolds, R.	Pit.	S	.248	130	323	35	80	116	14	2	6	51	7	0	4	0	20	3	62	15	2	5	.359	.288	4
Rijo, J.	Cin.	R	.054	49	37	2	2	5	0	0	1	1	0	4	0	0	0	0	14	0	0	0	.135	.054	1
Riles, E.	S.F.	L	.294	79	187	26	55	75	7	2	3	28	4	0	4	0	10	2	33	1	2	5	.401	.323	3
Ritchie, W.	Phi.	L	....	19	0	0	0	0	0	0	0	0	0	0	0	0	0	0	0	0	0	0	....	....	0
Rivera, L.	Mon.	R	.224	123	371	35	83	118	17	3	4	30	5	3	3	1	24	4	69	3	4	9	.318	.271	19
Roberts, L.	S.D.	S	.333	5	9	1	3	3	0	0	0	0	0	0	0	0	1	0	2	0	2	0	.333	.400	1
Robinson, D.	S.F.	R	.173	52	52	2	9	14	2	0	1	4	0	2	0	0	2	0	12	0	0	1	.269	.204	3
Robinson, J.	Pit.	R	.188	75	16	0	3	3	0	0	0	1	0	5	0	0	1	0	7	0	0	0	.188	.235	0
Robinson, R.	Cin.	R	.200	17	25	1	5	6	1	0	0	1	0	1	0	0	0	0	8	0	0	0	.240	.200	3

Rodriguez, R.	Pit.	R	.200	2	5	1	1	3	0	1	0	1	0	0	0	0	0	0	2	0	0	0	.600	.200	0
Roenicke, G.	Atl.	R	.228	49	114	11	26	34	5	0	1	7	1	0	0	0	8	0	15	0	0	4	.298	.279	0
Roenicke, R.	Cin.	S	.135	14	37	4	5	6	1	0	0	5	0	0	0	1	4	0	8	0	0	1	.162	.238	0
Roomes, R.	Chi.	R	.188	17	16	3	3	3	0	0	0	0	0	0	0	0	0	0	4	0	1	0	.188	.188	1
Royster, J.	Atl.	R	.176	68	102	8	18	21	3	0	0	1	0	3	0	0	6	1	16	0	0	2	.206	.222	1
Rucker, D.	Pit.	L	.000	31	2	0	0	0	0	0	0	0	0	0	0	0	0	0	2	0	0	0	.000	.000	1
Ruffin, B.	Phi.	S	.121	55	33	3	4	4	0	0	0	0	0	0	0	0	3	0	15	0	0	0	.121	.194	2
Runge, P.	Atl.	R	.211	52	76	11	16	21	5	0	0	7	1	0	1	0	14	0	21	0	0	4	.276	.330	1
Russell, J.	Phi.	R	.245	22	49	5	12	19	1	0	2	4	0	0	0	1	3	0	15	0	0	2	.388	.302	5
Ryan, N.	Hou.	R	.057	33	70	1	4	4	0	0	0	2	1	7	0	0	4	0	34	0	0	1	.057	.108	4
Sabo, C.	Cin.	R	.271	137	538	74	146	223	40	2	11	44	8	5	4	6	29	1	52	46	14	12	.414	.314	14
Salazar, A.	Chi.	R	.250	34	60	4	15	18	1	1	0	1	0	2	0	0	1	1	11	0	0	1	.300	.262	3
Samuel, J.	Phi.	R	.243	157	629	68	153	239	32	9	12	67	8	0	5	12	39	6	151	33	10	8	.380	.298	16
Samuels, R.	S.F.	L	.000	15	3	0	0	0	0	0	0	0	0	0	0	0	0	0	2	0	0	0	.000	.000	0
Sandberg, R.	Chi.	R	.264	155	618	77	163	259	23	8	19	69	9	1	5	1	54	3	91	25	10	14	.419	.322	11
Sanderson, S.	Chi.	R	....	11	0	0	0	0	0	0	0	0	0	0	0	0	0	0	0	0	0	0	....	....	0
Santiago, B.	S.D.	R	.248	139	492	49	122	178	22	2	10	46	4	5	5	1	24	2	82	15	7	18	.362	.282	12
Santovenia, N.	Mon.	R	.236	92	309	26	73	121	20	2	8	41	4	4	4	3	24	3	77	2	3	4	.392	.294	9
Sasser, M.	N.Y.	L	.285	60	123	9	35	50	10	1	1	17	2	0	2	0	6	4	9	0	0	4	.407	.313	6
Sauveur, R.	Mon.	L	....	4	0	0	0	0	0	0	0	0	0	0	0	0	0	0	0	0	0	0	....	....	0
Sax, S.	L.A.	R	.277	160	632	70	175	217	19	4	5	57	6	7	2	1	45	6	51	42	12	11	.343	.325	14
Scherrer, B.	Phi.	L	....	8	0	0	0	0	0	0	0	0	0	0	0	0	0	0	0	0	0	0	....	....	0
Schiraldi, C.	Chi.	R	.100	29	60	4	6	7	1	0	0	5	2	4	1	0	1	0	26	0	0	0	.117	.113	4
Schmidt, M.	Phi.	R	.249	108	390	52	97	158	21	2	12	62	6	0	6	6	49	10	42	3	0	11	.405	.337	19
Scioscia, M.	L.A.	L	.257	130	408	29	105	132	18	0	3	35	4	3	3	0	38	12	31	0	3	14	.324	.318	7
Scott, M.	Hou.	R	.085	32	71	1	6	7	1	0	0	5	0	7	0	0	1	0	27	0	0	0	.099	.097	0
Sebra, B.	Phi.	R	.000	3	5	0	0	0	0	0	0	0	0	0	0	0	0	0	0	0	0	0	.000	.000	0
Service, D.	Phi.	R	....	5	0	0	0	0	0	0	0	0	0	0	0	0	0	0	0	0	0	0	....	....	0
Sharperson, M.	L.A.	R	.271	46	59	8	16	17	1	0	0	4	0	2	1	1	1	0	12	0	1	1	.288	.290	2
Shelby, J.	L.A.	S	.263	140	494	65	130	195	23	6	10	64	12	1	6	0	44	5	128	16	5	13	.395	.320	6
Show, E.	S.D.	R	.148	32	81	5	12	13	1	0	0	4	0	5	0	0	1	0	27	0	0	0	.160	.159	1
Sierra, C.	S.D.-Cin.	R	.000	16	4	0	0	0	0	0	0	0	0	0	0	0	0	0	4	0	0	0	.000	.000	0
Simmons, T.	Atl.	S	.196	78	107	6	21	33	6	0	2	11	2	0	1	0	15	2	9	0	0	4	.308	.293	3
Smajstrla, C.	Hou.	S	.000	8	3	2	0	0	0	0	0	0	0	0	0	0	0	0	1	0	0	0	.000	.000	0

Batter	Team	Bats	Avg	G	AB	R	H	TB	2B	3B	HR	RBI	GW	SH	SF	HB	BB	IBB	SO	SB	CS	GI DP	SLG	OBP	E
Smiley, J.	Pit.	L	.079	34	63	2	5	6	1	0	0	1	1	7	0	0	3	0	30	0	0	0	.095	.121	0
Smith, B.	Mon.	R	.109	32	55	0	6	7	1	0	0	2	1	8	0	0	2	0	21	0	0	0	.127	.140	2
Smith, D.	Hou.	R	.000	51	2	0	0	0	0	0	0	0	0	0	0	0	0	0	1	0	0	1	.000	.000	0
Smith, L.	Atl.	R	.237	43	114	14	27	39	3	0	3	9	1	0	1	0	10	0	25	4	2	0	.342	.296	2
Smith, M.	Mon.	R	.000	5	2	0	0	0	0	0	0	0	0	0	0	0	0	0	1	0	0	0	.000	.000	0
Smith, O.	St.L.	S	.270	153	575	80	155	193	27	1	3	51	9	12	7	1	74	2	43	57	9	7	.336	.350	22
Smith, P.	Atl.	R	.113	32	53	2	6	7	1	0	0	0	0	8	0	0	1	0	11	0	0	1	.132	.130	3
Smith, Z.	Atl.	L	.167	27	42	3	7	8	1	0	0	0	0	7	0	0	1	0	8	0	0	0	.190	.186	1
Smoltz, J.	Atl.	R	.118	12	17	1	2	3	1	0	0	0	0	3	0	0	1	0	8	0	0	0	.176	.167	0
Snider, V.	Cin.	L	.214	11	28	4	6	10	1	0	1	6	1	0	1	0	0	0	13	0	1	0	.357	.207	0
Sorensen, L.	S.F.	R	.000	12	1	0	0	0	0	0	0	0	0	1	0	0	0	0	0	0	0	0	.000	.000	0
Soto, M.	Cin.	R	.045	14	22	1	1	1	0	0	0	1	0	4	0	0	3	0	7	0	0	1	.045	.160	3
Speier, C.	S.F.	R	.216	82	171	26	37	57	9	1	3	18	1	5	1	1	23	2	39	3	3	7	.333	.311	3
Spilman, H.	S.F.-Hou.	L	.156	47	45	4	7	13	1	1	1	3	1	0	0	0	4	1	9	0	0	0	.289	.224	1
St. Claire, R	Mon.-Cin.	R	.000	16	1	0	0	0	0	0	0	0	0	0	0	0	0	0	1	0	0	0	.000	.000	0
Strawberry, D.	N.Y.	L	.269	153	543	101	146	296	27	3	39	101	15	0	9	3	85	21	127	29	14	6	.545	.366	9
Stubbs, F.	L.A.	L	.223	115	242	30	54	91	13	0	8	34	5	2	5	1	23	3	61	11	3	4	.376	.288	13
Sundberg, J.	Chi.	R	.241	24	54	8	13	20	1	0	2	9	0	3	1	0	8	0	15	0	0	1	.370	.333	0
Sutcliffe, R.	Chi.	L	.160	33	75	8	12	20	5	0	1	6	0	4	2	1	3	0	18	1	0	0	.267	.198	3
Sutter, B.	Atl.	R	.000	38	1	0	0	0	0	0	0	0	0	0	0	0	1	0	1	0	0	0	.000	.500	2
Sutton, D.	L.A.	R	.087	16	23	1	2	2	0	0	0	1	0	6	0	0	1	0	6	0	0	0	.087	.125	1
Tejada, W.	Mon.	R	.267	8	15	1	4	6	2	0	0	2	0	0	1	0	0	0	4	0	0	0	.400	.250	0
Tekulve, K.	Phi.	R	.000	70	2	0	0	0	0	0	0	0	0	0	0	0	0	0	2	0	0	0	.000	.000	0
Templeton, G.	S.D.	S	.249	110	362	35	90	128	15	7	3	36	3	7	3	0	20	10	50	8	2	6	.354	.286	16
Terry, S.	St.L.	R	.250	51	28	5	7	8	1	0	0	2	1	5	0	0	1	0	7	0	0	0	.286	.276	0
Teufel, T.	N.Y.	R	.234	90	273	35	64	96	20	0	4	31	3	2	4	1	29	1	41	0	1	6	.352	.306	7
Tewksbury, B.	Chi.	R	.000	1	2	0	0	0	0	0	0	0	0	0	0	0	0	0	0	0	0	0	.000	.000	0
Thomas, A.	Atl.	R	.252	153	606	54	153	218	22	2	13	68	4	0	6	1	14	6	95	7	3	17	.360	.268	29
Thompson, M.	Phi.	L	.288	122	378	53	109	135	16	2	2	33	2	2	3	1	39	6	59	17	9	8	.357	.354	5
Thompson, R.	S.F.	R	.264	138	477	66	126	183	24	6	7	48	5	14	5	4	40	0	111	14	5	7	.384	.323	14
Thon, D.	S.D.	R	.264	95	258	36	68	87	12	2	1	18	3	2	2	1	33	0	49	19	4	4	.337	.347	12

Tillman, K.	S.F.	R	.250	4	4	1	1	4	0	0	1	3	0	0	0	0	2	0	1	0	0	0	1.000	.500	0
Treadway, J.	Cin.	L	.252	103	301	30	76	109	19	4	2	23	3	4	6	3	27	7	30	2	0	4	.362	.315	8
Trevino, A.	Hou.	R	.249	78	193	19	48	71	17	0	2	13	1	3	0	3	24	4	29	5	2	8	.368	.341	9
Trillo, M.	Chi.	R	.250	76	164	15	41	49	5	0	1	14	3	4	1	0	8	0	32	2	0	2	.299	.283	3
Tudor, J.	St.L.-L.A.	L	.085	32	59	0	5	5	0	0	0	0	0	7	0	0	4	0	24	0	0	1	.085	.143	0
Turner, S.	Phi.	L	.171	18	35	1	6	6	0	0	0	1	0	0	0	0	5	0	9	0	0	1	.171	.275	1
Uribe, J.	S.F.	S	.252	141	493	47	124	157	10	7	3	35	10	4	2	0	36	10	69	14	10	3	.318	.301	19
Valenzuela, F.	L.A.	L	.182	23	44	2	8	10	2	0	0	1	0	7	0	0	1	0	5	0	0	0	.227	.200	1
Van Slyke, A.	Pit.	L	.288	154	587	101	169	297	23	15	25	100	16	1	13	1	57	2	126	30	9	8	.506	.345	4
Varsho, G.	Chi.	L	.274	46	73	6	20	23	3	0	0	5	0	0	1	0	1	0	6	5	0	0	.315	.280	3
Virgil, O.	Atl.	R	.256	107	320	23	82	119	10	0	9	31	4	2	1	5	22	1	54	2	0	10	.372	.313	5
Walk, B.	Pit.	R	.087	34	69	3	6	7	1	0	0	5	0	3	0	2	2	0	31	0	1	0	.101	.137	3
Walker, D.	St.L.	L	.182	24	22	1	4	5	1	0	0	3	1	0	0	0	2	0	7	0	0	1	.227	.250	0
Wallach, T.	Mon.	R	.257	159	592	52	152	230	32	5	12	69	6	0	7	3	38	7	88	2	6	19	.389	.302	18
Walling, D.	Hou.-St.L.	L	.239	84	234	22	56	76	13	2	1	21	2	1	0	0	17	3	25	2	0	3	.325	.291	9
Walter, G.	N.Y.	L	....	19	0	0	0	0	0	0	0	0	0	0	0	0	0	0	0	0	0	0	....	....	0
Wasinger, M.	S.F.	R	.000	3	2	1	0	0	0	0	0	0	0	0	0	0	0	0	0	0	0	0	.000	.000	0
Webster, M.	Mon.-Chi.	S	.260	151	523	69	136	186	16	8	6	39	4	5	4	8	55	2	87	22	14	5	.356	.337	6
West, D.	N.Y.	L	1.000	2	2	1	2	3	1	0	0	0	0	0	0	0	0	0	0	0	0	0	1.500	1.000	0
Whitson, E.	S.D.	R	.167	34	66	4	11	14	3	0	0	3	0	9	0	0	1	0	23	0	0	0	.212	.179	4
Williams, F.	Cin.	R	.000	60	1	0	0	0	0	0	0	0	0	0	0	0	0	0	1	0	0	0	.000	.000	4
Williams, M.	S.F.	R	.205	52	156	17	32	64	6	1	8	19	3	3	1	2	8	0	41	0	1	7	.410	.251	7
Wilson, G.	Pit.	R	.270	37	126	11	34	48	8	0	2	15	1	2	2	1	3	1	18	0	0	4	.381	.288	1
Wilson, M.	N.Y.	S	.296	112	378	61	112	163	17	5	8	41	3	1	2	2	27	2	63	15	4	12	.431	.345	5
Wilson, T.	S.F.	L	.286	4	7	1	2	2	0	0	0	0	0	1	0	0	0	0	2	0	0	0	.286	.286	0
Winningham, H.	Mon.-Cin.	L	.232	100	203	16	47	58	3	4	0	21	3	3	2	0	17	1	45	12	8	2	.286	.288	1
Woodson, T.	L.A.	R	.249	65	173	15	43	58	4	1	3	15	4	0	2	1	7	1	32	1	2	4	.335	.279	6
Worrell, T.	St.L.	R	.000	68	6	1	0	0	0	0	0	0	0	0	0	0	1	0	5	0	0	0	.000	.143	0
Wrona, R.	Chi.	R	.000	4	6	0	0	0	0	0	0	0	0	0	0	0	0	0	1	0	0	0	.000	.000	0
Wynne, M.	S.D.	L	.264	128	333	37	88	142	13	4	11	42	5	3	2	0	31	2	62	3	4	3	.426	.325	3
Youmans, F.	Mon.	R	.154	14	26	2	4	5	1	0	0	3	0	0	1	0	0	0	12	0	0	0	.192	.148	1
Young, G.	Hou.	S	.257	149	576	79	148	187	21	9	0	37	4	5	5	3	66	1	66	65	27	10	.325	.334	3
Young, M.	Phi.	S	.226	75	146	13	33	50	14	0	1	14	1	0	2	1	26	1	43	0	0	1	.342	.343	5
Youngblood, J.	S.F.	R	.252	83	123	12	31	35	4	0	0	16	2	2	3	1	10	0	17	1	1	5	.285	.307	1

CLUB BATTING

Club	AVG	G	AB	R	OR	H	TB	2B	3B	HR	GS	RBI	SH	SF	HP	BB	IBB	SO	SB	CS	GIDP	LOB	SHO	SLG	OBP
Chicago	.261	163	5675	660	694	1481	2174	262	46	113	3	612	57	46	21	403	58	910	120	46	109	1136	13	.383	.310
New York	.256	160	5408	703	532	1387	2142	251	24	152	3	659	65	56	32	544	79	842	140	51	94	1138	6	.396	.325
Montreal	.251	163	5573	628	592	1400	2077	260	48	107	2	575	66	44	32	454	71	1053	189	89	120	1081	12	.373	.309
St. Louis	.249	162	5518	578	633	1373	1859	207	33	71	0	536	105	48	22	484	61	827	234	64	110	1174	16	.337	.309
San Francisco	.248	162	5450	670	626	1353	2007	227	44	113	2	629	91	51	33	550	71	1023	121	78	96	1130	14	.368	.318
Los Angeles	.248	162	5431	628	544	1346	1910	217	25	99	2	587	95	50	32	437	65	947	131	46	118	1075	10	.352	.305
San Diego	.247	161	5366	594	583	1325	1882	205	35	94	3	566	106	45	21	494	59	892	123	50	117	1109	11	.351	.311
Pittsburgh	.247	160	5379	651	616	1327	1987	240	45	110	0	619	66	60	32	553	65	947	119	60	97	1137	10	.369	.317
Cincinnati	.246	161	5426	641	596	1334	1996	246	25	122	1	588	69	51	37	479	60	922	207	56	99	1075	14	.368	.309
Houston	.244	162	5494	617	631	1338	1927	239	31	96	4	575	77	44	38	474	67	840	198	71	103	1087	14	.351	.306
Atlanta	.242	160	5440	555	741	1319	1891	228	28	96	0	527	74	46	21	432	59	848	95	69	136	1038	17	.348	.298
Philadelphia	.240	162	5403	597	734	1294	1920	246	31	106	1	567	67	48	47	489	51	981	112	49	106	1115	16	.355	.306
Totals	.248	969	65563	7522	7522	16277	23772	2828	415	1279	21	7040	938	589	368	5793	766	11032	1789	729	1305	13295	153	.363	.310

Pitching

INDIVIDUAL PITCHING LEADERS

Games Won	23	Hershiser, L.A. & Jackson, Cin.
Games Lost	17	Glavine, Atl.
Won-Lost Percentage	.870	Cone, N.Y.
Earned Run Average	2.18	Magrane, St.L.
Games	76	Murphy, Cin.
Games Started	36	Browning, Cin. & Reuschel, S.F.
Complete Games	15	Hershiser, L.A. & Jackson, Cin.
Games Finished	61	Franco, Cin.
Shutouts	8	Hershiser, L.A.
Saves	39	Franco, Cin.
Innings	267	Hershiser, L.A.
Hits	279	Mahler, Atl.
Batsmen Faced	1068	Hershiser, L.A.
Runs	125	Mahler, Atl.
Earned Runs	102	Mahler, Atl.
Home Runs	36	Browning, Cin.
Sacrifice Hits	19	Mahler, Atl.
Sacrifice Flies	14	Reuschel, S.F.
Hit Batsmen	11	K. Gross, Phi.
Bases on Balls	89	K. Gross, Phi.
Intentional Bases on Balls	16	Maddux, Chi.
Strikeouts	228	Ryan, Hou.
Wild Pitches	13	Walk, Pit.
Balks	10	Cone, N.Y., De. Martinez & Perez, Mon.
Games Won, Consecutive	10	Agosto, Hou. (April 29-August 22)
Games Lost, Consecutive	7	Glavine, Atl. (June 15-Aug. 7) & Rawley, Phi. (June 23-Aug. 4)

TOP FIFTEEN QUALIFIERS FOR EARNED RUN AVERAGE CHAMPIONSHIP

Pitcher	Team	Thrs	W	L	ERA	G	GS	CG	SHO	GF	SV	IP	H	TBF	R	ER	HR	SH	SF	HB	BB	IBB	SO	WP	BK	OPP AVG
Magrane, J.	St.L.	L	5	9	2.18	24	24	4	3	0	0	165.1	133	677	57	40	6	8	4	2	51	4	100	8	8	.217
Cone, D.	N.Y.	R	20	3	2.22	35	28	8	4	0	0	231.1	178	936	67	57	10	11	5	4	80	7	213	10	10	.213
Hershiser, O.	L.A.	R	23	8	2.26	35	34	15	8	1	1	267.0	208	1068	73	67	18	9	6	4	73	10	178	6	5	.213
Tudor, J.	St.L.-L.A.	L	10	8	2.32	30	30	5	1	0	0	197.2	189	794	60	51	10	12	5	1	41	7	87	0	3	.257
Rijo, J.	Cin.	R	13	8	2.39	49	19	0	0	12	0	162.0	120	653	47	43	7	8	5	3	63	7	160	1	4	.209
Perez, P.	Mon.	R	12	8	2.44	27	27	4	2	0	0	188.0	133	741	59	51	15	10	3	7	44	6	131	5	10	.196
Robinson, D.	S.F.	R	10	5	2.45	51	19	3	2	19	6	176.2	152	725	63	48	11	7	8	3	49	12	122	4	2	.231
Walk, B.	Pit.	R	12	10	2.71	32	32	1	1	0	0	212.2	183	881	75	64	6	14	5	2	65	5	81	13	9	.230
Martinez, D.	Mon.	R	15	13	2.72	34	34	9	2	0	0	235.1	215	968	94	71	21	2	6	6	55	3	120	5	10	.239
Jackson, D.	Cin.	L	23	8	2.73	35	35	15	6	0	0	260.2	206	1034	86	79	13	13	5	2	71	6	161	5	2	.218
Ojeda, B.	N.Y.	L	10	13	2.88	29	29	5	5	0	0	190.1	158	752	74	61	6	6	6	4	33	2	133	4	7	.225
Belcher, T.	L.A.	R	12	6	2.91	36	27	4	1	5	4	179.2	143	719	65	58	8	6	1	2	51	7	152	4	0	.217
Leary, T.	L.A.	R	17	11	2.91	35	34	9	6	0	0	228.2	201	932	87	74	13	7	3	6	56	4	180	9	6	.234
Scott, M.	Hou.	R	14	8	2.92	32	32	8	5	0	0	218.2	162	875	74	71	19	16	4	8	53	6	190	1	1	.204
Deshaies, J.	Hou.	L	11	14	3.00	31	31	3	2	0	0	207.0	164	847	77	69	20	8	13	2	72	5	127	1	6	.218
Smith, B.	Mon.	R	12	10	3.00	32	32	1	0	0	0	198.0	179	791	79	66	15	7	6	10	32	2	122	2	5	.243